™

Colonel John Coburn

COBURN'S BRIGADE

85th Indiana, 33rd Indiana,
19th Michigan, and 22nd Wisconsin
in the Western Civil War

FRANK J. WELCHER

AND

LARRY G. LIGGET

Guild Press of Indiana
Carmel, IN 46032

Library of Congress Number 99-71524

ISBN: 1-57860-070-7

Contents

List of Maps

Preface

Historians who have thoroughly covered many aspects of the Civil War lately have neglected one of the more important units of the armies—the brigade. The army camped, marched, and fought in brigades. A brigade was much like a miniature army, consisting of a commanding officer and his aides, an ordnance and commissary department, medical staff, quartermasters' department, inspector, and so on. Perhaps historians have hesitated to write about the brigade because they are often difficult to follow. With few exceptions, the assignments of regiments to a brigade were not permanent. Coburn's brigade was one such exception.

In October 1862, while near Lexington, Kentucky, the 85th Indiana, the 33rd Indiana, the 19th Michigan, and the 22nd Wisconsin regiments were assigned to a brigade to be commanded by Colonel John Coburn. These four regiments remained in the same brigade, though later commanded by Colonel Daniel Dustin, until they were mustered out in June 1865, and thus shared the same experiences for nearly three years of the war.

They worked at construction of fortifications and building bridges, supplying labor for the quartermasters' department, and performing the usual camp duties—including almost ceaseless drill. They were frequently sent out on foraging expeditions and on reconnaissances into enemy territory, and this sometimes led to skirmishing and small engagements. Coburn's brigade fought gallantly often, but they also performed many mundane duties that were usual to army routine, especially in the Western Army.

The soldiers who performed this very useful service generally received far less attention than those who fought the big battles. It is important to note their contribution because no major Union army could have moved far in those days without the support of such regiments and brigades, and in this way alone they contributed significantly to the outcome of the war. John Coburn's brigade was composed of lesser known regiments that spent much of their time in the rear areas.

Although the noncombat role of Coburn's brigade has been emphasized, it must be remembered that it was seriously engaged at Thompson's Station in Tennessee, Resaca, Georgia, Peach Tree Creek in Georgia and Averasboro in North Carolina. Although the brigade has been stigmatized for many decades because it surrendered, our thesis is that the men generally performed well in *all* these battles, despite their capture by superior numbers of the enemy at Thompson's Station.

The authors hope that as you read this book, you will feel that you have traveled a few miles with John Coburn's brigade. You will watch them grow from green-but-determined boys at Thompson's Station, to sage, deliberate hard-fighting men at Atlanta, across Georgia, and through the Carolinas. Perhaps you will wonder what the men thought and how they felt as they saw Libby Prison for the second time, at the War's end. The story of this brigade, Coburn's brigade, is genuinely representative of the Western soldier during the war.

Frank J. Welcher, Indianapolis
Larry G. Ligget, Terre Haute

Acknowledgments

In researching this book we met many exceptional people who helped us in countless ways. Here, we endeavor to express our thanks to some of them.

The staff of the Library of the Indiana Historical Society with whom we came in contact were extremely kind and helpful, but we wish to thank particularly Alexandra S. Gressitt, Curator of Manuscripts and Archives; Susan Sutton, Coordinator of Visual Reference Services, Paul Brockman, Archivist; and Eric Mundell, Head of Reference Services.

We spent much time in the Indiana State Library. There, we were treated with courtesy and kindness and received much valuable information. Those particularly deserving of thanks and commendation include the following: Martha Wright, Reference Librarian of the Indiana Division; Larry Hathaway, Manuscript Section, Indiana Division; Carol Kruszewski, Loan Librarian; Pamela Wasmer, Manuscript Librarian, Indiana Division; Stephen E. Towne, Archivist; Cynthia St. Martin, Reference Librarian, Indiana State Library; and Barney Thompson of the Indiana Division.

Thanks are also due to George Heerman, Reference Librarian, and Jane Ehrenhart of the Reference Division of the Illinois State Historical Library at Springfield, Illinois, for providing biographical information on Colonel Daniel Dustin.

Harriet Liston Webb of Beaverton, Oregon, author of *Write To Me Often*, from the Webco Press of Beaverton, Oregon, provided interesting information about Colonel John P. Baird.

Richard S. Skidmore, editor of *The Alford Brothers*, published by the Nugget Press of Hanover, Indiana, gave permission to use material about Camp Vigo taken from his book.

Margery E. Katz, Library Consultant, and James L. Hanson, Reference Librarian, of the State Historical Society of Wisconsin provided much useful information about the 22nd Wisconsin Regiment, the Utley-Bloodgood feud, and biographical material about Colonel Utley and Lieutenant Colonel Bloodgood.

The following have been of great help in supplying information about people, places, and events occurring in Vigo County, Indiana, during the Civil War: B. Michael McCormick, Terre Haute attorney and Vigo County Historian; the reference staff of the Vigo County Public Library;

David Lewis, research assistant, Vigo County Public Library; and Susan Dehler, Special Collections Archivist, Vigo County Public Library. Jane McCauley graciously provided information about Major John P. Dufficy of the 35th Indiana Regiment.

We would like to thank Randy and Elizabeth "Liddy" Wright for their assistance regarding John P. Dowd of the 85th Indiana. The staff of the Rockville Public Library assisted us in every way, as we spent hours reading and researching *The Rockville Republican* and other sources. Mr. Perry Neet of Catlin, Indiana, was very generous in providing us with information and materials about his ancestor, William Neet. Mr. James Goforth of Dana, Indiana, kindly gave us permission to examine materials regarding Captain Caleb Bales, and Company D of the 85th Indiana

Thanks to Flo Sinsheimer, Reference Librarian, Scarsdale Public Library, Scarsdale, New York, for valuable information about the life of Alexander B. Crane.

Our special thanks to Joseph W. Quigley, MD of Indianapolis for interpreting some of the Civil War period disorders into modern medical terms.

David Slay of Rome, Georgia, and Ronald Bachman of Falls Church, Virginia, fielded questions, provided research assistance, and made excellent recommendations on several occasions. We are sincerely grateful for their assistance.

Craig Dunn, of Kokomo, Indiana, kindly allowed us to use many photographs from his comprehensive collection.

We are especially indebted to John and Sue Oden, Dr. and Mrs. William J. Darby, Doug and Jan Darby, Martha Ragan, and Tim Neal of Thompson's Station, Tennessee. They gave their time, answered our questions, and allowed us to walk their property in our efforts to better understand the Battlefield. We are most appreciative for their consideration and friendship.

Mr. Richard Warwick, editor of *Williamson County Historical Society Journal*, Franklin, Tennessee, spoke with us about the hanging of Orton Williams and Walter Peter and provided us with a copy of their superb publication containing an article about Franklin's Hanging Tree.

Likewise, Alice Algood of the Maury County Historical Society, Columbia, Tennessee, gave us permission to use materials regarding Orton Williams and Walter Peter, taken from *Frank H. Smith's History of Maury County.*

We are indebted to the staff of the Allen County Public Library. Researching in the ACPL genealogy department is a delightful experience because theirs is truly an exceptional collection. We also wish to express our gratitude to Lisa Ann Libby, rare books stacks supervisor, The Huntington Library for providing a copy of Herron's *Reminiscences of the Eighty-Fifth Indiana Volunteer Infantry*. The staff of the Tudor Place Foundation, Washington, D.C., was most helpful in furnishing us information about Orton Williams and Walter Peter, and we extend our appreciation to Leni Preston, Fran White, and Anne Webb for their attention to our requests.

A project of this scope usually consumes the family members of the authors as well. Frank Welcher expresses special thanks to his lovely wife, Helen, for her constant support and for her efforts to make his work less burdensome, and also to his son, Robert B. Welcher, who unfailingly assisted with the computer problems that arose while preparing this manuscript, for his help in arranging the reference lists and proofreading some sections. Without his assistance, the task of writing this book would have been far more difficult.

Likewise, Larry Ligget extends appreciation to his beloved wife, Lucinda, who lent her exceptional expertise as a genealogist on several occasions and cheerfully assisted in innumerable other ways. Larry's son, Kristopher, also an ardent student of the Civil War, was a constant source of inspiration and enthusiasm for this work. They shared many long walks together, earnestly and joyfully contemplating John Coburn's brigade.

Chapter One

ORGANIZATION OF THE REGIMENTS
OF THE BRIGADE

Coburn's brigade, organized in Kentucky in October 1862, consisted of four volunteer infantry regiments: the 33rd Indiana, the 85th Indiana, the 19th Michigan, and the 22nd Wisconsin. The 33rd Indiana was the first to be organized, formed from troops responding to Lincoln's second call for volunteers, issued May 3, 1861 (the first was April 15, 1861.) The other three regiments were all organized during the summer of 1862 with men enlisting after Lincoln's third call, issued August 4, 1862.

ORGANIZATION OF THE 85TH INDIANA VOLUNTEERS

When the Civil War began in April of 1861, there were few people in the North who did not believe that it would soon end in a Union victory. It was not to be. After the disastrous Battle of Bull Run, Major General George B. McClellan's Army of the Potomac moved to the Peninsula in Virginia and advanced toward Richmond, and Major General Ulysses S. Grant's Army of the Tennessee and Major General Don Carlos Buell's Army of the Ohio fought the Battle of Shiloh and then advanced on Corinth, Mississippi. Clearly, there was no immediate prospect of peace.

As a result of the heavy fighting that spring, a shortage of manpower developed in the North, and on July 1, President Abraham Lincoln decided to call for 300,000 troops. In response to this call, on July 7, Governor Oliver P. Morton of Indiana authorized the organization of eleven new three-year regiments, one from each of the congressional districts of the state. As a result of this directive, the 65th through the 75th Indiana regiments were organized as follows:[1]

REGIMENT	DISTRICT	ORGANIZED AT	DATE OF MUSTER IN
65th Indiana	First	Princeton	August 20, 1862
66th Indiana	Second	New Albany	August 19, 1862
67th Indiana	Third	Madison	August 20, 1862
68th Indiana	Fourth	Greensburg	August 19, 1862
69th Indiana	Fifth	Richmond	August 19, 1862
70th Indiana	Sixth	Indianapolis	August 12, 1862
71st Indiana	Seventh	Terre Haute	August 18, 1862

72nd Indiana	Eighth	Lafayette	August 16, 1862
73rd Indiana	Ninth	South Bend	August 16, 1862
74th Indiana	Tenth	Fort Wayne	August 21, 1862
75th Indiana	Eleventh	Wabash	August 19, 1862

At about the time of Lincoln's call for troops, the military situation in Tennessee and Kentucky which had been relatively quiescent became active. On June 17 General Braxton Bragg, who was then at Tupelo, Mississippi, after the evacuation of Corinth, relieved General Pierre G. T. Beauregard from command of the Confederate Western Department, including the Army of the Mississippi. Bragg soon decided to move northward across Tennessee with his army and invade Kentucky. He hoped to reach the Ohio River at Louisville and, if possible, at Cincinnati. According to the plan, Confederate forces were to advance in two columns: Major General E. Kirby Smith with his reinforced command in East Tennessee from Knoxville, Tennessee, into Eastern Kentucky; and Bragg, after transferring his army to Chattanooga, across Tennessee into Kentucky.[2]

The opening moves of this campaign were made by Confederate cavalry commanded by Colonel John Hunt Morgan and Brigadier General Nathan B. Forrest. Morgan, moving first, left Knoxville with his cavalry brigade July 4, and during the next three days he moved westward about one hundred miles to Sparta, Tennessee. There he turned northward, crossed the Cumberland River at Celina, and continued northwest through Tompkinsville and Glasgow to Cave City. From there he moved northeast through Lawrenceburg to Georgetown, north of Lexington, and on to Cynthiana. At that point Morgan turned back toward Tennessee. He passed through Paris, Richmond, Somerset, and Monticello in Kentucky and finally halted and went into camp July 27 at Sparta, Tennessee.[3]

The news of Morgan's raid caused a great flurry of activity in Indiana and the surrounding states. There were at that time very few Federal troops available in Indiana, but troops of the Indiana Legion were called out along the Ohio River. Then, between August 13 and August 22, all eleven of the new Indiana regiments organized under Morton's call for troops of July 7 were mustered in and left the state for Kentucky. The 66th, 69th, 71st, and 73rd moved to Lexington and were later assigned to the Army of Kentucky. The 67th, 68th, 70th, 74th, and 75th regiments went to Louisville. Upon arriving there the 67th and 68th Indiana were assigned to the Army of Kentucky, and the 74th and 75th to the Army of the Ohio. The 70th Indiana was assigned to the District of Louisville, Department of the Ohio. The 65th Indiana moved to Henderson and was assigned to the District of Western Kentucky, Department of the Ohio. The 72nd Indiana moved to Lebanon, Kentucky, and was later assigned to the Army of the Ohio.[4]

On August 13, as a further response to Lincoln's call for troops, Governor Morton authorized the organization of eleven more three-year regiments:

REGIMENT	DISTRICT	ORGANIZED AT	DATE OF MUSTER IN
79th Indiana	Sixth	Indianapolis	September 2, 1862
80th Indiana	First	Princeton	September 5, 1862
81st Indiana	Second	New Albany	August 29, 1862
82nd Indiana	Third	Madison	August 30, 1862
83rd Indiana	Fourth	Lawrenceburg	September 9, 1862
84th Indiana	Fifth	Richmond	September 3, 1862
85th Indiana	Seventh	Terre Haute	September 2, 1862
86th Indiana	Eighth	Lafayette	September 4, 1862
87th Indiana	Ninth	South Bend	August 28, 1862
88th Indiana	Tenth	Fort Wayne	August 29, 1862
89th Indiana	Eleventh	Wabash	August 28, 1862

August 13 John P. Baird of Terre Haute was granted authority to organize the 85th Indiana Volunteers.[5]

The above regiments, except the 83rd Indiana, left Indiana for Kentucky during the period August 28-September 9. The 79th, 81st, 82nd, 85th, 87th, 88th, and 89th went to Louisville; and the 80th, 84th, and 86th to Covington, Kentucky, where they served in the defenses south of Cincinnati. The 79th, 80th, 81st, 82nd, 86th, 87th, and 88th Indiana were later assigned to the Army of the Ohio; and the 84th and 85th to the Army of Kentucky. The 89th Indiana moved up from Louisville to Munfordville, Department of the Ohio, and was captured there September 17. The 83rd moved to Memphis in the Department of the Tennessee and later joined Major General William T. Sherman's Yazoo River Expedition against Vicksburg, Mississippi, December 20, 1862-January 2, 1863.[6]

The men of the 85th Indiana, one of the regiments of Coburn's brigade, were recruited from the Seventh Congressional District, which consisted of the counties of Clay, Greene, Owen, Parke, Putnam, Sullivan, Vermillion, and Vigo. The ten companies of the regiment, from west central Indiana and other counties of the state, were as follows:

Company A from Parke County (and Montgomery and Owen counties)
Company B from Vigo County (and Clay, Dubois, Marion, Parke, and Vanderburgh counties)
Company C from Vigo County (and Morgan and Wayne counties)

Company D from Parke and Vermillion counties (Allen and Marion counties)

Company E from Vigo County (and Boone, Clay, and Randolph counties)

Company F from Vigo County (and Bartholomew, Blackford, Montgomery, Putnam, and Rush counties)

Company G from Parke and Vigo counties (and Cass, Clay, Lake, Montgomery, Owen, Putnam, and Vermillion counties)

Company H from Sullivan County (and Marion and Vigo counties)

Company I from Clay County (and Lake, Owen, and Vigo counties)

Company K from Clay and Greene counties (and Boone, Lake, Marion, and Putnam counties)

Note: The names of the counties which furnished only a relatively few recruits to the companies indicated are enclosed in parenthesis.[7]

Typical of regiments organized in 1862, some recruits came from well beyond the state. Approximately fifty-five men enlisted from Illinois, Ohio, Kentucky, Pennsylvania, and New York. About forty-five of these were from Illinois, and they came principally from the central and east central part of that state.[8]

Most of the recruits who filled the ranks of the 85th Indiana were country and small-town boys who were generally good citizens and later proved to be good and intelligent soldiers. These small towns and the surrounding country depended on churches and schools for their cultural life, and corn and pork were sold to the South for their very existence.

Captain Abner Floyd organized Company A at Annapolis, Parke County, in August 1862. Annapolis was a typical Midwestern small post town situated near Sugar Creek, seven miles north of Rockville, the county seat. A church, Literary Institution, The McClure Institute, Library Association, Western Manual Labor School, Masonic Lodge, four stores, one hotel, and two woolen mills in the town marked it as having a cultural as well as mercantile life in the heart of the prairie cornfields. When enrollment was completed, the company marched to Rockville, where it arrived August 8.[9]

Captain Francis Brooks organized Company B at Terre Haute, Vigo County, in August 1862. On August 16 David Philips of Montezuma came into Camp Dick Thompson at Terre Haute with forty-two men of Company K, which he had attempted to organize in Parke County. Philips was unable to recruit the required number for the company,and consequently, his command was consolidated with the company of Captain Brooks of Terre Haute. In the election of officers, Brooks was chosen as captain of the combined companies, which were designated as Company B.[10]

Captain Alexander B. Crane organized Company C at Terre Haute in August 1862. With a history dating to French times in Indiana, Terre Haute was, in Civil War times, a flourishing pork packing and mill town near the Wabash River, with a population of about 8,600. Culturally, it had its own Lyceums, many ladies aid societies, and more than one hotel.[11]

Captain William Reeder organized Company D at Clinton, Vermillion County, in August 1862. It then marched to Terre Haute, arriving there August 12.[12]

Captain Jefferson E. Brant organized Company E at Prairieton, Vigo County, in August 1862. It marched seven miles to Terre Haute and arrived there August 17.[13]

Captain William D. Weir organized Company F at Middletown (or Prairie Creek), Vigo County, in July 1862. It too traveled to Terre Haute fourteen miles away and arrived there July 28.[14]

Captain Ellery C. Davis organized Company G in August 1862 at Otter Creek, in Vigo County, six miles from Terre Haute. It arrived at Terre Haute August 14.[15]

Captain William T. Crawford organized Company H at Sullivan, Sullivan County, in August 1862. It then marched to Terre Haute, a distance of twenty-six miles, and arrived August 15.[16]

Captain Caleb Nash organized Company I at Terre Haute in August 1862.[17]

Captain Lewis Puckett organized Company K at Coffee, Indiana. This was a small post village in southwestern Clay County, located about one mile west of Eel River and on the Worthington and Terre Haute stage route, about eighteen miles from Bowling Green, the county seat. A post office and a grocery store and several other buildings lined the main street of Coffee. When enrollment was completed the company marched to Terre Haute, a distance of about twenty-two miles, arriving there August 13.[18]

When the companies were filled by recruiting, they were ordered to rendezvous at Camp Dick Thompson in Terre Haute, the second rendezvous camp organized in that town. The first was Camp Vigo, located on the north side of town.[19] In the summer of 1862 the rendevous camp was moved to what was then the new fairgrounds, about two miles east of the city, and renamed Camp Dick Thompson in honor of Richard W. Thompson, a prominent citizen of Terre Haute[20] who served in politics in the state senate, and U.S. Congress.[21]

When the Civil War broke out in 1861, Thompson became active in military affairs in the state, and on November 1, 1861, was assigned command of the organized militia in the counties of Vigo, Clay, Owen, Greene, and Sullivan, in the district in which the 85th Indiana was recruited.[22]

By an order dated July 8, 1862, Governor Morton appointed Thompson as commandant of the new camp bearing his name, with the rank of captain, and assigned to him the task of recruiting and organizing the regiments that were to assemble there. In addition to the work of recruiting, Thompson was also responsible for equipping and training the troops. The 85th Indiana was the second regiment organized at Camp Dick Thompson.[23]

On September 1 John P. Baird was commissioned colonel of the 85th and assigned command of the regiment. Baird was born January 5, 1830, on the old Baird farm on Simpson Creek in Spencer County, Kentucky, about eight miles from Taylorville. His father, Stephen Baird, was a native of Ireland and his mother, Sarah, was born in Spencer County. In 1832 Stephen Baird sold his property in Kentucky and moved to Indiana, eventually settling in Southeastern Vigo County.

John Baird spent most of his youth on the farm and was educated in the neighborhood schools. At the age of eighteen, he entered Franklin College, in Franklin, Indiana, and remained there for two years. He then moved to Terre Haute, where he found employment under Charles T. Noble, circuit clerk. In 1851 and 1852 he attended law school at the State University in Bloomington; on March 10, 1852, he was admitted to the bar.

In April 1852 he formed a partnership with William D. Griswold, who retired from practice two years later and turned over to Baird his office, library, and an extensive practice. Baird formed a new partnership with Salmon Wright and was later associated with Edward E. Bassett, with the office on Main Street of Terre Haute.[24]

During August of 1862, Dick Thompson, mounted on a horse, drilled the men during the day; in the afternoons the families of many of the soldiers treated the men to visits and frequent picnic dinners.[25]

Meantime, at the front, the early signs of a possible invasion of Tennessee were being closely watched by Brigadier General George W. Morgan, commander of the forces at Cumberland Gap, and by General Buell, who was with his Army of the Ohio in south central Tennessee. These officers were promptly reporting their findings to the War Department and to the military authorities in Kentucky, Indiana, and Ohio. Receiving the reports of Morgan and Buell, the Secretary of War urgently appealed to Indiana to make every effort to fill its quota of 21,250 men called for in July. On August 9 Governor Morton replied that the men would be ready in twenty days.[26]

The expected enemy invasion began at 4:00 AM on August 14, when Kirby Smith left Knoxville with his Confederate Army of Kentucky, moving northward to Big Creek Gap. After crossing the Cumberland Mountains at Rogers' Gap, he entered Barboursville in eastern Kentucky August 18.[27]

To oppose Smith's advance, many of the newly organized regiments and a number of generals were ordered to Kentucky. Among the latter was Major General Lewis (Lew) Wallace, later to write the famous novel *Ben Hur*, who, on August 20, was assigned command of all Union troops at Lexington, Kentucky. There was some confusion because of his high rank, but Wallace waived his rank and accepted the appointment.[28]

The Department of the Ohio was re-established August 19, 1862, and four days later Major General Horatio G. Wright assumed command. The new department consisted of the states of Illinois, Indiana, Michigan, Ohio, and Wisconsin and that part of Kentucky lying east of the Tennessee River. Wright's principal function was to coordinate the Union efforts to repel the Confederate invasion of Kentucky. The many new troops, just recruited, would soon be on their way to Kentucky, and upon their arrival there they would be put in camp, fed, drilled, and equipped for field service. They would also be organized into brigades and divisions. All of this was a part of Wright's job.[29]

August 24 Major General William Nelson arrived at Lexington from the Army of the Ohio, at that time in Tennessee, and relieved Wallace of command. Wallace immediately went north to Cincinnati, where, on September 1, 1862, he was assigned command of the troops at that city and those who were arriving.[30]

The second phase of the Confederate invasion began on August 27-28, as Bragg crossed the Tennessee River at Chattanooga with his Confederate Army of the Mississippi and began his march northward across Tennessee toward Kentucky.[31]

August 30 Kirby Smith, advancing from Barboursville by way of Big Hill, met and defeated at Richmond, Kentucky a small Union army consisting of two brigades of new troops and commanded that day by Brigadier General Mahlon D. Manson. From there Smith moved on northward and occupied Lexington September 2. Troops sent forward from Lexington occupied Frankfort the next day. The incendiary situation was about to break into flame.[32]

On the day that Smith occupied Lexington, September 2, the 85th Indiana Regiment was mustered into the United States service at Terre Haute. The men received their advance pay and bounty that afternoon with orders to leave the next day for Indianapolis.[33]

Baird assumed command of the regiment and prepared to start with it toward Covington, Kentucky, to help defend Cincinnati from Bragg's and Kirby Smith's advancing armies.[34]

The officers of the regiment at that time were as follows:[35]

RANK AND NAME	DATE OF COMMISSION	DATE OF MUSTER IN
Col. John P. Baird	Sept. 4, 1862	Sept. 4, 1862
Lt. Col. Alexander B. Crane	Sept. 4, 1862	Sept. 4, 1862
Maj. Robert E. Craig	Sept. 4, 1862	Sept. 4, 1862
Adj. Hiram L. Tillotson	Sept. 1, 1862	Sept. 2, 1862
QM. William C. Lupton	Sept. 5, 1862	Sept. 5, 1862
Chap. Philip B. Cook	Sept. 4, 1862	Sept. 8,1862
Surg. Wilson Hobbs	Sept. 4, 1862	Sept. 4, 1862
Asst. Surg. William W. Johnson	Sept. 4, 1862	Sept. 4, 1862

CAPTAINS

A—Abner F. Floyd	Aug. 8, 1862	Sept. 4, 1862
B—Francis Brooks	Aug. 21, 1862	Sept. 2, 1862
C—Alexander B. Crane	Aug. 15, 1862	Sept. 2, 1862,
D—William Reeder	Aug. 8, 1862	Sept. 2, 1862
E—Jefferson E. Brant	Aug. 19, 1862	Sept. 2, 1862
F—William D. Weir	Aug. 15, 1862	Sept. 2, 1862
G—Ellery C. Davis	Aug. 15, 1862	Sept. 2, 1862
H—William T. Crawford	Aug. 15, 1862	Sept. 2, 1862
I—Caleb Nash	Aug. 16, 1862	Sept. 2, 1862
K—Lewis Puckett	Aug. 12, 1862	Sept. 2, 1862

Note: Elijah Adamson of Bowling Green was commissioned as quartermaster August 16, 1862, but this was revoked. John M. Coleman of Spencer was commissioned August 27, but he declined to serve. David C. Stillwagen was then commissioned September 5, but he too declined to serve. William C. Lupton of Indianapolis became quartermaster September 5.

The men who enlisted in the 85th Indiana were somewhat older and more mature than those who entered the service in 1861. They believed when they enlisted that the war would soon end. On the contrary, the men of the

85th who left Camp Dick Thompson in 1862 were generally convinced the war would last a long time and would be bitterly fought. They would soon be tested in that conviction.[36]

ORGANIZATION OF THE 19TH MICHIGAN VOLUNTEERS

In the neighboring state of Michigan, young men in the seven counties of the Second Congressional District, located in the southwestern part of the state, were joining the 19th Michigan Volunteers. Recruits were from Berrien, Cass, St. Joseph, and Branch counties, which extended eastward from Lake Michigan along the Indiana state line; from Van Buren and Kalamazoo counties, just to the north; from Allegan County, bordering the lake; and north of Van Buren County.[37]

Recruitment for the ten companies of the regiment officially began July 15, at the following places: Company A at Dowagiac, Company B at Allegan, companies C and H at Coldwater, Company D at Constantine, Company E at Sturgis, companies F and K at Kalamazoo, Company G at South Haven, and Company I at St. Joseph. By mid-August most companies had completed their recruitment and had begun training under the direction of the recruiting officers while they awaited orders to assemble at Dowagiac, a town in Cass county on the Michigan Central Railroad.[38]

Late in July 1862 Governor Austin Blair appointed Henry C. Gilbert colonel and assigned him to the command of the 19th Michigan Regiment. Gilbert was born in Onondaga County, New York, July 14, 1818. In 1841 he moved to Michigan. Gilbert, a successful lawyer, was also active in politics. He served as prosecuting attorney of Branch County for six years, in 1850 becoming an attorney for the Michigan Southern Railroad Company. In that capacity he worked at procuring a right-of-way through Branch County and the neighboring counties through which the line was to pass. Gilbert also was appointed Indian agent for the Northwest Territory during the administration of President Franklin Pierce. He was a successful businessman financially interested in a number of enterprises, including the *Sentinel*, a newspaper in Coldwater, a saw mill, and a flour mill. By the outbreak of the Civil War, he had become a wealthy man. He was married in 1843 and was the father of four boys and four girls.[39]

Gilbert arrived at Dowagiac August 10 and immediately began preparations for an encampment to receive, train, and care for the new recruits. When this work was completed, he ordered the ten companies to assemble at Camp Willcox, named in honor of Colonel Orlando B. Willcox, who commanded the 1st Michigan regiment at the First Battle of Bull Run. Wounded and captured, Willcox was confined in Confederate prisons until released August 19, 1862, when he was commissioned brigadier general.[40]

While at Camp Willcox, the new recruits were, for the first time, subjected to military discipline and were drilled by squad, company, and regiment. They were also instructed in guard mounting and dress parade.[41]

The 19th Michigan was mustered into United States service September 5, to serve for three years. At about 4:00 PM September 14, the regiment left Dowagiac and started its journey toward Cincinnati, to meet with the other regiments that would eventually become a part of Coburn's brigade.[42]

Some of the early officers of the 19th Michigan Regiment were as follows:[43]

OFFICER	HOMETOWN	OCCUPATION
Col. Henry Gilbert	Coldwater	Lawyer
Lt. Col. David Bacon	Niles	Lawyer
Maj. William B. Shafter	Galesburg	Teacher
Adj. Hamlet B. Adams	Coldwater	Lawyer
QM Warren Chapman	St. Joseph	Lumberman
Surgeon William E. Clark	Dowagiac	Doctor
Asst. Surgeon John Bennitt	Centerville	Doctor
2nd Asst. Surgeon,		
Leander Tompkins	Cassopolis	Doctor
Chaplain Israel Cogshall	Coldwater	Minister

CAPTAINS	HOMETOWN	OCCUPATION
A–Joel H. Smith	Pokagon	Businessman
B–Elisha Bassett	Allegan	Merchant
C–Charles P. Lincoln	Coldwater	Lawyer
D–Hazen Brown	Constantine	
E–John J. Baker	Sturgis	
F–Charles Thompson	Kalamazoo	Lawyer
G–Charles Bigelow	South Haven	
H–George H. White	Coldwater	Nurseryman
I–Richard Lysaght	St. Joseph	Grocer
K–Phelix Duffie	Kalamazoo	Hotel Keeper

Note: Because of ill health David Bacon was unable to exercise command; Major William R. Shafter was promoted to Lieutenant Colonel.

ORGANIZATION OF THE 22ND WISCONSIN VOLUNTEERS

The ten companies of the 22nd Wisconsin, raised in response to President Lincoln's call of July 2, 1862, for 300,000 additional troops, were recruited from the counties of Rock, Racine, Green, and Walworth in Wisconsin, located in the extreme southeastern part of the state. The companies of the regiment were organized at the following places: Company A at Racine, Company B at Beloit, Company C at Geneva, Company D at Delevan, Company E at Janesville, Company F at Racine, Company G at Monroe, Company H at Burlington, Company I at Beloit, and Company K at Jefferson.

The 22nd rendezvoused August 25 at Camp Utley at Racine. There the organization of the regiment was effected during the latter part of the month. The recruits spent several weeks in rudimentary infantry drill, interspersed with speeches by visiting dignitaries. The regiment was mustered into the United States service under Colonel William L. Utley September 2 to serve for three years, and left WisconsinSeptember 16 and moved to Cincinnati, Ohio.[44]

Officers were as follows:[45]

Col. William L. Utley
Lieut. Col. Edward Bloodgood
Maj. E. D. Murray
Adj. William Bones
QM. John E. Holmes
Surg. George W. Bicknell
1st Asst. Surg. C. S. Blanchard
2nd Asst. Surg. Jerome Burbank

CAPTAINS

A—George R. Williamson
B—Thomas B. Northrup
C—Charles W. Smith
D—Alphons G. Kellam
E—Isaac Miles
F—Owen Griffiths
G—James Bintliff
H—Gustavus Goodrich
I—Warren Hodgdon
K—G. E. Bingham

Utley was born at Monson, Massachusetts, July 10, 1814. His father was engaged in the cotton business, but in 1818 the business failed and his father moved with his family to the "Western Reserve" in Ohio, which was then an unbroken wilderness. At that time William was four years old, and for the next seventeen years he lived a pioneer life. Such education that he received was in a log schoolhouse or through the teaching of his father and mother. When he was twenty-one he went to New York, where he studied portrait painting and played the violin at a dancing school run by his uncle.

He did not remain there long but started moving about with no permanent location. In 1839 he married Louisa Wing, and they had three children. Utley finally decided to seek his fortune in the West, and in 1844 he settled in Racine, Wisconsin, where he established himself as an artist and musician and then as a hotel keeper.

In 1848 Utley began his political career, abandoning his former Democratic sentiments and becoming identified with the Free-Soil, or Republican, movement. In that year he was elected marshal of Racine, and in 1850 to the legislature. He was reelected in 1851. Governor Leonard J. Farwell appointed him adjutant general of the state in 1852. In 1860 he was elected to the state senate, and at the outbreak of the Rebellion in 1861, Governor Alexander Randall reappointed him adjutant general. Within six months he had assembled and placed in the field 30,000 men. He resigned when Governor Harvey took office and resumed his seat in the Senate. When the session ended he returned home, and a short time later Governor Edward Salomon commissioned him colonel and directed him to raise a regiment in ten days. At the end of that time, he reported at Madison with enough men to form two regiments. He was then assigned command of one of these, which was designated the 22nd Wisconsin.[46]

ORGANIZATION OF THE 33RD INDIANA VOLUNTEERS

The 33rd Indiana had been raised under an earlier call for troops and was already well seasoned when it joined the new regiments assembled in Kentucky, near Cincinnati, during Bragg's and Kirby Smith's invasion of that state.

Back in July 1861, when the regiment had been recruited, the rendezvous for the companies was at Camp Morton, located on the Fairground, south of Fall Creek at the northern edge of Indianapolis. Major Thomas J. Wood of the regular army was specially detailed by the War Department to organize the regiments from the companies reporting to Camp Morton and to muster the troops into the United States service.[47]

In his *History of the Thirty-Third Indiana Veteran Volunteer Infantry*, John

R. McBride described life at Camp Morton in the fall of 1861, and it was fairly typical of the experiences of the men of the other regiments of Coburn's brigade:

> The barracks in which the men were quartered were rudely constructed out of rough lumber and contained upper and lower berths, open in front, and provided with plenty of straw. It did not take long for the boys to adapt themselves to the new conditions. The beds, made of straw and boards, together with the blankets furnished by Uncle Sam and those supplied by friends, tended to benefit rather than impair them physically, and the hardtack and bacon, beans and pork, mixed vegetables, coffee, etc., were devoured with as much satisfaction as the food of former days served by the skillful hand of the wife or mother. The boys soon realized that the free and easy life at their homes was vastly different from the restraints which now environed them, but they cheerfully accepted the new order of things. Each company was divided into squads or messes and placed in charge, generally, of non-commissioned officers, and, if possible, made up of old acquaintances and friends. From reveille in the morning until taps at night, daily, each soldier had to perform certain routine duties. They had to take turns in drawing rations, fetching water, and cooking the meals, and in standing guard and doing police duty about camp. From none of these could they escape, except through sickness. These duties were all necessary incidents of camp life, and had to be, and generally were cheerfully, performed. In addition to these, the drill in the manual of arms and company movements were not neglected.[48]

Recruiting for the companies that were later to form the 33rd Indiana Infantry, a three-year regiment, began in July 1861. They were recruited and assembled as follows:

Company A was previously a Home Guard company composed of men living in Adams, Ashland, Gregg, and Jefferson townships in the northwestern corner of Morgan County and it had been organized at the village of Hall in that county; Company B was recruited in Knox County; Company C was recruited in Morgan County and was named the "Lyon Guards"; Company D was organized near Smithland in Shelby County and was designated as the "Dumont Guards"; Company E was assembled from men living in Marion, Owen, and Putnam counties; Company F was organized at Princeton, in Gibson County; Company G was recruited at Columbus, in Bartholomew County; Company H was recruited in Morgan County; Company I was formed at Hope, in Bartholomew County, and was organized as the "Hope Guards"; and Company K was organized at Williamsport in Warren County.[49] Now these disparate groups would coalesce in Kentucky.

August 28 Captain Edward T. McCrea arrived at Camp Morton with his Company D, and Major General John Love of the Indiana Legion, who was then in command of the military camps at Indianapolis, directed him to take his company to Camp Sullivan in that city and to assume command of the camp and of all troops that were later to be sent there.

Camp Sullivan was located at the old state fairgrounds (present-day Military Park). In a short time eight other companies reported to McCrea at Camp Sullivan. On September 16, John Coburn was commissioned colonel and was assigned command of the new 33rd Indiana Regiment, formed from these nine companies. The regiment mustered into the United States service that same day. At 11:30 am September 29, it left Indianapolis by rail for Louisville, Kentucky, and arrived there that evening and took up quarters in the Boone tobacco warehouse ready to begin its military career in the early days of the war in Kentucky.

The name of John Coburn is significant as the man who later organized and then commanded the brigade commonly known as Coburn's brigade. It is informative to know more about this man who was destined to tie together all these disparate groups of soldiers, just beginning to think of themselves as a fighting unit.

John Coburn was born in Indianapolis on October 27, 1825. His father, Henry P. Coburn, was a native of Massachusetts, and his mother Sarah Malott Coburn was a native of Kentucky. Henry Coburn was raised on a farm; from there he went to Harvard College, graduating in 1812. He was admitted to the bar in Massachusetts and then moved west and located at Corydon, soon to be the capital of Indiana. John's father moved to Indianapolis in 1824 and died there in 1854. His mother died in 1886.

John Coburn received a good education in Indianapolis and then entered Wabash College, graduating with honors in 1846. After reading law, he was admitted to the bar of the Supreme Court in 1849, and he became active in politics, serving in the Indiana Legislature in 1851. The following year Coburn was on the Whig electoral ticket in the Winfield Scott campaign for the presidency.

In 1852 he married Caroline Test, a first-cousin to Lew Wallace and the daughter of Charles H. Test of Centerville, Indiana. Coburn practiced law in Marion and adjacent counties until 1859, when he was made Judge of the Court of Common Pleas. With the outbreak of the Civil War, Coburn resigned this position and was appointed colonel of the 33rd Indiana Infantry Regiment.[51]

The 33rd Indiana served in Kentucky at Camp Dick Robinson, Camp Wildcat, Crab Orchard, Mill Springs, and at Lexington during the fall and winter of 1861-1862. Then, by an order of March 26, 1862, George W. Morgan was assigned command of a new Seventh Division, Army of the Ohio, which was to concentrate at Cumberland Ford, Kentucky, and attempt the capture of Cumberland Gap. The 33rd Indiana was assigned to this division. By April 1 most of Morgan's division had assembled in the vicinity of Cumberland Ford, but the 33rd Indiana did not leave Lexington until April 11, and it did not join the division until April 28. It was then assigned to the Twenty-Seventh Brigade of Seventh Division, which also included Colonel John C. Cochran's 14th Kentucky and Colonel William J. Landram's 19th Kentucky infantry regiments. Upon his arrival at Cumberland Ford, Coburn assumed command of the Twenty-Seventh Brigade, but was relieved a few days later by Brigadier General Absalom Baird. When all preparations were completed, Morgan advanced with his division and occupied Cumberland Gap June 1862.[52]

On August 17 during E. Kirby Smith's advance into Kentucky, troops belonging to Smith's command in East Tennessee moved against Cumberland Gap, and Morgan was soon under siege. Unable to receive supplies, he ordered the evacuation of the Gap on September 16, and with his division he then marched northward through Kentucky toward the Ohio River.[53]

Henry C. Gilbert, Colonel of the 19th Michigan Regiment, was a harsh critic of John Coburn and his action at Thompson's Station.

Dr. Wilson Hobbs, surgeon of the 85th Indiana Regiment, was well thought of by the men. Hobbs' account of the Williams/Peter events appeared on the front page of *Harper's Weekly*, July 4, 1863.

Jefferson Brant, Captain of Co. E, 85thIndiana Infantry, was promoted to major, lieutenant colonel, and briefly commanded the regiment.

John P. Baird, Colonel of the 85th Indiana Regiment, was said to be one of the most able lawyers that ever practiced at the Terre Haute bar.

John McBride, historian of the 33rd Indiana, and the last adjutant of the regiment.

Robert F. Bence, Asst. Surgeon and later Surgeon of the 33rd Indiana Regiment, was John Coburn's brother-in-law.

Levin Miller, with the rank of major, commanded the 33rd Indiana Regiment during the Atlanta campaign,

Frank Crawford, the first Union soldier to enter Atlanta following Hood's evacuation of the city.

Indiana Governor Oliver Perry Morton was a skillful politican and was regarded by many as the foremost of the war governors.

Charles C. Gilbert, commander of the post at Franklin, Tennessee, ordered an expedition of Coburn's brigade to reconnoiter south towards Spring Hill and Columbia. They soon encountered the forces of Earl Van Dorn.

On October 7, 1862, Gordon Granger assumed command of all United States forces then operating in Kentucky on the line of the Licking River, and extending from the Ohio River southward in the direction of Lexington.

Alpheus S. Williams, a Yale graduate, fought in the east, performed well at Chancellorsville and Gettysburg, and later commanded a division in the XX Corps.

Chapter 2

On Duty In Kentucky

The defeat of the Federal forces at Richmond, Kentucky, by E. Kirby Smith, and his subsequent occupation of Lexington and Frankfort, caused great concern in the states north of the Ohio River, and the authorities in those states made every effort to complete the organization of the new regiments then forming and to send them to the front as rapidly as possible. When they were finally mustered in, they moved south to Cincinnati and Louisville, and the regiments arriving at Cincinnati quickly crossed the Ohio River and went into camp in the vicinity of Covington and Newport in Kentucky.

The Licking River, which rises in the southeastern part of Kentucky, flows generally to the north and west, past Falmouth, and empties into the Ohio River at Covington. At its lower end the valley is about two miles wide, and there the river runs close to the eastern side. An irregular series of steep ravines, some two hundred to three hundred yards apart, run eastward across the wider, western part of the valley and down to the Licking River. These ravines divide that part of the valley into an irregular series of plateaus, on which many of the new regiments made their camps.[1]

When the new regiments first began to arrive at Cincinnati from the North, there was no competent officer of high rank to take command of the large force that was then beginning to assemble across the Ohio River in Kentucky. As has been said, on September 6, 1862, Major General Horatio G. Wright, commanding the Department of the Ohio, with headquarters at Cincinnati, assigned Major General Lewis (Lew) Wallace to that duty. Wright also directed him to organize into brigades the regiments that had been mustered into service and were encamped around Covington and Newport and to prepare these regiments for field service. He also ordered Wallace to furnish such daily work details from his command as might be required by the engineers in charge of the defensive works south of the river. Lieutenant Colonel Sidney Burbank of the 13th United States Infantry relieved Wallace as the military commander of Cincinnati, and Wallace moved to Covington, where he established his headquarters and assumed his new duties.[2]

The course of the Ohio River in the vicinity of Cincinnati made the construction of an effective defensive line for the protection of the city a comparatively simple matter. The river flowed northward to the east of Cincinnati, and then westward past the southern edge of the city before bearing off to the southwest. Thus, the counties of Boone, Kenton, and Campbell in Kentucky extended northward to form a sort of peninsula south of Cincinnati. It was possible to form a defensive line across this peninsula from the Ohio River below Cincinnati and back to the river above the city.

This line began near the village of Bromley, about three-fourths of a mile below Ludlow, Kentucky, and about three miles below Cincinnati, and it ran to the southeast to Fort Mitchel, on the Lexington pike, where it turned to the east to the Ohio River. It ended at Lee Battery, which was situated on an overlook in The Highlands (later Fort Thomas), known as Crown Point. The main line consisted of gun emplacements and rifle pits crowning the hilltops and ridges of that part of Kentucky for a distance of about ten miles, but there were also numerous outlying forts and batteries. The Licking River, which flowed from south to north, divided this line, but a pontoon bridge was laid across the river about three miles from its mouth to provide communication between the two parts.[3]

At 5:00 PM September 3 the day after they were mustered in at Terre Haute, the men of the 85th Indiana boarded the cars and began their trip by rail to Indianapolis. They arrived late that evening and slept in the Union Depot that night. The next day they moved to Camp Morton, about three miles north of the city. The regiment left the same day, September 4, because of lice; at any rate the men were issued new clothes. The next day they were equipped and armed with bayonets, swords, and Belgian muskets.

When this work was completed, the regiment moved to Cincinnati, where it arrived September 7. There the men were treated to a substantial and delicious meal, prepared by the women of the city, with barrels of ice water placed conveniently about the area. That afternoon the men crossed the river into Kentucky and marched to Camp Mitchel, or Sweet Potato Hill, where they went into camp about three miles south of Covington. The meal in Cincinnati was the last such meal that the men would have in a long time. Samuel H. Mattox of Company C, in a letter home, wrote "This is the hilliest country I ever saw, in fact it is nothing but hills and hollows and rocks."[4]

At about the same time that the 85th Indiana had been sent to Cincinnati, twenty-four pieces of artillery, 3,000 stand of arms, 31,136 rounds of artillery ammunition, and 3,365,000 musket cartridges were forwarded to Cincinnati and Covington from the State Arsenal at Indianapolis by special train.[5]

On September 10 the correspondent of *The Daily Wabash Express* (initials J.T.P.), who accompanied the regiment to Kentucky, wrote the following report for the paper from near Covington:

> Here we are encamped among the hills of "Old Kentucky," our rear protected by a sweet potato patch and the Ohio River—our front, by a brigade of Ohio and Michigan troops, while we have all creation for a bedroom—not having slept under cover but once since leaving camp "Dick Thompson." The 85th "squatted" upon these knobs—down which we slide in the night—on the 7th inst. On the 8th the "long roll" was suddenly beat, the men fell into line and marched off, leaving about seventy-five men in camp, and your correspondent has not seen them since. We hear, however, that they are about five miles to the south-east of us, in company with several thousand other troops, barring the advance of the rebels, who are said to be within eight miles of them.
>
> I have made two attempts to reach the regiment, but have been turned back each time; this morning, however, we have the assurance of joining the regiment to-day.

In this report the correspondent further says:

> I might as well come to the point at once: we are expecting a battle within the week, and Surgeon Hobbs requests me to ask the ladies of Terre Haute to prepare lint and bandages immediately and forward them to the address of Wilson Hobbs, Surgeon 85th Regiment Ind. Vol., near Covington, Kentucky. The sanitary condition of the 85th is—according to the surgeon's report—as follows: Left at Indianapolis thirty, five of whom have since joined the regiment; six at Cincinnati, eighteen at Camp Mitchell and fifteen at Camp King.[6]

The next day, the following notice appeared in the paper:[7]

> SPECIAL CALL.—The Ladies Union Aid Society will meet at Mrs. J. D. Early's on Tuesday next, at 1 PM to prepare Lint, Bandages, &., in a response to a late call, for use of the 85th Indiana, and other troops in the field.
>
> Let each bring whatever they can contribute of old linen or muslin, to be made into lint.
>
> A full attendance of members, and all others interested in the welfare of our soldiers, is requested.
>
> Mrs. J. P. Usher, Pres.
Mrs. H. J. Keeler, Sec.

Not everyone thought "linting" helpful. *The Express* carried the following item in its September 29 issue:

> A writer in the *Boston Post* says of lint: Every ounce of lint sent the army does mischief. It's [sic]only use is to cover up the blunders of bad surgery. It is seldom used by the best Surgeons here. In the army it is crowded into wounds by men who know no other way to stop hemorrhage, and there it remains until it becomes filled with filth and maggots. It retains the discharges till they putrify, and produce an intolerable stench. The termination of its work is the death of the patient.[8]

While in camp in Kentucky, the 85th Indiana was engaged in guard, picket, and fatigue duty along the Licking River and near Latonia Springs (Latonia). The men spent the days largely in drilling and working on the fortifications, and during the nights were frequently interrupted in their sleep to answer the long roll. Camp life was difficult at first, because the regiment had not yet been supplied with tents, and the men were forced to sleep unprotected on the ground.[9]

Shortly after arriving in Kentucky, the 85th Indiana moved to Camp Lew Wallace, located on high hills along the south bank of the Ohio River in the present-day Crescent Springs area of Kentucky. It was about five miles down river from the pontoon bridge at Cincinnati and a little more than two miles west and a little north of Fort Mitchel, Kentucky.

Off limits at Camp Lew Wallace was a little store where, according to a soldier who was stationed there, the men could buy sweet milk for three cents a pint and cider for four cents. Pies, though available, were too expensive at ten cents each. The camp was also located on a sweet potato patch, which was good news to the hungry men who were encamped there. Water, however was a problem, because the well was almost a mile distant and downhill from the camp. Not only was the distance great, but the men were forced to carry the water all the way back up the hill to camp.[10]

On September 25 the regiment received the long-awaited tents. The men provided for their comfort by placing corn stalks on the floor of the tents, and that night, for the first time, they slept under cover. Their sleep, however, was interrupted by drums, the shouting of captains, and the noise caused by men hurrying to take their positions in line of battle. Then the men waited, and continued to wait, but no enemy appeared. They were still waiting when the gray dawn began to light up the eastern sky and the order came to return to quarters and remain under arms. They all then enjoyed a breakfast of flint crackers, fried bacon, and hot coffee. That morning all was calm. In general, after receiving their tents, the health of the men began to improve. On October 6 Surgeon Wilson Hobbs reported that there were twenty-three men sick in the hospital, forty-four in their quarters, fifteen in the general hospital.[11]

On September 12 Captain Brooks of Company B, from Vigo and Parke counties, wrote a rather lengthy letter to the *Express*:

> . . . Since we have been in Kentucky, we have been constantly in a line of battle sleeping upon our arms at night and preparing by day for the most sudden attack that might be made, although no battle has yet occurred beyond the killing of some pickets as they are gradually driven in behind the fortifications. It is considered certain by the best military authority that Kirby Smith is moving upon Cincinnati with an immense force of rebel troops, the main body of which is about twenty miles distant, and it may be that before these lines reach you, the great battle of the West has been fought defending Northern soil and strength and courage of this immense mass of raw troops and state militia has been most severely tested.
>
> Our regiments should be better drilled before going into action, but whenever it goes into action you may expect to hear a good report of its courage and determination. A letter from the 85th would be incomplete if it failed to speak in the highest terms of the young Col. Baird, whose popularity with the troops is unbounded. The men believe that he will lead them bravely and skillfully through the trials and dangers of this campaign. Our Lieut. Col. Crane is cool and steady, always on duty and fast displaying military qualities of a good soldier.[12]

A private letter from an officer of the regiment written at Camp Wallace September 19 and published in the *Daily Wabash Express*, September 26 was more realistic:

> . . . We arrived in Cincinnati Sunday Morning, and were ordered to Kentucky immediately. We were sent four miles out on the Lexington Pike and quartered one night in the woods. When we came to issue our ammunition, we found our cartridges would not fit our guns; we drew more, and got another supply that would not fit, and the next day we were ordered in line of battle without ammunition; then marched three miles and slept on our arms at Camp King. Next day we marched across the Licking River where we camped two days in the mud; up to this time we had neither knapsacks or haversacks, and the men slept one night in the open air without blankets or anything to eat.
>
> Here one indefatigable Quartermaster overtook us with . . . ammu-

nition to fit the guns.

The 85th Indiana was placed in a temporary brigade created by Lew Wallace to defend Cincinnati. With four other regiments, it was organized as the Third Brigade of the Cincinnati Defenses, commanded by Brigadier General Stanhope, an Ohio officer who was assisting Wallace. William Herron of the 85th Indiana wrote back to say that, after testing the regiment, Stanhope had placed it on the extreme right, the post of honor and danger.[13]

The 19th Michigan and the 22nd Wisconsin arrived at Cincinnati a short time after the 85th Indiana, and thus three of the four regiments that were to form Coburn's brigade were with Wallace's forces around the city.

After leaving Dowagiac September 14, the 19th Michigan had come by rail through Michigan City, Lafayette, Indianapolis, Shelbyville, and Lawrenceburg in Indiana, and the train finally arrived at Cincinnati about 8:00 PM, September 15. The next day the regiment moved west by rail to a place called Gravel Pit, Ohio, on the Ohio-Indiana state line, where the men disembarked and went into camp. The Ohio River was quite shallow at this point, and one of the duties of the 19th Michigan was to guard this crossing. The regiment was also assigned the task of picketing and guarding the other crossings of the Ohio River from Cincinnati to a point west of Lawrenceburg, a distance of about twenty-two miles.[14]

September 16 the 22nd Wisconsin had received orders to move by rail to Cincinnati. It arrived there the following evening and was quartered in a former German beer garden. The regiment remained there until September 22 when it was ordered to Kentucky. At noon that day, the men had their last dinner in Cincinnati at the Fifth Street Market, and then they started for the Ohio River.[15]

Meantime, Wallace, desperately trying to prepare for the defense of Cincinnati, had found that ferrying troops across the river from Ohio to Kentucky was not satisfactory, and he ordered the construction of a pontoon bridge, which was to be formed by lashing empty coal barges together, side by side, and anchoring them on both banks. The 22nd Wisconsin crossed the river on this bridge and entered Covington, Kentucky. While the troops were passing through Cincinnati and Covington, they marched in regular order, with the bands playing. At about a half mile south of the city, the order "Arms at Will" was given, and the men were no longer required to keep step, and could carry their arms as they wished.[16]

About sundown, the regiment halted for the night on a high hill near the Lexington pike about three miles south of Covington. It was quite cold that evening, but the men got out their blankets and overcoats and passed a fairly comfortable night on a barren and dusty former campground.[17]

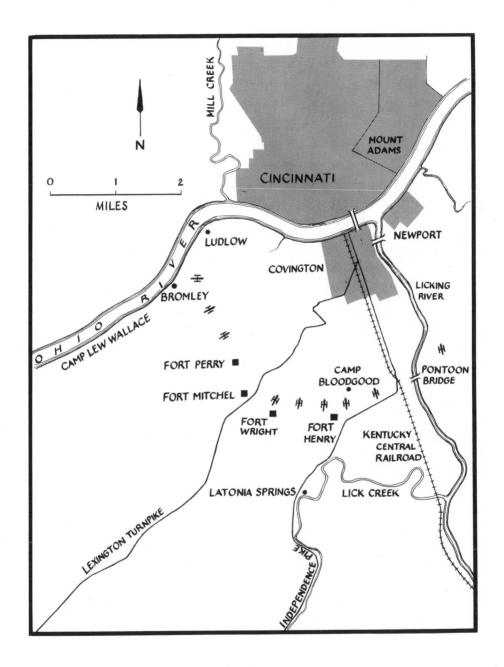

Defenses of Cincinnati

The camp was a little south of Fort Mitchel and on the opposite side of the pike. The fort was an earthwork, extending on both sides of the pike, in front of which for about a mile all the trees had been cut down to give an unobstructed view and a clear range for the guns. Both Fort Mitchel and the later nearby town of Fort Mitchell were so named to honor the memory of Major General Ormsby McKnight Mitchel. The name of the town, however was misspelled, and for this reason the name of the fort is also frequently incorrectly called Fort Mitchell.[18]

On the afternoon of September 24, the 22nd Wisconsin marched back to a point about a mile east of Fort Mitchel, and there, on a hilltop covered with grass and trees, established a new camp called Camp Bloodgood for Lieutenant Colonel Edward Bloodgood of that regiment.[19]

On the morning of September 25, companies A, D, and F, of the 22nd Wisconsin, under the command of Bloodgood, moved out for duty on the picket line. They marched back to Fort Mitchel, then south about a mile on the Lexington pike, and halted about a mile south of the fort. There Bloodgood posted his pickets along a road that crossed the pike at a right angle. Most of the houses in the area were deserted, and while off duty the men visited orchards and fields of sweet potatoes. Headquarters was established at the foot of a large haystack, and some of the men had a soft bed to sleep on for the first time since leaving Racine.

September 26 the pickets of the 22nd Wisconsin were relieved without having seen the enemy, and they returned to the hill where they had camped. The regiment remained in camp there for about ten days, spending much of the time in drill and camp duties.[20]

When the 22nd Wisconsin arrived in Kentucky, it received orders to report to Brigadier General Andrew J. Smith, and on October 7 broke camp and moved to Camp Smith on the Lexington pike. There, on October 16, the regiment was attached to Colonel Peter T. Swaine's Second Brigade of Brigadier General Stephen G. Burbridge's First Division of Major General Gordon Granger's Army of Kentucky.[21]

In the early part of September 1862, Horatio G. Wright reported that there were 40,000 troops in the vicinity of Cincinnati, with the numbers changing daily, and he needed a number of good generals before they could be organized into an effective fighting force. During the month, the following officers were sent to command troops near Covington.[22]

Gordon Granger, who was commanding a division in the Army of the Mississippi near Corinth, was ordered to reinforce the Union forces in

Kentucky with a brigade of his division. After a brief stop in Louisville, Granger moved on without his brigade to Cincinnati, where he arrived September 12. On September 17 he was assigned to duty in the Department of the Ohio.[23]

On September 7 Brigadier General Andrew J. Smith, who had been Halleck's chief of cavalry at Corinth, Mississippi, was ordered to report to General Wright in Cincinnati, and there, on September 9, he was assigned to duty with Wallace in Covington.[24]

September 15, Brigadier General Quincy A. Gillmore, then serving in South Carolina, was ordered to Cincinnati, where he was assigned command of the Union forces at Florence, Kentucky, just south of Covington.[25]

Andrew J. Smith relieved Wallace on September 18, in command of the United States forces in the vicinity of Newport and Covington in Kentucky. Wallace was then ordered to Columbus, Ohio.[26] September 29 Wright ordered Burbridge, who was then in Cincinnati, to report to Andrew J. Smith at Covington. [27]

As the Union forces, including the regiments soon to make up Coburn's brigade, gathered around Cincinnati during September 1862, Bragg's Confederate Army of Mississippi steadily moved northward through Tennessee and Kentucky toward Louisville. At Lexington, Kentucky, E. Kirby Smith divided his army, sending Brigadier General Henry Heth's Second Division of the Department of East Tennessee northward to threaten Cincinnati, and the other two brigades to Shelbyville, where they would be in position to move on Louisville if Bragg approached that city. Smith remained with the rest of his command at Lexington to await the arrival of Bragg's army.[28]

Heth was at Cynthiana, Kentucky, September 7, 1862, with orders to move northward and threaten Covington. On September 10 however, he was ordered not to attack unless supported by a force commanded by General Humphrey Marshall, who had been ordered forward from Abingdon, Virginia. The next day, when it became apparent that Marshall would not arrive for some time, Heth was ordered not to risk battle but to withdraw to the vicinity of Falmouth and Williamstown. Heth reached Walton, about eighteen miles south of Cincinnati, and then, conforming to orders, he began to withdraw his division on September 13. He first retired slowly to the vicinity of Williamstown and Falmouth, and then moved further back and reached Georgetown a few days later.[29]

One of the major concerns of the administration and the military authorities in the North during the Confederate invasion of Kentucky was the absence from the state of Major General Don Carlos Buell's Army of the Ohio. At the beginning of the invasion, Buell's army was along the Memphis and Charleston Railroad, with headquarters at Huntsville, Alabama, and with some troops in south central Tennessee. Buell had reached his headquarters on his return along the Memphis and Charleston Railroad from Corinth. Cautious and strong-willed, Buell moved only when sorely pressed or ordered. He did not seem to sense how vulnerable he was.

When General Braxton Bragg began his advance from Chattanooga, the Army of the Ohio moved from northern Alabama into south central Tennessee, and Buell established his headquarters at Decherd, Tennessee. Buell made no effort to stop Bragg's army as it moved forward into Kentucky, but he did keep pace as it marched north. On September 5, the same day that Bragg arrived at Sparta, Tennessee, Buell's army reached Murfreesboro. Buell then moved on to Nashville and remained there until he was certain that Bragg did not intend to attack that city. Bragg did not move toward Nashville, but instead marched northward from Sparta and on September 12 reached Glasgow, Kentucky. That same day, after leaving sufficient troops to defend Nashville, Buell left the city with the rest of his army and marched toward Bowling Green, Kentucky.[30]

On September 14 an advance brigade of Bragg's army arrived in front of the Union works at Munfordville, Kentucky, which were defended by troops commanded by Colonel John T. Wilder. The brigade unwisely attacked and was strongly repulsed with serious losses. Bragg then moved up with his entire army from Glasgow and, with help from Brigadier General Nathan B. Forrest's cavalry, surrounded the defenses of Munfordville. The garrison finally surrendered on September 17, and two days later, when Buell's army approached from the direction of Bowling Green, Bragg moved toward Bardstown, Kentucky, where he arrived September 22, 1862. By marching to the east toward Bardstown, Bragg left the road to the north unguarded, and Buell promptly marched toward Louisville. His leading troops arrived there September 25, and by September 29 the Army of the Ohio was safely within the defenses of Louisville.[31]

Buell immediately reorganized his Army of the Ohio into three corps, commanded as follows: First Corps, Major General Alexander McD. McCook; Second Corps, Major General Thomas L. Crittenden; and Third Corps, Major General Charles C. Gilbert. Major General George H. Thomas was assigned as second in command of the army.[32]

September 28 Bragg left Major General Leonidas Polk in command of the Confederate Army of the Mississippi at Bardstown and hurried on with his staff to Lexington to join E. Kirby Smith. From that place, on October 2 Bragg ordered Polk to move with his army to Lexington, and directed Smith to concentrate his forces at the same place for a celebration to accompany the inauguration of Richard Hawes as the Confederate Governor of Kentucky.[33]

On October 1 Buell began his advance against the Confederate forces in Kentucky, which was to end with their departure from the state. He sent Brigadier General Joshua W. Sill's division of McCook's corps and Brigadier General Ebenezer Dumont's unattached division eastward toward Frankfort, and with the rest of his command he moved southward toward Bardstown, where Bragg's army was encamped.

Polk marched his Confederates from Bardstown on October 3, but, being aware of the presence of Sill's and Dumont's forces on the Frankfort road, he moved toward Perryville, Kentucky, instead of in the direction of Lexington as ordered. Arriving at Perryville, Polk left there a part of his command and moved on with the rest to Harrodsburg. When Buell reached Bardstown and learned of Polk's departure, he immediately followed toward Perryville with Gilbert's corps and arrived east of the town on the evening of October 7. The other two corps came up during the night and the next day. Bragg, learning of Gilbert's arrival at Perryville, sent Polk back with a division to reinforce the troops left there and to attack Gilbert. The Battle of Perryville was fought October 8, after which Bragg and Kirby Smith began the Rebel withdrawal from Kentucky and started on the long march back to Knoxville, unmolested by Federal forces.[34]

Meanwhile, on October 3, George W. Morgan, whose division had been struggling northward through Kentucky after its evacuation of Cumberland Gap, finally arrived on the Ohio River at Greenup (Greenupsburg), Kentucky. There he crossed the river into Ohio, and, marching by way of Portsmouth, moved to Oak Hill (also called Portland), where he went into camp.[35]

On October 7 Granger, who had recently arrived from Mississippi, assumed command of all United States forces then operating in Kentucky on the line of the Licking River and extending from the Ohio River southward in the direction of Lexington. Wright designated Granger's command as the Army of Kentucky, Department of the Ohio. As new regiments, batteries, and detachments arrived from the several states of the department, they were incorporated into, and organized with, the forces of Granger's command that were already assembled around Covington and Newport. Granger established his headquarters at Covington.[36]

Wright had assigned Andrew J. Smith to the command of the United States forces at Covington, directing him to move forward with his troops as soon as preparations were completed and to take positions at Falmouth, about thirty miles south of Covington, and also at such points on the road from Falmouth to Williamstown that he found suitable for encampments. Wright further ordered Smith to occupy Williamstown with a force sufficient to watch and hold the roads running into that town. Burbridge's division, which included the force near Walton, was to march on the Lexington pike, and Green Clay Smith's division was to take the Falmouth Road, passing through Independence.[37]

October 8, 1862, Burbridge, leading the advance, moved out with his First Division on the road toward Williamstown. Colonel Utley's 22nd Wisconsin Regiment moved south with this column to Williamstown as a part of Swaine's Second Brigade of Burbridge's division. Also that day, Green Clay Smith's division marched southward through Independence. October 9, it went into camp at Falmouth. Colonel Baird's 85th Indiana marched south from near Latonia with Smith's division as a part of Colonel Frederick W. Moore's First Brigade, and October 9 it arrived at Falmouth and camped with the brigade, building railroad bridges and doing provost and picket duty. The regiment's principal occupation, however, was drilling—drilling by squads began before breakfast, then company drill lasted from 10:00 to 11:00 AM, and battalion drill from 2:00 to 4:00 PM. Dress parade was held each day at sundown. John B. Dowd of the 85th Indiana noted that every evening many young ladies of the community visited the camp of the regiment to watch the dress parade, which they seemed to enjoy very much.[38]

Granger did not accompany the Advance, Army of Kentucky on its march to Falmouth and Williamstown, but remained at Covington to complete the organization of his army. October 10 Wright relieved Absalom Baird from duty with Morgan's division, then at Oak Hill, Ohio, and ordered him to report with his staff to Granger. Baird reported at Granger's headquarters the next day and was assigned command of all the troops then in and around Covington, with orders to organize them and prepare them for the field. The troops under his command later became the Third Division, Army of Kentucky. When Baird left Oak Hill for Covington, Colonel Coburn of the 33rd Indiana assumed command of his Twenty-Seventh Brigade of Morgan's division, and Lieutenant Colonel James M. Henderson assumed command of the 33rd Indiana.[39]

At the beginning of the Civil War, Henderson was teaching in what was then the Morton Academy at Princeton, Indiana. When hostilities began, Henderson enrolled and became captain of a company of infantry organized at Princeton, which became Company F of the 33rd Indiana, with Henderson as its lieutenant colonel.[40]

October 11 Major General Jacob D. Cox relieved Gillmore, who was then at Point Pleasant, Virginia, in temporary command of the District of Western Virginia. Gillmore returned to Cincinnati, where he was ordered to Covington to report to Granger. On October 13 Andrew J. Smith, commanding the Advance Forces, assigned Gillmore to the command of the First Division, Army of Kentucky, which consisted of all United States forces then present in the neighborhood of Williamstown. Gillmore assumed command, relieving Burbridge the next day.[41]

October 13 the 22nd Wisconsin marched to Camp Gilmer on Eagle Creek, and it remained there in camp for three days.[42]

The 19th Michigan Regiment, on duty along the Ohio River west of Cincinnati, did not accompany the initial advance of Granger's army, but on October 14 it moved to Cincinnati by rail, then crossed the river on the pontoon bridge and went into camp in the valley of the Licking River, about two miles south of Covington.[43]

Also October 14, at Wright's direction, George W. Morgan ordered the 33rd Indiana, 14th Kentucky, 19th Kentucky, and the 9th Ohio Battery, all under the command of Coburn, to move from Oak Hill to Cincinnati. Wright also directed the remainder of Morgan's force to move to Point Pleasant, West Virginia. October 15 Wright ordered the commanding officers of the 14th Kentucky and 33rd Indiana, who had just arrived in Cincinnati, to cross the Ohio River to Covington and report to Granger.[44]

The organization of Granger's Army of Kentucky, as of October 16, 1862, was as follows:[45]

First Division, Quincy A. Gillmore
    Second Brigade, Peter T. Swaine
    Third Brigade, Charles C. Doolittle

Second Division, Green Clay Smith
    First Brigade, Frederick Moore
    Second Brigade, Joseph W. Vance

Third Division, Absalom Baird
    No brigade organization given.

Note: In this organization the 22nd Wisconsin was attached to Swaine's brigade, the 85th Indiana to Moore's brigade, and the 19th Michigan to Baird's division. The 33rd Indiana had not yet joined the army.

October 16 Granger began to move his army forward in two columns from its advanced positions south of Covington. Gillmore's First Division advanced on the Lexington pike from Williamstown toward Georgetown, and on October 24 Green Clay Smith's Second Division left Falmouth and marched toward Cynthiana on the road that ran near the Covington and Lexington Railroad (The Kentucky Central Railroad). The 85th Indiana marched with Frederick W. Moore's brigade of Smith's division to

Cynthiana, and after its arrival there it moved on and went into camp near
Paris, Kentucky.[46]

Harvey Reid, in his *The View from Headquarters*, describes the following
incident:

> Our camp here [Williamstown] was in the rear of a large farm
> house, and to gain the turnpike, we passed through the barnyard and
> a lane. Our regiment marching out, halted in the lane, the rear guard
> opposite the negro quarters. They had stood there but a few minutes,
> when a "darkey" boy, about 17 years old, ran out and expressed a de-
> sire to go with us. The guard boys immediately took him into the ranks,
> put an overcoat on him, drew a large glazed havelock over his cap, gave
> him a gun, and he was a soldier as natural as life. His master soon
> missed him, came around to the negro quarters and asked another
> darkey, "Whar's George." (I have it from the darkey himself) "I tole
> him, 'I dun no' an' I was alookin at George all de time." He then went
> to the barn to look for "George" and this darkey and George's little
> brother (about 14) took the opportunity to decamp also. They were
> dressed in the same way, and placed in the middle of the ranks, closely
> surrounded by the boys, while "Massa" was looking around in the
> wagons, and up and down the ranks to find his "niggers." When the
> column started, Major [Edward D.] Murray, fearful that he ["Massa"]
> should recognize them as they passed by him, engaged him in con-
> versation, and attracted his attention in another direction as they were
> passing, He ["Massa"] mounted a horse and followed the troops to
> Williamstown, two miles distant, and, while passing the rear guard of
> our regiment at rest, he might have seen three soldiers sitting with their
> faces to the fence, surrounded by a crowd of others, so disposed as
> almost to hide them, all talking and laughing most unconcernedly, but
> if he saw them he mistrusted nothing and after swearing around
> Williamstown a while, went back home 3 niggers poorer. . . . George
> and his brother Johnnie are now in our company, Johnnie being the
> Captain's waiter, and George belongs, for the present, to the rest of
> the Company. "Abe" is in Company B . . . .[47]

On October 18 Gillmore was at Jones, on the Lexington pike, and on
the other road, Green Clay Smith was at Cynthiana with a part of his division. The next day Gillmore moved south from Jones toward Big Eagle
Creek and Georgetown, and arrived that day near Big Eagle Creek. The
22nd Wisconsin accompanied this column. Also that day, October 19, Green
Clay Smith had the 85th Indiana, three hundred cavalry, and a section of
artillery at Paris; two regiments at Cynthiana; and the rest of his division at
Falmouth.[48]

In Kentucky

October 18 Absalom Baird left Covington with his Third Division, Army of Kentucky, including the 33rd Indiana and the 19th Michigan, and moved toward Lexington. The 19th Michigan left its camps south of Covington and, passing through Florence and Crittenden, reached Falmouth October 21.[49]

On October 20 and 21 the 22nd Wisconsin moved with Gillmore's division to Georgetown.[50]

October 24 the final day of the march to Lexington, was a rough day for the men of the 22nd Wisconsin. There had been significant traffic on the pike between Georgetown and Lexington; and, as the morning wore on, the sun became hotter and a very high wind came up. The dust was so thick that the men could scarcely see the length of a company.[51]

The regiment passed on through Lexington, with its many fine stores and public buildings, and appeared to have been quite a wealthy city. It finally went into camp at the fairground southwest of the city.[52]

On the morning of October 24 the 19th Michigan resumed its march in a southwesterly direction along the line of the railroad, and, passing through Cynthiana and Paris, it went into camp near Lexington October 28.[53]

On October 27 Granger established his headquarters at Lexington and placed Gillmore in command of the city.[54]

When the 33rd Indiana arrived at Covington from Ohio it was badly in need of new clothing and equipment of all kinds. When these were supplied, the regiment set out to join the Army of Kentucky. It arrived at Georgetown, near Lexington, October 30.[55]

When the soldiers left their encampments around Covington and moved southward into the interior of Kentucky, it became more difficult for them to receive news from home. A couple of announcements that appeared in the *Daily Wabash Express* indicate one of the methods used to send mail to the men of the 85th Indiana while on this march.

> Maj. Wm. C. Lupton, who is in the city [Terre Haute], requests us to say to the friends of the 85th Regiment that any letters left at the store of Simeon Cory for the members of that regiment, before 3 o'clock this afternoon [October 14, 1862], will be taken to them.[56]
>
> James A. Modesitt, Quartermaster Sergeant of the 85th Regiment, who is now here [Terre Haute], will return to his regiment on Monday of next week. We are requested to say that he will take all letters and small packages which those having friends in the regiment may desire to send, if left at the jewelry establishment of Mr. Tillatson, previous to the time of his departure.[57]

As the army approached Lexington, the autumn weather became disagreeable. On October 25, while the 85th Indiana was in camp near Paris, Kentucky, it began to sleet and snow. Captain Jefferson E. Brant of the 85th Indiana wrote:

> We awoke in the morning to see what we had never seen in Kentucky in October the whole face of nature around us veiled in the snows of the approaching winter. We shivered around our Camp-fire until about 9:00 o'clock when we struck tents and started through snows and wind and spent a Sabbath as we had never spent it before.
>
> We marched 14 miles before night, trudging through mud most of the way nearly shoe mouth deep.
>
> Last night was the coldest since we left home. The ground was frozen hard this morning when we started on our march but the sun came out and the snow melted in a hurry.[58]

The men of the 22nd Wisconsin built fireplaces by digging a hole in the corner of the tent and covering it with sheet iron, if available, or with flat stones. They then extended the hole or trench to the outside of the tent and built there a chimney of sod.[59]

October 30 the 22nd Wisconsin marched from its camp at the fairground southwest of Lexington to join the 85th Indiana, the 19th Michigan, and the 33rd Indiana regiments, which were at Sandersville, about three miles north of Lexington. That day these four regiments were organized into a new brigade, which was assigned to Colonel Coburn.[60]

By the end of October 1862 all of the troops that earlier had assembled near Covington had moved on to positions at Lexington and Frankfort and at other posts in that part of the state. Only one regiment remained at Covington. According to the commissary, rations were issued October 30 to seventy-three infantry regiments of the Army of Kentucky within twenty-five miles of Lexington.[61]

This initial march of the army from Covington to Lexington, with full equipment, was one of great hardship for the men. The country just south of Covington was very rough and difficult, with the road running over a long succession of hills so steep that it was often necessary to double the mule teams. At times the soldiers had to push the heavily laden wagons up the slopes. At the same time other soldiers moved along with the wagons carrying stones to chock the wheels during the frequent halts.

To add to the difficulties of the march, there had been no rain in that part of Kentucky for several months. As a result, water for the men and animals was very difficult to find. When water was available it was often barely fit to drink. The men marched through clouds of dust during the entire day.

In addition, the men were forced to carry a burden of about forty pounds: one Springfield rifled musket, ten pounds; one cartridge belt and box, three pounds; forty rounds of cartridges, five pounds; one knapsack and strap, three pounds; one blanket, three pounds; one great coat, four pounds; one poncho, two pounds; one canteen with water, two pounds; one haversack with three days rations, three pounds; one shirt, one pair of drawers, one pair of socks, two pounds; and incidentals, three pounds.

Many of the marching men were forced to fall out of the ranks because of exhaustion, illness, and sore feet; and units from the columns were detached to pick up these stragglers. Later, some of the soldiers were permitted to place their packs on the wagons, and some of men were carried on the wagons and in ambulances. In the 19th Michigan, for example, from forty to eighty men were excused every day from carrying knapsacks because of ill health; ten or twelve rode in ambulances; and sometimes as many as forty men rode on the wagons. The two-horse ambulance used at that time carried eight or nine men, seated on benches, and, of course, the driver.[62]

When the 85th Indiana was encamped at Falmouth more than one hundred of the men were in the hospitals. By this time, however, the soldiers had, or were getting, tents and had been drilling, marching, doing picket and provost duty, and building bridges. As a result they were better prepared for field duty.[63]

The tents used early in the war were of two types: the "A," or wedge tent, and the Sibley tent. The "A" tent could accommodate five or six men. Both types of tents were carried on wagons and were therefore unsuitable for the rapid movement of troops. They were eventually replaced by the shelter tent, or pup tent; and the Sibley tent was used thereafter for permanent camp and garrison use.[64]

At Lexington, Granger completely reorganized his Army of Kentucky as follows:

First Division, Andrew J. Smith
  First Brigade, Stephen G. Burbridge
    83rd, 96th, and 118th Ohio, and 23rd Wisconsin
  Second Brigade, William J. Landram
    77th, 97th, and 108th Illinois, and 19th Kentucky

Second Division, Quincy A. Gillmore
  First Brigade, Green Clay Smith
    112th Illinois, 18th and 22nd Michigan, and 45th Ohio

Second Brigade, Samuel A. Gilbert
   44th, 100th, 103rd, and 104th Ohio

Third Division, Absalom Baird
   First Brigade, John Coburn
      33rd and 85th Indiana, 19th Michigan, and 22nd Wisconsin
   Second Brigade, Peter T. Swaine
      92nd, 96th, and 115th Illinois, and 14th Kentucky [65]

Coburn's new First Brigade of Third Division was commonly referred to by his name, although later it would be given other designations and at various times would be commanded by other officers. These same four regiments would continue to serve together until the end of the war.

While the brigade was encamped near Lexington, some of the officers became involved in problems relating to runaway slaves. Colonel Baird of the 85th Indiana Regiment acquired a young Negro to act as his body servant, but under the laws of Kentucky this boy was soon taken from Baird and confined in the jail at Paris. Baird threatened to use his regiment to secure the release of his servant, but he was restrained from taking such action by General Absalom Baird. After the owner of the slave reclaimed him and took him away, Colonel Baird sent Captain William T. Crawford of Company H to follow the boy, basing his claim on the disloyalty of the owner. The boy was then brought back and continued to serve as Colonel Baird's servant without further trouble until a few weeks later when he was taken across the Ohio River into Indiana. Finally, the owner of the runaway slave, who was notoriously disloyal, sued Baird for compensation. With the help of a lawyer, Baird won the suit.[66]

A runaway slave, who had been given refuge in the camp of Colonel Utley's 22nd Wisconsin, was found by his owner, but Utley refused to give him up. The slave was still with the 22nd Wisconsin when the regiment left the state and moved into Tennessee. The owner sued Utley in the United States Court in Kentucky, and when Utley was served with the process, he allowed judgment to go by default against him. (After the war, when Utley had returned to Racine, Wisconsin, he was again sued and was compelled to pay the judgment. Later, Congress passed an act to reimburse Utley for the money spent in this case).[67]

After Bragg's and E. Kirby Smith's departure, General Wright decided to leave Granger's army in Central Kentucky to prevent Confederate forces from moving back into the state, and on November 7 he ordered Granger to move south and cover the country between Cumberland Gap and Big Creek Gap. Four days later, Wright ordered Granger to occupy Danville or

Harrodsburg with a Northern regiment from Baird's division.[68]

November 10 Wright directed Andrew J. Smith to move with his First Division, Army of Kentucky, which was then at Nicholasville, Kentucky, to Memphis, Tennessee. After Smith's departure, the Federeal Army of Kentucky consisted of only Gillmore's and Absalom Baird's divisions, which were encamped near Lexington.[69]

Granger ordered Baird to move with his division, to which Coburn's new brigade belonged, to replace Smith's division at Nicholasville. Baird moved promptly, and November 13 Coburn's First brigade struck its tents in the Blue Grass region around Lexington and moved there that day. Nicholasville was then the terminus of the Cincinnati and Southern Railroad and therefore of considerable military importance. After an untroubled march of fifteen miles, the brigade arrived at mid-afternoon and again went into camp. The troops were not cheered by the appearance of the town of about 2,000 inhabitants, which was dirty, old, and dilapidated.[70]

On September 12 Swaine's 99th Ohio regiment was transferred from his Second Brigade, Third Division of the Army of Kentucky to the Army of the Ohio, with Swaine remaining in command of the Second Brigade. Later, however, Swaine was sent to rejoin his regiment, and Colonel John C. Cochran of the 14th Kentucky relieved him in command of the brigade.[71]

Baird established headquarters of his Third Division at Nicholasville, although the 115th Illinois regiment of Cochran's Second Brigade was absent at Richmond, Kentucky, and 92nd Illinois regiment was at Mount Sterling.[72]

While the 85th Indiana was encamped with the rest of Third Division near Nicholasville, there were about two hundred Negroes within the Union lines. To avoid further difficulties involving the local citizens and runaway slaves, Lieutenant Colonel Alexander B. Crane of the 85th Indiana, acting as provost marshal, issued orders that no one was to go out of the town.[73]

Despite these precautions, Colonel Baird seems to have created a problem by attempting to send a Negro home with his wife, who was visiting him at Nicholasville at that time. This event is described by William Neet, a private in the 85th Indiana, in a letter written to his wife, Eliza, in late November 1862.

> . . . Since i commenced this letter well I must tell you that our colonel beard [Baird] is about or has got in a Snap by undertakeing to Send a negro home with his wife[.] She started with him and was taken up by a regiment of Kentucky Union Soldiers [18th Kentucky] and the darky was put in jail and the woman [Mrs. Baird] sent back and last night the colonel raised the regiment [85th Indiana] and if there had been wood and water to of run the cars through they would have had a general row but they had

to come back to quarters without any fite [.] . . . you had better believe the Col was warm and as tight [drunk] *as warm*[.][74]

November 17 Granger was assigned command of the District of Central Kentucky, with headquarters at Lexington.[75]

In late November and December 1862, Company A of the 22nd Wisconsin of Coburn's brigade was detached to Hickman's Bridge on the Kentucky River to guard the crossing there. The company rejoined the regiment at Danville December 27.

December 1, while the 85th Indiana was still at Nicholasville, Jessie Burr Crawford, the wife of Adjutant Francis C. Crawford, on behalf of the ladies of Terre Haute, presented to the regiment a beautiful regimental flag. Following the presentation, the brigade had its first grand review in which the four infantry regiments, two batteries, and a detachment of cavalry took part. These were reviewed by General Wright and General Baird.[76]

By Thanksgiving Day 1862, which was about three months after the regiments of Coburn's brigade, except the 33rd Indiana, had been mustered in, the men had spent all their money. The last pay that the men of the 85th Indiana had received was August 14, 1862, at Camp Dick Thompson and amounted to two dollars premium and twenty-five dollars bounty. On September 12, at Dowagiac, the men of the 19th Michigan had received an advance bounty of twenty-five dollars, but had received nothing since.[77] United States Army Regulations mandated that the troops were to be paid so that the arrears should not at any time exceed two months unless circumstances made it impossible.[78]

Colonel Gilbert of the 19th Michigan, noted in a letter dated December 5 that at that time there was not ten dollars in the entire regiment. Some of the men wrote to their wives asking for money, and further asking them to borrow money if necessary to sustain them until the paymaster arrived.[79]

The reporter from *The Daily Wabash Express* who was with the 85th Indiana sent the following report:

> We are looking anxiously for the Paymaster, but he hasn't turned up yet, and to reveal the painful truth, the regiment is dead broke, financially crushed; green backs have taken wings and fled, to be known only among the things that were, and as for small change, if one of our men found a piece of the filthy lucre about him he would be as much of a curiosity as an honest army contractor. The only circulating medium we have are Shannon's Sutler Checks, and it is amusing to see the look of disappointment on a well dressed officer's face when a newsboy refuses a Sutler's Check for a Cincinnati paper; the . . .

washer-woman refuses to take them for washing and there is a profusion of tightly buttoned coats, but then what is the use of a clean shirt— it will get dirty again.[80]

Some pay was forthcoming January 1 when the paymaster arrived at Danville and paid each of the men $20.85 for two months of service. When debts had been paid, the men sent money home to their families, and were left with but little cash.[81]

December 10 the 33rd Indiana and 85th Indiana of Coburn's brigade left Nicholasville and marched by way of Camp Dick Robinson to Danville, Kentucky. Two days later General Absalom Baird followed and established headquarters of his Third Division, Army of Kentucky at that place. Also present were the 92nd and 96th Illinois regiments of Cochran's brigade of the division. December 14 Coburn, with the 19th Michigan and the 22nd Wisconsin of his brigade, followed the other two regiments of the brigade to Danville. While there, the 85th Indiana furnished heavy detachments for picket and guard duty and also for the protection of the bridges over the Kentucky River and the Dick's River.[82]

On December 13 Company I of the 85th Indiana was ordered to guard the bridge over Dick's River, about five miles from Danville. It remained there until ordered to Nicholasville December 26, and it arrived there the next day.[83]

During the latter part of their stay in Kentucky, in the early, cold winter of 1862, the men of Coburn's brigade suffered severely from exposure and sickness. The hospitals were filled with men afflicted with measles, typhoid fever, diarrhea, pneumonia, and colds that developed into pneumonia.[84]

The extent of this problem is illustrated by the reports from the 85th Indiana and the 19th Michigan. During its stay in Kentucky, the 85th Indiana lost fifty-three men by death from disease. One man died at Covington, eight at Lexington, seven at Nicholasville, twenty-eight at Danville, one at Camp Dennison, one at Hickman's Bridge, and seven at places not recorded. In addition, four men died in the hospital at Danville after the brigade departed for Tennessee.[85]

Early in December 1862, while the brigade was at Nicholasville, the surgeon of the 19th Michigan reported that 160 men and five officers of the regiment were sick. According to this report, seventeen men were in the post hospital at Nicholasville, twenty-three were in the regimental hospital, and thirty men were sick in their tents but were able to walk to the hospital for medicine. In addition, there were ninety men sick in hospitals in the rear at Lexington, Covington, and Cincinnati.

During the stay of the 19th Michigan in Kentucky, thirty-four men died of disease. The regiment suffered its first loss at Gravel Pit, Ohio, on October 5 while on duty along the Ohio River, and six more men died that month. Four more died in November; sixteen in December, mostly at Nicholasville; and seven in January 1863. Three more men, who had been left behind when the brigade moved to Nashville, Tennessee, died in February 1863.[86]

Similarly, Chaplain Bradley of the 22nd Wisconsin reported that during the regiment's stay at Nicholasville and Danville, there were times when there were hardly enough men who were well to take care of the sick. He further added that the water was not fit to drink.[87]

There was sickness in all regiments of the army, but the new regiments generally suffered most from the communicable diseases, because they had not at that time been in the field long enough to have developed the necessary immunity against such diseases. For example, on November 13, 1861, the 33rd Indiana marched to Crab Orchard, Kentucky. Soon after the march began, a heavy, cold rain set in and it continued to pour for the next few days. Less than a month after this march, 511 men of the 33rd Indiana were sick and in hospitals, and by the end of the following month sixty-two of these men had died of disease. By comparison, however, during the fall and winter of 1862, only two men of that regiment died at Nicholasville and one died at Covington.[88]

On December 22 John Hunt Morgan set out from Alexandria, Tennessee, with about 3,100 men on his Second Kentucky Raid. He crossed the Cumberland River at Sand Shoals Ford that evening and moved toward Glasgow for a raid on the Louisville and Nashville Railroad. He arrived at Glasgow December 24 and continued on through Munfordville to Elizabethtown, which he captured December 27, with about 650 prisoners. The next day Morgan moved to Muldraugh's Hill, where he burned the large trestles on the railroad, and then moved back through Springfield, Columbia, and Burkesville toward Tennessee. He recrossed the Cumberland River January 2, 1863, and halted at Smithfield three days later.[89]

When Morgan appeared in Kentucky, Colonel William A. Hoskins, commanding the post of Lebanon, Kentucky, feared a movement in his direction, so he telegraphed Absalom Baird at Danville for reinforcements of infantry and a battery. On Christmas Day, in response to Hoskins' request, Baird ordered Lieutenant Colonel James M. Henderson to march the next day with the 85th Indiana, the 19th Michigan, and a battery of artillery to Munfordville, Kentucky.[90]

In a typical march, such as the one to be made by Henderson, it was difficult to have a regiment on the road early in the morning. The men needed time to prepare coffee and eat breakfast, and everything needed on the march had to be packed up and loaded on the approximately thirty wagons needed for a regiment. About sixty mules had to be harnessed and hitched to these wagons. If the night was dark, and it was dark before Henderson's march began, fires were built so men could see. At Danville a barrel of salt pork was set on fire and this illuminated the entire camp. There were further delays that morning when some of the troops were forced to wait for the road ahead to clear before they could pass through the town, so it was fully 9:00 AM, December 26 before Henderson's entire column was on the move toward Lebanon.[91]

Shortly after the march started, it began to rain, and all that day it continued to come down in torrents. Finally, after plodding through the mud and rain for fourteen miles, and covering less than one-third of the distance to Lebanon, the men camped, wet and tired, near the battlefield of Perryville. The 85th Indiana camped in a little valley at the foot of a high hill. The men soon had their tents up, and, using straw from a nearby stack, had fixed comfortable beds for the night. They had finished their evening meal and were relaxing when the skies opened with one of the hardest rains that many of the men could remember. In just a few minutes, water stood in many of the tents six inches deep, causing the men to hurry to higher ground. Finally, after the water had drained out of the tents, they carried in rails and put them on the ground inside, covering the rails with straw and blankets. They slept well for the rest of the night.

Ironically, about nine o'clock that night a courier arrived from Danville with a dispatch from General Granger ordering Henderson to return with his command to Danville.[92]

On December 28 a short time after Henderson's return, Baird issued new orders directing him to move again toward Lebanon, this time with the 33rd Indiana and the 19th Michigan. The column was scheduled to march at 7:30 AM, but at 5:30 AM these orders were countermanded; the 33rd Indiana and the 22nd Wisconsin regiments were directed to march instead. The following day these two regiments moved to within a few miles of Lebanon but then were ordered back to Danville. After marching about three miles in the direction of Danville, orders were again changed; the two regiments were directed to move back toward Lebanon. Finally, when Wright learned that there was already a sufficient force in the area to deal with Morgan, he ordered the 33rd Indiana and the 22nd Wisconsin regiments to return to Danville, where they arrived after an absence of three days.[93]

A short time after the 33rd Indiana returned to Danville, Company I was detached and sent to the Hickman's Bridge over the Kentucky River. For three weeks, this company cut and erected poles for a telegraph line from Nicholasville to the Dick's River Bridge, one mile west of Camp Dick Robinson. Company I remained in the vicinity of Hickman's Bridge until January 22, 1863, when it rejoined the regiment at Danville.[94]

During the rest of their stay in Kentucky, the men of Coburn's brigade were engaged only in routine activities, such as drilling, picket and guard duty, and inspections.

One event worthy of mention was a "Grand Military Mule Race," which took place January 1, 1863. The following program was issued to the soldiers:[95]

GRAND MILITARY MULE RACE, to take place on the drill ground, back of the 85th Indiana, January 1, 1863.

First Race, 10 o'clock AM, mile heat, running, 16 mules to be entered. Purse $2.

Second Race, 10 1/2 AM, mile heat, running, 16 mules to be entered, one from each team. Purse $2.

Third Race, 11 AM, mile heat, slow race, each competitor to ride his neighbor's mule, 16 mules to be entered. Purse $1.

JUDGES—Brig. Gen. [Colonel] Coburn, Col. Gilbert, 19th Michigan, and Col. Baird, 85th Indiana.

COURSE MANAGERS—Major Craig and Adjutant Crawford of the 85th Indiana.

RULES OF THE COURSE—No liquor allowed on the Course. Drunkenness severely punished. Betting except in sutler's checks forbidden—Strict military discipline will be enforced.

The soldiers assembled at about 10:00 AM, and the band of the 22nd Wisconsin entertained them as they waited for the race to begin. Then a bugle sounded, and sixteen untrained mules started down the track. The efforts to keep them on course were largely futile; most of them bolted off in the direction of the place they were last fed. Only four mules could be kept on the track to finish the race. Jimmy Wilson of Rockville, a member of Company B, won the first purse.[96]

Finally, on January 26, 1863, the regiments of Coburn's brigade completed their service in Kentucky and left Danville for Louisville on their way to reinforce Rosecrans' army in Tennessee.

The arduous responsibility of command is reflected in John Coburn's countenance.

Colonel John Coburn

Chapter 3

Movement to Tennessee

After Brigadier General Nathan B. Forrest returned to Tennessee from his raid into Kentucky, Major General Henry W. Halleck, General in Chief of the Army, concluded that the only way to prevent such disturbances in Kentucky was to provide for the certain defeat of Major General Braxton Bragg's army in Tennessee. With this in mind, on January 10, 1863, Halleck directed Major General Horatio G. Wright, commanding the Department of the Ohio, to secure the Louisville and Nashville Railroad, concentrate sufficient forces at a few points to deal with any disturbances in the department, and send all available forces to Major General William S. Rosecrans, commanding the Department of the Cumberland, at Murfreesboro.[1]

January 20 General Wright announced the composition of the force that was to be sent to Tennessee and assigned Major General Gordon Granger to its command. Many of the troops selected to accompany Granger were taken from his Army of Kentucky, and these consisted of Brigadier General Absalom Baird's Third Division; the 18th and 24th Kentucky regiments from Brigadier General Quincy A. Gillmore's Second Division; three batteries; and the 2nd Michigan, 9th Pennsylvania, 6th Kentucky, and 9th Kentucky cavalry regiments. Other troops selected were Colonel William P. Reid's infantry brigade, which was at New Haven, Kentucky; four regiments from West Virginia under Brigadier General George Crook; the 78th Illinois Infantry; and the 12th and 16th Kentucky infantry regiments. These troops were to assemble at Louisville as soon as possible and were then to move by way of the Ohio and Cumberland rivers to Nashville as soon as transportation could be provided.[2]

January 25 Granger, at his headquarters at Lexington, turned over the command of the District of Central Kentucky to Gillmore, and the next day began the movement of his troops toward Louisville.[3]

Colonel John Coburn's First Brigade of Baird's Third Division, Army of Kentucky, was included in the troops to accompany Granger to Tennessee, and on January 26, the brigade left Danville and marched north through Nicholasville and Camp Dick Robinson en route to Louisville. The route followed by Coburn's brigade ran generally through Harrodsburg, Hardensville, Claysville (Clay Village), Simpsonville, and Shelbyville to Louisville.

Snow and sleet fell on the men as they marched through slush and mud. Nevertheless, they completed their march of about seventy-five miles and arrived at Louisville January 30 after only four and a half days on the road.[4]

At the time, this was considered a rapid march. It is interesting to note, however, that a man walking alone could have reached Louisville from Danville in two to two and a half days, but a soldier marching in a regiment or brigade moves much slower. When a soldier marches in the ranks, his movements are governed by those of a thousand or many thousands of other men. He does not stop to rest when he is tired, but only when told to do so, and he may not be rested when orders come to move on. His heavy and tightly buttoned clothing, a belt and shoulder straps, a gun, and heavy loads suspended from his shoulders further interfere with his movements. The general rate of "heavy marching" is about two miles per hour, with a rest of ten minutes every hour. This is least fatiguing to the soldier.[5]

The Kentucky Negro question was reaching a fever pitch. Before Granger's column reached Louisville, slave owners who were looking for escaped slaves stated that they would take every slave found with the troops as they marched through the city, even if they had to use force to do so. When the brigade began its march the next day, the men were ordered to fix bayonets, and they continued on through the city without interruption to the steamboat landing at Portland, across the Ohio River from New Albany.[6]

Some Negroes who had accompanied the 85th Indiana from Danville were taken on board the transports with the soldiers, but orders soon came to put them ashore. After some protesting, this order was obeyed, but Mrs. Caroline Coburn, who was present with the regiment, aided in concealing some of the officers' servants in a room by covering them with saddles and harnesses that had been stored there. Some of the men of the 85th Indiana assisted Mrs. Coburn in getting the servants across the Ohio River into Indiana.[7]

Beginning on February 1 the 85th Indiana, and the other regiments of Coburn's brigade, embarked with the rest of the army for the long journey down the Ohio River to the mouth of the Cumberland River and then up that river to Nashville. The transports left Louisville as they were ready, with instructions to rendezvous at Fort Donelson.

The fleet consisted of fifty-four transports, all that were available at Louisville, six gunboats, and a number of barges. Except for the very large *Jacob Strader*, the transports were lashed together in pairs, with the gunboat *Lexington* in the lead, and another gunboat bringing up the rear. Aboard the flagship *Prioress* were General Baird and his staff and fourteen paymasters with about $4,000,000. The *Prioress* was lashed to the *Hazel Dell*, which contained the Signal Corps, and these transports were in the center of the fleet—in a column steaming in close order, about two and one-half miles long with Coburn's brigade dispersed as follows: the 33rd Indiana, with a part of the rest of the brigade, took passage on the *Ella Faber* and the *Horizon*; the 19th Michigan was on the *Ohio No. 3*; the 85th Indiana was on the *Fort Wayne* and *Horizon;* and the 22nd Wisconsin traveled on the *Champion*, with the men occupying every available space.[8]

The sight of the long line of vessels, loaded to the gunnels, carrying the army to Nashville, was one to be long remembered. Bands played lively music as the boats moved along the river on their trip of 340 miles to the mouth of the Cumberland River and then over two hundred miles up to Nashville.[9]

It was far from a pleasant trip, however, and many of the men had to sleep on crowded, freezing decks.[10]

After the arrival of the fleet at Nashville, on February 24, 1863, William Neet of the 85th Indiana wrote of this part of the trip as follows:

> . . . *the river trip was a hard trip on the boys[.] it was in time of that cold spell the first week of the month and it was not one bit better than it would be laying in the barn with all the doors open and the floor wet and froze[.] well they piled up just like hogs and of a morning they was covered completely with frost and snow but I got to lay in the cabin but on the floor and I would have like to have that privilege all the time[.]*[11]

The fleet arrived at Evansville about noon on February 3 to gather supplies and remove the sick to hospitals. This done, the convoy resumed its course down the Ohio and reached the mouth of the Cumberland that night. The boats immediately began taking on fuel, but before they were finished, orders arrived to hurry on up the Cumberland to Fort Donelson.[12]

February 3 Confederate Brigadier General Joseph Wheeler arrived near Fort Donelson with his cavalry command, Brigadier General John A. Wharton's brigade and a part of Nathan B. Forrest's brigade. That afternoon Wheeler advanced and attacked Colonel Abner C. Harding's 83rd Illinois Infantry, which occupied a strong position at the town of Dover near Fort Donelson. After some severe fighting, this attack was repulsed, and late that evening Wheeler withdrew to await the coming of morning to renew the attack. Granger's transports and the gunboats arrived at Fort Donelson the next morning, and, when Wheeler learned that reinforcements and gunboats had arrived, he withdrew his command under heavy fire from the gunboats and moved to the south.[13]

The fleet remained at Fort Donelson for two days and then continued on its journey toward Nashville. Before leaving, all men were put under arms and carried cartridge boxes filled with ammunition. The gunboats moved ahead of the transports and everyone was ready for action, but there was no further interruption. The fleet arrived at Nashville February 7-8. The 22nd Wisconsin lost one man who fell overboard from the *Champion* and was drowned.[14]

Before the troops could go ashore, it was necessary to reassemble the wagons, which had been taken apart for the trip, and to unload the vessels and load the wagons with everything brought from Kentucky.[15]

Because so many soldiers had camped near the city and left behind so much filth, it was difficult for the men of Coburn's brigade to find decent campsites, but they finally disembarked and marched to a point about three miles south of Nashville, where they pitched their tents and camped for the night on the Franklin pike.[16]

Before the war, Nashville, situated on the south bank of the Cumberland River, was a lovely city of about 30,000 inhabitants. In the suburbs were many fine homes with beautiful gardens and delightful parks. When Granger's men arrived, however, all of this had been largely destroyed by the occupying armies, and the entire city was one great military camp.

Surgeon Wilson Hobbs of the 85th Indiana, in a letter home, described the city of Nashville at the time of the arrival of Coburn's brigade.

> . . . its happy homes are desolate; peaceful industry and enterprise have deserted its busy streets; the demon of war has made complete conquest of the city, and has made her and her beautiful environs one grand encampment for armed men. Her institutions of learning, places of public worship, and more spacious mansions, are hospitals for the sick and wounded, and prisons for her disloyal citizens. Her storehouses and streets are filled with army supplies and "tramping squadrons."
>
> A respectable lady is not found on the streets—of females, only negroes and prostitutes.—But few wooden fences are left for miles away, and even they are melting in our camp fires.—The stone fences are many of them demolished to facilitate military evolutions . . . from every hill top for miles around . . . foundations of fine homes have been removed to procure sites for forts.
>
> . . . The parks, for years cultivated with improved husbandry, around palatial residences, are hewn down and shaped and fitted into forts and breastworks. . . . [17]

Very few of the inhabitants remained in the city; they had been forced to move out into the country to obtain food. Some soldiers of the 22nd Wisconsin found only one public house open, and they reported that it would have been unfit to enter in any other city they had ever been. A breakfast that was barely edible cost one dollar. The streets of the city were narrow and indescribably dirty, and there was virtually no business except that done through the United States Government.[18]

Coburn's brigade remained near Nashville until February 21, when it marched to Brentwood, Tennessee, a small station on the railroad, about midway between Nashville and Franklin. The brigade went into camp there on the northern edge of what might properly be called a "no man's land." There was so much activity by Rebel cavalry and guerrillas in the country to the south that the men were ordered to be in a constant state of readiness for an attack. Every day each regiment of the brigade mounted a guard of forty-eight men and their officers to protect the camp. In addition, a detachment of forty men and officers were sent to guard a nearby bridge, and another thirty-five officers and men were detailed as pickets. Two or three times a week, each regiment sent out two companies with wagons and an escort on foraging expeditions; a section of Aleshire's 18th Ohio Battery was sent out with each foraging party.[19]

Samuel Mattox, a soldier of the 85th Indiana, described the area around Brentwood ". . . as a beautiful part of the world, but the families are suffering here for the necessities of life. The rebels armies have passed through here so much they have stripped them of everything they have. What they did leave belonged to the Secesh and I would not be surprised if we took what they have before we leave here."[20]

By 1862 the people from Indiana, who had once rallied to the call, solemnly came to realize that this war was the most difficult struggle ever encountered by Americans. Citizens and politicians were expressing their unrest by questioning the way the war was being managed, and the unity and nonpartisanship shared at the beginning of the war had turned into dissent and heated political warfare. Issues of the continuing privations and losses in the war, the newly instituted draft, and a political struggle of Oliver Perry Morton with rebellious Democrat legislators in Indiana caused the men of the 33rd and 85th Indiana regiments, then in the field at Brentwood, Tennessee, to reaffirm their confidence in, and fidelity toward, the Governor, the State of Indiana, and the Union. Near the end of February 1863, an overwhelming majority of noncommissioned officers and men of the 85th Indiana passed and adopted a declaration reflecting their position, which was that they were ready at the call of the government to go home and stamp out all treasonable activity in the state.

In summarizing the reactions of the officers and men of the 85th Indiana to the resolutions, *The Daily Wabash Express* offered the following information: Of the company officers of the 85th Indiana, thirteen were Democrats and seventeen Republicans. The regiment also had dissenters, and perhaps this discord, plus the fact that so many members of the 85th Indiana were known to be Democrats, further caused them to express their loyalty toward governor, state, and country. Out of the thirty-nine commissioned officers, thirty-three endorsed the resolutions, four were away from the regiment at the time of ratification, and two officers, Captain William T. Stark of Company C and Captain William D. Weir of Company F, refused to endorse them. (It was reported that Captain Stark was under arrest on a charge of encouraging desertions within his company.) The four who were absent were captains Abner Floyd and Lewis Puckett and lieutenants Hiram L. Tillotson and Jacob F. Hoke, and they had no opportunity to see the resolutions. All privates and noncommissioned officers endorsed them.[21]

The brigade remained at Brentwood, doing picket duty and guarding the railroad until March 2, 1863. Coburn then received orders to move at once to Franklin, Tennessee, which was threatened by a cavalry force under Major General Earl Van Dorn at Columbia, Tennessee. The brigade left its camps at Brentwood about mid-afternoon of that day and moved south on the Columbia pike toward Franklin, about ten miles distant. As the column approached the town and the enemy, the troops became more vigilant. They were kept under arms and issued more ammunition.[22]

The enemy had burned a bridge over the Little Harpeth River north of Franklin, and this caused some delay, but finally Coburn was able to cross. At about 10:00 that night, the brigade moved into Franklin and reported to Brigadier General Charles C. Gilbert, commanding the U. S. Forces at that post. Coburn left behind Company B of the 33rd Indiana, Company D of the 85th Indiana, Company D of the 19th Michigan, and companies E and F of the 22nd Wisconsin to protect the river crossing in the event that he might be forced to retreat.[23]

Coburn's brigade remained in camp all the next day, with the 85th Indiana encamped on Harpeth Heights. It is interesting to note that at that time, after about six months in the service, sixty men of the 85th Indiana had died, although the regiment had not been in combat. The challenge of battle, however, was just around the corner.[24]

Chapter 4

Battle of Thompson's Station

On the morning of March 3, 1863, Major General William S. Rosecrans, commanding the Department of the Cumberland at Murfreesboro, sent through his chief of staff, James A. Garfield, later President of the United States, the following order to the commander of the United States forces at Franklin, Tennessee:[1]

Franklin, Tenn., March 3, 1863

Brig. Gen. C. C. Gilbert:

> The general commanding directs you to send a brigade and a sufficient cavalry force to-morrow on the Columbia pike as far as Spring Hill. Send out a party from there toward Columbia, and one through to Raleigh Springs, on the Lewisburg pike. A cavalry force from here will communicate with your party at that place some time during the day after to-morrow. We desire to know what is in our front. Take a forage train along. Have you any news?
>
> J. A. Garfield
Brigadier-General and Chief of Staff

Gilbert received Garfield's order that evening, and at 11:00 that night, issued the following order for the march the next day:[2]

Special Order No. 15.   Head Quarters United States Forces, In Camp near Franklin Tennessee, March 3, 1863

> VI. Colonel [John] Coburn, with his brigade and battery and 600 cavalry, will to-morrow morning, at 8 o'clock, proceed along the Columbia pike as far as Spring Hill, and send out a party from there toward Columbia and one through to Raleigh Springs, on the Lewisburg pike, where a cavalry force from Murfreesboro will communicate with it on the ensuing day.

VII. Colonel [Archibald P.] Campbell will furnish the cavalry from the three regiments. Colonel [Oliver H.] Payne, one hundred and twenty-fourth Ohio, with his regiment, will report to Colonel Coburn, to accompany this command. Four days rations will be taken, two in the haversacks and two in the wagons.

A forage train of eighty wagons will accompany the expedition. Only 4 wagons to the regiment and 2 to the battery will be allowed.

By order of Brigadier-General Gilbert
George R. Speed
Lieutenant and Acting Assistant Adjutant General

The infantry accompanying the expedition consisted of Colonel John P. Baird's 85th Indiana, Lieutenant Colonel James M. Henderson's 33rd Indiana, Colonel Henry C. Gilbert's 19th Michigan, and Colonel William L. Utley's 22nd Wisconsin, all belonging to Coburn's brigade; and Payne's 124th Ohio Infantry, which belonged to a brigade at the post of Franklin. (At that time Lieutenant Colonel James Pickands was in command of the regiment, while Payne was in command of the brigade.) The six hundred cavalrymen were detached from the 9th Pennsylvania, 4th Kentucky, and 2nd Michigan regiments, all commanded by Colonel Thomas J. Jordan of the 9th Pennsylvania Cavalry. For artillery, Gilbert selected Captain Charles C. Aleshire's 18th Battery, Ohio Light Artillery, with six Rodman rifled guns. Coburn commanded the entire force of 2,837 officers and men. Captain William Reeder's Company D of the 85th Indiana Regiment was left to guard the camp and did not accompany the expedition.[3]

Marching in Coburn's brigade that day there were 1,845 effective men: 606 men in the 33rd Indiana, not including those on details and absent sick, 330 men in the 85th Indiana, 378 in the 22nd Wisconsin, and 531 in the 19th Michigan.[4]

About 9:00 on the morning of March 4 the entire command moved out from its camps near Franklin and marched southward on the Columbia Turnpike toward Spring Hill. The order of march that day, from front to back, was as follows: 2nd Michigan Cavalry, 33rd Indiana, Coburn and his staff, three guns of Aleshire's battery, 22nd Wisconsin, 19th Michigan, and the 124th Ohio on the left of the 22nd Wisconsin, later to support the artillery. The 85th Indiana, though disgruntled by this assignment, was placed in rear of the wagon train, with a company of the 9th Pennsylvania cavalry and the rest of Aleshire's guns. This force remained there during the day guarding the train.[5]

The men were in light marching order that morning, without knapsacks or tents, and in good spirits. Coburn, in his report, stated that the weather was "cool and favorable," the road was good, and the column moved rapidly forward. Others, however, who marched with the brigade that morning have left a different impression of the weather. A private in Company A of the 85th Indiana noted that the morning was very cold and snowing; a private in Company I of the 33rd Indiana also wrote that the morning of March 4 was cloudy, cold, and snowing; and Harvey Reid, a soldier of the 22nd Wisconsin, described that morning as "freezing cold." The country ahead was rough with a succession of swells and ridges ranging from fifty to two hundred feet in height, and, except directly along the line of the road, the men could see no more than a half mile to their front.[6]

Meanwhile, early in January 1863, General Joseph E. Johnston had ordered Major General Earl Van Dorn to move with his available cavalry in northern Mississippi to Middle Tennessee to aid Braxton Bragg in opposing any advance of the Union forces in that area. The head of Van Dorn's column arrived at Columbia, Tennessee, February 20, 1863, and there it joined Brigadier General Nathan B. Forrest's cavalry brigade, which had been encamped there for some time. Van Dorn's command then consisted of four cavalry brigades of fifteen regiments and four batteries of artillery, first designated as Van Dorn's Cavalry division and later as First Cavalry Corps. Van Dorn then led his command across the Duck River and a short time later encamped near Thompson's Station, with pickets well to the front toward Franklin to watch for any Federal movement from that direction.[7]

On the morning of March 4, Van Dorn set out with Brigadier General William H. Jackson's division of his command on a forced reconnaissance toward Franklin. Thus, he was moving directly toward Coburn's column, marching south from Franklin on the same road.[8]

At 10:30, after advancing about four miles, Coburn's skirmishers encountered the advance of Jackson's column. Coburn immediately directed Jordan to deploy his cavalry and advance to the right of the turnpike. At the same time, he formed the 33rd Indiana, the 22nd Wisconsin, and a section of artillery on the right of the road, and placed the 19th Michigan and the 124th Ohio, with two sections of artillery, on the left of the road. The 85th Indiana was about a half mile to the rear with the trains.[9]

Aleshire opened fire with his four guns on the left of the turnpike about 10:40 AM and the enemy immediately replied. This exchange of artillery fire continued for some time, and Coburn ordered one of the sections to move to the left to protect that flank. While this movement was in progress, one of the guns was disabled when the axle-tree broke down. It was sent back to Franklin for repairs.[10]

Aleshire's battery continued in action for more than a half hour, then gradually ceased firing, after which the 33rd Indiana, the 19th Michigan, and the 22nd Wisconsin resumed their advance. They soon reached the hill on which the enemy had been posted, and there, for the first time, Coburn's men could see Van Dorn's position. The brigade occupied a small cluster of houses in the hollow between the hill and another high hill farther south, and the enemy's battery was placed to the left of these houses.[11]

Skirmishers of the 33rd Indiana and the 19th Michigan pressed on; when they reached the top of the high hill beyond the houses, they found that the enemy had departed.[12]

Coburn soon learned, however, that the enemy force, stronger than he had at first thought, was then attempting to flank him by way of the Lewisburg pike, about a mile to his left. He ordered his advanced forces to retire to their original positions. When this movement was completed, the men stacked arms and began to gather fence rails and start fires for boiling coffee. Coburn remained in this position about three hours, awaiting orders from General Gilbert in Franklin. During this time the men ate their evening meal.[13]

At about 2:00 PM, Coburn sent a messenger to Gilbert to report what had happened that day and to ask for instructions. He also suggested that the large train of about one hundred wagons might cause difficulties in his future movements. During the three-hour wait mentioned above, Coburn received Gilbert's response to his message. Gilbert did not send any instructions for Coburn's guidance, but he did send him the following order regarding the wagons: "I suppose you understand the object of the move; if forage train is likely to prove an embarrassment, send it back and go ahead."[14]

At about 5:00 PM, Colonel Baird, whose 85th Indiana was still guarding the train, started the wagons on the road toward Franklin, with thirty-nine of them filled with forage. This left Coburn with forty baggage wagons, loaded with camp equipage and ammunition.[15]

Later that afternoon, Coburn sent a second note to Gilbert:

> We are on the Columbia Road, and have repulsed a force of about 2,000 to 3,000 rebel cavalry. They have disappeared in front and are now flanking us on our left—that is on the Lewisburg Pike. They are now nearer than we are to Franklin. What shall I do? I think we can advance, but there will be a force in our rear.[16]

That evening as Coburn's men advanced, they passed through the small group of houses in the hollow mentioned above and found a man lying dead along the road near the gate in front of one of the houses. He had not been shot, but his face was covered with blood, which apparently had come from his nose. Seeing this death that had probably been caused by the concussion of a shell had a sobering effect on the men.[17]

It was near sundown when Jordan's cavalry scouts came in to report that they had found no enemy within two or three miles of Coburn's position. Coburn advanced his men about two miles to the high hill mentioned earlier and halted. From the information he had received up to 5:00 PM, Coburn believed that there was an enemy force not far ahead, but because of the lateness of the hour, he decided not to attack that day. He then ordered his brigade into camp for the night on the ground previously occupied by the enemy, with a strong picket in front of the camp. The men slept on their arms that night. The casualties for the brigade that day were two men slightly wounded. The 85th Indiana was not engaged.[18]

Soon after daylight March 5, two Negro boys about twelve years old, servants of officers in Van Dorn's army who had escaped, came into the Union lines with information about the strength of the enemy forces on the road ahead. They reported that Van Dorn and his entire command were just south of Thompson's Station. The boys were sent to Colonel Baird's headquarters, and later that morning they were sent on by Coburn to tell their story to General Gilbert at Franklin. Gilbert discredited this report, probably because it came from a "citizen-soldier," in whom he had little faith.

Coburn had no further communication with Gilbert that day and was, therefore, forced to make his own decision about what to do on the morrow. Although his situation was precarious, he believed his only choice was to move ahead as ordered.[19]

Coburn's troops were up and under arms at 4:00 AM, March 5, and at about 8:00 the brigade resumed its advance toward Spring Hill. Before describing the movements and activities of the troops that day, it will be helpful to describe briefly some of the more important features of the country ahead. For the most part it was broken and hilly and, in many places, covered with trees. It was not thickly populated, and the scattered farms were irregular in shape because of the hills and ravines. The occasional farmhouses along the road were occupied only by women and children, who watched the Union soldiers march by with obvious dislike.[20]

The Columbia Turnpike, on which Coburn's command was marching that morning, ran generally southward from where Coburn's brigade had bivouacked the night before. About a mile and a quarter farther south the turnpike came up to the crest of a high ridge, which crossed the road at nearly a right angle, running east and west. This ridge was broken up into a series of hills or knolls, some of which, on the east side of the road, were covered with thick growths of cedar. This ridge, on which Coburn later formed his command in line of battle, will be called the "first ridge" to avoid confusing it with other ridges crossing the road.[21]

As the turnpike approached the first ridge, it crossed a field on the floor of a valley lying between two ranges of hills until it came to a gap, no wider than an ordinary street, in the ridge at the end of the field. The road then ran through the gap.[22]

The Tennessee and Alabama (Central Alabama) Railroad ran south from Franklin, not far from the turnpike, and about one-fourth of a mile from the first ridge. It came up beside the road and ran along close beside it for several hundred yards through the gap, between two high hills that formed a part of the main ridge.[23]

On the south side of the first ridge, the ground sloped down onto an open plain or field, which was about a half mile wide and semicircular in shape. Much of this plain was under cultivation, and was crossed by about six lines of rail fence and one or two stone walls, which seriously impeded the passage of troops as they advanced.[24]

The road to Spring Hill ran south across this field, and the railroad curved to the right, past Thompson's Station, a small village consisting of a railroad depot and a few Negro huts. The station was situated near the middle of the field, about three hundred yards west of the turnpike and about five hundred yards south of the first ridge.

On the south side of the plain, beyond Thompson's Station, a row of hills formed a second ridge about three-fourths of a mile south of the first ridge. Thompson's Station was situated in the valley nearly halfway between the two ridges. Beyond the station and the open field was a thick woods. It was at this second ridge that Van Dorn formed his troops in line of battle to await the arrival of Coburn's brigade.[25]

The enemy troops facing Coburn that morning consisted of Forrest's cavalry brigade and William H. Jackson's Second Division of Van Dorn's First Confederate Cavalry Corps. Jackson's division was composed of the brigades of Brigadier General Frank C. Armstrong and Colonel John W. Whitfield. Brigadier General George B. Cosby's brigade of Brigadier General William T. Martin's First Division arrived later in the day, near the end of the battle.[26]

Jackson's division was in position on the second ridge, which crossed the Columbia Turnpike south of Thompson's Station. Whitfield's Texas brigade was positioned on the left, Armstrong's brigade was on the right, and Forrest's brigade, which was on the same line, extended out into the open fields to the right of Jackson's line. Captain Houston King's 2nd Battery, Missouri Light Artillery, was posted on the ridge on the extreme Confederate left, where it commanded the valley in front of Van Dorn's position for about a half mile. Jackson had advanced sharpshooters into the buildings near the depot at Thompson's Station and had formed a line of skirmishers along the railroad.[27]

As noted above, Coburn's command left its bivouac of the night before at 8:00 AM, March 5, and resumed its march toward Spring Hill. Troopers of Jordan's cavalry covered the front and flanks of the column. The 4th Kentucky Cavalry watched the Carter's Creek turnpike on the right and the Lewisburg road on the left, while the 9th Pennsylvania and 2nd Michigan cavalry moved out as flankers and skirmishers. One gun of Aleshire's battery advanced with the cavalry that morning, and Aleshire with the remaining four guns followed the 22nd Wisconsin Infantry, the leading regiment that day. The other regiments of Coburn's column followed Aleshire's battery in the following order: 19th Michigan, 85th Indiana, 33rd Indiana, and the 124th Ohio, which was in the rear with the wagon train. The skirmishers, carefully advancing through the woods for about a mile on each side of the road, became engaged soon after the advance began.[28]

When the 22nd Wisconsin arrived at a point about three-fourths of a mile from Thompson's Station, enemy artillery of Captain Huston King's battery opened fire. Utley immediately ordered his regiment, and the brigade, to halt and await orders from Coburn, who was up ahead on the road. The Wisconsin troops quickly climbed the fence at the side of the road and lay down in a field to escape the enemy fire. A short time later, orders arrived from Coburn for the brigade to continue its advance, and at about 10:00 AM, after marching about one-half mile, it arrived on the crest of the first ridge, or line of hills, north of Thompson's Station.[29]

When the head of Coburn's column came up to the crest of this ridge, King's battery again opened fire, and Coburn ordered Aleshire to place three guns of his 18th Ohio Battery on a hill to the left of the turnpike and the other two guns on the ridge to the right of the road. In this position, the guns were about fifty feet above the valley, commanding the fields, roads, and woods to their front.[30]

About 10:30 AM Coburn posted his infantry in line of battle to support the artillery. The 22nd Wisconsin, which was the leading infantry regiment that morning, was sent to the left to support the three guns that had been placed on the hill to the left of the turnpike. The regiment was formed behind a stone wall that ran in front of and a little to the left of the guns. In front of the guns was a small hill that was covered with cedar thickets.

The 19th Michigan was also placed to the left of the turnpike and to the left of 22nd Wisconsin. There, the men sought shelter from the Confederate artillery behind the same stone wall that covered the 22nd Wisconsin. The 33rd Indiana was deployed in line of battle on the ridge west of the turnpike to support the right of the two guns on that side of the road, and the 85th Indiana was formed to the right and rear of the 33rd Indiana, within supporting distance of the guns. That part of the ridge to the east of the turnpike, on which the 19th and 22nd was formed, was somewhat lower than the ridge west of the road where the 33rd and 85th Indiana regiments were posted.[31]

Some companies of Jordan's dismounted cavalry occupied a strong position in a dense thicket of cedars on the crest of a knoll some distance to the left of the 19th Michigan and 22nd Wisconsin, and the remainder of the cavalry was in position just to the rear of this knoll.[32]

The 124th Ohio was about one-third mile to the rear of the first ridge, where it was left to guard the trains.[33]

Shortly after Coburn's troops had taken position on the first ridge, King's battery opened fire, and Colonel Baird ordered his men of the 85th Indiana to lie down under the shelter of the crest of the hill.[34]

At about 11:30 AM, Henderson sent forward three companies of his 33rd Indiana to drive back to their main line the enemy's sharpshooters at Thompson's Station and the skirmishers along the railroad.[35]

About a half hour later, Coburn ordered the rest of the 33rd Indiana and the 85th Indiana, both under the command of Colonel Baird, to advance to Thompson's Station and take position there under cover of the depot and other buildings of the village. Coburn also ordered Baird to charge King's battery if it appeared that he would be successful.[36]

The advance of these two regiments is described by Baird as follows:

> These two regiments marched out from the cover of the hills, in columns of companies about six hundred yards, under a galling fire from the enemy's batteries, we being in plain view and having fences to tear down as we went, and wholly unable to return the fire by a single shot.[37]

When Baird's men reached the depot, they found Jackson's dismounted cavalry posted in the woods at the foot of the second ridge, directly between the depot and King's battery. These troops consisted of Whitfield's brigade and Colonel Samuel G. Earle's 3rd Arkansas Cavalry Regiment of Armstrong's brigade, which held the center and left of Jackson's line. They were strongly protected by a long stone wall, some fences, and thick underbrush.[38]

After an hour's cannonading, Baird's two regiments were ordered to charge and capture King's battery on their right. The men advanced at the double quick across a muddy cornfield and began climbing the hill toward the stone wall. When they had arrived within about two hundred yards of the wall, the enemy opened with a heavy fire and forced the men to fall back. Some of them took shelter behind the railroad embankment, which at that point ran nearly east and west in front of the depot, and others lay down under the cover of the buildings and fences about the depot.[39]

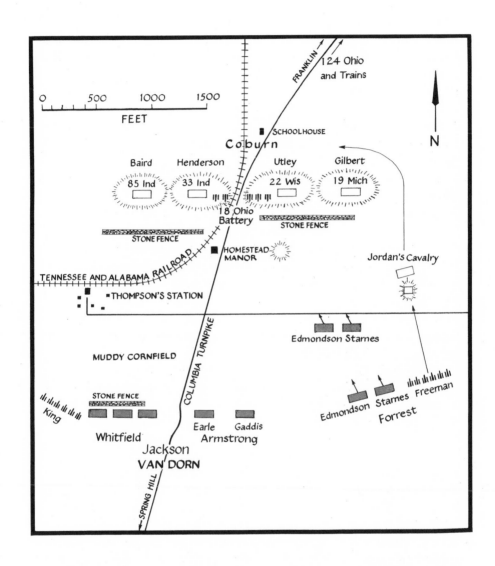

Battle of Thompson's Station, Morning, March 5, 1863

At about the same time that Coburn discovered the strength of the enemy beyond the station, he learned that a strong force of about one thousand enemy cavalry was advancing on his left, about one mile distant, near the Lewisburg pike. He immediately sent First Lieutenant Edwin I. Bachman of the 33rd Indiana, a member of his staff, with orders for Baird to retire to his original position on the first ridge. Coburn also ordered Jordan to bring up two companies of his cavalry to support the 33rd and 85th Indiana regiments as they retired across the field toward the ridge. Jordan departed, apparently to carry out his orders, but, oddly, he did not support the two Indiana regiments, and Coburn did not see him again that day, although he sent for him.[40]

Baird's two regiments moved back from the station in open order, and, while thus exposed, were subjected to heavy musketry fire and the fire from two pieces of King's artillery. John W. Whitfield's Confederate brigade and Colonel S. G. Earle's 3rd Arkansas Regiment pursued Baird's men vigorously as they sought to regain their former position on the first ridge, but, in spite of the enemy's efforts to prevent their escape, the Federals succeeded in reaching the crest in time to form in line of battle to the west of the turnpike. The left of the 33rd Indiana rested near the two guns of Aleshire's battery, and the 85th Indiana extended the line to the right, from the right flank of the 33rd Indiana. Whitfield and Earle crossed a stone wall at the foot of the first ridge and immediately launched an attack against the two Indiana regiments on the crest, but the attack was repulsed just short of the summit. Whitfield and Earle then fell back into the valley to make a stand behind the buildings and depot of Thompson's Station. They soon re-formed their men and were ready for a second attempt to drive the Indiana regiments from the ridge. The 85th Indiana lost two men killed and four wounded while crossing and recrossing the field during the attack.[41]

Elwood Hunt of Company A of the 85th Indiana, tells about the fighting at the crest of the ridge, in letter published in the *Rockville Tribune*, January 17, 1906:

> Captain Floyd of our Company A seized a gun and saying, "I can't stand this any longer, boys," fired the first shot, and where without orders, the company voluntarily turned and poured the first volley into the ranks of the enemy only a few feet distant.

Hunt further said that Adjutant Crawford, ". . . was there on his bob-tail bay horse, as he was always in the thickest of the fight." On arriving at the top of the ridge, Hunt was wounded in the elbow, tells of the following incident:

. . . I came face to face with Colonel Baird, sitting on his black stallion cheering on and directing his men, and what he was saying may be inferred from what he said to me. As I approached him I said, "Colonel, I am wounded, what shall I do?" Only understanding the last part of my remark, he answered me saying, "Just turn around there my boy and give them hell."

In his letter, Hunt also tells of his experiences in passing to the rear on his way to the hospital. This story is of particular interest because it provides some insight into incidents that happened during a Civil War battle other than killing.

. . . a mounted cavalryman, who was holding several horses of his comrades, who were dismounted and in line to the east of the pike, seeing my condition led a big horse up to the fence I had climbed upon, took my gun and helped me mount while some other wounded men mounted the other horses he was holding. He then started in a full run saying, "Follow me boys and I will take you out of this," which he did by coming back on the pike northward, in front of the enemy coming in from the east and firing upon us and the dismounted men, who were at this moment falling back to the pike.

Hunt also adds, significantly, "Here we also passed a company of cavalry already mounted and ready to retreat." He then continues his story of the horseholder.

As soon as we had passed the firing line and out of danger, he ordered us off and went galloping back with his horses to his company.

Hunt had not yet concluded the account of his wounding. He and others then walked on for a mile or two and then they came to a temporary hospital Dr. Hobbs had established at a large farmhouse. He then tells what happened:

. . . the Doctor met me in the yard as I walked up to the house. He ripped open my coat sleeve to see my wound and said, "Go to the house. I will be in presently and dress your wound."

During Baird's advance to Thompson's Station, Aleshire's guns kept up a steady fire, but, on being ordered to fire more slowly and carefully, they soon ceased firing altogether, and as Baird's men began to fall back toward the ridge, the guns began to leave their position.[42]

Coburn was properly concerned about the enemy column that had been seen moving to his left, and a short time after the 33rd and 85th Indiana had repulsed the attack on their front, he began to reorganize his defense. He ordered Colonel Baird to change the front of the 85th Indiana from south to east and to move forward in rear of the 33rd Indiana and take position parallel to and facing the railroad and the turnpike to prevent the enemy from advancing westward from the turnpike. Baird and the 85th Indiana set out on this mission immediately, leaving the 33rd Indiana in position alone on the ridge, facing south.[43]

The Confederate force that Coburn had observed moving to his left was Forrest's cavalry brigade, with six guns of Captain Samuel L. Freeman's Tennessee Battery. Forrest arrived with his command in front and to the left of the 19th Michigan and the 22nd Wisconsin about a half hour after these regiments had taken position on the first ridge to the Union left of the turnpike.

Forrest sent forward Colonel James W. Starnes' 4th [also called 3rd] Tennessee Cavalry and Colonel J. H. Edmondson's regiment to drive off the dismounted Union troopers who occupied the cedar knoll mentioned above. At the same time, he advanced with the rest of his command against Jordan's mounted force, which quickly withdrew to the rear of the infantry line. Forrest then sent forward Freeman's battery to occupy the hill just vacated by the Union cavalry. This was on the extreme Confederate right, far in advance of Forrest's first position, and from which point it completely commanded the left of Coburn's line. Freeman's Confederate battery opened fire at about the same time that Baird's regiments were ordered to withdraw from Thompson's Station.[44] The first shell struck the ground in the midst of the men of Company E of the 19th Michigan, but it failed to explode and fortunately no one was injured.[45]

Freeman's fire enfiladed the line of the 19th Michigan, and Colonel Gilbert, seeing that his position was much too exposed, ordered his regiment to form in column by division, close order, and move to the right and rear to a new position under the three guns of Aleshire's 18th Ohio Battery east of the turnpike. He then ordered the men to lie down to escape the effects of enemy fire. The artillerymen on the hill above Gilbert's new position turned their guns to face Freeman's battery and they opened fire.[46]

Gilbert's movement of his 19th Michigan occurred at about the same time that Jackson's division was pursuing the 33rd and 85th Indiana across the field from Thompson's Station and the subsequent attack on the two regiments when they reached the ridge west of the turnpike.[47]

As the Union right was being attacked, and before a serious attack had been made on the left, Jordan's cavalry disappeared, and Aleshire's artillery followed soon after. The departure of the cavalry and the artillery was a serious matter, and clearly some parts of Coburn's defense were at this point wanting. Immediately after Freeman opened fire on the 19th Michigan, Aleshire came up to Coburn and with much excitement, reported that his battery was out of ammunition and that it could not withstand the enemy's fire. Coburn sent Lieutenant Hamlet B. Adams of his staff to investigate. Adams tells of the incident as follows:

> . . . Colonel Coburn directed me to ascertain from the officers in charge of each ammunition box of the entire battery how much ammunition there was remaining. I did so, and reported to Colonel Coburn that there were 230 rounds of shell and 70 of canister. I also gave orders to the officers not to move the battery or any portion without orders.

So there was ammunition after all. What had Aleshire meant? After about twenty minutes of firing, Aleshire, without orders, withdrew the three guns from the hill above the 19th Michigan and sent them back down the pike to the rear. At about the same time, the two guns posted on the left of the 33rd Indiana started down the hill. When Coburn observed this movement, he ordered the men to hold their position and resume firing, but they ignored this order and moved on down to the pike and started northward toward the rear. Adams and Bachman, Coburn's two staff officers, who were on the ground at that time, attempted to rally the artillery and put it in position to assist in covering a retreat, if that became necessary. Adams was able to put a part of the artillery in position, but it soon departed, under orders from Jordan and Aleshire, without firing a shot at the enemy who were then pushing forward around Coburn's left flank. Neither the artillery nor the cavalry was seen on the field again that day.[48]

When the guns supporting the Union left departed, the 19th Michigan was left in an exposed position, and Colonel Gilbert moved the regiment a little to the right and around the hill from which the guns had just been withdrawn. He then took up a new position on the hill near, and facing, the turnpike and directly in rear of the 22nd Wisconsin.[49]

It should be noted that when the 19th Michigan first took position it was formed in a column by division, in which the companies were in columns two abreast. This became significant because, while this formation was well suited for the movement of the regiment, it was possible to mass a front of only two companies if attacked from either the front or rear. Surprisingly, although expecting an attack, the regiment was later left in a column by division formation in its new position.[50]

At about the same time that Gilbert moved his regiment, Utley learned that the enemy was approaching the front of his 22nd Wisconsin in large numbers just beyond the cedar-covered hill on his front. Utley immediately realized that the best place to receive this attack was from the cedar-covered hill; but it was also clear that if he advanced to that position his line would be raked from end to end by Freeman's artillery. He then decided that his only course was to fall back with his regiment to the hill in his rear and take the position recently occupied by Aleshire's guns east of the pike.[51]

Utley ordered Lieutenant Colonel Edward Bloodgood, who was on the right of the position occupied by the 22nd Wisconsin, to lead the regiment by the right flank to the brow of the hill just vacated by Aleshire's guns and to form a new line. When this movement was completed, the 22nd Wisconsin was in line, facing left and around the brow of the hill, and the 19th Michigan was in its rear some sixty paces down the slope and toward the right. The movements of these two regiments brought the two wings of Coburn's line closer together.[52]

At about the same time that Freeman commenced firing, Van Dorn ordered attacks on both the Union right and left, directing Forrest to move forward and, if possible, get in rear of the left of the 22nd Wisconsin and the 19th Michigan. He ordered Jackson to make a second attack on the ridge held by the 33rd and 85th Indiana regiments.[53]

To execute his order, Forrest dismounted Edmondson's and Starnes' regiments and placed Edmondson on the left and Starnes on the right of his line. He also directed Colonel Jacob B. Biffle and Lieutenant Colonel E. B. Trezevant, the latter commanding Colonel N. N. Cox's regiment that day, to form their regiments on the extreme Confederate right near the Lewisburg pike. This took more time than expected because when the orders came for these two regiments to move, they were dismounted and about two miles distant, and the men were about a half mile in advance of their horses. Biffle and Trezevant were directed to keep pickets and videttes well out on the pike to give early warning of the approach of Union troops from that direction.[54]

When Whitfield's Confederates were ready to make a second attack on the ridge held by the 33rd and 85th Indiana regiments, Armstrong's brigade came up, dismounted, and formed a line to the left of Forrest's brigade and on the right of Whitfield's line.[55]

On the Confederate right, as soon as Edmondson and Starnes had deployed their commands, Forrest's men moved forward to attack the 22nd Wisconsin and the 19th Michigan regiments.[56]

Because of its position in rear of the hill on which Aleshire's three guns had been posted, and also because of its positioning, the 19th Michigan was compelled to face Forrest's attacking force by the rear rank, and, as a result, only two or three companies of the regiment were able to return an effective fire as the enemy approached. The 22nd Wisconsin, however, was able to hold its position until Gilbert brought over two companies from the extreme right of his 19th Michigan to support the 22nd Wisconsin, and together they held their position on the hill for about twenty minutes.[57]

When the first enemy charge struck the line of the 22nd Wisconsin, Bloodgood fell back without orders, taking with him, from the right wing of the regiment, Company A and a large part of Company D, a total of about 150 men. When Utley saw Bloodgood leaving his position on the hill, he ordered him to halt, but because of the sounds of battle, Bloodgood apparently did not hear him. Then Utley, not having anyone to send after Bloodgood, ran down the hill himself in an attempt to stop him and bring his two companies back into line. The men of the regiment who had remained on the hill, however, believing that Utley too was falling back, quickly broke and followed, leaving the hill undefended.[58]

Utley finally reached the railroad, and there he was able to halt his men and form a line. He immediately began preparations to retake the hill, but then he saw a part of his regiment, again headed by Bloodgood, in full retreat northward on the turnpike. This left Utley with his weakened force on the extreme left of the Union line, where he could accomplish little. Only about thirty minutes had elapsed since the first enemy attack on the regiment's position on the hill.[59]

Shortly after the 22nd Wisconsin had fallen back from the hill to its position near the railroad, Coburn ordered the 19th Michigan, on the hill, to cross to the west side of the turnpike. There, it was to take a new position, with a slight change of front, on the crest of the ridge to the left of the 33rd Indiana. By chance, this was the same position to which the 85th Indiana had been assigned and which it was then approaching. When the line was completed, the right of the 19th Michigan rested on the hill near where Aleshire's two guns had formerly stood, near the left of the 33rd Indiana, and its left rested near a schoolhouse farther to the north on a ridge.[60]

When Colonel Baird's 85th Indiana reached its designated position after moving eastward from the right of Coburn's line, it found that the 19th Michigan was forming on the ground it was to have occupied. Baird then formed his regiment in line facing east with its right connecting with the 19th Michigan at the schoolhouse, facing the pike and railroad. What remained of the 22nd Wisconsin was beyond the 85th Indiana to the north. The line held by the 19th Michigan, and the 85th Indiana was at a right angle to that occupied by the 33rd Indiana, which was on the crest of the ridge where it had first formed, facing south.[61]

A short time after the 85th Indiana had taken its new position, Armstrong's Confederates attacked along the pike in an attempt to break Coburn's line at the point between the 19th Michigan and the 33rd Indiana. At about the same time, Whitfield's Rebels, advancing on the left of Armstrong, again

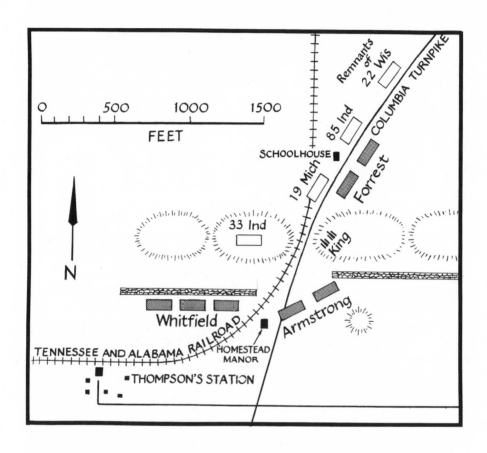

Battle of Thompson's Station, Afternoon, March 5, 1863

attacked the ridge held by the 33rd Indiana. Whitfield's men advanced in an irregular line through the woods, from tree to tree, and Baird's men, similarly protected by trees, resisted firmly. There was a fierce struggle for the crest of the hill, and at times the fighting was hand to hand, but finally, for the second time, Whitfield's troops were driven back to the foot of the hill, where they took protection behind the stone wall. The enemy suffered considerable loss in this attack, including Colonel Earle, who was killed.[62]

The fighting in front of the 33rd Indiana and the 19th Michigan was later described by Baird as follows:

> Our lines were hardly formed—the men laying down behind the crest of the hill—till Armstrong's brigade charged from the east, and the Texans from the south. The fighting was terrific. We reserved our fire until they were within thirty paces. Three times they gallantly charged up the hill from the east, and thrice we forced them back. In one of their charges the 19th Michigan captured the colors of the 4th Mississippi, and four prisoners, and we were so near each other that one man was shot by the soldiers of the 85th from the window of a school house as he was trying to get in the door.
>
> During the time one battery was throwing shells at us, and having got possession of the hill on the east of the road [from which the 19th Michigan and the 22nd Wisconsin had withdrawn], they [two pieces of King's battery] hurled grape and canister at short range like hail. Old soldiers on both sides say they never saw hotter work while it lasted.[63]

The Michigan troops kept up a heavy fire for some time from behind trees, and finally fixed bayonets and launched a furious charge. They drove Armstrong's brigade back down the hill to the stone fence, behind which Whitfield's Texan brigade was in line to the west of the road. In the hand-to-hand fighting that followed, a sergeant of Company C of the 19th Michigan jumped on the stone wall, bayoneted the color bearer, and brought away the flag of Whitfield's brigade. Whitfield's brigade then fell back to Thompson's Station.[64]

Captain Charles P. Lincoln of Company C, 19th Michigan Infantry, describes an act of bravery that he observed during this heated action:

> Here an incident illustrating personal courage and our admiration of it occurred. In the flight of the Texan brigade, an officer of Van Dorn's staff, well mounted, the last to retreat, stopped in his flight to protect with his horse and his person a wounded soldier from our fire, and to assist him from the field. This act of courage elicited a cheer

from many of our men, and an order "to cease firing at that officer."[65]

At this time Coburn's regiments were in line as follows: the 33rd Indiana remained in its position on the ridge, facing south, and the other regiments were on a line at a right angle to the 33rd Indiana, parallel to the railroad and facing east. The 19th Michigan was on the left of the 33rd, and the 85th Indiana was on the left of the 19th Michigan, with what was left of Utley's 22nd Wisconsin beyond the 85th Indiana to the north.[66]

Utley felt that the troops of the 22nd Wisconsin remaining with him were too few to recapture the hill, and that they probably would be unable to hold their position along the railroad if attacked, so he fell back with the remnant of his regiment over the hills to the left of the 85th Indiana. Bloodgood, with a few of his men, ultimately escaped to Franklin with the cavalry and artillery. The men with Utley became separated in the underbrush and a cane brake, and a few escaped, but the rest were soon surrounded and captured.[67]

The fighting on the Union left had lasted about one hour, giving time for Confederate Colonel Biffle and Lieutenant Colonel Trezevant to bring their regiments up to the front. Upon their arrival, they attacked and dispersed some of Coburn's troops moving on the pike and then formed in line on the Confederate right of the pike. Later, Forrest directed them to move to the rear of Coburn's brigade, and to take position between it and Franklin.[68]

Some time after Forrest's attack on the Union left began, Coburn ordered the train to turn back and return to Franklin. The cavalry, artillery, and 124th Ohio Infantry retired and took with them the ambulance train and the ammunition train; the rest of the brigade continued to hold the enemy for two hours after the ambulances had gone.[69]

When the fighting on the ridge ended with the repulse of Armstrong's and Whitfield's brigades by the 19th Michigan, the 85th Indiana, and the 33rd Indiana, Coburn's brigade changed front to the north and moved out by the left flank about three hundred yards into the woods on the crest of another line of hills. This brought the 85th Indiana once again on the extreme right of the brigade line.[70]

Here Coburn's men met Forrest's cavalry, which had gained the rear of their former positions by coming through the hills to the east. Forrest's troops occupied the entire slope of a deep ravine that lay directly to Coburn's front; its steep side was difficult to ascend. They were posted behind fences, trees, and in other favorable positions on a line that extended eastward from the left of Coburn's position, across the road, and to the right and rear of his position. Cosby's brigade of Martin's Confederate division finally arrived on the field, and it was placed in rear of the right of Coburn's line.[71]

Coburn then realized that he was nearly surrounded. Further fighting would be fruitless. His feelings at the time are best expressed in his own words as they appear in his report of the battle.

> . . . The brigade was formed in line, bayonets fixed, and all things made ready for a charge, under a galling fire, which cost us some of our best men. The men would willingly have made the desperate venture without a shot in their cartridge-boxes. Nothing remained but to give the word to charge.
>
> I was convinced that a massacre would ensue to little purpose; that a few might escape, but that many would fall in a vain struggle for life with unequal weapons. I ordered a surrender. I believed it was justified by the circumstances.

The surrender took place at about 4:00 PM.[72] This was, of course, a crushing event for the men of the brigade, who had fought well against superior numbers for about five hours. But in the end they had no choice. Coburn's brigade entered the battle that day with only 1845 effectives, both officers and men. There were about six hundred cavalry present, although they performed very little useful service, with Pickands' regiment numbering about four hundred men, but they were guarding the trains and not engaged. Van Dorn's forces, at the beginning of the battle, consisted of about 5,300 men, and Martin arrived later with about seven hundred men, bringing the Confederate total to about 6,000 men.

Colonel Baird's 85th Indiana took into action 303 non-commissioned officers and men, losing thirteen men killed and twenty-one severely wounded. Among the killed were Captain Abner Floyd of Company A; Corporal Salmon Lusk, also of Company A; and Sergeant Lloyd W. Conaway of Company I. It was particularly devastating to the men that Salmon Lusk, the pet and pride of Company A, was killed near the end of the battle, shot through the heart by a rebel bullet, and that Abner Floyd was mortally wounded by the last fire of the enemy. Floyd was left on a bed of straw in the hut of a Negro at Thompson's Station, where he had been taken, dying from loss of blood.

It is interesting to note that Floyd approached Elwood Hunt after the latter had been wounded but was still fighting. Seeing that Hunt was wounded, Floyd took off his haversack and hung it over Hunt's shoulder, saying, "Here Elwood, take this and go back, you are badly wounded, there is something to eat and you may need it; I will not have further use for it." As it turned out, he did not.

In addition to the actual losses in battle, the 85th Indiana also lost thirty men who died of exposure and mistreatment while in captivity, and one officer and five men were so disabled from the same causes that they were unfit for further service. Captain Lewis Puckett of Company K suffered a broken leg. Thus the total officers and men killed and wounded was thirty-four, and the number who died and were disabled was thirty-six, making the total loss resulting from the battle seventy officers and men.[73]

In the other three regiments of Coburn's brigade, the 33rd Indiana lost seventeen killed, fourteen mortally wounded, thirty-two severely wounded, and thirty-seven slightly wounded. The 22nd Wisconsin lost seven killed and nineteen wounded. The 19th Michigan lost twenty killed, thirteen mortally wounded, forty-two severely wounded, thirty-seven slightly wounded, and one missing.[74]

A battle that ends in defeat is always difficult to accept for those who lose, and a defeat that ends in surrender is even more so, because the officers and men who were engaged generally feel that they were stigmatized by their behavior. Indeed, this might in some degree be true. Certainly, there may be other explanations for what happened to the regiments of Coburn's brigade after the men had been exchanged and returned to the army in June 1863, but they were then assigned to garrison duty and as guards along the Nashville and Chattanooga Railroad. They saw no further active field service until the beginning of Sherman's campaign against Atlanta in May of 1864. The stigma seems to have been quite definite, and conscious on the part of higher-ups.

Naturally, one of the first things that the officers and men of Coburn's brigade did after their capture was to begin a determined effort to find out what had happened to cause the loss of so many good soldiers. The officers who managed to avoid surrender at Thompson's Station and who made their way back to Franklin were quick to provide excuses for their shortcomings and to defend their actions during the battle. Those who were captured and later confined in Libby Prison were equally energetic in attempting to fix the blame for their troubles on someone else. And of course, a battlefield has many fronts, many phases, and many observers, all of whom have their own points of view.[75]

Among the officers and men of the infantry there was, with good reason, the general feeling that the artillery and cavalry support units had let them down and were to blame for the disaster. The behavior of the artillery and cavalry during the battle has already been described, based on the best evidence available. But nothing has been said of the statements made by Jordan, commanding Coburn's cavalry, and Aleshire, commanding the 18th Ohio Battery. An uncritical reading of the offical reports of Jordan and

Aleshire leaves the reader with the impression that they both fought stubbornly throughout the day, but that they were unable to prevent the encirclement and ultimate surrender of Coburn's brigade. A careful reading, however, reveals that this simply is not what happened.

Both Jordan and Aleshire appear to have been trying to conceal what actually occured that day. The truth is that the infantry performed fairly well for green troops, but the cavalry and the artillery performed dismally.

Jordan tells the story of his part in the battle in his report to Gordon Granger, written at Franklin on March 6. He begins by expressing his opinion that Coburn's decision to advance the 33rd and 85th Indiana regiments to silence the Confederate battery in the woods beyond to Thompson's Station was a mistake. Then, referring to Coburn's order for the two regiments to retire to their former position, he continued:

> But it was then too late; the avalanche had been started, and came sweeping down upon it [the retiring column], while from behind a stone fence near the railroad a perfect storm of lead was thrown upon it [the retreating column]. Seeing that all was lost, I was ordered by Colonel Coburn to call in my cavalry and form it in such position as to cover his retreat.[76]

Jordan then said that he proceeded to execute his orders by forming his cavalry in rear of a small strip of woods about one-fourth mile in rear of Aleshire's battery. He further said that upon arrival there he saw the enemy infantry moving from the hill on which Freeman's battery stood in order to cut off his retreat and to capture Aleshire's guns and the wagon train.[77]

Continuing, he said that he directed a part of his cavalry to dismount and take advantage of such cover as fences and irregularities as the ground offered and to hold off Forrest's attack until he could withdraw the battery and be joined by Coburn's infantry. Then, to quote from his report, he added:

> . . . I at once ordered the battery to withdraw from the hill to the left of our position, as a swarm of rebel infantry were about to inclose it, and then dashed off to a hill on the right and withdrew the two pieces stationed there, and just in time, as the rebel line was within 60 yards of them and they entirely unprotected, the infantry, under Colonel Coburn, having retreated through the hills to the right of our position and in a directly opposite direction from the point I was holding to cover its retreat. After getting the guns under my protection, I waited (though my whole line was engaged with the enemy) at least fifteen minutes, hoping that Colonel Coburn would still come toward me, when, finding that the firing on my right was receding, while that

on my left was approaching, and nothing but stubborn resistance could save my flank, I ordered the retreat to begin.

For 2 miles my men sustained, with unflinching bravery, the repeated assaults of more than three times their number, while others could be seen at double-quick still farther toward my rear. As I withdrew my men from one position, I had at once to place them in new ones to repel fresh attacks.

. . . After about 2 1/2 miles, the enemy's infantry withdrew, finding that they were foiled in cutting off my retreat.

Had Colonel Coburn retreated by the Franklin road, not a man would have been lost. My column never moved a step till long after he [Coburn] was out of sight on the hills to my right.[78]

Jordan's statements are supported, in part, by Aleshire, who said in his report:

The conduct of the cavalry, under the command of Colonel Jordan, during the whole time, and particularly the retreat, was unexceptionable. Had it not been for their repeated efforts to drive back the enemy, neither my battery nor the wagon train could possibly have been saved.[79]

There are reasons to believe, however, that Jordan's claims of hard fighting by the cavalry were greatly exaggerated, if not totally fabricated. First of all, the reports show that out of a cavalry force of about six hundred men, only three were killed, one mortally wounded, six severely wounded, and ten slightly wounded, for a total of twenty casualties. By comparison, the 33rd Indiana lost a total of one hundred and nine men and the 19th Michigan one hudred forty-three. The losses sustained by the Union cavalry do not indicate hard fighting.[80]

Further, Colonel Gilbert of the 19th Michigan said in his report:

I beg leave to state, as a matter within my own personal knowledge, that our battery, the Eighteenth Ohio, Captain Aleshire, and the cavalry, under the command of Colonel Jordan, Ninth Pennsylvania, rendered no assistance after the infantry were engaged.[81]

Finally, the statement made by Jordan that he was attacked by three times his number while retreating for a distance of two miles is not supported by Confederate reports. Van Dorn certainly was not particularly impressed with the performance of Jordan's cavalry during the battle. He simply says, "The Federal cavalry, with one regiment of infantry, after offering some resistance, taking battery and baggage train with them, precipitately left the field." Further, Forrest makes no mention at all in his report of any pursuit of Jordan by his cavalry.[82]

In concluding his report, Jordan made a surprising statement. He said that on the retreat toward Franklin, he learned for the first time that an infantry regiment which had not been engaged was retreating from the field of battle ahead of the wagon train. It is difficult to believe that he was unaware of the presence of the 124th Ohio Regiment with Coburn's column that day, but, accepting that as true, his next statement is even more surprising. He said: "Had it [124th Ohio] remained upon the ground or sent to me for orders, I could not only have safely covered the retreat, but have given the enemy such a chastisement as would have made him more cautious in the future."[83]

Jordan's statement that he was unaware of the presence of Pickands' 124th Ohio becomes the more difficult to understand when we read Pickands' report of the battle. In this he makes the following statement:

> Near the close of the action, the train-master informed me that . . . he had been ordered to turn the train and move rapidly to the rear. At the same time vedettes, which were posted on a hill to the left of the road, instructed me that a heavy force was moving around the hill to cut off our retreat. The cavalry was then retreating, and I immediately caused the train and my regiment to move rapidly to the rear; but I was overtaken by a member of your [Coburn's] staff, with an order for me to halt at a favorable position for the posting of the battery [Aleshire's], allow the trains to pass on, and await the arrival of the battery. These instructions were obeyed, the halt being made at the brick church, where I remained until after the battery had taken position in front of my regiment, when Colonel Jordan, commanding the cavalry, ordered me to retreat. The train retreated in perfect order, without the loss of a single man or wagon.[84]

One further comment about Jordan's behavior: Coburn ordered him to prepare for a retreat early in the battle, there is no record to indicate that Jordan made any attempt to communicate with Coburn, his commander, again that day.[85]

Aleshire, too, had some interesting things to say in his report about the withdrawal of his guns. He said that after the 33rd and 85th Indiana regiments retired from Thompson's Station, two rebel regiments came up from the buildings near the station and charged his two guns that were in action west of the pike, and that he opened on them with canister. Aleshire further said that Colonel Jordan came up at about that time and ordered him to withdraw his three guns from the left, which he did, and then, after leaving them on the pike, he rode back to the remaining two guns on the hill on the right. Jordan ordered Aleshire to withdraw these guns also to and take them back to where the artillery had fought the day before and cover the retreat.[86]

Aleshire further said:

> ...When I rode back to the guns on the right, commanded by Lieutenant McCafferty, Colonel Coburn brought a regiment of infantry on my left to support me. They fired but one volley, and fell back in disorder. Colonel Coburn went to my right again, and I saw him no more. As the two regiments that charged this battery came close, I fired double-shotted canister into their ranks. I did not withdraw these guns until the infantry had all left, and do not think that the charge of the enemy was more than 60 yards from me when I ordered Lieutenant McCafferty to retire. The charge of the enemy on the left almost surrounded him as he came down the hill into the pike.[87]

This account implies that Aleshire did not immediately comply with Jordan's orders, but stayed on as long as he could, firing canister, and, in so doing, barely escaped capture. Aleshire's battery suffered no losses during the battle, which does not indicate hard and close fighting by the artillery.[88]

Aleshire's statement that he was left without infantry support and fought alone against two enemy regiments advancing from Thompson's Station is simply preposterous. The 33rd Indiana regiment fought alongside the two guns west of the pike and remained there until after the enemy had been driven back down the hill a second time. Similarly, the three guns on the hill east of the pike departed long before the 22nd Wisconsin and the 19th Michigan fell back to the west side of the road. Aleshire also stated that the three guns were nearly surrounded by the enemy as they were withdrawing from the hill east of the pike, but in fact the guns were gone before Forrest began his attack on the Union left flank.[89]

Soon after Freeman's battery opened on Coburn's left flank, Aleshire, who was quite excited, aooroached Coburn to report that he was out of ammunition and could not withstand the enemy's fire. At that time, the three guns on the left of the pike had already, by Aleshire's direction, moved down onto the pike without orders from Coburn. Coburn immediately sent Lieutenant Adams of his staff to ask the officers in charge of each ammunition box of the entire battery how much ammunition they then had. Adams did so and reported to Coburn that there were with the battery 230 rounds of shell and seventy rounds of canister, thus completely refuting Aleshire. Aleshire clearly had other motives for retiring.[90]

Both Van Dorn and Forrest, in their reports, clearly contradict Aleshire's statement that he did not withdraw his artillery until all of Coburn's infantry had left the line on the ridge. They both state that Forrest did not begin his movement around the Union left until the artillery had been withdrawn. In his report Van Dorn says:

> . . . The enemy's [Union] battery, which had been stationed on the turnpike, was withdrawn from the cross-fire of this [Freeman's] and King's battery, and did not return to the field. And now General Forrest was ordered to take the enemy in the rear.[91]

Forrest, in his report, agrees with Van Dorn. He says:

> . . . I found two regiments of infantry and a regiment of the Federal cavalry posted behind a stone fence to the left of their artillery. A few shells from my guns [Freeman's] drove them from their position to the right of their battery and into the pike. I then ordered a fire opened on their battery, and, after about 20 rounds, drove it from its position, retreating by the pike toward Franklin. At this time I was ordered to move forward, and, if possible, get in rear of the enemy.[92]

An extreme case of "battlefield nerves" better translated as cowardice seems to have been involved. Colonel Gilbert of the 19th Michigan tells of an interesting meeting that took place on the morning before the battle began, and this sheds some light on Aleshire's eagerness to fight that day. Gilbert's report contains the following statement:

> . . . early in the day [March 5, 1863], before any firing commenced on either side, Captain Aleshire attempted to retreat with his battery. He met Colonel Baird, of the Eighty-fifth Indiana, and myself on the turnpike, as we were advancing. We halted him, and ascertained from him that he was going back with his battery without orders. We protested against it, telling him he would create panic among our men; but he persisted, and would have done so had we permitted it; but just at this juncture he received your [Coburn's] order to take position, and reluctantly turned about.[93]

Colonel Baird, in a letter written in Libby Prison and delivered to Terre Haute by Major John P. Dufficy of the 35th Indiana Volunteers tells much the same story.

. . . I here [before reaching the gap in the first ridge] discovered that our battery, the 18th Ohio, was commanded by an arrant coward, for upon the first shot being fired he turned his guns back and started for Franklin, and it was with difficulty that Colonel Gilbert of the 19th Michigan, and your correspondent, kept him from running clear away.[94]

Thus all reports point to a weak performance by Jordan's cavalry, and, worse, outright cowardice and disobedience of orders on the part of Aleshire, whose behavior contributed in some degree to the loss of the battle.

Perhaps the strangest part of Aleshire's report relates to an event that, according to him, occurred during the retreat. He says:

After all of my battery had arrived safely in the pike, in obedience to orders from Colonel Jordan, I was retreating, when some one came to me and told me that Brigadier General [Charles C.] Gilbert was on a hill (pointing it out to me), and desired to see me. I halted my battery and reported to him, and he ordered me on to Franklin, and afterward over the river.[95]

There appears to be no confirmation of the statement that General Charles C. Gilbert left Franklin during the Battle of Thompson's Station and rode out toward the battlefield.

If the culpability for the failure at Thompson's Station seems to lie, at least in part, at the feet of the artillery and cavalry, it does pave the way for the exoneration of the infantry. Generally, the infantry regiments of Coburn's brigade fought well at Thompson's Station. This is especially notable, because, with the exception of the 33rd Indiana, they had not previously been engaged in battle. It is doubtful that they could have gained a victory even with good cavalry and artillery support, but it is possible that they might have been able to retire safely to Franklin if they had been properly covered.

Although it may not have affected greatly the outcome of the battle of Thompson's Station, the conduct of Bloodgood, second in command of Utley's 22nd Wisconsin, during the fighting was at least questionable—and a precursor of difficulties to come with him.

The participation of the 22nd Wisconsin in the battle, as described above, is based largely on the report of Colonel Utley of that regiment. In his report Utley stated that shortly after Freeman's Confederate battery opened fire and Forrest's dismounted cavalry attacked, Bloodgood, without orders, led one company of the regiment and most of another off to the left and out of the action. It is also a matter of record that Bloodgood finally led these troops off the field altogether, and with them accompanied Jordan's cavalry, Aleshire's artillery, and the trains to Franklin.[96]

Bloodgood, however, in his official report, written March 8, gives a different account of what happened during Forrest's attack. He says:

> A few minutes before this, our battery had moved from the hill into the pike, being very nearly out of ammunition. Colonel Coburn, finding himself severely pressed, sent for the Nineteenth Michigan Regiment to assist him. The Twenty-second Wisconsin Regiment was left alone, with the enemy pressing in front and right flank, and on our left a regiment of infantry, with one piece of artillery and a small body of cavalry, was pressing forward around the hill to take possession of the pike in our rear.
>
> Our regiment then fell back across the pike to the railroad. Here we received orders from one of Colonel Coburn's aides to move down the pike and check the enemy, if possible, from closing on our rear. The order was given, but before we could reach the point indicated, a portion of the regiment, including the colonel and adjutant, were cut off. The portion that escaped formed line and opened fire upon the enemy, but our force being so small, we were compelled to retire with the cavalry.[97]

Bloodgood's claim that he retired under orders is refuted by Adams, one of the two aides who delivered messages for Coburn that day. In his report, Adams includes the following statement:

> . . . At the time the Twenty-Second Wisconsin received the first charge, Lieutenant-Colonel Bloodgood, of that regiment, with about 150 men from the regiment, retired from the field and moved off, by the left flank, with the retreating party. I cannot believe that Lieutenant-Colonel Bloodgood had orders from Colonel Coburn or any other person to move; at least, if he did, no member of his [Colonel Coburn's] staff had any knowledge of it, and they were at that time on the ground. If there were any orders from any one for Lieutenant Colonel Bloodgood to move, they were not to retire, and there was nothing to prevent him from going to any part of the field for fifteen minutes after he left, as the remainder of the regiment, under Colonel Utley, with the Nineteenth Michigan, held the top of the hill that length of time.[98]

It is important to note that on March 5, a few hours after the battle had ended, and three days before his official report, Bloodgood wrote to his brother but said nothing of having received orders to retreat. Quite the contrary, he wrote:

> In the confusion we could get no orders; each regiment had to look out for themselves. . . . I sent word down the line to the Colonel [Utley] to move the regiment in that direction by the flank. . . . I gave the order, as there was no time to hesitate.[99]

Utley, in his report, speaks of this incident of having received an order from his lieutenant colonel as follows: ". . . During the engagement the lieutenant colonel [Bloodgood], from his safe retreat, annoyed me by sending word to me to retreat."[100]

And now, what of the commander? How should history evaluate Coburn's performance? According to some observers, Coburn performed well during the battle, showing great bravery and good leadership. Others were quite critical of his performance. James A. Garfield, Rosecrans' chief of staff, referred to Coburn as a fool and Colonel Gilbert of the 19th Michigan said that he was incompetent.[101]

In a message to Rosecrans at Franklin, March 6, Granger, referring to the defeat at Thompson's Station, had this to say:

> . . . If anyone is to blame, it is Colonel Coburn, in not keeping General Gilbert advised, and in not approaching the enemy with sufficient caution so as to ascertain his position and strength before attacking three or four time his own numbers in their chosen position.[102]

Coburn does appear to merit some criticism, especially that of Granger in stating that he had not used proper caution in his advance. Coburn's instructions clearly indicated that his was a reconnaissance mission, and by allowing his command to become engaged in battle he went beyond his instructions. It would be unfair, however, to accept all this criticism as deserved without considering some of apparent weaknesses in General Gilbert's own conduct that day.[103]

Coburn was engaged less than ten miles from Franklin, and General Gilbert could hear the artillery fire during the day, but he did not send reinforcements and he did not send any instructions to Coburn for his guidance. This was not unnoticed at army headquarters. Frank S. Bond, aide-de-camp to General Rosecrans, wrote to Gilbert on the day of the battle, saying: "The General Commanding directs me to say that he regrets exceedingly that you did not support Coburn and help to bring off the infantry."[104]

There is another matter, too, for which Gilbert should perhaps share a part of the blame for what happened that day. For some reason, Coburn felt that after he had started on his reconnaissance mission, he had no option but to continue his advance toward Spring Hill, even after his encounter with the enemy on March 4. The way that Coburn interpreted his orders may or may not have been Gilbert's fault, but it was certainly responsible for the fighting that occurred the next day, and the defeat that followed.[105]

On March 9, 1863, John McRae, chaplain of the 33rd Indiana, of Bloomington, Indiana, wrote a letter from Franklin, Tennessee, to Governor Oliver P. Morton of Indiana, which was published in the March 13 issue of *The Indianapolis Journal* and was reprinted March 16 in *The New Albany Ledger*. This letter contains some interesting information that may or may not shed light on Gilbert's handling of the Thompson's Station affair. The letter reads, in part, as follows:

Franklin, Tenn, March 9, 1863

Gov. Morton: I think it but justice to Col. Coburn and the brave men of his command in the late unfortunate affair at Thompson's Station, eight miles south of Franklin, Tennessee, to publish the following statement of facts, obtained on the spot. Wednesday, the 4th of March, the brigade under the command of Col. Coburn had several skirmishes with the rebels under the command of Van Dorn. Thursday morning Col. Coburn being satisfied that the enemy had been largely re-enforced through the night, sent an Orderly to Gen. Gilbert asking re-enforcements.

To this request General Gilbert said "Colonel Coburn must be scared," and wrote the following order: "Your force is sufficient; move forward." Colonel Coburn, rather than disobey the order of his superior officer, advanced to meet the enemy, . . .[106]

Reverend G. S. Bradley, Chaplain of the 22nd Wisconsin Regiment, in his book *The Star Corps* makes a statement that is almost identical to that made by John McRae in his letter to Governor Morton. It appears likely that the two accounts have been taken from the same source. There appears to be no official confirmation of the statements made by McRae and Bradley, and in fact the records generally tend to refute them, but they are included here for whatever historical value they may have.[107]

Thompson's Station was not the first time that Gilbert had been criticized for failing to support troops in battle. He commanded a corps at the Battle of Perryville, and he won a brevet for his conduct there. But he was strongly condemned by the Buell Commission, which was convened to investigate that campaign, for his failure to support Major General Alexander McD. McCook's hard-pressed corps during the battle. Because of this, the Senate failed to act upon Gilbert's nomination as Brigadier General, and on March 4 his commission expired. He was not reappointed, and on that date he reverted to his regular army rank of captain. He did not see field service again, and during the rest of the war he served only on administrative duties.[108]

Later, on March 25, Bloodgood, commanding a force consisting of a part of the 33rd Indiana, 19th Michigan, and 22nd Wisconsin of Coburn's brigade, surrendered to Nathan B. Forrest at Brentwood, Tennessee. The men were marched to Tullahoma and from there sent by rail to Richmond. They entered Libby Prison April 8 and 9, but were soon exchanged.[109]

On July 3, 1864, during Sherman's Atlanta Campaign, Utley became engaged in an serious quarrel with Bloodgood and left the service. Despite the criticism of his conduct at Thompson's Station and of his surrender at Brentwood, Bloodgood assumed command of the 22nd Wisconsin and remained in command of the regiment until the end of the war. But the shadow had been cast.[110]

Lastly, in considering the factors in the Northern loss of the battle and the surrender of Coburn's brigade, one should consider one of the opponents, Nathan Bedford Forrest. No one who faced him, either at Thompson's Station or elsewhere, considered him anything other than the boldest and most original commander that the South could offer. The odds were strongly against a commander having Forrest in front, beside, of behind him, even with a strong performance.

On the south side of the plain, beyond Thompson's Station, a row of hills formed a ridge and there Van Dorn formed his troops in line of battle to await the arrival of Coburn's brigade.

No one who faced Nathan Bedford Forrest, either at Thompson's Station or elsewhere, considered him anything other than the boldest and most original commander that the South could offer.

William T. Ward was given command of a brigade of Butterfield's Third Division, XX Corps, and when Butterfield left the army, Ward assumed command of the division.

Braxton Bragg-controversial commander of the Confederate forces in Tennessee.

Colonel William L. Utley of the 22nd Wisconsin Regiment, at the outbreak of the Civil War was the Adjutant General of the State of Wisconsin.

State Historical Society of Wisconsin/ Whi (X3) 2380

Lieutenant Colonel Bloodgood of the 22nd Wisconsin managed to escape capture at Thompson's Station, but a few weeks later was captured at Brentwood by Forrest's command, without firing a gun.

State Historical Society of Wisconsin/ Whi (X3) 18312

Louis D. Watkins became colonel of the 6th Kentucky Cavalry in February, 1863 and played an important part in the capture of Orton Williams and Walter Peter.

Major John Dufficy of the 35th Indiana was captured at Stones River and sent to Libby Prison.

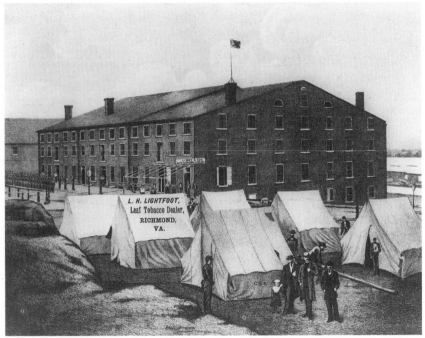

Libby Prison as it looked during the time Coburn's brigade was "in residence."

Andrew McClure, of Company A, 85th Indiana Regiment, wrote illuminating letters to the *Parke County Republican*.

William T. Crawford, from Sullivan County, Indiana, was the captain of Co. H, 85th Indiana Regiment, and eventually was made major.

Caleb Bales became the captain of Company D, 85th Ind. Regiment June 10, 1863.

Abner Floyd, Captain of Company A, 85th Indiana, fell mortally wounded at Thompson's Station, Tennessee.

During the late afternoon of June 8, 1863, Colonel John Baird of the 85th Indiana observed two uniformed strangers ride up to his tent at Franklin. Thus Orton Williams (seated) and Walter Peter began their unfortunate road to execution.

History of the Eighty-fifth Ind. Regiment Elwood Hunt (Silas Elwood) received a serious gunshot wound in his left arm during the fighting at Thompson's Station, and was discharged June 8, 1863. He later became a well-known attorney in Rockville, Indiana.

While at Libby Prison, a stressed-out August Willich shouted, "Stop Mr. Chaplin, stop the damned prayer."

Homestead Manor was built between 1809 and 1819 by Francis Giddens, Revolutionary War gunsmith from Virginia. The house served as a refuge for neighbors during the Battle of Thompson's Station in 1863. Alice Thompson, 17-year-old daughter of Dr. and Mrs. Elijah Thompson, dashed out of the cellar to recover the 3rd Arkansas Regimental colors from the fallen color-bearer. The manor was listed on the National Register of Historic Places in 1977.

Chapter 5

Journey to Libby Prison

After the firing ended at Thompson's Station on the evening of March 5, 1863, the men of Colonel John Coburn's brigade lay down their arms, took off their empty cartridge boxes, and awaited whatever fate had in store for them. In a short time, Brigadier General Nathan B. Forrest came forward under a flag of truce, and the formalities of the surrender took place immediately. Major General Earl Van Dorn also greeted Coburn, and then the 1,221 surrendered men were immediately marched off the field, leaving behind their dead and wounded.

Lieutenant Colonel James Gordon, with his 4th Mississippi Cavalry, which had suffered severely in the battle that day, was detailed to escort the prisoners to Tullahoma, Tennessee, a distance of about seventy-five miles. The prisoners passed through the brigades of Forrest, George B. Cosby, Frank C. Armstrong, and John W. Whitfield and then moved on to Spring Hill, at midnight reaching the Duck River opposite Columbia, Tennessee, twenty miles from the battlefield. There they crossed the river on ferries and moved into the town. The oath was administered: men pledged not to take up arms again until properly exchanged. The prisoners were put under the shelter of some covered hog and cattle pens for the night without food.[1]

Private Harvey Baker, Company H of the 33rd Indiana, who was wounded during the battle, has given the following account of the first few days of his captivity.

I lay on the battlefield till 12 o'clock at night when four colored men carried me to a school-house, where I remained until 6 o'clock a. m., and was then taken to Spring Hill. At night, with eight other wounded men, I was removed in a wagon to Columbia. We traveled all night in a dreary rain, reaching Duck River about daylight; crossed on a ferry-boat, but in doing so a rope broke and the boat drifted down stream about one-fourth of a mile, where we landed, and reached Columbia on the 8th. During my stay at Columbia forty-three men had either their arms or legs amputated, of whom forty died. Had it not been for the interference of some ladies my leg would have been amputated, and it was through the kindness of these same ladies that I was enabled to again reach the Union lines. My meals were generally supplied by the loyal ladies of Columbia and consisted chiefly of mush. I did, however, have one good meal. Captain Puckett, a sick Confederate, occupied a room near mine. He was generously taken care of by friends. His room was not generally known by the servants, and on one occasion one of them, with a steaming hot dinner, stopped at my room and inquired for Captain Puckett. I claimed the honor of being said captain, and the result was that I was favored with the first and only "square meal" during my sojourn in rebel hands.[2]

At early dawn, March 6, the men of the 85th Indiana had their first Confederate rations, consisting of less than half a ration of fat bacon and cornbread cooked on the outside just enough to hold the meal on the inside. Toward noon, the prisoners started their march toward Tullahoma in a dismal rain, and camped that night in the woods near the village of Lewisburg after a march of about twenty miles.[3]

The next morning the men were given a small quantity of bread made of salt, flour, and water, the only bread received until the men arrived at Shelbyville.[4]

About noon, March 7 the brigade continued the march toward Tullahoma, passing through Farmington and moving on to the northeast to Shelbyville, where it arrived two days later. There the men were confined for a few hours in the circular courthouse yard. A large crowd turned out to see the prisoners, and among them were many people loyal to the Union. Some of these handed food to the men through the palings of the fence, and little boys and girls brought pies and cakes to sell, but gave them instead to the hungry men.[5]

No rations were issued at Shelbyville; the men needed Confederate money to buy food, which they obtained by selling their knives, watches, and other valuables. These items were of far less use to them now than food that they could purchase.[6]

The prisoners waited at Shelbyville for one day before receiving another small quantity of the heavy flour bread. Late in the day on March 8, the prisoners left Shelbyville and camped a few miles from town for the night, then hurried on to Tullahoma, where General Braxton Bragg had his headquarters. They arrived there about sunset March 11.

The march from Shelbyville was a terrible experience for the men. Indeed, during the entire five days of the march from Columbia to Tullahoma, a cold drizzling March rain fell almost every day and night, with the men forced to go into camp unprotected each night soaked to the skin. The country between Shelbyville and Tullahoma was generally flat and mostly marshy, and the rains had filled the streams, causing many of them to overflow onto the adjacent bottom land. Bridges had been washed away, and the men often waded in water up to their waists, frequently barely able to keep their heads above water.[7]

When the brigade reached Tullahoma, the enlisted men were marched to a vacant lot, formerly used as a mule pen until the mud became so deep that the animals had to be removed. On this area was some brush, and the guards had scattered a few piles of green oak logs. Some of the sick were placed on the piles of brush to keep them out of the mud and water that night. The officers were put in the shell of an old building, affording some shelter from the driving rain that continued to fall that day and night.[8]

There was nothing for the men to sit upon, and no rest was possible. The woods, dry wood, and buildings nearby, were forbidden. A ration of raw bacon and raw meal was issued to the men by their heartless guards, but they had no fuel and no vessels for cooking, so it was thrown away.

Private James G. Bain of the 33rd Indiana has described the conditions of the encampment that night as follows:

How the night was passed it is hard to tell and harder to believe; but each little pile of smoking chunks was surrounded by as many soldiers as could huddle about it, and while they took turns on their hands and knees puffing and blowing the fire to keep it alive, the others would form a circle, one behind the other, and as close as they could get and march thus in close order round and round the fire, the dense smoke of which would gradually infuse a little warmth into the inside of the circle, and the tramping would keep up the circulation, and when the side away from the fire became so chilled that they could stand it no longer they would about face, bringing the outside to the inside and continue the tramping round and round until compelled to change again. As they would become exhausted, they would slip out of the circle, one and two at a time, and tumble down on the little piles of brush in the mud and at once drop to sleep; but they had to be watched, and after sleeping ten or fifteen minutes had to be aroused and forced into line to keep from freezing to death. About 10 o'clock PM, a half pint of meal was issued to each man, no vessels nor means of cooking it were provided. Some of the boys who had tin cups, dipped up nasty, dirty water from holes in the enclosure and tried to make mush, but there wasn't fire enough to more than warm it, and most of them ate their meal dry, and hungered for more. Before midnight the rain ceased and it turned colder, and later in the night "spit" snow, until by morning the mud was frozen a quarter or half an inch deep. The officers fared little better, being separated and quartered in a warehouse.[9]

Colonel Gordon, whose command was a combat unit, did the best that he could for the prisoners while on the march, but he left them at Tullahoma under the care of noncombatant troops, who had acquired no respect for their adversaries. Fighting men on both sides generally tended to respect one another because they had so much in common. Gordon had nothing to do with the mistreatment of the men after they reached Tullahoma. Colonel William L. Utley, in his report of the battle, spoke of Gordon as follows:

> . . . It gives me pleasure to say of Colonel Gordon that he treated the officers with extreme kindness, and did everything possible for the men. I believe he did everything in his power to furnish the men with suitable rations. They were not to be had, and he could not help it. The prisoners had got to be put through; there was no postponement because of the weather.[10]

Colonel Henry C. Gilbert of the 19th Michigan also spoke very highly of Colonel Gordon, and when the prisoners boarded the train for Chattanooga, Colonel Gilbert gave his sword and saddle to Gordon.[11]

On the morning after the prisoners had arrived at Tullahoma, they were marched to a train that was to carry them to Chattanooga. Before departing, however, both officers and men were required by the provost marshal to place in piles their overcoats, blankets, haversacks, canteens, leggings, and extra clothing. According to Bragg, this was done in retaliation for an order by Major General William S. Rosecrans that stripped Federal uniforms from Confederate soldiers. Colonel Coburn vigorously protested this order and demanded to see Bragg personally, but this request was denied. Later, Rosecrans vehemently denied that any such order had ever been given.[12]

Alvin D. May, Company H of the 33rd Indiana, who was an orderly of Coburn's staff gives more details:

> In all of General [Colonel] Coburn's transactions with his men we were satisfied that he was doing his duty toward us most conscientiously. He never left the boys in camp to put up in a comfortable hotel. He said his place was with the boys in camp. When we were captured General Bragg ordered the men to give up their overcoats. General Coburn argued against this in vain. General Bragg said to him, "General, we are not going to deprive you of your overcoat, you are to keep it." At this General Coburn indignantly pulled off his overcoat and threw it on the ground saying, "I'll be d—— if I take any better treatment than is given to my boys!"[13]

Upon arriving at the station, the men, who were cold, half starved, and without sleep or rest, were crowded into boxcars or on open flat cars, which were without seats and were started for Chattanooga. The floors of some of the cars were covered with wet manure. The officers were assigned to some old dilapidated passenger cars.

The prisoners traveled that day to Chattanooga, where they were placed, without food, in a large frame building that had just been erected as a hospital. The next day, about noon, the men were finally fed with plenty of good bread, which was remembered as being the best food they had been given while in the Confederacy.[14]

The brigade remained at Chattanooga for a day and a night. At the request of Coburn, the surgeons were permitted to look after the men, and although it was impossible to get necessary supplies, these medical officers did everything they could. Nevertheless, a number of the men died from exposure and wounds.[15]

From Chattanooga the prisoners moved by rail to Knoxville. For the first few hours after arriving there, the Union people of the town brought food to the men and talked to them, but then the Confederate soldiers drove these sympathetic helpers away. The prisoners stood all night, guarded in an open muddy space, although nearby there were large sheds and other buildings where they might have been sheltered. At this point, the exposure and the hardships of the trip began to tell on the men, and many who were unable to continue were left behind.[16]

The men of the 85th Indiana left Knoxville and moved with the rest of the prisoners by rail to Bristol, Tennessee, where miserable mistreatment continued. Among other indignities, all interaction with civilians was forbidden, and enemy physicians were not permitted to visit sick prisoners. Some men who had died were buried at Bristol, but many of the sick attempted to continue the journey, hoping for better treatment.[17]

The prisoners arrived at Lynchburg, Virginia, March 12 and 13. Though there was ample shelter near the railroad, the men were marched to the fairground and were quartered for several days in extreme discomfort in open sheds. Many of the sick were taken to hospitals, and some died there. Among the sick was Sergeant Francis A. Remington of Company G of the 85th Indiana, from Terre Haute, who lingered for many weeks and finally died at Richmond. In his dying moments he shouted until he could only whisper, and he asked his comrade John Singhoss to tell his wife and children that he had died as he had lived, a Christian, and that he had died for his country.[18]

Some of the prisoners arrived at Richmond March 16, and the rest left Lynchburg March 16 and 17 in very bad weather, in broken and partially open boxcars without food, water, or rest, completely chilled by the cold weather. While en route, the train was delayed in the mountains and in the midst of a dense forest until March 20, with a snowfall covering the area to a depth of twelve to fifteen inches, and from March 19 to March 21, the men had no fire, no shelter, no food, and no water. They awaited their fate in desperation.[19]

Finally, on March 21, just sixteen days from the date of their capture, the last of the prisoners arrived in Richmond, and in the early light of morning they had their first view of Libby Prison. This grim old building, four stories high, formerly housing the L. Libby & Son Ship Chandlers & Grocers, was located near the James River on the western half of the block bounded by Cary and Dock streets at 20th Street. When Coburn's brigade arrived, the building and the surrounding ground were covered with snow. It was here that the officers and men of Coburn's brigade were to be confined until exchanged some weeks later.[20]

Chapter 6

Libby Prison

Upon entering Libby prison on that grim March day, each man was registered and then searched for money, arms, and tools that could be used for escape. If a man was fortunate enough to have money, he was permitted to keep five dollars for his personal use, but was required to turn over anything greater than that amount to a man named Dick Turner to hold for him until needed. When a man had spent the five dollars, he was allowed to withdraw more money, but not more than five dollars at a time. While on the way to prison, Colonel John P. Baird sold his gold watch and used the money to provide loans to those who had the greatest need.

Dick Turner has been sometimes confused with Major Thomas P. Turner, the commandant of the prison, but Richard P. Turner was a private in the Confederate army who had been detailed for duty in the prison as a turnkey. When the war ended, both Dick Turner and Major Thomas P. Turner were arrested for mistreatment of the prisoners and were themselves confined in Libby Prison.[1]

When preliminaries were completed, the officers and the enlisted men were separated for the duration of their confinement. The fates of both were somewhat different for the three weeks they were confinded, but both suffered awfully.[2]

The men were crowded by the hundreds in a room like cattle in a pen, without fires or lights, and, although the season was bitterly cold, none of the windows in the prison were closed with glass. No visitors were allowed; further, much of the correspondence that could have served as some connection with the outside world was withheld or destroyed.[3]

The men slept on the bare floors in double rows, with their feet almost touching in the center of the rows. Twice each day they were formed in ranks and were made to stand there while an arrogant Rebel sergeant counted them. The sick were cursed and abused when they were unable to "fall in" for roll call, and one soldier was taken downstairs and forced to "mark time" for thirteen hours for spitting out the window onto the sidewalk below.[4]

The food issued to the men, twice daily, consisted of a half pound of bread per man each day and about one-fourth ration of corned beef, or mule meat as it has also been called. When the meat was brought in for distribution to the men, the room was filled with a rotten, disagreeable odor. The men sometimes boiled the meat in water to remove, at least in part, the taint caused by spoilage. Peas and flour were usually issued with the meat, and from these the men made soup. Occasionally, too, there was a ration of rice or black beans. The above was the allowance for two days, but it was so scant that it was usually consumed in one meal. At no time did the prisoners receive good meat, vegetables, sugar, or coffee. If a man had Confederate money he could purchase food from peddlers, but only at very high prices. Water was scarce and polluted, and at one time it was cut off completely for two days, apparently as a punitive measure against the prisoners. This was particularly difficult for the men, because some of their food was very salty. Guards would provide water at the price of one dollar a pail.[5]

Each officer received two filthy, lousy, thin blankets, and each enlisted man one. The prisoners had no change of clothing and no water, soap, or facilities for washing their blankets or what clothes they had.[6]

Vermin ruled Libby Prison. Everything around the men was literally covered with these creatures. It was a common occurrence to see ten to fifteen men with their shirts off hunting lice.[7]

The lice were not regarded simply as a nuisance, although they certainly were that; prolonged exposure to their activity was actually life threatening. Not having any change of clothing or water for cleansing purposes, the men became so infested with lice that rest and sleep became virtually impossible.[8]

Lieutenant James N. Hill, Company E, 33rd Indiana, who was wounded at Thompson's Station, wrote:

> . . . I was in Libby only about three weeks, and ten days more would
> have ended my life. I was worn out and starved. My flesh was all wasted
> away, and lice literally swarmed all over me. The surgeon on board the
> vessel at City Point said the lice would have killed me in another week
> if nothing else had been the matter.[9]

To add to the woes of both officers and men, the guards at Libby Prison were, as a rule, insolent and indifferent. Latrines were completely unsatisfactory and their stench was overpowering in the living quarters.[10]

Many men were already ill when they arrived in prison because of the cruel treatment to which they had been subjected during the sixteen days of the journey from Thompson's Station to Richmond. During this period they had been exposed much of the time to cold and rainy weather, had little or no rest, and only limited quantities of poor food. Colonel John Coburn reported more than fifty of his men died in prison because of these barbarities. Others survived for only a few days after their exchange, and many more were disabled for life.[11]

In addition to those who suffered on the trip to Richmond, many quickly became ill because of the abominable conditions in the prison, and they suffered greatly from such disorders as scurvy, itch, erysipelas, sore throat, rheumatism, diarrhea, fever, lockjaw, and delirium. Many died of disease while in the prison without consolation from their officers, who were not permitted to visit these dying men.[12]

Coburn says:

> Earnestly pleading for the privilege, I, with other officers, was denied a visit to the faithful and dying men who had followed us during the war, though the distance of but 10 feet separated us. No intercourse was allowed. A list of the dead was refused, asked for in the most respectful terms. The only accounts we have are from their fellow sufferers in the hospitals.[13]

Every morning a wagon backed up to the door of the prison basement, which fronted on Dock Street, to carry away those who had died during the night. These unfortunate men were not placed in coffins, but were piled on the wagon, largely without clothes, and hauled away for burial. About half of them were placed in graves marked "Unknown." Ned McGahee and Tyra Hunt of Company E, along with many other men of the 85th Indiana, were taken away in this manner.[14]

The enlisted men were prisoners only twenty to twenty-five days, but more than ten percent of them died from the effects of exposure, and many more were never again fit for duty. It is interesting to note that the chances of dying from the effects of prison life were about twenty-six in one hundred, while in battle the chances were about three in one hundred.[15]

The men found various ways to relieve the monotony of prison life. Some who were artistic carved objects, such as knitting needles, Odd Fellows, and Masonic emblems, and finger rings from beef bones. Some of the men played games; others studied, sang songs, and argued and debated, while still others marched in double file around and around the room. They had the opportunity to write home, but few, if any, letters were ever forwarded to their destinations.[16]

Every Sunday morning while in prison, Captain (Reverend) Jefferson E. Brant of Company E conducted church services and preached, while a Captain Buckley of Pittsburgh, Pennsylvania, led the singing, using some old books that were found in the prison. This was no doubt a source of solace to many of the prisoners. Many of the officers listened and participated, while the rest whittled and played cards.[17]

As noted above, the conditions of prison life for the officers were about the same as those for the enlisted men, but they were handled somewhat differently. There were about sixty officers of all ranks in the detachment of prisoners to which the officers of the 85th Indiana belonged, and they were immediately organized into messes. The officers on the brigade and regimental staffs constituted one mess, and the line officers of each regiment separately made up the others.[18]

The fifteen officers of the 85th Indiana were issued eight loaves of bread. Each man received one-half loaf, and half of this was placed in soup. All were very hungry, and when the soup was ladled out, each man watched carefully to see that he got his fair share.[19]

The officers of the 85th Indiana were placed in the south room on the third floor of the prison, along with 150 other officers. Altogether there were 212 officers in that room, including Brigadier General August Willich, who had been captured December 31, 1862, at the Battle of Stones River while commanding a brigade in Rosecrans' Army of the Cumberland. He had been confined there for more than five months, and at times was irritable beyond endurance. He remained in a corner by himself and paced back and forth like a caged animal.[20]

After two weeks of confinement in the third floor room, sixty-six captains were transferred to a room just above the basement. At the east end of this room was the guard room, separated from the prisoners' room by a board partition. Conditions were somewhat improved by this move, but the filth and vermin continued unabated. In the lower room officers of different ranks, from colonels on down, were added until the total number was about one hundred.[21]

Finally the day came when negotiations were complete and the enlisted men began to leave prison. The first of Coburn's brigade, about four hundred men, were exchanged April 1, 1863, and the rest followed during the next two weeks. The men were moved by rail from Richmond to City Point, where the formal exchange took place: the name of a Confederate soldier and that of a Union soldier would be called out. The former would then start from the boat on which he had been brought south to City Point, and the latter would start from the wharf at the same time. They would pass on the way, and the exchange was thus completed. The exchanged Union soldiers were then transported on the boat *Metamora* from City Point to Annapolis, Maryland, where they arrived and landed April 1, 1863. That day the men were given new blankets and the next day they were given new clothing. The regiment remained there until April 6 and then boarded the steamer *North America* for the trip up the Chesapeake Bay to Baltimore.[22]

At Baltimore the sick and wounded were placed in hospitals and were well cared for, but some, whose health had been totally destroyed, lingered awhile and then died. The rest of the men were issued new clothing and were then sent on to Camp Chase at Columbus, Ohio, a trip that required three days and four nights. From the Camp Chase parole camp, the 85th and 33rd Indiana moved on to Indianapolis; the 22nd Wisconsin to Benton Barracks at Saint Louis, Missouri;, but the 19th Michigan remained for a time at Camp Chase. Many of the men who were denied leave, however, simply left and returned to their homes in Michigan.[23]

The officers' turn came next. Captain Brant of the 85th Indiana gives the following account of their release:

> About midnight [at Libby Prison], preceding May 5, just two months after our capture, the prison Adjutant came in and called "Attention!" We were soon all awake, and then he said: "All whose names are called will be ready to come out in the morning." While that roll was being called, the handshaking, congratulations and exhibitions of joy exceeded that of any religious revival I ever witnessed. Strong men wept for joy and shook hands round and round.
>
> As the day dawned we were on a train of flat cars crossing a long bridge and were soon in the green woods and scenting the flowers as the dew drops sparkled on the grass in the early sunlight. Out of the dingy windows of old Libby we had looked across James River upon the fields and woodlands and longed to be free. Now it was becoming a reality. At Petersburg we were switched onto the Appomattox R. R. and rounding the curve at City Point we came in sight of "Old Glory", as she waved over the flag of truce boat [*State of Maine*] that was to carry us home. Many of our number had not seen the old flag for many months, and the sight caused a sensation like an electric shock, beginning at the crown of the head and going out at the toes and fingertips. Such cheering we never expect to hear again. As we were going to the boat, Gen. Willich took off his old hat and saluted the flag of his adopted country, pausing a few moments gazing upon the old flag, he saluted more gracefully than the first time. Moving up a few steps and doffing his old hat again he bowed lower than ever as in adoration, and then I forgave him for all his fretfulness and profanity while in prison.[24]

This was not the first time that Willich expressed his patriotism and love for his country. John Coburn, in a letter written in his own hand, tells of the following incident:

> *Many of us* [officers confined in Libby Prison] *were piously inclined and upon an intimation of the prison officers that a clergyman would visit us—a request was made for one to come on & have prayers. Upon his arrival all assembled at a place in the room indicated by him. A familiar hymn was sung, in which most of us joined; certainly every one who could sing. He then offered up a prayer; some kneeling; some standing; all silent and reverent as if in a sacred temple. It was deliverd in beautiful, touching and even elequent words. Supplictions were offered by him for all men for all the unfortunate, for the sick and the wounded and those cast in prison, in feeling and touching terms. Then changing the subject he prayed for all those in authority—for the President and his cabinet, for the army in the field, and for the success of the Rebel Cause. Suddenly Gen Willich who stood near him, with a look of indignation turned upon him & said in deep ringing tones that hushed the preacher, "Stop Mr Chaplain stop the damned prayer." It did stop, and the meeting was broken up; we turned our backs upon the author of this ill-timed and ill-placed prayer and he, without another word, found the door.* [25]

When the officers were finally on board the *State of Maine* after their exchange, they moved to the north, the beginning of their journey home. It wasn't long until they were enjoying full rations of bread, boiled ham, and coffee. The men sang as they steamed out of Hampton Roads and into Chesapeake Bay for the run up to Annapolis. Upon their arrival there, they disembarked at the wharf and marched to the quartermaster's office, where they drew blankets, and then to Camp Parole. The next day they discarded their vermin-infested clothes and received new uniforms. The officers were restored to duty May 8, and leave was granted to all who wished it.[26]

Colonel Baird of the 85th Indiana had been exchanged some three weeks before the other officers left Libby Prison, and he had been ordered to Tennessee, where he was assigned command of the troops at Franklin, which included some men of the 85th Indiana who had not been present at Thompson's Station.[27]

While in Libby Prison, Captain Caleb Nash of Company I became so ill with scurvy that he was placed in the hospital. When the officers were released, Nash was carried in the arms of men to the cars and onto the boat. He was placed in a hospital at Annapolis, and he died there about a week later, leaving a wife and small children.[28]

Chapter 7

Franklin, Tennessee

March 1863-June 1863

Major General Earl Van Dorn's cavalry remained in Middle Tennessee for a few months after the defeat and capture of Colonel John Coburn's brigade at Thompson's Station March 5, 1863. It continued to threaten Major General Gordon Granger's forces at Franklin. This town, south of Nashville, was an important post, situated on the extreme right flank of Major General William S. Rosecrans Army of the Cumberland. It was a key point in the defenses of Nashville. The greater part of Rosecrans' army was encamped in the vicinity of Murfreesboro.

The Federal forces at Franklin had been greatly reduced by the capture of Coburn's brigade at Thompson's Station, but some of its units had escaped from the battlefield and made their way safely back to Franklin. These consisted of companies A, B, and I of the 22nd Wisconsin, under the command of Lieutenant Colonel Edward Bloodgood, Lieutenant Colonel James Pickands' 124th Ohio Infantry, Colonel Thomas J. Jordan's cavalry, and the discredited Captain Charles C. Aleshire's 18th Ohio Battery. In addition, some troops of Coburn's brigade had been left behind with the convalescents to guard the regimental camps and stores: Captain William Reeder's Company D of the 85th Indiana, Captain John T. Freeland's Company B of the 33rd Indiana, Captain Hazen Brown's Company D of the 19th Michigan (Note: Captain Brown had resigned January 1, 1863), and Captain Owen Griffith's Company F of the 22nd Wisconsin.[1]

The 85th Indiana took into action at Thompson's Station 303 officers, non-commissioned officers, and men. It lost in the battle one officer killed and two wounded, and twelve men killed and nineteen wounded. In addition, thirty men died from exposure and ill treatment while in captivity, and one officer and five men were disabled from the same causes. Thus the total loss for that part of the regiment that fought at Thompson's Station was seventy, which means only 233 officers and men survived the battle.

In addition to Captain Reeder's Company D of the 85th Indiana Regiment, there were other men of the 85th Indiana, who, because of their health, had been unable to accompany the regiment when it marched to Thompson's Station. These men, belonging to all companies of the regiment, were consolidated into two temporary companies, and these companies, together with

Reeder's Company D, were still called the 85th Indiana. Lieutenant Caleb Bales commanded Company D in place of Reeder, who commanded what remained of the 85th Indiana. The remnant of this regiment was put in charge of the pontoon bridge there and also was engaged in building a stationary bridge across the Harpeth River.[2]

The detachment of the 33rd Indiana not present at Thompson's Station, including Captain John T. Freeland's Company B, numbered about two hundred men. Most of this detachment was stationed on Rosser's Knob, about one mile north of Franklin, but a detail had been sent to Fort Granger to man the siege guns, and they were in action during Van Dorn's attack.[3]

The troops at Franklin were reinforced immediately after the battle of Thompson's Station, when General Gordon Granger arrived from Nashville with Brigadier General Absalom Baird's Third Division of his Army of Kentucky. Granger assumed command of the United States forces at Franklin, which then consisted of Absalom Baird's and General Charles C. Gilbert's divisions.[4]

On March 8 Captain Elisha B. Bassett, as the senior officer of the 19th Michigan, was ordered to move with Company D of that regiment and to guard the railroad bridge over the Little Harpeth River, about two miles south of Brentwood. This force was later reinforced when it was joined by the remnants of the regiment that had escaped at Thompson's Station, and by others who had been left in camp at Franklin before the battle because of sickness.[5]

Also on March 8 Bloodgood was ordered to take companies A, B, F, and I of the 22nd Wisconsin, which had escaped capture at Thompson's Station, to Brentwood to guard the railroad station there. On March 11 the camp of the 22nd Wisconsin was moved to a grassy area, well shaded by trees and about one-fourth mile from the station. The next day a detail of men cut down the trees around the camp to form an abatis for protection against an enemy attack.[6]

A misty rain was falling on the cold and cloudy morning of March 24 and, because the cooking fires had been extinguished by a rain that had fallen during the previous night, breakfast had been delayed. Finally, however, the food was prepared, and as the men of the 22nd Wisconsin were finishing their morning meal, the long roll sounded; they learned that the enemy had passed the camp of the 19th Michigan, about two miles to the south, and was approaching Bloodgood's position. The companies marched out of camp. They were formed and deployed as skirmishers, and completely surrounded the camp. This done, they moved out and took position, with companies A and H, both under the command of Captain Francis Mead of Company A, covering the southwest corner of the camp. Mead advanced through the woods, and, after proceeding about a half mile, observed Confederate horsemen some distance to his front. He immediately ordered his men to fall back and form a line in front of the abatis.

The enemy force approaching Bloodgood's camp at Brentwood was General Nathan B. Forrest's cavalry division, the brigades of Colonel James W. Starnes and Brigadier General Frank C. Armstrong. Forrest had been given divisional command shortly after the Battle of Thompson's Station.[7]

To the south of the camp there was a low hill, with the crest about fifty yards in front of the abatis. Companies B and I were deployed across the pike at this point, and it was here that the enemy attacked. There was brisk fire for about ten minutes, and the two companies fell back to the abatis. When companies B and I were leaving the hill, another enemy column appeared around its western base, moving directly toward Company A and toward Company F, which was to the right of Company A.[8]

A messenger sent by Forrest, bearing a flag of truce, informed Bloodgood that he was completely surrounded and demanded an immediate surrender. Bloodgood soon discovered that he was indeed surrounded, and he surrendered his force of 521 men without firing a single shot.[9]

Forrest left a part of his command to send off the prisoners and captured arms and wagons; and, with 4th Mississippi and 10th Tennessee cavalry regiments and Captain Samuel L. Freeman's artillery, he moved down to the stockade at the bridge over the Little Harpeth, two miles south of Brentwood, which was held by troops of the 19th Michigan under Bassett. When Freeman opened with one of his guns, Bassett surrendered his command of 230 men.[10]

General Gordon Granger, commanding the Army of Kentucky with headquarters at Franklin, reacted angrily to the surrender of the troops at Brentwood and at the Little Harpeth River, by referring to them as "our milk and water soldiers." He concluded his report of the incident as follows:

> From all that I can ascertain, Lieutenant-Colonel Bloodgood surrendered Brentwood, and Captain Bassett the stockade, unnecessarily, and without having a man either killed or wounded. Had they fought for one hour, our cavalry and infantry would have arrived on the spot and cut the rebels to pieces. I visited the stockade in person, and found it very strong—capable of holding 200 men—and it could easily have been defended for a long time, but not a mark of a bullet could be discovered on it.[11]

Actually there were three men wounded, all from the 22nd Wisconsin, but two of these woundings were accidental and occurred when the men carelessly attempted to break up their loaded rifles.[12]

The men captured at and near Brentwood were immediately marched southward on their way toward captivity in Richmond, along the same route as those captured at Thompson's Station; they arrived at Libby Prison on April 8 and 9. They were not there long. The men of the 19th Michigan spent just two days in Richmond and were then exchanged and sent north April 11, 1863. The prisoners of the 22nd Wisconsin were exchanged at City Point April 23. Bloodgood, when exchanged, was ordered to report to his regiment at Benton Barracks, Missouri. It appears that Bassett never rejoined the 19th Michigan regiment after he was captured, and he was dismissed from the service June 23 for cowardice at the Battle of Thompson's Station.[13] According to Anderson, in his history of the 19th Michigan Regiment, Bassett took cover behind a tree at Thompson's Station and refused to command his company, turning it over to Lieutenant Samuel Hubbard.[14]

A few days after Bloodgood's surrender, Second Lieutenant Caleb Bales, then commanding Company D of the 85th Indiana at Franklin, was sent up to Brentwood to watch the road junction at that point. A short time later, Bales received word that he was in danger of being surrounded by the enemy, and he immediately started his command back toward Franklin. He was soon overtaken by a part of Van Dorn's cavalry, but his men fired into the advance guard and caused it to halt. The enemy quickly came up in greater numbers, and Bales then divided his small force into two parts and sent them to the fence lines on both sides of the road. Keeping the men inside of the fences, he kept up a running fight until his company arrived safely inside the Federal lines at Franklin. In this engagement Bales did not lose a man. Captain William Reeder, commander of Company D of the 85th Indiana, resigned June 10 and Bales was promoted to captain of the company.[15]

When Bales returned from Brentwood to Franklin, he found that Colonel John P. Baird of the 85th Indiana had returned to the army and was in command of the post. Captain Jefferson E. Brant made the following comment: "Some three weeks before the other officers were exchanged, Col. Baird in a way peculiar to himself, was exchanged and . . . was in command at Franklin."[16]

This statement appears to imply Brant believed Baird may have used some questionable influence in securing his early release. It is interesting to note, however, that shortly after Baird's death in Terre Haute, Lieutenant Colonel Alexander B. Crane, then in New York, wrote a letter to the Terre Haute Bar, dated March 14, 1881, and addressed to General Charles Cruft. In this letter Crane explained Baird's early release as follows:

In Libby Prison at the time the 85th Indiana was confined there, was Thomas C. Fletcher, a radical Republican, who was colonel of the 31st

Missouri regiment. Fletcher had been wounded and captured at Chickasaw Bayou, near Vicksburg, Mississippi, in late December 1862. Fletcher's name was drawn for exchange, but because of his political beliefs he had made many enemies at Richmond, and some of them did not want him released. He had already been taken from Libby in preparation for exchange when his enemies were finally able to halt the proceedings, and Fletcher was thereupon returned to the prison about midnight.

It was then necessary to find a replacement for Fletcher, and Baird's name was called, because he was alphabetically the first colonel on the exchange list. Baird, who had been sleeping beside Crane under a piece of carpet, was then awakened and told of his good fortune, He immediately arose, and, giving his carpet to Crane, said good-bye and a few minutes later left Libby Prison.[17]

Baird was paroled at City Point, Virginia, April 12, and two days later reported at Camp Parole, Maryland. He arrived at Camp Morton, Indianapolis, Indiana, April 19, and was sent to Franklin, Tennessee, where he assumed command of the post.[18] He was not involved in any intrigue to secure his release before his men.

April 10 Van Dorn advanced with his cavalry from Spring Hill and made an effort, although apparently not a serious one, to capture Franklin. A few days earlier Granger had received information from Murfreesboro and Triune that such an attack was imminent, and he had disposed his troops so as to protect the town. His command consisted of General Baird's and General Gilbert's divisions; Brigadier General Green Clay Smith's Cavalry Brigade; a cavalry force of about 1,600 men under Major General David S. Stanley; and four guns in Fort Granger, northeast of Franklin. The guns were two 24-pounder siege guns and two 3-inch rifled guns from Aleshire's 18th Ohio Battery. Granger sent Stanley's command out on the Murfreesboro road about four miles from Franklin and placed Smith's brigade in reserve to support Stanley if necessary. He posted Absalom Baird's division to watch the fords of the Harpeth below Franklin and held Gilbert's division in reserve where it could meet any attack on its front or reinforce either flank.[19]

After leaving Spring Hill, Van Dorn moved northward along the Columbia pike with Forrest's and Brigadier General William H. Jackson's cavalry divisions and Freeman's battery. When he arrived at a point about three miles from Franklin, Van Dorn divided his command, sending Forrest with his division across to the Lewisburg pike. Forrest advanced on the pike toward Franklin with Armstrong's brigade in front and Starnes following about two miles to the rear. Van Dorn with Jackson's division advanced toward

Franklin along the Columbia pike. The two roads converged to enter the town from the south on parallel streets.[20]

Jackson's cavalry soon became engaged with the Federal pickets and drove them in shortly after noon. When the enemy reached the southern outskirts of Franklin, they met the 40th Ohio Regiment, serving on guard duty that day. At about the same time, Armstrong came up to the Federal infantry in the outskirts of Franklin, where the Lewisburg pike approaches the town. The pickets and the 40th Ohio held up the enemy advance for some time, but they were finally driven back into the houses and the fort on the other side of the Harpeth River. Some of the enemy forced their way into the town, but they were either killed or captured. Granger then ordered the guns in the fort to open fire on a part of the enemy who were forming in an open field, and soon forced them to retire to the cover of a woods.[21]

When Stanley heard the Confederate firing at Franklin, he promptly crossed the Harpeth River at Hughes' Ford and attacked Starnes brigade and Freeman's battery on the Lewisburg pike. Van Dorn then realized that he was in a precarious position, and, after attacking and driving Stanley back across the Harpeth, he retired toward Spring Hill.[22]

The units of Coburn's brigade still at Franklin, including Reeder's Company D of the 85th Indiana, were not engaged in the fighting that day.

During Van Dorn's attack on Franklin, Captain William T. Crawford, Company H of the 85th Indiana, became involved in an interesting incident. While the regiment was on the march from Brentwood to Franklin, early in March 1863 he became so sick that he was unable to walk. Dr. Wilson Hobbs, surgeon of the regiment, directed him to mount his horse and ride until the regiment reached Franklin, which it did on the night of March 4.

The next day, when Coburn received orders to move southward with his brigade on a reconnaissance toward Spring Hill, Crawford got out of bed and started to rejoin his regiment. He was so sick, however, that he could not stand, and he was forced to return to his bed, where he remained until April 9. The doctors believed that they had done all they could for him and felt that he would not recover. Surgeon Hobbs then said to Crawford, "Capt., we have done all we can for you, and if you have any special word to send back to your wife, we will gladly inform her." Captain Crawford felt that he was born to see the end of the rebellion and said, "Write to my wife, that I am very sick, but will get well and will live to see this rebellion wiped out."

Jefferson E. Brant, in his history of the 85th Indiana, tells of the rest of this incident as follows:

> . . . Dr. Cliff who had been a physician in the Rebel army lived in Franklin, Tenn. and came to the home of Mrs. Hoffman where the

Captain was being treated for typhoid pneumonia fever and becoming interested in the welfare of Capt. Crawford [Dr. Cliff] gave him some medicine after the other Doctors gave him up, and in a few days the Captain took a turn for the better and was able to get to the fireplace by the aid of a hickory cane which Dr. Cliff had presented him. The next day after the Captain had walked from his bed to the fireplace, Van Dorn's forces made an attack on the Union forces, then defending the town of Franklin. When the attack began, the Captain resolved to get to his command, which was at Fort Granger, just east of the town, about one-half mile. He buckled on his sword and started for his command; as the house where he was sick was about half way between the Union picket lines and Fort Granger. When he was about half-way between the town and Fort Granger, about three hundred cavalry horses came dashing through the town toward the Union fort, about every tenth horse had a rider. In the rear of all these horses, five rebels rode up to Capt. Crawford and demanded his sword, and with oaths said they would blow out his d—n brains if he did not surrender his sword at once. The Captain said, : "Boys, you have got the drop on me and if you must have my sword I will unbuckle it." "Be quick", was the response and "get up behind me", said the leader. "I'll not do it," said the Captain, and with another oath the leader said. "I'll leave you here"— bringing his revolver down to shoot the Captain in the head. That hickory cane given by Dr. Cliff the day before, served as a good protector to Capt. Crawford, for with it he knocked the revolver out of the Rebel leader's hand and at the same instant the Union boys on the other side of the Harpeth River, which flows at the base of the hill at Fort Granger, fired a volley at the five Rebels, who had surrounded the Captain, shooting the leader through his jaw, and he fell off his horse at the Captain's feet. Another who had his carbine pointed at the Captain's head was shot through his right arm; a third man was shot through the side; a fourth man had his horse shot from under him; and the fifth man threw up his hands and begged our men not to kill him. They hallowed to him to hurry over the pontoon bridge to where the Union men were stationed or they would shoot h—l out of him. He ran across to the Union forces, and Capt. Caleb Bales ran across the pontoon bridge where Captain Crawford was, and helped him over to where the Union forces were stationed; . . ..

The men who had rescued Captain Crawford were Captain Bales, Tom Reed, and about ten men who had seen Captain Crawford approaching the bridge and had started forward at a double quick to help him. Bridge guard, George Kidle of Company I, 85th Indiana, fired at the group surrounding

Crawford, striking the leader in the jaw, and another bridge guard of the 40th Ohio shot the man who had his carbine pointed at Crawford's head in the right arm. When Crawford crossed the river to the safety of the fort, he weighed only ninety-eight pounds, but his health improved steadily, and he was later able to resume command of his company.[23]

At this point Van Dorn disappears from the history of Coburn's brigade and from the Civil War. He was shot and killed at his headquarters at Spring Hill, Tennessee, May 7, 1863, by Dr. George B. Peters, who later claimed that Van Dorn had "violated the sanctity of his home."[24]

While Granger was in command of the post of Franklin, he was very popular with his men but was hated by most of the inhabitants of the town. At the time of its occupation, its population numbered about 1,500, and of these only six were Union families. The Union families were allowed to go anywhere they wished within the Union lines. On the other hand, the Southern sympathizers, both men and women, were forbidden to leave the town under penalty of being arrested as spies. Unless they could prove that they had been loyal citizens of the United States, they were told that they had no privileges. Private William Herron of Company C, 85th Indiana, on April 25, 1863, described the suffering of the non-loyal citizens:

> The misery and suffering of the rebels can hardly be imagined. They have no firewood, and in two weeks more will have nothing to eat. Not a market wagon is allowed to enter the town. All the rebels are engaged in cutting down their fruit and ornamental trees for firewood. In many cases the owners were destroying their fences and outhouses for the same purpose. The half dozen Union families, by order of General Granger, are supplied with firewood by the soldiers, and the necessaries of life they are permitted to procure of the Quartermasters at Government rates. Under no consideration are the rebels to pass any of the picket lines, unless making oath that they will not return until the termination of the war.[25]

It has been noted that the men of Coburn's brigade who had been captured at Thompson's Station were exchanged during the first two weeks of April 1863, and the officers of the brigade were released May 5. Rosecrans, commander of the Army of the Cumberland, wanted the exchanged troops to return to the army as soon as possible, so that they could be re-equipped and made ready for field operations. On May 31 he informed Major General Henry W. Halleck, at Washington, that Coburn's brigade was much scattered, and he inquired by whose orders this had been done. On June 6

Brigadier General Milo S. Hascall, commanding the District of Indiana at Indianapolis, reported to Rosecrans that a great many men of Coburn's brigade had simply left Camp Chase and had gone home, and that when the men from Indiana had arrived at Indianapolis Governor Oliver P. Morton asked for and received authority to grant them a furlough for ten days.

Hascall also reported that the scattered men were being collected and clothed and placed in readiness for the field, and that for the past three or four days he had been forwarding those who were ready to return to the army. He had placed Coburn in command of a camp for the exchanged men in Indianapolis, and all men reporting there would be forwarded to Tennessee as soon as they were ready.[26]

Corporal Samuel Coble's experiences after leaving Camp Chase are perhaps typical for most of the men of the 85th Indiana. He arrived at Camp Chase April 9 and remained there until June 20, and then traveled by rail to Indianapolis. He stayed at Camp Morton until furloughed, and from May 4 to May 14, he was at his home at Bridgeton, Indiana. He then returned to Indianapolis, where he and the rest of the men drew guns May 18 and received pay for four months May 21. With these duties completed, he went back to his home, without furlough, and remained there June 1-4. He left there June 4 and arrived at Indianapolis the next morning, finally departing Indianapolis with the regiment June 9 and arriving at Franklin, Tennessee, June 12.[27]

By an order of June 8 Rosecrans reorganized the Army of the Cumberland by assigning Granger to the command of a newly constituted Reserve Corps, which included Coburn's brigade. Granger's headquarters at that time was at Triune, Tennessee, and his new corps was organized as follows:[28]

Reserve Corps, Gordon Granger

First Division, Absalom Baird
  First Brigade, Thomas E. Champion
  Second Brigade, William P. Reid
  Third Brigade, John Coburn
Second Division, James D. Morgan
  First Brigade, Robert F. Smith
  Second Brigade, Daniel McCook
  Third Brigade, Charles C. Doolittle
Third Division, Robert S. Granger
  First Brigade, Sanders D. Bruce
  Second Brigade, William T. Ward

The men of Coburn's brigade rejoined the army at Franklin, Tennessee, during the early part of June 1863, finally together again and ready for duty after having been widely scattered for a period of more than three months.

On June 8 upon learning that the 33rd and 85th Indiana regiments were soon to depart for Tennessee, the ladies of Indianapolis gave a farewell picnic, attended by the soldiers and many citizens of the city. After the dinner, the band of the 71st Indiana played for a time, and a sword was then presented to Colonel Coburn by his friends. The soldiers of the 85th Indiana left Indianapolis for Franklin the next day, rejoining the brigade there June 12.[29]

The men of the 33rd Indiana rejoined the brigade at Franklin June 18 but Coburn was kept on duty at Indianapolis for two months after his return from Libby Prison. Colonel Utley, and later Colonel Gilbert, were commanding the brigade during his absence.[30]

A little after noon June 8 the reorganized 19th Michigan Regiment left Camp Chase and marched to Columbus, Ohio, a short distance away. It remained there until about dusk, and then the men boarded the train for Cincinnati. During the afternoon they received four month's back pay, and by the time the train pulled out some of the men were quite drunk. The train arrived at Cincinnati early the next morning, and then, after a short delay, they boarded a steamer and moved off down the Ohio River. After a layover of twenty-four hours at Louisville, the regiment moved on to Nashville on a train of cattle cars and arrived there during the afternoon of June 11. There the men moved into a large unfurnished building for the night.[31]

The next day the regiment encamped outside the city and drew new Enfield rifled muskets, accouterments, and dog tents, to replace the old Sibley tents that had been captured at Thompson's Station. Then the regiment moved on to Franklin June 18.[32]

The town and the county surrounding it had changed dramatically since the regiment last saw it about five months earlier. The countryside, which had then been richly covered with trees and prosperous, rolling farms, was barren and desolate. Buildings had been burned, and fortifications had been built all around the town. There were also many deserted campsites, with all the attendant unpleasantness of such places.[33]

After the release of the 22nd Wisconsin from Libby Prison, a rendezvous was established at Benton Barracks, Saint Louis, where the regiment was reorganized and re-equipped for field duty. On June 12 it left Camp Gamble, in the suburbs of Saint Louis, and marched down to the Mississippi River, crossed on a ferry boat, and marched to the Ohio and Mississippi Railroad depot on "Bloody Island." The men boarded the cars at 4:00 PM and arrived at Mitchell, Indiana, at noon the next day. At Mitchell they boarded cars of the Chicago and New Albany Railroad and arrived at New

Albany a little after sunset, taking quarters for the night in the depot.

The next morning the regiment crossed the Ohio River on a ferry to Portland, about three miles below Louisville, and then marched through heat and dust to the Louisville and Nashville Railroad depot. It moved southward on freight cars through Bowling Green, Kentucky, and reached Nashville a little after noon June 15, 1863. After Bloodgood arrived and ordered the men to go into camp until he could draw teams and wagons and otherwise prepare for the field, they then moved out about a mile to the southwest of town and pitched tents. The regiment was directed to join Granger's Reserve Corps at Triune, Tennessee.[34]

As a result of the disastrous affair at Thompson's Station, a serious rift had inevitably developed between Utley and Bloodgood. On June 17 Utley arrived at Nashville but did not come out to the camp of the 22nd Wisconsin that day. He finally arrived at the camp about sundown the next day, and later that evening he called all the line officers to his tent and asked that they not take sides in the controversy between him and Bloodgood. This meeting resulted in some unpleasantness, and, despite his plea, the men did take sides.[35]

The next morning, before the guards took their places, Utley came out and gave them some instructions. He said in effect that under Bloodgood the men had been pampered. Bloodgood had been lenient, permitting the men on those hot days to stand with their guns on the ground if they wished. From then on, Utley told them, they would be subjected to stricter discipline. He ordered the guards to walk their beats all the time, while carrying their guns in proper position, saluting their officers, and conforming to all regulations. This order added to the ill feelings among the men.[36]

Bloodgood completed his work in Nashville and returned to the regiment June 19. He and Utley did not shake hands when they met, but they did discuss their troubles; there was no reconciliation.[37]

On the morning of June 22 the 22nd Wisconsin left camp near Nashville and began its march toward Franklin. At 2:00 PM the regiment arrived within a half mile of Colonel Baird's headquarters of the post of Franklin, and it was then halted while preparations were made for its reception. After a wait of about an hour, Utley was informed that all was ready and the column resumed its march. With bands playing, the regiment ascended a ridge on which stood the house used by Baird as his headquarters, and the men saw before them, drawn up in line along the road, the 33rd Indiana, 85th Indiana, and the 19th Michigan—the other regiments of Coburn's brigade. The regiments were standing at "present arms," and the 22nd Wisconsin acknowledged the honor by marching with shouldered arms and the officers carrying their swords at "present." With the arrival of the 22nd Wisconsin at Franklin, Coburn's brigade, troubled by the disaster at Thompson's Station with some of the men still experienceing the awful trials of Libby Prison, was reunited.[38]

When Utley arrived at Franklin, he assumed temporary command of Coburn's brigade as the ranking colonel. As regiments of this brigade arrived at Franklin, there were present at the post the 33rd and 85 Indiana regiments, the 19th Michigan, the 22nd Wisconsin, the 78th Illinois Infantry, and the 5th and 6th Kentucky Cavalry. The 78th Illinois, however, soon left for Triune.[39]

On July 1 line officers of the 22nd Wisconsin requested by petition that Utley resign as colonel of the regiment for incompetency and inefficiency. The petition, signed by twenty-three of the twenty-seven line officers and by the quartermaster, was presented to Utley that evening. When Utley reported this matter to Colonel Baird of the 85th Indiana, commander of the post, Baird ordered every signer to be placed under arrest and sent an officer to take their swords, leaving the regiment with only four of the original line officers.[40]

Because of events shaping up elsewhere in central Tennessee during the latter part of June 1863, the regiments of Coburn's brigade were soon to be called to other duties at Triune and Murfreesboro. The experiences of the regiments during the last three months, beginning with the Battle of Thompson's Station and ending with their return to the army after confinement in Libby Prison, had not been conducive to good discipline. The men needed to be made fit for fighting again. The last days spent by the 85th Indiana at Franklin were occupied with picket duty, daily drills, a strict observance of reveille and taps, and other routine duties.

The men were assigned to picket a line that was three miles in length, extending from the Harpeth River on the northwest, around Franklin on the south, and back to the river on the southeast. Heavy details were required to cover this extended and difficult line.[41]

In a letter home, written June 22, Captain Brant of the 85th Indiana said: "We are having pretty heavy picketing to do. Ten men from my company are out today . . . watching on picket amid the sparkling lightening bugs and screams of numberless frogs during the doleful nights make one think of home as a paradise." [42]

Apparently frogs had some significance to the soldiers other than that of being noisy. Private Neet of Company G of the 85th Indiana wrote to his wife: ". . . the boys have got to ketching bull frogs and eating them[.] they are called a big dish[.] me and one of the boys went up the [Harpeth] river yesterday but we could not find any frogs[.]" [43]

While the 85th Indiana was on this picket duty, flooding from a heavy rain washed away the two bridges across the river, interrupting communications between the camp of the regiment and Franklin until a foot bridge could be constructed.[44]

HANGING OF THE SPIES AT FRANKLIN
JUNE 8-9, 1863

In early June 1863, most of Coburn's brigade had not yet returned to Tennessee from confinement at Libby Prison. The members of the brigade remaining at Franklin experienced one of the most extraordinary events of their service and of the war itself. It all began innocently enough during the late afternoon of June 8. Colonel John P. Baird of the 85th Indiana, commanding the post of Franklin, was seated in front of his tent at Fort Granger, chatting with Lieutenant Colonel Carter Van Vleck of the 78th Illinois Infantry, which was a part of the garrison of Franklin, when two strangers in uniform rode up and spoke to them. The older of the two, who did all the talking, introduced himself as Colonel Lawrence W. Auton of the Army of the Potomac, and his younger companion as Major Dunlop, an assistant inspector of Western troops. Auton then stated that both of them had been assigned to the War Department as inspectors general and that they were there to inspect defenses, outposts, and local troops in Tennessee. They had just come from Rosecrans' headquarters of the Army of the Cumberland at Murfreesboro and stopped briefly at Granger's headquarters at Triune.[45]

Both men had on civilian overcoats but wore Federal regulation pants and caps covered with white flannel havelocks. Auton explained his attire to Colonel Baird as follows:

> . . . he had missed the road from Murfreesborough to this point [Franklin], got too near Eagleville, and run into rebel pickets, had his orderly shot, and lost his coat containing his money; that he wanted some money and a pass to Nashville; . . .[46]

Although it was not known at the time, it is certain that the men were not wearing Confederate uniforms when they crossed the Union lines, because they paused to visit the home of Judge Randal M. Ewing in Franklin before going on the Fort Granger. In a reminiscence, Judge Ewing wrote as follows:

> *These two officers were splendidly mounted and equipped; they were fine looking men, who would attract attention in any assemblage. They wore military caps with a cape cover to the cap that protected the neck [a havelock]. They were in Federal uniform. . . .*[47]

The men presented the following papers to Baird, who examined them and found them to be in order. [48]

Document 1.

War Department, Adjt. Gen.'s Office
Washington, May 25, 1863
Special Order No. 140

IV. Col. Lawrence W. Auton, cavalry, United State Army and acting special inspector-general, is hereby relieved from duty along the
"Line of the Potomac." He will immediately proceed to the West, and
minutely inspect the Department of the Ohio and the Department of
the Cumberland, in accordance with special instructions. . . .

V. Maj. George Dunlop, assistant quartermaster is hereby relieved
from duty in this city. He will report immediately to Col. Auton for
duty.

By order of the Secretary of War:

E. D. Townsend

Document 2.

Col. L. W. Auton, Cavalry, Special Inspector-General:

Colonel: The major-general commanding desires me to say to you
that he desires that, if you can spare the time at present, you will inspect his outposts before drawing up your report for the War Department at Washington City. All commanding officers of outposts will
aid you in this matter to the best of their ability. The general desires
me to give his respects to you.

I remain, very respectfully, your obedient servant,

J. A. Garfield

Document 3.

Headquarters Department of the Cumberland,
Murfreesborough, May 30, 1863

All guards and outposts will immediately pass without delay Colonel Auton and his assistant, Major Dunlop.

By command of Major-General Rosecrans:

J. A. Garfield

Document 4.

Headquarters United States Forces
Nashville, Tenn. June 5, 1863

All officers in command of troops belonging to these forces will give every assistance in their power to Col. L. W. Auton, special inspector-general, under direct orders from the Secretary of War.

By command of General [James D.] Morgan

Jno. Pratt,

Assistant Adjutant-General

At that time Baird saw no reason to suspect that the two men were other than what they claimed to be, and indeed, at their request, loaned them the fifty dollars, which they promised to repay as soon as they reached their destination. Just at dark, they prepared to depart, saying that they were going to Nashville. Before leaving, at their request, Baird gave them the countersign for the night so that they could pass through the lines on their way north.[49]

Baird was completely charmed by the two men, but Van Vleck was disturbed by a number of the circumstances attending their visit, one of which was they declined an invitation to spend the night at Fort Granger, hurrying off near dark for the long ride of about eighteen miles to Nashville. Van Vleck was not asked for his opinion while the strangers were at Baird's headquarters, but after they had departed he expressed his doubts to fellow officers. He came to the conclusion that they were spies, and Captain William T. Crawford of the 85th Indiana, who had heard Van Vleck's comments, concurred in this opinion. Baird, after listening to Van Vleck's misgivings, began to have second thoughts himself.

At about that time, Colonel Louis D. Watkins of the 6th Kentucky Cavalry, rode up, and Baird related the story to him. Baird then asked Watkins if he believed that the two men were spies, and the latter replied emphatically that he did. Baird then directed him to follow and arrest them as quickly as possible. The two men had moved off rapidly, however, and Watkins, not having time to call a guard, set out in pursuit with only an orderly of his command. Watkins directed the orderly to unsling his carbine and to fire without further orders if the two men made any suspicious moves on being stopped.

Watkins caught up with them a little less than a half mile from Baird's headquarters, just before they reached the picket line at Spencer Creek. He explained to them that, because it was dangerous for them to travel alone outside the Union lines, he had been sent to ask that they return to Baird's headquarters, where they were to await an escort. Despite their feelings, the two men could not very well refuse, and they accompanied Watkins back to his tent at the cavalry camp in the woods near Fort Granger. There he placed them under a heavy guard. Apparently they did not suspect that they were prisoners until the guard was placed at the door. A short time later, Watkins took them to Colonel Baird under a strong guard.[50]

The two men became uneasy and protested vigorously at being so treated, and then Baird informed them that he suspected them, and they were under arrest. He further stated they would be held as prisoners until he could determine their true character.

There was to be no sleep at headquarters that night. Baird immediately telegraphed Brigadier General James A. Garfield, General Rosecrans' chief of staff at Murfreesboro, as follows:

> Is there any such inspector-general as Lawrence Orton, colonel U.S. Army, and assistant, Major Dunlop? If so, please describe their personal appearance, and answer immediately.[51]

Garfield's reply was sent at 10:15 PM and arrived at Baird's headquarters about midnight. He said:

> There are no such men as Insp. Gen. Lawrence Orton, colonel U. S. Army, and assistant, Major Dunlop, in this army, nor in any army, so far as we know. Why do you ask?[52]

Baird explained:

> Two men came in camp about dark, dressed in our uniform, with horses and equipments to correspond, saying that they were Colonel Orton, inspector-general, and Major Dunlop, assistant, having an order from Adjutant-General [Edward D.]Townsend and your order to inspect all posts, but their conduct was so singular that we have arrested them, and they insisted that it was important to go to Nashvile to-night. The one representing himself as Colonel Orton [W. Orton Williams] is probably a regular officer of the old army, but Colonel Watkins, commanding cavalry here, in whom I have the utmost confidence, is of opinion that they are spies, who have either forged or captured their orders. They can give no consistent account of their conduct.
>
>   . . . If these men are spies, it seems to me that it is important that I should know it, because [Nathan B.] Forrest must be awaiting their progress.[53]

Garfield replied to Baird at midnight, June 8, 1863, as follows:

> The two men are no doubt spies. Call a drum-head court-martial to-night, and if they are found to be spies, hang them in the morning, without fail. No such men have been accredited from these headquarters.[54]

A further investigation revealed additional incriminating evidence. Lieutenant Henry C. Wharton of the Corps of Engineers came up from Triune and, after viewing the prisoners, stated that they had never been to Triune as they claimed, and that he had noticed, after an examination of the stranger's orders, that they had not been written on War Department paper; therefore, their papers were forgeries.[55]

Baird then ordered that the prisoners be searched. "Major Dunlop" consented without opposition, but "Colonel Auton" protested and went so far as to reach for his arms, but resistance was useless and both submitted to the search. When the major's sword was drawn from its scabbard, his captors found etched upon it "Lt. W. G. Peter, C.S.A." The newly discovered Lieutenant Peter was also found to be wearing a Confederate cap that had been covered by the white flannel havelock.

There was still more evidence against the prisoners—Colonel Auton, who also wore a havelock to conceal his military headgear, was wearing the correct shoulder straps of his supposed rank, but they were not those of a staff officer serving in the War Department.[56]

When confronted with such evidence, both men admitted that they were Confederate officers, but strongly denied that they were spies or had been engaged in spying. Orton tried to explain why they were there by saying that they had been in the vicinity only having a good time and that they had made a bet with fellow officers that they could borrow fifty dollars from Baird and return that same evening. This story made little impression on his captors.[57]

Some time after midnight Baird sent still another message to Garfield containing an appeal from Orton:

> General Garfield, Chief of Staff:
>
> Will you not have any clemency for the son of Captain Williams, who fell at Monterey, Mexico? As my dying speech, I protest our innocence as spies. Save also my friend.
> Lawrence W. Orton
> (Formerly W. Orton Williams.)

I send this as a dying request. The men are condemned, and we are preparing for execution. They also prefer to be shot. If you can answer before I get ready, do.

J. P. Baird[58]

The court-martial was convened at 3:00 AM June 9 and consisted of Colonel Thomas J. Jordan, 9th Pennsylvania Cavalry, president; Lieutenant Colonel Carter Van Vleck, 78th Illinois Infantry; Lieutenant Colonel William T. Hoblitzel, 5th Kentucky Cavalry; Captain William T. Crawford, 85th Indiana Infantry; and Lieutenant Henry C. Wharton, Judge advocate. Captain Edward Davis of Company G, 85th Indiana read the charges and specifications.[59]

At 4:40 on the morning of June 9, the following order was sent from Rosecrans' headquarters at Murfreesboro:

Col. J. P. Baird, Franklin:

The general commanding directs that the two spies, if found guilty, be hung at once, thus placing it beyond the possibility of Forrest's profiting by the information they have gained.

Frank S. Bond
Major and Aide de Camp.[60]

The case was decided before daylight June 9, and the prisoners were found guilty of the charge of being spies, and they were informed that they must prepare for immediate death by hanging.[61]

Rosecrans approved the finding, and Baird issued the following order:

. . . by order of Major General Rosecrans, the prisoners will be executed immediately by hanging by the neck till they are dead.

Captain [Julius] Alexander [of the 7th Kentucky Cavalry], provost marshal, will carry out the sentence into execution.[62]

The gallows for the execution was constructed in a wild cherry tree, not far from the depot, and in a very public place. It appears to have been formed by nailing a braced crossbar to a tree, then suspending the ropes and nooses from this bar until they reached to within eight feet of the ground. Finally they placed a cart under the nooses to serve as a platform. Two poplar coffins were nearby.

A little after 9:00 AM the entire garrison was called out and formed around the place of execution. At 9:20 AM the guards conducted the prisoners to the scaffold, where they took their places on the cart. The provost marshal then tied a new handkerchief over the face of each man and adjusted the ropes. What happened next is described by a man of the 85th Indiana who simply signs his name as "D" in a letter to *The Rockville Tribune*, written after the war.

> While these men were convicted of being spies, yet they died as bravely as ever human beings died. They requested that their hands be not tied. The request was granted, and before they were swung off they embraced each other; the scene brought tears to the eyes of all who witnessed it. A cart was placed under the limb of a tree, to which the ropes were made fast. The[y] were placed standing on the cart, the nooses were placed on their necks and the cart drawn from under them. The knot of one did not slip around under the ear, but caught under his chin, whereupon the poor victim reached up and caught hold of the rope and slipped the noose around under his ear, then let go and hung until dead. It was a sad, sad sight, but one of the necessary cruelties of war.[63]

Dr. Forester, surgeon of 6th Kentucky Cavalry, Dr. Samuel C. Moss of the 78th Illinois Infantry, and Captain Jefferson E. Brant of Company E, 85th Indiana Regiment, had been detailed to examine the bodies, and after a wait of twenty minutes they found that there were no further signs of life. At thirty minutes the bodies were cut down and placed in the coffins in full dress. Both men were buried in the same grave.[64]

The following communications marked the end of the official proceedings:

Headquarters Post, Franklin, Tenn., June 9, 1863

Capt. J[ulius]. H. Alexander. Seventh Kentucky Regiment Cavalry, provost-marshal of Franklin, Tenn., by virtue of the above proceedings and order, carried the sentence into execution by hanging said prisoners by the neck until they were dead.

J. H. Alexander
Captain and Provost-Marshal[65]

Baird then notified Rosecrans as follows:

The men have been tried, found guilty, and executed, in compliance with your order. There is no appearance of the enemy yet.

I am ever yours, &c.,

J. P. Baird

Colonel, Commanding Post[66]

When the true identities of the men became known, it was found that Colonel "Lawrence W. Auton" had been known earlier as Colonel William Orton Williams, but later he had taken the name of his brother, and was, at the time of his capture, known asLawrence Orton Williams. "Major Dunlop" was Lieutenant Walter G. Peter, familiarly known as "Gip."

Colonel Williams was from Georgetown, D.C., and was the son of Captain William George Williams, who had died of wounds received at Monterey in the Mexican War. Colonel Williams was a captain of cavalry in the regular army when the war broke out and was, at that time, aide-de-camp and private secretary to General Winfield Scott. Orton Williams was also said to be a first cousin to Robert E. Lee, who would later command the Confederate Army in Virginia, but in fact he was not related to Lee. Orton's mother, America Peter Williams, was, however, a first cousin to Mary Anne Custis, Robert E. Lee's wife.

Williams joined the Confederate army and was, for a time, on General Braxton Bragg's staff as chief of artillery. But at the time of his death he was Bragg's inspector general.

At the time, little was known about Walter G. Peter other than that he was Colonel Williams' adjutant. Later, however, it was found that his uncle, Thomas Peter, had married Martha Parke Custis, granddaughter of Martha Custis Washington. Thus Walter Peter was a first cousin, once removed, to Orton Williams.[67]

It is an interesting coincidence that Colonel Watkins of the 6th Kentucky Cavalry and Williams knew one another, because they both had served in the 2nd United States Cavalry before the war. Although Williams recognized Watkins when he was brought to Baird's headquarters, Watkins did not recognize "Colonel Auton" until the latter's true identity became known.

The real reason for Williams' and Peter's entering the Union lines as spies has never been determined. Williams' superiors later claimed that he acted on his own responsibility, without any orders from them. He had commanded a brigade in William T. Martin's Confederate cavalry division, and had been stationed near Franklin, where he had been placed to observe the town's Federal garrison.

In a communication to Rosecrans' chief of staff, dated June 9, 1863,

Colonel Baird reported:

> . . . The officers I executed this morning, in my opinion, were not ordinary spies, and had some mission more important than finding out my situation. They came near dark, asked no questions about forces, and did not attempt to inspect works, and, after they confessed, insisted that they were not spies in the ordinary sense, and that they wanted no information about this place. Said they were going to Canada and something about Europe; not clear. We found on them memorandum of commanding officers and their assistant adjutant-generals in Northern States. Though they admitted the justice of the sentence and died like soldiers, they would not disclose their true object. Their conduct was very singular, indeed; I can make nothing of it.
>
> J. P. Baird
Colonel, Commanding[68]

On June 17, 1863, a short article was published in *The Indianapolis Daily Journal.*

> —Col. Baird, 85th Indiana, has issued a general order presenting to Colonel Lewis D. Watkins, 6th Kentucky Cavalry, the horse, equipments and sabre, which belonged to Col. Williams, lately executed as a spy in the Confederate service.[69]

The execution of the spies troubled Colonel Baird, both then and for years afterward. It was to be his nemesis. June 16, 1864, during the Atlanta Campaign, he would resign and go home, and some years after the war he would enter voluntarily, the Indiana Hospital for the Insane in Indianapolis where he died March 7, 1881. General Charles Cruft, his old law partner, later stated that the hanging of the spies at Franklin had preyed on his mind and possibly accounted for, at least in part, his mental problems.[70]

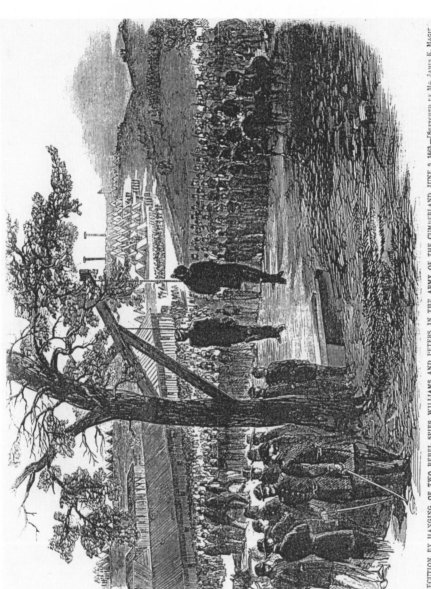

EXECUTION, BY HANGING, OF TWO REBEL SPIES, WILLIAMS AND PETERS, IN THE ARMY OF THE CUMBERLAND, JUNE 9, 1863.—[SKETCHED BY MR. JAMES K. MAGIE

Harper's Weekly

Chapter 8

Guarding the Nashville and Chattanooga Railroad

After the defeat of General Braxton Bragg's army at the Battle of Stones River, Major General William S. Rosecrans put his Army of the Cumberland in camp around Murfreesboro, and, despite constant urging from Lincoln and Halleck in Washington to advance against the enemy, he remained there for about six months until he felt that the army was again ready for active field operations.

Meanwhile, Bragg had retreated with his Army of Tennessee to a strong defensive position behind a range of hills north of the Duck River in Tennessee. His infantry occupied a line that ran from Shelbyville on the Confederate left, through Wartrace, and to Fairfield on the right. The cavalry extended the flanks to Columbia on the left and McMinnville on the right. To approach Bragg's line, it was necessary to move along roads that passed through the range of hills at a series of strongly fortified gaps. Bragg's headquarters was at Tullahoma, on the Nashville and Chattanooga Railroad, which passed through Bell Buckle Gap.[1]

Finally, on June 23, when his preparations had been completed, Rosecrans began his long awaited advance at the beginning of the Tullahoma or Middle Tennessee Campaign. This brilliantly planned and executed campaign was ended successfully when Bragg evacuated Tullahoma June 30 and retired with his army to Chattanooga, where it went into camp on July 8.

In considering how best to drive Bragg's army from its positions in front of Tullahoma, Rosecrans concluded that a frontal attack against General Leonidas Polk's strong position at Shelbyville would be too costly to attempt; he decided instead on a flanking movement. He would feint in the direction of Shelbyville with a part of his force and advance with the rest of his army through Hoover's Gap to Manchester, beyond Bragg's right flank, hoping to force Bragg to withdraw farther south.

According to this plan, Major General Gordon Granger's Reserve Corps, with a cavalry force from Major General David S. Stanley's Cavalry Corps, were to move toward the left of Bragg's line as a feint designed to hold Polk's

Confederate corps at Shelbyville. The cavalry consisted of Brigadier General Robert B. Mitchell's First Division and Colonel Robert H. G. Minty's First Brigade of Brigadier General John B. Turchin's Second Division. Rosecrans was to move with the rest of the army against the right of Bragg's line, held by Lieutenant General William J. Hardee's corps, and attempt to pass his flank in the direction of Manchester.[2]

Late on the night of June 22, Rosecrans ordered Granger to move the next day with his entire command, then at Triune, to Salem, a village about five miles to the southwest of Murfreesboro on the road to Versailles. He explained to Granger that this opening move of the Tullahoma Campaign was a permanent move and directed him to break up the post at Triune and to remove all stores that had been accumulated there. He ordered that all the sick be sent to Nashville and all extra baggage to Murfreesboro. On June 23 Granger marched as ordered, with Brigadier General Absalom Baird's First Division of his Reserve Corps and Brigadier General John M. Brannan's Third Division of Fourteenth Corps, and arrived at Salem that evening.[3]

It has been noted earlier that in the organization of Granger's Reserve Corps, Army of the Cumberland, on June 8, 1863, the designation of Colonel John Coburn's brigade had been changed to Third Brigade of Absalom Baird's First Division, Reserve Corps, commanded temporarily by Colonel William L. Utley while Coburn was still absent on detached duty in Indianapolis.[4]

Coburn's brigade was active during the Tullahoma Campaign, but the regiments were not at the front with the advance troops. Apparently because of their misfortune at Thompson's Station, the regiments of the brigade spent their time as escorts for the army trains, repairing railroads, and as garrison troops for posts in the rear. The regiments of the brigade were not at Triune when Granger began his advance, but were just completing their assembly at Franklin following release from Libby Prison. About noon on June 23, however, the 19th Michigan and the 33rd Indiana regiments, together with the 5th and 6th Kentucky Cavalry regiments, left Franklin for Triune and completed the fourteen mile march at dusk that day.[5]

They were assigned to guard a wagon train that was to leave for Murfreesboro loaded with supplies for Rosecrans' army. The train, consisting of three hundred wagons, each pulled by six mules, moved out in a pouring rain and over terrible roads. The wagons could scarcely be moved without the help of the men, and at the end of six hours of hard work the train was forced to halt for the night, after having covered only three miles. The men and train, however, finally reached Murfreesboro on June 26.[6]

On June 24, 1863, while Granger was moving with the cavalry and Baird's division (less Coburn's brigade) to threaten Polk's position at Shelbyville,

Rosecrans began his advance from Murfreesboro with the rest of his Army of the Cumberland. His movement was directed against the right of Bragg's line, held by Hardee's Confederate corps. Major General George H. Thomas, with the three divisions of his Fourteenth Corps which were then with him, advanced toward Hoover's Gap and Manchester; Major General Alexander McD. McCook's Twentieth Corps moved out on different roads toward Millersburg and Liberty Gap; and Major General Thomas L. Crittenden's Twenty-First Corps moved by roads to the left of Thomas toward Manchester, Tennessee.[7]

Major General Joseph J. Reynolds' Fourth Division was leading Thomas' corps that day, and toward evening Colonel John T. Wilder's First Brigade of mounted infantry arrived at Hoover's Gap, sixteen miles from Murfreesboro. Wilder immediately advanced and drove a cavalry force of Brigadier General John A. Wharton's division of Major General Joseph Wheeler's Cavalry Corps from the gap and continued on for about a mile to McBride's Creek. He then moved back to a strong position at the southern end of the gap. Enemy infantry, consisting of Brigadier General William C. Bate's and Brigadier General Bushrod Johnson's brigades of Major General Alexander P. Stewart's division of William J. Hardee's corps, attempted to retake the gap but were repulsed. About 4:00 PM, Reynolds arrived with the other two brigades of his division and extended Wilder's line on both sides of the gap.[8]

Brigadier General Richard W. Johnson's Second Division of McCook's corps marched through the little town of Millersburg and arrived at Liberty Gap, a short distance beyond, that afternoon. Brigadier General August Willich's brigade advanced about 5:15, and, after passing through the gap, halted for the night. The rest of the division came up during the night to support Willich, while the other two divisions of Twentieth Corps camped that night at Millersburg.[9]

Early on the morning of June 24, Brannan, on Granger's orders, moved with his division from Salem to Christiana, a town on the Nashville and Chattanooga Railroad, ten miles south of Murfreesboro. Upon arriving there he relieved Major General Philip H. Sheridan's Third Division of Twentieth Corps, which moved on and camped at Millersburg, in the vicinity of Liberty Gap. Brannan remained at Christiana until relieved by Baird's division, which had come up from Salem, and Brannan then moved out two miles toward Millersburg and went into camp. Granger halted his command at Christiana to await further orders.[10]

Colonel Henry C. Gilbert of the 19th Michigan assumed command of Coburn's brigade on June 24, relieving Utley, who had been in temporary command of the brigade during the absence of Coburn in Indianapolis.[11]

On June 25 Brannan was relieved from further duty with the Reserve

South Central Tennessee

Corps and was ordered to report with his Third Division to Fourteenth Corps, his proper corps. Brannan remained at the Ross farm at Christiana until about 11:00 that morning and then advanced to Hoover's Mill and camped for the night.[12]

On June 25 the rest of Fourteenth Corps came up to Hoover's Gap, and Thomas continued to hold his position there during the day. McCook's troops were engaged at Liberty Gap most of the day, but they held their positions and repulsed all attempts to dislodge them.[13]

At about 10:30 AM, June 26, Major General Lovell H. Rousseau's division and Brannan's division of Thomas' corps attacked toward Beech Grove at the southern end of Hoover's Gap and, with reinforcements, drove the enemy back toward Fairfield. When Reynolds' division advanced on the left of Thomas' line, it encountered no resistance, because the enemy had been driven back toward Fairfield. Wilder moved up the road toward Manchester and seized Matt's Hollow, a narrow defile through which the road passed. Reynolds' division also moved toward the Manchester road as ordered. Thus, by that evening Thomas had cleared Hoover's Gap and his men were encamped for the night along the road to Manchester.[14]

Three brigades of Twentieth Corps remained at Liberty Gap June 26, 1863, but the rest of the corps moved that day to Hoover's Gap. Crittenden continued his advance toward Manchester. Granger, with Absalom Baird's division of the Reserve Corps, remained in camp near Christiana, where he was joined by Mitchell's cavalry division and Stanley with Minty's cavalry brigade.[15]

Late on June 26 Bragg learned that Union forces had turned his right flank at Hoover's Gap, and that his line was no longer tenable. Accordingly, at 11:00 that night he ordered Polk and Hardee to move back the next morning and concentrate their forces at Tullahoma. This movement was completed on the afternoon of June 28.[16]

Rosecrans continued his advance on June 27, reaching Manchester, beyond Bragg's right flank. Reynolds' Fourth Division of Thomas' corps occupied the town that morning, a part of Major General James S. Negley's division came in that evening, and the rest of the corps arrived during the night. Crittenden's corps and McCook's corps joined Thomas' corps at Manchester June 28. Rosecrans then began preparations for an advance on Tullahoma.[17]

Early on the morning of June 27 Granger left Christiana with Stanley's cavalry and Absalom Baird's division of his Reserve Corps and marched toward Fosterville with orders to drive the enemy cavalry from Guy's Gap. The cavalry moved out in front, and Baird's infantry followed in close support. The cavalry finally succeeded in driving the enemy back toward Shelbyville, and Granger, leaving Baird to hold the gap, pushed on with the cavalry until 6:00 PM, when he arrived in front of the enemy's works, about three miles from the town. The cavalry then charged and drove Major General Joseph Wheeler's cavalry back across the Duck River, on the south side of Shelbyville. It was near dark, and, pursuit being impossible, Granger halted for the night. The next morning he ordered Stanley to move with his cavalry to join Rosecrans at Manchester, and he then returned with Baird's division to his camp at Christiana.[18]

Meanwhile, the 19th Michigan and the 33rd Indiana of Coburn's brigade had been active. The men of the 19th Michigan were not permitted to rest after their arduous trip with the wagon trains from Triune to Murfreesboro. They were up early the next morning, June 27, and at 5:00 AM marched out of Murfreesboro guarding an ammunition train bound for the front. The regiment reached Guy's Gap, south of Fosterville, June 29, and rejoined Baird's division. It went into camp at Guy's Gap, near the Murfreesboro and Shelbyville pike. Generally, its purpose was to defend the gap and the signal station located there, but a part of the regiment was engaged in cutting ties and repairing the railroad toward Shelbyville, a branch of the Nashville and Chattanooga Railroad that ran from Wartrace to Shelbyville.[19]

The 33rd Indiana remained at Murfreesboro for three days after its arrival there with the trains from Triune, and on June 29 it marched to Christiana. Lieutenant Colonel James M. Henderson, commanding the regiment, halted there to feed five hundred Confederate prisoners being held at the town and then continued on southward with the regiment, reaching Guy's Gap at midnight. The 33rd Indiana then rejoined Baird's division of the Reserve Corps and moved on to Shelbyville and returned to Guy's Gap.[20]

The enemy had recently destroyed the railroad south from Fosterville to Wartrace. While the 33rd Indiana was at Guy's Gap, Henderson sent a detachment of 150 men of the regiment and the same number of Negroes, all under the command of Lieutenant William W. Hollingsworth, to put it back in running order. John McBride tells of the following incident:

> . . . While the men were engaged in chopping down trees to work up into ties, the rebel owner of the land demanded them to stop, but Sam Strain, of Company F [of the 33rd Indiana], settled matters by insisting on hanging the man. He was not seen afterward.[21]

Bragg learned on June 30, 1863, that the Federals were in strong force at Manchester, and that night he fell back from Tullahoma to the south side of Elk River, near Decherd and Winchester. He then withdrew to Cowan, where he formed a defensive line at the foot of the mountain. On July 3, 1863, however, Bragg began crossing the mountains by way of University

Place and retired to Chattanooga, where he arrived during the first week of July 1863.[22]

Rosecrans, after learning that Bragg had evacuated Tullahoma, issued orders for pursuit July 1, 1863. The Army of the Cumberland moved forward from the vicinity of Manchester to a general line running through Winchester, Decherd, and Cowan, and there, on July 5, all major movements ended. Rosecrans ordered the army into camp to await the arrival of supplies and to prepare for a further advance toward Chattanooga.[23]

Supplies were virtually non-existent in the region occupied by the Army of the Cumberland at the close of the Tullahoma Campaign. To prepare for a further advance toward Chattanooga it was necessary to bring from Nashville food and supplies of all kinds to sustain the army on its march. The Nashville and Chattanooga Railroad had to be put in running order and protected.[24]

Guarding the railroad was no picnic for the soldiers who were stationed in detachments along the line at bridges, trestles, tunnels, and other sensitive points. Raids were frequent; the enemy usually burned bridges or derailed trains and then moved on, but they rarely remained at any one point long enough to bring on a serious engagement. In addition to defensive activities, the men were engaged in the arduous work of keeping the road in repair. The road had never been well constructed, and trains ran off the track almost daily. The track ran through rough country, but to minimize the cost of cuts and fills it followed rather closely the natural surface of the land. The maximum grade was two percent (106 feet to the mile). The track, which had been in use for twelve years, was made of light inverted U or bridge rail laid on cedar stringers seven inches thick. Only gradually were the stringers replaced by cross-ties. To make matters worse, everything needed by the entire army as it moved south was carried over this single track railroad. A very large force was required to repair and protect it. Coburn's brigade was assigned this duty.[25]

Friday afternoon, July 3, Colonel John P. Baird's 85th Indiana left Fort Granger, just to the northeast of Franklin, on the Harpeth River, and marched toward Murfreesboro. It advanced only five miles the first day, over a rough and hilly road, and halted when darkness made further progress impossible. The regiment spent the night in a wheat field, using the newly shocked wheat for bedding, then resumed the march July 4 on a very hot day. After a march of fourteen miles, they bivouacked in the woods for the night. The regiment reached the vicinity of Murfreesboro the following evening and encamped about one-half mile southeast of town.

This proved to be a very unpleasant campground. The greater part of the Army of the Cumberland had been encamped in this area for about six months after the Battle of Stones River, and the country about the town was a scene of complete desolation. There was not a fence left standing, and the stench from the old camps, and from the battlefield to the north was almost unbearable.

Companies A and D were assigned to duty in the city—A as a prison guard and D as patrol guard handling rebel prisoners.[26]

On July 3 the 14th Michigan arrived at Franklin from Nashville, relieving Utley's 22nd Wisconsin from duty at that post. Upon being relieved, Utley was ordered to Murfreesboro with his regiment. Originally, the 22nd Wisconsin was to have gone directly to Guy's Gap and join the 19th Michigan and the 33rd Indiana, but the arrest of the line officers, which rendered the regiment unfit for field service, necessitated a change of plan.[27]

Because of the very hot weather, the 22nd Wisconsin waited until about 5:00 PM on July 3 to begin its march. The roads between Franklin and Murfreesboro were very bad, and the regiment covered only six miles that day. The next day the march continued over what one of the men described as "one of the worst roads in the world," and the men camped that night seven miles east of Triune and nine miles from Murfreesboro.[28]

July 5 was another day of difficult marching over hills, rocks, muddy roads, and wading streams. The 85th Indiana halted about three miles from Murfreesboro to cook dinner while Colonel Baird, who accompanied the column, left for Murfreesboro to report the arrival of his command and to select a campground. Baird returned about 3:00 PM, and the 22nd Wisconsin again moved forward. The men finally pitched their tents just outside the town on the Shelbyville pike.[29]

It should be noted here that the march of the 22nd Wisconsin from Franklin to Murfreesboro was totally without order. With most of their officers under arrest, the men did exactly what they pleased, wandering through the fields looking for blackberries, occupying the full width of the road, and being disorderly. Colonel Utley attempted to restore order but without success, and he finally remarked "that they are demoralized as H–l."[30]

On July 11 a paper was prepared preferring charges against Utley. He was charged with cowardice, incompetency, conduct prejudicial to discipline and good order, and conduct unbecoming to an officer and a gentleman. The charges were signed by the captains who had earlier signed the petition requesting his resignation and also by captains George H. Brown and Wallace H. Jennings.[31]

Rosecrans was at Murfreesboro July 14, while on a tour of inspection of the posts of his department, and there he was informed of the serious situation existing in the 22nd Wisconsin. This discussion resulted in an order late that afternoon, through Granger, releasing from arrest, temporarily, the officers arrested for signing the petition, but he did not release Bloodgood, who had been under arrest for some time for his conduct at Thompson's Station.[32]

On the night of July 7 Colonel Coburn finally completed his work in Indiana and started south to rejoin the army. He arrived at Murfreesboro July 13 and assumed command of his brigade, relieving Colonel Gilbert, who had been in temporary charge during his absence.[33]

Granger moved his headquarters to Nashville on July 18 and left Coburn in command at Murfreesboro. Also that day, the 33rd Indiana left Guy's Gap and returned to Murfreesboro. The night before the regiment left, a captain and a private were killed only a short distance from their camp. This sad affair is described by John R. McBride in his *History of the Thirty-Third Indiana Veteran Volunteer Infantry* as follows:

The day previous to leaving Guy's Gap Captain [Israel C.] Dille and Private Lothario C. Jones, both of Company G, took some chickens to a house outside of the lines to have them cooked for the next day's march. They did not return. The following day after the regiment moved out Lieutenant [John C.] Maze [of Company D], dressed in citizen's clothes, with Lieutenant [William W.] Hollingsworth [of Company B] and a detail of about forty men in hailing distance, went to the house and pretended to the woman, who was the only person about, that he was making his way to the rebel lines, and through her learned that Dille and Jones were killed by a captain and another man. At first Maze discredited her story. To prove it, she showed him the blood where they had been lying, and then modified her statement by saying that her two sons and a neighbor had killed them. Lieutenant Maze then said, "I have got you now," and at a signal the detachment under Hollingsworth rode up. They then took charge of the woman and all the Negroes about the house and in the neighborhood, and also the old man who did the shooting. They urged him to tell what they did with Captain Dille and Jones, but he would not. They then hung him up with gun-straps, but he would not speak. They then received orders to go to Murfreesborough, where the entire party was placed in jail. Shortly after, the woman took sick, and believing that she would die, sent for Maze and Hollingsworth and repeated her first statement. In a short time the regiment moved again to the front, and the disappearance of the two men remained a mystery thereafter, but

it was believed that the first statement made by the woman was correct.[34]

July 18 the 19th Michigan broke camp and moved about four miles to
Fosterville, a sorry village that had been almost completely destroyed during the war. Military occupation of the village was a very unpleasant duty,
because the surrounding region was infested with bushwhackers and guerrillas, making it dangerous for the men to wander far from camp except in
large groups. The 10th Illinois Regiment finally arrived at Fosterville and
relieved the 19th Michigan from duty there, and on July 23 the latter made
a hot and dusty march of fourteen miles to Murfreesboro.[35]

William Neet of the 85th Indiana, then at Murfreesboro, emphasized
the bushwhacker problem in a letter written July 18, 1863, as follows:

> . . . we have been out on a general blackberry picking this afternoon[.]
> there was about 50 or 60 of us went and we got several bushel and picked
> with our guns in our hands[.] we went out about 3 or 4 miles and the whole
> country looks like a prairie[.] It is about as good land as I ever seen and we
> seen only one little fence while we was out and that was a little patch of 2
> or 3 acres around a cabbin where there was some negroes lived i reckon for
> i did not see a white person while I was out but some darkys at most every
> place[.][36]

By the end of the month, the four regiments of Coburn's brigade were
united at Murfreesboro, with Coburn again in command. While there, the
men of the brigade, in addition to their duties in guarding the railroad, spent
much of their time in regimental and brigade drill, which greatly improved
the quality of the troops.[37]

During the summer and fall of 1863, while the 85th Indiana was in camp
near Murfreesboro, many of the soldiers became homesick, and a number
of them applied for furloughs. None were granted. Finally, Private William M. Jackman, whose home was near Catlin, in Parke County, Indiana,
decided to write directly to President Lincoln. He sent the following letter:

> murfresboro, tense.

> dear abe I want a furlo, my great grandfather fit in the war of the
> rivolution and he never deserted or had a furlo and my grandfather fit in
> the war of 1812 and he never diserted or had a furlo and my father and his
> two brothers were in the war of mexeco and neither of them ever diserted or
> had a furlo now dear abe I dont want to be the furst jackman to disert but

I want to be the furst jackman to git a furlo.

william m jackman

Lincoln was apparently touched by Jackman's simple logic and honesty, and after a time his application for a furlough came back to Colonel Coburn with the President's endorsement, instructing the colonel that if Jackman had a good record to return the application with a statement to that effect, and that he would receive a furlough. Coburn returned the application with positive certification. A few days later an order from Lincoln came through the regular channels to Colonel Baird of the 85th Indiana, bearing the endorsements of generals Henry W. Halleck, Ulysses S. Grant, George H. Thomas, Gordon Granger, William T. Ward, and Colonel John Coburn. The furlough was immediately granted, and Jackman went home for a visit.

Jackman's success prompted a number of other soldiers to write Mr. Lincoln requesting "furlo's." Finally, to put an end to this problem, Colonel Baird issued an order to place under arrest any soldier who should in the future make a similar request. None did. [38]

Samuel H. Mattox was a private in Company C of the 85th Indiana, but because of ill health, he spent much of his time in service in military hospitals. In his letters to his family in Terre Haute, he frequently gives considerable insight into army life in hospitals and behind the lines. When the 85th Indiana began its duty guarding the railroad in Tennessee, Mattox was in the hospital in New Albany, Indiana, where he had been sent early in May 1863. One example of his problems is illustrated in a letter to his wife, dated May 12, 1863:

> *. . . I want you to send me about five dollars. I want it to buy my tobacco and some paper and envelopes and stamps and buy me some milk and butter once in a while. They dont give milk and butter to anyone here only the sick ones* [apparently at that time he was not very sick]*.* "

On June 6, 1863, after receiving ten dollars, he wrote her about the cost of food as follows:

> *. . . I think I will have plenty of money to do me now till I make a draw. Butter was 35 cents a pound, when I first came here, but it has come down to 20 cents now, so I dont think it would pay to express any to me, any how I can get sweet milk at 5 cents a quart and buttermilk at 10 cents a gallon. I went to market this morning and saw some new potatoes and cabbage in market, but if we get any, we have to buy for we have no such things at the table.*[39]

The high cost of food prompted many of the soldiers to do a little foraging on their own. Private Neet of the 85th Indiana wrote his wife from Murfreesboro, August 16, 1863, the following:

> . . . *i must tell you that I got my haversack most full of tomatoes this morning out in the woods close where I was on picket[.] they grow where the soldiers was camped last year[.] I think this is a good country for vegetables[.] . . .*[40]

Mattox finally left the hospital at New Albany and rejoined his regiment at Murfreesboro. He traveled by train from Nashville to Murfreesboro and relates the following harrowing experience, which shows the difficulties of travel "on the cars" at that time:

> *We left Nashville at 6 o'clock in the morning and there was a train ahead of us. It ran out about 10 miles from town and it being very heavily loaded, stalled being considerably up grade. It was right at a turn in the road, when our train came up and not seeing it they ran right into it. It spoiled two cars and injured the engine considerably. Three men, two who were brothers and the third a cousin were sitting on the platform. They were instantly crushed to death. One Lieut. stepped to the door to tell them to 'get up from there and he got his leg broken. There were a good many riding on the top and I was one* [the cars were full of supplies], *but was on the hind most car. A great many saw they were going to strike and jumped off. Some three or four were crippled by so doing. I stuck to the top and did not get injured in the least. After three hours work, we got started again. We ran on the balance of day and when we stopped that night, a young man by the name of Wm. Dubagh got his foot caught between the bumpers of the cars and crushed it off or so badly it had to be taken off. He had come with me all the way from New Albany.*[41]

During the last three weeks of July and the early part of August 1863, Rosecrans brought up supplies from Nashville and otherwise prepared his army for a further advance on Chattanooga and Bragg's army. This preparation was a slow and laborious operation, and Rosecrans refused to move until he was satisfied that the army was ready. The authorities in Washington had, for some time, been urging, without success—there was talk in Washington about his removal—that Rosecrans renew his advance against Bragg's army, and finally, on August 4 Major General Henry W. Halleck, General in Chief of the Army, sent him a peremptory order to move forward without further delay.[42]

In response to this order, the Army of the Cumberland left its camps August 16 and moved forward toward the Tennessee River, where it arrived

August 21. The next week was spent building bridges and otherwise preparing to cross, and the troops began crossing the river August 29 at Caperton's Ferry, Shellmound, Battle Creek, and Bridgeport.[43]

Absalom Baird, commander of First Division of Granger's Reserve Corps, to which Coburn's brigade belonged, left the army on an extended leave after the close of the Tullahoma Campaign, and during his absence Brigadier General Walter C. Whitaker assumed temporary command of the division. Finally, on August 11, because Baird was still absent, Granger ordered Brigadier General James B. Steedman to relieve Baird and assume permanent command of First Division.[44]

When Rosecrans' army left its camps August 16, 1863, and began its march toward the Tennessee River and Chattanooga, Steedman's division remained in Tennessee to help guard the Nashville and Chattanooga Railroad. Steedman established his headquarters at Murfreesboro.[45]

In August 1863 an examining board was constituted in Nashville, Tennessee, for men seeking commissions as officers in the colored regiments then being organized in the Department of the Cumberland. Lieutenant Colonel Alexander B. Crane was detached from the 85th Indiana and assigned to serve on this board and was absent from the regiment for many weeks.[46]

Bloodgood's trial by court-martial began at Murfreesboro August 31, convened to examine both his conduct at the Battle of Thompson's Station and the surrender of his command at Brentwood.[47]

On September 3 headquarters of Coburn's Third Brigade of Steedman's division was at Murfreesboro with the four regiments of the brigade also in camp there. Headquarters of Colonel Thomas E. Champion's First Brigade of the division was at Estill Springs, headquarters of Colonel William P. Reid's Second Brigade at Shelbyville.[48]

A few days later, Steedman began to move south with Champion's and Reid's brigades, and September 10 he arrived at Bridgeport, Alabama. Two days later he resumed his march toward Chattanooga, and, passing through Shellmound he arrived at Rossville September 14. Steedman's command was later engaged at the Battle of Chickamauga, September 20, 1863.[49]

When Steedman departed from Murfreesboro with his division for Bridgeport, he left behind at Murfreesboro Coburn's brigade to guard the Nashville and Chattanooga Railroad south of that point. The brigade was temporarily broken up and widely scattered, as troops were assigned by companies or detachments to the various posts along the line of the railroad. Coburn established his headquarters at Tullahoma.[50]

On September 5 the 85th Indiana left Murfreesboro and moved south on its assignment to guard the railroad from Christiana to Duck River Bridge. Captain Jefferson E. Brant's Company E halted at Christiana, where it was to be on guard south to Fosterville, and Francis M. Rude's Company F took post at Fosterville. The rest of the regiment continued on to Wartrace, where it arrived the next day. From there Josiah H. Sherman's Company A and William T. Crawford's Company H advanced to the Duck River, eleven miles south of Wartrace, to guard the railroad bridge at that place, and Francis Brooks' Company B moved to the Garrison Fork of Duck River, three miles south of Wartrace. Thomas Grimes' Company C, Caleb Bales' Company D, Ellery C. Davis' Company G, Caleb Nash's Company H, and Lewis Puckett's Company I were also sent to Duck River Bridge. Headquarters of the regiment was established at Wartrace, a small village consisting of a railroad station, one or two stores, and a bake shop. It was a good place to camp.[51] While at Wartrace, about fifty men of the 85th Indiana were mounted to hunt guerrillas and bushwhackers, and some men served with the artillery.[52]

A minister, Jefferson E. Brant, was in charge of Company E at Christiana instead of serving as a chaplain. Brant was born in Tuscarawas County in Ohio, February 27, 1837. He moved to Indiana and attended Asbury College in Greencastle, Indiana (now DePauw University), where he graduated in the class of 1860. He was married on August 8, 1858, to Mary A. McAllister. After completing his work at DePauw, he became a minister, and in 1861, at the outbreak of the Civil War, he was at Prairieton, Indiana. A year later he became captain of Company E of the 85th Indiana, which was then being formed in the Seventh Congressional District, and he served in that regiment until the end of the war.[53]

First Lieutenant Henry R. Ingraham of Company A has given a brief description of the stockade occupied by Company B of the 85th Indiana at the Garrison Fork bridge, one mile south of Wartrace. This stockade, in which the company camped, was very similar to many of the fortifications constructed along the road. It was located on top of a high hill overlooking the railroad bridge and was about sixty feet square. Timbers from twelve to eighteen inches in diameter were set upright in the ground, close together, to form a wall about eight feet high. A row of loop holes was cut on each of the four sides so it could serve as a watch tower and a secure defensive position.[54]

The 33rd Indiana remained at Murfreesboro until September 6, 1863, then traveled by train to Tullahoma, where the troops were scattered in detachments along the railroad as far south as Decherd. The men of the regiment were stationed at six different posts as follows: Companies B, E, F, and I were on garrison duty at Tullahoma; Company D was, for a time, at Manchester, but was then ordered to join the companies at Tullahoma; Company A was at Estill Springs, near Elk River Bridge; companies H and K were at Decherd; Company C was at Cowan, at the north end of the

Cowan Tunnel; and Company G was at Tracy City guarding coal mines in the vicinity. Tracy City was not on the railroad. The 33rd Indiana remained at these locations for about two months.[55]

During September 1863, only the 19th Michigan and 22nd Wisconsin regiments, both under the command of Colonel Utley, were at or near Murfreesboro. Although secure at this post, and spared the horrors of the Battle of Chickamauga, the men suffered severely from the intense summer heat, and this, combined with a lack of fresh meat and vegetables, caused much sickness. Picket duty during this time was very heavy, requiring one entire regiment each day.[56]

First Lieutenant Frank D. Baldwin, commanding Company D of the 19th Michigan, was ordered to take post at a stockade on Stones River, about three miles south of Murfreesboro, where it was to guard a bridge on the Nashville and Chattanooga Railroad. Companies A and E of the 19th Michigan were also detached and sent to the Duck River to guard the bridge there.[57]

Meanwhile, by September 4 the Army of the Cumberland had completed its crossing of the Tennessee River, and on September 9 troops of Crittenden's Twenty-First Corps occupied Chattanooga. Thomas' Fourteenth Corps and McCook's Twentieth Corps crossed the mountains and advanced into Lookout Valley (also called Wills' Valley). Thomas then moved through Stevens' Gap into McLemore's Cove to Chickamauga Creek, and McCook continued on south along the valley and then moved through Winston's Gap toward Alpine, Georgia.[58]

Rosecrans then learned that Bragg was not retreating as he had previously believed, but that he was instead concentrating his army in front of Thomas' and Crittenden's corps. He immediately issued orders for his army to assemble along Chickamauga Creek, and soon thereafter, on September 19 and 20, 1863, Bragg attacked and defeated the Army of the Cumberland at the Battle of Chickamauga and drove it back to Chattanooga. There Rosecrans took up a strong defensive line about the town, but he was soon under siege when Bragg moved up and occupied Lookout Mountain and Missionary Ridge. Rosecrans' army was in desperate circumstances, because he was unable to bring up adequate food and supplies for the men and animals. At this point the protection of the Nashville and Chattanooga Railroad, the job of Coburn's brigade, became increasingly important, because it was imperative that supplies for the army be brought forward as far as possible.[59]

During the evening of September 23, Lieutenant Colonel Jacob M. Thornburgh rode into the camp of Brant's Company E, 85th Indiana, at Christiana with about two hundred men of his 4th East Tennessee Cavalry. They had with them four prisoners, one of whom they turned over to the corporal of the guard. Next morning no prisoners left with them. About 9:00 AM a little girl came into camp and reported that three men were hanging in the woods not far away. The child then led a party of the 85th Indiana to the spot where the dead men were hanging. They were cut down and placed in a fence corner, where they remained until some of their friends came from about six miles to the east to claim their bodies. During the night cavalrymen came to the stockade and asked to take the prisoner that they had turned over to Brant's men, but the corporal of the guard refused to turn this one man over to them without orders, and the prisoner's life was thus saved. He was then sent to Colonel Baird's headquarters at Wartrace and was paroled. Just why the men were hanged is not recorded; it may have been that they were bushwhackers and therefore deserving of this fate, or possibly that they would have been a burden to fast-moving cavalry and were simply eliminated. These were hard times.[60]

Problems with Negroes continued. September 15, 1863, while at Christiana, Captain Brant, of the 85th Indiana, wrote the following letter:

> Yesterday morning we had some visible evidence of the inhumanity of slavery. A mulatto woman came to us about daylight with a pair of handcuffs on, and her head was cut and the blood had run down her neck beside her face and one eye was terribly burned and bruised and all this because she wanted to go to a Union man's house to work and get money to buy her some clothes. We sent for the key and took off her handcuffs, and her mistress who gave up the key, confessed that her husband in a rage had done as stated. And had locked her up. She managed to escape by a window and after wandering over rocks and in the woods overnight reported to us. In accordance with the Mosaic Scripture we unloosened her shackles and let her go free. Then sent her where she wanted to go. This is one among the many, many like inhumanities toward slaves. But the days of this 'sum of all villianies' are about ended.[61]

After the Battle of Chickamauga, Confederate General Joseph Wheeler, commanding the cavalry of the Army of Tennessee, left Bragg's army near Chattanooga with the divisions of Brigadier General John A. Wharton and Brigadier General William T. Martin and started on a raid against Rosecrans' communications in Tennessee. In a controversial order dated September 28, 1863, Bragg directed Forrest to turn over the troops of his command to Wheeler, and these too were to join the expedition.[62]

Wheeler began his movement September 30 moving up the left bank of the Tennessee River to Cottonport, about thirty-five miles northeast of Chattanooga, to join the three brigades of Forrest's former command, a cavalry division commanded by Brigadier General H. B. Davidson. Wheeler crossed the Tennessee River and moved into the Sequatchie Valley, where early on the morning of October 2 he captured and burned a large Federal wagon train at Anderson's Cross Roads. During the night he crossed the Cumberland Mountains and moved on to McMinnville, Tennessee. There he captured Major Michael L. Patterson and his 4th Tennessee Infantry, which was garrisoning the post, and then destroyed the town, a locomotive, a train of cars, and a railroad bridge over Hickory Creek. When this work was completed, Wheeler marched toward Murfreesboro. After making a demonstration on the town during the morning of October 5 he moved south along the Shelbyville pike to Stones River.[63]

About 7:30 that morning, troops of Wheeler's command appeared in front of the stockade that had been built on Stones River to guard the Nashville and Chattanooga Railroad bridge at that point, garrisoned by Baldwin's Company D of the 19th Michigan Infantry. At 9:00 AM an officer approached the stockade under a flag of truce and demanded the surrender of the post. Baldwin refused, but after being subjected to artillery fire for some time, he surrendered at 10:40 AM. The men laid down their arms and were then marched to the Shelbyville pike.

Wheeler's men spent most of the day cutting down the bridge, burning the timber, and destroying three miles of track south of the river. They then took Baldwin's men to a point near Guy's Gap, where they were released unconditionally at sundown. Baldwin returned to the stockade with his men that night and continued on to Murfreesboro the next day.[64]

After capturing Baldwin's command at Stones River, Wheeler moved on toward Christiana, garrisoned by Brant's Company E of the 85th Indiana. Brant has left a description of what happened there as follows:

> During the first week at Christiana under the direction of Captain Brant a star-shaped wooden stockade was built as a protection against assaults of guerrilla bands. There was a water tank and telegraph office here and just North of the stockade the country road leading down West to the Shelbyville Pike, 3/4 mile away, crossed the rail road. The ground was flat, and about the little town of a dozen houses were woods excepting to the North and West.[65]

> For several days the colored people had been reporting to the Captain that the country was full of guerrillas. Gen. Wheeler had made his celebrated raid; burning up a wagon train in Sequatchie Valley; cap-

tured a regiment of our troops at McMinnville; and on the morning of Oct. 5th made a feint on Murfreesboro. We could hear the cannonading. All these facts were reported to Col. Baird and Col. Coburn and by them to General [Gordon] Granger who ordered Captain Brant to wait until a train from the South would take him off.

In the meantime the rail road to the south was pried up so as to throw the train off the track and in a little while after the telegraph wires were cut.

About that time the rebel Cavalry made their appearance on the road leading to the Shelbyville Pike. The Captain ordered his men into the stockade and stationed a man near the rail road to watch for artillery. When they were deploying around us a Lieutenant and a Sergeant were sent in under a flag of truce demanding a surrender. The Captain refused saying "we will fight and see about that." About the time we were well surrounded and the firing was going on from the port holes from the inside and rebel bullets were rattling against the stockade outside; the guard came in reporting that they were bringing up artillery. The Captain at once waved a white handkerchief and taking sergeant [Otis J.] Gunn met the same Lieutenant and Sergeant and asked if they had Artillery. On being answered they had, the Captain asked to see the guns, fearing a bluff. Following the Lieutenant to where the country road crossed the rail road he met General [Colonel Thomas] Harrison who was commanding this Texan Brigade who saluted him calling him "Captain Brant". The Captain said "I came to ask you if you have artillery," and he replied "we have". Then pointing down the road within 200 yards of the stockade to where two twelve pound parrots glistened in the sun-light, but out of sight from the stockade, General Harrison said "do you see them?", and laughed as though he enjoyed what was no joke to us. The Captain said "I hope you will treat my men as well as possible". The General said "March your men out, Captain,—March your men out."[66]

Brant surrendered his command, because the stockade could not withstand artillery fire, and the fifty men of the garrison marched out and stacked their arms. The enemy burned the stockade and destroyed the water tank and telegraph station, and they also took some commissary stores and ammunition. The lieutenants lost their side arms, overcoats, and blankets; and the enlisted men lost knapsacks, overcoats, and blankets. Captain Brant was permitted to keep his sword, side arms, and pay rolls.[67]

During the evening after the surrender of the post of Christiana, Wheeler's men threatened to hang three men of the 85th Indiana in retaliation for the hanging of the three men near the stockade by Thornburgh's East Tennessee cavalry, but did not carry out the threat. The prisoners were marched some eight miles to Guy's Gap, where they went into camp. Brant tells of the following incident that occurred that night:

> . . . about 11:00 o'clock [PM] some Texas officers [of Colonel Harrison's brigade] sent for Capt. Brant, Lieutenants [Orrin] [Mc]Anderson and [John] Gunn and had them eat with them out of our own mess kit and our own hardtack, meat and coffee they had taken from us. That was a joke that we enjoyed, for we were very hungry.[68]

The next morning, the men of the 85th Indiana who had been captured at Christiana were paroled and sent back to Murfreesboro. They were ordered to proceed to Camp Chase in Ohio, but upon arriving at Louisville, they were sent back to Nashville and then on to Wartrace. They remained there for some time while awaiting orders from Rosecrans. There was some question as to whether the men had been legally exchanged, and many of them objected to taking up arms again until they were certain that the exchange was legal. Finally, it was decided that the parole was not in accord with the cartel between the Federal and Confederate governments; still, the men were ordered back to duty. All obeyed except privates Marvin B. Harris of Pimento and James E. Railsback of Terre Haute, who deserted because of this order.[69]

Meantime, Coburn, who was at Tullahoma, and Colonel Baird of the 85th Indiana, at Wartrace, had been informed of the ranging abroad of Wheeler's cavalry, and they reported this information to Granger at Chattanooga. During the morning of October 5, 1863, Granger ordered Coburn to evacuate Fosterville and Christiana and take the troops guarding those posts to Murfreesboro. The train that was to effect the evacuation started from Wartrace, took aboard Company F of the 85th Indiana at Fosterville, and was on its way to Christiana when word was received that the post had been surrendered. The train then immediately returned to Wartrace with the company from Fosterville.[70]

Also that afternoon Granger, who believed that it was his first duty to hold the Duck River Bridge and certainly irritated at the surrendering of the outpost, sent the following order to the commanding officer at Wartrace: "Move your troops at once to Duck River Bridge, and hold that point until every man is sacrificed." Colonel Baird, the commanding officer, promptly obeyed and left the works at Wartrace at 5:00 PM. He arrived at Duck River at 7:00 that evening with eight companies of the 85th Indiana and one piece of artillery. Baird assumed command of the post of Duck River Bridge and reported to Coburn that the road had been evacuated north of Duck River.

Later, the 28th and 147th Pennsylvania regiments of Brigadier General John W. Geary's division of Twelfth Corps, which was just arriving in Tennessee, also reported at Duck River Bridge and went into camp.[71]

Early in October 1863 Coburn's brigade received some much needed help in guarding the railroad. On September 23 at a meeting held in Washington, President Abraham Lincoln and Secretary of War Edwin M. Stanton decided to send the Eleventh Corps and Twelfth Corps of the Army of the Potomac to aid in relieving Rosecrans' Army of the Cumberland, then penned up in Chattanooga. Major General Joseph Hooker was placed in command of both corps.[72]

The movement of these corps to the west began two days later, and by October 2 the last of Eleventh Corps, together with a few regiments of Twelfth Corps, had arrived in Alabama. The rest of Twelfth Corps was still moving forward by rail and was then approaching Nashville. The next day Rosecrans informed Hooker at Stevenson, Alabama, that enemy cavalry had started on a heavy raid against the Nashville and Chattanooga Railroad and instructed Hooker to halt Major General Henry W. Slocum and his Twelfth Corps on the line of the railroad. On October 4 Rosecrans ordered Hooker to station detachments of Twelfth Corps along the railroad from Nashville to Bridgeport, Alabama, to secure the line against the expected cavalry raid.[73]

In another order, issued October 4, Hooker assigned to Slocum the task of guarding the railroad south from Wartrace to Tantalon, about five miles southeast of Cowan, with his Twelfth Corps. This order was not carried out, however, until October 13 because for a time the troops of Twelfth Corps were being shifted around to various places in an attempt to prevent Wheeler from destroying the railroad.[74]

Except for the few regiments that had arrived at Bridgeport with Eleventh Corps, troops of Slocum's Twelfth Corps did not reach Nashville until the morning of October 5. Brigadier General William T. Ward, commanding the Second Brigade in Brigadier General Robert S. Granger's Third Division of the Reserve Corps, met the 98th and 149th New York and the 5th Ohio regiments there and took them by train to Murfreesboro. The troops at Murfreesboro at that time consisted of the 19th Michigan and the 22nd Wisconsin of Coburn's brigade, both commanded by Colonel Utley of the 22nd Wisconsin. Later that day, Brigadier General Alpheus S. Williams and General Geary, commanding the First Division and Second Division of Twelfth Corps, respectively, arrived, and by the next day between 4,000 and 5,000 men of Twelfth Corps had reached Murfreesboro.[75]

On October 6 Williams started his division southward from Murfreesboro along the railroad toward Bridgeport, Alabama, and that day Brigadier General Joseph F. Knipe's First Brigade and two regiments of Brigadier General Thomas H. Ruger's Third Brigade reached Tullahoma. The other four regiments of Ruger's brigade were halted at Decherd to await transportation. Geary and his Second Division remained at Murfreesboro.[76]

While Williams was moving south with his division to protect the railroad from Wheeler's raiders, Slocum was detained at Nashville, where he was engaged in forwarding equipment, trains, and supplies for his Twelfth Corps. When Hooker, at Stevenson, Alabama, became aware that Wheeler was on the railroad between Slocum and the troops south of Wartrace, he decided that no officer present with these troops was capable of exercising proper command, and on the morning of October 6, he issued the following order to Major General Daniel Butterfield, his chief of staff:

> You will proceed without delay to Decherd and assume command of Twelfth Corps and of all troops in that district, and, after leaving a sufficient number to protect the bridges and stations along the line of the railroad, proceed at once with the residue to disperse and destroy any rebel force you may find along the road between Duck River and Murfreesboro. . . .

Butterfield left Stevenson at 10:00 that morning and moved up to Decherd and then on to Tullahoma.[77]

Meanwhile, on the evening of October 5, Hooker, through Butterfield, had ordered Coburn to put two good regiments on a train and move up to Christiana and drive away Wheeler's raiders. Butterfield also added gratuitously that "This should have been done without waiting for orders." Coburn received Hooker's order about midnight. Hooker was unaware that the post of Christiana had been captured several hours before the order was issued, and that Coburn had been unable to send any troops toward Christiana, because no train had gone north on the railroad that day. Two Ohio regiments of Colonel Charles Candy's First Brigade of Geary's division were then at Tullahoma and were ready to go, but no train was available. Finally, at 1:00 AM October 6 a train arrived from Normandy, and a short time later Coburn started north with three hundred men of the 66th Ohio, one hundred men of the 7th Ohio, and one gun of the 9th Battery, Ohio Light Artillery.[78]

When he arrived at Duck River, Coburn learned that the railroad had been evacuated as far north as Murfreesboro and was then in possession of Wheeler's cavalry. To avoid a possible ambush on the road ahead, Coburn sent forward Colonel Baird in the direction of Christiana with about fifteen mounted men of his command, and gave orders to Colonel Robert Galbraith with about two hundred men of his 1st Middle Tennessee Cavalry, to scout the country toward Shelbyville.[79]

About noon, October 6, Baird, who was out in front, sent back word from

Wartrace that no enemy troops were there, and Coburn then decided to go on to that point. Before starting, he sent Baird and Galbraith on a scout toward Shelbyville. Coburn transferred his men to another train, leaving the gun behind, and moved up to within about one-half mile of Wartrace. At that point a local resident came in and reported that the enemy were in the town and that it would not be safe to take the train in. Coburn stopped the train and sent forward a messenger to verify the man's statement. The messenger soon returned and reported that he had been fired at as he approached the town.[80]

Coburn had to decide whether to continue on, as ordered, or to return to Duck River Bridge. He finally chose the latter course, and he gave his reasons in his report, written October 10, as follows:

> . . . With these uncertainties [the whereabouts of Galbraith and Baird] before me, and not knowing anything whatever of the country or the road, and having the amplest information that General Wheeler was on the road or near it with a force numbering from 10,000 to 15,000, I thought it unwise to unload the men from the train and await the coming of the enemy. I had every reason to believe the enemy to be in force, since only twenty-six hours before he had been about 16 miles north on the railroad, and would probably come in the direction of Wartrace. In addition I did not consider the holding of the road at that place of paramount importance, there being but a small bridge a mile south on Garrison's Creek. The important point being Duck River Bridge, I felt sustained in this decision by the fact that Maj. Gen. Gordon Granger had himself, by ordering its [the Garrison Creek Bridge] evacuation the day before, held it to be a comparatively unimportant point. His order was to hold Duck River Bridge at all events. With Colonels Baird and Galbraith gone, and with my command away, I felt that Duck River Bridge would be very unsafe as against the force which General Wheeler might at any hour bring against it. I resolved at once to return without running the risk of a contest, which might result in the loss of my command, of Colonels Baird's and Galbraith's mounted men, and the Duck River Bridge beside, the force being thus separated miles apart.
>
> To get from the train was at once to assume the whole responsibility, for then the forces would be effectually divided, with no hope of uniting before both places could be attacked. I decided to take care of the main point, the creek bridge being a slight loss, while if the large bridge at the river fell the damage would be almost irreparable.

Accordingly, Coburn finally returned to Duck River, and he took with him Company B of the 85th Indiana that he had ordered up to guard the Garrison Fork bridge.[81]

Coburn's reasons for not remaining at Wartrace and protecting the Garrison Fork bridge would have been convincing if his orders had been discretionary, but they appear not to have been. As a result, he was subjected to considerable criticism. Moreover, there is the possibility that Coburn's caution in not advancing beyond Wartrace might have been related to the capture of his brigade at Thompson's Station earlier in the year. If Coburn was indeed thinking of being caught and overwhelmed, he was probably more cautious about the loss of another command than he otherwise would have been.

It is interesting to note that when the Garrison Fork bridge was later destroyed, it was repaired shortly after daylight October 9, 1863, six hours before the bridge south of Murfreesboro at Stones River was rebuilt and the track repaired. Thus, the evacuation of Wartrace, and the subsequent destruction of the Garrison Fork bridge, does not appear to have been responsible for any delay in the opening of rail communications between Nashville and Stevenson.[82]

When Coburn arrived back at Duck River, he received no information as to the whereabouts of Baird and Galbraith, and he ordered his men to remain on the train until cavalry arrived. About two hours later, Colonel William W. Lowe, commanding the Third Brigade of Brigadier General George Crook's Second Cavalry Division, came up with the 5th Iowa and a part of the 3rd Ohio cavalry regiments, and together they then moved forward toward Wartrace. When the train carrying Coburn's two regiments moved up to within one half mile of the Garrison Fork, they found that the enemy was in possession of the bridge, which was already in flames. Coburn ordered his men off the cars, formed them in line, and advanced toward the bridge. The enemy then departed pursued by Lowe's cavalry, which passed Coburn's infantry at the bridge and moved on through Wartrace toward Shelbyville.[83]

Coburn returned to Duck River bridge and reported to Butterfield, who had by that time arrived there. On Butterfield's orders, Coburn remained at Duck River bridge, in command of the forces there, until there was no further danger of an attack, and he then returned to Tullahoma.[84]

Both Hooker and Butterfield were highly critical of the performance of Coburn and of his brigade in defending the railroad during Wheeler's raid. On the evening of October 6 Hooker wrote to Butterfield at Duck River as follows:

> ...I can scarcely retain the chagrin and mortification I feel at what you write me of the abandonment of Wartrace and the burning of the

bridge. It does not appear that a gun was fired in the defense of either. Women would not act so badly. I hope that you will learn all the particulars, that the guilty may be brought to punishment. There ought to be infantry enough on the road to cut up the rebel cavalry. For God's sake have the bridge repaired as speedily as possible. If you have an opportunity, telegraph Granger and ask if he gave such orders.[85]

Butterfield shared Hooker's displeasure at the lack of Federal resistance to Wheeler's attack on the railroad, and, after Wheeler had departed, ordered an investigation of Baldwin's conduct in surrendering at the Stones River bridge. He also recommended the dismissal of Coburn from the service for not defending the Garrison Fork Bridge and severely criticized Colonel Baird for withdrawing from Wartrace to Duck River. No one was convicted in the investigations that followed.[86]

Given the perspective of hindsight and knowledge of all complications of the situation Hooker's—and Butterfield's—reaction seem overly harsh, and apparently the investigative authorities thought so too. The situation along the railroads in Tennessee was complex because of Wheeler's rapid and unpredictable movements and the lack of reliable communications, and Coburn and others opposing Wheeler probably did the best they could. Thompson's Station was not forgotten—Coburn's past performance, or the prevailing interpretation of what had occurred there, was conditioning the present reaction at command headquarters. Coburn could do no right. Thus are reputations built, or destroyed, in war.

After Wheeler had departed, Butterfield arranged for the rebuilding of the bridge at Garrison's Fork and the bridge at Stones River, and the repair of the track. At 4:00 PM October 9, when this work was completed and the track was again open between Nashville and Stevenson, Butterfield turned over the command of Twelfth Corps to Slocum at Murfreesboro and returned to Stevenson.[87]

Shortly after Wheeler began his raid at Chattanooga, Crook, with his cavalry division of the Army of the Cumberland and Colonel Abram O. Miller, with Colonel Wilder's brigade of mounted infantry, started up the Sequatchie Valley in pursuit. Brigadier General Robert B. Mitchell, Chief of Cavalry of the Department of the Cumberland with Colonel Edward M. McCook's First Cavalry Division, followed close behind. They passed through McMinnville and Murfreesboro and then took the road to Shelbyville.[88]

On October 6 Mitchell's two divisions joined about seven miles from Shelbyville and camped there for the night. The next day Mitchell moved toward Shelbyville, learning before he reached the town that Wheeler had divided his command into three columns: one had moved to the left the day before to attack Wartrace, another had marched on the direct road to Shelbyville, and the third had moved to the right toward Unionville. He also learned that the column that had taken Wartrace had destroyed the Garrison Fork bridge and returned during the night to Shelbyville, where it had rejoined the main command.[89]

That day, October 6, Wheeler captured and destroyed large quantities of stores of all kinds at Shelbyville, and that night Davidson's cavalry division camped on Duck River near Warner's Bridge, Martin's division two miles farther down the river, and Wharton's division two miles below Martin's.[90]

The next morning in a heavy rain, Crook pursued the enemy and, near Farmington, defeated a force consisting of Davidson's and Martin's divisions, inflicting serious losses.[91]

Mitchell's cavalry continued the pursuit despite bad weather and severe fighting, but Wheeler was finally able to withdraw across the Tennessee River near Rogersville on October 9. His rear guard lost ninety-five men at Sugar Creek, near Pulaski, Tennessee.[92]

Philip D. Roddey was to have moved north at the same time as Wheeler with a cavalry brigade from Alabama to cooperate with Wheeler. Roddey crossed the Tennessee River near Larkin's Landing and Guntersville, but not until October 7 and 8. He then moved northward through Vienna, Maysville, and New Market to Salem, Tennessee. He remained there a short time, and then started back toward Huntsville, Alabama.[93]

After the departure of Wheeler and Roddey from Tennessee, the regiments of Coburn's brigade resumed their usual duties of guarding bridges, tunnels, water tanks and other railroad installations, and garrisoning posts along the Nashville and Chattanooga Railroad.

In a major organizational change October 9, 1863, Granger's Reserve Corps was discontinued. The next day Granger assumed command of a newly created Fourth Corps, Army of the Cumberland. This corps was formed by the consolidation of Twentieth Corps and Twenty First Corps. The First and Second brigades of Steedman's former First Division, Reserve Corps, then near Chattanooga, were assigned to Fourteenth Corps, and Coburn's Third Brigade was left at Tullahoma as an unassigned brigade. It remained on duty there during October and November of 1863.[94]

For some time, Coburn had been understandably concerned about the widely scattered condition of his brigade. On October 9, while at Tullahoma, he closed a communication to Seth B. Moe, assistant adjutant general of Steedman's First Division, Granger's Reserve Corps:

> The brigade is much scattered and at almost every post but this [Tullahoma] my command is under a ranking officer of some other brigade or regiment. This is unpleasant to officers and men. Will you have us occupy exclusively a certain number of posts, or get us out of the business entirely?
>
> [William T.] Ward's, [James D.] Morgan's, and R. [Robert S.] Granger's men are in front of us by the thousand. I desire to go on; so do the men. We will cheerfully do duty anywhere, but would rather be with our friends than distributed over 100 miles of mountain and plain.[95]

Steedman referred this request to Granger, commanding the Reserve Corps (he assumed command of Fourth Corps the next day), who wrote the following endorsement: "I respectfully request that Colonel Coburn's brigade be relieved and brought to the front. It has an old grudge to settle in the Thompson's Station affair."[96]

It certainly did. The men of Coburn's brigade felt that most of them had fought bravely at Thompson's Station and had endured the torment of Libby Prison, and that they were entitled to be recognized as first class soldiers. Granger, close to the facts of the situation, understood this. This view was obviously not shared by all the generals, but there would be plenty of time for the brigade to demonstrate its fighting qualities.

On October 10, the day after Wheeler recrossed the Tennessee River at the end of his raid, Williams moved headquarters of his division of Twelfth Corps from Murfreesboro to Decherd. Knipe's brigade was on the railroad at Decherd and Cowan, and Ruger's brigade was at Christiana, but it marched that day to Tullahoma and Elk River Bridge. Geary's division of Twelfth Corps remained at Murfreesboro.[97]

Slocum assumed command of all United States Forces along the Nashville and Chattanooga Railroad from Murfreesboro to Tantalon on October 13, and a short time later he moved his headquarters to Wartrace.[98]

On October 15 he reported the position of his troops as follows: headquarters of Williams's First Division was at Decherd, with his troops at Decherd, Cowan, Tullahoma, Elk River and Estill Springs. Headquarters of Geary's Second Division was at Murfreesboro, with his troops at Duck River, between Wartrace and Bell Buckle, Garrison's Fork Bridge, Normandy, Murfreesboro, Christiana, Fosterville, and Millersburg. The 85th Indiana was also at Wartrace at that time.[99]

General Ulysses S. Grant, who was then at the Galt House in Louisville, Kentucky, was assigned command of the newly created Military Division of the Mississippi on October 17, and General William T. Sherman was assigned to replace Grant in command of the Army of the Tennessee. One of Grant's first acts in his new assignment was to relieve Rosecrans of his command of the Department and Army of the Cumberland and to replace him with General Thomas. A short time later Grant left Louisville for Chattanooga, and he arrived about dark October 23, 1863.[100]

When Bragg's army followed the Army of the Cumberland to Chattanooga after the Battle of Chickamauga, it had occupied positions on Missionary Ridge and Lookout Mountain that forced Rosecrans to bring in supplies from Stevenson, Alabama, by wagon train over a sixty-mile detour. This route ran up to the Sequatchie Valley, then over Walden's Ridge, and finally down to the north bank of the Tennessee River, opposite Chattanooga. About mid-October the rains set in, and the roads became so bad that eight days were required to make the trip. It became clear that something had to be done soon.[101]

Brigadier General William Farrar ("Baldy") Smith, chief engineer of the Army of the Cumberland, had prepared a plan for opening a shorter supply line that ran by way of Kelley's Ferry and Brown's Ferry; when Grant arrived he approved the plan and put Smith in charge of the operations. At 3:00 AM, October 27, a picked force under Brigadier General William B. Hazen captured Brown's Ferry, and a bridge was then laid across the river. Hooker had left Geary's division at Wauhatchie to guard the road, and during the night of October 28 and 29, the enemy attempted to drive back this isolated division. They failed in this attempt, and the next day, with the new road open, supplies began to move into Chattanooga.[102]

Coburn directed Colonel Gilbert to move with his 19th Michigan Regiment from Murfreesboro. He had been stationed there for about three months. His new headquarters was at McMinnville, which was a supply base for operations in that part of Tennessee and also was the terminus of McMinnville and Manchester Railroad running through Manchester and connecting with the Nashville and Chattanooga Railroad at Tullahoma. The regiment was also to hold the important gap through the Cumberland Mountains, east of the town.[103]

By October 23 all regiments from the Army of the Potomac had left Murfreesboro for Lookout Valley, near Chattanooga, and with the departure of the 19th Michigan, Colonel Utley was again in command of the post.[104]

The 19th Michigan arrived at McMinnville October 25 about three weeks after Wheeler had passed through on his raid against the Nashville and Chattanooga Railroad. Colonel Gilbert found the town in a terrible condition, without a single place of business open. Nearly all the shops, stores, and houses on the main street were vacant and filthy—Wheeler had carried off or destroyed almost everything of value. After Wheeler left, 1st East Tennessee Cavalry was sent there to garrison the town, and they were little better than the enemy. The cavalry stabled their horses in the Court House with the men using the houses as quarters, and when they left after Gilbert's arrival they did not clean out their quarters or those of the horses. Gilbert promptly put soldiers of his 19th Michigan, and also Negroes, to work cleaning up the place.[105]

Supply was a problem for a time, because the railroad bridge at Hickory Creek, three miles out of town, had been destroyed, and also some track. Two or three days were required for a mule train to make a trip to Murfreesboro, fifty miles distant, and back. The men rebuilt the bridge, however, and repaired the track, and soon had the trains running again.[106]

Duty at this remote outpost was extremely difficult. The entire area was infested with guerrillas and bushwhackers, and there was also a constant warfare between the rebel sympathizers and the East Tennesseeans who supported the Union. These partisans were engaged in robbing, pillaging, and murdering, and guards and workmen were often subjected to sharpshooter fire. Despite all this activity, however, the troops of the garrison of McMinnville, the 19th Michigan of Coburn's brigade, suffered virtually no military casualties.[107]

October 26 Slocum assumed command of all the troops assigned for the defense of the railroad from Murfreesboro to Bridgeport, including the latter two towns.[108]

With the arrival of Twelfth Corps on the railroad, a confusing command situation soon surfaced. Coburn's brigade had previously been assigned the duty of guarding the railroad, and this order had not been rescinded. Consequently, Coburn's troops continued to occupy posts along the railroad also held by troops of Twelfth Corps. In a letter to Colonel Hiram C. Rodgers, assistant adjutant general of Twelfth Corps, dated November 3, 1863, Alpheus S. Williams explained the anomalous position of Coburn and his command, and then continued:

. . . The scattered companies of the Thirty Third Indiana are of little service, excepting the company at Tracy City, and the one at the trestle below this [Tullahoma]. They are at points held by detachments of my division, and with their different notions of duty, and a most unaccountable prejudice, do not cheerfully cooperate with us.

Colonel Coburn, as a brigade commander in a different corps, I fancy, thinks his rights somewhat intrenched upon, and his officers and men, generally, sympathize in the feeling. If his brigade, or two or three regiments, could be concentrated on either flank of this division and take adjacent posts, the service of guarding the railroad would be much better performed. He might relieve two or three regiments of this division, which could take the posts he now occupies. As it now stands part of Coburn's is a sort of military *imperium in imperio* [a state within a state], which works badly.[109]

Finally, Coburn received orders to concentrate the detachments of the regiments of his brigade, and on November 5 he ordered the 33rd Indiana to assemble at Christiana, Tennessee. The four companies of the regiment at Tullahoma, marching by way of Shelbyville, reached Christiana the next day and went into camp. The other companies moved to Christiana by rail. A short time later the men began to construct winter quarters.[110]

Company C of the 33rd Indiana was the first company of the regiment of Coburn's brigade to arrive at Christiana, finding there Colonel William Cogswell's 2nd Massachusetts Regiment of Slocum's Twelfth Corps. This immediately resulted in another conflict of authority. Captain Charles Day of Company C had not been ordered to report to anyone upon his arrival, and he refused to submit to Cogswell's authority. This problem was soon resolved, however, but it was typical of the overlapping command situation of the troops along the Nashville and Chattanooga Railroad at that time.[111]

About November 6, companies and detachments of the 85th Indiana, which had been guarding the railroad from Christiana to Duck River Bridge, assembled at Fosterville. There the men constructed good plank shanties, made from demolished houses, to serve as winter quarters. Four men shared a shanty, and each had a comfortable fireplace. Samuel Mattox and his companions put a big schoolhouse stove in their shanty, and were as comfortable as if at home. The men had good clothing, plenty to eat, much to do, and no one was sick—but they had received no pay since June 30, 1863.[112]

Mattox wrote later to say that their food consisted of hard crackers, flour, beef, pork, coffee, tea, sugar, molasses, pepper, beans, and hominy. The men were also issued soap and candles. Sometimes they traded their sugar for buttermilk and vegetables. Mattox got twenty-five cents for sugar. Butter cost twenty-five cents per pound, milk ten cents per quart, potatoes two dollars per bushel, turnips one dollar per bushel, and apples ten cents per dozen, but they were very scarce.[113]

While at Fosterville the men spent their time in drilling and guarding the railroad for a distance of two or three miles to the north and south of the town.[114]

During the regiment's stay at Fosterville, the men fitted up an old storeroom for church services and held a revival lasting about five weeks. As a result, there were more than a hundred conversions, and a regimental church was organized. Many of the converts would face being killed or wounded during the Atlanta Campaign the following summer, so they probably needed the strength to be gained from this religious experience.[115]

Unfortunately, as morale was rebuilding, the problems that had almost destroyed the 22nd Wisconsin had not yet been resolved. The Bloodgood court-martial had ended September 19, and the decision of the court was sent to Rosecrans for his examination. It was not until October 31, however, that the decision was announced: Bloodgood would be dismissed from the service.[116]

On November 3 and 4 a paper was circulated in the 22nd Wisconsin by Private Alexander T. Smith that was to be presented to Bloodgood. This paper, which was signed by most of the enlisted men of the regiment, expressed their very high regard for Bloodgood's qualities as an officer. Coburn, who had been at Tullahoma, arrived at Murfreesboro November 6, and took command of the post, relieving Utley, who returned to his regiment. Utley had heard of the paper, and the next day he sent for Smith and asked to see it. Smith complied, and Reid has recorded what happened next.

> . . . "Don't you know that this a treasonable act, sir," thundered the Colonel. "You poor, lousy calves that I have pulled up by the tails, and now you turn around and butt at me. But your heads are so soft that you don't hurt me any." He went to Colonel Coburn and told him about it, but Colonel Coburn told him that he had had trouble enough with the 22nd and didn't want to hear anything more [about] this matter— that *Mr.* Bloodgood was a citizen now, and the boys had a perfect right to say anything they pleased about him, and that he (Utley) had better let the matter drop just where it was.[117]

Citizen Bloodgood went to Washington in an attempt to obtain aid from the two Wisconsin senators.[118]

The District of Nashville was created November 10, 1863, to include the defenses of the Nashville and Chattanooga Railroad to the Duck River.

Major General Lovell H. Rousseau was assigned command of the district, and later Brigadier General Horatio P. Van Cleve was assigned command of the post of Murfreesboro. The troops then under Van Cleve's command consisted of Coburn's brigade and some unattached regiments.[119]

Meanwhile, Grant had been assembling his forces for an attempt to drive Bragg's army from its positions about Chattanooga. These included the Fourth, Eleventh, Twelfth, and Fourteenth Corps of the Army of the Cumberland, which were already at or near Chattanooga and four divisions of Sherman's Army of the Tennessee which had been ordered to move east from the Mississippi River in late September 1863.[120]

Sherman's divisions began arriving near Chattanooga November 20, and by November 23, 1863, three of his divisions had crossed the Tennessee River at Brown's Ferry and were in position on the west bank of the river opposite the mouth of Chickamauga Creek. During the night and the next morning these divisions again crossed the river and moved forward to attack the northern end of Missionary Ridge. Sherman made some progress that day but his advance was soon stopped.[121]

Early on the morning of November 24 Hooker moved forward and attacked the enemy's positions on Lookout Mountain, with Brigadier General Peter J. Osterhaus' division of Fifteenth Corps, Brigadier General Charles Cruft's division of Fourth Corps, and Geary's division of Twelfth Corps. Hooker encountered strong opposition, and there was severe fighting during the day, but the enemy withdrew from the mountain that night.[122]

Sherman renewed his attack along Missionary Ridge on the morning of November 25, but it accomplished little. Meantime, Hooker had crossed the valley of Chattanooga Creek, from Lookout Mountain to Rossville, and had started an attack against the Confederate left flank on Missionary Ridge. That afternoon, Grant ordered Thomas, with the divisions of Absalom Baird, Thomas J. Wood, Philip H. Sheridan, and Richard W. Johnson, to advance and carry the enemy's rifle pits at the base of Missionary Ridge. Nothing more was intended. Thomas' men quickly drove the enemy from their rifle pits and back up the hill, and then, without halting, and without orders, in one of the most remarkable assaults of the war, they charged up the ridge and drove the enemy from the top and down into the valley beyond.

Grant observed the attack from Orchard Knob, a low hill east of Chattanooga, and between the town and Missionary Ridge. He became visibly upset when the men did not halt at the base of the ridge as he had expected, and he promised that someone would pay if the attack was unsuccessful. The attack was successful, however, and Chattanooga was completely freed of the enemy. After his defeat, Bragg led his army back to Dalton, Georgia, and went into camp.[123]

On January 2, 1864, a new division was organized at Nashville from Ward's brigade, Post of Nashville, District of Nashville, and Coburn's brigade of Van Cleve's post of Murfreesboro. Ward was assigned command of the division, with headquarters at Nashville, and Colonel Benjamin Harrison was assigned command of Ward's brigade which was designated as First Brigade, with Coburn's brigade as Second Brigade. On January 16, 1864, this division was designated as First Division, Eleventh Corps, and was organized as follows:

> First Division, Eleventh Corps, William T. Ward
>   First Brigade, Benjamin Harrison
>   Second Brigade, John Coburn

The composition of Coburn's brigade was unchanged by this reorganization. It still consisted of the 33rd Indiana, 85th Indiana, 19th Michigan, and 22nd Wisconsin regiments, who were burdened with a poor reputation but earnestly wishing for combat duty and were attempting to redeem themselves.[124]

Colonel Baird of the 85th Indiana was granted a leave of absence on January 16, 1864. Lieutenant Colonel Crane had been absent for many weeks, serving on an examining board for commissions as officers in the Black regiments then being organized. Because of Crane's absence, Captain Brant assumed command of the regiment.[125]

In January 1864 several officers of the beleaguered 22nd Wisconsin resigned. Lieutenant George Bauman, Lieutenant Frank P. Lawrence of Company A, and captains Darwin R. May of Company C and Perry W. Tracy of Company I took their leave. Adjutant William Bones was under arrest, awaiting court-martial. And, as if there was not enough turmoil, Bloodgood arrived at Murfreesboro February 4 and informed Utley that he had been reinstated. Utley, however, refused to recognize his claim.[126]

On February 11 Utley received an order issued by Ward, the division commander. The line officers who had opposed Utley might resign within four days and avoid trial by court-martial. Utley then sent word to Captain Burgess of Company E, Captain Griffith of Company F, and Adjutant Conrick and Lieutenant Kingman of Company C that charges against them had been drawn, and that they might resign within four days, as the order stated, if they so chose. They all resigned, leaving as the only captains with the regiment Francis Mead of Company A and Alphons G. Kellam of Company D.[127]

On December 14 Colonel Baird, then at Fosterville, wrote to Brigadier General William D. Whipple, assistant adjutant general on General Thomas' staff, asking for a leave of twenty days, because he was the principal witness in a case to be tried at Terre Haute, Indiana, January 6, 1864. The case was important because it involved about ten thousand dollars. In asking for this leave, he stated that he had been in the service sixteen months and had never been absent from his command. The leave was granted, and Baird departed December 15.[128]

Baird returned to his command February 7, 1864, after an absence of twenty-four days, in some trouble for a time because he was four days late, but this problem was soon resolved.[129]

In his letter to Whipple, written December 14, 1863, Baird informed him that his 85th Indiana regiment was below minimum strength, and December 19 he again wrote Whipple from Fosterville as follows:

> I respectfully ask that Lt. Col. A. B. Crane 85 Reg of Indiana Vol Infantry be relieved from duty on the Board of Examiners for applicants for commands in the colored Regts now sitting at Nashville.
>
> I am the only Field officer present with the regiment. The Major is detailed and will probably never return to the Regiment.
>
> My Adjutant is also detailed on the staff of the Brigade commander.
>
> With no Field officers and only a detailed Adjutant the duty is heavy on me. Especially as I have command of a Post.
>
> Col. Crane has been absent from his regiment for six months. Not consistent with the good of the service. I earnestly request that he be returned to his regiment.[130]

February 22, 1864, Hooker ordered Benjamin Harrison to move with his First Brigade of Ward's First Division from Nashville to Bridgeport, Alabama, and upon arriving there to report to Major General Oliver O. Howard, commanding Eleventh Corps. Harrison left Nashville the next day and arrived February 29 at Tullahoma, where the brigade stayed until March 2, and then, with division headquarters, continued on to Wauhatchie, Tennessee, in Lookout Valley. It arrived there March 10 and by Howard's orders went into camp.[131]

When Harrison's brigade left Nashville, Major General Lovell H. Rousseau, commanding the District of Nashville, ordered the regiments of Coburn's brigade to take post as follows: the 33rd Indiana and 22nd Wisconsin at Nashville, the 85th Indiana at La Vergne (LaVergne) on the Nashville and Chattanooga Railroad, and the 19th Michigan at McMinnville. The 19th Michigan was already at McMinnville, and the other three regiments then moved to their assigned positions.[132]

About February 23, after enjoying the fine camp at Fosterville for about two months, the 85th Indiana moved back by way of Murfreesboro to La Vergne, Tennessee, on the Nashville and Chattanooga Railroad. There the regiment was refitted with arms and clothing in preparation for the coming summer campaign and welcomed a number of recruits.[133]

While at La Vergne, Company G of the 85th Indiana became for a time mounted infantry. William Neet of this company wrote to his wife, Eliza, March 3, 1864:

> *Eliza I must tell you that our company is mounted[.]We all have horse to take care of[.] I have a first rate gray mare and a first rate traveler but our wooden saddles is rather hard but I guess our rumps is tollerble tuff for we have done nothing much this winter but set on them[.] we don't have any standing picket to doo [.] now we do patroleing the railroad and doo the forageing and running about and the other companies does the picketing and you know that soots your billy[.]*

Neet further stated:

> *. . . we have good quarters here better than we had at fosterville[.] our tents are made of seder logs hewed generly about 10 by 14 ft[.] brick chimneys and some of them have brick floors[.] ourn has a brick floor and the chimney is built up in one corner and the fire place is stuck out in the house[.] It looks funy but it's a good make shift[.] we have bin having quite a bluster here[.] . . .*[134]

The 22nd Wisconsin, which had been on garrison duty at Murfreesboro since July 3, 1863, moved February 24, 1864, for Nashville. It reached La Vergne that afternoon and continued on to Nashville the next day, where it went into camp about a half mile from Fort Negley on the Franklin pike.[135]

On February 26 the 23rd Missouri Regiment of Van Cleve's Second Brigade of Rousseau's District of Nashville relieved the 33rd Indiana of Coburn's brigade at Christiana, and the latter then moved to Nashville and went into camp.[136]

Disease continued to plague the regiments of Coburn's brigade in the cold February weather. On March 13, while the 85th Indiana was at La Vergne, Tennessee, Surgeon Wilson Hobbs wrote a letter to his wife, in which he explained the treatment of measles.

> *. . . little medicine is needed, but great care in regards to taking cold. Many soldiers have lost their lives by this means. . . . .The greatest danger lie in injury to the lungs by inflamation in the air tube. Cool water and cool air should be avoided. The bowels kept open by oil or salt and warm tea such as peneroyal or something of the kind is most that is wanted*

*We give often if the fever is not great whiskey, especially after the erup-
tion appears.*[137]

About March 5 Thomas, commanding the Army of the Cumberland,
recognized Bloodgood as reinstated and ordered him to report for duty, and
on March 11 Utley, whose wife was seriously ill, started for home. He left
Bloodgood, his bitter adversary, in command of the 22nd Wisconsin. Utley,
however, would be back.[138]

In order to obtain more men for the armies in the field, General Orders
No. 376, Adjutant General's Office, dated November 21, 1863, authorized
the granting of furloughs of at least thirty days to volunteers then in service
who re-enlisted before the expiration of their original enlistment. If three-
fourths of a veteran regiment re-enlisted, officers were to take the volunteers so enlisted home as a group. The Veteran Volunteer Act, which was
enacted early in 1864, provided that any man who re-enlisted would have
free transportation home, a month's furlough, and a bounty of $400.[139]

The 33rd Indiana was eligible for veteran service, and mid-December
1863 authority was given to renew its service, with Captain Henry C.
Johnson of Company K designated as the recruiting officer.

In order to preserve the organization of the regiment, it was necessary
for three-fourths of the men to re-enlist and to be sworn in. Re-enlistments
were very slow at first, and by January 1, 1864, only about fifty men had
enrolled. Many of the enlisted men did not wish to re-enlist unless they were
assured that they would be allowed to select their own officers, as they had
done when they first entered the service. Governor Morton and Colonel
Coburn discussed this problem with the commissioned officers, and nearly
all of them agreed that they would leave the service and would allow those
who re-enlisted to choose their own officers. This caused an increase in re-
enlistments, but by the end of the month the goal had not yet been met.
Coburn again addressed the regiment, and it produced some results, but in
early February it appeared that the regiment would not reorganize. Once
more, on February 13 Coburn spoke to the regiment and this proved effective, and the continued organization of the regiment was assured. By February 15 the men who chose to do so were re-enlisted as veterans. On February 23 the regiment was mustered in and left Christiana for Nashville
February 26. The 33rd Indiana was in Nashville from February 29 until
March 25, when Coburn, with those men who had re-enlisted, left Nashville for Indiana and a leave of thirty days.

The 252 non-veterans of the 33rd Indiana, who had not re-enlisted, were
left behind and were temporarily attached to the 85th Indiana, which was
in camp at La Vergne.[140]

Major Robert E. Craig of the 85th Indiana, who was serving as Provost Marshal on the staff of General Horatio P. Van Cleve, died suddenly On April 2 at Murfreesboro. He was succeeded as major by Jefferson E. Brant.[141]

On April 15, 1864, a report on the death of Major Craig was included in the *Indianapolis Daily Journal*, stating that the major was a special favorite with the command and was "every bit a gentleman." The report included a letter written under the direction of General Van Cleve and addressed to the commanding officer of the 85th Regiment:

> . . . the General [Van Cleve] tenders his sympathy to the associates of Major Craig in his regiment, and to his afflicted family, and embraces this opportunity of testifying to his untarnished character as a gentlemen and efficiency as an officer.

This is in quite a contrast to a comment made by William Neet of the 85th Indiana in a letter home, written at Nashville, Tennessee, April 3, 1864:

> . . . *our Major, Kreg [Craig], died nite before last at Murfreesboro[.] was found dead in bed in the morn at 7 oclock[.] he was a drinking man supposed killed his self[.] maby that will be warning to some of the rest of our officers[.] they are half or more drunkards[.] whiskey and wimmen is most they care for[.]*[142]

As a part of the preparations for Sherman's advance into Georgia on April 12 Thomas ordered Coburn to move with his brigade to Lookout Valley near Chattanooga, and report to Joseph Hooker, commanding Twentieth Corps. At that time, the troops of the 85th Indiana and the non-veterans of the 33rd Indiana were in position along the Nashville and Chattanooga Railroad between Nashville and Murfreesboro with five companies at La Vergne.

The 22nd Wisconsin was at Nashville and the 19th Michigan was at McMinnville, and the veterans of the 33rd Indiana were home on leave.[143]

Chapter 9

Atlanta Campaign
Rocky Face Ridge to Cassville

In the spring of 1864, the armies of the United States began operating under new direction. On March 1, 1864, Congress revived the rank of lieutenant general, and on March 9 President Abraham Lincoln presented Major General Ulysses Grant with the commission of this newly created rank. The next day Grant was given the command of the Armies of the United States.[1]

After his meeting with the President, Grant returned to Nashville to confer with Major General William T. Sherman, who had been left in command of the Military Division of the Mississippi. Grant formally assumed his new command March 17 and returned to Washington March 23, after which he went on to Culpeper Court House, Virginia, where he established his headquarters with Major General George G. Meade's Army of the Potomac.[2]

Grant issued orders April 9 for the operations of the armies in the spring and summer of 1864. According to his plan, Meade's Army of the Potomac was to move against General Robert E. Lee's Confederate army in Virginia; Sherman's combined armies of the Cumberland, the Ohio, and the Tennessee were to advance against Joseph E. Johnston's army in Georgia; Major General Nathaniel P. Banks' army in the Department of the Gulf was to move on Mobile, Alabama; Major General Franz Sigel's army of the Department of West Virginia would march south in the Shenandoah Valley; and Major General Benjamin F. Butler's Army of the James was to advance on Richmond from the south side of the James River. The armies were to begin their advance during the first week of May 1864.[3]

One of the first steps taken by Grant in preparing for the upcoming offensive operations was to order every man who could be spared from duty in the rear areas sent to the front as quickly as possible. He directed the generals commanding the departments of the army, the defenses of Washington, and the posts of New York City, Saint Louis, Cincinnati, and Saint Paul to forward all surplus troops, especially infantry, to the field armies at the front.[4]

Colonel John Coburn's Second Brigade, First Division, Eleventh Corps was one of the units in the Department of the Cumberland that could be spared. Relieved from duty in Middle Tennessee it was ordered to join the army that Sherman was assembling near Chattanooga for the invasion of Georgia.[5]

April 12 Major General George H. Thomas, commanding the Department of the Cumberland, ordered Major General Lovell H. Rousseau, in charge of the District of Nashville, to relieve from duty along the line of the Nashville and Chattanooga Railroad the 23rd Missouri, the 85th Indiana, and the detachment of the 33rd Indiana. These regiments were to be replaced by troops from the garrison of Nashville as far as Murfreesboro and by troops from the garrison of Murfreesboro on south to a point about two and one-half miles north of Bell Buckle, Tennessee. When the 23rd Missouri was relieved from its positions between Stones River and Fosterville, it moved to McMinnville and relieved the 19th Michigan from duty at that place. The 19th Michigan then left on its march to the front to rejoin the other regiments of the brigade in Lookout Valley.[6]

On April 14 (ordered April 4, 1864) a new Twentieth Corps, consisting of three divisions, was organized by the consolidation of Eleventh Corps and Twelfth Corps, Army of the Cumberland. Major General Joseph Hooker was assigned command. The three divisions were organized as follows:

First Division, Twentieth Corps was formed from Brigadier General Alpheus S. Williams' First Division, Twelfth Corps and a brigade of Eleventh Corps. Williams remained in command.

Second Division was formed from Brigadier General John W. Geary's Second Division, Twelfth Corps and a brigade from Eleventh Corps. Geary remained in command of the division.

Third Division was formed by the consolidation of Brigadier General William T. Ward's First Division, Eleventh Corps; Colonel James Wood's Second Brigade, Second Division, Eleventh Corps; and the 20th Connecticut and 26th Wisconsin regiments. Major General Daniel Butterfield was assigned command of Third Division. In this reorganization the designation of Coburn's brigade was changed from Second Brigade, First Division, Eleventh Corps to Second Brigade, Third Division, Twentieth Corps.

The organization of Butterfield's division was as follows:

Third Division, Daniel Butterfield
    First Brigade, William T. Ward
    Second Brigade, Samuel Ross, to May 9, 1864, John Coburn
    Third Brigade, James Wood, Jr.[7]

The order of April 14 announcing the organization of Twentieth Corps, assigned the 5th Connecticut to Second Brigade, Third Division because of the absence of the 33rd Indiana, then on veteran's leave in Indiana. On April 16, however, the 5th Connecticut was transferred to First Brigade, First Division, Twentieth Corps, and Colonel Samuel Ross' 20th Connecticut of First Brigade, First Division, Twentieth Corps, was assigned to Coburn's brigade of Butterfield's division. By this order Coburn's brigade consisted of the 20th Connecticut, 85th Indiana, 19th Michigan, 22nd Wisconsin and the detachment of 33rd Indiana.[8]

Colonel John P. Baird returned to the army about April 5 from leave of absence in Indiana and resumed command of the 85th Indiana. The regiment left La Vergne, Tennessee, April 20, and started on its long march to the front at Chattanooga, reaching Fosterville two days later and arriving at Tullahoma April 25. From there it followed the railroad to Cowan, Tennessee and then marched across the mountains. This part of the journey was described in a letter written by Captain Jefferson E. Brant to his family at home as follows:

> We left the rail road at Cowen [Cowan] and crossed the mountains by way of University place. We camped one night on the mountains.
>
> The ascent was no small undertaking, being by the windings nearly three miles. The road, rocky and rough. We followed the mountain tableland for nearly twenty miles. There are but few houses, the land is covered by timber, mostly chestnut. The descent was as difficult as the ascent—yesterday, and the day before the road winding and rough. Some places very steep. We camped last night in Sweeden's cave [Cove] or valley near to the greatest spring I ever saw. Rising up at the mountain base as clear as crystal in a basin some forty or fifty feet across, and runs down the valley in a large stream or creek. Our Camp near this spring was one of the finest we ever had. The scenery was grand.[9]

The men, breathing the crisp and exhilarating mountain air, experienced no serious difficulties on the march, and only one man was forced to ride in an ambulance. The regiment reached Bridgeport, Alabama, on April 29 and finally arrived at its destination in Lookout Valley May 2.[10]

The 19th Michigan left McMinnville April 21 and then moved south to join the other regiments of Coburn's brigade in Lookout Valley near Chattanooga. The regiment passed through Hillsboro two days later, forded the Elk River, and arrived at Cowan early on the morning of April 25. There Colonel Ross' 20th Connecticut, which had been stationed at and near Cowan for some time guarding the railroad and which had recently been assigned to Coburn's brigade, joined the 19th Michigan. Ross, as senior officer, assumed command of Coburn's brigade during the absence of the latter in Indiana.[11]

The 19th Michigan rested at Cowan for two days and then, accompanied by the 20th Connecticut, moved south, crossed the Cumberland Mountains, and marched to Bridgeport, Alabama, where they crossed the Tennessee River. Proceeding along the railroad to Lookout Valley, they went into camp April 30 a few miles south of Chattanooga.[12]

Colonel William L. Utley returned to the army from his home in Wisconsin and rejoined the 22nd Wisconsin at Nashville April 9, 1864. The regiment left Nashville April 19 and the next day joined the 85th Indiana and the detachment of the 33rd Indiana at La Vergne. On April 21 the 22nd Wisconsin marched through the battlefield of Stones River and the town of Murfreesboro and camped that night on the same ground it had occupied the past summer.[13]

The 22th Wisconsin marched to Decherd and on April 27 arrived at Cowan station at the foot of the Cumberland Mountains. There was some indications of rain that day, and Colonel Ross, commanding the brigade, ordered Utley to march with his regiment up the mountain that afternoon. They camped that night at a place called University, a station on the Tracy City Branch Railroad. Utley continued on down the mountain, passed through Sweden's Cove and reached Bridgeport, Alabama, April 29. The regiment reached Lookout Valley May 1, after a march of 143 miles in thirteen days and joined the brigade near Wauhatchie, Tennessee, where it went into camp.[14]

The time spent by the brigade in Lookout Valley was used to prepare for the march into Georgia. The 85th Indiana shipped home all surplus baggage, leaving each regiment only one wagon. Within a few weeks the men had thrown away or otherwise disposed of all overcoats and extra blankets. The regiment was then ready for the campaign for Atlanta, which was soon to begin. Captain Brant wrote, in a letter home, that "We are allowed three teams for the regiment, one hand trunk for the officers, two blankets apiece, one shelter tent apiece, and a few cooking utensils."[15]

THE OPENING MOVES

During April 1864 the troops assigned to accompany Sherman on his advance into Georgia were rather widely scattered over a region extending from Knoxville in the east to Nashville and Huntsville in the west. A partial concentration was then effected, and on May 1, just before the movement of the armies to the front was to begin, the various units were located as follows:

Major General John M. Schofield's Army of the Ohio (Twenty-Third Corps) was concentrating at Charleston, Tennessee.[16]

Major General John A. Logan's Fifteenth Corps and Major General Grenville M. Dodge's Left Wing, Sixteenth Corps of Major General James B. McPherson's Army of the Tennessee were guarding the railroad from Nashville to Huntsville, Alabama, and from Huntsville to Stevenson, Alabama. Major General Frank P. Blair's, Seventeenth Corps was at Cairo, Illinois.[17]

Major General Oliver O. Howard's Fourth Corps of Thomas' Army of the Cumberland was at and near Cleveland, Tennessee.[18]

Brigadier General Richard W. Johnson's First Division of Major General John M. Palmer's Fourteenth Corps was at Graysville, Georgia; Brigadier General Jefferson C. Davis' Second Division was at McAfee's Church near Rossville, Georgia; and Brigadier General Absalom Baird's Third Division was near Ringgold, Georgia.[19]

Williams' First Division of Hooker's Twentieth Corps, which had been guarding the Nashville and Chattanooga Railroad, was concentrated in the valley opposite Bridgeport, Alabama. Geary's Second Division was somewhat scattered, with Colonel Charles Candy's First Brigade at Bridgeport, Colonel Adolphus Buschbeck's Second Brigade near the base of Lookout Mountain in Lookout Valley, and Colonel David Ireland's Third Brigade at Stevenson, Alabama, and on the railroad westward to Anderson, Tennessee. Butterfield's Third Division was in Lookout Valley, except Coburn's brigade (commanded by Colonel Ross), which was en route to that place from Middle Tennessee.[20]

The first step necessary to carry out Sherman's plan for the capture of Atlanta was to assemble his scattered forces at the front and put them into position for the initial advance, which was to begin May 5, 1864. He issued orders May 1 for the three armies under his command to move forward to be in position to begin the advance on the assigned date as follows:

Schofield's Army of the Ohio (Twenty-Third Corps) was to move forward from its positions in East Tennessee on the left of Sherman's line to Cleveland, Tennessee, north of Dalton.[21]

Thomas was to move forward on the Dalton road in the center of Sherman's army and concentrate his Army of the Cumberland near Ringgold, Georgia. There his command was to face toward Rocky Face Ridge, with Fourth Corps on the left, Fourteenth Corps in the center, and Twentieth Corps on the right.[22]

McPherson was to move his Army of the Tennessee from its positions guarding the railroad in the rear of Sherman's army and bring the scattered units together at Chattanooga. He would then be in position to advance on the right of Sherman's army in the direction of Resaca, Georgia.[23]

Thomas began his movements on May 2, and that day Davis' Second Division of Fourteenth Corps marched from Graysville and joined Absalom Baird's Third Division of the same corps at Ringgold. Also that day, Butterfield, with William T. Ward's First Brigade and Colonel James Wood's Third Brigade of his Third Division, Twentieth Corps, marched toward Lee and Gordon's Mills on Chickamauga Creek. The two brigades broke camp in Lookout Valley early that morning, crossed Lookout Valley, with Ward's brigade in front, and then marched on the Chattanooga road around the foot of Lookout Mountain. From there they crossed Chattanooga Valley, passed through Rossville, and arrived at Lee and Gordon's Mills and went into camp between 2:00 and 4:00 that afternoon. The last of Ross' Second Brigade, which had been on the march from Nashville, La Vergne, Cowan, and McMinnville, arrived in Lookout Valley that day.[24]

May 3 Schofield marched with the three divisions of his Twenty-Third Corps from Charleston to Cleveland, Tennessee, and Johnson's division of Fourteenth Corps closed up on the other two divisions of the corps at Ringgold. Williams' division of Twentieth Corps arrived that day in Chattanooga Valley at the eastern end of Lookout Mountain, and reported to Hooker.[25]

Also that morning, Ross moved with his brigade, less the 33rd Indiana, from Lookout Valley and, following the route of the other two brigades of Butterfield's division, went into camp on the Chickamauga battlefield that night. Coburn, with his Veteran 33rd Indiana Regiment, left Indianapolis for the front that day, while Butterfield's division remained at Lee and Gordon's Mills.[26]

Surgeon Wilson Hobbs of the 85th Indiana described his visit to the Battlefield of Chickamauga as follows:

> *After we went into camp yesterday evening nearly the whole brigade went on the battlefield so far as the time would allow and all that has been said about the treatment of our dead is true. I saw several places where our men have been only partially buried with the skull and feet uncovered. They dug no trench to bury these men in but threw a little dirt over them as they lay, and left them so. We did not till this morning see the ground where the hard fighting was when we marched over it. . . . I saw several trees not*

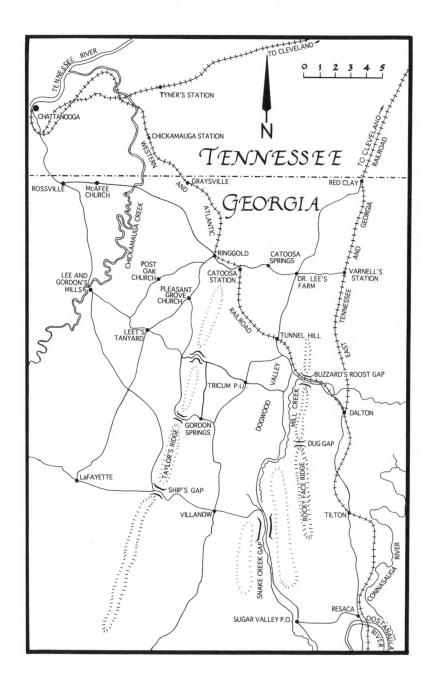

Atlanta Campaign, Chattanooga to Resaca

larger than my body with 7 bullet holes in them and either one of them would have killed or wounded a man. I saw many trees hit with cannon balls and shell twice . . . taking out a piece of them and many trees shot through and broken off by them. A cannon ball or shell will go through an oak tree 2 feet through if the tree is green. I ought to have said that our men buried over many bodies they saw exposed.[27]

May 4, a sultry day, Sherman's troops continued to move forward to their assigned positions. Schofield advanced with his Twenty-Third Corps from Cleveland to Red Clay, Georgia. Howard's Fourth Corps, with Brigadier General Edward M. McCook's First Cavalry Division of the Army of the Cumberland on the left, advanced to Catoosa Springs, where it took position on the left of Fourteenth Corps. Thus, except for Hooker's Twentieth Corps, Thomas had his command in readiness to open the campaign.[28]

That morning Williams' division of Twentieth Corps marched from Chattanooga to Lee and Gordon's Mills and camped there for the night. Geary's division marched from Bridgeport, Alabama, toward Chattanooga. It passed through Wauhatchie and Lookout Valley, crossed Lookout Mountain, and camped that night in Chattanooga Valley. Daniel Butterfield, with Ward's brigade, Ross' brigade, and Wood's brigade of his division, marched from near Lee and Gordon's Mills to Pleasant Grove Church, which was near Taylor's Ridge, about three miles from Ringgold.[29]

May 5, 1864, was the date that had been set for the opening of the campaign in Georgia, but this was changed to May 7 to enable the last troops to reach the front. The Army of the Tennessee was not yet up but was drawing near. Dodge's Left Wing, Sixteenth Corps, arrived at Chattanooga May 5 and Logan's Fifteenth Corps arrived during the night and the next morning. The part of Blair's Seventeenth Corps designated to take part in the Atlanta Campaign was organizing in Cairo, Illinois, at that time.[30]

Hooker's corps was still getting into position May 5. Williams' division moved to Pleasant Grove Church, three miles southwest of Ringgold, and Ross' brigade of Butterfield's division advanced to Leet's Tanyard (or Tannery). The 22nd Wisconsin of Ross' brigade remained in camp near the base of Taylor's Ridge during the day. That day Geary's division marched by way of Rossville toward Lee and Gordon's Mills, but because of heavy traffic it changed direction and camped that night about four miles from Ringgold at Post Oak Church.[31]

On May 6 Hooker's corps was in its assigned positions and ready to move out the following day, at the beginning of the campaign for Atlanta. Williams' division was in camp near Pleasant Grove Church, Geary's division marched to Pea Vine Church and went into camp, and Butterfield's division was in camp near Leet's Tanyard.[32]

Ross' brigade moved into Dogwood Valley that day, and it then advanced in line to Dogwood Ridge, which was covered with woods and dense underbrush. Here the brigade halted, with the 85th Indiana on the right center of the line, and the men then constructed works facing toward Buzzard Roost Gap (also called Buzzard's Roost Gap and Mill Creek Gap) about four miles distant. The 85th remained in camp here until May 11 doing heavy picket duty.[33]

On May 6 the Army of the Tennessee marched from Chattanooga to Lee and Gordon's Mills, taking position on the right of Twentieth Corps.[34]

DEMONSTRATION AT ROCKY FACE RIDGE, GEORGIA

May 7, conforming with Sherman's revised orders, the Army of the Ohio, the Army of the Cumberland, and the Army of the Tennessee moved forward against Johnston's Confederate lines at Dalton. The Army of the Ohio left Red Clay and formed a line north of Dalton. This line connected on the right with the Army of the Cumberland at Dr. Lee's farm, near Tunnel Hill, and extended to the left in the direction of the East Tennessee and Georgia Railroad at Varnell's Station.[35]

As the Army of the Tennessee advanced from Chattanooga, it followed Hooker's route as far as Lee and Gordon's Mills, turning there to the right and marching towards Ship's Gap and Villanow. McPherson's orders were to be near Gordon's Gap on the night of May 7, and the next day he was to continue on by way of Villanow and Snake Creek Gap toward the Western and Atlantic Railroad at Resaca. McPherson halted that night at a point west of Gordon's Springs.[36]

Thomas' Army of the Cumberland advanced May 7 and closed up toward the enemy's positions at Rocky Face Ridge. Howard's Fourth Corps moved from Catoosa Springs to Dr. Lee's house, and Palmer's Fourteenth Corps advanced from Ringgold on the main road to Tunnel Hill.[37]

Williams' and Geary's divisions of Hooker's Twentieth Corps crossed Taylor's Ridge at Nickajack Gap that day and moved down into Dogwood Valley. Williams' division encamped that night at Trickum (or Trickum P.O.). Geary moved with his division to Gordon's Springs, where he detached Ireland's Third Brigade, and then moved on with his other two brigades and arrived at Thornton's farm on the Rome road about dark. After being detached, Ireland's brigade joined Brigadier General Judson Kil-patrick's Third Cavalry Division of the Army of the Cumberland for an advance on Villanow. Butterfield's division marched early that morning from Leet's Tanyard and passed through Gordon's Springs Gap and Gordon's Springs in Dogwood Valley. Ross' brigade was already in position on the ridge facing Buzzard Roost Gap, and the other two brigades camped near the junction of the Gordon's Springs and Dalton Road and the Villanow and Ringgold road, near Trickum. Butterfield's headquarters was at a point where the Gordon's Springs road branched off to Villanow.[38]

During the period May 7 through 10, Fourth Corps, Fourteenth Corps, and Twenty-Third Corps demonstrated against Tunnel Hill and Rocky Face Ridge, and there was sharp fighting at Buzzard Roost Gap and Dug Gap on May 8 and 9.[39]

The Army of the Tennessee continued its advance toward Resaca May 8. Fifteenth Corps marched from its camps at the western entrance of Gordon's Springs Gap, passing through Villanow and camping that night at the northern entrance of Snake Creek Gap. Left Wing, Sixteenth Corps, reached Ship's Gap that day and camped in the gap.[40]

Also on May 8 Williams' and Butterfield's divisions of Hooker's Twentieth Corps remained in their positions of the night before, but Geary's division advanced into Mill Creek Valley at the foot of Rocky Face Ridge (also called Chattoogata Ridge) and launched an attack on the enemy's positions at Dug Gap. Geary's men advanced up the gap toward the summit, with sharp fighting that lasted nearly all day, but that evening they withdrew to the foot of the ridge and went into camp near the Babb house on Mill Creek.[41]

On the morning of May 9, with Dodge leading, the Army of the Tennessee advanced toward Resaca. After arriving near the town, however, McPherson decided that the enemy's position was too strong to attack. He withdrew and went into camp for the night between Snake Creek Gap and Sugar Valley.[42]

May 9 the divisions of Hooker's corps remained in the positions occupied the day before. Schofield made a strong demonstration against the enemy's right flank as a diversion for the operations of the rest of the army through Snake Creek Gap.[43]

Meanwhile, on May 3, at the end of their leave, the veterans of the 33rd Indiana had left Indianapolis, Indiana, on their return to the army; they arrived at Chattanooga May 7. From there they marched through the Chickamauga battlefield and rejoined the brigade at Trickum, Georgia, in Dogwood Valley May 9. That day Colonel John Coburn relieved Ross in command of his brigade, and Ross resumed command of the 20th Connecticut Regiment.[44]

While the 33rd Indiana was in Indianapolis, just before the Atlanta Campaign began, Lieutenant Colonel James M. Henderson lost the use of his voice and was unable to perform his duties during the remainder of his time of service. Major Levin T. Miller assumed command of the 33rd Indiana and was in command when the regiment arrived in Georgia. It went into camp at Trickum and remained there until May 11, when it marched with the division to Snake Creek Gap.[45]

At 1:00 AM May 10, Williams marched with his division from Trickum and reached Snake Creek Gap at 8:00 that morning. After Williams reported to McPherson, he took position with Brigadier General Joseph F. Knipe's and Colonel James S. Robinson's brigades at the northern entrance to the gap. He also moved Brigadier General Thomas H. Ruger's brigade through the gap to act as a reserve behind the lines occupied by the Army of the Tennessee.[46]

Geary was directed to remain with his division in front of Dug Gap until relieved by Edward M. McCook's cavalry division, and Butterfield was ordered to move with his division to Snake Creek Gap the next day.[47]

At 1:15 on the morning of May 10, in anticipation of the movement of the army toward Resaca, Samuel Ross received an order directing him to gain possession of and to hold a trail known as Boyd's Trail, which was located between Buzzard Roost Gap and Dug Gap. Ross' command consisted of the 20th Connecticut, under Lieutenant Colonel Philo B. Buckingham and Colonel Henry C. Gilbert's 19th Michigan of Coburn's brigade. After a march of about four miles, Ross reached Boyd's Trail about 4:00 AM. He advanced his command, and by 8:00 AM had driven the enemy's pickets and their reserve back up the trail to the top of Rocky Face Ridge. Ross then established a picket line across the trail and placed the main body of his command on a hill that commanded the main road and much of the trail that ran down the ridge to the point where it joined the main road. Ross fortified his position so as to be able to hold it against large numbers of the enemy. Ross was directed to remain there until relieved, and then to move to Snake Creek Gap, where he would join the rest of the brigade. On May 11 Geary sent the 33rd New Jersey of his Second Brigade to relieve Ross' two regiments at Boyd's Trail, and Ross then moved with them to Snake Creek Gap to rejoin the brigade.[48]

That day, Butterfield's division marched to Snake Creek Gap. The head of the column reached the northern entrance at 8:00 AM. Butterfield then put his brigades in camp along the five-mile length of the gap and put them to work clearing, repairing, and widening the road so as to make it a double track road for the passage of troops and trains. Butterfield's instructions were as follows: "The two wagon roads must be well made, filled in with stone, ditched when necessary, and a clear path cut on the east side of the gap throughout for infantry, with bridges for crossing the creek. . . ." Coburn's brigade was placed at the northern end of the gap near Williams' headquarters, Ward's brigade was near the center of the gap, and Wood's brigade was at the southern end.[49]

May 11, 1864, Sherman issued orders for a general movement of the army, which was to begin at daybreak the next morning. Howard's Fourth Corps was to remain in position to cover the movement of the rest of the army. Major General George Stoneman's cavalry division of the Army of the Ohio was to replace Twenty-Third Corps on the line north of Dalton, and then the rest of the Army of the Cumberland and the Twenty-Third Corps were to march by the right flank through Snake Creek Gap to join the rest of the army.[50]

At sunrise May 12 Thomas, with Palmer's corps, began his movement southward, closely followed by Schofield's Twenty-Third Corps. That same morning McCook's cavalry division relieved Geary's division in Mill Creek valley, and Geary marched through Snake Creek Gap and camped a short distance east of the southern entrance. At the end of the day, Sherman's entire army was concentrated close to McPherson's position near the southern end of the gap, facing Resaca. The troops had ten days' rations, with three days' food cooked and in their haversacks. All baggage had been left in the rear near Ringgold, and the men, including general officers, had no tents. The army was traveling light.[51]

General Joseph E. Johnston evacuated Dalton on the night of May 12 and moved south with his army to a new position north and west of Resaca, where he was again in front of Sherman's army.[52]

Butterfield's division continued its work on the road through Snake Creek Gap during the morning of May 12, but that afternoon Ward's and Wood's brigades and the 85th Indiana, 19th Michigan, and 22nd Wisconsin of Coburn's brigade marched out from the gap about three miles and camped in rear of the Army of the Tennessee. The 33rd Indiana and the 20th Connecticut of Coburn's brigade continued their work on the road until about midnight and then moved out from the gap and rejoined the brigade.[53]

On the morning of May 13, Howard learned that Johnston had evacuated his positions during the night; he then advanced with his Fourth Corps through Dalton and followed the retiring Confederates toward Resaca. He camped that night in Sugar Creek Valley, with the head of his column about nine miles south of Dalton.[54]

BATTLE OF RESACA, GEORGIA
MAY 14-15, 1864

Palmer's Fourteenth Corps moved out May 13, 1864, from its camp near Snake Creek Gap and marched to a point two miles to the northeast of Hooker's position, which was on the road about two and a half miles west of Resaca. It then moved eastward, north of the Resaca road and parallel to it, toward the Western and Atlantic Railroad. Palmer found the enemy strongly posted on a range of hills west of the railroad; he spent the rest of the day skirmishing without further progress.[55]

Schofield's Army of the Ohio marched through Snake Creek Gap that day and moved to the northeast, finally taking position on the left of Fourteenth Corps.[56]

May 12 Hooker had ordered his division commanders to mass their commands by 7:00 on the morning of May 13 on the right of the Resaca road at a point where McPherson's entrenchments crossed the road, with Butterfield on the right, Williams in the center, and Geary on the left.[57]

Hooker's divisions moved forward as ordered on the morning of May 13, and they were in their assigned positions by that afternoon. Butterfield's division on the right formed in line of battle on the left of McPherson's Fifteenth Corps. Butterfield then moved forward about a mile and a half, to the rear of a division of Fifteenth Corps, whose men were skirmishing with the enemy.[58]

Ward's brigade arrived on the left of Fifteenth Corps about 1:00 PM and formed in line of battle. Later it advanced and formed in battalions en masse in an open field in rear of Brigadier General William Harrow's division of Fifteenth Corps.[59]

About 2:00 PM Coburn's brigade, the left brigade of Butterfield's division, went into position in rear of Fifteenth Corps. That evening, the 85th Indiana faced the enemy's works from south of Tilton, Georgia, with companies A and B of the regiment out in front as skirmishers for the brigade.[60]

Wood's brigade moved up and formed in line of battle, but it later moved back to the rear of the left of Fifteenth Corps, where it was held in reserve, in column by division.[61]

About dusk that evening Hooker moved his Twentieth Corps to the left and front about one and a half miles to support Johnson's division of Fourteenth Corps. Because of the thick woods and the difficulty in finding Johnson's line in the dark, it was not until early on the morning of May 14 that Butterfield had his troops in position. Coburn's brigade finally went into camp that night in rear of a part of Palmer's corps. Wood's brigade took position on the left of Fifteenth Corps and connected on its left with Ward's brigade, which had relieved Brigadier General John H. King's brigade of Fourteenth Corps.[62]

On the morning of May 14 Williams massed his division in rear of Butterfield's division, which was in line of battle facing the enemy forces in front of Resaca. About 4:30 that afternoon, Williams' division, with Geary's division following, marched to the left, passing in rear of Fourteenth Corps, Twenty-Third Corps, and Fourth Corps, to support the left of Fourth Corps, which was then heavily engaged some miles distant. The enemy had attacked Howard's corps about 4:00 PM with the divisions of Major General Carter

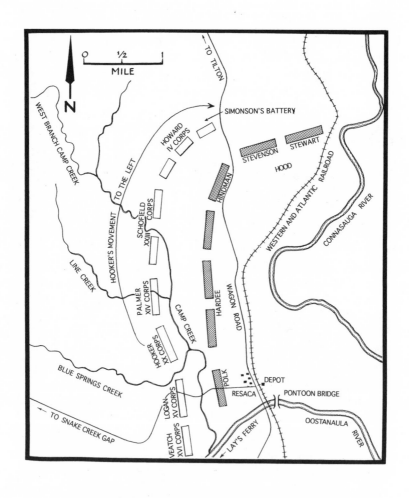

Battle of Resaca, May 14 - 15, 1864

L. Stevenson and Major General Alexander P. Stewart of Lieutenant General John B. Hood's Confederate corps. Williams arrived at his assigned position along the Dalton and Resaca road about 6:00 PM and deployed; soon thereafter Hood called off his unsuccessful attack. Geary did not get his division into position until after dark.[63]

Butterfield's division did not accompany Williams' and Geary's divisions of Twentieth Corps to the left of Sherman's line but remained with Palmer's Fourteenth Corps May 14. That day Coburn's brigade of Butterfield's division advanced to the front and left about four hundred yards and relieved Brigadier General William P. Carlin's brigade of Johnson's division. The brigade camped in that position during the night, on the left of the division. The enemy was entrenched in front of Coburn's brigade on a low, wooded ridge beyond the narrow and cleared valley of Camp Creek. The 85th Indiana moved forward a few hundred yards and relieved a regiment of Fourteenth Corps, then built works on the right of the brigade, working by reliefs until 3:00 AM May 15. Fourteenth Corps was heavily engaged with the enemy during the day, but Hooker had been instructed by Thomas to avoid an engagement unless Palmer was driving the enemy.[64]

Early on the morning of May 15 Butterfield's division pulled out of the line along Camp Creek and followed the route taken by Williams' and Geary's divisions the day before. Butterfield marched to the left about two miles and formed his division in line on the left of the Dalton and Resaca road. It was on high ground near a point where Morris Creek crossed the road. Geary moved his division to the right about three-fourths of a mile and formed his brigades in column for an attack. Ireland's brigade was in front, Buschbeck's brigade was next, and Candy's brigade was in rear of Buschbeck. When this deployment was completed, Hooker's corps was in line as follows: Geary's division was on the right, Butterfield's division in the center, and Williams' division on the left.[65]

Hooker's preparations were made for an attack on the right of the Confederate line, which was held by Hood's corps. Butterfield was to make the attack and was to be supported by Geary. Williams' division was to cover and protect the left of the attacking divisions. The column of attack was to be formed on Ward's brigade, with Coburn's brigade advancing in support of Ward on the right and Wood's brigade on the left. Ward's brigade, with a front of one regiment, was to attack a small enemy earthwork on a hill near the enemy's main line, on the far side of a valley.[66]

Butterfield formed his division as directed approximately one mile from the enemy's works about noon, and he then began his advance. When Coburn reached his assigned position, he was unable to deploy his brigade as ordered, because a part of Fourth Corps was too close on his right. Therefore, he formed his brigade in a column of battalions directly in rear of Ward's brigade.[67]

A short time later, Butterfield ordered John Coburn to form his brigade in two lines, immediately in rear of Ward's brigade. Coburn placed John P. Baird's 85th Indiana on the right of his first line and Henry C. Gilbert's 19th Michigan on the left. Samuel Ross' 20th Connecticut was placed on the right of the second line and William L. Utley's 22nd Wisconsin was on the left of this line. Levin T. Miller's 33rd Indiana was in reserve, in rear of the 22nd Wisconsin.[68]

While the above changes in the disposition of his regiments were being effected, Coburn received an order to advance as rapidly as possible and to support Ward's brigade, which was then advancing on the enemy's works. The order for Ward to advance was given after an attack by James Wood's brigade of Butterfield's division had ended.[69]

Ward's brigade advanced up a narrow and steep-sided ravine, thickly covered with low, bushy trees, sloping sharply upward to the crest of a ridge or line of hills. The slope on the far side of this ridge was an open field that ran down into a valley, with the ground rising to another ridge on the far side of the valley. The enemy's entrenched main line ran along this second ridge. A short distance in front of this line, in a commanding position on a small hill, was the earthwork that Ward was ordered to attack. It was occupied by Max Van Den Corput's Confederate battery of four guns, covering much of the ground over which Butterfield's and Geary's troops would have to pass in the attack.[70]

When Ward's brigade, leading the attack, came into the open field on the slope of the ridge, it immediately advanced toward the earthwork from which the four guns were firing. Benjamin Harrison's 70th Indiana, the leading regiment of the brigade, soon arrived in front of the earthwork. After a sharp fight, the men drove the defenders back to their main line, leaving their guns behind. The earthwork was open at the back, making it impossible for the men to enter and bring off the captured guns because of the heavy enemy fire from the main line.[71]

Other troops also aided in taking the earthwork and preventing its recapture. Colonel George A. Cobham, commanding the 111th Pennsylvania of Geary's division, moved down the slope of the ridge, across the valley, and up toward that part of the enemy's line held by the three divisions of John B. Hood's corps. When Cobham arrived within about fifteen yards of the battery, he directed his men to halt and lie down and open fire, an action which aided in silencing the enemy firing the guns. Cobham held his position from about 12:30 PM until dark, and during this time the right of his regiment covered the guns and helped prevent any approach by the enemy to draw them off. Geary also sent forward ten other regiments of his division to support Cobham. Troops of Coburn's brigade of Butterfield's

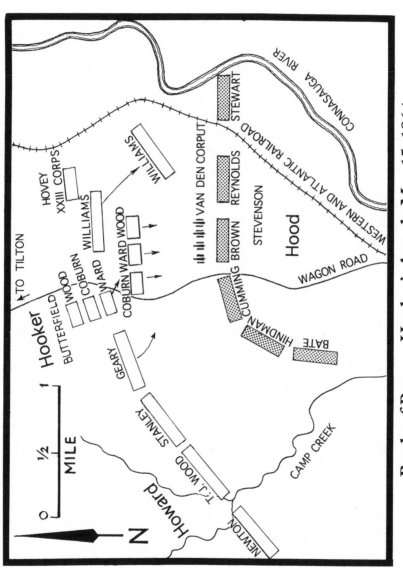

Battle of Resaca, Hooker's Attack, May 15, 1864

division arrived at the front at about the same time as Ward and Cobham, and they too took part in the attack at and near the earthwork.[72]

Coburn's men, experiencing difficulty maintaining their line as they followed Ward's brigade up the ravine, soon were faced with another problem when they ran into Geary's division. Geary's men were marching by the left flank in several columns; in this formation, they passed through Coburn's brigade, completely breaking up Coburn's advancing lines. This prevented the regimental commanders from seeing all of their own troops, and they were, therefore, for a time, unable to exercise proper control over them. Also, because of the intermingling of the men of the two commands, some of Coburn's men moved on with Geary, and some of Geary's division joined Coburn as he moved ahead. Despite all the confusion, however, Coburn's brigade finally arrived on the crest of the ridge. There, the men immediately came under a heavy fire from the enemy artillery.[73]

Because of the confusion that had occurred in moving up the ravine, and also because of a misunderstanding of orders, Coburn's attack from the crest of the ridge did not take place as planned. When the brigade moved out to attack, the right of the line advanced across the open field and across the valley, and the left moved forward along the woods to the left. There was a general intermingling of the men of the regiments, but generally the 85th and 33rd Indiana continued on straight ahead, and the 19th Michigan, 22nd Wisconsin, and the 20th Connecticut moved off to the left. Ahead of the 33rd and 85th Indiana there were several lines of troops of Geary's division, formed in various ways, all lying down and firing over other lines farther in advance. Confronted with this situation, the two Indiana regiments could advance no farther with any semblance of order, and Colonel Baird decided to halt and await orders while he re-formed the two regiments in a good position. Major Miller, commanding the 33rd Indiana, reported to Baird in the absence of any commanding officer.[74]

The three regiments of Coburn's brigade which had moved to the left from the crest of the ridge also took part in the fighting around the battery, and some of the men of the 19th Michigan and the 22nd Wisconsin moved up to the enemy's works. Early in the action, Colonel Gilbert of the 19th Michigan was mortally wounded, and Major Eli A. Griffin succeeded him in command of the regiment.[75]

Shortly after Coburn arrived near the enemy's works, Ward was wounded, and Coburn assumed command of the troops of the brigade present at that point. He made three attempts to capture the breastworks, but all failed. He held his ground close up to the works.[76]

Washington L. Jones, who participated in the charge at Resaca with Company E of the 85th Indiana, later stated that his most vivid memory of the fight was when the regiment charged:

As they advanced, a soldier horribly wounded in the hip, his clothing saturated with blood, came staggering back. When he saw the charging troops, he drew himself up as far as possible, shouted encouragement to the comrades, saying, "Go on boys and hurry, they are needing you at the front."[77]

About 4:00 PM the 33rd Indiana moved back to a ridge to the left and rear of its advanced position, and later the entire brigade joined the 33rd Indiana on the ridge. About 5:00 PM, Stewart's Confederate division made another attempt to turn the left flank of Hooker's line and struck the position held by the 33rd Indiana; but that regiment, assisted by some troops of Geary's division, repulsed the attack.[78]

During the fighting that day, Coburn's brigade lost one officer killed and seven wounded, and twenty-six men killed and 191 wounded. Only one man was reported missing. In the fighting near the enemy's earthworks, Sergeant William A. Richardson, Company D of the 85th Indiana, was killed, and Corporal James Andrews of the same company was mortally wounded.[79]

There has been considerable controversy about who removed the four captured guns from the earthwork and brought them back safely into Union lines. Lieutenant Colonel Robert L. Kilpatrick claimed that his 5th Ohio Regiment of Geary's division performed this task, and it is probably true that some of his men did take part in this operation. It appears, however, that men of several regiments had some part in bringing the guns back, and that an account given by Lieutenant Colonel Philo P. Buckingham of the 20th Connecticut of Coburn's brigade is correct. Buckingham later said that after dark May 15, he was detailed with two companies of the 20th Connecticut and two companies from each of the other regiments of Coburn's brigade to gain possession of the four guns that had been abandoned by the enemy in the earthwork and, if possible, to remove them during the night. It was not possible to bring them out through the open rear of the works because of enemy fire, but Buckingham's men, aided by some men of Cobham's command, cut an opening in the front of the works and, with the aid of ropes, pulled the guns out and by 2:00 AM, May 16, they had brought them safely into Union lines.[80]

The fighting ended at dark, and much of the night was spent constructing defensive works on the positions gained in the fighting that day. These were unnecessary, however, because at daylight the next morning it was found that the enemy had departed during the night.

Coburn's men had much to be proud of for their conduct at the Battle of Resaca. In the midst of major confusion, they had fought well, advancing with courage and helping capture the enemy's guns.

Resaca to Cassville, Georgia

On May 15, 1864, while Hooker's battle on the Union left was in progress, Joseph E. Johnston learned that Federal Brigadier General Thomas W. Sweeny's division of the Army of the Tennessee had crossed to the south side of the Oostanaula River on a pontoon bridge near Lay's Ferry and was threatening his communications with Atlanta. Faced with this danger, Johnston ordered his Confederates to withdraw from the lines at Resaca and, during the night, to move back across the Oostanaula River and march southward toward Calhoun, Georgia. Johnston had hoped to establish there a suitable position from which he could successfully engage a part of Sherman's army as it moved forward in pursuit. Upon arriving at Calhoun, however, Johnston found the terrain unsatisfactory for his purpose, and he moved on south to Adairsville, where there was a more defensible position.[81]

When Sherman discovered, early on the morning of May 16, that Johnston's army had retired during the night and was then moving south, he started his entire army in immediate pursuit on a wide front. McPherson's Army of the Tennessee moved forward that day on roads to the right and crossed the Oostanaula River at Lay's Ferry; George H. Thomas, with Fourth Corps and Fourteenth Corps of the Army of the Cumberland, except Davis' division of Fourteenth Corps, moved up to Resaca in preparation for crossing the river. Howard's Fourth Corps was able to cross the river that day, and it moved forward along the direct road to Kingston as far as Calhoun, where it camped for the night. Davis' division, which was detached, moved down the west bank of the Oostanaula River May 16 and occupied Rome, Georgia, the next day.[82]

On the morning of May 16, Schofield's Army of the Ohio and Hooker's Twentieth Corps advanced by obscure roads on the left of the army. There was some confusion about the routes to be taken by Hooker's Twentieth Corps and Schofield's Twenty-Third Corps, causing a delay in starting their pursuit. Schofield's corps was on the left of Sherman's line at Resaca that morning, with its left resting on the Connesauga River. It was ordered to move eastward, cross the Connesauga River between Resaca and Tilton, and march on to the Coosawattee River. These two rivers come together at Newtown a few miles southeast of Resaca to form the Oostanaula river.[83]

Hooker's orders were to follow the Newtown road with his corps and cross the Oostanaula in the southward bend of that river near Newtown. By some error, however, Geary's division, which was leading Hooker's corps that morning, took the route that had been assigned to Schofield.[84]

Because Geary's division, and later the other divisions of the corps, was on the road that Schofield was to have used, Schofield's troops marched to the southeast and forded the Connesauga at Fite's Ferry, some two miles below Echota. The artillery and the wagons were ferried over in a small boat. The crossing provided some laughter for the men. The water in the river was about waist deep, and the men stripped off all their clothes and waded across, holding clothes and arms above their heads. After crossing the Coosawattee, Schofield marched further up the river to Field's Mill where he crossed the river on May 17.[85]

From Field's Mill, Schofield took the Cassville road and passed through Big Spring to Marsteller's Mill. From Marsteller's Mill he marched on the Sallacoa Road directly toward Johnston's right flank at Cassville, arriving there on May 18, 1864. At the same time, McCook's and Stoneman's cavalries were also approaching the right of Johnston's line on the Canton Road.

May 16, 1864, Geary's division marched to within a mile of Resaca and then proceeded eastward to Fite's Ferry, where it arrived about 9:00 AM. Geary then crossed the Connesauga River, a part of the division moving over on a ferry boat and the rest at the ford a short distance below. The division marched to the Coosawattee River at Bryant's (or McClure's) Ferry, arriving late in the day. It crossed the river that night and rested on the south bank the following morning while the rest of the corps came up and crossed.[86]

Williams' division left the battlefield on the morning of May 15 and with the rest of the corps, crossed the Connesauga River above Resaca. It bivouacked that night at Bryant's (or McClure's) Ford on the Coosawattee River in preparation for crossing that river the next morning.[87]

Coburn's brigade, which was continuing to march with Butterfield's division, arrived at Field's Mill (or Field's Ferry) about at 11:00 PM and immediately began crossing the river on a ferry boat. The 33rd Indiana, which was the rear regiment of the brigade that day, was finally across by 3:00 AM May 17. The men, exhausted by the fighting, marching, and hard work of the past few days, were ordered into camp near the river for some much needed rest.[88]

May 17 Fourth Corps and Fourteenth Corps followed directly along the road and the railroad in the center of Sherman's line. Palmer, with the divisions of Richard W. Johnson and Absalom Baird of his Fourteenth Corps, crossed the Oostanaula River and marched southward along the railroad in pursuit of Johnston's army. These divisions passed through Calhoun on the road to Adairsville, and bivouacked at 11:30 that night about seven miles south of Calhoun, on the left of Baird's division.[89]

Brigadier General John Newton's and Major General David S. Stanley's divisions of Fourth Corps marched along the wagon road, and Brigadier General Thomas J. Wood's division advanced on the right along the railroad.[90]

After resting until about 2:00 PM May 17, Coburn's brigade broke camp and marched with Butterfield's division until 10:00 PM and then halted for

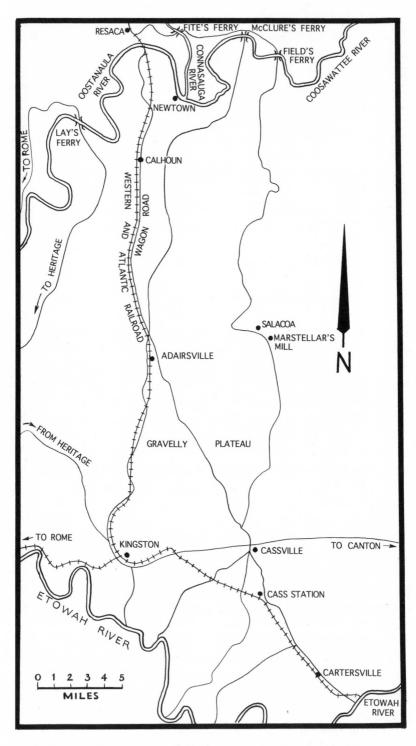

Atlanta Campaign, Resaca to the Etowah River

the night to the east of Calhoun. Companies A, D, E, and H of the 85th Indiana were detailed as ordnance train guard that day.[91]

May 18 Palmer marched through Adairsville with the divisions of Johnson and Baird and bivouacked at midnight on the railroad, within three miles of Kingston.[92]

Butterfield's division marched with the corps that day toward Cassville, with many of the men falling out along the road because of the heat. When the advance troops of the division found enemy forces on their front, the 22nd Wisconsin of Coburn's brigade was left with the train as a guard, going into camp with the train at 11:00 that night.[93]

The rest of the brigade continued on with the division and, after a march of twenty-one miles, encamped on Gravelly Plateau, about four miles north of Cassville. The 33rd and 85th Indiana regiments were then sent back about two and a half miles to guard a road that intersected the road to Cassville on the right. At this point Butterfield's division was leading the corps, with Geary's division following and Williams' division marching at the rear.[94]

About 11:00 AM May 19, the 20th Connecticut and the 19th Michigan, both under the command of Buckingham, were detached from Coburn's brigade and ordered to report to Butterfield, who was then about two miles distant in the direction of Kingston with Ward's and Wood's brigades.[95]

The 33rd Indiana and the 85th Indiana, having completed guard duty on the road to the rear, were ordered to take position on the Cassville road and to fortify and hold it if attacked. These two regiments remained behind with brigade headquarters. The 22nd Wisconsin was still with the train, and, fearing an attack by enemy cavalry, enclosed the train in a breastwork.[96]

About 2:00 PM May 19 Butterfield's division made a demonstration with infantry and artillery, with the 19th Michigan and the 20th Connecticut covering the right flank and supporting the artillery. At that time, Butterfield's division was near the Price house on the Cassville and Kingston road. Geary's division was on the right of Butterfield, with its right connecting with Fourth Corps, and Williams' division was on the left of Butterfield. Butterfield advanced about one-half mile and then swung around toward Cassville, with the enemy retiring as he moved forward. Ross, with the 19th Michigan and the 20th Connecticut regiments on the right, advanced with the division to the road near the Seminary, the name given to a brick school house on the road.[97]

At 2:00 PM Coburn ordered the 33rd Indiana and the 85th Indiana regiments to move forward from their position on the Cassville road and to join the division; he then proceeded to the front and assumed command of the two regiments under Ross. At 4:00 PM the 33rd and 85th Indiana rejoined the division, which was then advancing. These two regiments were hurried forward and were placed on the right and rear of the division, which had arrived at a point about one-half mile west of Cassville.[98]

At about this time, the 19th Michigan and the 20th Connecticut were ordered to support a battery which had taken position on a hill, commanding the enemy's line of entrenchments on the hills to the east, beyond Cassville. The 33rd Indiana and the 85th Indiana were moved forward to form a second line in rear of the other two regiments of the brigade.[99]

At dusk the 19th Michigan and the 20th Connecticut, supported by the 33rd Indiana and the 85th Indiana, moved into Cassville, which they occupied after a brief skirmish. They advanced to the crest of a hill overlooking the town and threw up breastworks, staying the night in reserve.[100]

Howard's Fourth Corps moved on May 18 six miles and camped on Connasene Creek.[101] It reached Kingston at 8:00 the following morning, and there the head of the column turned toward Cassville. Near that town the corps deployed, with Hooker's Twentieth Corps on the left and Palmer's Fourteenth Corps on the right.[102]

May 19 the two divisions of Palmer's Fourteenth Corps marched into Kingston. Absalom Baird's division, leading that morning, passed through the town and then took position on a range of hills south of the town, moving out to the east of the town and taking position on the right of Fourth Corps. About 2:30 PM Johnson's division moved out to the south of Kingston to seize Gillem's Bridge over the Etowah River, but on arriving at the bridge he found Brigadier General Kenner Garrard's cavalry division already there. Johnson then took a position covering the approaches to the bridge and camped for the night.[103]

During the night of May 19 Johnston withdrew his troops from the works on the hills beyond Cassville and marched back through Cartersville and across the Etowah River, establishing his army in a strong defensive position along the eastern bank of the river near the railroad crossing.[104]

At 10:00 on the morning of May 20, Knipe's First Brigade of Williams' division relieved Coburn's brigade at Cassville, and Coburn moved westward for about a mile and a half toward Kingston and went into camp with the rest of Butterfield's division.[105]

Sherman's army remained in camp along the north side of the Etowah River until May 23, while he completed preparations for his next movement toward Atlanta.

Francis C. Crawford of Company G, 85th Indiana, describes the nerve-wracking situation for Union soldiers during the advance on Cassville:

> Of the many situations that confront the soldier on an active campaign, I think that of advancing under the enemy's picket fire with the uncertainty of there being any force behind them, and the prob-

ability of any moment being drawn into a general engagement, is the most trying to the individual.

Of such was the situation that confronted our brigade of Sherman's Army in advancing on the little town of Cassville during the Atlanta Campaign. The country over which we were to advance was a dry table-land (designated in orders as "Gravelly-Plateau"). It was covered with a scattering growth of timber with very little under-brush to obstruct the view. The trees were hardly enough in growth to cover a skirmisher and I know to a man on horse-back they appeared as mere saplings. The advance during the whole day was spasmodic, a hundred yards at a time, one-fourth mile–and one half of a mile and between long waits without the relief of a place to rest. The incessant pop, pop of the skirmishers, sometimes in sight, and then far in advance, would be occasionally varied by a sharp rattle of infantry fire, either to our right or left and then the boom of a field-gun at still farther distance kept ones nerves on a constant strain, that fatigued, not only the mind, but every muscle of the body.

Late in the afternoon, we had halted on a ridge which we called Seminary Ridge, on account of a brick school house which stood on the road. In advance one half or three quarters of a mile was another ridge and in the valley between them was the village of Cassville. Considerable firing was being kept up by our skirmishers and the enemy, who seemed to have made a stand on the ridge beyond the town, but at long range and harmless.

It was here that an incident occurred which illustrates the mental strain we had been under all day. While riding up the road to the school house, I met a man of my own regiment, whom I knew to be a good soldier, and a brave man, and whom I had seen active on the skirmish-line all day. He was coming back from the Front and shaking all over like a person with the ague. I called him by name and asked him, "why, have you been hit?" He put his hand on the shoulder of my horse and looked up with tears in his eyes and said, "no, but I'm just scared to death, can't I go back?" I gave him some message as an excuse back to the wagon train. Next day he was in front and all right, as ever.

Just at dusk an order came for us to occupy the town and there being no troops of ours in sight on either flank, our Brigade Commander decided to push forward two regiments, and hold the other two in the ridge, which was done, by a dash across the open space and into the shelter of the houses of the town calling out a few ineffectual shots from the enemy on the hill beyond. The village was rather a long town, built on three streets running parallel with the ridges and in the center was a stone Courthouse the only stone or brick building there.

Behind this the General and his Staff took quarters and so close were we to the enemy that we could hear them digging and throwing up entrenchments, hear them placing cannon in position, and an occasional command given. To caution our men to keep silent was unnecessary. They knew the situation: that we were far in advance of our right and left connections, if indeed we had any; that we were within 150 or 100 yards of the enemy's entrenched line of artillery, with no protection save small wooden buildings, more dangerous, perhaps, than the open field. And thus the suspense of the day was being prolonged into the night and intensified.

Along about midnight or after, all sounds ceased and darkness and the most absolute silence hung like an inevitable pall over us. About 3:00 AM I went under orders to find Division Head Quarters or some one to whom to report the situation, and fortunately struck General Thomas's Head Quarters, who informed me that if they had not gone they would before morning or if not, the flanking Corps "would have them in a tight place." He then gave me orders to General Coburn to have the town searched and ascertain what troops had been there or had passed through. On getting back to the Court house I was instructed to search the houses for anyone who could give information. Up to this time not a man, woman or child had been seen, nor a dog, not even a cat. So calling a couple of men I set out on a tour of Burglary, and indeed I did feel something like a burglar as we went prowling through the rooms and climbing stairs, by the light of a match shaded in the hand. Some of the houses we found unlocked and all showing signs of hasty departure. Some had evidently made hasty selections of articles to be carried away, indicated by open drawers and things scattered about on the floors. Others had fled evidently upon the first alarm, as in one house we found a full coffee pot and only part of the cups filled, some plates filled and others empty, a few chairs overturned and the door open, showing how the horrors of war had come like an earthquake shock.

Our search through the town was fruitless, and having reached the last house on the south end and found nothing in it, we were about to give up the search, when one of my men called to me that he had heard voices. Going around we found a slanting door covering the entrance to a cellar, I believe the only one in town[.] [T]hrowing this open, I demanded if there was anyone there, whereupon there was some exclamations of either terror or relief with one or two cries from children, and then there came pouring up into the gray of morning (which by this time was quite visible) some 15 or 20 women, girls, and children who had spent the long and miserable night cooped up in this small space, dreading the coming of day, for they knew that the "Rebs" intended to fight here. They all looked wan, terror stricken and speechless, until one elderly women asked me if they would be harmed and began begging protection. Just then I heard a shout from the front and then another followed by a general cheer and I at once knew that another last ditch had been abandoned. I assured them that there would be no battle over the town and that the safest place would be at their homes, upon which they all began to talk at once and shake off the evidences of their long vigil in the cellar.[106]

(Crawford, in the above account of his experiences at Cassville, refers to "General Coburn," but at that time his rank was Colonel Coburn. He was not promoted to the rank of Brevet Brigadier General until the omnibus bill of March 13, 1865. Thereafter, especially after the War, he was properly referred to by his men as General Coburn.)

With the withdrawal of Johnston's army from Cassville, and the Union occupation of the town, Sherman had demonstrated his ability to move his army well into the interior of Georgia, and he was then preparing his orders for continuing his march toward the Etowah River.

During the early stages of the movement on Atlanta, Coburn's brigade had done well, and its performance at Resaca, in the attack on the right of Johnston's line, though unsuccessful, was very creditable. The brigade was beginning to gain the respect of their superiors, and they would add greatly to this feeling of respectability when they reached Peach Tree Creek later in the campaign.

Chapter 10

Atlanta Campaign

Cassville to Acworth

Major General William T. Sherman was aware of the great strength of the position held by General Joseph E. Johnston's army along the eastern bank of the Etowah River, and, in planning his next move beyond Cassville, he decided against an attempt to force a crossing at that point because of the high casualties that would almost certainly be incurred. Instead, he ordered another flanking movement to the right, this time in the direction of Dallas, Georgia. By taking this route he could cross the river with little or no opposition and move beyond Johnston's left flank and thus force him out of his strong position along the river. When this had been accomplished, Sherman could move back to his line of supplies on the railroad and continue his advance toward Atlanta.[1]

The early part of this march would prove difficult because of the nature of the terrain and the problem of obtaining supplies for the army after leaving the railroad. The country south of the Etowah River, through which the army was to pass, was very rugged and mountainous, densely wooded, and traversed by many streams. There were only a few poor and obscure roads crossing this region, and this, together with all the other obstacles, would make the passage of men and trains a very difficult task.[2]

When Sherman started his advance toward Atlanta, he had ordered that the soldiers prepare cooked rations for four days and leave all baggage behind. Some basic supplies were issued to the army when it reached Snake Creek Gap and these where to last until it reached the Etowah River, where supplies were brought forward by rail. The Resaca bridge had been rebuilt in three days, and on May 22 rations for twenty days had been issued to the divisions. When the army left the line of the railroad at Cassville and crossed the Etowah on its march toward Dallas, it carried twenty days' rations in the haversacks of the men and in wagons. Kingston was established as the base of supplies and was to serve as such until the army again reached the railroad somewhere south of Allatoona Pass.[3]

Day-by-day existence while on the march was at all times difficult for both officers and men. The only shelter for division and brigade headquarters was a tent fly, a single sheet of light canvas. A company pack mule carried only the simple cooking utensils and other items that experience had shown to be the most needed when the men were in camp without mess kits. The mule, driven by a Negro servant, could keep close to the company on the march, both on and off the roads, and it was generally fairly close up to the line when the men were under fire.[4]

The private soldier carried with him his shelter tent or a rubber blanket, and when in the field two men combined their two tents to provide fairly good protection from the weather. The private's haversack contained his rations, with a small tin coffee pot and a canteen attached to his belt. The ration of meat, bread, coffee, and sugar was generally fairly large and of good quality in 1864 in the Northern Army, except when the army was operating in difficult country and distant from its line of communication, as was the case after crossing the Etowah River.[5]

Even the general officers lived under trying conditions during the march toward Dallas and then back to the railroad at Acworth. Their life was complicated by the fact that there was much business and clerical work to transact. Brigadier General Jacob D. Cox, commanding a division in Twenty-Third Corps, has offered the following comments about affairs at division headquarters:

> . . . Necessity was the mother of invention, and at Cartersville the mess at a division headquarters boasted that, beginning with nothing, they had accumulated a kit consisting of a tin plate, four tin cups without handles, three round oyster cans doing duty as cups, two sardine boxes for extra plates, and a coffee pot! Pocket knives were the only cutlery needed, and for dishes nothing could be better than one of the solid crackers commonly known as "hard tack." This outfit they declared was luxurious compared with that of the General-in-Chief.[6]

Sherman left garrisons at Kingston and Rome and put his army in motion toward Dallas May 23. As before, the men marched in three columns on a wide front. Major General James B. McPherson, with Major General John A. Logan's Fifteenth Corps and Major General Grenville M. Dodge's Left Wing, Sixteenth Corps of the Army of the Tennessee, crossed the Etowah River near Kingston and camped that night near Van Wert on Euharlee Creek. Major General Frank P. Blair had assumed command of Seventeenth Corps at Cairo May 4, 1864, and by May 23 he had concentrated two of its divisions at Huntsville, Alabama, but had not yet joined Sherman's army.[7]

Major General George H. Thomas' instructions were to move his Army

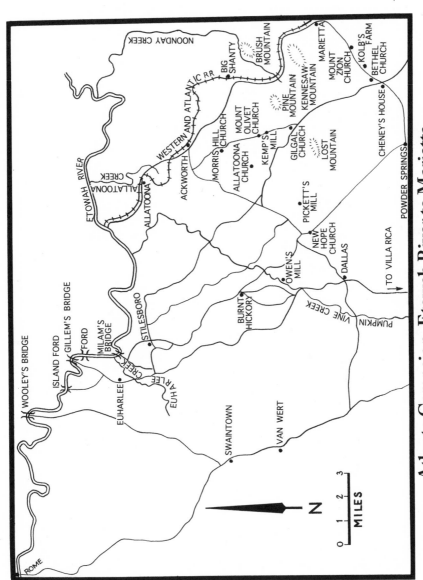

Atlanta Campaign, Etowah River to Marietta

of the Cumberland, beginning on the morning of May 23, on Dallas by way of Euharlee and Stilesboro. Brigadier General Jefferson C. Davis' division of Major General John M. Palmer's Fourteenth Corps, which was then at Rome, Georgia, was to wait until it was relieved by troops from the Army of the Tennessee, and then march to Van Wert and Dallas.[8]

Thomas left his camps near Cassville and moved almost due south to the Etowah River, where Major General Oliver O. Howard's Fourth Corps and Palmer's corps crossed that afternoon at the bridges on the direct road from Kingston to Euharlee. Instead of waiting to cross his Twentieth Corps, including Coburn's brigade, at these bridges, however, Major General Joseph Hooker became impatient and moved farther to the left and crossed on a pontoon bridge that had been laid for Major General John M. Schofield's Army of the Ohio (Twenty-Third Corps) at Milam's Bridge. This was to complicate matters a short time later.[9]

Thomas crossed the river that afternoon and camped for the night on the high ground about one and one-half miles beyond the crossing. Palmer, with Brigadier General Richard W. Johnson's and Brigadier General Absalom Baird's divisions of Fourteenth Corps, camped on Euharlee Creek near the Burnt Hickory road. Davis' division remained at Rome until the following day and then moved to Euharlee Creek.[10]

Schofield's Army of the Ohio, following Thomas to the Etowah River that afternoon, was delayed in crossing by troops of Hooker's corps of the Army of the Cumberland and was forced to remain north of the river that night. The men marched with twenty days' supplies in haversacks and wagons, under orders to be in position on the left flank of the main army, near Dallas, Georgia.[11]

May 24 the Army of the Tennessee continued its march, passing through Van Wert toward Dallas, and camped that night near a branch of Raccoon Creek.[12]

That morning Brigadier General John W. Geary's Second Division of Hooker's corps crossed Raccoon Creek on the Allatoona road and took position so as to cover the road running up the creek. It remained there until about noon, when it was relieved by troops of Schofield's command. Hooker, with Brigadier General Alpheus S. Williams' First Division and Major General Daniel Butterfield's Third Division of his corps, preceded by Brigadier General Edward M. McCook's cavalry division of the Army of the Cumberland, marched on through Euharlee and Stilesboro to Burnt Hickory, the name of a place on the old Kentucky stock road where a large Hickory tree once stood. Travelers on the road often stopped there and built their fires at the base of the tree, and in time it became known as Burnt Hickory. There were a few houses scattered along the road, but there was no village at this point. The troops camped that night in a heavy storm.[13]

Colonel John Coburn's Second Brigade marched with Butterfield's division that day. Colonel Samuel Ross' 20th Connecticut of the brigade was detached to serve as guard for the ordnance and supply trains of the division. It remained on this duty until June 13, 1864. May 26 Ross was transferred with his regiment from Second Brigade to Third Brigade of Butterfield's division, and Coburn was then again in command of the four regiments that had for so long comprised his brigade.[14]

On the morning of May 24 Schofield followed Hooker's Twentieth Corps across the Etowah River, and about noon, with Major General George Stoneman's cavalry division of the Army of the Ohio covering the advance, he marched southward on the Allatoona road. He soon came up and relieved Geary's division, which then moved on and rejoined Twentieth Corps near Burnt Hickory. Schofield continued on to Sligh's (Sly's) Mills, at the forks of the roads running to Acworth and Burnt Hickory.[15]

Meanwhile, when the important information that Sherman's army was crossing the Etowah River had been communicated to General Johnston, he immediately began to re-position his troops to meet the threat of this flanking movement. He ordered Lieutenant General William J. Hardee to march with his corps by way of New Hope Church to the Stilesboro and Dallas road, and Lieutenant General Leonidas Polk to move with his corps in the same direction, but a little farther to the south. Lieutenant General John B. Hood's corps would follow the next day. By May 25 Johnston had his entire command in a good defensive position in front of and covering the road from Dallas to Acworth. Hardee's corps was on the left, east of Dallas; Hood's corps was on the right, with its center at New Hope Church, about four miles north of Dallas; and Polk was in the center between Hardee and Hood.[16]

Advancing on the right of Sherman's command, the Army of the Tennessee arrived within about two miles of Dallas on the evening of May 25 and camped on Pumpkin Vine Creek. On the left, the Army of the Ohio remained in camp near Burnt Hickory, but the Army of the Cumberland, moving forward in the center, had a more eventful day.[17]

BATTLE OF NEW HOPE CHURCH
MAY 25, 1864

May 25, 1864, Thomas resumed his march from Burnt Hickory on several roads. Fourth Corps and Fourteenth Corps made a detour to the right with the intention of reaching the road from Van Wert to Dallas three or four miles west of Dallas. Twentieth Corps moved directly toward Dallas, with Geary's division marching in the center on the main road and with Butterfield's division, including Coburn's brigade and Williams' division, advancing on country roads on the left and right of Geary, respectively. There were showers during the day; the weather and the poor condition of the roads had a depressing effect on the men.[18]

When Geary reached Pumpkin Vine Creek near Owen's Mills he found the bridge on fire and enemy cavalry in position across the creek. The enemy soon withdrew, however, and Geary repaired the bridge in preparation for crossing. The presence of enemy cavalry led Hooker to believe that a strong force of Johnston's command was somewhere in the direction of New Hope Church, and he ordered Geary to move on and take the fork of the road that ran in that direction.[19]

It has been noted that when Johnston moved his army back from the Etowah River to oppose Sherman's flanking movement, Hood's corps was placed in line in the vicinity of New Hope Church. This church was located at the junction of three roads that ran in from Acworth, Marietta, and Dallas. In front of the church there was a valley covered with woods along the road with open fields a short distance to the north. A branch of Pumpkin Vine Creek flowed through this valley in a northeasterly direction, and the ground on both sides sloped upward to elevations of about fifty feet above the valley floor. In the vicinity of New Hope Church the creek ran parallel to Hood's line, which was located along the crest of the ridge on the eastern side of the valley.[20]

After crossing Pumpkin Vine Creek, Geary's Second Division moved out on the road that ran to New Hope Church, as ordered, and near the Hawkins house, about a mile and a half from the bridge. There the division's skirmishers became heavily engaged. Almost immediately the enemy charged Geary's line and were repulsed, and Geary continued his advance for another half mile, attacking and driving a heavy force of the enemy before him. After some time he arrived on the ridge on the west side of the valley mentioned above, taking position in front of Hood's main defensive line. At that point he was some distance ahead of all supporting troops, and he ordered his men to throw up a breastwork of logs to provide temporary cover.[21]

When Sherman heard the sounds of Geary's engagement, he hastened to the front and directed Hooker to call in his other two divisions from the right and left to support Geary. He further ordered that when they arrived they were to attack and develop the enemy force on their respective fronts. Butterfield's division, which had marched from near Burnt Hickory that morning, arrived at Pumpkin Vine Creek during the late afternoon, crossed the creek, and moved up to a position on the left and rear of Geary's division.[22]

Williams' division had already reached a point not far from Dallas when the general received Sherman's order to close up on the rest of the corps.

Williams immediately turned back and marched to Owen's Mills, where he followed Geary's and Butterfield's divisions across Pumpkin Vine Creek. At about 5:00 PM Williams came up in rear of the other two massed divisions of Hooker's corps, and then passed to the front and took position on the right of Geary. Thus by about 5:00 PM all of Hooker's divisions were on the field, with Williams' division on the right of Geary and Butterfield's division to the left and rear of Geary.[23]

The country through which Hooker's troops advanced that evening consisted of a succession of ridges that were about twenty to fifty feet in height, with intervening valleys. The entire area was covered by an unbroken forest, including both slopes of the valley in front of Hood's main line at New Hope Church.[24]

Colonel James Wood's Third Brigade was the first brigade of Butterfield's Third Division of Twentieth Corps to arrive on the field. Butterfield ordered Wood to support Williams' First Division in an attack the corps was preparing to launch to drive the enemy back. Wood formed his brigade in line of battle by battalion in mass and then advanced for a time in rear of Williams' division. Wood was soon ordered to cross to the left side of the road for the attack, and after this movement was completed, to move up with his brigade and connect with the left of Williams' line.[25]

Coburn's Second Brigade of Butterfield's division arrived near the field a short time after Wood's brigade, and it crossed Pumpkin Vine Creek and marched out about a half mile on the road toward New Hope Church and halted. The 33rd Indiana, which was leading the brigade when it reached the front, was formed in column of division on the right of the road and then moved forward about a mile through the forest with the rest of the brigade in support of Wood's brigade.

When Wood's brigade moved off to the left of the road in his advance that evening, Coburn was ordered to move to the front. After advancing through the woods for about three hundred yards, he came unexpectedly under rapid artillery fire and at once deployed his brigade in two lines. He placed Major Eli A. Griffin's 19th Michigan on the left of Major Levin T. Miller's 33rd Indiana, and Miller's regiment thus formed the right of Coburn's first line and the 19th Michigan the left. Colonel John P. Baird's 85th Indiana came up in rear of the 33rd Indiana and took position on the right of the second line. Colonel William L. Utley's 22nd Wisconsin remained in rear of the brigade on the left of the 85th Indiana and was not engaged that day. When the deployment was completed, the brigade advanced a short distance and then again halted.[26]

About dusk Colonel Baird ordered the men of the 85th Indiana to lie down to escape the enemy fire, which at this point was very severe, and they held this position during most of the night.[27]

A short time later, having been ordered to relieve Colonel James S. Robinson's Third Brigade of Williams' division, Coburn again moved forward with his brigade. He had not gone far, however, when Hooker ordered the 19th Michigan to move to the left and relieve a hard pressed regiment of Williams' division. The 33rd Indiana continued its advance to the front to relieve the men of Robinson's brigade, as ordered, with the 85th Indiana and the 22nd Wisconsin held in reserve.[28]

Arriving at the front, Coburn was unable to find Robinson's brigade, which had given way earlier and fallen back. He did find on the first line Brigadier General Joseph F. Knipe's brigade of Williams' division nearly out of ammunition. Coburn relieved the 46th Pennsylvania of Knipe's brigade, all that he could replace with only his 33rd Indiana. When the Pennsylvania regiment had departed, the 33rd Indiana took its place. The 19th Michigan, which had moved over from the right, relieved the 141st New York of Knipe's brigade.

The 33rd Indiana passed through Knipe's line and soon silenced the enemy's musketry fire, which had been increasing in intensity. During its advance, the 33rd Indiana was subjected to heavy artillery fire consisting of shells, grape, canister, and even railroad spikes. Near dusk the 33rd Indiana was ordered to cease firing and to lie down. The fighting ended at dark, but the men worked on through in the darkness and a heavy, cold rain, throwing up breastworks of logs and limbs, and anything else that was handy.[29]

When Butterfield's division formed for the attack late in the afternoon of May 25, Brigadier General William T. Ward's First Brigade was placed in rear of Coburn's and Wood's brigades, and it was not engaged.[30]

Hooker's divisions attacked Hood's position several times on a brigade front, with the rear brigades relieving those in front by passing lines. The enemy works were too strong to carry, however, and when the fighting ended at dark, Hooker's men retired to the crest of the ridge from which they had launched their attack.[31]

In the midst of the fighting that day, a violent thunderstorm struck the area, followed by a pouring rain that lasted throughout the night. It was an eerie experience for the men that evening, with sounds of thunder mingling with roars of artillery and almost continuous musketry fire, while they fought desperately in blinding rain in the darkening woods.[32]

Jefferson E. Brant, in his *History of the Eighty-Fifth Indiana*, describes the regiment's activities that day:

> On Wednesday morning May 25, we moved on over hills and hollows and in thick woods, and by four or five o'clock we came to the scene of the cannonading and musketry. One hundred had been killed and wounded in the first division.

Our division, the 3rd, was immediately placed in position and moved on through the dense woods, in line of battle. About sun down we encountered the enemy, who poured deadly volleys into the regiment in advance. Our boys, however, moved on and gave volley for volley, driving the enemy before them. The fighting was as fierce as any we have been in hearing of during this campaign.

Night ended the conflict, leaving us the vantage ground. Our losses were severe, as the enemy lay in the brush until our columns were well up. They used their artillery with deadly effect. Our regiment was in the third line, but we lost six wounded. Night set in and it commenced raining and the thick darkness of that quiet but doleful night, in the Dallas woods, will not soon be forgotten.[33]

During the night of May 25 Colonel Baird of the 85th Indiana was nearly captured. He moved out in the darkness to examine the ground in his front, and he was soon halted by an enemy picket. Baird asked, "Who are you," and the picket replied, "Mississippi regiment." Baird then replied "I am officer of the guard" and quickly turned away and made his way back to the regiment.[34]

In the fighting at New Hope Church, Coburn's brigade lost one officer and seven men killed and seven officers and 101 men wounded, for a total of 116. Many of the wounded died later. Although not engaged, the 85th Indiana lost Corporal Thomas Files of Company E and six men who were wounded by enemy fire.[35]

Brigadier General John Newton's Second Division of Howard's Fourth Corps came up during the fighting, and by about 6:00 PM, at Hooker's request, had taken position on the left of Twentieth Corps. By the morning of May 26, the other divisions of Fourth Corps had arrived and extended the Union lines farther to the left.[36]

May 26 the Army of the Tennessee marched through Dallas and took position east of the town, facing Hardee's corps. Davis' division of Palmer's Fourteenth Corps, which had advanced from Rome by way of Van Wert to Dallas, took position with the Army of the Tennessee, east of Dallas.[37]

Schofield, who had been ordered forward with his Army of the Ohio (Twenty-Third Corps) during the fighting at New Hope Church, finally arrived on the morning of May 26 and placed his corps on the left of Howard's Fourth Corps.[38]

At 1:00 AM May 26 Johnson's division of Palmer's corps resumed its march from Raccoon Creek and reached Burnt Hickory before daylight. It continued on and halted about two miles to the south. At 11:30 AM it resumed the march and early in the afternoon halted in rear of Fourth Corps, about three miles east of Pumpkin Vine Creek. Absalom Baird's division of Palmer's corps remained near Burnt Hickory, guarding the trains, until the end of the month.[39]

Hooker's Twentieth Corps remained in position in front of New Hope Church until June 1. Butterfield's Third Division continued to hold the position it had occupied at the end of the fighting, but there were some changes in the disposition of the troops of the division during the next few days after the battle. In Coburn's Second Brigade of Third Division the 19th Michigan was relieved at 1:00 in the morning of May 26 but the other regiments of the brigade remained out in front all night. At about 3:00 AM the 22nd Wisconsin moved to the right and relieved the 33rd Indiana, which then moved to the rear about one hundred yards. The men built fires and made coffee, and details were sent out for ammunition and rations. Also about 3:00 AM the 85th Indiana moved forward into the front line and relieved the 123rd New York of Knipe's brigade, Williams' division. The men then built breastworks about 150 to 200 yards in front of the enemy line and endured an almost continual skirmish fire. About dark that day, Coburn's brigade was relieved, and it moved to the right and took position in rear of Ward's brigade of Butterfield's division.[40]

BATTLE OF PICKETT'S MILL
MAY 26, 1864

On May 27 Sherman decided to attempt to turn the right flank of Johnston's army and, for this purpose, he ordered Brigadier General Thomas J. Wood's division of Howard's corps, Johnson's division of Palmer's corps, and Brigadier General Nathaniel C. McLean's brigade of Schofield's Twenty-Third Corps to move out beyond the extreme left flank of the Union army and to find a suitable point to attack beyond the enemy's line of entrenchments. Wood and Johnson finally attacked near Pickett's Mill, but instead of striking a lightly held position they encountered a strong force of the enemy, and the attack was repulsed with a Federal loss of about 1,500 men. McLean's brigade was of no help in the fighting that day. Although the attack failed to turn the Confederate right, the ground gained by this movement proved to be helpful during the extension of Sherman's line toward the Acworth road which began a few days later.[41]

Other than the battle at Pickett's Mill, there was little change in the positions of Sherman's troops on May 27. Coburn's brigade of Butterfield's division moved forward that day and occupied the line held by Ward's brigade, and Ward then moved forward fifty to one hundred yards and fortified a new line. Coburn remained in this position until the evening of May 30.[42]

The fighting of the past few days convinced Sherman that Johnston's entire army was on his front in a strongly entrenched position, and that any attempt to dislodge it would be costly and probably unsuccessful. With this in mind, he decided on another flanking movement, this time to his left. His plan was to pass by Johnston's right flank and to gain possession of the Acworth road.[43]

Accordingly, on May 28 Sherman issued instructions for the movements of the army. He directed McPherson to relieve Davis' division of Fourteenth Corps, then temporarily attached to the Army of the Tennessee east of Dallas, and to send it back to Thomas' Army of the Cumberland. At the same time, he ordered McPherson to extend the line of his army to the left and relieve a part of Hooker's corps, which was then to replace Schofield's corps on the line. When Schofield was relieved, he was to move beyond the Army of the Cumberland and again occupy the extreme left flank of the army.[44]

During the afternoon of May 28, while McPherson was preparing to execute his part of Sherman's plan, he was strongly attacked by Hardee's corps. The attack was repulsed, but, because of the threat posed by this action, Davis was unable to withdraw from McPherson's line that day as ordered. Sherman's movement was further delayed when Hardee delivered another unsuccessful attack late the next day.[45]

There was little change in position of the army May 30 but Coburn's brigade moved up to the front and relieved Ward's brigade on Butterfield's line.[46]

Finally, on June 1 Sherman began his movement to the left. That day Stoneman's cavalry moved into the east end of Allatoona Pass, and Brigadier General Kenner Garrard's cavalry division of the Army of the Cumberland pushed around by the rear to the west end of the pass. Then, with his cavalry in a strong position to protect the workers, Sherman ordered that the railroad bridge across the Etowah be rebuilt at once and the railroad be repaired from Kingston to the Etowah River.[47]

Early on the morning of June 1 McPherson relieved Hooker's corps on the line near New Hope Church, and Hooker marched to the northwest about four miles, passing by the rear of Fourth Corps, Fourteenth Corps, and Twenty-Third Corps. He camped in line that night on a rocky ridge in rear and to the left of Twenty-Third Corps. Butterfield's division, to which Coburn's brigade belonged, was on the right, Geary's division was in the center, with Williams' division on the left.[48]

The weather took a turn for the worse on June 2. Early that morning rain began to fall and it continued all that day. At first the troops enjoyed the rain, because it offered some relief from the heat and humidity, but when the rain continued to fall through the night and almost every day during the rest of the month of June, the movements of the army were greatly impaired.[49]

Despite the rain, Sherman resumed his flanking movement to the left that day. Schofield, after being relieved by Palmer's corps, marched with his three divisions to the vicinity of Burnt Church, at the crossing of the Allatoona road and the road running from Burnt Hickory to Marietta. At that point Schofield formed his corps in line, with his left on the Marietta road, and waited until Hooker's Twentieth Corps moved up in support.

Schofield then moved forward steadily against some opposition for about a mile and a half until he crossed Allatoona Creek near the Dallas and Acworth road, where he halted and entrenched. Hooker followed Schofield's movement in support and put Butterfield's division en echelon on the left of Schofield's line. Butterfield placed Coburn's brigade on the front line of his division, where it threw up works, with Ward's brigade forming the second line, and Wood's brigade in reserve. Here Levin T. Miller, commanding the 33rd Indiana, was struck above the left eye by a piece of shell, and Captain Edward T. McCrea assumed temporary command of the regiment while Miller went back to the hospital to have the wound dressed.[50]

While Schofield and Hooker were advancing on the extreme left, Absalom Baird's and Johnson's divisions of Fourteenth Corps pushed out beyond Pickett's Mill, and by the end of the day Sherman's entire line had been extended to the left for about three miles, with all divisions on the line in contact with one another.[51]

June 3 Schofield shifted his corps to the left, which placed his left division, commanded by Brigadier General Alvin P. Hovey, beyond the Confederate right flank. When Hovey advanced toward the Dallas and Acworth road near Allatoona Church, he completely turned Johnston's position, thus causing him to abandon the works in front of Twenty-Third Corps and to fall back. Johnston took position on a new line of entrenchments, a continuation of the line at Pickett's Mill, facing north.[52]

Coburn's brigade moved to the northeast that day, with Butterfield's division on his left, toward Acworth in support of Hovey. It camped that night near Morris Hill Church on the extreme left of the entire army. The 22nd Wisconsin was utilized as artillery support. Geary and Williams remained in their camps June 3 and 4, but on June 4 Butterfield moved into the works left vacant when Hovey advanced.[53]

Johnston had decided to abandon his lines at New Hope Church June 3. The next day he moved out to the right with his whole army and established a new line extending from Lost Mountain on the left, past Pine Mountain to Brush Mountain, two or three miles north of Kennesaw Mountain, on the right. This line ran to the east and a little north from Lost Mountain and covered Marietta and the roads leading to the Chattahoochee River. The withdrawal that night was carried out under abominable conditions. It was very dark and the rain continued to fall, turning the red-clay roads into paths of soft mud from a few inches to at least a foot in depth. As the Confederates marched back, they stumbled and fell, and many lost their shoes in the mud. Teamsters often called for aid in extricating wagons that had become stuck.[54]

When Sherman learned that Johnston had retired, he ordered his army to march at once toward the Western and Atlantic Railroad near Acworth. He directed Schofield to hold his position for a time to cover the passage of the hospitals and trains and directed Thomas to move with the Army of the Cumberland and follow Hooker's corps, which was to advance on the extreme left of Sherman's line. At daylight June 5, Logan's Fifteenth Corps of McPherson's Army of the Tennessee marched by way of Burnt Church toward Acworth, arriving at the latter place on the morning of June 6. Logan's corps then moved out about two miles and took position to command the Marietta road. Meanwhile, Blair had been marching to the front with his Seventeenth Corps from Huntsville, Alabama, and on June 8 he joined Logan's Fifteenth Corps at Ackworth. The Army of the Tennessee remained near Ackworth until June 10.[55]

June 6, after Johnston had retired, Hooker moved his command to the vicinity of the McLean house on the Sandtown road, near its intersection with the Burnt Hickory and Marietta road about three miles southwest of Acworth. Butterfield's division marched on the Acworth and Sandtown road and took position at Mount Olivet Church near Kemp's Mill. That same day, Geary's and Williams' divisions also moved up and the corps took position, with Geary's division on the left at the Hull farm, Butterfield's division in the center, and Williams' division on the right.[56]

Howard's Fourth Corps went into camp on the left of Geary's division on the Acworth and Sandtown road, about two miles from Acworth, and Palmer's Fourteenth Corps camped in front of Pine Mountain, with his left resting on Proctor's Creek.[57]

Captain Jefferson E. Brant, commanding Company E of the 85th Indiana, had been suffering from "camp diarrhea" for the past month, and finally, on June 6 he was sent to the Third Division field hospital at Acworth and then back to the hospital at Lookout Mountain. While there he wrote a letter in which he made the following observations about hospital life:

> Here in the hospital on every side are wounded in every conceivable way, some with limbs off. Just across the hall is a young Lieutenant with his right hand off and with his left he is nursing the stump very good naturedly. In the next room is an old Kentucky Captain badly wounded in the leg, sitting up in bed. Looks badly but is cheerful, and reads his testament. It is wonderful how patient these wounded heroes bear their sufferings.

Brant further stated that a hospital was the most tiresome and monotonous place in the army, and that he was happy to leave when the time came. He rejoined his command July 10, when the army arrived at the Chattahoochee River.[58]

June 7 through 9 was spent by the entire army in establishing depots at Allatoona and bringing up and distributing supplies.

Schofield's command remained in position on the right of Sherman's army from June 4 to June 8, while the rest of the army completed its movement toward the railroad near Acworth. At this time Hovey, dissatisfied with his command, left the army and returned to Indiana. The two brigades of his First Division were temporarily assigned to the Second and Third divisions of the corps, and on August 11 First Division was discontinued and the assignment of the two brigades was made permanent.[59]

During the time the army was moving toward the railroad at Acworth, the difficulties of supplying its far-flung divisions became painfully obvious, largely because of a shortage of transportation. Sometimes food for the troops arrived two or three days late, and then only a part of a ration was issued to each man. John R. McBride of the 33rd Indiana tells of an incident that occurred during one of these occasions when General Hooker happened to pass Coburn's brigade.

> . . . Some of the men called out, "Hardtack! Hardtack!" The demands began to multiply so rapidly that all soldiers in Hooker's presence repeated it. He inquired of General Butterfield what it all meant. Butterfield said that the men needed provisions and that transportation was scarce. General Hooker knew that rations were plentiful at a place in the rear near by and asked Butterfield why those wagons, standing near them, were unused. Butterfield told him they were his

headquarters wagons, whereupon Hooker ordered them unloaded and sent for provisions. Before the day was over the men got additional rations, and that is one of the reasons why he was such a favorite with the men.[60]

The following account, taken from McBride's *History of the Thirty-Third Indiana Volunteer Infantry*, illustrates some of the problems faced by quartermasters in supplying the army in which Coburn's brigade served during Sherman's Atlanta Campaign:

About the 1st of June, 1864, Lieutenant [Edwin I.] Bachman was riding at the head of the train of thirty-five six-mule teams, as quartermaster of [Coburn's] Second Brigade, Third Division, Twentieth Corps. The division quartermaster told him that he had a nice job for him. When asked what it was, he answered: "Building a bridge!" Lieutenant Bachman told him that he was no bridge builder. He then replied: "The chief quartermaster, General [Lieutenant Colonel William G.] Le Duc, ordered him to build it, and he knew that he (Bachman) could superintend the work better than he himself could."

Lieutenant Bachman was well aware that the brigade would be out of rations the next day and, as it had been doing heavy marching and fighting, fully realized the importance of immediate and vigorous action.

The river was a swift-running stream and a place where an island divided it, near the center, was selected for the bridge site. The building of the first bridge from the bank to the island was allotted to Bachman and the chief quartermaster was to build the other—from the island to the opposite bank. Two companies of the Thirty-Third Indiana were detailed to build the bridge. Eight axes were secured and sixteen experienced choppers were detailed to take turns in cutting down the necessary timber. Lieutenant Bachman estimated the bridge to be about forty feet in length and had four logs cut sixty feet long. It was wonderful how the Hoosier soldier boys made the chips fly! Handspikes were cut by others and sixty men then carried the logs to the place where needed. They would pick up the pine logs with ease, march up in good order, then wade into the water nearly up to their armpits, and lay the logs so that the small end rested on the shore and the butt end on the island. Rails were driven down in the center until they passed under the logs, which kept them from going down too much for the heavily-loaded wagons. After the four logs were in place, cross ties were needed, and a new rail fence, nearby, supplied the material. Pine branches were used to smooth up the work, and then a sufficient quantity of dirt was shoveled on to complete the bridge. The entire structure was built in two hours.

Lieutenant Bachman's bridge was built two hours before the chief quartermaster's, and the first wagon that passed over the latter's bridge broke down, so that the movement of the train was delayed two hours more, and the crossing was not accomplished till about 10 o'clock at night. After crossing, the movement was made through woods and over hills, and the teams had to stop frequently for repairs to be made to the roads by the light of lanterns. This was in the Dallas Hills. The chief quartermaster paid Lieutenant Bachman the deservedly high compliment that his teams were the best in Sherman's army. This magnificent condition of the teams, it is but justice to say, was largely due to the teamsters. The mules were kept in good order, living apparently upon one-quarter rations. Lieutenant Bachman did not understand how it could be done until he learned that his drivers foraged among other trains at night.

The next day Bachman proceeded with his train, and marched continuously until four o'clock in the afternoon, when he halted in the vicinity of Pumpkin Vine Creek. The road ahead was strongly picketed and it was with some difficulty that he received permission to pass through the troops holding the road at one o'clock the following morning. What happened next is best told by Bachman:

I then ordered my best wagon master to get the drivers of five wagons that were loaded with the proper provisions to prepare for the night's march; also six extra men with axes, shovels, and ropes that might be needed. We had been on the go two days and one night, and this was our second night. At midnight we started, well equipped with lanterns. We found that, to get the wagons on the rail bridge, we would have to let them down an embankment about ten feet, and, as the bank was too steep, it had to be shoveled off to an incline. It took all the drivers and helpers to let one of these wagons down with ropes, and after one was down I rode across with my old gray, as no team of mine would refuse to follow him, and we landed safely on the other side in sand, in which the wheels sank half way to the hubs. It was a pretty sight to see those mules get down to work and draw the wagon through the sand a distance of perhaps a hundred feet. All the teams were gotten over safely and then we commenced climbing the first hill, which was steep and slippery. On descending the hill both hind wheels of the wagon were locked, and the fourth wagon slipped off the road, but lodged against a tree, which kept it from upsetting. Ropes were fastened to the side to keep it from turning over and twelve mules were hitched to the rear end of it, when it was drawn up into the road and run down the hill by hand. The rear wagon was run against a log at the bottom of the hill in such position that the log had to be cut in two before the wagon could be extricated. We finally reached the vicinity of the brigade, and Lieutenant Harbert went to headquarters to get a detail of men to carry the rations. In the meantime we prepared a breakfast for those who came after the rations. This done, I observed General Sherman coming—I supposed to order me placed under arrest for bringing the teams so near the line of battle. We formed a good line, saluted him, which he returned, and walked on down to the spring and took out a cup, towel, and tooth brush, and was soon brushing his teeth, took a good wash and then returned.

Lieutenant Harbert and the men soon arrived, and how they did enjoy that breakfast! Hot coffee goes right to the spot on such occasions, and we felt repaid for all the hardships we had gone through during the past two days and nights without sleep.

The other two brigades of our division had been out of provisions two days, but our boys were generous and helped them out.[61]

Foraging, of course, supplemented late-arriving or meager supplies. The headquarters cook of the 85th Indiana informed Sergeant Major John B. Dowd of the regiment that there was no meat. Dowd, with a squad of volunteers, left camp and soon found a smokehouse full of meat. When he demanded the key, the owner refused to give it. Dowd glared at him and said in a firm voice: "Sir, the American army must be fed!" Dowd's men went back to camp with a good supply of ham.[62]

On June 4 Butterfield, commanding Third Division, Twentieth Corps, to which Coburn's brigade belonged, attempted to improve on the methods of preparing food in his command. He ordered that two men be detailed from each company to do the cooking, but because most cooking utensils had been left at Chattanooga at the beginning of the campaign, the cooking was very poorly done and the food was frequently indigestible. Until the army reached Marietta, the food consisted almost entirely of hard bread, salt pork or bacon, fresh beef, and sugar and coffee. After arriving at Marietta, however, commissary supplies of all kinds were more plentiful.[63]

Chapter 11

Atlanta Campaign

Acworth to the Chattahoochee River

By June 9, 1864, Sherman's army had been resupplied and made ready for further field service and was ready to move out of its camps at and near Acworth to resume the advance toward the Chattahoochee River.[1]

Sherman's new field of operations lay between the Etowah River and the Chattahoochee, with its features largely determined by the general course of the mountain range that extended across the area from the northeast to the southwest. The most dominant features of the country were four isolated hills or mountains. Two of these, Brush Mountain and Pine Mountain, were about three hundred feet high, Lost Mountain was about five hundred feet high, and Kennesaw Mountain, off to the east near Brush Mountain, was about seven hundred feet high.

The country extending from the bases of these mountains was very rough and consisted of a confusion of hills, gullies, and ravines, through which a number of small streams flowed in winding courses. In the dry seasons these streams were of little consequence, but because of the constant rains since June 2, the whole countryside was a vast sea of mud, with the streams overflowing with water running fast and deep.

When General Joseph E. Johnston retired from the Dallas-New Hope Church-Pickett's Mill line, he took position on a slightly curved new line running for about ten miles from Brush Mountain on the right to Lost Mountain on the left. The mountains were key points on this line and were occupied by the enemy and strongly fortified. From their summits, observers could note all Union movements below and report them immediately to army headquarters. Earthworks had been constructed between and along the forward slopes of the mountains, and artillery had been placed on the highest ground so that the guns commanded all approaches to the new positions.

Lieutenant General John B. Hood's corps held the right of Johnston's line, which ran along Brush Mountain to the northeast of the Western and Atlantic Railroad. Lieutenant General Leonidas Polk's corps was next to Hood, covering the railroad southward and holding the center of the Con-

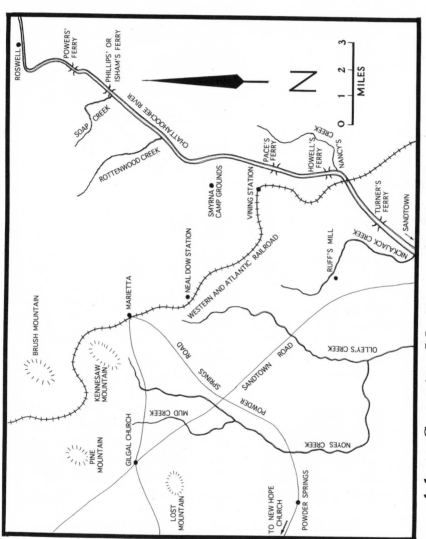

Atlanta Campaign, Marietta to the Chattahoochee River

federate line. Lieutenant General William J. Hardee's corps held the line to the left of Polk and extended generally to the southwest to Gilgal Church.

Major General William B. Bate's division of Hardee's corps also occupied Pine Mountain, which was about equidistant from Brush Mountain and Lost Mountain, and about one mile in front of Johnston's main line. Two Confederate brigades were also in position in forward field works to the left of Pine Mountain and across the Sandtown road.

The passage of the army through this rugged, muddy countryside was slow and laborious. Guns and wagons bogged down and were extricated only with great difficulty, and in a short time many of the roads were completely obliterated.

On June 9 squadrons of Federal cavalry moved toward Marietta, about eight miles to the southeast of Acworth, to examine the country ahead, and by evening they had located the enemy on their fortified line running from Brush Mountain to Lost Mountain. All was then in readiness for the beginning of Sherman's march toward the Chattahoochee the next day.[2]

The next morning Major General John M. Schofield's Army of the Ohio (or Twenty-Third Corps) advanced on the right of Sherman's army toward the enemy's main line, which was along the east bank of Allatoona Creek. It halted on a new line on the right of the Army of the Cumberland, about one-half mile north of Gilgal Church (known locally as Hardshell Church), and during the next five days closed up on the enemy's works.[3]

On the left of Sherman's army, Major General James B. McPherson's Army of the Tennessee, with Major General John A. Logan's Fifteenth Corps in the lead, marched down the Acworth and Marietta road toward Big Shanty. About a mile south of Big Shanty, Logan's advance encountered enemy skirmishers, but continued to move forward for about a mile and a half until it encountered a stronger force and halted for the day.

The next morning, June 11, McPherson moved forward for nearly a mile and came up to Johnston's main line at Brush Mountain. He then formed his corps in line, with Major General Frank P. Blair's Seventeenth Corps on the left, Fifteenth Corps in the center, and Major General Grenville M. Dodge's Left Wing, Sixteenth Corps, on the right. The Army of the Tennessee remained in this position until June 19.[4]

Major General George H. Thomas' Army of the Cumberland also advanced June 10 with Major General John M. Palmer's Fourteenth Corps moving forward on the right of the Army of the Tennessee. Major General Oliver O. Howard's Fourth Corps moved up on the Burnt Hickory and Marietta road on the right of Palmer and formed directly in front of Pine Mountain.[5]

Major General Joseph Hooker's Twentieth Corps remained in camp June 10. The next day it moved to the left about a mile and a half and connected with Fourth Corps, facing Pine Mountain.[6]

June 11 the engineers completed the railroad bridge over the Etowah River, which had been destroyed by the enemy, and supplies for the army were then brought up by rail as far as Big Shanty.[7]

That day Palmer and Howard moved to the left to a new line, a little in advance of the one occupied the day before. Palmer's left was on the railroad, where it connected with McPherson's right corps.[8]

There were no movements of the army June 12 and 13 because of the incessant rains, but on June 14 the rains let up, and Sherman ordered the army to advance along the whole front and get as close to the enemy works as possible. That day Palmer's corps and the left of Howard's corps pushed forward into the angle between Pine Mountain and the Confederate lines to the east of the mountain and threatened to cut off the enemy forces holding the mountain from the rest of the Confederate line.[9]

On the morning of June 14, General Polk was killed on Pine Mountain by an artillery shell, and Confederate Major General William W. Loring assumed command of his corps.[10]

That night Hardee ordered Bate to withdraw his division from their advanced position on Pine Mountain and to retire to the main Confederate line. At three o'clock the next morning skirmishers of Major General David S. Stanley's division of Fourth Corps moved up and occupied the vacated mountain top.[11]

When Sherman learned that Johnston had abandoned his position at Pine Mountain, he directed Thomas to move forward June 15, with Howard's Fourth Corps and Hooker's Twentieth Corps of his Army of the Cumberland and to attack the enemy's main line.[12]

At 11:00 AM that day, Thomas ordered Howard to move southward to the left of Pine Mountain and be ready to attack at 2:00 PM. He also directed Hooker to advance on the right of Fourth Corps and to the right of Pine Mountain, against the enemy's position. Both Howard and Hooker established their corps within one hundred yards of the enemy's main line.[13]

At noon Brigadier General John W. Geary's Second Division of Hooker's corps marched in a southeasterly direction for about a mile to the right of Pine Mountain, and not far from it. Geary then halted with his skirmishers, connecting with the skirmishers of Howard's Fourth Corps at the base of Pine Mountain, about three-fourths of a mile to the left.[14]

While Geary was getting his troops in position, Sherman issued orders for a general attack on enemy works at 2:00 that afternoon. Geary was to advance against Johnston's line directly on his front, with Fourth Corps attacking on Geary's left. Major General Daniel Butterfield's Third Division of Twentieth Corps was to attack on Geary's right.[15]

At the appointed time, Howard's Fourth Corps moved forward. By late evening it had driven the enemy back into their main works, which were found to be very strong. Howard halted and fortified his new position. Palmer's Fourteenth Corps, on the left of Howard, was formed in column en masse for an assault but did not attack that day.[16]

Geary began his attack at 2:15 PM and pushed forward with sharp fighting over very rough and tumbled ridges, until he came up close to a strong enemy position situated on a high ridge. There, after some severe fighting, he drove the enemy back into his main line. Geary succeeded in getting up close to this line, but it was then nearly dark and the fighting ended for the day.[17]

That afternoon Brigadier General Alpheus S. Williams advanced his First Division of Twentieth Corps on the right of Geary, and at 4:00 PM, after crossing a deep ravine, massed the division in rear of Geary's right reserve brigade. Soon after Geary's attack started, Williams sent two of his brigades forward to cover Geary's flanks and placed the third brigade in rear of Geary's left center as a reserve.[18]

Butterfield's division of Twentieth Corps had remained in its camps at Mount Olivet Church, near Kemp's Sawmill, until June 15. That day it joined in the general advance of the army. About two and a half miles ahead of Butterfield's camps, near Gilgal Church, Major General Patrick R. Cleburne's Confederate division occupied a strong line of entrenchments across the Sandtown road, with artillery support. Butterfield marched to the southeast on the Sandtown road to Gilgal Church, and halted on the left side of the road near Cleburne's line, forming his division in line of battle, with Brigadier General William T. Ward's First Brigade on the front line, Colonel John Coburn's Second Brigade on the second line, and Colonel James Wood's Third Brigade on the third line.[19]

Immediately in front of Butterfield's division was a large cleared field about three-fourths of a mile wide, and beyond was a woods held by enemy skirmishers. Butterfield directed Ward to move his brigade forward into the field and to take position on a row of hills in front of the woods. When this new line was formed, Butterfield ordered Ward to move forward into the woods.[20]

After advancing his line about 150 yards into the woods, Ward halted along a road. During this advance, the enemy opened with heavy fire on the left of the line and also on Geary's division, which was advancing on the left of Ward. While halted along the road, skirmishers returned to report that the enemy was present in heavy force about five hundred to six hundred yards ahead in the woods, protected by a strong line of breastworks. Despite this report, Butterfield believed that only skirmishers held the works, and he ordered Ward to attack and drive them out.[21]

It was near dusk when Ward began his attack, soon coming under a brisk fire which became a murderous fire of artillery and musketry as the brigade approached the enemy's position about two hundred yards to its front. Then, as Ward continued his advance, the Confederate artillery opened with eight pieces on his front and a battery on each flank. Under this hail of fire, it was impossible to advance farther.[22]

One of Ward's regiments had not yet come up because of difficulties in crossing a deep ravine and passing through thick underbrush, but it finally arrived at dark and took its place in line. The enemy attacked Ward's brigade twice that evening but was repulsed each time.[23]

As Ward moved forward, Coburn's brigade followed him across the field and into the woods, with the regiments in line from right to left as follows: Major Eli A. Griffin's 19th Michigan, Colonel John P. Baird's 85th Indiana, Major Levin T. Miller's 33rd Indiana, and Colonel William L. Utley's 22nd Wisconsin. In advancing through the woods, a part of the brigade crossed a deep ravine, and still farther forward the ground sloped upward to a broken ridge that was covered with trees.[24]

At dusk, as Ward's brigade was running out of ammunition, Coburn was ordered to move up with his brigade and relieve them. The 85th Indiana and the 19th Michigan took the place of that part of Ward's brigade which had moved to the right of the Sandtown road, and the 33rd Indiana and 22nd Wisconsin relieved the troops on the left of the road. When the exchange was completed, Ward moved his brigade to the left and connected with Williams' division. During the fighting on the right of the road that evening, Major Griffin was mortally wounded, and Captain John A. Baker succeeded him in command of the 19th Michigan. Geary's and Butterfield's divisions lost about seven hundred casualties that afternoon.[25]

Finally, darkness began to settle over the battlefield. The troops on the left of the road worked all through the night on breastworks, and the troops on the right of the road moved to the left of the brigade, where they too fortified their new positions. When this movement was completed, the 33rd Indiana and eight companies of the 22nd Wisconsin held the front of the brigade line; the rest of the brigade refused on the left along the edge of a ravine. A part of the 85th Indiana was on the far side of the ravine on the extreme left of the line. By morning, Coburn's men had constructed strong works within two hundred yards of the enemy's works. Wood's brigade followed Coburn into the woods and bivouacked for the night, but it was not engaged.[26]

On June 15 while Hooker's corps was moving up against the enemy's line to the right of Pine Mountain, Schofield's Twenty-Third Corps was advancing on Hooker's right. Finding Johnston's left flank unprotected, Schofield moved with the right of Hascall's division well into the rear of this flank. At the same time, Cox's division advanced in the center, and after a brief but spirited resistance the enemy withdrew.[27]

The Army of the Cumberland was relatively inactive on June 16, with Howard and Hooker remaining in the positions that they had gained the day before. Skirmishers of both corps were kept close to the enemy's works, keeping up a steady fire all day. Palmer advanced his line a short distance to improve his position.

Schofield's Twenty-Third Corps, which was advancing on the right of Butterfield's division, continued to exert pressure on the left of Johnston's line, which ran from Lost Mountain to Gilgal Church, and finally succeeded in turning Johnston's left flank by enfilading Cleburne's line with well-placed artillery on high ground. Schofield thus secured the Burnt Hickory road and the Dallas road, both of which ran to Marietta.[28]

By the evening of June 16, Johnston was aware that he could no longer hold his present position, and at 10:00 PM, Hardee began withdrawing his four divisions from their entrenchments to a new line on the hills along the east side of Mud Creek. This new line left the old line near the right of Hardee's former position, and, bending back to the south, followed the east bank of the creek to a point beyond the direct road that ran by way of Lost Mountain from New Hope Church to Marietta. Hardee accomplished his withdrawal by swinging back his extreme left to a point three miles in rear of its original position. Hood's and Loring's corps remained in their works on the old line, facing northwest.[29]

In the new Confederate line there was a vulnerable angle at the point where Hardee's and Loring's lines connected. Johnston knew that he could delay, but not stop, Sherman's advance on the Mud Creek line. He directed his engineers to construct a new line closer to Marietta and to include Kennesaw Mountain in his defenses.[30]

About 1:00 AM June 17 Geary's skirmishers found that Hardee had abandoned his position during the night, and Geary moved up and occupied the vacated works with his entire division. Later in the morning, Thomas and Schofield moved out in pursuit of Hardee, swinging around to the southeast until their skirmishers came up to his new line on the hills behind Mud Creek.[31]

Hooker's corps marched to the southeast at 10:00 AM, with Williams' division on the left, Geary's division in the center, and Butterfield's division on the right. Near the Darby house, Geary's division filed to the left and formed his brigades on the low ground between the Darby house and Mud Creek. At the same time, Schofield's Army of the Ohio, coming up from Lost Mountain, took position on the right of Geary, with his left resting on the Marietta and Dallas road.[32]

Williams' division, advancing on the left of Geary, took position with its left resting on the Burnt Hickory and Marietta road near the Kirk house, where it connected with Howard's Fourth Corps.[33]

At noon June 17 Butterfield's division moved forward, with Coburn's brigade in advance and the 85th Indiana out in front as skirmishers. The brigade followed Geary through the woods and into a large cleared field, where it formed in line between Geary's division on the right and Williams' division on the left about four hundred yards from the enemy's works. Ward's brigade and Colonel James Wood's brigade were held in reserve in rear of the line held by Williams, Coburn, and Geary. When in position, Hooker's corps was in front of the left of Hardee's corps near the Darby house. Hooker's right was a little in advance of the Darby house, on the Sandtown road about five miles due west of Marietta.[34]

An exchange of artillery fire followed, lasting for about one hour, while Thomas deployed his troops in preparation for crossing Mud Creek in an attempt to turn Hardee's left flank. Heavy rain caused the creek to overflow its banks, and almost all further operations were suspended until June 19.[35]

During the night of June 18 Johnston pulled his divisions out of the Mud Creek line, and the next morning began a new line which had as its key position Kennesaw Mountain. Believing that Johnston was falling back to the Chattahoochee River, Sherman immediately started his entire army in pursuit in the direction of Marietta. It was not long, however, before Sherman found that he had been mistaken. When his columns advanced along the Burnt Hickory road, the Sandtown road, and the Dallas road they came up in front of the new and strongly defended Kennesaw Mountain line about six miles in length, extending both to the right and left of Kennesaw Mountain, covering the railroad and the roads running into Marietta. The front of this line was protected by several creeks, which, because of the heavy rains, had overflowed their banks and covered parts of the adjacent valleys.[36]

Hood's corps held the high ground to the east of the railroad, which ran to the northeast at this point, between Brush Mountain and Kennesaw Mountain. Loring's corps occupied Kennesaw Mountain, and Hardee's corps, which was on the Confederate left, connected with Loring at the base of the mountain. On the Confederate right Noonday Creek flowed across the front of Hood's corps, and on the right, in front of Hardee's corps, Noyes' Creek and Ward Creek (or John Ward Creek) were significant barriers.[37]

On June 19 after Johnston's withdrawal to the Kennesaw Mountain line, Sherman slowly advanced his army against their outposts and forward defensive positions, and pushed back the defenders toward their main line. McPherson's Army of the Tennessee made limited attacks threatening Johnston's right flank. Thomas kept his Army of the Cumberland close up to the enemy's center, and at the same time began shifting his divisions to the right, toward the enemy's left flank. This movement not only threatened Johnston's left flank, but also provided for better cooperation with

Schofield's Army of the Ohio on the extreme Union right. At that time Schofield was advancing along the Sandtown road toward the crossing of Noyes' Creek to be in position to pass beyond Johnston's left flank. There was heavy skirmishing along the line all that day.[38]

Rain had poured down continuously on Sherman's struggling men since the beginning of the month, and the whole country had been turned into a morass, with all the streams swollen and overflowing their banks. The roads had been obliterated by the passage of the trains as they struggled to keep up with the army, making passage even more difficult.[39]

Nevertheless, on June 19 Howard, marching on the Burnt Hickory and Marietta road, came up with the enemy posted on ridges a short distance west of Marietta. Palmer moved up close to Kennesaw Mountain on the left of Howard.[40]

Also that day, Hooker, who was advancing on the Dallas and Marietta road, moved up to Noyes' Creek and found the enemy strongly posted on a line of ridges on the far side. Williams' division, advancing on the left of the corps, crossed the overflowing creek and pushed forward two or three miles to the front of Johnston's new position. Geary's division also moved up to Noyes' Creek but was detained there for some time while the men constructed a bridge. Geary finally crossed the stream and encountered enemy skirmishers about three-fourths of a mile beyond. He continued his advance, however, and found the Confederate main works. Geary then put his division in line across the road on the right of Williams.[41]

Butterfield's division also advanced on the morning of June 19. Wood's brigade was in front, Ward's brigade followed, and Coburn's brigade, which marched at 10:00 AM, brought up the rear. When enemy pickets halted the column, Wood formed his brigade in line of battle to the right of the road and advanced until he came up close to the enemy's works. There he was halted by enemy skirmishers. Ward's brigade also advanced and formed in line with Jones' brigade. Coburn was delayed for a few hours at a branch of Noyes' Creek because the high waters had washed away the bridges and covered the road. Finally, however, after crossing the stream, Coburn formed his brigade in line of battle on a wooded ridge about one-half mile to the right of the road and in rear of Wood's and Ward's brigades. Butterfield advanced his division about three-fourths of a mile until he found the enemy on his front and right flank. At that time, Butterfield's division was on the right of Geary and was separated from the latter by a small branch of Noyes' Creek. Butterfield halted until dark and then withdrew James Wood's brigade to a position behind Coburn, about one hundred yards to the rear. All movements that day were made in a pouring rain and with almost constant skirmishing.[42]

On June 20 there were some changes in the positions of Hooker's Twentieth Corps. That morning, troops of Fourth Corps relieved Williams' division, which then moved to the right of Butterfield's division, and later to the right and front to the Atkinson plantation, where it connected with Schofield's corps.[43]

At dark that evening, a brigade of Fourth Corps moved to the right and relieved Colonel Candy's First Brigade and Colonel David Ireland's Third Brigade of Geary's division, which then moved to the right of Butterfield's division. Colonel Patrick H. Jones' brigade of Geary's division remained in position to the left of Butterfield and was thus separated from the other two brigades.[44]

There was little change in Butterfield's position June 20. Coburn's brigade moved forward and to the left; connecting with Geary's division, it built a new line of works. Ward's and James Wood's brigades remained on the line that they had occupied the day before.[45]

Early on the morning of June 21, Jones' brigade of Geary's division was relieved on the left of Butterfield and then rejoined the other brigades of the division to form a continuous line, which connected on the right with Williams' division.[46]

Only Coburn's brigade of Butterfield's division made any significant change in position that day. Brigadier General Nathan Kimball's First Brigade of Newton's division came up and relieved Coburn's brigade, and a short time later the two brigades moved forward and formed in line, with Coburn on the right of Kimball. Coburn then constructed a new line of works about one-half mile in advance of his former position.[47]

Howard's Fourth Corps and Palmer's Fourteenth Corps also advanced that day about five hundred yards under a heavy enemy fire to a new position where Fourteenth Corps connected on its left with Howard's corps.[48]

The next morning the sun was shining brightly, and the army rejoiced. For almost a month the men had marched, eaten, slept, and fought in rain or a sea of mud and stood in trenches that were knee-deep in water. Sometimes, for days at a time, they were unable to take off and dry wet clothes. As a result, hundreds of men were forced to go to the rear each day suffering from rheumatism, pneumonia, and influenza. Many of the men also left the ranks unable to perform their duties as soldiers as a result of the mental and physical strain imposed by the terrible conditions under which they lived.[49]

That sunny morning Hooker again advanced his corps. About 8:00 AM, Butterfield's division, on the left of the corps, moved to attack a hill on its front. Wood's brigade moved out first, supported by Coburn's brigade. After advancing about a mile and a half, Wood found the enemy in position on a high ridge with a strong skirmish line out in front. As Wood's brigade advanced, the 22nd Wisconsin and 33rd Indiana of Coburn's brigade moved forward and formed in line of battle on its left. After a short but vigorous resistance, the enemy fell back to another ridge to the left of Butterfield's front. A short time later, because Howard's line had not moved up with Butterfield's division, Coburn's regiments came under a heavy flank fire on their left. The left of the 33rd Indiana was refused at once, and Coburn brought up the 19th Michigan and the 85th Indiana and placed them on the left of the 33rd Indiana. Coburn's regiments were then in line from left to right as follows: 85th Indiana, 19th Michigan, 33rd Indiana, and 22nd Wisconsin. This line faced to the left, except on the extreme left, where it faced to the front. Coburn's brigade was engaged in serious fighting for a time, and then, at Coburn's request, Kimball brought up his brigade and formed on the left of the 85th Indiana. About 3:00 PM the enemy launched a vigorous attack on Coburn's front, but it was repulsed, and then Butterfield entrenched on his new position. At 5:00 PM Coburn's brigade was relieved by Kimball's brigade and Brigadier General Charles G. Harker's Third Brigade, both of Newton's division.[50]

BATTLE OF KOLB'S FARM
JUNE 22, 1864

On the morning of June 22 Geary's division of Hooker's corps advanced about a mile and entrenched on a commanding ridge on the right of Butterfield. Williams' division also advanced, with skirmishing, to a position on the right of Geary, with its right resting on the Powder Springs and Marietta road at the Peter Valentine Kolb house. Williams massed his brigades in the woods, with Brigadier General Thomas H. Ruger's Second Brigade on the right, Brigadier General Joseph F. Knipe's First Brigade in the center, and Colonel James S. Robinson's Third Brigade on the left.[51]

Also that day Schofield crossed Noyes' Creek in force, and Cox then advanced with his Third Division on the Sandtown road to its intersection with the Powder Springs and Marietta road at the Cheney place. Hascall moved up on the road toward Marietta with his Second Division and took position on the right of Hooker's corps, making the connection at the Kolb farm.[52]

When Johnston learned that Schofield was moving southward on the Sandtown road toward his left flank, he directed Hood to transfer his corps from its position on the right flank of the Confederate line to the opposite flank. On the rainy night of June 21, Hood's three divisions left their trenches east of Kennesaw Mountain and marched to the left through Marietta and then out on the Powder Springs road about three miles to Mount Zion Church, halting on the left of Hardee's corps.[53]

The next morning Hood deployed his troops on a ridge that crossed the road at an angle, about one mile east of Kolb's farm, with Major General Thomas C. Hindman's division on the right, Major General Carter L. Stevenson's division in the center, and Major General Alexander P. Stewart's division on the left, in reserve.[54]

At 5:00 PM Hood launched a vigorous attack on Williams' division, but the attack was repulsed. For all practical purposes the battle of Kolb's Farm was over, but Hood continued to send his men forward until dark, when he finally withdrew after a loss of nearly one thousand men. Geary supported Williams' division during this attack with heavy artillery fire that continued until dark.[55]

Late on June 22 Brigadier General John H. King's First Division of Palmer's Fourteenth Corps relieved Stanley's division of Howard's Fourth Corps. Stanley then moved to the right of Howard's line and relieved Butterfield's division of Hooker's Twentieth Corps. Then, with Coburn's brigade in the lead, Butterfield marched about two miles to the right to support Williams' division in its fight with Hood. The division halted in rear of Williams' line that night, and, after a rest of four hours, Coburn's brigade moved up to the immediate rear of Knipe's brigade. The losses in Coburn's brigade that day were one officer killed, four wounded, five men killed and fifty-three wounded.[56]

According to an item appearing in *The Union Democrat*, July 1, 1864, Lieutenant Mortimer Denny of Company G, 85th Indiana Regiment, was seriously wounded July 23 (his military record says July 22). He was taken to an officers' hospital in Chattanooga, Tennessee, and appeared to be doing well, but he died there of his wounds on August 19, 1864.

There was little change in the positions of the units of Sherman's army during the next two days except by Butterfield's division. At 9:00 AM, June 23, Butterfield moved to the right about three-fourths of a mile, with Coburn's brigade in the lead; he then moved eastward on the Powder Springs and Marietta road to a point beyond Scribner's Female Institute. Coburn took position on the left of the road and on the immediate left of Hascall's division of Twenty-Third Corps. The brigade formed in a single line and immediately threw up earthworks. At that point Coburn's brigade was on the front line, within musket range of the enemy's works, and three miles west of Marietta. It remained in camp there until the evening of June 26.[57]

James Wood's brigade of Butterfield's division also moved to the right and took position in line of battle, with its right resting on the Powder Springs and Marietta road, thus forming a second line in rear of Coburn. On the evening of June 26 Ward's brigade moved up and relieved Coburn's brigade on the front line, and Coburn moved back and went into camp a short distance to the rear. Wood occupied his position until June 27; before dawn he moved back and formed a new line to the rear of its former position on the right of Knipe's brigade of Williams' division, with his right resting on the Powder Springs road.[58]

BATTLE OF KENNESAW MOUNTAIN, GEORGIA
JUNE 27, 1864

After the engagement at Kolb's Farm, Sherman considered a change in his plans of operation. Instead of continuing the flanking movements that had characterized his advance thus far, he weighed the advantages and disadvantages of launching a frontal attack in an attempt to break through Johnston's line. The weather was decidedly unfit for marching. He believed that Johnston had weakened his center as he had extended his lines, and he further believed that he had extended his own line as far as he safely could.[59]

On June 24 Sherman issued the order for a general assault to be made three days later. The next day he began preparations for the attack by relieving Brigadier General Jefferson C. Davis' Second Division of Palmer's corps, which was on the extreme left of the Army of the Cumberland, by a division of Sixteenth Corps, Army of the Tennessee, and then moving Davis to the right and rear of Howard's Fourth Corps, where it arrived by dawn June 26, 1864.[60]

That day Brigadier General Absalom Baird's Third Division of Palmer's corps was also relieved by troops of the Army of the Tennessee and moved to a position in reserve near Davis' division, thus placing Davis' and Baird's divisions on the right of Howard's Fourth Corps. Schofield attempted to divert Johnston's attention from the impending battle by advancing Jacob Cox's division of his Twenty-Third Corps to Olley's Creek, about one mile south of the Cheney house.[61]

According to Sherman's plan, the main effort in the attack was to be made by Thomas against the center of Johnston's line, south and west of Kennesaw Mountain, and south of the Dallas and Marietta road. Hooker's corps was to be held in readiness to support Howard's and Palmer's troops if needed. McPherson, on the left of Thomas, was to make a secondary attack at Kennesaw Mountain. Schofield was to make a demonstration on his right to threaten the roads leading to Marietta from the north and to attract the enemy's attention in that direction.[62]

At about 8:15 AM, McPherson began his secondary attack on Kennesaw Mountain, but it was soon stopped all along the line. At 9:00 AM, Thomas began the main attack by advancing the divisions of Brigadier General John Newton, Davis, Stanley, Baird, and Brigadier General Thomas J. Wood against that part of the Confederate line held by the right of Hardee's corps south of the mountain.[63]

Harker's Third Brigade of Newton's division, Colonel John G. Mitchell's Second Brigade and Colonel Daniel McCook's Third Brigade of Davis' division struck the right of Major General Benjamin F. Cheatham's line at what is sometimes called the "Dead Angle." The divisions of Newton and Davis drove the enemy into his main line of works and gained some forward positions, which they were able to hold, but they were unable to break through. In this assault, Thomas suffered an estimated loss of about three thousand men, and McPherson about 850 men.[64]

When the Union artillery opened at the beginning of this Battle of Kennesaw Mountain June 27, 1864, Coburn was ordered to have his brigade ready to move at once, but it was not called upon during the day.[65]

On the day of the battle, Butterfield ordered Coburn and James Wood to report to Ward, whom he placed in temporary command of the division, but during the evening Butterfield resumed command. On June 29, 1864, however, Butterfield departed on leave of absence, and he did not again return to the army. Ward, as the senior officer, assumed command of Third Division, Twentieth Corps, and Colonel Benjamin Harrison of the 70th Indiana Regiment took charge of Ward's First Brigade.[66]

Harvey Reid, who first saw Ward at Murfreesboro in October 1863, has given us the following unflattering description of the future commander of Third Division, Twentieth Corps as he appeared then:

He is the roughest looking old fellow I ever saw. When he came off the train and during the entire day he wore a blue private's overcoat, dirty and almost ragged, a black hat that looked as if its owner had been in a "free fight" and had received several punches in the head—a common black scabbard sword with a gilt belt that had seen so much service that the leather was red in places and his face and figure corresponded with his attire. In person he was short, stocky, and almost corpulent. From beneath his battered hat long iron-gray uncombed locks depended nearly to his chin on one side, while the other was cut so short as to be scarcely visible under the hat–a string of iron-gray whiskers ran under his chin. . . . Face bronzed almost to Indian darkness.[67]

Though he may have been rough in appearance, Ward was a very capable officer. Born in Amelia County, Virginia, August 9, 1808, he later moved to Kentucky, where he was educated and practiced law. He served in the Mexican War and in the Kentucky legislature, and then as a representative in Congress. Ward was commissioned a brigadier general of volunteers September 18, 1861, and first served as commander at several posts in Kentucky. At the beginning of the Atlanta Campaign, Ward was given command of a brigade in Butterfield's Third Division, Twentieth Corps. When Butterfield left the army, Ward assumed command of the division.[68]

After the Battle of Kennesaw Mountain, James Wood's brigade held its position on the right of Williams' division until June 30, 1864; it then relieved Ward's brigade on the front line of Butterfield's division. Earlier, Coburn's brigade had held this part of the line; when relieved, it moved farther to the rear and went into camp. While there, the men washed their clothes, cleaned their weapons and equipment, and awaited orders.[69]

Geary's division held its advanced position in front of Hooker's line until after dark June 30, when it was relieved by Absalom Baird's division of Fourteenth Corps. Geary moved to the right about two and one-half miles and relieved Hascall's division of Schofield's corps in the works beyond Powder Springs and the Marietta road. Hascall rejoined Schofield, who at that time occupied a strong position extending from a ridge beyond Olley's Creek on the left to some hills near Nickajack Creek, where the road from Marietta to Sandtown ran into the road on which Schofield had been marching.[70]

The Army of the Tennessee and the Army of the Cumberland remained quietly in their camps near Kennesaw Mountain during July 1 and 2, while Sherman considered his next movement. He finally decided that following the failure of his attack at Kennesaw Mountain, he would resume his flanking movement by the right flank. To carry out this plan, he ordered McPherson to withdraw his Army of the Tennessee from its position on the left of the line in front of Kennesaw Mountain, move south in rear of the Army of the Cumberland and the Army of the Ohio, and take position on the right of the Army of the Ohio. There it would be on the extreme right of the army and would threaten the Western and Atlantic Railroad and the Chattahoochee River crossings in rear of Johnston's army.[71]

McPherson began his movement at 4:00 AM, July 2, by sending a division of Logan's Fifteenth Corps down the Sandtown road to support Schofield, and at nine o'clock that evening Blair's Seventeenth Corps, followed by Dodge's Left Wing, Sixteenth Corps, followed Smith. Logan, with the other three divisions of Fifteenth Corps, remained in their works near Kennesaw Mountain that day.[72]

By July 2 Johnston realized that he could no longer remain in his present position and ordered the evacuation of Marietta. During the night he withdrew his troops from the lines in front of the town and moved south on the main road toward Atlanta. Instead of continuing on to the Chattahoochee River as expected, Johnston halted four miles southeast of Marietta in a previously prepared position on a ridge that extended across the railroad at Smyrna Camp Ground. His line was about six miles in length and was protected on the right by Rottenwood Creek and on the left by Nickajack Creek.[73]

Early on the morning of July 3 when Sherman learned that Johnston had departed, he ordered his army commanders to make a vigorous pursuit, beginning at daylight the next morning. Thomas, with the Army of the Cumberland, was to follow the enemy along the railroad, with Schofield's Army of the Ohio moving on his right and McPherson's Army of the Tennessee on the right of Schofield.[74]

Thomas' Army of the Cumberland was to follow Johnston, with Palmer's Fourteenth Corps moving south along the railroad on the main road to Atlanta, Howard's Fourth Corps on the left of Palmer, and Hooker's Twentieth Corps on the right.[75]

On the morning of July 3, a very hot and humid day, Hooker's corps moved eastward toward the railroad from its camps near Kolb's Farm. Coburn's brigade marched with Ward's division (formerly Butterfield's) on the Powder Springs road, with Williams' division marching on the left of Ward and Geary's division advancing on the right. The road ran through difficult country toward Neal Dow's Station on the railroad.[76]

About a mile and a half from Marietta, Hooker's divisions turned to the south, with Ward marching on the Turner's Ferry road, Williams' division following Ward, and Geary's division advancing to the right of Ward. At 4:00 PM, after advancing about two miles, Hooker came up in front of Johnston's new position and went into camp, with Ward's division on the left near the railroad, Williams' division in the center, and Geary's division on the right.[77]

Early that morning Coburn's brigade continued its march with Ward's division on the Marietta road to the intersection of the Sandtown road, which was three-fourths of a mile from Marietta. It then moved southward on that road for a little more than a mile when it came up to Geary's division moving eastward at right angles to the direction of Coburn's column. After passing Geary's division, Coburn moved about five miles to the south to a point close to the enemy's works on the left, where the brigade halted, formed in two lines, and fortified its position.[78]

At 4:00 PM, Ward's division crossed a branch of Nickajack Creek and camped for the night about seven miles south and west of Marietta. Coburn formed his brigade, with the 19th Michigan in front as skirmishers, the 22nd Wisconsin and 85th Indiana on the first line, and the 33rd Indiana on a second line.[79]

By dark July 3, Thomas' three corps were all up in front of Johnston's new line, and the skirmishers had worked their way up into position near his breastworks.[80]

The Army of the Tennessee also moved forward on July 3, and by the evening of July 4, it was in position near Nickajack Creek, with Sixteenth Corps in the center, Seventeenth Corps on the right, and Fifteenth Corps on the left.[81]

When the last of McPherson's troops departed from the left of Sherman's line, Brigadier General Kenner Garrard was left with his Second Cavalry Division of the Army of the Cumberland to cover the roads to Marietta running near the railroad.[82]

Thomas spent the day of July 4 readjusting his lines and driving the enemy skirmishers back into their main works. About 2:00 PM, Ward and Williams moved their divisions to the right of Geary, and the latter extended his line to connect with the right of Fourteenth Corps. Ward moved off toward Nickajack Creek and took position near Sixteenth Corps and Twenty-Third Corps. Williams moved about two miles to the right, taking position between Geary and Ward.[83]

McPherson's Army of the Tennessee spent the day of July 4 getting into position near Nickajack Creek, with Sixteenth Corps in the center, Seventeenth Corps on the right, and Fifteenth Corps on the left. This movement so threatened the left flank of the enemy's Smyrna Camp Ground line that Johnston withdrew his army on the night of July 4 and fell back about three miles to another previously prepared position near the Chattahoochee River. By dawn the next morning the Confederates were established in their new position, which ran in a curving line from near Howell's Ferry on the right to a point covering Mason and Turner's Ferry on the left.[84]

Early on July 5 when Sherman learned that Johnston had fallen back toward the river, he advanced his army on a broad front, with Thomas moving along the main road to Atlanta, and McPherson, on his right, marching toward Mason and Turner's Ferry. Schofield massed his divisions in rear of McPherson. Major General George Stoneman's cavalry pushed forward toward Sandtown to the right of Army of the Tennessee.[85]

Thomas advanced his army that day in three columns: Howard, on the left, came up to the Chattahoochee River near Pace's Ferry; Palmer, in the center, arrived in front of Johnston's new line, about one mile from the river; and Hooker's corps advanced on the right.[86]

Geary's division of Hooker's corps marched to the south and east over a succession of rough and densely wooded ridges without regular roads, and they crossed Nickajack Creek at Ruff's Mill. Geary then moved toward Turner's Ferry, with Palmer on his left and McPherson on his right. Williams' and Ward's divisions of the corps followed Geary. About 3:00 PM, Geary arrived near the enemy line and massed his division in the woods, with his right connecting with the Army of the Tennessee by pickets. There was no connection on his left with Fourteenth Corps, which was across Nickajack Creek.[87]

Williams' division marched across fields to the Turner's Ferry road, just in rear of the enemy's vacated works. After an exhausting march through a rough and broken country, part of the time on this crowded road and part of the time over paths, it took position on a high ridge overlooking a part of Johnston's new line. Williams posted a strong picket line along Nickajack Creek, close to the enemy's line. Ward's division, which also had a very fatiguing march, followed Williams' ordnance train on the Turner's Ferry road, crossed Nickajack Creek, and camped that night on a high range of hills on the left of the road and in rear of Williams and Geary. Stoneman's cavalry was farther to the right toward Sandtown.[88]

That day, from a hill just in rear of Vining's Station, Sherman and troops of Twentieth Corps could see for the first time the houses and other buildings in the city of Atlanta, about nine miles distant to their front, with all of the valley of the Chattahoochee lying between them.[89]

Garrard moved July 5 with his cavalry division from south of Marietta to Roswell and the next day destroyed the important cotton, wool, and paper mills located there.[90]

Early on the morning of July 5 Blair's Seventeenth Corps advanced to the Chattahoochee River at Howell's Ferry and the mouth of Nickajack Creek, and it moved along that creek within five hundred yards of Johnston's breastworks.[91]

On July 6 Palmer's and Howard's corps remained in the positions taken the day before, but Hooker's corps crossed the Nickajack and moved up to the enemy's works. Williams' division crossed the creek and formed on the right of Palmer's corps and threw up breastworks. Geary and Ward extended to and connected with the Army of the Ohio. At 3:00 PM Brigadier General Peter J. Osterhaus' First Division of Logan's corps relieved Geary's division, which then moved northward and followed Williams to the ridge road that ran to Vining's Station. Then, moving eastward, it camped in the woods east of the Nickajack. Ward's division moved two miles to the east and camped on a line in front of the enemy's works on the Chattahoochee River on the same range of hills it had held the night before. Ward's brigades were in line with Colonel Benjamin Harrison's First Brigade on the left, Colonel James Wood's Third Brigade in the center, and Colonel John Coburn's Second Brigade on the right. Geary's division was on the right of Ward, and Williams' division was on the left of Ward.[92]

Early on the morning of July 7, 1864, Geary moved two miles to the south and formed his division on the right of Ward, connecting on the right with Osterhaus' division of Fifteenth Corps at Nickajack Creek. Hooker's divisions were then in line with Williams on the left, Ward in the center, and Geary on the right. They remained in these positions until July 17. During this time the men rested, received supplies, and prepared for the next phase of the advance toward Atlanta. The railroad had been sufficiently repaired by July 7 so that supplies could be brought up directly to Sherman's lines.[93]

An inspection of Johnston's position convinced Sherman that it was too strong to attack, and on July 6 he ordered Schofield to move with his infantry to Smyrna Camp Ground and to prepare for crossing the Chattahoochee River at some place between Pace's Ferry and Roswell. The next day he sent Schofield to look for a suitable place upstream for the crossing, and Schofield decided on the mouth of Soap Creek (Phillip's Ferry), which flows into the river six or seven miles above Pace's Ferry. There on July 8 and 9 Schofield crossed his two divisions, commanded by Brigadier General Jacob D. Cox and Brigadier General Milo S. Hascall, and established a beachhead on the far side of the river.[94]

July 9 Howard sent Newton's Second Division of his Fourth Corps to Roswell to support Garrard; McPherson sent Dodge's corps to Roswell by way of Marietta.[95]

During the night of July 9 Johnston withdrew his troops from the lines north of the Chattahoochee and moved across the river in the direction of Atlanta. By the next morning the enemy engineers had removed the pontoon bridges, and the rear guard had retired after burning the railroad and wagon bridges.[96]

The next day Sherman's skirmishers confronted the enemy's skirmishers on the opposite bank of the river. For a time the pickets on both sides of the river agreed to an armistice, and there was friendly conversation, visiting, trading of coffee and tobacco, and exchanging of newspapers. Men of both armies swam on opposite sides of the river. In one recorded conversation, a Confederate soldier asked, "Who commands the army across the river?" A Union soldier said, "General Sherman." "Well, he commands ours too," said the first soldier, "for every time you are ordered to move, we move too." Another Confederate complained, "You'uns don't fight we'uns fair. You'uns go around and fight us on the end." This truce did not last long, however, because officers on both sides issued orders forbidding fraternization.[97]

During the brief period of fraternization, a Confederate soldier invited one of the men of the 85th Indiana to come over; he asked him to write a letter to his sweetheart in Kingston, Georgia. The man of the 85th then brought the letter back with him and showed it to John P. Baird, his regimental commander. The latter read the letter, endorsed it as "examined and approved," and forwarded it by mail.[98]

During the week of July 10-17, 1864, Sherman continued his efforts to get his army across the Chattahoochee River. In the Army of the Tennessee, Dodge crossed the river with his Left Wing, Sixteenth Corps, at Roswell and joined Newton's division of Fourth Corps. On the opposite flank of Sherman's line, Blair's Seventeenth Corps remained near Nickajack Creek. On the evening of July 12, Logan's Fifteenth Corps followed Dodge to Roswell, where it arrived the next morning. July 15, 1864, it crossed to the south side of the river and joined Newton and Dodge. Blair, who had been detached to await the return of Stoneman's cavalry from a movement down river, followed Logan to Roswell July 16. It then crossed the Chattahoochee the next day. The Army of the Tennessee was assembled on the south bank.[99]

In Thomas' Army of the Cumberland, Howard left Newton's division of his Fourth Corps with Dodge at Roswell, and moved with Stanley's and Thomas J. Wood's divisions to a position near the mouth of Soap Creek, where he was within supporting distance of Schofield. On July 12 Howard crossed the Chattahoochee at Powers' Ferry with these two divisions and then took position on the right of the Army of the Ohio.[100]

Palmer's and Hooker's corps remained in front of Johnston's abandoned works until July 17, afterwards crossing the Chattahoochee River. A short time after 11:00 that morning, Palmer began crossing the river at Pace's Ferry; he then advanced to a point near Kyle's Bridge over Nancy's Creek, a tributary of Peach Tree Creek, where he halted for the night.

Hooker's corps remained in its camps until that afternoon, then marched down to Pace's Ferry and followed Palmer across the river to the south bank. From there it marched in an easterly direction for about two or three miles and camped that night on the left of Palmer's corps, within about a mile of Nancy's Creek. Thomas' corps were in line, with Howard on the left, Hooker in the center, and Palmer on the right.[101]

When Hooker's corps moved that day, Coburn's brigade marched from its camps in an easterly direction, passing Vining's Station on the railroad and moved down to the river at Pace's Ferry. The river, spanned by two parallel pontoon bridges, was about 150 yards wide at that point. To facilitate the passage, the front rank men went to the bridge on the right and the rear rank to the one on the left. After crossing the river, the brigade marched about three miles and went into camp on the crest of a ridge not far from Nancy's Creek.[102]

That same morning, the Army of the Tennessee, on the left of Sherman's line, began its advance toward Atlanta. Blair's Seventeenth Corps crossed the Chattahoochee near Roswell and joined the other two corps of the army. Together they moved southward on the Roswell and Decatur road. In the evening the head of the column reached Nancy's Creek near Cross Keys. There the army went into camp for the night.[103]

Earlier on July 5 as Sherman's army was approaching the Chattahoochee River, Colonel William L. Utley of the 22nd Wisconsin, after his long and bitter controversy with his lieutenant colonel, Edward Bloodgood, finally resigned and left the service. He gave ill health as his reason for leaving. Utley was indeed not well at the time and had trouble keeping up with the regiment, but the real reason probably went deeper than that. For one thing, Utley had never been on good terms with Butterfield and had recently acquired an intense dislike for him. Then there was his long and bitter controversy with Bloodgood. Before Utley left the regiment Bloodgood had told a friend that Utley had resigned to avoid a court-martial for incompetency. This story was repeated, and soon, on July 2, Utley learned of it. He went to Bloodgood and demanded to know if he was the source of the story; he received an evasive answer. The conversation grew more heated and finally, after Utley had made some abusive accusations, Bloodgood called him a liar. Utley then struck him and nearly knocked him down. Bloodgood made no response and the affair ended, but Utley left that same evening for Chattanooga, where he waited for the papers approving his resignation.[104]

Edward Bloodgood, who became the new commander of the 22nd Wisconsin, was born at Fort Holton, Maine, May 12, 1831, where his father, a West Point graduate, was stationed as an officer in the United States Army. Bloodgood was educated at Albany, New York, and then moved with his family to Milwaukee, Wisconsin, in 1854. After the fall of Fort Sumter in 1861, he served as sergeant major in the 1st Wisconsin infantry until mustered out August 21, 1861. He was appointed captain in the 1st Wisconsin October 18, 1861, and resigned August 4, 1862. He was appointed lieutenant colonel of the 22nd Wisconsin regiment September 1, 1862, the time of its formation. As noted previously, Bloodgood had been dismissed from the service October 9, 1863, but was reinstated December 28, 1863. He served with his regiment during the rest of the war until muster out June 12, 1865.[105]

Also in July, Coburn lost another of his regimental commanders. On the 17th, as the army was crossing the Chattahoochee River, Colonel John P. Baird of the 85th Indiana became ill, and Lieutenant Colonel Alexander B. Crane assumed temporary command of the regiment. Finally, on July

20, 1864, because of failing health, Baird resigned and left the army. Crane took permanent charge of the regiment.[106]

It appears that Baird was suffering from various conditions caused by the stress of a long war. This stress resulted in a condition known today as a "spastic colon," which caused a severe cramping of the bowel and lower abdominable pains. He also had what is now called "benign prostatic enlargement." According to Assistant Surgeon W. V. Wiles, at times these conditions caused much inconvenience, intense suffering, and mental depression, and left him unable to perform the duties of his office.[107]

Alexander B. Crane, who replaced Baird in command of the 85th Indiana, was born April 23, 1833, in Berkley, Massachusetts. He was the son of Abiel Briggs Crane and Emma Tisdale Crane. Crane was privately tutored by his pastor and later entered Amherst College, where he graduated in the class of 1854. After moving to Terre Haute, Indiana, he studied law in the office of Richard W. Thompson, a leader of the state bar, who later became Secretary of the Navy in the Cabinet of Rutherford B. Hayes. Crane was admitted to the bar in Terre Haute in 1856 and later practiced law in that city. He also served as district attorney of Vigo County. When the Civil War began, Crane and John P. Baird helped raise and organize the 85th Indiana regiment, and Crane was mustered in as lieutenant colonel of the regiment September 4, 1862. He was promoted colonel July 21, 1864, and he served with the regiment throughout the war.

In addition to his service in the field, Crane also served as provost marshal, judge advocate, and member of a commission to examine officers for Colored regiments. As judge advocate, while his regiment was on duty in Kentucky, he set what was regarded as a precedent when he rendered a decision that a Negro had the right to testify in court.[108]

Captain Ellery C. Davis of Company G resigned July 30, also because of disability. The regimental adjutant, Francis C. Crawford, assumed command of the company.[109]

There were reports that Baird was a heavy drinker, and on at least two occasions it was definitely stated that he was drunk while in command of his regiment in the presence of the enemy. On June 12, 1863—three days after the hanging of Walter Peter and Orton Williams—Horace Maynard, the pro-Union Attorney General for the State of Tennessee, then at Nashville, wrote the following letter to General Rosecrans, commanding the Department and Army of the Cumberland:

> *General,*
> *I have heard a statement, apparently well founded, that, if true, you ought to know, & if false, is very prejudicial to the party concerned.*
> *It is that Col. Baird, in command at Franklin, is consistently and ha-*

bitually intoxicated; that during the recent attack upon that post, he was so drunk as to be unable to give commands to his men.

You will surely agree with me, that the command of our outpost is not a fit place for a drunken, incompetent, or unfaithful officer. Our misfortunes in this department lost some [illegible] from this cause, and surely admonish us against repetition of this latest blunder.

Of this officer I know nothing personally, and have taken the trouble to communicate a matter to you, which seems to me to be of public concern.

> *I am very respectfully your Obt. Servt.*
> *Horace Maynard*[110]

In his diary, Samuel C. Harrison, a musician in the 85th Indiana, recounts the following episode, which occurred during the advance of the brigade beyond Noyes' Creek during the Atlanta Campaign: "In the evening [of June 20], Col. Baird was drunk and took his regiment in front of the works nearly to the skirmish line. Brigade officers succeeded in getting them back."[111]

Alexander Baxter Crane, lieutenant colonel of the 85th Indiana, commanded the regiment after John Baird's resignation. It was falsely reported that Crane had been killed, and Jefferson Brant wrote home saying he prayed Crane had not been killed "for our regiment could ill-afford to lose so good an officer as Col. Crane. He has few equals anywhere, I think, in the army."

History of the Eighty-fifth Ind. Regiment

Chapter 12

Atlanta Campaign
Closing in on Atlanta

General Joseph E. Johnston withdrew his army from the west side of the Chattahoochee River during the night of July 9, 1864, and the next day established a new entrenched outer defensive line in front of Atlanta, located on high ground a mile or more south of Peach Tree Creek. It began on the Western and Atlantic Railroad, about two miles from the river, and extended eastward some six miles to the junction of Pea Vine Creek and Peach Tree Creek, there turning to the south and ending at the Georgia Railroad between Atlanta and Decatur. In addition to this outer line, a very strong inner line of works surrounded Atlanta at a distance of approximately a mile and a fourth to a mile and a half from the center of the city.[1]

July 18, the day after Major General George H. Thomas' Army of the Cumberland had crossed to the south bank of the Chattahoochee River in preparation for the final advance on Atlanta, President Jefferson Davis ordered some important changes in the higher command of the Confederate Army of Tennessee. Johnston was relieved from command of the army, and General John B. Hood was assigned in his place. With the elevation of Hood to army command, Major General Benjamin F. Cheatham was assigned command of Hood's former corps. In another change, Lieutenant General Alexander P. Stewart relieved Major General William W. Loring in command of Leonidas Polk's former corps. Lieutenant General William J. Hardee remained in command of his corps. Under the new arrangement, Stewart's corps held the left of Hood's line, south of Peach Tree Creek, between the Marietta and Pace's Ferry roads. Hardee's corps extended the line eastward from the right of Stewart to the point where the line turned to the south. Cheatham's corps was on the right of Hood's line, facing east toward Decatur.[2]

On July 18 Major General William T. Sherman, with all of his army then on the south side of the Chattahoochee River, resumed his advance toward Atlanta, with Thomas' Army of the Cumberland on the right, Major General John M. Schofield's Army of the Ohio in the center, and Major General James B. McPherson's Army of the Tennessee on the left.

Sherman's plan called for Thomas to move on the roads from Pace's Ferry and Phillip's Ferry directly on Atlanta, with his left following the road by Buck Head (present day Buckhead), thus covering the Western and Atlantic Railroad while the bridge over the Chattahoochee was being rebuilt and fortified.[3]

McPherson's Army of the Tennessee, which had marched from near Roswell to Cross Keys the day before, was to continue its march and strike the Georgia Railroad in the vicinity of Stone Mountain. Brigadier General Kenner Garrard's Second Cavalry Division of the Army of the Cumberland was to move out in front of McPherson. Schofield's Army of the Ohio, which was about midway between Thomas and McPherson, was to march by way of Cross Keys toward Decatur, east of Atlanta.[4]

July 18 the Army of the Cumberland crossed Nancy's Creek and marched eastward toward Buck Head. That evening it took position in front of the Old Peach Tree Creek road running from Turner's Ferry to Decatur. Major General Oliver O. Howard's Fourth Corps moved directly to Buck Head, arriving about noon, and took position on the left of the town, along the road to Decatur. Major General John M. Palmer's Fourteenth Corps was on the right, with its right resting near the junction of Nancy's Creek and Peach Tree Creek. Major General Joseph Hooker's Twentieth Corps, at the center of the army, marched along a road that ran between Howard and Palmer.[5]

Brigadier General Alpheus S. Williams' First Division of Hooker's corps moved forward during the afternoon of July 18, and that evening took position along the Buck Head and Turner's Ferry road, connecting with Howard's corps on the left. Brigadier General William T. Ward's Third Division also moved up close to Buck Head and camped that night on the right of the road, next to Fourth Corps, which was already at Buck Head. Brigadier General John W. Geary's Second Division followed Ward and encamped at the junction of the Turner's Ferry and Decatur road with the Howell's Mill road, about one mile west of Buck Head.[6]

Schofield continued his march on July 19 and at about 3:00 PM Brigadier General Milo S. Hascall's Second Division of the Army of the Ohio entered Decatur. Brigadier General Jacob D. Cox's Third Division took position about four miles northeast of Atlanta and about a mile and a half from the main line of Confederate defenses. Also that day, McPherson's Army of the Tennessee moved westward along the railroad toward Atlanta, destroying track as it advanced, and that evening it concentrated at Decatur. When McPherson's troops arrived at Decatur, Hascall withdrew and took position in rear of Cox, in reserve.[7]

Thomas' orders for July 19 were to hold fast with his right near Howell's Mill and to swing forward with his left and cross Peach Tree Creek. He was to connect on the left with Schofield, approaching from the north. Early that morning Howard moved southward with his Fourth Corps along the main road from Buck Head to Atlanta and reached the crossing of Peach Tree Creek about 6:30 AM. There he found that the bridge had been destroyed and enemy troops in position on the far side of the creek. During the afternoon Major General David S. Stanley's First Division and Brigadier General Thomas J. Wood's Third Division forced crossings of the creek, and by dark they had effected lodgments on the south bank. Brigadier General John Newton's Second Division moved up to Peach Tree Creek in support of Wood.[8]

On the left of Thomas' line, Brigadier General Jefferson C. Davis' Second Division of Palmer's corps crossed Peach Tree Creek below Howell's Mill and then built a bridge for the other divisions of the corps to cross the next day.[9]

That morning, July 19, Geary's division advanced about two miles on the road running by Howell's Mill and occupied a hill overlooking the mill about three-fourths of a mile from Howell's Mill. His skirmishers connected with those of Fourth Corps on the left.

Geary then made preparations to cross Peach Tree Creek, which was about twenty feet wide and quite deep, with marshy banks and a muddy bottom. Along both banks were narrow strips of cleared land, which, from Geary's right, became wider and finally extended out into open country in front of Fourth Corps to the left. On both sides of the valley, steep and irregular hills were densely covered with timber. There were no roads or bridges crossing the creek on the front of Geary's division.

After the pioneer corps built a footbridge over the creek, Geary crossed and moved forward for about one-fourth mile and halted in front of the enemy's picket line.[10]

During the afternoon of July 19, Williams moved his division southward toward the front and camped that night on the north side of Peach Tree Creek, above Howell's Mill. Ward's division, with Coburn's brigade, remained in its camps that day and spent the time building bridges across Peach Tree Creek.[11]

That evening Thomas ordered Hooker to cross the rest of his corps to the south side of Peach Tree Creek where Geary had crossed and then to move out toward Atlanta.[12]

BATTLE OF PEACH TREE CREEK
JULY 20, 1864

July 20 Sherman's army continued its efforts to close in inexorably on Atlanta. On the far left, McPherson advanced in two columns from Decatur to within about two and a half miles of the city. Major General John A. Logan's Fifteenth Corps, followed by Major General Grenville M. Dodge's Sixteenth Corps, took the direct road, and Major General Frank P. Blair's Seventeenth Corps marched on a road to the south. Both corps entrenched on a line facing Cheatham's works in front of Atlanta, with Logan on the right and Blair on the left. Schofield's Army of the Ohio, which was on the right of McPherson, advanced about a mile and a half toward Atlanta, and when Dodge's corps came up it covered the interval between Logan and Schofield.[13]

At daylight July 20, by Sherman's orders, Stanley's and Wood's divisions of Howard's corps moved to the left to connect with Schofield, and Newton's Second Division was left to hold a position on the Buck Head and Atlanta road, on the left of Hooker's corps. Newton's division was detached that day from Howard's command and received its orders direct from Thomas.[14]

Thomas ordered Newton to remain in position until Hooker's corps had crossed Peach Tree Creek and effected a junction with his division, and then to advance on the main road toward Atlanta. The junction was completed about 1:00 PM, and at that time Newton sent forward a strong line of skirmishers to drive the enemy from the first ridge on his front and to hold it. When the skirmishers had occupied the ridge, Newton advanced his division to the skirmish line, where he placed Brigadier General Nathan Kimball's First Brigade on the right of the road and Colonel John W. Blake's Second Brigade on the left. Both brigades began to throw up barricades of logs and rails. Brigadier General Luther P. Bradley halted his Third Brigade in order of march along the road in rear of the other two brigades. When these dispositions were completed, Newton prepared to resume his advance, but he soon found the enemy in force on his front. Thomas ordered him to remain where he was for the rest of the day and entrench his position, which was about one-half mile south of Peach Tree Creek. His left flank extended toward Clear Creek, with his line covering the crossroad that ran to Collier's Mill.[15]

Early on the morning of July 20 Hooker ordered Williams' division to cross Peach Tree Creek in rear of Geary's position and then to move up to Geary's right. He also directed Ward's division to cross the creek and support Geary and Williams. Williams crossed to the south bank of Peach Tree Creek on Geary's bridge, and then marched to the right on a farm road along a wooded ridge toward the house of H. Embry, where the direct road from

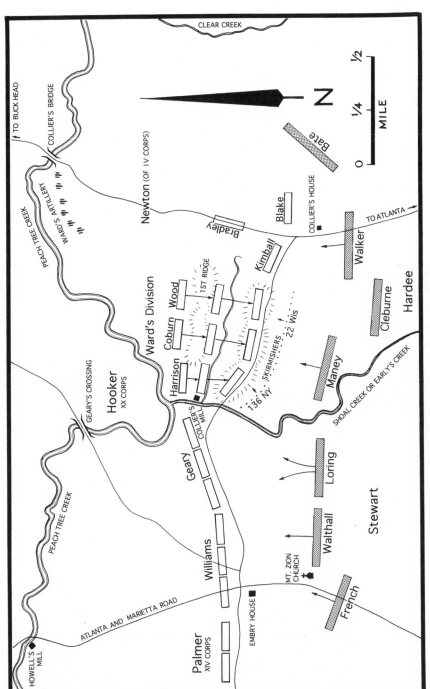

Battle of Peach Tree Creek, July 20, 1864

Howell's Mill joins the road from Geary's bridge. There he halted at a group of deserted houses about six hundred yards from Embry's and massed his brigades on the road.[16]

On the morning of July 20, Ward's orders were changed; instead of supporting Williams and Geary, he was directed to fill the gap that existed between Newton's and Geary's divisions. At 7:00 that morning, Ward's brigades left their camps and moved slowly southward through the woods by different routes. At about 11:00 Colonel John Coburn's Second Brigade, which was at the head of the column, crossed Peach Tree Creek on the bridge used earlier by Newton. By noon the entire division was over, and formed in column of division en masse in rear of Newton's position.[17]

The Battle of Peach Tree Creek was fought that afternoon. In order to understand better the part played by Ward's division and Coburn's brigade in that battle, a brief description of the country to the south of the creek, which Ward was later to occupy, should be noted in some detail. On this part of its course the creek was a narrow, muddy stream about forty feet wide and from four to twelve feet deep, impassable except at the bridges. On the south side of the creek, a flat stretch of cleared bottom land extended from the right of Newton's division to the left of Geary's division, averaging about two hundred yards in width.

Along the south side of the valley, the ground sloped upward for about four hundred yards to a ridge, some seventy feet in height, which ran roughly parallel to the creek. The slopes of this ridge in front of Ward's division were generally cleared, and except on the left, where there was a thick growth of pine, the greater part was covered with a thin growth of young pines, sassafras, and briars. This ridge was occupied by enemy skirmishers.

Beyond this first ridge was a narrow ravine, with banks about thirty feet high, and filled with tangled wood. Along the bottom of this ravine a small stream ran west into Shoal Creek, a tributary of Peach Tree Creek. Collier's Mill was on Shoal Creek, near the Collier's Mill road (or Collier road). Shoal Creek ran through a fairly deep valley between the positions occupied by the divisions of Geary and Ward. In this valley there was some open country along the stream, especially near Collier's Mill.

Beyond the ravine on the far side of the first ridge, the ground rose again for about two hundred yards to the crest of a second ridge that was higher and longer than the first. This ridge had been cleared and cultivated and was bare of trees, but the slope was partly covered with brush. Along the crest of this ridge, sometimes called the Collier Ridge, the Collier Mill road ran westward from the Buck Head and Atlanta road, at Newton's position, past Collier's Mill, and on to the Chattahoochee River. A rail fence ran along the road on the top of this ridge. To the south of the crest, was an open field about one-third to one-half mile wide, and on the far side of the field was a woods in which the enemy was entrenched.[18]

After Ward had crossed Peach Tree Creek and had halted in rear of Newton for a short rest, he ordered Lieutenant Colonel Edward Bloodgood's 22nd Wisconsin, which was leading Coburn's brigade that day, and Lieutenant Colonel Lester B. Faulkner's 136th New York of Colonel James Wood's Third Brigade forward as skirmishers. They advanced to the crest of first ridge, with the 22nd Wisconsin on the left, connecting with Newton's division and the 136th New York on the right, connecting with Geary's division.[19]

Ward advanced from Peach Tree Creek into a cornfield, some two hundred yards from the creek, and deployed his division on the bottom land at the foot of the first ridge. Colonel Harrison's First Brigade was on the right, next to Geary's division, Colonel Coburn's Second Brigade was in the center, and Colonel Wood's Third Brigade was on the left of the division and to the right of Newton's division. The distance from Ward's line in the valley to the ravine between the two ridges to his front was about 350 yards.[20]

Coburn formed his regiments in line of battle as follows: The 85th Indiana, then commanded by Lieutenant Colonel Alexander B. Crane, was on the right, next to Harrison's brigade; Major Levin T. Miller's 33rd Indiana was on the left, connecting with Colonel Wood's brigade; and Captain John J. Baker's 19th Michigan on the second line, was in the rear of the 85th Indiana. The 22nd Wisconsin, as noted, was out in front as skirmishers.[21]

When Harrison moved his brigade forward to his place in line, he found that Geary's left was resting on the cornfield and that Geary's division had already taken position on the crest of a hill that he was to occupy. Harrison also found that Coburn's brigade had already been formed, and that he had been left with only sufficient room for one regiment in the interval between Coburn and Geary. He reported this situation to Ward, who ordered each of his brigade commanders to pull one regiment out of the front line and to place it on a second line, so the brigades could close to the left, enabling Harrison to bring two more regiments into the first line.[22]

When Harrison's brigade was finally deployed, the front line was within about three hundred yards of Collier's Mill, to the right of the so-called first ridge, with Ward's division in line at its base. James Wood deployed his brigade on the left of Coburn and on the right of Newton. When the deployment of Ward's division was completed, the brigade commanders were instructed to remain in their position at the foot of the ridge and await further orders.[23]

About 10:00 AM July 20 Geary's skirmishers, supported by Colonel Charles Candy's First Brigade, advanced from near Peach Tree Creek, and Colonel Patrick H. Jones's Second Brigade followed Candy. Colonel David Ireland's Third Brigade also moved forward. These troops advanced about a mile, crossed two ridges, and then attacked and drove the enemy skirmishers from a third ridge and from a cornfield to the right of the ridge. Candy's brigade occupied this ridge about noon, and then constructed a barricade of rails for protection.[24]

About eighty yards to the left of Geary's line was Shoal Creek, and beyond this stream was the first ridge, along the lower slope of which, in the valley of Peach Tree Creek, Ward's division was deployed. While Geary was getting in position, Ward's skirmishers were moving up the northern slope of this ridge, and a short time later, supported by some of Geary's artillery, they occupied the crest. To Geary's left was the open field occupied by Ward's division before the battle that day.[25]

When Geary formed his line, Williams' division was about five hundred yards in rear of Geary's right. About 3:30 PM, Williams heard sounds of heavy musketry firing, beginning on the right of Fourth Corps and rolling with increased volume in the direction of Williams' position. Williams then moved his division forward and formed on the right of Geary. All divisions of Joseph Hooker's Twentieth Corps were then across Peach Tree Creek and in position on the ridges to the south.[26]

Earlier, when Johnston had retired across the Chattahoochee River, July 10, he had moved into a new line of entrenchments constructed in preparation for an expected battle at Peach Tree Creek. He believed that during the Union advance east of the Chattahoochee River, Sherman would divide his army; when that happened, Johnston planned to strike and destroy the separated wings. His best opportunity, he thought, would come when Thomas' Army of the Cumberland was divided during the crossing of Peach Tree Creek. Hood later claimed that he had no knowledge of Johnston's plans, but nevertheless, shortly after he assumed command of the army, he issued orders for an attack on Thomas' army while it was crossing Peach Tree Creek.

According to Hood's plan, Hardee and Stewart were to make the attack, and Cheatham's corps was to remain in position on the right, facing the Army of the Tennessee and the Army of the Ohio. The attack was to begin on the right of Hardee's line, en echelon at intervals of two hundred yards, against the left of the Army of the Cumberland. Major General William B. Bate's Confederate division, on the right of Hardee's line, was to attack first, followed, in order to the left, by the divisions of Major General William H. T. Walker, Brigadier General George Maney, Major General William W. Loring, Brigadier General Edward C. Walthall, and Major General Samuel G. French.[27]

The attack was to begin at 1:00 PM July 20, but because McPherson was advancing toward Atlanta from the east more rapidly than had been expected, Hood delayed his attack while he made some readjustments in his line. All was ready at 2:00 PM, but then, by mistake, Loring attacked first at 2:45 PM, although at that time Bate had not yet moved. Loring's right brigade, commanded by Brigadier General Winfield S. Featherston advanced to the Confederate right of Collier's Mill toward the front of Ward's division, and his left brigade, under Brigadier General Thomas M. Scott, moved toward the front held by Harrison's brigade of Ward's division, and the left of Geary's line.[28]

Ward sent forward Bloodgood's 22nd Wisconsin that morning as skirmishers; it moved up to the crest of the first ridge, where it halted briefly. Then, about noon, it crossed the ravine that extended along its front and moved up to the crest of the second ridge (Collier Ridge). Bloodgood moved his men forward at the double-quick, firing as they ran. When they reached the top of the ridge, they took position behind the fence that ran along the Collier Mill road. In this position they covered the division front. The three reserve companies of the regiment entrenched in the ravine at the foot of the ridge.[29]

A little after 2:45 PM, the first line of Featherston's Confederate brigade emerged from the woods and started rapidly across the wide field toward Bloodgood's skirmishers, who were behind the rail fence. Featherston's first line was followed by two other lines. Bloodgood immediately sent back to brigade headquarters for support and prepared to slow the enemy advance. The 22nd Wisconsin opened fire when the enemy left the cover of the woods and kept up a steady fire as they crossed the field. The regiment continued to hold its position until its line was broken on both the right and left and canister from Geary's batteries on their right began falling among the men. Finally, when Featherston's men were within about thirty feet of the skirmishers' rifle pits, Bloodgood, to avoid capture, gave the order to fall back into the ravine and rally on the reserves.[30]

About 3:00 or 3:30 PM, private Henry Crist of the 33rd Indiana, who had been out on the front near the skirmish line picking blackberries, came in and reported to Coburn that the enemy was advancing. Coburn quickly asked Ward's permission to move his brigade to a better position on the ridge to his front. Ward informed Coburn that such movement was contrary to Hooker's orders, but he went on to say that if the enemy should attack he was authorized to advance. Ward's brigade commanders discussed the situation, and a short time later the whole division moved up the slope of the first ridge, with James Wood's brigade on the left, Coburn's brigade in the center, and Harrison's brigade on the right. Coburn's brigade advanced with the 85th Indiana on the right, the 33rd Indiana on the left, and the 19th Michigan in rear of the other two regiments. Upon reaching the crest of the ridge, the division halted briefly before continuing.[31]

Hardee, who was to have attacked first, did not begin his advance until about 3:15 or 3:30 PM, and by that time Bate's Confederate division was moving out and marching to the northwest along Clear Creek through dense woods and thick underbrush. As it happened, Bate moved into the gap created that morning when Stanley's and Thomas J. Wood's divisions were shifted to the east to connect with Schofield's Army of the Ohio, and he passed by the left flank of Newton's division without encountering any opposition. Because of the time lost by Bate while attempting to find Newton's left flank, it was Walker's division of Hardee's corps, advancing on the left of Bate, while he was on the west side of the Buck Head and Atlanta road, that first came up against Newton's main line. The Federals immediately opened with artillery and musketry, but the enemy came on, and Brigadier General Clement H. Stevens' brigade captured a part of the works on Newton's right. Stevens was soon driven back, however, and was mortally wounded.[32]

Bate's brigade veered off to the left as it advanced, and it soon ran into Bradley's reserve brigade, to the left and rear of Newton's main line. Bate promptly attacked but was repulsed by Bradley's men. The Confederate second attack, delivered a short time later, was also beaten back. Bradley's brigade was greatly aided in repelling Bate's attacks by Captain Wilbur A. Goodspeed's battery of Newton's division and Ward's artillery, which had been left behind when the division advanced from Peach Tree Creek earlier that day. Thomas used Ward's guns to sweep the valley of Clear Creek, through which Bate's men were advancing. A part of Bate's division spent the afternoon wandering about in the brush and woods and was not engaged.[33]

As Hood's attack shifted to the left, as originally planned, Maney's division of Hardee's corps came up to continue Walker's assault, launching a heavy attack on Kimball's brigade. Kimball's right flank was not fully protected—at that time Ward's line was several hundred yards to the right and rear of that part of the line, thus leaving a gap between Kimball's right and Ward's left. When Maney came up and attacked, his line overlapped Kimball's right flank, but Kimball quickly refused the right of his line and drove Maney's men laterally in front of Ward's division, which was then advancing to connect with Newton. At about that time, the 20th Connecticut of James Wood's brigade reached the crest of the ridge, opening with deadly fire that aided the repulse of Maney. Kimball held his position against repeated enemy charges until the fighting ended that evening.[34]

At the time of Maney's advance, Loring's division attacked on his left, but, after some initial success it was driven back. Featherston's brigade charged against the line held by Ward's division, and Scott's brigade struck at the junction of Ward's and Geary's divisions.

When Coburn reached the crest of the first ridge with his brigade of

Ward's division, he ordered the 33rd Indiana to move forward into the ravine beyond. A little later the 85th Indiana and the 19th Michigan moved down and joined it there. At about the same time the skirmishers of Bloodgood's 22nd Wisconsin joined the rest of the brigade in the ravine. Coburn's four regiments were together again fighting for survival. James Wood's brigade came into the ravine on the left of Coburn's line, and Harrison's brigade moved up on its right.[35]

Following closely behind Bloodgood's retiring skirmishers, Featherston's Confederate brigade of Loring's division came over the crest of Collier Ridge and rushed down the slope toward Ward's men in the ravine. All three of Ward's brigades immediately opened with heavy and sustained fire, which checked the attack and caused the enemy to recoil in some confusion. Ward's entire line counterattacked and drove the enemy back up the slope and over the ridge.[36]

On reaching the crest of the ridge, a part of Coburn's brigade advanced beyond the Collier Mill road and took position, while the rest of the brigade remained in line along the road. Both lines immediately strengthened their positions by throwing up barricades of rails. A large force of rebels advanced against Coburn's left flank; two companies of the 33rd Indiana were refused to face left and to protect that flank. A short time later, however, Wood's brigade came up and connected on its right with Coburn's line—thereafter Coburn's left flank was in no danger. Harrison's brigade moved onto Collier Ridge, forming on the right of Coburn. The Confederates attempted several times to advance that evening but they were unable to do so. The Federals held the high ground.[37]

When James Wood advanced with his brigade on the left of Coburn to meet Featherston's attack, he passed over the first ridge and moved down into the ravine on the other side. His men then charged up the slope of Collier Ridge and drove the enemy over the crest and into the valley beyond. Just as the left of Wood's line reached the crest, a part of Maney's troops were attempting to pass around Newton's right flank, but a volley from the 20th Connecticut caused this column to break and fall back.[38]

James Wood's men took positions behind the partially destroyed rail fence along the road, keeping up a constant and continuous fire. The enemy made one or two ineffectual attempts to renew the attack and then fell back to their main line of works.[39]

When Loring launched his attack, Harrison ordered the three regiments of his brigade on the left of Shoal Creek to advance and attack Confederate forces that were then coming down the slope of Collier Ridge. These regiments immediately advanced, against strong opposition, and pushed the rebels back over the ridge.[40]

While the regiments on the left of Shoal Creek were getting into position, Harrison brought forward the two regiments to the right of the creek to cover the left of Geary's line and to connect with the right of Harrison's line. These two regiments were not engaged at close quarters, but they aided Geary in repulsing Loring's attack on the left of Geary's line. Loring's Confederates rallied after being driven from the ridge; several times they attempted to renew the attack before dark, but each time they were repulsed.[41]

Loring's left brigade, commanded by Scott, advanced on the right of Featherston. When the right wing crossed Collier Ridge, it was struck by heavy artillery fire from Geary's batteries on its left and deadly infantry fire on its front. It was driven back with fearful losses. That evening the ground around Collier's Mill was strewn with the dead and wounded of Scott's Rebel brigade. The left wing of Scott's line also moved up Collier Ridge, directly in front of Geary's line, but it too was forced back down the slope.[42]

About 4:00 PM, after Scott began his attack, Walthall's Confederate division of Stewart's corps advanced through difficult country, with Colonel Edward A. O'Neal's brigade on the right and Brigadier General Daniel Reynolds' brigade on the left. O'Neal's brigade moved into a ravine that ran between the right of Geary's division and the left of Williams' division, but Geary soon checked the advance. O'Neal made three unsuccessful attempts on Geary's line but continued fighting until the battle ended at dark.[43]

Williams was still advancing his division when, at about 3:30 PM, he first heard the sounds of firing to his left. He promptly deployed and prepared for action. His left rested on the ravine that separated him from the right of Geary's division, and on the right he was separated from Palmer's Fourteenth Corps by another ravine. The center of Williams' line ran across the high ground between the two ravines.[44]

A short time after O'Neal's attack on Geary's line, Reynolds advanced along the ridge and attacked on the front and right of Williams's line. He attempted to gain the rear of Williams' division but was driven back.[45]

Brigadier General William Quarles' brigade, next in order to Hood's left, was unable to get in position, and it did not attack that day.

At dusk, the men of Hardee's and Stewart's Confederate corps returned to their works, and the Battle of Peach Tree Creek was over.

Ward's division played a very significant role in the Union victory that day. Coburn personally deserved credit for his part in the victorious effort, together with that of the other brigade commanders, in moving the division forward to meet the enemy attack that afternoon. John R. McBride, quartermaster sergeant and later adjutant of the 33rd Indiana, later wrote of the battle as follows:

> The position held by the enemy was obstinately contested by them, and at times the conflict was hand to hand; but the onslaught of Ward's

Third Division was so terrific and well-directed that the enemy was overwhelmed, dismayed and demoralized. Three or four distinct charges were made by the enemy and as often he was gallantly repulsed.

Prisoners and Enfield rifles were captured by the wholesale, and some battle flags were taken by the Second Brigade. Some of the men of the 33rd Indiana and 19th Michigan captured a rebel flag, but gave it to some officer unknown to them to take care of, but who the officer was was never known, except that he was serving upon the division staff. Private Thomas J. Williamson, of the 85th Indiana, picked up a rebel flag, waved it three times, and then threw it down, because he could not carry it and fire his gun at the same time. The flags thus captured were most probably picked up and retained by stragglers of some other commands.

. . . The fighting lasted about four hours and was the severest the regiment [33rd Indiana] and brigade [Coburn's brigade] had participated in during the campaign. Throughout the entire conflict Coburn's Second Brigade never wavered, never hesitated, but pressed forward until victory was fully assured.[46]

One of the more interesting accounts of the battle was the story of James H. Crabb, Company G of the 85th Indiana, as told to a reporter for *The Terre Haute Tribune* in its series "Memories of the Civil War," written in 1911. Crabb says that after advancing to the Collier Mill road on the second ridge:

> . . . three lines of Johnnies broke from the cover [of the woods] and it looked as though the whole of Confederate army was racing toward them across the open field, guns belching, officers' swords flashing and bayonets looking mean and ugly. The skirmishers held their ground as the fierce looking column advanced and heard their own columns coming up at a double quick from the rear. . . .
>
> The two columns were within fourteen feet of each other when the fighting began in earnest and during a period of time in which Crabb says he was able to shoot ten times in a fierce, bloody hand to hand conflict, when knives, bayonets, pistols, clubbed guns, swords, and even fists were used . . .
>
> [After the fighting ended] It was found that Company G had not lost a man, though it had held the hardest position. There was not one member of the company, however, who had not been struck by a bullet. Hats were shot through, guns bore the splotches of lead where the bullets had struck. Coats were shot through and such mementos of the flirts of death shown. . . .

The battle was over, but . . . the real battle came when that field of horror was witnessed. Along the fighting line where the hand to hand conflict had been, the dead and dying soldiers, blue and gray lying side by side, were piled everywhere, and directly on the fighting line the dead made a low wall of human flesh. Pitiful groans and pleadings for water, the first craving of the dying or badly wounded, was heard on every side and contortions of their sufferings could be seen grotesquely through the haze of smoke which covered the battleground. The Union soldiers in charge of the field gave aid, indiscriminately, to all the wounded, and honorable burial for the dead.[47]

Captain William T. Crawford of Company H of the 85th Indiana tells of another incident that occurred during the same charge:

. . . Though there was plenty of time for musketry fire as the Confederates were seen advancing, for some reason the fire was held and with crunching grind the two armies came together at bayonet points. Horrors of the field were sickening, . . . Rash and fearless the confederates threw themselves against the Union lines, bristling with bayonet points. Crawford saw a Confederate and Yankee deliberately run toward each other with bayonets set, and both weapons took effect, passing entirely through the bodies of each fighter. The black muzzles of the guns stuck out at the back of the men, locked in death, and held together by the grewsome bonds.[48]

The ferocity of the fighting on the front of Coburn's brigade, from which they emerged victorious, strongly attests to the bravery and fighting qualities of these soldiers, which were never questioned again. This was their greatest day.

Coburn's brigade entered the battle with 1,263 men with muskets and fifty-two officers. During the afternoon of July 20, it lost seven officers wounded, thirty-three men killed, 169 men wounded, and seven missing for a total of 216. Alexander B. Crane's 85th Indiana crossed Peach Tree Creek that day with sixteen field, staff, and line officers and 278 enlisted men. In the fighting that day the regiment lost three killed, thirty-two wounded, and three missing. Among the killed were Sergeant Mitchell C. Purcell of Company C, from Terre Haute, Indiana, and Sergeant Charles Ault of Company K, from Bateham, Indiana. Captain John J. Baker, commanding the 19th Michigan was wounded, and Captain David Anderson assumed command of the regiment.[49]

Captain William M. Meredith of the 70th Indiana made the following comment during a discussion of the Battle of Peach Tree Creek:

What impressed me most at the battle was the conspicuous gallantry of General [Colonel] Coburn. I have always held that he saved the Army of the Cumberland that day, and that, had it not been for his promptness, our brigade [Benjamin Harrison's] would have been surprised and driven into the creek.[50]

Coburn, in closing his report of the battle, had this to say of his command:

> ... To all officers and men are due the honors and gratitude earned by heroic valor and enthusiastic devotion to principle, and theirs are the laurels of a victory snatched from the trembling balance of battle which wavered on either hand of our division.[51]

The dismaying sense of failure and the blame that was attached to the brigade for what had happened at Thompson's Station had been laid to rest. The brigade had redeemed itself, not only in the eyes of the men themselves, for that had been accomplished during the many trying days of guarding the railroad and at the Battle of Resaca, but also in the eyes of the rest of the army for their performance at Peach Tree Creek, which was courageous and competent by anybody's standards.

Chapter 13

Atlanta Campaign
The Fall of Atlanta

The day after the Battle of Peach Tree Creek, July 21, 1864, Major General Joseph Hooker's Twentieth Corps and Brigadier General John Newton's Second Division of Major General Oliver O. Howard's Fourth Corps spent the day burying the dead, caring for the wounded, and attending to the usual camp duties. Major General John M. Palmer's Fourteenth Corps remained on the right of Twentieth Corps.[1]

Howard, whose Fourth Corps was somewhat scattered that morning, brought his divisions together into line on the left of Twentieth Corps; with Newton's division on the right, next to Twentieth Corps, Brigadier General Thomas J. Wood's Third Division in the center; and Major General David S. Stanley's First Division on the left.[2]

East of Atlanta, Major General James B. McPherson's Army of the Tennessee continued its advance on this key city. That evening Major General John A. Logan's Fifteenth Corps connected on McPherson's right with Major General John M. Schofield's Army of the Ohio (Twenty-Third Corps); Major General Frank P. Blair's Seventeenth Corps was on the left of Logan's corps, and Major General Grenville M. Dodge's Sixteenth Corps was largely in reserve.[3]

After his unsuccessful attack on Major General George H. Thomas' Army of the Cumberland at Peach Tree Creek July 20, General John B. Hood decided to make another attempt to destroy a part of Sherman's army. His plan this time was to send Lieutenant General William J. Hardee's corps and Major General Joseph Wheeler's cavalry corps by a long and circuitous route for an attack on the extreme left flank and rear of McPherson's Army of the Tennessee east of Atlanta. This attack was to be made early on the morning of July 22. That night, as a preliminary to the attack, Hood withdrew Lieutenant General Alexander P. Stewart's and Major General Benjamin F. Cheatham's corps from their old lines south of Peach Tree Creek to an inner line of works immediately about the city. At the same time he ordered Major General Gustavus W. Smiths' to move with his Georgia Militia from Poplar Springs, near the Atlanta and West Point Railroad, into the trenches on the east side of the inner defenses of Atlanta.[4]

During the night of July 21 Hardee withdrew his command from its old lines in front of the Army of the Cumberland and marched back through the streets of Atlanta until he reached the south side of the city. There he turned and marched eastward then northward, finally halting his leading troops on a line facing northwest, to wait for the rear of his corps to close up.[5]

Early on the morning of July 22, Union pickets, moving forward, found that Hood had withdrawn during the night from his entrenchments in front of the lines of Thomas and Schofield. Sherman immediately ordered a general advance of the army toward Atlanta.[6]

Schofield moved his Twenty-Third Corps forward to the front of the Howard house, where he strongly entrenched a new line. From this position Atlanta was clearly visible, and the enemy's fortifications around the city at this point were just across a deep valley, in which Lewis' Mill was located.[7]

July 22 Howard's Fourth Corps, on the right of Schofield, also advanced toward Atlanta, with Major General David S. Stanley's and Brigadier General Thomas J. Wood's divisions moving by different roads. They encountered the enemy's skirmishers about two miles from the center of the city and deployed. Newton's division came up along the Buck Head and Atlanta road and formed in rear of the other two divisions.[8]

Hooker's Twentieth Corps also advanced to the right of Howard and entrenched on a line about two miles from the center of the city. Brigadier General William T. Ward moved first with his Third Division on the Buck Head and Atlanta road. Colonel Benjamin Harrison's First Brigade, at the head of Ward's division that morning, moved out rapidly on the road for about three miles, with sharp skirmishing, until it came up against a strong force of the enemy. It then turned off from the road and moved obliquely to the right in a southwesterly direction and took position on a high ridge. Colonel John Coburn's Second Brigade and Colonel James Wood's Third Brigade followed Harrison, marching by the flank. When they arrived on the ridge, Coburn's brigade formed on the left of Harrison's line as Wood's brigade formed on the right. Coburn's brigade, which was then on the left of the Twentieth Corps line, connected with the right of Thomas J. Wood's division of Fourth Corps. Coburn immediately fortified his position and sent out skirmishers a half mile to the front.[9]

When Coburn moved forward on the morning of July 22 the formation of his brigade was of column by division in mass, right in front. Lieutenant Colonel Alexander B. Crane's 85th Indiana marched with the brigade that day, and about 10:00 AM took position on a hill to its left and to the left of Harrison's brigade.

When Coburn's brigade was in position, Lieutenant Colonel Edward Bloodgood's 22nd Wisconsin was in the center of the first line, Crane's 85th Indiana was on the right, and Captain David Anderson's 19th Michigan was on the left. Major Levin T. Miller's 33rd Indiana advanced at 9:00 AM and halted in reserve, in rear of the other regiments of the brigade.[10]

Brigadier General John W. Geary, with two of the brigades of his Second Division of Twentieth Corps left his camps at 6:00 AM July 22 and moved forward across rough and broken country in the direction of Atlanta. After marching about one mile, Geary crossed Hood's abandoned entrenchments, turned to the right, and came up to the road running from Howell's Mill to Atlanta. At that time Brigadier General Alpheus S. Williams' First Division of Twentieth Corps and Palmer's Fourteenth Corps were advancing on this road. When they had passed, Geary followed on that road to a point near its junction with the Marietta road. Geary's other brigade, advancing through the woods about a mile to the left, then came up and rejoined the division. At 10:00 AM, Geary took position on the ridge to the right of Ward, about a half mile east of the Howell's Mill road. Williams' division was on the right of Geary. The corps then erected a strong line of breastworks about two miles from the center of Atlanta. Skirmishing and artillery fire greeted Hooker's men as they got into position.[11]

When the work of occupying and fortifying their new positions was completed, Thomas' and Schofield's men held a connected line of entrenchments extending from Thomas' right flank, near the Western and Atlantic Railroad, to the works held by McPherson east of Atlanta. On this new line the corps of Sherman's army were in order from right to left as follows: Palmer's Fourteenth, Hooker's Twentieth, Howard's Fourth, Schofield's Twenty-Third, Logan's Fifteenth, Blair's Seventeenth, and Dodge's Sixteenth.

About noon July 22 Hood finally got his attack started on the left flank of the Army of the Tennessee. Hardee's divisions violently attacked Dodge's Sixteenth Corps and Blair's Seventeenth Corps, and, advancing on the left of Hardee, Cheatham launched a frontal attack on Logan's Fifteenth Corps. There was heavy fighting that lasted throughout the afternoon, and, although Hood's Confederates gained some initial successes, they had been stopped all along the line by the end of the day. Hood had suffered heavy losses, and he then fell back into his lines about Atlanta. McPherson was killed early in the fighting at the Battle of Atlanta, and Logan, as the senior corps commander, assumed temporary command of the Army of the Tennessee. Brigadier General Morgan L. Smith took temporary charge of Logan's Fifteenth Corps.[12]

July 23 the day after the Battle of Atlanta, Hooker ordered changes in his Twentieth Corps line: Ward shortened his line by advancing his division, and the next day Williams and Geary began construction of shorter and stronger lines. Geary occupied his new position, about six hundred yards in front of his former line, on the night of July 26. These changes so shortened the front held by Hooker's corps that during the afternoon of July 27, Ward's division was relieved by a part of Geary's division. Ward then moved to the right about a mile and formed in rear of Geary's line as a reserve. The Army of the Cumberland was in line with Howard's Fourth Corps on the left, Hooker's Twentieth Corps in the center, and Palmer's Fourteenth Corps on the right.[13]

Although Union forces had closely invested Atlanta on the north and east, Hood's lines of communication to the south and the southwest still remained open. That sitution would have to be corrected.

Sherman sent Major General George Stoneman on July 27 with his cavalry of the Army of the Ohio and Brigadier General Kenner Garrard's Second Division of the Cavalry Corps, Army of the Cumberland, out from Decatur on a raid to the Macon and Western Railroad between Griffin and Jonesboro. This attempt, however, ended in disaster when Stoneman was finally captured with about seven hundred of his men.[14]

Brigadier General Edward M. McCook also made an attempt on the railroad with his First Division, Cavalry Corps of the Army of the Cumberland. He left the Chattahoochee River below Sandtown July 27, but he had not gone far when he was surrounded and forced to fight his way back to the Union lines. During the raid he lost about five hundred men, his pack train, and a large number of horses. Neither raid resulted in any serious damage to the railroad.[15]

July 27 Howard assumed command of the Army of the Tennessee, and Logan, who had been in temporary command since July 22, resumed command of his Fifteenth Corps, relieving Morgan L. Smith. Also that day, Stanley relieved Howard in command of Fourth Corps, and Colonel William Grose assumed command of Stanley's former First Division, Fourth Corps. On July 28 Hooker, angered at having been passed over in favor of Howard in command of the Army of the Tennessee, asked to be relieved from further duty with Sherman's army. His request was granted, and Williams was assigned temporary command of Twentieth Corps until Major General Henry W. Slocum could arrive from Vicksburg.[16]

By July 25 the railroad from Chattanooga was in running order up to Thomas' camps, and Sherman was free to abandon the Roswell road as a line of supplies and to transfer the Army of the Tennessee from the extreme left of his army to the extreme right. Accordingly, he issued orders for Logan to move his army by successive corps to the right, directing Schofield to remain in position for the time being, to hold the left of the Union line.[17]

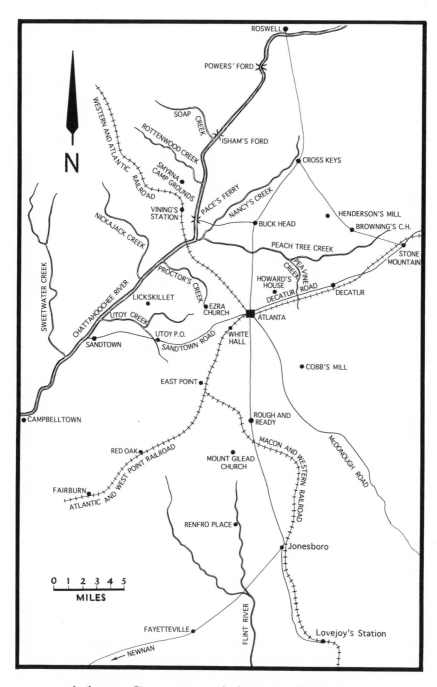

Atlanta Campaign, Atlanta and Vicinity

On the morning of July 27 Dodge's Sixteenth Corps, followed in order by Blair's Seventeenth Corps and Logan's Fifteenth Corps, moved to the right and, passing in rear of the Army of the Ohio and the Army of the Cumberland, took position on the right of Fourteenth Corps. Dodge's corps halted on the right of Palmer, facing east toward Atlanta; Blair's corps formed on the right of Dodge, extending Sherman's line to a point near Ezra Church; and Logan's corps took position on the right of Blair, near Ezra Church, facing south and southwest.[18]

A short time after the Army of the Tennessee began its march to the right, Hood, becoming aware of this movement, sent parts of Lieutenant General Stephen D. Lee's corps (formerly Hood's) and Stewart's corps to strike the flank of Howard's column as it arrived on the west side of Atlanta. On the afternoon of July 28, Lee's corps, followed by Stewart's corps, launched a Confederate attack on the Army of the Tennessee near Ezra Church, but instead of moving against an exposed flank, as they had expected to do, they came up in front of Logan's corps, which had taken position and entrenched on a line at right angles to that of the corps of Dodge and Blair. Logan, with help from the other two corps, managed to hold his ground and inflict a costly defeat on his attackers. The enemy lost about five thousand men killed, wounded, and missing, including General Stewart, Major General William W. Loring, Brigadier General John C. Brown, and Brigadier General George D. Johnston, who were among the wounded.[19]

At 5:00 PM that day, July 28, Ward's division marched to the right from its camps in rear of Geary's division to support Logan's corps in its battle near Ezra Church. The enemy's attacks were repulsed before Ward reached the battlefield, so Ward returned to his camps. The 33rd Indiana of Coburn's brigade did not accompany this movement, but remained in camp as a reserve for Geary's division.[20]

Sherman also ordered Brigadier General Jefferson C. Davis on July 28 to make a reconnaissance with his Second Division of Fourteenth Corps in the direction of Turners Ferry and East Point and, from there, to move toward the right of Howard's Army of the Tennessee. Williams ordered Ward to march with his Third Division of Twentieth Corps in support of Davis. (Brigadier General James D. Morgan commanded the division that day because Davis was ill.)

Morgan marched that day toward Turner's Ferry, but before this movement was completed Hood launched his attack on the Army of the Tennessee near Ezra Church; Morgan then moved to support Howard. The fighting ended before Morgan arrived, however, and he halted for the night. The next morning he moved his division up to the right of the Army of the Tennessee, extending Sherman's line farther to the right.[21]

About 10:00 AM July 29 Ward moved his division to the right, passing in rear of Fourteenth Corps and the Army of the Tennessee, halting for the night in rear of Morgan's (Davis') division. Coburn's brigade was on the right of Ward's division and therefore on the right of the army. Ward fortified his position near the Sandtown road, about six miles west of Atlanta and one mile in advance of the works of the Army of the Tennessee.[22]

The next day Ward moved about one-half mile farther to the right, to the right of Morgan, and again threw up strong works. Coburn's brigade was in the center of the division, with the 85th Indiana on the right of an advanced line and the 22nd Wisconsin on the left. The 33rd Indiana and the 19th Michigan camped in column of division about one-fourth mile to the rear of the other two regiments of the brigade. July 30 Morgan's brigade made a reconnaissance in front of Utoy Creek, but Ward's division remained in camp.[23]

When Stoneman's and McCook's cavalry raids against the railroads running into Atlanta ended in failure, Sherman ordered a further movement of his infantry to the right. Schofield's Army of the Ohio, which was then in position on the left of the Army of the Cumberland, marched out from its encampments on the night of August 1 to the extreme right of the Union line. The next day, Schofield moved up and entrenched on the banks of the North Fork of Utoy Creek in preparation for further operations against Hood's left flank. Howard then advanced his right flank to connect with the Army of the Ohio, thus gaining about one mile of new ground. At that time Ward, near Schofield's right, was ordered to support Schofield if the latter was attacked.[24]

August 2, however, Ward's division, on Sherman's orders, moved back about five miles to the left and camped near the railroad. James Wood's brigade marched at the head of the division, followed by Coburn's brigade and Colonel Benjamin Harrison's brigade. Ward's orders were to relieve Brigadier General Richard W. Johnson's First Division and Brigadier General Absalom Baird's Third Division of Palmer's corps at daylight the next morning.[25]

Baird and Johnson did not leave their positions until 10:00 AM August 3, when Ward's men moved in and took their place. When the replacement was completed, Harrison's brigade was on the left, connecting with Fourth Corps; Coburn's brigade was in the center, with the 85th Indiana in the center of the brigade line; and Colonel James Wood's brigade was on the right, connecting with Sixteenth Corps. Palmer's two divisions moved about five miles to the right and joined Morgan on the right of the Army of the Tennessee.[26]

Ward started a new line of works about two hundred yards in front of Palmer's former line and moved in August 5.[27]

Generally, accounts of the siege of Atlanta indicate that Ward's brigade spent most of its time marching and constructing fortifications, and that the men enjoyed a rather quiet time. Actually, however, there was almost continuous skirmishing and artillery fire, and sharpshooters were a constant and deadly threat. On August 5, 1864, Corporal Wesley A. Brown of Company D of the 85th Indiana was mortally wounded while carrying coffee from the rear to the front line, and August 13 Corporal Miles W. Ratcliff of Company A was killed by a sharpshooter as he was cooking dinner.[28]

In a letter home, Captain Jefferson E. Brant of Company E, then commanding the 85th Indiana, tells of his narrow escape during an artillery exchange as follows:

I must not omit to tell you of my narrow escape. The rebs were shelling us yesterday and a piece of shell passed into our tent, tearing a hole through an oil blanket and passing clear through the tent. If I had been sitting where I was before going out it would have no doubt hit me. I think about it and wonder why I was prompted to leave the spot when I did. Was it a providence or a coincidence? [First Lieutenant Hiram L.] Tillotson [of Company E, adjutant of the regiment], [Assistant Surgeon William V.] Wiles, and old Sergeant Major [Lewis W.] Wells were in the tent at the time.[29]

August 3 Sherman ordered Palmer to move forward with his Fourteenth Corps and cooperate with Schofield in an attempt to force a crossing of Utoy Creek. To facilitate this movement he placed Schofield in command of both his own Twenty-Third Corps and Fourteenth Corps. This arrangement caused Palmer to raise the question of rank, and during the ensuing controversy movements of the two corps were considerably delayed because of a lack of cooperation. Nevertheless, both corps crossed the creek with considerable difficulty and took position on the other side, with Palmer's corps on the left and Schofield's corps on the right.[30]

Hood was constructing a new line of entrenchments that ran along the Sandtown road. He placed Major General William B. Bate's division of Hardee's corps in these works, but he soon abandoned this position and moved to a new line, beginning near the North Fork of Utoy Creek, running southward across the Sandtown road for about a mile and a half, and then following the ridges beyond the southernmost branches of Utoy Creek until it reached the Atlanta and West Point railroad a mile beyond East Point.[31]

Finally, on August 7, because of the controversy over rank, Sherman relieved Palmer from command of Fourteenth Corps at his own request, and assigned Richard W. Johnson to the temporary command of the corps. Two days later, Sherman assigned Jefferson C. Davis to the command of Fourteenth Corps, and Davis assumed permanent command August 24.[32]

Also on August 7 Fourteenth Corps and Twenty-Third Corps pushed skirmishers up close to the enemy's fortifications, but at that point Sherman decided that he had extended his lines about as far as he safely could. He was then convinced that to force the evacuation of Atlanta, he would have to move south with his whole army. Before doing this, he ordered an exploratory artillery bombardment of the city. The guns opened fire August 10 and continued in action day and night for some time, causing fires and considerable destruction in Atlanta, but did not force the enemy to evacuate the forts and entrenched lines about the city.[33]

On August 9 Lieutenant Colonel Crane left for the North on leave, and Captain Brant assumed command of the 85th Indiana.[34] Brant was therefore in command of the regiment during the bombardment, and on August 24, about two weeks later, he wrote to his family about the artillery fire:

> We are still here in the trenches and all is quiet on the front, but this is not the case all along the line. Just up yonder on the railroad to our left Sherman's clock as the boys call it keeps its regular time of throwing 32 pound shells into Atlanta. About every twenty minutes it makes the ground tremble by its terrible click, and away goes a shell hissing and whizzing through the air like a locomotive letting off steam. While I write, the clock keeps striking, and my nerves quake although I have heard it for two weeks. This is what we call 'all quiet on the front'. Down yonder about one-half mile to the right is another irregular clock that throws either 40 or 64 pound balls, sending terrific and thunderous messages. Then away off almost out of hearing are other guns of various caliber that mingle in the dim, and occasionally varies the 'Quiet on the front'. Then just wait awhile and the rebs with their big guns from their forts over yonder let in, and show us that we haven't all the cannon on our side. As yet they have not favored us with their 'Camp Kettles' as the boys call them; but I can hear them as far as they go to the right of us plunging ahead at a 'yelling and demon-like rate'. . . .[35]

During the second week of August 1864, Sherman completed a final extention of his lines somewhat farther to the right, moving Schofield's corps out beyond the crossing of the Campbelltown road and the East Point road.[36]

Meantime, while Sherman was pushing the line out to the right, Fourth Corps and Twentieth Corps continued to hold their positions to the north and northwest of Atlanta. Coburn's brigade remained in camp during the period August 6-9, but on the night of August 9, 1864, engineers laid out a new line of works about three hundred yards in advance of the position then held by Coburn. The men started construction that night and continued work during the next two days, moving into the new entrenchments August 11.[37]

The 85th Indiana was in the fourth line of these new works. The other lines were about two hundred yards apart, with the first line within about two hundred yards of the enemy's works, although there were places where the front line and the enemy's line were only about one hundred yards apart.[38]

William Neet, a private in Company G of the 85th Indiana, in a letter to his wife, told something about life in the breastworks.

> *... we have had more men killed around our breastworks than we have in battle Just by flying balls that is shot at our skirmish lines. I have heard them pass me that had come I believe considerably over a mile. it appears like our boys has got so used to hearing them whizing around that they hardly notice them without they hit them. i have heard of 2 of our men gitting shot through the head while in their bunks asleep never knowed what hurt them. the other night while i was up on guard I thought that I would count the shots that was fired on the skirmish lines for one minute but at times they fired so fast I couldent count them but I think I counted a hundred shots in a minnet but they don't fire so all the time and some times faster.*[39]

Wheeler moved northward from Covington, Georgia, with eight Confederate cavalry brigades on August 10 on a raid to destroy railroads bringing forward supplies for Sherman's army from Nashville. Wheeler struck the Western and Atlantic Railroad north of Marietta at Cassville, Calhoun, and south of Dalton, before moving on into East Tennessee in search of forage. He had little effect on the outcome of the campaign.[40]

Believing that a cavalry raid on the Macon and Western Railroad might be successful while Wheeler was absent from Hood's army, Sherman sent Brigadier General Judson Kilpatrick on another expedition against Hood's communications south of Atlanta. On August 18 Kilpatrick left Sandtown with his Third Division, Cavalry Corps, Army of the Cumberland, and arrived at Jonesboro during the evening of the next day. After destroying about a mile of track, he was attacked by Hood's remaining cavalry commanded by Brigadier General Frank Armstrong and Brigadier General Lawrence S. (Sul) Ross. Kilpatrick moved out about midnight and rode southward to Lovejoy's Station, but he then had to fight his way through the enemy's lines, as had his predecessors, to reach Decatur August 22, without having accomplished his mission.[41]

After Kilpatrick's failure, Sherman was convinced that the cavalry alone could not cut Hood's lines of communications and that a strong force of infantry would be needed to accomplish this mission. He decided to put a plan in operation he had been considering for some time. He ordered the Twentieth Corps to move back to the Chattahoochee River to entrench a position there protecting the crossings of the river, and he directed the rest of his army to prepare for a march to the south of Atlanta.[42]

The opening moves of Sherman's new and final operation against Atlanta began on the night of August 25. At that time, Stanley's Fourth Corps, which then occupied the lines on the left of the army, left its entrenchments at dark and marched to the right, in rear of Williams' Twentieth Corps to begin its movement toward the south of Atlanta. After Stanley's departure, Garrard's dismounted cavalry moved into the lines vacated by Fourth Corps.[43]

Williams began the withdrawal of his Twentieth Corps from its line of entrenchments at about 8:00 PM, and that same day, he massed his troops about one-fourth to one-half mile in rear of his former position. Brigadier General Joseph F. Knipe's First Division, together with Colonel Harrison's brigade of Ward's division, assembled near the Montgomery's Ferry road; Geary's division near the Howell's Mill and Pace's Ferry road; and Ward, with Coburn's and James Wood's brigades of his division, near the Turner's Ferry road.[44]

Williams ordered his division commanders to begin their march toward the Chattahoochee River as soon as the rear of Fourth Corps had passed their respective positions. Knipe's First Division was to take position at Montgomery's Ferry to protect the railroad crossing and the bridges across the river; Geary's Second Division was to occupy the high ground about the bridge at Pace's Ferry; and Ward's Third Division was to hold the hills on the south side of the river at Turner's Ferry with Coburn's Second Brigade and James Wood's Third Brigade to protect the pontoon bridge at that point. Harrison's brigade accompanied Knipe that day.[45]

Because Fourth Corps was late in moving out of the way, it was not until early on the morning of August 26, 1864, that Williams' corps could begin its march to the Chattahoochee River.[46]

Knipe's division arrived on the river at Montgomery's Ferry at daybreak August 26 and took position across the Marietta road, east of the Chattahoochee River. Harrison's brigade of Ward's division was held in reserve for a time near the railroad bridge to determine whether the enemy was following Twentieth Corps.[47]

Geary did not move with his division until midnight August 25, arriving at Pace's Ferry at 4:00 the next morning and forming his brigades in line, with his right covering the bridge at the ferry and connecting on its left with Williams' division.[48]

Ward began his movement at 6:00 AM August 25, when Coburn sent his 33rd Indiana to Turner's Ferry on the Chattahoochee River to assist in the construction of fortifications for the new camp. The regiment arrived about noon and immediately started work. Coburn waited with the rest of the brigade until Fourth Corps had passed. He started toward Turner's Ferry at 8:00 that evening. Coburn's pickets, however, were not withdrawn until 2:00 the next morning.

The road taken by Coburn was crowded with wagons and troops, and the brigade did not arrive at the river until early on the morning of August 26. It then went into camp in a single line on the south side of the Turner's Ferry road, with its right resting on the river and its left on the road. The 85th Indiana was on the right center of this line. The men immediately began strengthening the works started by the 33rd Indiana.[49]

James Wood's brigade followed Coburn toward the Chattahoochee, arriving at Turner's Ferry that afternoon and taking position on the left of Coburn, with its left on the river and its right on the Turner's Ferry road.[50]

General Slocum arrived at the front from Vicksburg August 27 and assumed command of Twentieth Corps, relieving Williams, who resumed command of First Division. Knipe returned to his First Brigade of the division. Slocum then sent Harrison's brigade to the north side of the Chattahoochee to occupy Johnston's old line of works. Here he could cover the trains and the commissary and ordnance depots. Both of Harrison's flanks rested on the river.[51]

On the morning of August 27, Confederate Major General Samuel G. French, with Brigadier General Matthew D. Ector's brigade (commanded by Colonel William H. Young) and Brigadier General Claudius W. Sears' brigade, with a section of artillery, made a reconnaissance toward the Chattahoochee River. About 10:00 French appeared in front of Coburn's line, drove in the pickets and opened with his artillery. French made no serious infantry attack, and, satisfied with what he had learned, withdrew about noon.[52]

Meanwhile, Sherman continued his movement to the south of Atlanta. Stanley arrived on Utoy Creek August 26 and massed the divisions of his Fourth Corps in rear of Fourteenth Corps. At that time Fourteenth Corps was in position on Utoy Creek, west of Atlanta, and nearly opposite East Point. It was detached from the Army of the Cumberland and was acting under the orders of Schofield, commanding the Army of the Ohio. When General Davis assumed command of Fourteenth Corps, he withdrew his troops from their field works and went into bivouac on the south side of Utoy Creek, leaving his skirmishers to occupy the entrenchments.[53]

At 8:00 PM August 26 the three corps of Howard's Army of the Tennessee began to withdraw from their positions in front of Atlanta and march in two columns toward the Atlanta and West Point Railroad by roads to the west of Fourth Corps and Fourteenth Corps.

Logan's Fifteenth Corps, marching all night, arrived in the vicinity of Camp Creek early the next morning. Blair's Seventeenth Corps and Brigadier General Thomas E. G. Ransom's Sixteenth Corps, marching by way of Lickskillet and Dry Pond, also reached Camp Creek at about the same time. Ransom had assumed command of Sixteenth Corps when Dodge was wounded August 19.[54]

By the evening of August 27, all of Sherman's army except Twentieth Corps was en echelon along the Sandtown road between Atlanta and Sandtown. The next day, Fourth Corps and Fourteenth Corps of the Army of the Cumberland advanced to the Atlanta and West Point Railroad, near Red Oak. That evening, August 28, the Army of the Tennessee reached Fairburn, about five miles to the southwest of the Army of the Cumberland and on the same road.[55]

The armies of Howard and Thomas spent the day of August 29 destroying the railroad, and Schofield moved his Army of the Ohio four miles to the southeast of East Point.[56]

August 30 Sherman's army, except Schofield's Army of the Ohio, moved forward between the Macon and Western and the Atlanta and West Point railroads. The Army of the Tennessee marched that morning on two roads toward Jonesboro. Logan, followed by the trains, marched on the main road from Fairburn; and Ransom, followed by Blair, took a road to the right of the main road. Howard, with Logan's and Ransom's corps, reached the Flint River northwest of Jonesboro that day, and during the evening Logan crossed the river and took position on the east side. Ransom formed his corps in line on the west side of the river, opposite the right of Logan's line, facing south. Blair's corps arrived the next morning, but was held west of the river in readiness to move if needed.[57]

Back in Atlanta, when the direction of Sherman's latest movements became known, Hood ordered Hardee to move to Jonesboro with his own and Stephen D. Lee's corps and to attack Howard's forces the next morning. Major General Patrick R. Cleburne, commanding Hardee's corps, was in position at Jonesboro at 9:00 AM August 31, but Lee did not arrive until later that morning. Hardee was finally ready, and at 3:00 that afternoon he strongly attacked the Army of the Tennessee, but was repulsed with serious losses. The attack was pushed hard, but that evening the Confederates retired to within their lines.[58]

Farther north, on the morning of August 31, Schofield moved to the Macon and Western Railroad about one mile south of Rough and Ready. Stanley's Fourth Corps took a road that ran in the same direction but a little farther to the south and, after arriving on the railroad at 4:00 PM, began destroying track. Schofield's column reached the railroad about 3:00 PM, and marched northward to Rough and Ready, where Cox's division went into camp. Hascall's division, which followed Cox to the railroad, moved southward, destroying the track.[59]

By the night of August 31 Sherman knew that his troops held the railroad from Rough and Ready to a point near Jonesboro and that Hardee and Lee were in position in front of that town. Thomas then ordered Davis to march with Fourteenth Corps to the left of the Army of the Tennessee and to destroy as much track as he could. He also ordered Fourth Corps to move down the railroad and destroy the track until it reached Davis' corps. Sherman also ordered Schofield to tear up the track south of Rough and Ready.[60]

Hood, misunderstanding Cox's movement northward to Rough and Ready, believed that the Federals were moving on Atlanta from the south, and he ordered Lee to return with his corps to aid in defending the city. This left Hardee, with only his own corps, in an isolated position at Jonesboro.[61]

When Sherman learned on the afternoon of September 1 that Hardee was alone at Jonesboro, he immediately ordered Thomas to concentrate his Army of the Cumberland and, together with the Army of the Tennessee, attempt to surround and capture Hardee's corps. It was near 5:00 PM before any of his divisions were in position to attack, and the fighting ended at dark without decisive results.[62]

On September 1 Hood, learning that he had made a serious mistake in leaving Hardee's corps alone at Jonesboro, ordered Lee to take position to cover the withdrawal of Stewart's corps and Gustavus W. Smith's Georgia Militia from Atlanta. Stewart's corps and the militia began to leave about 5:00 PM that day, then the pickets were drawn in, and the evacuation was completed about 11:00 PM. Sometime after midnight, demolition details set fire to an ammunition train that had been left behind when the railroad was destroyed south of Atlanta, and a violent explosion rocked the city, causing considerable damage. Hardee also evacuated his position at Jonesboro that night, and on September 2 Hood's army was again assembled at Lovejoy's Station.[63]

Sherman at Jonesboro and Slocum at the Chattahoochee River heard the sounds of the explosions at Atlanta during the night, and early the next morning, September 2, Slocum sent out troops of his Twentieth Corps to find out what had happened. Ward, commanding the Third Division of Twentieth Corps, ordered Coburn to move out with nine hundred infantry from Turner's Ferry on a reconnaissance in the direction of the city. It was to be a portentous and memorable order, for it would allow men of Coburn's brigade to be the first into the city the North had waited so long to take.

Coburn took with him five hundred men from his Second Brigade as follows: five companies of the 85th Indiana, command by Captain William T. Crawford; seven companies of the 19th Michigan, commanded by Captain Frank D. Baldwin; some troops of the 22nd Wisconsin, commanded by Captain Oliver T. May; and a detachment of the 33rd Indiana, commanded by Lieutenant Benjamin H. Freeland. The other four hundred men were from Wood's Third Brigade, commanded by Captain Charles P. Wickham. In addition, twenty-five mounted men of Colonel Horace Capron's brigade of Stoneman's cavalry division moved out as an advance in front of the infantry, commanded by Captain Henry M. Scott of the 70th Indiana, who was acting assistant inspector general of Ward's division. Two hundred and forty men of the infantry also went forward as skirmishers and flankers for the main column.[64]

Coburn advanced without opposition until he reached the breastworks recently abandoned by Twentieth Corps. There was a brief delay there, caused by a slight skirmish with a few enemy mounted men. What happened next is best described by Coburn in his report of the occupation of Atlanta:

. . . we proceeded through the lines of the enemy's works, finding them abandoned. A brigade of enemy cavalry was found to be in the city and we advanced cautiously. I was met in the suburbs by Mr. [James M.] Calhoun, the Mayor, with a committee of citizens bearing a flag of truce. He surrendered the city to me, saying "he only asked protection for persons and property." This was at 11AM I asked him if the rebel cavalry was yet in the city. He replied that [Brigadier General Samuel W.] Ferguson's brigade was there, but on the point of leaving. I replied that my force was moving into the city and that unless that force retired there would be a fight in which neither person nor property would be safe, and that if necessary I would burn the houses of citizens to dislodge the enemy; that I did not otherwise intend to injure persons or property of the citizens unless used against us. I order my skirmishers to advance, and they proceeded through the city, the cavalry evacuating the place. . . . As we passed through the streets many of the citizens ran gladly out to meet us, welcoming us as deliverers from the despotism of the Confederacy; others regarded us with apprehension and begged us to be spared from robbery. I assured them they would be safe from this.

Coburn's losses on his reconnaissance to Atlanta were five killed and twenty-two wounded.[65]

And so, Coburn, with troops from his Second Brigade and from James

Wood's Third Brigade of Ward's division, with some cavalry, were the first to enter the fortress toward which all earlier efforts had been directed. It was a moment of glory and realization of unit pride.

Francis Crawford of the 85th Indiana accompanied Coburn's force toward Atlanta. According to a story told after the war, Crawford rode ahead of the skirmish line and into Atlanta on Center Street. When he reached the foot of a hill over which the street ran, he saw a troop of Confederate cavalry drawn up in line across the street, and they appeared ready to charge. Crawford then rode back and rejoined his men, but he had been inside the city proper, and thus it was claimed that a resident of Terre Haute, Indiana, was the first Union soldier to enter Atlanta after its evacuation.[66]

After the war, there were various claims that several officers were the first to enter Atlanta, and frequently in these accounts Coburn's name was not mentioned at all. Finally on December 31, 1888, G. M. Walrad, Editor of the *American Tribune* asked Coburn what actually happened that long-ago day in September 1864. Coburn replied, giving an account of the occupation of Atlanta, and concluding with the statement:

> . . . I have seen various accounts of this matter [other officers preceding Coburn into Atlanta], but like many works of fiction on the same subject, they do not agree with each other and contain very few grains of truth, and don't deserve contradiction.[67]

The other two divisions of Twentieth Corps also sent out reconnaissances toward Atlanta that morning, joining Coburn's troops in the city. When Slocum learned that his men had occupied Atlanta, he immediately ordered forward the greater part of his corps to take position in and around the city, and then proceeded there in person.[68]

In accordance with Slocum's orders, Ward ordered Lieutenant Colonel Bloodgood of the 22nd Wisconsin to move up from Turner's Ferry with five hundred men of Coburn's brigade to reinforce the troops in the city. Bloodgood arrived with his men at sunset, and the rest of the brigade under Major Levin T. Miller of the 33rd Indiana came up at 11:00 the next morning. Harrison's brigade, and that part of James Wood's brigade that had not gone forward that morning, remained on the Chattahoochee River for the time being. September 4, 1864, Wood moved with the rest of his brigade to Atlanta.[69]

Shortly after Slocum arrived in Atlanta, he ordered Coburn to move with his brigade, which was at that time in the old enemy works in the southeastern part of the city, to take position on the right of the Decatur road east of the city.[70]

September 2 and 3 Williams moved forward from the Chattahoochee to Atlanta the three brigades of his division and placed them in the old enemy's works north and east of the city.[71]

Geary's brigades entered Atlanta on September 2nd through the 4th, and occupied the enemy's works south and west of the city.[72]

On September 4 James Wood moved to Atlanta with his Third Brigade of Ward's division and the baggage train, relieving Mindil's brigade in the southern part of the city.[73]

The stronghold of Atlanta had finally fallen, and Coburn's brigade had played a significant role in the final phase of its fall. It had been a long and difficult campaign, and while the soldiers of the brigade were pleased with their accomplishments, they could not help looking back and remembering the price they had paid along the way.

According to Captain Jefferson E. Brant, who was commanding the 85th Indiana at the end of the Atlanta Campaign, the regiment left La Vergne Tennessee, in April 1864 with 650 men and arrived in Atlanta with 318. He states that there were 127 men killed and wounded during this period. The 85th Indiana lost during the period from May 2 to September 2, 1864, eleven men killed, three officers and 105 men wounded, and two missing, for a total of 121.[74]

Brant goes on to say in his *History of the Eighty-Fifth Indiana*:

> Just two years after our muster in at Camp Dick Thompson, Atlanta fell. On the 19th of April we left Lavergne, Tenn. and on May 4th we left Ringgold, Ga. for the campaign. For 120 days we were on the fighting line and 96 days of that time we were either under fire or within hearing of the boom of cannon or the rattle of musketry. Not a day without rations. General Hooker has sustained his reputation as a good feeder and a good fighter.[75]

Sherman, with the rest of the army, pursued the retreating Confederates from Jonesboro to the vicinity of Lovejoy's Station and skirmished for a time to develop their position. Then, during the period September 5-8, Sherman withdrew his army to the vicinity of Atlanta, where the men could rest while he prepared for his next campaign. Thomas' Army of the Cumberland occupied Atlanta, and Howard's Army of the Tennessee moved to East Point and went into camp, with Schofields' Army of the Ohio taking position at Decatur. The cavalry covered the front and flanks of the army.[76]

Chapter 14

Occupation of Atlanta

The organization of Twentieth Corps at the time of the occupation of Atlanta was as follows:

TWENTIETH CORPS, Major General Henry W. Slocum

First Division, Brigadier General Alpheus S. Williams
    First Brigade, Brigadier General Joseph F. Knipe
    Second Brigade, Brigadier General Thomas H. Ruger
    Third Brigade, Colonel Horace Boughton

Second Division, Brigadier General John W. Geary
    First Brigade, Colonel Ario Pardee, Jr.
    Second Brigade, Colonel George W. Mindil
    Third Brigade, Colonel David Ireland

(Note: David Ireland died of disease September 10, 1864, and he was succeeded in command of Third Brigade by Colonel Henry A. Barnum.)

Third Division, Brigadier General William T. Ward
    First Brigade, Colonel Benjamin Harrison
    Second Brigade, Colonel John Coburn
    Third Brigade, Colonel James Wood, Jr.[1]

It has been noted in the preceding chapter that after Hood evacuated Atlanta on September 2, 1864, troops of Slocum's Twentieth Corps, including Coburn's brigade, marched in and occupied the city, and that later the rest of the corps came up and moved into defensive positions along the old line of Confederate works about the city. From that time until the beginning of Sherman's march through Georgia in mid-November 1864, Twentieth Corps occupied Atlanta and the surrounding country for a distance of about one and a half miles.

When Slocum finally established his lines, the divisions of his corps were in position as follows:

Williams' First Division occupied the rebel works on the northeast side of Atlanta, north of the Decatur road.[2]

Geary's Second Division was south and west of Atlanta, with Mindil's Second Brigade on the right of the McDonough road, one mile south of the city; Ireland's Third Brigade was in line between the right of the Second Brigade and the Macon and Western Railroad, southwest of the city; and Pardee's First Brigade was to the right of Ireland's brigade and on the right of the railroad, west of Atlanta.[3]

Ward's Third Division was in line covering the east and southeast part of Atlanta. Coburn's Second Brigade was south of the Decatur road, east of Atlanta, and James Wood's Third Brigade was on the left of the McDonough road, connecting on its left with the right of Coburn's brigade and on its right with Mindil's brigade of Geary's division. Wood's brigade occupied the works originally built by the enemy south of the city and later abandoned. Harrison's First Brigade of Ward's division remained in the rear until September 16 to guard the bridges on the Chattahoochee and the supplies accumulated there, and it then moved up to Atlanta to rejoin the division. It remained in the suburbs of Atlanta until September 23, and then the brigade, under the command of Colonel Franklin C. Smith, moved to the Chattahoochee to guard the railroad bridge. Second Brigade, then commanded by Lieutenant Colonel Edward Bloodgood, and Third Brigade, commanded by Lieutenant Colonel Philo B. Buckingham, remained on picket duty, guarding the division front, which extended from the McDonough road on the right, where it connected with the pickets of Geary's division, to the Georgia Railroad on the left, where it connected with the pickets of Williams' division.[4]

A short time after the occupation of Atlanta by the Army of the Cumberland, the 19th Michigan was temporarily detached from Coburn's brigade and ordered to report to Colonel Amos Beckwith, chief commissary of subsistence, Military Division of the Mississippi. Beckwith assigned the regiment to guard and fatigue duty in the quartermaster and commissary departments, under the command of Colonel Nirom N. Crane of the 107th New York, who was commanding a Provisional Brigade in the city. Company B of the 19th Michigan was assigned to duty at the Soldiers' Home, and other companies guarded the depot. The rest of the men of the regiment worked at loading, unloading, and storing freight.[5]

From September 3 to October 4, the 85th Indiana was in position on the right of the Georgia Railroad, near the line of old rebel works covering Atlanta on the southeast. During this period the regiment changed position five times, but it finally went into camp on that part of the line of works near the city cemetery. It remained there during the occupation of Atlanta.[6]

When Sherman occupied Atlanta he decided to convert the city into a military garrison or depot, and to this end he ordered that all citizens and families leave as soon as possible.[7]

On September 8 Mayor James M. Calhoun addressed the following notice to the Citizens of Atlanta:

> Major General Sherman instructs me to say to you that you must all leave Atlanta; that as many of you as want to go North can do so, and that as many as want to go South can do so, and that all can take with them their movable property, servants included, if they want to go, but that no force is to be used, and that he will furnish transportation for persons and property as far as Rough and Ready, from whence it is expected General Hood will assist in carrying it on. Like transportation will be furnished for people and property going North, and it will be required that all things contemplated by this notice will be carried into execution as soon as possible . . . .
>
> James M. Calhoun
> Mayor[8]

George E. Farrington, quartermaster of the 85th Indiana, aided in removing the citizens of Atlanta to Rough and Ready. In a letter to his mother he describes his interesting experiences:

> *My dear Mother,*
> *As I have told you in previous letters, we have had an armistise for 10 days for the purpose of sending the rebel families into the rebel lines. On the morning of the 20th inst. I took charge of the Division train bound South for Dixie. I had 108 wagons loaded to the bows with household & kitchen furniture and the inmates of the house. We went to Rough and Ready Station on the Macon R.R. when we met the flag of truce and the rebel troops. As we hurried them down so fast the rebs could not keep up with their share of the task to receive them from us, so that I had to spend two days with them before I could get unloaded. We mingled freely with their officers and conversed on all matters, politics inclusive. I for a portion of the time was the only Federal Officer with them and at rebel Head Qrts with some ten or a dozen Confederate Officers. I spent the most of it Wednesday morning we played "wish," "Euchre" &c and had a very pleasant time generally. They were very courteous and polite, and studiously avoided mention of anything that might give offence to me. It was indeed a strange sight to see the Blue and Gray laughing & chatting away, as if old friends. It looked stranger however to see Rebel soldiers on duty, armed and equipped, pacing their*

beats. By invitation I dined with them, at the same time I gave them some sugar and coffee, which I assure you was acceptable for they had none at all (as far as I could see) We had corn bread and some mutton, which formed our dinner. By force of circumstances they live very plainly. Their officers were in full dress & looked very trim in their suit of Gray, which were apparently new. But the new did not bear the appearance of soldiers. Their uniform being of a light clay color and of coarse texture, & the worse for wear.

In company with a Confed Officer I witnessed their guard mounting & and them releiving their pickets. They all seem anxious to learn the news from the East, and just before we left them I read them Sec'y Stantons despatch to Gen Sherman, of Gen Sheridans victory, which I had just received from one of our officers. They looked very doleful and one asked me, "Lieut you have that officially"? I assured them that it might be relied on. Among their number was one Major Mason of Hoods staff, who is a regular "hale fellow well met", jolly, free & easy always, and is so considered I should judge, by their officers, for he seemed to be the leading spirit. When he heard it, he remarked, "I knew there was something up, no mail for several days". And continued "I'll go [to] the gulf, and climb a persimmon tree"! What then Major, I asked, "I will cut the tree off below me"! Most of them endeavored to appear confident and put on a bold front, but it is very evident they are very much depressed at their prospects. They know their losses, defeats and that our army is increasing daily, theirs is decreasing rapidly in numbers. We have plenty to eat, they have not, by their own acknowledgments. My friend, the Major, informed me that they fed over ten thousand citizens, while in this city, daily. I heard him remark, to a lady, in reply to some inquiry of hers, about where they would go & what they would do,-" Madam, God only knows, we cannot spare much now, and winter is approaching!" It is indeed a fearful prospect for the citizens of the South, and untold suffering will be felt among them, and is already manifesting itself. Every thing is taken for the army, what is left the citizens keep.

They expressed no desire to get rebel money from us, but were anxious to get "greenbacks": and they lay it by, as the Major says, "for a rainy day."[9]

General John B. Hood made no movement against Atlanta during the first month of its occupation, and Coburn's brigade and the rest of the army in and around the city were given an opportunity to rest and recuperate from the long and arduous campaign just completed. They served on guard and fatigue duty and made occasional reconnaissances into the surrounding country. The men were also issued clothing and equipment to put them in condition for future operations.[10]

While Sherman's forces were in camp in and about Atlanta, there were many changes in the organization of the divisions and brigades of the armies, necessitated by musterings out and regimental losses suffered during the grueling Atlanta Campaign.[11]

Taking advantage of the lull in the fighting, many of the officers left for their homes on leaves of absence, and there were others whose terms of service had expired; many units of the army were left under temporary commanders. For example, at one time three of the four regiments of Coburn's Second Brigade were under the command of captains, and the 85th Indiana was commanded by Major Jefferson E. Brant.[12]

On September 14 Major General John M. Schofield went north to East Tennessee and Kentucky on department business, leaving Brigadier General Jacob D. Cox in temporary command of the Army of the Ohio at Decatur.[13]

There were also several changes in the higher command of Ward's division during September 1864. On September 18, 1864, Benjamin Harrison left the army in Georgia, with orders to report to Governor Oliver P. Morton of Indiana for special duty, and Daniel Dustin, colonel of the 105th Illinois, assumed command of Harrison's First Brigade during his absence. On September 23 Ward departed on leave, and Colonel Daniel Dustin assumed command of Third Division. Franklin C. Smith, colonel of the 102nd Illinois regiment, assumed command of First Brigade.[14]

When Harrison arrived in Indianapolis, Morton directed him to work for the Republican party in the upcoming state and National elections of 1864. In addition, at Ward's request, he recruited soldiers for the 33rd Indiana, the 70th Indiana, and the 85th Indiana regiments.[15]

Harrison was unable to rejoin his brigade until it reached Raleigh, North Carolina, at the end of Sherman's Campaign of the Carolinas.[16]

The terms of enlistment of the non-veterans of the 33rd Indiana of Coburn's brigade expired September 16, 1864, but it was not until September 19 that the muster-out rolls were completed. On that date 143 enlisted men of the regiment were mustered out. According to an earlier order, none of the commissioned officers of the regiment were to be mustered out except those who had served three years from the date of first muster as officers. This order was later modified, however, and those officers who wished to resign were permitted to do so.

Colonel John Coburn first noticed the appearance of a slight hernia while on duty near Cumberland Gap in the summer of 1862, and it slowly became larger during the following months. Finally, while near Dallas, Georgia, during the Atlanta Campaign, it became much enlarged and quite painful. He reported to Dr. Wilson Hobbs, the Brigade Surgeon, for examination. He was advised to wear a truss constantly, which he did. Finally, however, he decided that he could no longer serve effectively in the field under such conditions and tendered his resignation.[17]

September 20 Colonel Coburn, Captain Edward T. McCrea, Captain Charles Day, First Lieutenant William J. Day, and Second Lieutenant Jefferson C. Farr—all of the 33rd Indiana—were mustered out, and the following day Coburn took leave of the regiment and of the brigade. On September 22 the officers of the 33rd Indiana, including Coburn, and the enlisted men who had just been mustered out, left on a train for Indianapolis. Lieutenant Colonel Bloodgood of the 22nd Wisconsin assumed command of the Second Brigade when Coburn departed, and Buckingham took command of Bloodgood's regiment. Major Levin T. Miller, commanding the 33rd Indiana Regiment, resigned the next day.[18]

James Wood departed on leave September 23, and the next day Buckingham assumed command of Wood's Third Brigade of Ward's division.[19]

Following the departure for home of the non-veterans of the 33rd Indiana, the regiment was reorganized, and new officers were selected. Captain James E. Burton of Company H was chosen to lead the regiment. He assumed command September 24, and on November 8 he received his commission as lieutenant colonel. He was re-mustered two days later.[20]

The parents of James E. Burton had moved from their home in Kentucky at an early date and settled near the town of Mount Tabor, about two miles southeast of the present-day town of Gosport, in what is now Monroe County, Indiana. It was here that Burton was born September 23, 1824. As a boy, he spent most of his time around his father's grist mill and farm and later became a merchant in Mount Tabor.

March 23, 1848, James was married to Cynthia A. Buskirk. He then sold his business interests and bought a farm a few miles to the north in Baker Township in Morgan County, Indiana. There he settled down and became a successful farmer, stock raiser, and trader.

At the outbreak of war, Burton raised a company from among his neighbors, and with it reported to Camp Morton in Indianapolis in August 1861. There he was elected and commissioned captain of the company, which was later designated as Company H of the 33rd Indiana Regiment. Burton was later given command of the regiment and remained in command until after the war, when he was mustered out July 21, 1865.[21]

On September 18, 1864, Hood began to leave Lovejoy's Station on a movement to destroy Sherman's line of communications with the North, which he hoped would force the withdrawal of Federal troops from Atlanta. On that day Hood moved his army westward to Palmetto Station, where he covered the Atlanta and West Point Railroad. When Hood left Lovejoy's Station, his three corps were commanded by Lieutenant General William J. Hardee, Lieutenant General Stephen D. Lee, and Lieutenant General Alexander P. Stewart. But on September 28 Major General Benjamin F. Cheatham relieved Hardee in command of his corps. Major General Joseph Wheeler commanded the cavalry, which had been substantially reinforced.[22]

The Left Wing of Sixteenth Corps, Army of the Tennessee, was discontinued September 22, and Brigadier General John M. Corse's Second Division, Sixteenth Corps, was transferred to Fifteenth Corps as Fourth Division, and Brigadier General John W. Fuller's Fourth Division, Sixteenth Corps was transferred to Seventeenth Corps as First Division.[23]

On September 21 Major General Nathan B. Forrest's cavalry crossed the Tennessee River below Florence, Alabama, and began a raid on the Tennessee and Alabama Railroad (Nashville and Decatur Railroad). He moved northward by way of Athens and Sulphur Creek Trestle and arrived in front of Pulaski September 27.[24]

When Sherman learned of Forrest's movement, he sent Brigadier General John Newton's Second Division of Fourth Corps to Chattanooga, and he sent Corse from East Point with his Fourth Division of Fifteenth Corps for Rome, Georgia, to oppose Forrest and help keep open the rail communications with Nashville.[25]

Thus, late in September 1864 Sherman was aware that Forrest was in middle Tennessee with his cavalry, and that Hood was apparently moving in that direction. He sent George H. Thomas, commanding the Army of the Cumberland, back to Chattanooga with Brigadier General James D. Morgan's Second Division of Fourteenth Corps to aid in the defense of Tennessee from possible invasion. Thomas went up September 29, and Morgan's division followed the same day. Thomas then moved on to Nashville October 3. He proceeded to organize the new troops arriving there and to make preliminary preparations to meet the expected enemy offensive.[26]

On September 30, 1864, Henry W. Slocum's Twentieth Corps was organized as follows:

First Division, Brigadier General Alpheus S. Williams
    First Brigade, Colonel Warren W. Packer
    Second Brigade, Colonel Ezra A. Carman
    Third Brigade, James S. Robinson

COLONEL JOHN COBURN'S FAREWELL ADDRESS

HEADQUARTERS SECOND BRIGADE,
THIRD DIVISION, TWENTIETH ARMY CORPS
ATLANTA, GEORGIA, SEPTEMBER 20, 1864

Soldiers of the Second Brigade:

My term of service has expired and I am about to be separated from you. We have been associated as a brigade almost two years. We have borne in that time all the burdens and endured all the trials and hardships of war together. This experience has made us friends—such friends as only suffering and toil together can make. In that time you have shared an eventful part in the great struggle of the age. In Tennessee, Kentucky, and Georgia you have nobly illustrated the history of your own states of Indiana, Michigan, and Wisconsin. That history cannot be written without a record of your calm patience, disciplined courage, and heroic daring. The bloody and desperate battle at Thompson Station in Tennessee gave early proof of your valor. While in the last campaign, at Resaca, Cassville, New Hope Church, Culp's Farm, Peach Tree Creek, and Atlanta you have, in the front of the fight, borne straight onward your victorious banners. At Resaca your flags were the first to wave on the enemy's ramparts, the fury of your onset redeemed the day's disaster, at Peach Tree Creek your charge rivaled the most famous feats of arms in the annals of war, and at Atlanta your ranks were the first to climb the works and take possession of that renowned city.

The Thirty-Third Indiana at Wild Cat fought the first battle and won the first victory gained by the Army of the Cumberland, and the united brigade fired the last shot at the flying foe as he fled from his stronghold in Atlanta.

But not alone in the stormy and fiery fight have you been tried. You have by long marches, by herculean labors on field-works, by cheerful obedience, by watching that knew no surprise, and by toil that knew no rest or weariness, eclipsed the fame of your daring in battle and placed high above the glitter of victorious arms the steady light of your solid virtues.

We have lived together as brethren in a great common cause. We part, our hearts glowing with the same patriotic ardor, and hereafter, when the war is over and the light of home is smiling around you, you will have no prouder memories than those associated with this brigade.

Your comrades in arms are sleeping beneath the clods in the valley from Ohio to Atlanta, and from Atlanta to Richmond. Faithful, patient, and brave, they have given to their country and God whatever martyrs and heroes can give, and as one by one they fell out from your glorious ranks they have added new testimony to the sacredness of your cause.

My friends and soldiers, farewell.

John Coburn, Colonel
Thirty-Third Indiana Volunteers, Commanding Brigade[27]

Second Division, Brigadier General John W. Geary
   First Brigade, Colonel John Flynn
   Second Brigade, Colonel Patrick H. Jones
   Third Brigade, Colonel Henry A. Barnum

Third Division, Colonel Daniel Dustin
   First Brigade, Colonel Franklin C. Smith
   Second Brigade, Lieutenant Colonel Edward Bloodgood
   Third Brigade, Lieutenant Colonel Philo B. Buckingham

The regiments of Second Brigade, Third Division were commanded as follows: 33rd Indiana, Captain James E. Burton; 85th Indiana, Major Jefferson E. Brant; 19th Michigan, Captain David J. Easton; and 22nd Wisconsin, Captain Alphonzo G. Kellam.[28]

HOOD'S MARCH NORTHWARD TOWARD TENNESSEE

Hood remained at Palmetto, Georgia, until September 29, 1864, and he then crossed the Chattahoochee River and marched toward Lost Mountain. He arrived there October 3, and the next day sent Stewart's corps on to the railroad at Ackworth and Big Shanty. Upon arriving there Stewart sent Major General Samuel G. French's division to destroy the railroad at Allatoona Pass, but this attempt was unsuccesful.[29]

Sherman was informed about October 1 that enemy cavalry was west of the Chattahoochee, and that one infantry corps was near Powder Springs. When he learned that the rest of the Confederate infantry was crossing to the west side of the Chattahoochee, he left Slocum's Twentieth Corps to hold Atlanta and the Chattahoochee River bridge, and on October 4 he started the rest of his army in pursuit of Hood. Sherman passed through Smyrna Camp Ground, moving the next day into a strong position near Kennesaw Mountain.[30]

On October 6 after the failed attempt to take Allatoona Pass, Hood's army moved westward, crossed the Coosa River near Coosaville, and then moved up the west bank of the Oostanaula River toward Resaca.[31]

When Sherman learned that Hood had moved on to the west, he advanced with his army through Allatoona Pass and reached Kingston October 10. He moved on to Rome the next day and arrived near the railroad at Resaca. Hood was unable to reach Resaca, but he by-passed the town and occupied Dalton October 13. He broke up the railroad in the area, and the next day moved on to the southwest toward Gadsden, Alabama.[32]

Sherman reached Resaca October 14, the day that Hood left Dalton, and moved with his army to Snake Creek Gap and across the mountains to the rear of the gap. About noon the enemy retired before Sherman's men arrived in rear of the gap.[33]

Both armies moved directly toward Lafayette, Georgia. After passing through that town, Hood continued on to the west and halted at Gadsden, Alabama. Sherman followed Hood as far as Gaylesville, Alabama, where he arrived October 21 and went into camp.[34] The next day Schofield, having completed his department business, rejoined the army at Gaylesville and resumed command of the Army of the Ohio (Twenty-Third Corps). Cox returned to the command of his division.[35]

On October 26 Sherman, while still at Gaylesville, received word that Hood's entire army was in the vicinity of Decatur, Alabama. A reconnaissance to Gadsden revealed that Hood had indeed departed and had moved on, first to the vicinity of Decatur, and then on to Florence, Alabama. Sherman, then concerned about the safety of Tennessee, detached Stanley with his Fourth Corps and ordered him to proceed to Chattanooga and then report to Thomas at Nashville.[36]

Sherman remained at Gaylesville until October 29 and then withdrew with his army toward Rome, Georgia. From there Sherman sent Schofield with his Twenty-Third Corps to join Thomas' forces at Nashville, and he also directed Davis to march with his Fourteenth Corps to Kingston, Georgia. The Army of the Tennessee then moved back by way of Dallas and Marietta to Smyrna Camp Ground, and on November 2 Sherman arrived at Kingston where he established his headquarters.[37]

When Sherman left Atlanta October 3 in pursuit of Hood's Army of Tennessee, he left behind only Slocum's Twentieth Corps to hold the Chattahoochee River bridge, the city of Atlanta, and the surrounding country for a distance of several miles. It should be noted, however, that the army corps marching northward in pursuit of Hood left behind large detachments of convalescents and unarmed men and a large part of their trains. Over twelve thousand men reported to the post commanders along with 405 horses and 3,564 mules—a force of men and animals that was almost equal in numbers to that of Twentieth Corps.[38]

The old Confederate line of entrenchments at Atlanta, which extended entirely around the city at a distance of about a mile and a half beyond the city limits, required a far larger force to defend than could be supplied by Twentieth Corps alone. Slocum immediately began work on a shorter line of interior defenses about the city, and this was continued day and night until completed.[39]

Most of Twentieth Corps took part in this work, carried out under the direction of Captain Orlando M. Poe. Details from Williams' First Division were sent to work on the fortifications. A number of regiments of this division were on duty in the city of Atlanta, and these sent out only small details for construction work, but Colonel James S. Robinson provided a daily detail of 350 men from Third Brigade, First Division, for this purpose.[40]

Men from Geary's Second Division also worked on the construction of the inner line of forts and rifle pits. Their camps, however, were still near the old outer line, which had been strengthened and improved by constructing abatis and by creating barriers from limbs and the cuttings of small trees. From October 3 until October 20, with the exception of a few days, one thousand men from the division worked daily strengthening the inner line.[41]

Bloodgood's Second Brigade, temporarily commanded by Brant, and Buckingham's Third Brigade of Dustin's Third Division furnished heavy details for construction of the new fortifications. Lieutenant Colonel Edwin H. Powers of the 55th Ohio of Buckingham's brigade was in charge of the working party.[42]

The 33rd Indiana provided a detail of 143 men to aid in strengthening the defenses of Atlanta; but during most of its stay at Atlanta the 19th Michigan was temporarily detached from the brigade, and the men of the regiment were assigned as provost guards and as laborers for the commissary department.[43]

From October 4 to October 16, the 85th Indiana of Brant's Second Brigade furnished from seventy to 110 men daily for work on the defenses and fifty enlisted men for picket duty on the long line covered by the regiment. There were no other troops on this line from the right of the First Division, Twentieth Corps, to the left of 33rd Indiana, a distance of at least one mile. During this period, the regiment was re-equipped and fully prepared for another campaign. Buckingham's brigade, encamped southeast of the city, also furnished large details for working parties on the fortifications and for picket duty.[44]

As Hood's army moved northward along the Western and Atlantic Railroad in October 1864, it destroyed some track and for a time cut off rail communications between Atlanta and Chattanooga. As a result, food for the men and animals of Twentieth Corps soon became scarce, and for several days the men were almost without meat. To secure food for the men and to prevent a total loss of the horses and mules, Slocum found it necessary to draw entirely on the surrounding country. Accordingly, during the month of October he sent out four large foraging expeditions from Atlanta; for three of these expeditions, Dustin's Third Division furnished one brigade.

No troops of Coburn's former brigade accompanied Geary's first expedition, which left Atlanta on the morning of October 11 and returned three days later with about six thousand bushels of corn and forage for the animals.[45]

Colonel Robinson commanded the second foraging expedition, which moved out into the country to the southeast of Atlanta. Robinson's command consisted of his own Third Brigade, First Division of Twentieth Corps, commanded by Lieutenant Colonel Edward S. Salomon; Colonel Patrick H. Jones' Second Brigade, Second Division; Bloodgood's Second Brigade, Third Division; Captain Thomas S. Sloan's Pennsylvania battery; and 733 wagons.

Robinson's column moved out on the Decatur road at 6:30 AM October 16 and went into camp near Flat Rock (called Flat Shoals by the area residents) at 8:00 PM.

The 85th Indiana, commanded by Brant, marched at the front of Bloodgood's (formerly Coburn's) brigade in the center of the wagon train to Flat Rock, where it camped for the night. The next day, the regiment was assigned to guard the train and to fill the wagons with forage. It marched with the brigade about four miles in the direction of Covington and filled its wagons before returning to Flat Rock for the night.

On October 18 the 85th Indiana and the brigade moved out to the south across Flat Rock Creek about five miles in the direction of Jonesboro, guarding the wagon train. They returned to Flat Rock that evening with loaded wagons.

The next day Robinson returned to Atlanta with about eight hundred wagons loaded with eleven thousand bushels of corn, forage, fresh pork, poultry, sweet potatoes, and other provisions.[46] The 85th Indiana marched at the rear of the brigade that day, in the center of the train, arriving at Atlanta about 8:00 PM, with some sixty wagons loaded with forage, some fresh meat, sweet potatoes, and other foods.[47]

No troops of Coburn's former command accompanied the third expedition, which started 6:00 AM, October 21 under the command of Dustin. This expedition returned with 928 wagons loaded with corn.[48]

Geary commanded the fourth expedition, which consisted of Robinson's Third Brigade, First Division; Colonel Henry A. Barnum's Third Brigade, Second Division, commanded by Lieutenant Colonel Koert S. Van Voorhis; Second Brigade, Third Division, commanded by Brant during the absence of Bloodgood, who was ill; two batteries of artillery under Captain Edmund

C. Bainbridge; 450 cavalry under Colonel Israel Garrard; and 672 wagons. Geary's expedition left Atlanta at 7:00 on the morning of October 26 and arrived at Decatur about 10:00 AM. Garrard's cavalry joined Geary's column on the march that day at Avery's Cross Roads.

From Stone Mountain, Geary marched through Lawrenceville to near Trickum's Cross Roads, where he spent the night. During the next two days Geary and Garrard filled their wagons, and then Geary began his return to Atlanta. He arrived there about 3:30 PM, bringing with him 9,300 bushels of corn, five loads of wheat, four bales of cotton, and about one hundred head of cattle.[49]

The 85th Indiana marched with Second Brigade, Third Division during Geary's fourth foraging expedition, and it was commanded by Captain Josiah H. Sherman of Company A during the absence of Brant, who was in temporary command of the brigade. When the expedition left Atlanta, the 85th Indiana marched at the head of the brigade and guarded the center of the train of 672 wagons. Companies B and G of the regiment marched in rear of 150 wagons of the second division of the train. After a march of twenty miles, the regiment camped for the night about four miles east of Stone Mountain. The next day a part of the train was left in park, and most of the 85th Indiana was left to guard these wagons. During the day, detachments of the regiment were sent out to load wagons, and all but one of these returned to camp that evening. A detachment of 110 men under Captain Orin McAnderson of Company E, which had been sent out some five miles southeast of Stone Mountain, did not come in that night. The regiment remained in camp on October 28 until 4:00 PM, and it then moved back with the brigade through the little town of Gibralter and went into camp on the Atlanta road about two miles beyond. Here the detachment under McAnderson rejoined the regiment about midnight with about fifty wagons loaded with forage. On October 29 the 85th Indiana, marching in rear of the brigade and in the center of the second division of the train, moved back to Atlanta, where it arrived about 5:00 PM. There were no losses reported for the regiment during the two expeditions in which it took part.[50]

In addition to these major foraging expeditions, small details of men frequently went in search of food during the stay of the army near Atlanta. Unfortunately, these expeditions did not always end happily. John R. McBride in his *History of the Thirty-Third Indiana* tells the following story:

> Harry Lyons of Company E and five others went out on such an expedition. While engaged in digging some sweet potatoes they were notified by a Negro that they were about to be surrounded by some bushwhackers. Harry, having confidence in the story, tried to get the boys away. They would not stir. He left them and on reaching the road

met one of the rebels with a large square and compass on his coat collar. He immediately gave the Masonic grand hailing sign and was permitted to escape. He reported the matter in camp to a cavalry company. A detachment went to the place and found the five remaining comrades, who had been killed and dragged to the road, with bayonets driven through their breasts.[51]

At the end of October 1864, only one of the nine brigade commanders of Twentieth Corps who were in command at the beginning of the month was still in charge of his brigade. This was Ario Pardee, who commanded First Brigade of Geary's Second Division. The organization of the corps at the end of October 1864, was as follows:

TWENTIETH CORPS, Major General Henry W. Slocum

First Division, Brigadier General Alpheus S. Williams
    First Brigade, Colonel James L. Selfridge
    Second Brigade, Colonel Ezra A. Carman
    Third Brigade, Colonel James S. Robinson

Second Division, Brigadier General John W. Geary
    First Brigade, Colonel Ario Pardee, Jr.
    Second Brigade, Colonel Patrick H. Jones
    Third Brigade, Colonel Henry A. Barnum

Third Division, Brigadier General William T. Ward
    First Brigade, Colonel Franklin C. Smith
    Second Brigade, Lieutenant Colonel Alexander B. Crane
    Third Brigade, Lieutenant Colonel Philo B. Buckingham[52]

About November 1, Lieutenant Colonel Alexander B. Crane, who had departed on leave August 9 and who had been promoted to colonel, returned after an absence of about three months and relieved Bloodgood in command of Second Brigade of Ward's division. Bloodgood resumed command of his regiment.[53]

On November 5 Crane's [Coburn's] brigade moved out with the rest of the corps on the McDonough road about three miles and went into camp for the night. At daylight the next morning a squad of Confederate cavalry attacked the brigade picket line, killing Hiram Like of Company B, 33rd Indiana Regiment. That afternoon, the troops returned to their original position near Atlanta. During these two days, the regiment received eight months' pay to August 31, 1864.[54]

While the presidential election of November 8 was of interest to the men of the 85th Indiana at Atlanta, they were unable to cast their votes because Indiana had no law, as did some states, which permitted men in the field to vote. Only some who were sick or wounded were granted furloughs to go home and vote. A poll was taken of 382 men of the regiment at Atlanta and, of these, 372 were for Abraham Lincoln. Joseph Glatthaar gives the unofficial vote as 309 for Lincoln and 15 for McClellan. Whichever figure is correct, the soldiers of the 85th Indiana were overwhelmingly in favor of Lincoln.[55]

Michigan was one of the nineteen states that permitted soldiers to vote in the field, and on November 8, 1864, 290 men of the 19th Michigan voted for Lincoln and 14 for McClellan.[56]

Early on the morning of November 9, the enemy opened with two guns that had been placed near the Decatur road, firing fifteen or twenty shells into the brigade lines, some bursting within and close to the encampment of the 85th Indiana. The brigade was immediately placed under arms, but the firing soon stopped and there was no further action on its front. Fortunately no one was injured.[57]

Colonel Dustin assumed command of Coburn's Second Brigade, Third Division, on November 9, relieving Lieutenant Colonel Crane, the ranking officer of the brigade. Dustin's regiment, the 105th Illinois, however, remained with First Brigade. Crane rejoined his regiment November 10, and the next day assumed command of the 85th Indiana, relieving Brant. Also on November 11 Brigadier General Nathaniel J. Jackson assumed command of First Division, Twentieth Corps.[58]

Daniel Dustin was born in Topsham, Vermont, October 5, 1820, to John Knight Dustin and Sallie Thompson Dustin. The boy grew to manhood on the farm at Topsham, and there he worked hard to obtain a good education. He served at times as a teacher in the district school, and he continued teaching at intervals while studying at Dartmouth. Dustin graduated from Dartmouth College November 18, 1846, and then began the practice of medicine in Corinth, Vermont.

In the spring of 1850, after gold was discovered in California, Dustin left Vermont for San Francisco, where he practiced medicine for a while and then went into the mining region looking for gold. Having little success, he went into merchandising, the practice of medicine, and surface mining. He served for a term in the California State Legislature. Finally, in

1858 he returned to New York, but soom moved to Sycamore, Illinois, where he became a partner in a business selling drugs and medicine.

At the outbreak of the Civil War, Dustin sold his interest in the business and assisted in raising the 8th Illinois Cavalry. He was commissioned captain of Company L of the regiment, which was assigned to the Army of the Potomac, and was engaged during the Seven Days Battles on the Peninsula.

In July 1862 Dustin resigned and returned home. There he assisted in raising the 105th Illinois Volunteers, which was mustered into service at Dixon, Illinois, September 2, 1862, with Dustin as its colonel. A short time later the regiment moved south and joined the Army of the Cumberland. As noted above, Dustin was assigned command of Coburn's old brigade when Coburn left the army, and he commanded this brigade until the end of the war.[59]

When Dustin assumed command of Second Brigade, Third Division on November 9, it consisted of the following: 33rd Indiana, James E. Burton commanding, 636 men; 22nd Wisconsin, Edward Bloodgood commanding, 711 men; 19th Michigan, John J. Baker commanding, 703 men; and 85th Indiana, Alexander B. Crane commanding, 640 men. The grand aggregate for the brigade was 2,690 men. Of this number, the total present was 1,531 men, and there were 1,222 muskets.[60]

Also on November 9 Colonel Samuel Ross of the 20th Connecticut rejoined Third Brigade, Third Division, and assumed command. He relieved Buckingham, who had assumed command September 23, when James Wood, Jr. departed on leave of absence.[61]

On September 20 Sherman suggested that the capture of Savannah, Georgia, should be one of the army's next objectives and that with the cooperation of the navy he would not hesitate to march across Georgia with an army of sixty thousand men to close that important port.[62]

Sherman proposed to Lieutenant General Ulysses S. Grant at City Point, Virginia, on October 9 that he, Sherman, break up the railroad south of Chattanooga and then move eastward with his army across Georgia through Milledgeville and Millen to Savannah. He further proposed that he completely destroy the railroads and everything of military value to the Confederacy during his march. It was also his intention to demonstrate to the southern people at home the real meaning of war.[63]

While at Gaylesville, Sherman learned that Hood's army was at Decatur, Alabama, and on October 26 he finally resolved that he would leave Thomas' reinforced command in Tennessee to oppose Hood—to return to Atlanta with the remainder of his army and, from there, march across Georgia. On October 27 and again on October 28 he expressed his opposition to moving with his army to Tennessee.[64]

Assuming that there would be no reasons for changing his plan, Sherman began preparations on November 1 for his march across Georgia. A full supply of clothing and equipment was issued to the men, and baggage was reduced to the least possible amount. He ordered that all surplus artillery, all baggage that would not be needed on the march, and all sick, wounded, and refugees be sent back to Chattanooga. He further ordered that Fourteenth Corps, Twentieth Corps, Fifteenth Corps, Seventeenth Corps, and Brigadier General Judson Kilpatrick's Third Cavalry Division, Army of the Cumberland, be put in the best possible condition for the long and difficult march ahead.

Finally, in a letter dated November 2 Grant authorized Sherman to proceed with his proposed movement, and at 10:30 PM November 7 Grant sent Sherman the following dispatch from City Point:

> Your dispatch of this evening received. I see no present reason for changing your plan; should any arise you will see it; or if I do, will inform you. I think everything here favorable now. Great good fortune attend you. I believe you will be eminently successful, and at worst can only make a march less fruitful of results than is hoped for.[65]

In a special field order dated November 9, 1864, Sherman divided his army into two wings as follows: a Right Wing to be commanded by Howard and a Left Wing, Army of Georgia to be commanded by Slocum. Slocum assumed command of the Left Wing November 11. Williams then assumed command of Twentieth Corps, and Nathaniel J. Jackson assumed command of Williams' First Division of Twentieth Corps. The two wings of the army were organized as follows:[66]

Right Wing (or Army of the Tennessee), Oliver O. Howard
    Fifteenth Corps, Peter J. Osterhaus
    Seventeenth Corps, Frank P. Blair

Left Wing, Henry W. Slocum
    Fourteenth Corps, Jefferson C. Davis
    Twentieth Corps, Alpheus S. Williams

At that time, Twentieth Corps consisted of three divisions, as follows:

Nathaniel J. Jackson's First Division; John W. Geary's Second Division; and William T. Ward's Third Division.

Ward's division was organized as follows:

First Brigade, Franklin C. Smith
Second Brigade, Daniel Dustin
Third Brigade, Samuel Ross

Dustin's brigade [Coburn's] consisted of the following regiments:

33rd Indiana, James F. Burton
85th Indiana, Alexander B. Crane
19th Michigan, John J. Baker
22nd Wisconsin, Edward Bloodgood[67]

All the preliminary preparations for the march through Georgia had been completed by November 11, and Sherman was ready for the final measures to be taken before he left Atlanta. He ordered Corse, still at Rome, to destroy the bridges there, plus all foundries, mills, shops, warehouses, and anything that could be useful to the enemy, and then to move with his division to Kingston. At the same time, Sherman ordered that the railroad in and about Atlanta and between the Chattahoochee and Etowah rivers be completely destroyed, and that all garrisons from Kingston northward draw back to Chattanooga and take with them all public property and railroad stock. The rails from Resaca back to Chattanooga were to be taken up and placed in storage for future needs.[68]

Also on November 11 Sherman ordered Orlando M. Poe, his chief engineer of the Military Division of the Mississippi, to use the engineer troops to destroy all railroads, railroad buildings, storehouses, machine shops, mills, and factories within the defenses of Atlanta so that thereafter the city would have no military value. This work continued through the four days and nights of November 13-16.[69]

Communications of the army with the rear were broken on November 12, and Sherman and his staff left Kingston for Atlanta. That evening Jefferson C. Davis evacuated Kingston, and the next morning the Fourteenth Corps began the destruction of the railroad from the Etowah River to Big Shanty. This work was completed late that night, and November 14 the corps moved forward and camped at the Chattahoochee River. The next morning it arrived at Atlanta.[70]

The last train departed from Atlanta November 13, and Slocum directed Williams, commanding his Twentieth Corps, to begin immediately the destruction of the track between Atlanta and the Chattahoochee River bridge and to bend the rails. The wagon and railway bridges were to be left until the arrival of Colonel George P. Buell from Chattanooga with his Pioneer Brigade and the pontoniers.[71]

Also that day Howard's Army of the Tennessee left Smyrna Camp Ground and began the final work of destruction of the railroad near the Chattahoochee. When this work was completed, the army moved on and assembled near White Hall, Georgia, just south of Atlanta. Thus, by November 14, 1864, all troops assigned to the march through Georgia had arrived at or near Atlanta.[72]

That day, just before the beginning of Sherman's march across Georgia, Dustin announced his brigade staff, which included the following officers of the 85th Indiana: Major Wilson Hobbs, surgeon in chief; Lieutenant William S. Harbert, acting commissary of subsistence; and Lieutenant Henry C. Brown, brigade ambulance officer.[73]

John Bell Hood was a great division commander, but failed in the test of Army command.

Patrick Cleburne was called the "Stonewall Jackson of the West."

William J. Hardee(above) and A. P. Stewart at Peach Tree Creek were to attack on the right of Hardee's line, *en echelon* at intervals of two hundred yards, against the left of the Army of the Cumberland.

Henry W. Slocum commanded the XX Corps after Hooker asked to be relieved.

Dan Butterfield commanded a division of the XX Corps and won brevets of brigadier and major general.

James E. Burton, from Mount Tabor, Indiana, became commander of the 33rd Indiana Regiment when Major Levin T. Miller resigned. Burton remained in command of the regiment until after the war.

William D. Weir, from Prairie Creek, Indiana, served as Captain of Company F, 85th Indiana Regiment.

Lawrence Burget, Company C, 85th Indiana, was shot in the nose during the Atlanta Campaign.

In an article written for the *Terre Haute Tribune*, dated November 16, 1913, George Farrington described how he and Colonel Louis Watkins were sent in pursuit of Orton Williams and Walter Peter, and overtook them outside Union lines.

Chapter 15

Sherman's March Through Georgia

By the evening of November 14, 1864, Major General William T. Sherman's Army of the Military Division of the Mississippi was ready to begin its march across Georgia to Savannah. Sherman planned to carry out his advance in three stages: the first would end when his armies reached Milledgeville, the second when he arrived at Millen, and the third when he reached the coast at Savannah. Sherman directed that each column be at Milledgeville by November 22. He expected little opposition to his march, because, after the departure of General John B. Hood's army for Tennessee, only Major General Joseph Wheeler's cavalry corps and Major General Gustavus W. Smith's ineffective Georgia Militia were left in Georgia.[1]

Each Wing of the army was to advance by roughly parallel routes separated by about twenty to thirty-five miles, with corps on separate roads. Militarily this was important, because the Right Wing was to move south and threaten Macon, and the Left Wing was to march eastward in the direction of Augusta. By so doing, Sherman hoped to conceal from the enemy his true destination, and thus force Lieutenant General William J. Hardee, commanding the Confederate Department of South Carolina, Georgia, and Florida, to divide his limited forces in Georgia to defend both cities. Hardee would thus be unable to concentrate forces and effectively oppose the assembly of Sherman's army at Milledgeville, his first objective.[2]

This march arrangement also had other benefits. By using several roads the army could move more rapidly, avoiding the congestion that would result if the troops and trains moved on only one or two roads. It also allowed the separate corps to forage for food over wider areas than they would if they traveled on the same road. Finally, by marching in this extended order, Sherman's men would leave behind a path of devastation about sixty miles wide and three hundred miles long in which virtually everything of military value would be destroyed.[3]

On the morning of November 15, Sherman's army began to leave Atlanta on its march across Georgia. Brigadier General Alpheus S. Williams' Twentieth Corps of Major General Henry W. Slocum's Left Wing moved first and marched eastward by way of Decatur and Stone Mountain in the direction of Madison and Augusta. Major General Peter J. Osterhaus' Fifteenth Corps and Major General Frank P. Blair's Seventeenth Corps of Major General Oliver O. Howard's Right Wing marched southward toward Jonesboro and Macon, and Brigadier General Judson Kilpatrick's Third Cavalry Division covered the right flank of the Right Wing.[4]

Slocum's orders were to destroy the railroad from Social Circle to Madison, burn the large and important railroad bridge across the Oconee River east of Madison, and then turn south and reach Millidgeville on the seventh day. Howard, with Kilpatrick's cavalry division, was to move toward Jonesboro and McDonough and then, after making a strong feint toward Macon, cross the Ocmulgee River near Planter's Mills and rendezvous seven days later in the vicinity of the town of Gordon.[5]

Twentieth Corps, accompanied by Slocum, marched out of Atlanta on the morning of November 15 with Brigadier General Nathaniel J. Jackson's First Division in the lead. It was followed by Brigadier General John W. Geary's Second Division, and Brigadier General William T. Ward's Third Division brought up the rear. Ward's division left Atlanta on the Decatur road at about 11:30 AM, and followed the trains of Jackson's and Geary's divisions. Colonel Daniel Dustin's Second Brigade (formerly Coburn's brigade) of Ward's division marched in the middle of the division that day. Halting at Decatur for an hour and a half for dinner, Ward's division then moved toward Stone Mountain. Before the war, Decatur was a town of about one thousand inhabitants, but when Ward's men passed through it was deserted and consisted largely of old, destroyed or empty houses. The march was frustrating for Ward's men because of the movements of the two divisions ahead. They would march about a half mile and then be forced to halt for as much as an hour before the road was cleared and they could continue.[6]

On November 14 before the march began, Captain Orlando M. Poe's engineers began their work of destruction on the railroads, railroad installations, and other public buildings in Atlanta. The masonry walls of many of the buildings were knocked down, and the wooden framing fell in on the rubble. Many items marked for destruction, such as old wagons, tents, bedding, equipment, and trash, were piled on the rubble and set on fire. The fire spread to a block of stores near the depot in the heart of the city, and the buildings burned all through the night of November 14. When the army moved out November 15, the city was still in flames, and the marching men could see the reddish glow of the burning city far into the night.[7]

On November 16 Slocum's Left Wing continued its march over bad roads, with the trains still slowing the progress of the infantry. Ward's division marched through the night of November 15, halting near Stone Mountain at 8:00 the next morning. It remained there for two hours while the troops had breakfast and then resumed its advance. Pushing past Jackson's division, it took its place in the center of the column, behind Geary's division. Ward crossed Yellow River about dark and camped at 8:00 that night near the river at Rock Bridge Post Office, about eight miles east of Stone Mountain, having marched twenty-five miles during the past two days.[8]

Lieutenant Colonel Alexander B. Crane's 85th Indiana left Atlanta with Dustin's brigade of Ward's division. The men, finally liberated from the boredom of camp life, were in a pleasant mood. Almost all of the men of the regiment were in excellent health; all of the sick had been sent to the rear before starting the march. Only four men left Atlanta in ambulances, but after a short time they too joined the marching columns.[9]

When the 85th Indiana left Atlanta, it was accompanied by a good wagon train loaded with ammunition and supplies, including rations of hardtack for twenty days, coffee and sugar for forty days, and double portions of salt for forty days. A herd of beef cattle sufficient for forty days' rations and forage for three days accompanied the column. While on the march the men added to their supplies by foraging. Fine carriages and farm wagons were driven into camp loaded with food and forage taken from the countryside. On the second day's march to Yellow River, forage and fresh foods became available, and on the third day sweet potatoes were found in large quantities.[10]

Brevet Major General Jefferson C. Davis' Fourteenth Corps of the Left Wing marched out of Atlanta November 16 and followed Twentieth Corps eastward.[11]

On November 17 Twentieth Corps marched at 5:00 AM, with the divisions marching in the same order as they had the day before. The weather was pleasant that day, but the march was tedious. The column passed through Sheffield and Summers' Mills, crossed Big Haynes and Little Haynes creeks, and Ward's division camped that night four miles from Social Circle. The rear units did not come up until early the next morning. Dustin's brigade, which began its march at 6:00 AM, did not go into camp until 3:00 AM, November 18.[12]

Early on the morning of November 18, 1864, Williams' Twentieth Corps resumed its march and struck the Georgia Railroad at Social Circle. Geary's division was still in the lead that day, and it was followed by Ward's division, with Jackson's division at the rear of the corps. The weather was fine and the roads excellent, but the country was poor, and water and supplies were scarce. When Ward's division reached Social Circle, Colonel Samuel Ross' Third Brigade was detached and sent to destroy the railroad track at Rutledge, about seven miles ahead. Colonel Franklin C. Smith's First Brigade and Dustin's Second Brigade continued with the division toward Rutledge, halting several times to pile fence rails on the track and set them afire. They destroyed about twelve miles of track before going into camp about six miles from Madison. The country through which Ward's division

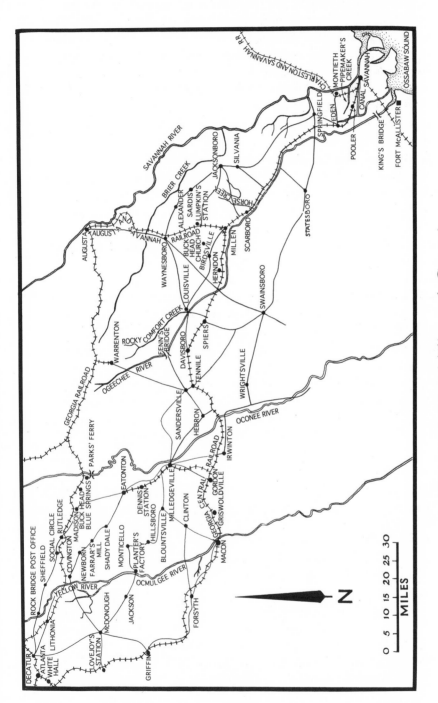

Sherman's March Through Georgia

passed that day had improved, and forage was abundant.[13]

During Sherman's march, a refined method of track destruction was used for destroying several miles of track at one time. A detachment of three thousand men was divided into three groups of one thousand. The first group moved up to the track, and each man grasped the end of one of the first one thousand ties. At an officer's order, the men lifted their ends of the ties and toppled the track upside down on the side of the railroad grade. After loosening the ties from the rails, the first group moved on to the next one thousand ties to repeat their routine.

The second group moved up to the overturned track, built piles of ties, and placed the rails over the piles of ties. By this time, the first group had turned over the second section of track and had moved on, and second group followed to build more piles of ties.

The third group, following the second, set fire to the piles of ties. When the rails had been heated until softened, the men carried them with tongs and wrapped them around the nearest trees. This done, the third group followed the other two to repeat its operations.[14]

Dustin's brigade, after two hours sleep, had breakfast and then resumed the march at 6:00 AM November 18. It passed through Social Circle early that morning and moved on toward Rutledge. Near that town it halted to destroy about two miles of track, then camped with the division about six miles west of Madison. During this part of the march, the men passed through one of the best agricultural regions in Georgia. Abundant supplies, such as hams and other meats, sweet potatoes and stored vegetables, and honey, were obtained from the many smokehouses, barns, farms, and gardens along the route.[15]

On the morning of November 19 Twentieth Corps moved with difficulty to Madison in a dense fog. At that point Geary's division was detached and sent, unencumbered by wagons, to destroy the railroad from Madison to the Oconee River, thirteen miles to the east. They were ordered to burn the railroad and wagon bridges over the river and make a feint on Augusta.[16]

Jackson's division, which had charge of the corps' wagon train that day, marched through Madison, Georgia, and camped four miles south of the town. Ward, with Dustin's and Ross' brigades, moved at 5:00 AM, and destroyed track to within about one-half mile of the Madison railroad station. Smith's brigade, which accompanied the trains that day, moved at 7:00 AM and passed through Madison and went into camp at about 4:30 PM, four miles east of the town on the road to Eatonton. Dustin's and Ross' brigades joined Smith's brigade at Madison, a beautiful and wealthy town, consisting of many fine residences set in large and pleasant grounds, usually surrounded by neatly built brick fences.[17]

As the 85th Indiana marched through the town, the bands played "Hail Columbia." Private property was not disturbed, but the depot and all railroad property were completely destroyed. The entire male population had left the town before Sherman's arrival. That evening the men ate fresh pork, mutton, duck, chicken, sweet potatoes, and sorghum molasses, all gathered up by foragers from the country through which the regiment had passed. During the first four days of the march, the regiment covered eighty miles and was then one hundred miles from Augusta and forty miles from Milledgeville.[18]

November 20 Twentieth Corps again took up the march on the road toward Eatonton, with Ward's division leading and Jackson's division following. Geary's division was still detached and at work destroying the railroad. It was a cloudy day, with rain beginning to fall at 5:00 PM. Ward's division camped at dark within two miles of Eatonton (Eatonton Factories).[19]

Dustin's brigade began its march that day at 6:00 AM and moved in rear of the division as train guard. Four men were assigned to each of the fifty wagons of the train. Dustin ordered the brigade into camp at dark, but because the men were deployed at such length along the train and because of the darkness of the night, they were able to reach the encampment only with great difficulty. On the march that day, the men frequently had to push the wagons to help the mules pull them up the many slopes.[20]

On November 21 Twentieth Corps moved at 5:00 AM on the road toward Milledgeville, with Third Division again in the lead and First Division following. Second Division had not yet returned from its work on the railroad. It rained during the preceding night and all of that day, and both troops and teams struggled to move forward through the rain along abominable roads.[21]

It was raining at 5:00 that morning when Ward's division, with Dustin's brigade in the lead, marched out and passed through Eatonton. This village was the terminus of a branch railroad that ran down to Gordon, where it connected with the main line of the Georgia Central Railroad. Lieutenant Henry C. Brown of the 85th Indiana described Eatonton as follows:

> . . . a small, old looking place, mostly deserted, where we captured a quantity of sugar, tobacco, and cigars, destroyed large quantity of cotton, cotton yarn factory, railroad buildings, and commenced destroying the old track, . . .[22]

The division went into camp that afternoon at 3:00 PM, on Little River, ten miles from Milledgeville, when it was detained by the crossing of the trains on the pontoon bridge. Resuming the march at 4:00 PM, the division continued on through the night.[23]

Also that day, Geary's division, having completed its destruction of the railroad as far as Buck Head and Swords (Blue Springs), marched back past Park's Ferry to Philadelphia Church, where it took the road toward Milledgeville to rejoin Twentieth Corps. It camped that night near Dennis Station on the branch railroad that ran from Eatonton to Gordon.[24]

November 22 Twentieth Corps resumed the march toward Milledgeville. The weather was bitterly cold that morning, and there was ice on the water a half inch thick. Jackson's division moved first and at Milledgeville camped on the east side of the Oconee River. Ward's division followed Jackson and camped on the west side of the river near the bridge.

Geary's division, which had not yet rejoined Twentieth Corps, marched from its camp of the night before to Dennis Station, where it came up in rear of the trains of the other two divisions. Geary moved on in rear of the trains to Milledgeville, where he crossed the Oconee River and camped on the left of Jackson's division.[25]

Ward slowly crossed Little River with Smith's and Ross' brigades and moved on toward Milledgeville, passing the corps trains on the way. Dustin remained in camp in charge of the trains. The men huddled around their campfires until about sundown, while waiting for the wagon train to cross the river. When Dustin's brigade finally crossed, the men had to wait until the pontoon bridge was taken up and ready to move before beginning their march to Milledgeville. The men then marched all night, with frequent halts because of the train. The advance regiment of the brigade reached Milledgeville about 10:00 PM November 22 and the rear regiment finally came in about 7:00 the following morning. The 85th Indiana arrived about 3:00 AM, November 23.[26]

Geary's division continued its march November 22 and at Dennis Station Geary found the trains of the other two divisions of the corps just passing on the road. He followed the trains to Little River and then hurried on to Milledgeville, arriving at dark. Finding the other two divisions of the corps already in camp, Geary crossed the Oconee River and encamped on the left of Jackson's First Division.[27]

Meanwhile, as Williams' Twentieth Corps advanced toward Milledgeville, Davis' Fourteenth Corps of the Left Wing marched toward the same destination. Davis' corps arrived in Atlanta from Kingston November 15 and camped that night in the suburbs. The next morning, accompanied by Sherman, it took the road eastward, passing through Decatur, Lithonia, and Covington. Davis's corps destroyed the railroad from Lithonia to Social

Circle and then veered off to the right and marched through Newborn and Shady Dale and went into camp near Eatonton on November 20.

Twentieth Corps was advancing from Madison that day on the main Milledgeville road, and Fourteenth Corps turned off to the right so that the two corps could march on separate roads. Fourteenth Corps moved in the direction of Milledgeville by way of Farrar's Mill and marched into Milledgeville on November 22, the same day that Williams' Twentieth Corps occupied the town.[28]

Slocum established his headquarters in the leading hotel of Milledgeville, the capitol of Georgia. When Sherman arrived a few days later he moved with all his camp equipage into the governor's mansion and set up his headquarters.[29]

While Slocum's Left Wing was marching toward Milledgeville, Howard's Right Wing kept pace to the south. On November 15 Howard moved south from White Hall, near Atlanta, toward Macon and Gordon, with Kilpatrick's cavalry division screening the right flank during the march.

Howard moved by different roads through McDonough, Planter's Factory, Monticello, Hillsboro, Clinton, Blountsville, and Irwinton to Gordon, Georgia, about sixteen miles south of Milledgeville. Howard's troops arrived there November 22, the same that that Twentieth Corps occupied Milledgeville.[30]

Brigadier General Charles C. Walcutt's Second Brigade of Brigadier General Charles R. Woods' division moved out also on November 22 on a demonstration against Griswoldville. About a mile and a half east of town, Walcutt and a part of Kilpatrick's cavalry encountered a body of troops of the Georgia State Militia under Major General Pleasant J. Phillips, who promptly attacked. Sadly, Walcutt's seasoned men opened fire on this collection of inexperienced older men and boys, who were easily repulsed with very serious losses, without affecting in any way the outcome of the campaign. Though a small affair, this was the only battle fought during Sherman's march through Georgia.[31]

Thus, on November 22 the first phase of Sherman's march ended exactly on schedule, with the Left Wing in possession of Milledgeville and the Right Wing near Gordon, a short distance to the south. The next day Sherman issued orders for the second phase of the march, which directed the army to move toward Millen. The Right Wing was to follow the line of the Georgia Central Railroad by roads to the south to a point opposite Sandersville, breaking up the railroad as it advanced. The Left Wing was to move from Milledgeville to the railroad opposite Sandersville and break up the railroad as far as the Ogeechee River. It was then to move on by way of Davisboro and Louisville in the direction of Millen.[32]

Kilpatrick's cavalry division, which was camped at Gordon November

23, was ordered to Milledgeville and then eastward by the most practicable route to break up the railroad between Millen and Augusta. Kilpatrick was also directed to make an attempt to rescue the prisoners of war confined at the Millen prison.[33]

November 23 was a very cold day, and Williams' corps remained in camp at Milledgeville. Lieutenant Henry C. Brown of the 85th Indiana provides a description of this city.

> ... The town is pleasantly located on the Oconee River, rather old-fashioned in style, containing few fine residences. The State House is not fine, though of good style of architecture for a Jewish Synagogue. It is built in a lot of ten acres, in which were also built an arsenal and armory, the latter containing about 4,000 small arms of various kinds, great Mississippi knives in abundance, and cords of long lances, all designed at one time or another to be used in extermination of the Yankees.

Lieutenant Brown also described the destruction of some of the buildings of Milledgeville.

> ... The Arsenal contained fixed and other ammunition, large and small, in great variety and abundance. The arms were piled up and burnt, together with the buildings, and a large amount of salt was taken to the banks of the Oconee and deposited in the bosom of the quiet little stream for safe keeping. The depot, a small brick building, was entirely sacked and strewn with the debris of an establishment that had just closed out to the lowest bidder, with few buyers. Upon the platform stood five or six lathes and other machinery that his Highness Brown could not get out of the way. ....

The penitentiary, also located at Milledgeville, was a large and massive building which burned during the night. Sherman's men plundered the State House and the State Library and also burned a powder magazine, other public buildings, and some shops. They burned the railroad and other railroad buildings and destroyed the track for about five miles in the direction of Gordon.[34]

At the time of Sherman's approach to Milledgevlle, the Georgia Legislature was in session, but as the Federal troops drew near the state capital, Governor Joseph E. Brown and the members of the legislature hurriedly left the city. The Union soldiers enjoyed their stay at Milledgeville. Some officers organized a mock session of the legislature in which the question of Georgia's secession from the Union was brought up and discussed. Colonel

James S. Robinson of the 82nd Ohio Infantry was elected speaker of the house, and a president of the senate was also elected. During this session, the mock legislature passed an act repealing the Ordnance of Secession.[35]

Captain Jefferson E. Brant of the 85th Indiana wrote of his visit to Milledgeville:

> ... I got Gibbon's famous fifth volume of the History of the "De-cline and Fall of the Roman Empire" from the books thrown out of the Library. That book, especially the fifteenth chapter, afforded Col. Crane and myself ground for debate the rest of that famous march. Here the Colonel got his fine Negro servant, "John", who by our help at Head Quarters learned to spell and read as he lay by the log fires at night and while resting on the way. John was among a thousand who made good use of his time and freedom. Here also came to us "Byron Ross" another mulatto fellow who proved himself a good man, and came home with us and afterward married in the colored settlement about Cloverland, Clay County, Indiana.[36]

November 24, in fine weather, Twentieth Corps left Milledgeville, crossed the Oconee River, and marched toward Hebron, with Jackson's division moving at the head of the column, Geary's division following, and Ward's division bringing up the rear. Ward's division marched at 6:00 AM, crossed the Oconee, and after proceeding a half mile, halted until 3:00 PM to allow Fourteenth Corps to pass. It then moved forward slowly on the Hebron road, greatly impeded by the trains, and camped near Gum Creek that night.[37]

Dustin's brigade marched in the center of Ward's division that day. The roads were in such terrible condition that the 85th Indiana spent most of the day making repairs and was able to cover only eight miles. The regiment halted for supper and then moved on again about dark, through swampy country with cold weather, fog, and darkness. Fences on both sides of the road for miles were set on fire, but the light of the burning rails did little to improve the visibility. As a result, the regiment did not get into camp at Buffalo Creek until 3:30 AM November 25, after moving only thirteen miles.[38]

Kilpatrick's cavalry reached Milledgeville November 24, crossed the Oconee River, and moved toward the city of Augusta.[39]

Davis' Fourteenth Corps began its march that morning on the right of Twentieth Corps. East of Milledgeville it moved to the left, crossed the Sandersville road, and then advanced on the left of Twentieth Corps through Black Spring in the direction of Sandersville.[40]

Williams continued his march November 25 with the divisions in the same order as the day before. At 6:00 AM, after a rest of three hours, Ward's division, still marching in the rear of the corps, moved out, passed through Hebron, and camped at mid-afternoon on Buffalo Creek. The bridge over the creek had been burned, so it was necessary for the column to wait for the pioneers to put down a pontoon bridge. The troops finally halted for the night on the farm of the man who was said to have burned the bridge. In retaliation they burned his house, other buildings, and fences. Dustin's brigade went into camp after all the trains except those belonging to Third Division had crossed the creek.[41]

That night the pioneers rebuilt the bridge over Buffalo Creek. The next morning Twentieth Corps crossed it and marched toward Sandersville, ten miles distant. Federal pickets skirmished with Wheeler's cavalry during the brisk, three-hour march, and upon arrival at Sandersville drove them from the town. When Williams' troops entered Sandersville, a few shots were fired at them from the courthouse. On Sherman's orders the engineers destroyed the building.[42]

Ward's division left its camps at 6:00 AM November 26 and marched in rear of the corps to Sandersville. It arrived about 2:00 PM and went into camp. Dustin's brigade broke camp at 6:00 AM, crossed Buffalo Creek at 10:00 AM, then waited for the pontoon bridge to be taken up. When all was ready, the brigade marched with the pontoon train toward Sandersville, where it arrived and went into camp at 4:30 that afternoon.[43]

The head of the column of Fourteenth Corps, marching on a parallel road to the left of that taken by Twentieth Corps, reached Sandersville at about the same time as the latter corps.[44]

During the afternoon of November 26, Jackson's and Geary's divisions of Twentieth Corps moved down to Tennille (Station No. 13) on the Georgia Central Railroad to destroy the road. Ward's division was left at Sandersville to cover the trains.[45]

Jackson's division marched along the Georgia Central Railroad to Davisboro (Station No. 12) the next day. Geary's division destroyed the track from Tennille to within six miles of Davisboro and then went into camp at Davisboro for the night. Ward's division, with the corps trains and artillery, marched directly to Davisboro, where they halted for the night. Dustin's Second Brigade broke camp at 7:00 that morning and marched in the center of Ward's division with the trains. It crossed to the south side of the railroad and arrived at Davisboro at about 7:00 PM.[46]

At Sandersville, Sherman, who had been traveling with the Left Wing, moved with his headquarters to join the Right Wing. He arrived at Tennille three miles south of Sandersville at 10:00 AM November 27, and from there he moved on with Blair's Seventeenth Corps.[47]

Twentieth Corps continued its advance in the direction of Millen on the morning of November 28. Jackson's division destroyed the Georgia Central Railroad as far as Spiers (Station No. 11), and Geary's division destroyed the track at, and west of, Davisboro. The country through which the track passed from Sandersville to Spiers was an enormous morass, known as Williamson's Creek, or Swamp.[48]

Ward's division moved with all the wagon trains and the artillery of the corps on the Louisville road and arrived on the Ogeechee River at noon. The bridge there had been destroyed, and the division halted again for the pontoniers and pioneers to construct a bridge.[49]

Dustin's brigade (Coburn's old brigade) marched at the head of the division that day, and when the 33rd Indiana, which was leading the brigade, came up to the river bank it was fired on by the enemy. The brigade moved to the left of the road into an open field, where the 33rd Indiana formed in line of battle on the front line. It remained in this position until late afternoon. Then the entire brigade moved back about one-fourth mile and formed in single line of battle, without further demonstration on the part of the enemy.[50]

On the morning of November 29 Twentieth Corps again moved forward, with the men of Jackson's and Geary's divisions destroying the railroad to the Ogeechee River and the railroad bridge there. At 2:00 PM, Ward, with his First Brigade, Third Brigade, and the trains, crossed the Ogeechee and Rocky Comfort Creek on pontoons and passed through Louisville. They camped that night southeast of the town on Big Creek, where the bridge had been destroyed. Dustin's Second Brigade was detained at the river until 10:00 PM by the crossing of the trains, and it then crossed and went into camp. It remained there during the night and the next day to guard the rear of the wagon train, the pontoon bridge, and the pontoon train.[51]

On November 30, an oppressively hot day, Ward's division of Twentieth Corps remained in camp all day, but Jackson's and Geary's divisions crossed the Ogeechee River at Coward's Bridge and encamped on the right of Ward's division.[52]

By Slocum's order, Dustin's Second Brigade remained in camp that day until 7:00 PM and then began crossing Rocky Comfort Creek with the pontoon train. It moved on, passing through Louisville at 9:00 PM, and finally went into camp after midnight December 1 near Dry Creek, three miles east of Louisville. The march that night has been described by John R. McBride, Adjutant of the 33rd Indiana:

> The regiment [33rd Indiana] . . . then marched through a swamp before reaching Louisville, and after going about a mile beyond the town crossed another pontoon bridge, and then plunged at once into another swamp that proved the most serious obstacle of the march.

Impenetrable darkness and fog rendered it impossible for the men to see each other, who could only be located by sound. The men had to march through mud and water, the latter in many places being waist deep, and to their confusion often tumbling over each other, and sometimes finding it difficult to extricate themselves from the mud. Those who were mounted could do nothing more than let the animals go as they pleased.[53]

Brant of the 85th Indiana also tells of some of the problems that night as the regiment crossed the swamp:

The fog was so dense that fire could not be seen further than ten rods. It was here that we fished poor Greenburg [Marks Greenbery] of Co. "I" out of the bog into which he had fallen and would have died in a little while had he not been helped out. Poor fellow, our only Jew, I can see him now as he lay helpless, appealing for help in that awful deep Gully. Men waded that night in mud knee deep. We moved in single file.[54]

During the period December 1-8 Williams' Twentieth Corps marched to the southeast through the country lying between the Ogeechee and Savannah rivers and along the Louisville and Savannah road. At 7:00 AM December 1, after a brief rest, the corps moved on through the swamp in the direction of Millen. Geary's division led the column that day, Jackson's division came next, and Ward's division brought up the rear. After crossing Dry Creek, the corps passed through the camp of Brigadier General William P. Carlin's First Division of Fourteenth Corps, then crossed Baker's Creek and camped about a mile and a half west of Bark Camp Creek.[55]

Ward's division remained in camp until 1:00 PM, then marched with the train of Kilpatrick's cavalry and the train of Carlin's division. Selfridge's brigade of Jackson's division assisted Ward in guarding the combined trains. Ward marched about eight miles, and his rear units did not come in to camp until about 3:00 AM December 2.[56]

Dustin's brigade remained in camp until 3:00 PM that day, waiting for the passage of the trains, then moved forward in the center of the division. After a march of four miles, it rested until 9:00 PM, and then marched another four miles. The brigade crossed Big Creek and went into camp at midnight, about one mile east of the crossing.[57]

On December 2, a cool and pleasant day, Williams' corps, accompanied by Slocum's headquarters, marched through Birdsville to Buck Head Creek, with Geary's division in the lead. Ward's division was still in the rear in charge of the same trains that it had guarded the day before. During the morning the division crossed Baker's Creek and then passed through one of the worst swamps that it had yet encountered. Quicksand added greatly to the difficulties in moving the trains along. During the afternoon the roads were generally better, and the division camped at dark near Jones' Creek, after a march of fifteen miles.[58]

While at Buck Head Church, a short distance north of Millen, someone informed Slocum that a planter named Bullard, living in the area, had been very active in recapturing escaped Union prisoners and returning them to Confederate authorities. In a short time, soldiers arrived at the Bullard plantation, where they burned his cotton gins, cribs, a cotton press, and a warehouse containing cotton valued at fifty thousand dollars. In parting, the soldiers informed Bullard that if he continued his activity of returning prisoners they would return and burn his house.[59]

Twentieth Corps marched toward Sylvania December 3, crossed the Augusta and Savannah Railroad (also called the Augusta and Millen Railroad) several miles north of Millen, and destroyed five miles of track before going into camp on Big Horse Creek. During the day the corps passed near the newly built and well designed Confederate prison at Millen (Camp Lawton), where ten thousand prisoners of war had been confined until a few days earlier, when they had been removed as Sherman's men approached.[60]

When Twentieth Corps resumed the march on the morning of December 3, Ward crossed Buck Head Creek with Franklin C. Smith's First Brigade and Ross' Third Brigade of his Third Division. He then moved ahead of Geary's Second division to take his place in rear of Jackson's First Division. Ward moved on to the Augusta and Savannah Railroad, where Smith's brigade was detached, to destroy the track. Ward passed to the right of the prison stockade with Ross' brigade and went into camp near Big Horse Creek. Smith's brigade came in about 11:00 that night after completing his work on the railroad.[61]

That morning, Carlin's train reported to its own division, and the cavalry train and Dustin's Second Brigade reported to Geary. When Dustin moved out at 7:00 AM, he was in charge of 240 wagons belonging to the cavalry, and his men were deployed along the train four paces apart. He crossed Buck Head Creek and reached Millen prison about noon. He halted there for about an hour and then moved on. The brigade crossed the Augusta and Savannah Railroad about dark and took the Sylvania road. Dustin finally camped at midnight, roughly four miles east of Millen. By that time the men were exhausted, hungry, and very much in need of sleep.[62]

On November 24 Kilpatrick arrived at Milledgeville from Gordon and then moved on rapidly toward Augusta, Georgia, to create the impression that this was Sherman's next destination. The next day, he crossed the

Ogeechee at the shoals, about twelve miles north of the Georgia Central Railroad, and arrived at Waynesboro November 26. The next day he moved on to Brier Creek.

Wheeler's cavalry, which had been following Kilpatrick during the march from Milledgeville, was pressing the Union cavalry so closely that Kilpatrick turned toward Waynesboro. He was attacked by Wheeler near Buck Head Church and forced to retire to Louisville to await infantry support.[63]

Meanwhile, Davis' Fourteenth Corps had also been moving toward Savannah, passing through Sandersville and arriving at Louisville November 28.[64]

Davis' Fourteenth Corps left Louisville December 1 and moved on toward Millen, camping on the night of December 2 two miles from Buck Head Bridge. The next day it moved to a point near Lumpkin's Station on the Savannah and Augusta Railroad.[65]

Howard's Right Wing had been keeping pace with the Left Wing as it moved toward Savannah. It left Gordon November 24 and marched eastward along the Georgia Central Railroad to Ball's Ferry on the Oconee River, where it arrived the next day.[66]

After crossing the river, Blair's corps moved along the present-day Georgia Highway 17, passing through Herndon, Millen, and Scarboro (Station No. 7), where it camped December 3. December 8 Blair was near Eden (Station No. 2) on the railroad, and the following day he moved on to Pooler (Station No. 1).[67]

Osterhaus' corps moved by roads to the south of that used by Blair and marched through Wrightsville, Sutherland's Mills, and Summerville. On December 10 he took position near King's Ferry in front of Savannah, on the extreme right of Sherman's line.[68]

With his army assembled in the vicinity of Millen early in December 1864, Sherman successfully completed the second stage of his march to the sea, and then, by his next march orders, he made it clear that his destination was Savannah. He destroyed the depot and other public property in Millen and on December 4 began the final phase of his campaign by advancing three of his corps on different roads down the narrowing space between the Savannah and Ogeechee rivers, directly toward Savannah. Davis' Fourteenth Corps took the Old Savannah Road (or Old River Road) along the west side of the Savannah River, through Sardis and Jacksonboro; Williams' Twentieth Corps advanced on the middle road by way of Springfield; and Blair's Seventeenth Corps followed the Georgia Central Railroad to Cameron, destroying the track as it advanced.[69]

Osterhaus, with Fifteenth Corps, marched on roads to the south and west of the Ogeechee River in two columns some two miles apart. Howard, in person, accompanied this corps. According to Osterhaus' marching orders, he was to cross to the east bank of the Ogeechee River opposite Eden (Station No. 2) on the Georgia Central Railroad and then join the other three corps on a line in front of Savannah.[70]

December 4, in beautiful weather, Twentieth Corps began its final advance toward Savannah, with the divisions marching in the same order as of the day before along the Louisville and Savannah road. The country through which it passed was flat, swampy, covered with pine timber, and sparsely settled. The roads were only lightly traveled. The march was not without interruption. On one occasion the enemy destroyed a dam that impounded a large body of water used to run a mill, and this forced the men to halt until the water subsided. After marching fifteen miles, the corps camped on the Little Ogeechee River. Ward's Third Division camped that night at the crossroads six miles from Sylvania. Dustin's Second Brigade of the division was still guarding the trains.[71]

During the period December 5-7, Twentieth Corps advanced by way of Turkey Creek to Springfield. The Confederates attempted to slow the march by felling timber across the roads, but corduroying the roads through the swamp consumed most of the time.

Geary moved at 6:30 on the morning of December 5 crossing Little Horse Creek, the South Fork of Little Ogeechee River, and the Little Ogeechee, covering twelve miles before going into camp. Ward moved at 7:00 AM, passed Jackson's division, and marched eight miles on the Springfield road before going into camp at 1:00 PM. Dustin's brigade, when relieved from its service with Geary's division, marched fifteen miles to rejoin Ward's division and went into camp at 7:00 PM. Jackson's division remained in camp until 3:00 PM, waiting for the other divisions to pass. It then took up the march over a road that was in such terrible condition that the men had covered only three miles when they halted for the night at 11:00 PM. During the day, Kilpatrick's cavalry advanced from Alexander to Jacksonboro, covering the rear of Fourteenth Corps.[72]

December 6 Williams' corps camped near Cowpens Creek. Ward's division marched in advance of the corps for a distance of fourteen miles and camped in a pine forest at 3:00 PM, ten miles northwest of Springfield. It continued its advance the next day, and, after marching ten miles through swampy country, the corps camped on Jack's Creek near Springfield. The pioneers cleared the road of trees that had been felled by the enemy and built a bridge over Jack's Creek during cloudy and sometimes rainy weather. Ward's division again marched at the head of the corps that day, and Dustin's brigade brought up the rear of the division. Franklin C. Smith's brigade went into Springfield, but the other two brigades camped about a mile west of the town.[73]

On December 8 Twentieth Corps moved forward toward Monteith (Station No. 10) on the Charleston and Savannah Railroad, with Geary's division in the lead, Jackson's division following, and Ward's division in the rear. Back at Madison on November 27, Ward's division had been given the responsibility of guarding all the corps' trains, which enabled the other two divisions to march unencumbered. Ward was still performing that duty as the corps moved out that day, with the men marching in single file along the trains. Most of the route was through pine forests, in which the men passed a number of plantation houses and obtained quite a large supply of potatoes, sugar cane, fodder, mutton, and poultry.[74]

Ward's division crossed Jack's Branch with the trains December 8 and then Ward massed his troops and parked the trains around Springfield to wait for Jackson's and Geary's divisions to pass. At 2:00 PM, the division again moved forward slowly with the trains, over terrible roads. After marching six miles, the head of the column went into camp at the forks of the road, but the men marching at the rear did not come in until 8:45 the next morning. Dustin's Second Brigade, marching in the center of the division that afternoon, did not go into camp until about 11:00 that night.[75]

On December 9 Twentieth Corps changed the direction of its line of march to the east. Jackson's division took the lead that morning, and shortly after leaving its camp turned left on the road from Eden to Montieth Station, arriving at Montieth Swamp about noon.[76]

This swamp, which was one of the worst encountered by the corps on its march, was about five miles west of Montieth Station and was about two miles wide where the road crossed. In the swamp the road was obstructed for nearly a mile by felled trees. The enemy had constructed two redoubts beyond the tree obstructions, and in one of these a piece of artillery commanded the road, preventing the removal of the cut trees. Jackson soon outflanked these works, however, and the enemy fled. The road was then quickly cleared, and Jackson's division crossed the swamp and camped on dry ground beyond. Geary's division, which had been following Jackson that day, then came up, crossed the swamp, and camped near Jackson's division.[77]

At 9:00 AM December 9 Ward's division, with Coburn's old brigade, also moved out from camp with orders to overtake Jackson's and Geary's divisions, if possible. Dustin's brigade, which had the lead that morning, broke camp at daylight and began its march toward Montieth Station. The 85th Indiana, under Lieutenant Colonel Crane, was detailed to move ahead and repair the road for the trains. It is interesting to note that as the men of the 85th Indiana moved out that morning, it was the first time since leaving Atlanta that they had been hungry and without rations.[78]

The work while passing through the swamp was arduous and constant, but was faithfully performed. McBride, in his *History of the Thirty-Third Indiana*, describes the details:

The roads were in the worst possible condition. The wheels would cut through to the hubs, and the wagons became widely scattered. In many instances the corduroy would be engulfed by the quicksands and water. From the time the army left Madison the duty of guarding the corps train had been turned wholly over to the Third division, Twentieth Corps, and while it was a place of great honor, for the capture or destruction of the supply train would have endangered the success of the movement, it entailed upon the men a vast amount of additional labor, in that they were often required to aid the mules by placing their own shoulders to the wheels.

Despite these difficulties, Ward's division advanced fifteen miles that day and went into camp that afternoon between the swamp and Montieth Station, in rear of the other two divisions of the corps.[79]

In his *History of the Eighty-Fifth Indiana*, Brant tells of an episode that probably occurred during the passage of Ward's Third Division of Twentieth Corps through Montieth Swamp. Captain Frank Rude, with his Company F of the 85th Indiana, was engaged in corduroying the road, when Ward rode up and stopped to watch the work. As usual, the general had been drinking when he spoke to Captain Rude:

. . . Captain, corduroy is good, its shaky down here. Corduroy is good, its shaky. The first wagon will go down, down, and the second wagon will go down to the hub, and the next wagon will go down to H-l. I tell you captain its shaky.

Brant then goes on to say:

After that in our regiment the boys called General Ward "Old Shaky." But with all his failings General Ward was a brave soldier. I am glad to record it—that after the war he reformed his life and joined the Methodist Church. He rests in peace with the silent majority.[80]

At times during December 9 the men of Williams' Twentieth Corps could hear the fire of artillery from the direction of Savannah, indicating that Howard's Right Wing was already in contact with the enemy.[81]

December 10 Williams' Twentieth Corps marched on to Montieth Station on the Charleston and Savannah Railroad, about ten miles from Savannah. Jackson's division was leading that morning and was followed by Ward's and Geary's divisions.

When Jackson arrived on the railroad his men began destroying the track. When Ward came up, Williams directed him to protect Jackson's working parties with his division. Ward formed Franklin C. Smith's First Brigade in line of battle near Cherokee Hill, and then the division moved forward without serious opposition until within about four and a half miles of Savannah, where it came up to a strong line of enemy works located behind swamps and artificial ponds. Jackson destroyed about three miles of track near Montieth Station before following Ward toward Savannah.[82]

When Ward came up to the enemy's main line, he halted and formed Smith's and Ross' brigades on the right of the Jonesboro road, where Ross connected on the right with Fourteenth Corps. Jackson brought up his division on the left of Ward's division.[83]

Dustin marched with his brigade to within five miles of Savannah on the Savannah and Augusta dirt road, crossed the Charleston and Savannah Railroad ten miles from Savannah, and then went into camp in reserve in rear of the other two brigades.[84]

Geary's division was put in charge of the corps trains that day, following the other two divisions toward Savannah. It arrived at Montieth Station about noon, and then moved forward and camped that night near Five-Mile Post. The trains then came up and parked in the woods nearby.[85]

Twentieth Corps remained generally in this position in front of the enemy's main line of defenses until December 21, when the enemy evacuated Savannah.[86]

December 11 Geary's division moved to the left and drove back the enemy pickets to their main works. Williams then established his Twentieth Corps in line of battle facing Savannah. The line began on the Savannah River, near Williamson's plantation, and ran to the southwest in advance of Pipemaker's Creek to the Charleston and Savannah Railroad, crossed the railroad and continued on to the Georgia Central Railroad, a few hundred yards from the junction of the two roads, connecting on the right with Fourteenth Corps. Ward's division was on the right of Williams' line, Jackson's division in the center, and Geary's division on the left.[87]

Also on December 11 Williams sent Captain Charles E. Winegar's Battery I, First New York Light Artillery to the Savannah River to block enemy traffic, and he directed Ward to send a regiment over to the river to support the battery. About dark Ward detached Lieutenant Colonel Edward Bloodgood's 22nd Wisconsin of Dustin's brigade and sent it to Gibbon's plantation on the river to protect the battery.[88]

At dark on December 11, the remaining regiments of Dustin's brigade moved forward from their position in reserve into the first line. When in position, Lieutenant Colonel James E. Burton's 33rd Indiana connected on the left with the right of Franklin C. Smith's First Brigade, Crane's 85th Indiana was in the center, and Baker's 19th Michigan connected on the right with the left of Ross' Third Brigade, midway between the dirt road and the railroad. The general direction of this line was north and south.[89]

Meanwhile, on December 3 Davis' Fourteenth Corps and Kilpatrick's cavalry had also resumed their march from Buck Head Bridge toward Savannah. It passed through Habersham and Lumpkin's Station and halted on December 5 at Jacksonboro, with the advance at Buck Creek Post Office. The next day Fourteenth Corps advanced about twenty miles on the river road and camped near Hudson's Ferry.[90]

From there it moved by way of Beaver Dam Creek, Ebenezer Church, and Cuylers plantation and arrived at Ten-Mile House December 10. There the corps yielded the road to Twentieth Corps, which was advancing from Montieth on a road that intersected the Augusta road.[91]

The next day Davis' corps moved down the Augusta road to a point near the Twentieth Corps, which was then in line in front of the enemy's works. There it relieved Seventeenth Corps, which was in position on the Louisville road and in the vicinity of the Ogeechee Canal. Thus on December 12 Fourteenth Corps was in line in front of the enemy works, where it connected on the left with Twentieth Corps near the Charleston and Savannah Railroad and on the right with Seventeenth Corps beyond the canal, near Lawton's plantation.[92]

By December 12 all four of Sherman's corps had come up and were in line, facing the Confederate fortifications covering Savannah. Twentieth Corps was on the left, next to the river, and then in order to the right were Fourteenth Corps, Seventeenth Corps, and Fifteenth Corps, the latter being on the extreme right of the army near King's Bridge.[93]

The defensive lines north of Savannah began at the mouth of a swampy creek that flowed into the Savannah River about three miles above the city and then followed generally along this creek to the head of a similar stream that ran into the Little Ogeechee River. These creeks greatly enhanced the strength of the line, being very marshy, bordered by rice fields, and flooded by tide water or by inland ponds. Water gates were used to control the water level. These were covered by Confederate heavy artillery. Further, the only entrances to the city were by five narrow causeways, two of them carrying the two railroads and the other three for the Augusta, the Louisville, and the Ogeechee dirt roads. All five of these avenues were commanded by Rebel heavy ordnance.[94]

At the time Twentieth Corps arrived near Savannah, food was very scarce, and in Dustin's brigade only one-third rations of crackers and potatoes were being issued to the men. Fortunately, the 22nd Wisconsin took possession of some rice mills on the upper end of Hutchinson's Island in the Savannah River and also the workers operating the mills. Lieutenant William S. Harbert, acting commissary of subsistence of Dustin's brigade, was put in charge of the mills, which he operated with details from the brigade. When all available rice had been hulled, it was sacked and carried on barges to the mainland, where it was distributed to the appreciative soldiers.[95]

Also on December 12 Winegar's battery, supported by the 22nd Wisconsin, attacked three boats attempting to pass the blockade. Two of the boats were armed. The unarmed boat was disabled and captured by Federal troops when it was abandoned by the other boats.[96]

When Sherman arrived near the coast, a Union fleet commanded by Rear Admiral John A. Dahlgren was in Ossabaw Sound, off the mouth of the Ogeechee River. With the fleet were ships carrying large quantities of food and supplies and a great amount of mail for the soldiers. Sherman, however, was unable to communicate with Dahlgren, because the Confederate Fort McAllister, located on the south bank of the Ogeechee River, prevented the passage of boats on the river. In order to obtain the much needed supplies from the fleet, Sherman sent Hazen's Second Division of Fifteenth Corps, with a battery of artillery and one section of another, to eliminate this barrier. Late in the afternoon of December 13, Hazen stormed and captured the fort, and in so doing sealed the fate of Savannah. A short time later, boats loaded with food and supplies were moving upriver, and the men were being supplied with greatly needed food and clothing.[97]

On the morning of December 14 Crane of the 85th Indiana reported to corps headquarters with his own regiment and the 19th Michigan for special duty. He took charge of twenty-four wagons and moved eight and a half miles beyond the lines, foraging for staves and rails for fuel to run the engines at the rice mills. He returned with the wagons fully loaded at 5:00 PM.[98]

On December 16 Jackson ordered Carman to move with his Second Brigade of First Division across the Savannah river to South Carolina to threaten the Charleston and Savannah Railroad. That very foggy morning, Dustin's brigade moved to the left of the Savannah and Augusta road, to a point about midway between the road and the river, occupying the partially completed works just vacated by Carman's brigade. In that position it connected on the right with Franklin C. Smith's First Brigade of Ward's division and on the left with Selfridge's First Brigade of Jackson's division. The picket line was established about five hundred yards in front of this line and about the same distance from the enemy's works. Dustin then held a long line, about seven hundred yards in length, with only the three regiments of the brigade that were with him at the time. (The 22nd Wisconsin was still on duty at Gibbon's plantation on the Savannah River.) Also at that time, Ward's division covered a front of about a mile and a half, with Ross' brigade on the right, Smith's brigade in the center, and Dustin's Second Brigade on the left.[99]

December 16 the men of the 85th Indiana received the last half-ration of the hardtack that the brigade had brought from Atlanta. The next day, however, they received the first mail from home and wrote the first letters to friends and family since leaving Atlanta. In the days that followed, a new supply line was opened between the fleet and the army by way of the Ogeechee River, and the men then received sufficient food and supplies of all kinds.[100]

December 20 Dustin began the construction of a new line about five hundred yards in advance of the one that he then held, and details from the regiments of the brigade were busily engaged at this work all that day and during the following night. This new line was near a marsh, beyond which was the fortified position of the enemy. A rice canal ran across this marsh, and if an attack were made it would be necessary to cross this canal. Bundles of cane and long poles as stringers would be used to build a foot bridge across the canal. Beyond the canal the enemy had cut and slashed timber to make an almost impassable barrier. During the night the Union artillery was put in position to open an attack the next day. At dawn the next morning, after a few hours sleep, the men of the 85th Indiana were up and ready for the order to begin their attack. This order never came. Captain Caleb Bales of Company D, of the 85th Indiana, who had been out on the picket line and had been in the enemy's works, came in to say "no enemy there."[101]

At 3:00 AM December 21 all firing ceased along the front of Geary's division, and when his pickets advanced they found the enemy rapidly withdrawing from their line of fortifications. Geary then took possession of the vacated works, sent a staff officer to inform Sherman of what had happened, and rapidly pushed on in the direction of Savannah. Hardee had abandoned the city during the night of December 20 and had withdrawn with his army into South Carolina. Just outside of Savannah, near the junction of the Louisville and Augusta roads, Geary met the mayor, with delegates from the board of aldermen, bearing a flag of truce. At about 4:30 AM, Geary received the surrender of the city. About dawn his division entered Savannah, and soon the National colors, together with those of the division, were hoisted over the dome of the Exchange and over the United States Custom House.[102]

Before daylight December 21 Ward learned that the Confederates had retired and that Geary's division was in the entrenchments. When Geary pushed on toward Savannah, Ward advanced his skirmish line and occupied these works with his division. The skirmish line of Dustin's brigade advanced that morning under the direction of Lieutenant Colonel Crane, brigade officer of the day. The brigade then moved up, with the 33rd Indiana leading, occupying the vacated works in front of the division. Dustin remained there for about two hours and then moved forward and took position at the center of Ward's Division, about one mile northwest of Savannah.[103]

At 11:00 AM that day, Williams ordered Ward to place his division in camp west of the canal, and Ward immediately moved forward and formed the division in line, with Samuel Ross' Third Brigade on the right, Daniel Dustin's Second Brigade (Coburn's old brigade) in the center, and Franklin C. Smith's First Brigade on the left. The wagon train was parked in rear of the division line.[104]

On December 22, after Geary's division had occupied Savannah, Sherman sent the following message:

> Savannah, Ga., December 22, 1864
> (Via Fort Monroe 6:45 PM, 25th)
>
> His Excellency President Lincoln:
> I beg to present you, as a Christmas gift, the city of Savannah, with 150 heavy guns and plenty ammunition, and also about 25,000 bales of cotton.
>
> W. T. Sherman
> Major-General[105]

One of Sherman's first acts was to appoint Geary as commander of the post of Savannah and to assign his division the duty of guarding and patrolling the city. Jackson's and Ward's divisions took position on the west side of Savannah, where they occupied a line from the Savannah River to the Georgia Central Railroad. They remained in these positions until the end of the month.[106]

At the beginning of the Savannah Campaign, the 85th Indiana left Atlanta with twenty-two officers and 313 men. The regiment arrived before Savannah without any casualties, with all the men in good health except three who had recently been sent to the hospital. The 22nd Wisconsin had 315 men present, with little sickness and no deaths.[107]

To give some idea of the effectiveness of the foragers during the march to the sea, and at the same time giving some idea of the extent of the personal dismay of those from whom the supplies were taken, Lieutenant Harbert, acting commissary of subsistence for Dustin's brigade, gives the following report of subsistence taken from the country during the campaign: 150 head of beef cattle; 475 sheep; eight thousand pounds of fresh pork; two thousand pounds of bacon; ten thousand pounds of poultry; 6,600 bushels of sweet potatoes; five thousand pounds of honey; thirty-three barrels of sorghum syrup; three thousand pounds of corn meal; and 2,300 pounds of flour. Lieutenant Lucius M. Wing, acting assistant quartermaster of the brigade, reported the following procured on the march: thirty-six horses; thirty-two mules; 99,312 pounds of corn; and 66,720 pounds of fodder.[108]

As Sherman's army advanced from Atlanta on its march through Georgia, the slaves all along the route learned of its approach long before the marching columns appeared, and many fell in behind the army and accompanied it as it moved eastward across Georgia. An estimated ten thousand were with the army when it arrived at Savannah, and seven thousand more were left at Fayetteville as the army marched northward through the Carolinas.[109]

McBride, in his *History of the Thirty-Third Indiana*, has left this comment:

> The Negroes continued to flock to the army. Some of them were utilized as servants, but the great mass was becoming an alarming incubus. Persuasions or threats did not deter them. Like an ancient plague of locusts, their numbers increased with each succeeding day. They had to be fed the same as the troops. Notwithstanding the anxiety occasioned by their presence they afforded considerable amusement to the army. Their plantation manners, thorough subordination, and plaintive songs; their natural love for the dance and frequent displays of strength rather touched the kindly nature of the great body of soldiers, and during the march the Negro was treated as humanely as circumstances would permit.[110]

FORAGING—SHERMAN'S "BUMMERS"

When the army left Atlanta, the number of horses and wagons had been reduced to the minimum needed for the transportation of the supplies then on hand, but soon after the march began additional supplies were obtained by foraging. Each company detailed a squad, each detachment a squad, and each headquarters a squad, and these, together with many individual soldiers, left the road at convenient points for the purpose of gathering provisions for the night. At first these men, and groups of men, moved out on foot and brought in what they could carry, but as the days passed these foragers (later called "Sherman's Bummers") rapidly became more effective. In a short time they had changed their methods and appropriated wagons, ox carts, and carriages from the farms along the route and enough mules and horses to carry all the supplies that they could gather over a far larger area.[111]

In addition to bringing in supplies, the activities of the foragers served another very useful military purpose. They were out on every road, all over the country, and in so moving they formed a complete curtain about the army, making it impossible for the enemy to determine whether the army was marching toward Augusta, Macon, or Savannah.[112]

Brant, in his *History of the Eighty-Fifth Indiana*, gives the following brief description of the foragers of the army:

They were our best all round men. They were supposed to be peculiarly fitted for foraging. As a class they were our alert soldiers, brave, discreet and audacious. Men who knew how to find out where the supplies were to be found, with an instinct almost unerring. They found sugar cured hams in new made graves marked by head and foot stones. With ramrods point down they could by punching find things eatable underground. Even under a hen roost to discover a box containing hams.

They could question a darkey and find out if the corn was hid in a swamp. They found wagon loads of sweet potatoes in barns and in the fields already gathered for our coming. Peanuts by the peck, yes by bushels and wagon loads. Hay and forage by the ton all along the way. Sometimes when our trains were not in reach they used farm wagons and buggies to carry things into camp . . . .

Then Sherman's Bummers were good fighters. They curtained our army, and kept the enemy guessing where the main force was to be found. They were on every main and by road, and at every house for miles beyond our main lines. . . . Some of these Bummers said their prayers every morning, and went out in a religious way. We were hungry and they fed us. Many of them were killed but their memory abides.

Had it not been for these religious and other kind of soldiers—called Bummers—we should have gone to bed hungry many times. Now after it is all over we rise up and call them blessed. Many have done well but in a way "thou excellest them all."[113]

This perspective is, of course, that of an officer in Sherman's army and is probably accurate, but it overlooks the terrible hardships and deprivations inflicted on the helpless women, children, and the elderly living in the path of the army. In marching across Georgia, Sherman's men left behind a path of destruction and desolation. They burned homes and buildings, destroyed fences and gardens, took all the horses, mules, and livestock, all the buggies and wagons that were needed for transportation, and left little or no food desperately needed by the people remaining in the region. They also allowed most of the slaves to follow the army from the plantations to seek their freedom. The immediate future for the residents in that part of the state was bleak indeed.

When the army moved northward from Savannah on its march through the Carolinas, the Bummers continued their work. During the early part of the march in South Carolina, Dustin organized a foraging party, which consisted of from fifty to eighty men under a commissary officer from each regiment of the brigade. So successful was this arrangement that, with few exceptions, neither men nor animals suffered from lack of food during the entire march. The efforts of these men were not merely gathering supplies, but there were frequent skirmishes, sometimes heavy, in which the rebels were driven back for considerable distances from the main column. Each night foragers came into camp loaded with provisions, and often with squads of prisoners captured during the day. Dustin further says that Lieutenant Worcester H. Morse of the 22nd Wisconsin, with a party of his own foragers, was the first to enter Fayetteville and drove the enemy rear guard from the town.[114]

Captain Francis C. Crawford, Company G, acting assistant adjutant general on Ward's staff during the Carolinas Campaign, told of an interesting incident that occurred during the march northward through the Carolinas. While on the march, Sherman's men frequently observed enemy troops hovering on their flanks and on their front, and there were almost daily encounters on some part of the line. As a result, the army moved with the vigilance necessary for a march in enemy territory, and it was always in readiness for a fight.

One bright sunny morning, Ward's division was leading the Twentieth Corps, with Dustin's brigade in front, when headquarters received word that the advance had encountered opposition, and had been fired on from a woods that bordered a sluggish stream which flowed across their front. Some days earlier Confederate forces had abandoned Charleston, South Carolina, and Sherman's columns had been cautioned to keep a sharp lookout for these troops, who, it was supposed, would position themselves across the Union line of advance. With this on his mind, Ward and his officers immediately jumped to the conclusion: "Here they are." Crawford then described what happened next as follows:

> The column was halted, wagons parked, pack mules ordered out of the way, information sent to Corps Head Quarters, and all preparations made for a fight.
>
> To the right and left of our front the ground was perfectly level and clear, but to the front, the view was completely shut off by the swamps full of trees and underbrush, except the cutting made by the road, which gave a narrow vista of a half a mile or so beyond a slightly rising background.
>
> Orders soon came to make the crossing, and the division was at once thrown into battle-array knapsacks were unslung and piled. Two brigades (the second, one of them) were deployed in double lines, Skirmishers detailed and thrown forward ready to advance. Musicians and hospital attendants together, behind their regiments. A battery came up on the run and went into line. Regimental flags and "Old Glory" were unfurled in the light breeze. At the center of each Regiment

Division, brigade and regimental commanders with their staffs, and the signal flags all in their places and in full sight, presenting in the bright sunshine, a sight that one seldom witnesses actual warfare.

After about one half hour, when all preparations for the attack had been completed, Crawford asked permission to join his old brigade (Dustin's) in the assault, and this was granted. He then rode down toward his old regiment, the 85th Indiana. Crawford continues his description of this affair:

> ...When in crossing the line of view of the vista through the swamp a most ludicrous scene was presented on the rising ground beyond, putting an end to all this "pomp and circumstance of glorious war."
>
> On the rising ground beyond the swamp, very leisurely strolling along, was a squad of "Sherman's Bummers" who had crossed at some point to our left and as we afterwards learned, had exchanged shots with a few of the enemy's scouts, driving them off but not thinking enough of it to report to anyone. As such occurrences frequently happened to those brave but rather disorderly advance guards.
>
> Much disappointment was expressed at not having a chance to engage the enemy. But I think a feeling of relief was also felt. For not withstanding how brave and heroic the soldier may be, he is always glad when it is over.[115]

When Sherman's soldiers moved into their camps around Goldsboro, later in the campaign, all foragers were ordered to turn in their horses and the men to rejoin their regiments. Their foraging days were over.

When Dustin's brigade marched into the lines about Savannah, the regiments could be well-satisfied with a job well done. They had not distinguished themselves in battle while crossing Georgia, for there had been no serious fighting during that time, but they had corduroyed, slogged through swamps, torn up railroads, and occupied abandoned towns without complaint. Such were the opportunities for soldierly service in Sherman's army in 1864; any man who attacked Lee's army on the hills at Fredericksburg in December 1862 would gladly have changed places with one of Sherman's soldiers, if that were possible. In war, however, circumstances determine a soldier's assignments, and it is his duty to do the best he can.

In closing his report of the Savannah Campaign, Colonel Dustin expressed his satisfaction with the soldiers under his command as follows:

> ... I am exceedingly well pleased with the brigade, and do not hesitate to pronounce it one of which any brigade commander may well be proud. The Twenty-second Wisconsin, Nineteenth Michigan,

and the Eighty-fifth Indiana must be reckoned among the best troops in the service. For the well-known bravery in the face of the enemy of the Thirty-third Indiana Veteran Volunteers, it will always be entitled to honorable mention. For its laxity in discipline, the present officers are by no means wholly responsible. The evil is of long standing, and therefore difficult to eradicate. The men are generally possessed of noble impulses, with pride and ambition to secure a good reputation in all that pertains to a true soldier; . . . [116]

Daniel Dustin, originally the colonel of the 105th Illinois, assumed command of John Coburn's brigade when Coburn was mustered out, due to medical reasons, on September 20, 1864.

USAMHI

Chapter 16

Occupation of Savannah

On December 22, 1864, General William T. Sherman with his staff and escort entered Savannah and moved into the Pulaski House. Sherman had stayed in this hotel many years earlier when he was on duty as a captain in the United States Army. After a short stay there, however, at the invitation of Mr. Charles Green, a wealthy English merchant, Sherman took up quarters in the Green's fine home. In fact, Mr. Green urged Sherman to accept his invitation because he was certain that some other general would move into his home, and he preferred Sherman as his guest.[1]

Major Henry Hitchcock, Assistant Adjutant General and Military Secretary on Sherman's staff, described the Green home as ". . . a fine house and very handsomely furnished. In the wide hall there were some very handsome pieces of statuary and banana trees growing in tubs. In the various rooms of the house there were several fine pictures, books of engravings, and other items of interest."[2]

During the short time that Sherman's army was at and near Savannah, it was refitted and prepared for a march northward through the Carolinas. Although there was much work to do, Captain Jefferson E. Brant of the 85th Indiana said: "Our short stay in that City, eating oysters and sleeping on beds of Spanish moss was a luxury." It was Brant's opinion that the people of Savannah were pleased to be back in the Union.[3]

There is a well known story that one Sunday while in Savannah Sherman attended church and the bishop asked if he might pray for Jefferson Davis and the Confederacy. Sherman is said to have replied "Yes, that Jeff. Davis and the Confederate Government needed praying for." This story, however, is probably not true. Captain Brant, who also attended church there that day, gave his own version of what happened:

> On Christmas Sunday morning George Farrington, Quartermaster of the 85th Indiana, and the writer [Brant] heard the Episcopal service read but no reference to either President or Government. That Bishop was not certain whose hands he would fall into. The sermon was dry but the singing excellent. The aristocracy of the City was there.

General Sherman was there and a large number of the elite of the army in full uniforms—shoulder strapped gentlemen of every grade from two stars to second Lieutenants. But above all a host of the truly noble of the army—the private soldiers. The basket collection beat anything I ever witnessed. I saw one hundred dollar Confederate bills spread out in the basket; that kind of money was cheap; but I saw many greenbacks in that basket. We felt grateful that we could attend church, and that collection was an expression of gratitude.[4]

Further, Hitchcock, who was with Sherman that Sunday, stated that when the minister was reading the service and came to the prayer for the President of the United States, which was in the prayer book, he simply omitted the prayer and moved on to the Litany without pause.[5]

In his *Memoirs*, Sherman writes about the Union occupation of Savannah as follows:

As the division of Major-General John W. Geary, of the Twentieth Corps, was the first to enter Savannah, that officer was appointed to command the place, or to act as a sort of governor. He very soon established a good police, maintained admirable order, and I doubt if Savannah, either before or since, has had a better government than during our stay. The guard-mountings and parades, as well as the greater reviews, became the daily resorts of the ladies, to hear the music of our excellent bands; schools were opened, and the churches every Sunday were well filled with most devout and respectful congregations; stores were reopened, and markets for provisions, meat, wood, etc., were established, so that each family, regardless of race, color, or opinion, could procure all the necessaries and even luxuries of life, provided they had money. Of course, many families were actually destitute of this, and to these were issued stores from our own stock of supplies. I remember to have given to Dr. Arnold, the Mayor, an order for the contents of a large warehouse of rice, which he confided to a committee of gentlemen, who went north (to Boston), and soon returned with one or more cargoes of flour, hams, sugar, coffee, etc. for gratuitous distribution, which relieved the most pressing wants until the revival of trade and business enabled the people to provide for themselves.[6]

On Christmas Day, while the 85th Indiana was at Savannah, Hiram S. Tillotson resigned and departed for home. Tillotson was formerly first lieutenant of Company F of the 85th Indiana Regiment. He assisted in organizing the company at Middletown (present-day Prairie Creek) in Vigo

County and was later promoted to adjutant of the regiment. Upon his return home he resumed his old trade as a harness maker.[7]

Sherman reviewed the Twentieth Corps December 30, probably to strengthen a sense of pride and confidence in the men which his presence inspired. Brant noted: "We had a grand review of the whole army under the shadow of the Pulaski monument and marched before General Sherman on Water Street where we could look out upon the ocean [Savannah River].[8]

After William J. Hardee evacuated Savannah December 21, Sherman put his army into camps around the city. Henry W. Slocum's Left Wing occupied a line that extended from the Savannah River at a point about one and a half miles northwest of the city to Milepost No. 7 on the Ogeechee Canal. Alpheus S. Williams' Twentieth Corps was on the left and Jefferson C. Davis' Fourteenth Corps was on the right of Slocum's line. John W. Geary's Second Division, Twentieth Corps, occupied the city of Savannah. Oliver O. Howard's Right Wing held the line from the right of Fourteenth Corps to Fort McAllister, southwest of Savannah. The troops remained generally in these positions until the army began its crossing of the Savannah River on its movement into South Carolina.[9]

Shortly after the occupation of Savannah, Sherman directed Colonel Orlando M. Poe, chief engineer of the Military Division of the Mississippi, to select and entrench a new line to defend such stores, depots, and materials that would be left there when Sherman's army departed from the city on its march northward. Poe reconnoitered and laid off a new line of parapets to enable a comparatively small garrison of about five thousand men to hold the place. This done, he put to work a heavy detail of soldiers on this new line.[10]

Brevet Brigadier General Langdon C. Easton, chief quartermaster, and Colonel Amos Beckwith, chief commissary of subsistence, had organized a complete depot of supplies, but, although vessels arrived almost daily with mail and provisions, it was some time before the army was prepared to move out on a new and hazardous campaign. In time, however, the work of preparation was completed and Sherman was ready to resume the march northward.[11]

Pocotaligo Depot, where Sherman began his march through the Carolinas.

Chapter 17

Carolinas Campaign

Savannah to Fayetteville

Early in December 1864, as Major General William T. Sherman's army was approaching Savannah and the capture of that city seemed assured, Major General George G. Meade's Army of the Potomac was facing General Robert E. Lee's Army of Northern Virginia in its defensive works at Petersburg, Virginia. Meade's army was having difficulty breaking the siege. At that point Grant began a discussion of plans with Sherman for bringing his Western armies to Virginia to cooperate with Meade in defeating Lee's army. Grant first proposed bringing Sherman's army northward by sea, but this idea was rejected because of the difficulty in obtaining the necessary transportation.[1]

December 18 Sherman proposed that he march northward through the Carolinas and destroy everything of military value in South Carolina, as he had done in Georgia. Grant approved this proposal and asked Sherman for more information about his plans. Sherman replied on the day before Christmas that he proposed to move on Branchville, South Carolina, ignoring Augusta and Charleston, and march to the Charleston and Wilmington Railroad at some point between the Santee and Cape Fear rivers. Then, after capturing Wilmington, he would move on toward Raleigh, North Carolina. The plan was later modified somewhat when Wilmington was occupied February 22 by Union Forces in North Carolina. Raleigh, however, remained an objective on Sherman's proposed line of march.[2]

Sherman was authorized on January 2, 1865, to march north with his entire army by land, and he at once began preparations. His first step was to establish a foothold on the South Carolina side of the Savannah River, and he selected Hardeeville as the rendezvous for the Left Wing and Pocotaligo for the Right Wing.[3]

At that time, the army was still organized in two wings and a cavalry division as follows:

Right Wing (Army of the Tennessee), Major General Oliver O. Howard
    Fifteenth Corps, Major General Peter J. Osterhaus
    Seventeenth Corps, Major General Frank P. Blair, Jr.

(Note: John A. Logan resumed command of Fifteenth Corps January 8, 1865, relieving Osterhaus.)

Left Wing, Major General Henry W. Slocum
 Fourteenth Corps, Brevet Major General Jefferson C. Davis
 Twentieth Corps, Brigadier General Alpheus S. Williams

Third Cavalry Division, Brigadier General Judson Kilpatrick

Alpheus S. Williams' Twentieth Corps was organized as follows:

First Division, Brigadier General Nathaniel J. Jackson
 First Brigade, Colonel James L. Selfridge
 Second Brigade, Colonel Ezra A. Carman
 Third Brigade, Colonel James S. Robinson

Second Division, Brigadier General John W. Geary
 First Brigade, Colonel Ario Pardee, Jr., to March 30;
  George W. Mindil
 Second Brigade, George W. Mindil to March 30;
  Colonel Patrick H. Jones
 Third Brigade, Colonel Henry A. Barnum

Third Division, Brigadier General William T. Ward
 First Brigade, Colonel Henry Case
 Second Brigade, Colonel Daniel Dustin
 Third Brigade, Colonel Samuel Ross

During the Carolinas Campaign, Daniel Dustin's Second Brigade of Ward's Third Division was organized as follows:

33rd Indiana, Lieutenant Colonel James E. Burton
85th Indiana, Lieutenant Colonel Alexander B. Crane
19th Michigan, Lieutenant Colonel John J. Baker, became sick at
 Hardee's plantation. Major David Anderson
22nd Wisconsin, Captain Darwin R. May, Captain George H. Brown
 Lieutenant Colonel Edward Bloodgood [4]

During the march through the Carolinas, many of the officers of Sherman's army were assigned brevet rank. Those so assigned in Twentieth Corps were as follows:

To rank of Brevet Major General: January 12, 1865, Alpheus S. Williams and John W. Geary; February 24, William T. Ward. Jefferson C. Davis had been so assigned August 8, 1864, and Judson Kilpatrick of the cavalry was also assigned the rank Brevet Major General January 12, 1865.

To rank of Brevet Brigadier General: January 12, 1865, Henry A. Barnum, William Cogswell, and Ario Pardee; March 16, James L. Selfridge, William Hawley, and Daniel Dustin of Coburn's old brigade.[5]

At the beginning of the march into South Carolina, the strength of Sherman's army was about sixty thousand officers and men and sixty-eight guns. His trains consisted of about 2,500 wagons, with six mules for each wagon, and about six hundred ambulances, each drawn by two horses. The wagons contained sufficient ammunition for a major battle, forage for about seven days, and provisions for twenty days. The latter consisted largely of bread, sugar, coffee, and salt. For fresh meat, the men would depend primarily on a herd of cattle driven along with the army, and on such cattle, hogs, and poultry as might be found along the line of march.[6]

THE OPENING MOVEMENTS

Sherman's opening movements were planned to confuse the enemy as to his true objectives. With this in mind, he transferred General Howard's Right Wing by sea to Beaufort, South Carolina, with orders to move out and occupy Pocotaligo, in position to advance on Charleston. General Slocum's Left Wing and Judson Kilpatrick's cavalry division were to cross the Savannah River at Savannah and at Sister's Ferry, from which points they were to march toward Augusta, Georgia. When these opening moves were completed, the two wings of the army were to advance on Columbia, South Carolina.[7]

Sherman's first step was to send Alpheus S. Williams with his Twentieth Corps to effect a lodgment on the north bank of the Savannah River. On December 30 Williams ordered William T. Ward to move the next day with his Third Division of the corps and cross the channel to Hutchinson's Island in the Savannah River. Ward was then to cross the second channel of the river into South Carolina on a bridge to be constructed there.[8]

Ward moved at 6:30 the next morning, as ordered, but upon arriving on Hutchinson's Island he found that little or no progress had been made on bridging the second channel. A cold rain fell that day, and the men who had not been issued new clothing suffered severely. Nevertheless, Ward obtained some small boats, and, after much labor and under the fire of enemy, mounted troops on the far side of the river and crossed a part of Colonel Henry Case's brigade. Unable to cross the rest of his command that night, he withdrew the men who had already crossed and put the brigade in camp on the island. Because of the severity of the weather, Dustin's brigade and Samuel Ross' brigade of Ward's division, which had also moved forward, were allowed to return to their camps, about a mile and a half northwest of Savannah.[9]

In his *History of the Thirty-Third Indiana Regiment*, John R. McBride tells of the following interesting incident that occurred during the Federal occupation of Hutchinson's Island:

> While the pontoniers were engaged in laying pontoons from Hutchinson's Island to the South Carolina shore in a storm of wind and snow and under fire of the enemy's sharpshooters, the Thirty-third Indiana was stationed near by as a support. Harry Lyons, of Company E, was anxious to know where the bullets came from and climbed a tree for that purpose. He had no sooner gained the top of the tree when he became a target for the sharpshooters and made great haste to descend. His comrades wanted to know the cause of his hurry, and he replied that the "Johnnies were making it too hot for him." He thought the conversation was conducted in a low tone of voice. Now, then, the sequel: A quarter of a century afterward, while Lyons was in Southwestern Missouri he was relating the circumstances and he had hardly begun when one of the listeners checked him and related the story himself, repeating every word of the conversation alluded to. The listener was one of the sharpshooters on the South Carolina shore. Strange, but true.[10]

Early on the morning of January 1, 1865, Case's entire brigade, with great labor, crossed the second channel by means of three small boats, and it then moved immediately to the Cheves' plantation, which was some six miles from the crossing. The small enemy forces that were on the road fell back as the brigade advanced.[11]

At about 3:00 PM that day, Dustin's and Ross' brigades again crossed to Hutchinson's Island and reached the second channel about dark. Lieutenant Colonel John J. Baker crossed his 19th Michigan of Dustin's brigade in small boats, and the other three regiments of the brigade and Ross' brigade were ferried over on the steamer *Planter*, going into camp early on the morning of January 2, 1865, at Screven's Ferry, on the river bank opposite

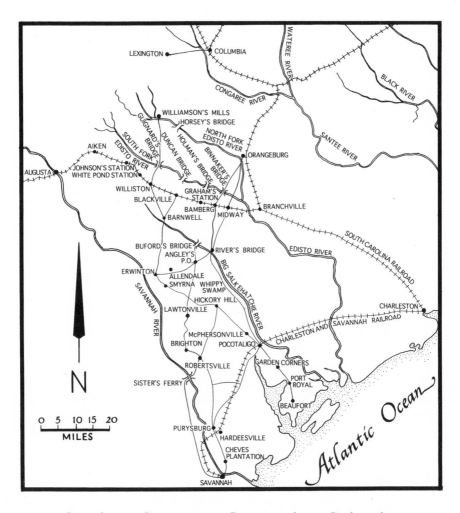

Carolinas Campaign, Savannah to Columbia

Savannah. During the rest of the day, scows carried the transportation and baggage of the division across the river.[12]

December 27, 1864, Grant, at City Point, Virginia, wrote a letter to Sherman, which included the following instructions:

> Without waiting further directions, then, you may make your prepa-rations to start on your northern expedition without delay. Break up the railroads in South and North Carolina, and join the armies oper-ating against Richmond as soon as you can. I will leave out all sugges-tions about the route you should take, knowing that your information, gained daily in the course of events, will be better than any that can be obtained now.[13]

Dustin's and Ross' brigades of Ward's division moved north on January 4 about seven miles from Screven's Ferry and occupied some old Rebel works at Hardee's plantation. Also that day Case's brigade of the same division marched from the Cheves' plantation to join the other two brigades at Hardee's plantation. Ward's division remained there for almost two weeks, drilling, erecting camps, scouting the country as far as New River and Red Bluff and repairing the road leading back to the river. Dustin's brigade fur-nished daily details of from sixty to one hundred men for this purpose. During much of the time spent at the plantation, Lieutenant Colonel Alexander B. Crane of the 85th Indiana commanded the Second Brigade while Dustin was on detached duty in Savannah.[14]

Meanwhile, on January 3 Howard began to move his Right Wing (Army of the Tennessee) into South Carolina. That day, Major General Frank P. Blair's Seventeenth Corps moved by sea from Savannah to Beaufort, South Carolina, and January 14 it was established at Pocotaligo on the Charles-ton and Savannah Railroad. Major General John Logan's Fifteenth Corps (less Brevet Major General John M. Corse's Fourth Division) followed Blair and by January 28 was in position at Garden's Corners and Port Royal. Corse was under orders to move his division by land and join the rest of the corps in South Carolina. After delays caused by floods and bad roads, Sherman directed Corse to join Slocum's Left Wing and march by way of Sister's Ferry. Corse arrived at Sister's Ferry and reported to Slocum January 30.[15]

Sherman left Savannah January 21 with his staff and moved by sea for Beaufort, arriving there January 23. He moved on to Pocotaligo two days later and then rode out to examine the country through which he planned to move the Right Wing at the beginning of its march through South Caro-lina.[16]

Ward's division marched on January 17 to Hardeeville over roads that had been obstructed with fallen timber. There Ward halted with his First

Brigade and Third Brigade and established division headquarters. Dustin's Second Brigade moved on about three miles up the river to Purysburg, an old steamboat landing on the Savannah River, about twenty-five miles above Savannah. This place could scarcely be called a town, for it consisted of only a few buildings, a brick kiln, and an old fort. All the local inhabitants had departed except one black family.[17]

Dustin's brigade went into camp that night at Purysburg on the low ground near the river, and there the men pitched their tents, put their bunks on stakes, and settled in for a night's sleep. This, however, was not to be. The water in the river was rising because of the recent heavy rains, and at the same time the tide was coming in from the sea; about midnight the men were awakened to find that their tents were about six to eight inches deep in water. In the camp of the 85th Indiana, the men waded out, but Lieutenant Colonel Crane and Quartermaster George E. Farrington were in deeper water and horses were sent in to bring them out.

After this experience, the brigade moved to higher ground and established a much better camp. All but three of the twenty houses of Purysburg had been abandoned, and the men tore them down and used the lumber to make walls and floors for the tents, using the bricks from their chimneys to build fireplaces. The men also found some rocking chairs, and for the next two weeks many of them sat by their fireplaces, smoked their pipes, read the daily papers, and wrote letters home. At that time the men were generally in a good mood; the end of the war was not far off, and they knew it.[18]

There was a dark side to that, however. In a letter home, Captain Jefferson E. Brant of the 85th Indiana wrote to his family that "Our boys seem to think they have special privileges in South Carolina, to take what they want and destroy the balance." Sherman's army was determined to punish South Carolina for the firing on Fort Sumter and for being the first state to pass an ordinance of secession.[19]

On the march to Purysburg, Lieutenant Colonel John J. Baker became ill and returned to Savannah, leaving Major David Anderson in command of the 19th Michigan. Baker was in the hospital for three months and then returned to his regiment in late March. Within a week of his return, he was injured by a fall from his horse and spent the rest of the war in a hospital. Also at about this time, Lieutenant Colonel Edward Bloodgood left for home because of a heart condition, and he did not rejoin the regiment until April 6. Captain Francis Mead commanded the 22nd Wisconsin during his absence.[20]

On January 18 and 19 Dustin sent out two reconnaissances, which reported the presence of small enemy forces on the roads to Grahamsville and Robertsville. Further reconnaissances were sent out by Dustin's brigade and the other brigades of Ward's division January 23-25.[21]

On the night of January 19, 1865, the steam-tug *General Lee* arrived at Purysburg with one hunded thousand rations, and the next day details from Dustin's brigade unloaded the food onto the river bank. Two days later, the *General Lee* returned with quartermaster stores, and these too were unloaded by details from the brigade. On January 26 Dustin's men unloaded quartermaster and commissary stores from the steamer *Jeff Davis*.[22]

Brigadier General Nathaniel J. Jackson's First Division of Twentieth Corps remained near Savannah until January 17, then broke camp and crossed the Savannah River and marched by way of Cheves' plantation and Hardeeville, and arrived at Purysburg January 19, 1865. There both his division and Ward's division could draw supplies that had been sent up the Savannah River.[23]

In preparing his plans for the campaign, Sherman intended that Howard's Right Wing be at Pocotaligo by January 15 and that Slocum's Left Wing be at Robertsville at about the same time. From these points, the army would begin its march north through South Carolina.[24]

Williams' Twentieth Corps was to move up the north side of the Savannah River to Robertsville, and Brevet Major General Jefferson C. Davis' Fourteenth Corps was to march on the Georgia side of the river to Sister's Ferry, where it was to cross the river and join Twentieth Corps at Robertsville. Brevet Major General John W. Geary's Second Division of Twentieth Corps did not accompany the other two divisions of the corps when they marched to Purysburg, but remained in Savannah on garrison duty until relieved. Earlier, on January 5, 1865, Major General Cuvier Grover's Second Division of Nineteenth Corps, then in the Shenandoah Valley, had been ordered to Savannah, where it arrived January 17 and 18 and relieved Geary's division January 19.[25]

Very heavy rains began to fall that day, however, and they continued day and night until January 23. As a result, the river overflowed, flooding the country on both sides of the river, covering the roads and rendering them impassable for both troops and trains. The floods swept away a large part of the causeway from Savannah to Hardeeville; Geary was forced to remain near Savannah until January 25. On that date, Williams ordered Geary to march the next day and to follow Fourteenth Corps along the south side of the river to Sister's Ferry, which he did but was delayed until January 27.[26]

Ward's division remained in camp at Purysburg until January 29 and then moved out on the road to Robertsville, a small place of about twenty houses, the only public building being a church.[27] Dustin's brigade broke camp at 7:00 AM and marched with the division, but the 33rd Indiana was left behind at Purysburg to guard the stores awaiting transportation. Progress was slow because much of the road was blocked to some extent by felled timber, but the column marched sixteen miles that day and camped for the night about two miles northwest of the W. F. Roberts plantation. Dustin's brigade resumed its march with the division January 30, camping at Robertsville about noon.[28]

Ward's and Jackson's divisions were then about eight miles north and a little east of Sister's Ferry, and about twenty miles west and a little south of Howard's Right Wing at Pocotaligo.

Dustin sent out foraging parties January 30 under Lieutenant Darwin B. Otis of Company C of the 85th Indiana and Lieutenant Stephen Knowles of the 22nd Wisconsin, and while on this service Bradford Hale of Company E of the 85th Indiana was captured. According to the historian of the 85th Indiana, the foragers were getting too reckless, and Hale's capture was a much needed lesson for the men. Hale experienced the horrors of prison life and did not get back until the war had ended. January 31 Quartermaster Farrington of the 85th Indiana went out on a more successful foraging expedition, which returned the next day with ten wagon loads of corn.[29]

That part of Sherman's army ordered to assemble under the command of Slocum and cross the Savannah River at Sister's Ferry included Davis' Fourteenth Corps, Geary's division of Twentieth Corps, Corse's division of Fifteenth Corps, and Judson Kilpatrick's cavalry division. By the end of January 1864 they were all in position and ready to cross.[30]

Also by the end of the month Williams, with Jackson's and Ward's divisions of Twentieth Corps, had moved to Robertsville, three miles from Sister's Ferry, on the South Carolina side of the river.[31]

January 30 at Sister's Ferry, Lieutenant Colonel Joseph Moore's 58th Indiana, serving as pontoniers for Slocum's Left Wing, constructed a pontoon bridge seven hundred feet long over the Savannah River at the site of the old ferry. At that time, however, nearly all the country bordering the river was inundated by flood water, and beyond the bridge, on the north side of the river, the road was under water for a distance of about two miles, and in some places was ten to twelve feet deep.

Heavy details were sent across the river to prepare the road for the passage of the troops and trains after they had crossed the bridge, and during the next five days the men were engaged in removing obstructions left by the enemy on the road, corduroying, and building bridges, including a trestle bridge one thousand feet long.[32]

ADVANCE OF THE ARMY TO THE SOUTH CAROLINA RAILROAD

On February 1 Howard's Right Wing left Pocotaligo and McPhersonville and began its march northward toward the South Carolina Railroad. Fifteenth Corps marched by way of Hickory Hill, Angley's Post Office, and Buford's Bridge at the Big Salkehatchie, and from there to Bamberg on the railroad, where it arrived February 7.[33]

Seventeenth Corps moved by way of Whippy Swamp and Angley's Post Office to River's Bridge on the Big Salkehatchie, and then on to Midway, about four miles west of Bamberg on the South Carolina Railroad, arriving there February 7.[34]

Williams remained at Robertsville with the divisions of Jackson and Ward on February 1, but at 7:00 the next morning he marched in a northerly direction on the Barnwell road in the direction of Graham's Station (present-day Denmark) on the South Carolina Railroad. Ward's division marched at the head of the column that day with Jackson's division following, but from then on, until they reached Graham Station, each division took the lead on alternate days.[35]

February 2 Colonel Henry Case's First Brigade marched toward Lawton-ville at the head of Ward's division, with Colonel Dustin's Second Brigade following and Brevet Brigadier General William Cogswell's Third Brigade bringing up the rear. Colonel Ross had departed on leave January 16, and Cogswell had relieved him in command of Third Brigade.

Case advanced for about eight miles, with some skirmishing, and at about 2:30 PM arrived within a mile of Lawtonville. There he encountered about five hundred Rebel cavalry and some artillery deployed behind a barricade in a dense swamp. After some difficulty, Case pushed forward and drove the enemy back through Lawtonville.

When Case first found the enemy on his front and had deployed his brigade, Ward placed Dustin's brigade on the left of Case and Cogswell's brigade on the left of Dustin. Crane's 85th Indiana moved to the front, and, after deploying, advanced with the whole line as the enemy retired. The regiment suffered no casualties in this skirmish.[36]

The day after the fighting near Lawtonville, Captain Brant made the following interesting entry in his diary:

> Feb. 3rd. marched at 7 am and launched out into the unknown dangers of a great campaign. We have 320 men in the 85th Indiana but they were worth more than the nine hundred we had when we left Covington, Kentucky. Then our boys were grumbling, now they fall into line cheerfully and march from 18 to 25 miles a day. Such are the men of this army and they are invincible.[37]

Williams halted his command for the night near Lawtonville, which consisted of several chimneys of burnt houses scattered along the road and a church that was about half demolished.[38]

At this point the 33rd Indiana, left earlier at Purysburg to guard the stores left there when Dustin's brigade moved to Robertsville, came up and rejoined the brigade.[39]

At Lawtonville the Twentieth Corps was in a part of South Carolina where the ground was very treacherous. The surface was covered with pine needles and appeared to be solid enough for passage of troops, but when a horse attempted to ride over it, the ground gave way and the animal would sink into quicksand. Captain Brant, of the 85th Indiana, tells of the following incident:

> An object lesson was presented one day by an animal of the kind Baalaam rode, who was loaded down with a mess kit. The soldier leading him undertook to cross one of those boggy places. In doing so the Jack began to go down rear end foremost, at every effort to get out he sank deeper, and the last I saw of that Jack his head, neck and ears were out and the leader trying to pull him out, presenting a most ludicrous appearance. As to the outcome I can't tell. Such was the kind of roads we had to corduroy in order to get our trains over. The Pioneer Corps were insufficient for the work so we had as a regiment to take our turns in that kind of work.[40]

On February 3 the day Slocum's command began to cross the Savannah River at Sister's Ferry, Williams resumed his march from Lawtonville toward the South Carolina Railroad. He camped that night at Duck Branch P.O. and marched next day to the left, over a crossroad to Smyrna, in order to pass around the Coosawhatchie Swamp. He then moved on to Allendale P.O., where the corps went into camp. Dustin's brigade, still guarding the trains, marched in the rear of the division that day.[41]

On February 5 Williams continued his march in a northerly direction, leaving the Barnwell road on the left, and camped that night in rear of Fifteenth Corps near Buford's Bridge on the Big Salkehatchie River. The river at this point was wide, deep, and swampy; and the crossing, which was over a half mile in length, consisted of a succession of twenty-two small bridges, averaging about twenty-five feet in length, with intervening causeways.[42]

The next day Ward's division, followed by Jackson's division, crossed the swamps and streams of the Big Salkehatchie at Buford's Bridge. There it turned left along Bird's Creek to avoid the route of Fifteenth Corps, then north to Nimmon's Cross Roads, and finally east to the Little Salkehatchie.[43]

On February 7 Williams' Twentieth Corps crossed the rain-swollen Little Salkehatchie and reached the South Carolina Railroad a mile and a half east of Graham's Station. Dustin's brigade, deployed on the trains during the march that day, moved very slowly over terrible roads by way of Dowling's and Patterson's to within one-half mile of the South Carolina Railroad, and the men straggled into camp late that night.[44]

While Fifteenth Corps, Seventeenth Corps, and Twentieth Corps were marching northward toward the railroad, Slocum's command at Sister's Ferry crossed the Savannah River and marched northward to rejoin the rest of the army.

On February 3 work on the road that ran from the Savannah River at Sister's Ferry to the high ground to the north was completed, and that evening Kilpatrick's cavalry began crossing the bridge and moving into South Carolina. From then on, troops and trains were moving constantly, night and day, but because of the poor condition of the roads the rear of the column did not leave Georgia until the evening of February 5.[45]

After crossing the Savannah River, Kilpatrick's cavalry moved on to the South Carolina Railroad at Blackville, arriving there February 7 and driving a brigade of Joseph Wheeler's Confederate cavalry from the town.[46]

After crossing the river, Davis' Fourteenth Corps began its march toward the railroad, passing through Robertsville, Brighton, and Barnwell, and on February 11 reached the South Carolina Railroad between Williston and White Pond.[47]

On February 4 Geary's division started from Sister's Ferry on their way to rejoin Twentieth Corps. It passed through Robertsville and Lawtonville, crossing the Coosawhatchie Swamp and the Big Salkahatchie at Buford's Bridge and arriving near Blackville on the South Carolina Railroad on February 9.[48]

Corse followed Geary through Robertsville to the point where Geary turned off to the left on the road to Lawtonville. There Corse departed from the Left Wing and continued to the north to find Fifteenth Corps.[49]

Thus, by February 7 most of Sherman's army was along the South Carolina Railroad at Midway, Bamberg, and Graham's Station. Geary's Second Division of Twentieth Corps was approaching Blackville, and Fourteenth Corps was marching toward Barnwell. During the next three days, the army was engaged in destroying the track and other installations on the railroad.

The Right Wing was at work on the right of the army, tearing up the track for a total distance of twenty-four miles from the Edisto River to Blackville. At the same time, Jackson's and Ward's divisions of Twentieth Corps worked on the track west of Graham's Station, but they camped that night at the station.[50]

Early on the morning of February 8, to protect these working parties, Ward directed Dustin to send Lieutenant Colonel Burton, with his 33rd Indiana regiment, back to the Patterson house to guard the crossroads at that place. He was to remain there until 5:00 PM, and then rejoin the brigade. Dustin also sent Lieutenant Colonel Crane, with the 85th Indiana, about two and a half miles north of the railroad to cover the roads intersecting at that place. Crane was also under orders to rejoin the brigade at 5:00 PM. The 19th Michigan and the 22nd Wisconsin moved on about three miles to the west to Graham's Station on the railroad to guard the trains that were parked there for the night. The 33rd Indiana and the 85th Indiana rejoined the brigade that night as ordered. Before returning to the brigade, however, Crane sent out scouts five miles to the Edisto River. They found no enemy on the south bank of the river.[51]

February 8 the 85th Indiana spent several hours on the rice plantation, where the men enjoyed a bountiful meal of fresh meat, sweet potatoes, and molasses. They also found a Negro who could read his New Testament, which they seemed to think highly unusual in South Carolina.[52]

The next day, in a sprinkling of snow, Ward's Third Division and Jackson's First Division of Twentieth Corps left their camps at Graham's Station and moved westward eight miles along the railroad to Blackville. On the march that day, Dustin's brigade moved in the center of Ward's division, deployed along the trains. The trains halted at Blackville; Dustin's brigade moved on about two miles west of the town and replaced Kilpatrick's cavalry, who were engaged in destroying the track. The brigade destroyed two miles of track and went into camp four miles west of Blackville. The 85th Indiana destroyed 1,900 feet of track in only two hours that day. In his report of this day's work, Dustin described the operation:

> . . . Each regiment and company being directed to destroy a certain portion of the road, the entire brigade went to work with great energy; piles of ties were made of ten or twelve each, then set on fire and the rails laid across; as they became heated the rails would bend of their own weight, and while they were yet hot they were twisted until made utterly useless. Never was a railroad more effectually destroyed.[53]

On the night of February 9 Ward's division was along the railroad from Blackville to a point four miles to the west.[54] Jackson's division marched thirteen miles that day, passing through Blackville, and bivouacked four miles west of that place at Station No. 96. [55]

February 9, while Ward's and Jackson's divisions were marching to Blackville, Geary's Second Division of Twentieth Corps arrived within a mile of the town and rejoined the other two divisions of the corps. Geary reported to Williams, the corps commander; and Slocum, who was with Geary's division that day, assumed immediate direction of the Left Wing.[56]

The next day Ward's and Jackson's divisions continued the work of destroying the railroad westward from Blackville. Case's brigade encamped that night at Williston, ten miles west of Blackville, Dustin's brigade two miles west of Williston, and Cogswell's brigade advanced to White Pond Station, three miles beyond Williston. Cogswell then destroyed the railroad for more than two miles beyond White Pond. Altogether, Ward's division destroyed the railroad and large quantities of cotton from Graham's Station to a point beyond White Pond. Dustin's brigade destroyed two miles of the railroad between mileposts No. 101 and No. 103 from Charleston. The 85th Indiana thoroughly destroyed a half mile of track in an hour and a quarter, and that evening the men enjoyed a good meal of fresh meat, sweet potatoes, and honey.[57]

February 10 Jackson's division moved to Station No. 96 (present-day Elko), seven miles west of Blackville, where it destroyed the track for two and a half miles beyond the station.[58]

Kilpatrick's cavalry remained on the railroad destroying track at Blackville, Johnson's Station, and Williston Station until the night of February 12, when Sherman began his march northward toward Columbia, South Carolina. Kilpatrick then picketed the left of the army on the north bank of the South Edisto River to watch for Wheeler's cavalry.[59]

ADVANCE OF THE ARMY TOWARD COLUMBIA AND WINNSBORO

On February 10 Sherman learned from reports of his generals that within a few days his entire army would be united along the line of the South Carolina Railroad, and that the track and installations would be sufficiently damaged that the line would be out of operation for some time to come. Sherman issued orders for the march to be resumed the next day toward Columbia. According to these orders, Howard's Right Wing was to move from Midway and Graham's Station by way of Orangeburg to Columbia, and Slocum's Left Wing was to leave the railroad west of Blackville and march by way of Lexington to Columbia. Kilpatrick's cavalry was to continue its demonstrations against Augusta until Slocum began his march northward, and then he was to move in cooperation with Slocum and protect the left flank of the Left Wing.[60]

Howard's two corps moved northward on February 9, crossed the South Edisto River, and moved on to Orangeburg. There they crossed the North Edisto and headed straight for Columbia. Fifteenth Corps reached the Broad River about four miles above Columbia February 16 and Seventeenth Corps halted on the south bank of the Congaree, opposite the city. The Saluda and the Broad rivers unite just above Columbia to form the Congaree.[61]

Corse's Fourth Division of Fifteenth Corps, which had followed Geary's division of Twentieth Corps as far as the Lawtonville road, finally rejoined the corps at Poplar Springs February 11.[62]

Meanwhile, Slocum's Left Wing had also left the line of the railroad and had started toward Columbia. February 11 Ward moved back with his division from its advanced position on the railroad to Williston, and then marched nine miles to the north to Guignard's Bridge over the South Edisto River. On the march from Williston, Dustin's brigade was leading the division, and immediately upon reaching the river Dustin sent Lieutenant Colonel Crane across with his 85th Indiana to guard the approaches from the north. Companies A, D, and F were sent over first, and they took position in the abandoned Confederate works. In crossing the river, the men waded in ice-cold water that had overflowed the banks to depths ranging from knee deep to neck deep. The other regiments of the brigade went into camp, but they furnished heavy details for gathering materials for rebuilding the bridge burned by the enemy.[63]

On February 10 Geary's division and Jackson's division of Twentieth Corps moved from the railroad to Duncan's Bridge on the South Edisto and crossed to the north bank that evening. February 12 they resumed their march in the direction of Columbia, after being delayed at Jeffcoat's Bridge on the North Edisto, where they were compelled to wait until the next morning.[64]

Ward's division made a difficult crossing of the South Edisto February 12. The river had overflowed its banks, and they were again forced to wade for about two-thirds of a mile in ice-cold water that was nearly up to their hips. After reaching higher ground, the division moved forward about seven miles and came up to the Blackville and Columbia road, on which the trains were moving, and halted some three miles south of the North Edisto. Ward then joined the other two divisions of Twentieth Corps near Jeffcoat's Bridge. During the march that day, Jefferson E. Brant of the 85th Indiana, while passing a fine mansion, saw Captain Francis (Frank) C. Crawford dancing a tune on the keys of a piano, but he observed that "it really didn't matter because a short time later the mansion was in flames."[65]

February 13 Williams, with his Twentieth Corps reunited, crossed the North Edisto and resumed its march toward Columbia. John W. Geary's division crossed at daylight and halted about a mile from the river for breakfast and to allow Ward's and Jackson's divisions to pass. Williams moved on by way of Jones' Cross Roads and Columbia Cross Roads, arriving within two miles of Lexington two days later. During the march, Ward's division was in front, Jackson's division following, and Geary's division bringing up the rear.[66]

Meanwhile, Davis' Fourteenth Corps, following Ward's division, had crossed the South Edisto at Guignard's Bridge February 13 and moved on by way of Horsey's Bridge on the North Edisto to Lexington, where it joined

Twentieth Corps two days later. February 16 both corps marched toward Columbia, Fourteenth Corps moving by the Lexington road and Twentieth Corps by a road to the right.[67]

During the march that day, Ward's division moved at the head of Twentieth Corps on the direct road to Columbia, with Daniel Dustin's brigade in the center of the column. They camped that night at Howell's Mills. The division continued the march February 14, 1865, and the following night camped on Congaree Creek, two miles from Lexington. Dustin's brigade marched in rear of the division that day, guarding the trains. Because of nearly impassable roads the trains were late in getting into camp. February 16 the corps continued on the direct road to Columbia, passing Lexington on the left of the line of march, and went into camp a mile from the Congaree River and within view of Columbia. Ward's division was in front that day, with Dustin's brigade in the center of the division. Also that day Howard's Right Wing arrived on the south bank of the Congaree River, opposite Columbia, and some of Howard's men could be seen from Dustin's camp.[68]

Brant describes the approach to Columbia February 16:

> ... Marched at 7:00 AM on Columbia road, and about 2:00 PM came in sight of this beautiful city two and a half miles distant. Expected a battle but was happily disappointed. This city is situated on the north side of the Congaree and on the ground sloping southward to the river. Its broad streets, stately towers and proud capital loomed up grandly to the Army as it filed over the hills opposite.
>
> The four army corps were all massed during the evening on the south side of the river within the space of four square miles; and to the people of Columbia must have presented a military display seldom witnessed. The meeting of the Army here was a master stroke of the great General who was at the head of this army. In the evening two pieces of artillery were planted in the open field, and threw shot and shells alternately at the few Rebels remaining there. In this doomed city was passed the first ordinance of secession, and now the day of judgment had come. As the shots fell in their midst and our army cheered, the bands played "Hail Columbia" and the "Star Spangled Banner". Such a scene and such surroundings were enough to satisfy the most ambitious soldier. During the night the whole army camped opposite the city.[69]

On February 17 Logan's Fifteenth Corps crossed the Broad River on a pontoon bridge and moved into Columbia. Leaving Colonel George A. Stone's Third Brigade, First Division, Fifteenth Corps to occupy the city, the rest of the corps moved on through that afternoon and out on the Camden and Winnsboro roads to the Columbia and South Carolina Railroad. Blair's Seventeenth Corps followed Fifteenth Corps across the pontoon bridge over the Broad River and encamped about a mile and a half north of Columbia.

Soon after dark that night, a fire broke out in the city. Howard's troops, who were then in Columbia, attempted to put out the fire. The rest of Brevet Major General Charles Woods' First division of Fifteenth Corps was called in to help, but it was not until 3:00 or 4:00 the next morning that the fire was brought under control. By that time, about half of the city was totally destroyed.[70]

Naturally, people and city officials of Columbia were outraged. As is usual under such circumstances, there have been different opinions as to the origin of the fire. The Confederates promptly accused Sherman's troops of starting the fire, and Union officers have attempted to prove otherwise. General Howard, a highly moral man who was in the city that day, would be expected to give an honest statement about what happened in Columbia that afternoon and night. Howard gives his account:

> Side by side Sherman and I entered the city and traversed the main streets. . . . I noticed that our own troops were unusually demonstrative in cheering for Sherman, and learned that traders and negroes had carried buckets of whiskey to them wishing to please and pacify the men. The soldiers had worked all night and marched to Columbia without breakfast. Numbers of [Colonel George A.] Stone's brigade were thus excited and soon intoxicated.
>
> Somebody [perhaps Wade Hampton] had caused to be taken nearly all the cotton which was stored in the city and arranged it in long rows in the main streets, and then set it on fire. Certainly this was done before any of our men reached the city. The Confederate officers were themselves under orders to destroy the cotton to keep it from falling into our hands. . . . The wind was blowing a hurricane all the morning so that the fire quickly spread; as soon as one or two houses had caught and began to burn, the flames extended to the others.
>
> . . . There were many imprisoned people—negroes, Union prisoners of war, and State convicts—who were let loose by our men. There were also criminal classes and drunken soldiers. All these elements, doubtless, were soon engaged in making bad matters worse, against my wishes and the orders of the other commanders. The ensuing great damage was originally owing to the fires set by the Confederate authorities.[71]

In his report of the Carolinas Campaign, Howard included the following comments about the wind at Columbia that day:

> ... The ground was dry, the wind blowing hard, so that the dust almost blinded us.
>
> ... [as we entered the city] In the main street was a large quantity of cotton partially consumed by fire. Some men were at work trying to extinguish the fire with a very poor engine. We remarked that the loose cotton was blown about in every direction, and the shade trees were so completely covered with bits of cotton as to remind me of a grove in Maine after a snow storm.[72]

Colonel Stone, whose brigade of Fifteenth Corps was the first to enter Columbia and remained to occupy the city, tells a somewhat different story as follows:

> I was absent from the brigade about an hour in placing the flag on the state-house, and when I rejoined my command found a great number of the men drunk. It was discovered that this was caused by hundreds of negroes who swarmed the streets on the approach of the troops and gave them all kinds of liquors from buckets, bottles, demijohns, etc. The men had slept none the night before, and but little the night before that, and many of them had no supper the night before, and none of them breakfast that morning, hence the speedy effect of the liquor.
>
> ... About 8 o'clock the city was fired in a number of places by some of our escaped prisoners and citizens (I am satisfied I can prove this), and as some of the fire originated in basements stored full of cotton it was impossible to extinguish it.[73]

Howard's Left Wing remained in the vicinity of Columbia February 18 and 19, destroying public buildings and everything of military value including the Charlotte and South Carolina Railroad to the north and the Columbia Branch of the South Carolina Railroad south of the city.[74]

February 20 Howard resumed his movement northward. Logan's Fifteenth Corps marched toward Peay's Ferry on the Catawba (or Wateree) River and arrived there February 22. Blair's Seventeenth Corps moved from Columbia toward Winnsboro, destroying the track as he advanced. He arrived at Winnsboro February 22 and joined Williams' Twentieth Corps, which was engaged in the same work. The next day Blair joined Fifteenth Corps at Peay's Ferry as the latter was crossing the Catawba River on the pontoon bridge.[75]

Earlier, on February 16, when Slocum's Left Wing had arrived within a few miles of Columbia, Sherman learned that the city was undefended and that there would be no fighting at that place. He therefore ordered Slocum to cross the Saluda River at Mount Zion Church and push on to Winnsboro. Davis' Fourteenth Corps marched immediately by way of Mount Zion Church and halted on the Broad River at Freshley's Mills.[76]

Kilpatrick's cavalry followed Fourteenth Corps across the Saluda and moved off to the left in the direction of Alston, South Carolina.[77]

On February 17 Williams' Twentieth Corps marched to Mount Zion Church in rear of Fourteenth Corps. Ward's division marched at the rear of Williams' column that day and Dustin's brigade moved with the division trains. Williams' trains crossed the Saluda that night, and his corps followed them across the river the next morning.

Dustin's brigade covered the passage of the corps February 18. They were over the river by noon. Ward's division waited until 1:40 PM, when the pontoon bridge was taken up, then marched in a northeasterly direction for eleven miles to Metts' Mills. Dustin's brigade guarded a large part of the train during the march. Twentieth Corps moved up behind Fourteenth Corps and camped on the night of February 18 a mile and a half south of Rockville. During the day the soldiers heard rumors of the evacuation of Charleston and Wilmington.[78]

At daylight February 19 the engineers completed a pontoon bridge 640 feet long across the Broad River at Freshly's Ferry, and Slocum's command immediately began crossing the river. Fourteenth Corps crossed first and then, after destroying the Greenville and Columbia Railroad, running along the river bank, it moved by way of Thompson's Post Office and occupied Winnsboro without opposition February 21.[79]

February 19 Jackson's and Geary's divisions of Twentieth Corps marched to Freshly's Ferry, with Ward's division turning off to the left onto the Rockville road and following that road for three miles. Ward then relieved Carlin's division of Fourteenth Corps, which had been guarding a main road at Rockville while the troops and trains were moving northward toward Freshley's Ferry. About an hour later Ward directed Dustin to remain with his brigade at Rockville, and with his other two brigades moved to Freshly's Ferry and rejoined the corps. At 3:30 PM, troops of Geary's division relieved Dustin's brigade, which then marched to Freshly's Ferry and joined the rest of the division.[80]

Williams' corps crossed Broad River the next day and marched to the right on the Winnsboro road. Ward's division was at the rear of the column that day, with Dustin's brigade marching at the head of the division. After crossing the river and the Greenville and Columbia Railroad, the corps moved on and camped that night at Thompson's P.O., about ten miles from Winnsboro.[81]

February 21 Williams' Twentieth Corps joined Fourteenth Corps at Winnsboro. Before arriving there, Williams saw that some buildings were on fire, and he ordered Geary, whose division was leading the corps that day, to hurry forward a brigade to save the town, if possible. The fire was soon extinguished. Geary left Brevet Brigadier General Ario Pardee's brigade to occupy Winnsboro and put the other two brigades to work destroying the Charlotte and South Carolina Railroad toward White Oak, about seven miles to the north. Jackson's and Ward's divisions of the corps passed on through Winnsboro, flags flying and bands playing, and went into camp on Beaver Dam Creek, about three miles beyond on the Rocky Mount Road. The roads on which Slocum's Left Wing had been traveling during the past four days had been poor, and the rear of Ward's division, then with the train, was unable to reach camp before daylight of the succeeding day. It had been necessary to corduroy the road for the length of an entire days' march.[82]

Kilpatrick reached Alston on the Broad River on the evening of February 18 and moved on to Rocky Mount, where he was to cross the river.[83]

ADVANCE OF THE ARMY TO CHERAW AND FAYETTEVILLE

During Sherman's advance from Savannah to Winnsboro, the army had generally moved in a northerly direction, but at the latter point it turned to the right and marched eastward toward Cheraw, South Carolina, and Fayetteville, North Carolina. On February 22 Ward's and Jackson's divisions of Williams' Twentieth Corps advanced on the Rocky Mount road and went into camp at Rocky Mount Ferry on the Catawba (or Wateree) River at 5:00 PM. During the early part of the night, the pontoniers began to build a bridge across the river; about midnight, when it was completed, Dustin's brigade crossed over and moved out to repair the road on the other side. Dustin found that the road had been used but very little for many years and that it ran up a very steep slope from the river for about three-fourths of a mile. In his report of the Carolinas Campaign, Dustin described the preparations for the crossing:

> It became necessary first to cut an entire new road directly through a swamp, from the head of the pontoon bridge to the main road, for nearly one hundred yards, and next the same piece of road had to be corduroyed the entire distance. Numerous other places had also to be corduroyed. On account of the scarcity of poles and other suitable timber for this work a great number of rails were packed for the distance of one mile or more to complete the road. A large amount of work was also done upon the west side of the river, repairing the approaches

to the bridge, cutting down the bank, straightening the old road, and bridging a deep ravine which intersected the road, but by sunrise the next morning the wagons commenced crossing. Details were furnished from the brigade to assist in lifting the wagons up the steepest and most difficult portions of the hill until noon, when, being relieved, the brigade moved some four miles to Montgomery's plantation, where it rejoined the division and went into camp.

Dustin further said:

> Attention is here respectfully called to the fact that the exceedingly hard labor above enumerated was performed during one of the darkest nights of the season, without proper tools, without sleep or rest, and, above all, after having just completed a march of sixteen miles. The endurance of the men in this instance was heavily taxed, and they are deserving of especial commendation.[84]

By the morning of February 23, Ward's division was safely across the Catawba River, and Jackson's division crossed the next day. Both divisions then moved on and camped about five miles beyond the bridge. After breakfast on the morning of February 24 the 85th Indiana, which had remained near the river, moved out and went into camp, tired and sleepy, with the rest of the division. While there, the regiment filled the wagons assigned to it with flour, meal, and meat for nine days.[85]

Twentieth Corps moved out the next day on the Chesterfield road, with Jackson's division leading, Ward's division following Jackson, and Geary's division bringing up the rear. Rain had fallen during most of the previous night, and it continued through a part of the next morning. As a result, the roads were almost impassable, and the corps advanced only about three miles before halting for the night. Dustin's brigade moved out with the division at 8:00 AM, but after moving about a mile, the train was forced to halt while the road was repaired. It was necessary to corduroy the road with fence rails for about a mile, and most of the work was being done by men of the 85th Indiana, which was the leading regiment of the brigade that day. Dustin finally went into camp with his exhausted men after advancing only two miles.[86]

Kilpatrick's cavalry division arrived at Rocky Mount on the morning of February 24, and, after crossing the Catawba River, marched to Lancaster, where he demonstrated strongly while the army was crossing the river farther south. He then moved on to the Peedee River March 6.[87]

The crossing of the Catawba by Fourteenth Corps on February 24 was delayed when rising waters in the river swept away a large part of the bridge.

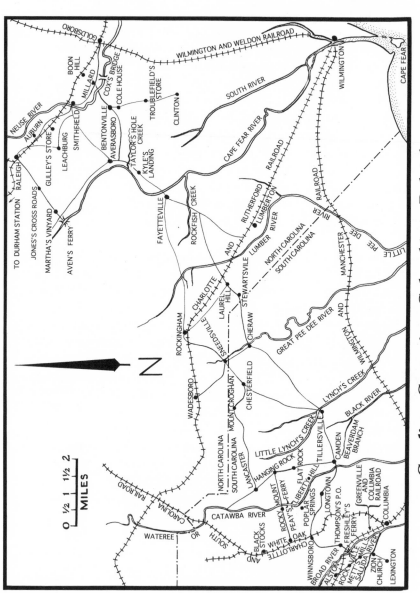

Carolinas Campaign, Columbia to Raleigh

The trains of Twentieth Corps and Morgan's division of Fourteenth Corps succeeded in crossing before the bridge was destroyed. Carlin's and Baird's divisions of Fourteenth Corps were forced to wait until the bridge could be rebuilt.[88]

Meanwhile, Howard's Right Wing had also been moving forward. February 22 Logan's Fifteenth Corps crossed the river on the pontoon bridge at Peay's Ferry and marched by way of Liberty Hill to the vicinity of Red Hill P.O., and Flat Rock Church. Blair's corps followed Logan's corps across during the day and night of February 23, despite terrible weather.[89]

February 24 both Logan and Blair attempted to continue the march toward Cheraw, but because of the weather and almost impassable roads, progress was slow. Howard was determined, however, and he struggled on, crossing Little Lynch's Creek, Big Lynch's Creek, and, passing through Newmarket, arriving with his Right Wing at Cheraw March 2-4.[90]

Sherman, who had been traveling with the Left Wing, joined the Right Wing at Cheraw March 4, and when Howard resumed his march toward Fayetteville, Sherman accompanied Fifteenth Corps.[91]

While Howard's Right Wing was moving slowly toward Cheraw, Slocum was still attempting to get his Left Wing across the Catawba River in preparation for its march toward Fayetteville. Heavy rains and bad roads kept Twentieth Corps and Fourteenth Corps in camp February 25 but the next day Twentieth Corps pushed on for eight miles to Hanging Rock, corduroying the road nearly all the way. Ward's division marched first that day, Geary's division followed, and Jackson's division brought up the rear. After marching eight miles through deep mud, Dustin's brigade camped that night on the Ingram plantation.[92]

The water in the Catawba began to fall February 27 and, after the bridge was repaired, Baird's and Carlin's divisions and the trains of Fourteenth Corps crossed the river. Morgan's division had already crossed at Rocky Mount February 24, before the bridge there was swept away. The engineers took up the bridge during the night of February 28.[93]

At Sherman's direction Fourteenth Corps proceeded by way of Hanging Rock and Mount Croghan to Sneedsville on the Pee Dee (Peedee) River, and Twentieth Corps marched to the same place by way of Chesterfield. Upon arrival at Sneedsville, the two corps prepared to cross the river and head for Fayetteville, North Carolina.[94]

During the afternoon of March 3 the leading troops of Fourteenth Corps reached Pegues' Ferry on the Pee Dee River and the rest of the corps came up the next day. The ferry was located three miles below Sneedsville and ten miles above Cheraw. The pontoniers immediately began construction of a bridge across the river.[95]

When the bridge was completed on the evening of March 6, Kilpatrick's cavalry division crossed the river and marched to Rockingham, and then on March 11 went into camp three miles from Fayetteville. He remained there until March 15, then moved up and crossed the Cape Fear River.[96]

Williams' Twentieth Corps resumed its march February 28 moving from Hanging Rock toward Chesterfield, with Jackson's and Geary's divisions leading and Ward's division about three miles to the rear. The corps advanced on the Chesterfield road by way of Clyburn's store, the bridge over Little Lynch's Creek, and Miller's Bridge on Big Lynch's Creek. The men camped for the night at and near Brewer's Cross Roads.[97]

On March 2 Jackson's division moved ahead, unencumbered, to secure the bridges over Thompson's Creek, and Geary and Ward followed with the trains. Jackson pushed on to within two miles of Chesterfield and halted when he came under a sharp fire from the skirmishers of Matthew C. Butler's Confederate cavalry. Jackson quickly drove the enemy back through Chesterfield and secured the two bridges across Thompson's Creek.[98]

The next day Jackson crossed the creek at Chesterfield and marched out on the road toward Cheraw. He had gone only a few miles, however, when Sherman, who was then with the Left Wing, learned that Howard's men had already reached Cheraw. He directed Slocum to march for Sneedsville and cross the Pee Dee River there. Jackson was recalled and sent to rejoin Twentieth Corps.

Sherman, who was riding with Twentieth Corps that morning, left the column near Chesterfield and moved on a crossroad to join the Right Wing at Cheraw.[99]

March 3 Ward's division moved on to Chesterfield, and Dustin ordered the 85th Indiana of his brigade to cross Thompson's Creek, opposite the town, and guard the bridge and roads in that direction. The other three regiments of the brigade encamped in a single line on the right of the town.

During the morning of March 4 all of Twentieth Corps moved to the vicinity of Sneedsville over very bad roads. Dustin's Second Brigade, leading Ward's division that day, crossed Thompson's Creek and marched northward on the Sneedsville road to the state line. It then moved on two miles into North Carolina and camped on the Grady plantation.[100]

During the evening of March 4, Captain Brant of the 85th Indiana went out with six men about six miles to secure a mill and grind grain. On the way, he met five officers who were escaped prisoners from Charlotte and who had been concealed for several days by a loyal white woman who lived near the mill. She had placed the men under a feather bed, and when the pursuers came to her home she was lying in the bed, pretending to be sick. The rebels did not disturb her, and the men then moved on to the Union lines. The men of the 85th took possession of the mill and ground the wheat and corn that they found there into flour and meal for the use of the regiment. The next morning Brant returned to camp, leaving Captain Orrin McAnderson of Company E with twenty bushels of wheat and twenty-seven bushels of corn at the mill.[101]

Brant tells of the following unhappy incident which occurred while the army was near Sneedsville:

> As indicating the heartlessness of soldiers during that time on the Sunday morning of March 5th, I came up to a house and barn where a soldier was just making off with the last sack of flour, while the woman with her children clinging to her were in sore distress saying, "there goes the last sack of flour we have", and the woman was wringing her hands saying that "she did not know where they were to look for anything to eat." I ordered the soldier to leave that last sack of flour but suspected that some other forager carried it away. Such are the vicissitudes of war. The innocent suffer with the guilty.[102]

Many of the men of Dustin's brigade expressed a great deal of interest in religion during the march through the Carolinas. Sunday, March 5, 1865, was a beautiful day, and Chaplain John McCrea of the 33rd Indiana preached to the largest audience ever assembled for worship in the brigade. A brigade Christian Association was formed that evening after a prayer and speaking meeting, led by Major Brant. There were 321 members enrolled in this organization before the final muster out the following June.[103]

Twentieth Corps remained in camp near Sneedsville March 5, 1865, and the next day the foragers returned from the mill with twenty-seven bushels of corn meal and seven hundred pounds of flour. A short time later the enemy recaptured the mill and with it several men from other regiments who had not yet departed.[104]

On March 6 with Sherman's permission, Williams' Twentieth Corps moved to Cheraw to cross the Pee Dee River on the pontoon bridge at that place. Williams arrived at Cheraw at about 1:00 PM and waited until 4:00 PM for Corse's division of Fifteenth Corps to clear the bridge. Then Williams' men followed Corse, and the corps and trains crossed during the night. Geary's division, leading the corps, camped four miles out from the river. Jackson's division followed Geary, and Ward's division crossed last.[105]

Davis' Fourteenth Corps crossed the Pee Dee March 7 and marched out toward Fayetteville. The next day Davis pushed on over the worst roads yet encountered on the march, and arrived near Fayetteville March 11.[106]

Meanwhile, farther to the right, Howard's Right Wing had also been closing in on Fayetteville. On March 4 Blair's corps crossed the Pee Dee River on a pontoon bridge at Cheraw, and Logan's corps followed the next day.[107]

Sherman remained in or near Cheraw until March 6 and then directed Howard to move his Right Wing by different roads toward Fayetteville. The two corps marched northward through Bennettsville and Brightsville, and on March 8 entered North Carolina, where Fifteenth Corps halted at Laurel Hill and Seventeenth Corps at Stewartsville.[108]

Early on the morning of March 11, as Howard was approaching Fayetteville, he ordered Captain William Duncan of his escort, in charge of the scouts, to take all available mounted men from Howard's headquarters and move forward toward Fayetteville. Duncan encountered the enemy's pickets just outside the town and drove them back through the town and across the Cape Fear River. At that time, Brigadier General Benjamin F. Potts, commanding the leading brigade of Brevet Major General Giles A. Smith's Fourth Division, Seventeenth Corps, moved up and entered the town.[109]

Fourteenth Corps was also moving into Fayetteville from the northwest at about the same time that Potts' brigade arrived. Sherman had directed that Fourteenth Corps was to occupy Fayetteville, and, accordingly, Howard withdrew Potts' brigade and put it in camp outside the town. Baird's division then moved into the city, and the other two divisions of Fourteenth Corps camped about two miles to the west on the plank road.[110]

Williams' Twentieth Corps was also moving with the army toward Fayetteville. After crossing the Pee Dee River at Cheraw, Sherman ordered Williams to move to the left on his march, so as to enter Fayetteville after Fourteenth Corps. On March 7 Williams moved forward fifteen miles and encamped at Mark's Station on the Wilmington, Charleston, and Rutherford Railroad.[111]

Dustin's brigade, which had arrived at Cheraw about sunset the day before, was assigned to cover the crossing of everything belonging to Twentieth Corps, and it remained behind near the town that night. The next morning, as the brigade passed through the town, the men found all the business houses in ashes and the railroad depot, cars, and engines destroyed. Dustin then moved over the Pee Dee on the pontoon bridge, passed the camps of Fifteenth Corps, and hurried forward to overtake the rest of Ward's division. After a march of nineteen miles through thinly settled country, the brigade camped that night at Laurel Hill near the Wilmington and Rockingham Railroad.[112]

After marching about five miles the next day, Williams' Twentieth Corps came up to Carlin's division, which was leading Fourteenth Corps on the Fayetteville road. Williams' men were then forced to build a new road for two miles, construct a bridge over Gum Creek, and corduroy the road across Gum Swamp. The order of march that day was Jackson's division first, Ward's division with the trains, and Geary's division in the rear. Jackson's division camped that night six miles from McFarland's Bridge at Lumber River, and

Geary's division camped about three-fourths of a mile in rear of Jackson.[113]

Dustin's brigade marched with Ward's division, which was guarding the trains that day. The roads were almost impassable because of heavy rain that afternoon, and the brigade was able to advance only eight miles before halting for the night. During the march that day, the brigade passed only two houses.[114]

At daylight March 9 Williams sent Jackson's division forward to repair the roads and bridges on the line of march. Because of the rains, Mill Creek had swollen to a large stream and Lumber River, with its overflow, required a bridge 150 feet in length to cross. Nevertheless, by 3:00 PM the bridges and corduroys were completed, and Jackson's division and the trains crossed the river. Two hours later the rain fell in torrents, inundating the countryside, causing the corduroy to float away and turning the roads into creeks and quagmires. The march of the corps that day was made through pine woods in the drenching rain. The fields were so saturated that the trains could not be parked. On the march of nine miles, the brigade passed only one house. Pitch on the trees and on the ground was, for some reason, on fire, and dense smoke from the burning pitch filled the woods. Before getting into camp, many of the teams became mired down, and the men worked in mud and rain until 10:00 that night, when, wet and weary, they went into camp about three miles from the Little Pee Dee.[115]

Progress was very slow March 10, 1865, another cold and rainy day, and Williams' entire corps worked to corduroy the road for the whole distance of ten miles to Rockfish Creek, where it arrived at 3:30 PM. The creek had overflowed its banks, and it was necessary to build a bridge 330 feet in length for the corps to cross. The pontoon was brought up, and with lumber from a vacant house, the bridge was completed during the night. On the march that day, Dustin's brigade supplied a detail of one hundred men to work with the pioneers in repairing the roads.[116]

The 85th Indiana marched with the brigade March 10, and at one point the men waded through a swamp for a mile and a half, where at times the water was waist deep. The regiment rested on the north side of the swamp until 2:00 PM, and then, deployed on the train of fifty wagons, it moved on slowly until 10:00 that night. On this part of the march, about half of the distance was on corduroyed roads. Because of the crossing of the swamp and marching with the train, the 85th Indiana covered only nine miles during the day; it went into camp twenty-three miles from Fayetteville.[117]

At 6:00 AM March 11 Williams sent Ward's division out ahead of the corps to corduroy and repair the road for the other two divisions, which followed a short time later. Dustin's brigade led the division that morning, with the 85th Indiana at the head of the brigade. Ward moved slowly forward until 10:00 AM. At that time, Slocum ordered Williams to halt his work on the road and to hurry forward with the pontoon train and two of his divisions, as a fight was expected in front of Fayetteville. Leaving Geary's division with the train, Williams moved toward Fayetteville with Ward's and Jackson's divisions and halted about 6:00 PM, within two miles of the city. Geary came up with the trains about midnight.[118]

March 12 was a great day for the men of the 85th Indiana: the gunboat *Pontiac* arrived from Wilmington on the Cape Fear River with the first mail they had received in weeks.[119]

Twentieth Corps remained in camp that day while awaiting the completion of a pontoon bridge for the Left Wing over the Cape Fear. This was being built just below the ruins of the road bridge burned by the enemy. The pontoon bridge was completed about 2:00 PM, and that night Morgan's division crossed the river. Carlin and the trains followed the next day, and the corps then camped on the east side of the river.[120]

The pontoniers laid a second bridge March 13 across the Cape Fear river for the Right Wing, opposite the Cade plantation, about a mile below Fayetteville, and that day and the next Howard's Right Wing crossed to the east bank.[121]

That same day Twentieth Corps marched in review order through Fayetteville, crossed the Cape Fear River on the pontoon bridge, and camped four miles out in the direction of Kyle's Landing. The 85th Indiana remained in camp until 3:00 PM that day, and then, deployed in single file on the ammunition train, crossed the river and marched two and a half miles before going into camp at 2:00 the next morning. March 15 the corps remained in camp.[122]

By this time, transports loaded with supplies had come up the river from Wilmington, North Carolina, to be transferred to the wagons of the army trains at Fayetteville.[123]

Chapter 18

Carolinas Campaign

Fayetteville to Goldsboro

By the morning of March 15, 1865, all of William T. Sherman's army had crossed the Cape Fear River at Fayetteville, except Brevet Major General Absalom Baird's Third Division of Fourteenth Corps, which had remained behind to destroy the arsenal and other buildings of military value. That day Sherman began the march toward Goldsboro, his next destination. After the work of destruction was completed, Baird's division crossed the river and, after taking up the two pontoon bridges, rejoined the army on its march the next day.[1]

During the advance of Sherman's army from Savannah to Fayetteville, it encountered only minor resistance, but this was about to change. When Sherman first moved into South Carolina, Confederate authorities began to assemble all their available forces to oppose his further progress. General Joseph E. Johnston had assumed command of all troops of General John B. Hood's former Confederate Army of Tennessee on February 25, and also of all troops in the Confederate Department of South Carolina, Georgia, and Florida. Johnston's forces were rather widely scattered, and the only troops he could quickly assemble to oppose Sherman consisted of the following: Lieutenant General William J. Hardee's corps, which was arriving at Cheraw from Charleston; General Braxton Bragg's troops from the Confederate Department of North Carolina; and Major General Carter L. Stevenson's corps from the Army of Tennessee, which was near Charlotte, North Carolina. In addition, Lieutenant General Alexander P. Stewart's and Major General Benjamin F. Cheatham's corps of the Army of Tennessee were advancing on the road between Newberry, South Carolina, and Charlotte, North Carolina.[2]

After Sherman's army marched into Fayetteville, Johnston ordered the concentration of his forces at Smithfield, North Carolina, about thirty miles northwest of Goldsboro. At that point he would be in position to oppose Sherman if he marched toward either Goldsboro or Raleigh.[3]

By the time Sherman arrived at Fayetteville, he knew that he could expect greater opposition than he had previously. To prevent an isolated corps from being attacked and destroyed, he decided to move toward Goldsboro with his corps marching within easy supporting distance of one another and with each corps protecting its own wagon train. Each wing was to advance with four divisions in light marching order and with only enough wagons to fight a battle. The general wagon train was to move by different roads under the convoy of the other divisions of the wings.[4]

The unencumbered troops of Major General Henry W. Slocum's Left Wing consisted of Brigadier General Nathaniel J. Jackson's First Division and Brevet Major General William T. Ward's Third Division of Brevet Major General Alpheus S. Williams' Twentieth Corps and Brigadier General William P. Carlin's First Division and Brevet Major General James D. Morgan's Second Division of Brevet Major General Jefferson C. Davis' Fourteenth Corps. These four divisions were to move by way of Kyle's Landing and Bentonville toward Goldsboro. Slocum's wagon train was to move on the direct road to Goldsboro, guarded by Brevet Major General John W. Geary's Second Division of Twentieth Corps and Baird's Third Division of Fourteenth Corps.[5]

The unencumbered divisions of Major General Oliver O. Howard's Right Wing consisted of the four divisions of Major General John A. Logan's Fifteenth Corps, and they moved on the next road south of the direct Goldsboro road. Major General Frank P. Blair's Seventeenth Corps marched with the wagons on a road that ran by way of Owensville.[6]

Battle of Averasboro
March 16, 1865

On the morning of March 15 Brevet Major General Judson Kilpatrick's Third Cavalry Division left Fayetteville and marched northward on the Raleigh road, which generally ran along the east bank of the Cape Fear River. Slocum's infantry, marching on muddy roads, followed Kilpatrick in the following order: Ward's and Jackson's divisions of Twentieth Corps, and then Morgan's and Carlin's divisions of Fourteenth Corp. Sherman accompanied Slocum on the march that day, and after advancing about thirteen miles these four divisions camped in a pine woods near Taylor's Hole Creek, a few miles in rear of Kilpatrick's position.

About 3:00 PM Kilpatrick encountered a strong force of Hardee's command in position about six miles from Averasboro. This was Brigadier General William B. Taliaferro's division of Hardee's corps, a part of the Confederate forces in the area commanded by General Johnston. Kilpatrick found this force too strong for his cavalry to attack, and he sent back for infantry support. Slocum then ordered forward Brevet Brigadier General

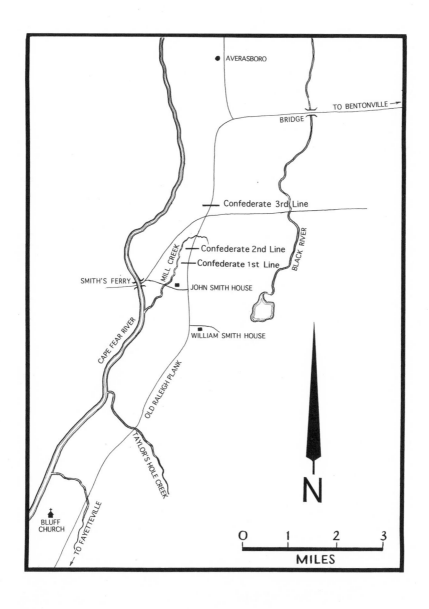

Battle of Averasboro, March 16, 1865, The Approach

William Hawley's Second Brigade of Jackson's division, which had encamped that evening at Bluff Church in a pouring rain. By 8:00 PM the brigade was again on the march, and, using burning pine knots to light the
way, struggled forward through the mud for about five miles. At 12:30 AM
March 15 Hawley arrived at the front and relieved Brevet Brigadier General Smith D. Atkins' Second Brigade of Kilpatrick's cavalry division.[7]

Also on February 15 Howard's four light divisions of Logan's corps advanced to South River, and the next day they crossed the river and moved
in the direction of Bentonville.[8]

At daylight March 16 Kilpatrick and Hawley advanced and drove the
enemy's skirmishers back into their line of works, but a short time later the
enemy attacked. For a time Kilpatrick was hard pressed, but he held his
ground.[9]

At 6:00 that morning, Ward's division began its march. The roads were
literally impassable without corduroying, and for about two miles the men
made repairs as they advanced. About 7:30 AM Williams heard heavy firing
to the north, and he ordered Ward to move forward with two of his brigades and support Hawley and the cavalry. After advancing about two miles,
Ward arrived at the scene of the action, and at 9:30 AM he began to deploy
in rear of Hawley's brigade. Brevet Brigadier General Daniel Dustin's Second Brigade (formerly Coburn's brigade) was leading the division that
morning, and the 85th Indiana was marching second in the brigade.

Ward placed Dustin's brigade on the right of the Raleigh road, in rear of
Hawley's brigade, and Brevet Brigadier General William Cogswell's Third
Brigade on the right of Dustin. A short time later, Colonel Henry Case's
First Brigade came up and took position on the right of Cogswell. When
the deployment was completed, Ward moved forward until he developed
the enemy's line. At that point, however, Dustin's brigade moved across the
road and relieved Colonel George E. Spencer's Third Brigade of Kilpatrick's
cavalry division, and Cogswell's brigade moved forward and relieved
Hawley's brigade. When relieved, Hawley took position on the right of
Cogswell.[10]

Jackson's other two brigades began to arrive, and they took position on
the right of Ward as they came up. When the division was in line, Hawley's
Second Brigade was on the left, Brigadier General James S. Robinson's Third
Brigade was in the center, and Brevet Brigadier General James L. Selfridge's
First Brigade was on the right. Kilpatrick's division then moved off to the
extreme right of Slocum's line, where he faced Major General Lafayette
McLaws' Confederate division.[11]

When Dustin moved his brigade across the Raleigh road he posted the
men behind some woods and the John Smith house and field, about five
hundred yards from the enemy's main line, which was plainly visible across

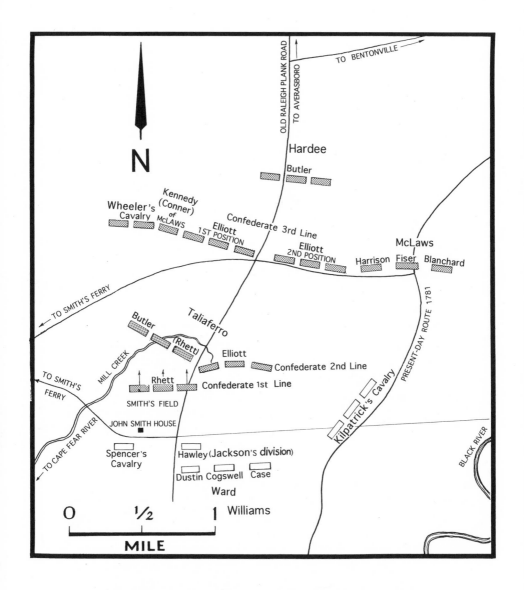

Battle of Averasboro, The Confrontation

the fields. He then sent Major David Anderson's 19th Michigan and Lieutenant Colonel Alexander B. Crane's 85th Indiana to occupy an advanced position about fifty yards in front of a small ravine. The 19th Michigan formed with its right resting on the Raleigh road, where it connected with Jackson's division, then forming on the right of the road. The 85th Indiana formed on the left of the 19th Michigan. Just when this line was completed, Dustin received orders to advance his other two regiments. Captain Darwin R. May's 22nd Wisconsin moved up on the left of the 85th Indiana, while Lieutenant Colonel James E. Burton's 33rd Indiana formed on the left of 22nd Wisconsin, extending the brigade line to the left into the woods. The other three regiments of the brigade were all in position on open ground.[12]

As Case was advancing his brigade on the right of Ward's division, he was directed to change direction and march to the left, passing the rear of Cogswell's and Dustin's brigades to a new position on the extreme left of Slocum's line. Upon arrival there, Case was directed to advance, while wheeling to the right, and to strike the enemy's exposed right flank. When Case appeared on the enemy's flank, Dustin and Cogswell were to advance with their brigades and attack the enemy on their front.

Earlier, Major John A. Reynolds, chief of artillery of Twentieth Corps, had placed three batteries of artillery in an excellent position on a slight elevation within five hundred yards of the Confederate breastworks and had opened fire with good effect. While the enemy were thus occupied by the artillery fire and by the musketry fire from Dustin's and Cogswell's advancing brigades, Case's brigade came down on their flank, his right striking just inside their line of works, and quickly drove them out on the run.[13]

About noon, soon after Case came up on his left, Dustin received orders to advance his brigade, and he promptly moved his line forward. The ground in front of the 19th Michigan and the 85th Indiana was open clear to the enemy's works. When these two regiments arrived within musket range of the works, Taliaferro's men opened with musket and artillery fire. The right wing of the 85th Indiana, being most exposed, suffered severely and doubled down on the left wing. By so doing it was partially sheltered by the woods and by some old buildings in front of the Smith house. A short time later, the brigade again moved forward at the double-quick and soon entered the enemy's works, capturing many prisoners and two pieces of artillery. The 19th Michigan entered first, with the other regiments of the brigade arriving in rapid succession from right to left. After gaining possession of the works, Dustin formed the 33rd Indiana and the 22nd Wisconsin in line facing to the left to prevent the enemy from approaching from that direction. These regiments were later withdrawn and placed in the main line when Morgan's division of Fourteenth Corps came up on the left.[14]

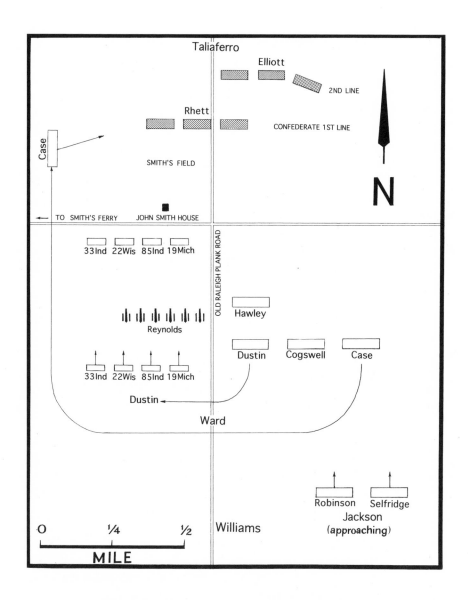

Battle of Averasboro, Ward's Attack

After being driven from their first line, Hardee's men fell back about a mile to a second line, where they made a brief stand and then fell back to a strong third line of entrenchments. Ward pushed on to the abandoned second line, with Cogswell's brigade on the right, Case's brigade on the left, and Dustin's brigade in reserve. Jackson's division moved up on the right of Ward.[15]

Williams then informed Ward that Morgan's division of Fourteenth Corps was moving up on his left, and Ward again moved forward for about a mile over swampy and overflowed ground until he found the enemy well entrenched in a position covering the Bentonville road. The flanks of this position rested on the swamps of Black River and a small tributary of the Cape Fear River. Ward's men drove the rebel skirmishers into their works and then pushed up to within a few hundred yards of the Confederate's third and last position. Upon arriving there, Dustin formed his brigade in two lines in reserve to Case's and Cogswell's brigades. At 3:00 PM Dustin relieved the skirmish line of Case's brigade with three companies of the 22nd Wisconsin and three companies of the 33rd Indiana.[16]

Williams had been ordered to await the arrival of Morgan's division before launching an attack, but because of the condition of the roads Morgan did not get in position until late in the afternoon. By that time the rain was again falling heavily; Slocum was forced to delay any further attack until morning.[17]

At dark the 85th Indiana took position between Cogswell's brigade on the right and Case's brigade on the left, and the men quickly threw up some works and prepared for the night. The other three regiments of Dustin's brigade formed the reserve. That night the skirmish line was formed by men of Dustin's brigade.[18]

Union casualties during the battle were reported as 682, and Hardee lost about five hundred men, many of them prisoners. Coburn's old brigade lost eight men killed and about forty-five wounded, one mortally. Of these, the 85th Indiana lost four killed and twenty-one wounded, one mortally. Also killed were Corporal William O. McCord of Company A and Theodore Latten of Company F. Sergeant David L. Huffman of Company I was mortally wounded and died at Goldsboro a few days after the battle.[19]

Hardee fought this battle as a delaying action with an inferior force to gain time for Johnston to assemble his scattered forces at Smithfield, North Carolina, and his men fought with determination to accomplish their mission. It was against this strong resistance that Slocum's Union forces attacked the enemy first line, held by the men of Alfred Rhett's brigade (commanded by Colonel William Butler). Dustin's (Coburn's) brigade advanced in the front line of this attack, starting from the buildings of the Smith farm and moving forward over open ground, and it was among the first units to enter the enemy's works. The 19th Michigan, the leading regiment of the brigade, was first inside the works. The brigade fought well in this engagement as it had at Thompson's Station, Resaca, and at the Battle of Peach Tree Creek. Finally, this string of successes gave the men tangible proof of the valor they knew they possessed.

BATTLE OF BENTONVILLE
MARCH 19-21, 1865

About 8:00 PM Hardee began to withdraw from his line in front of Averasboro, and by the next morning, March 17, he was well on his way to Smithfield. When Slocum learned that the enemy had departed during the night, he immediately issued orders for the Left Wing to resume its march toward Goldsboro. Kilpatrick's cavalry moved out on the road to Smithfield to cover the left and front of the infantry, and Davis' Fourteenth Corps, followed by Jackson's division of Williams' Twentieth Corps, marched from the vicinity of Averasboro toward Bentonville on the direct road to Cox's Bridge and Goldsboro. Fourteenth Corps advanced to Black River and halted there for three hours while the bridge was being rebuilt, then crossed the river and moved on about eight miles to Mingo Creek. Jackson's division, following in rear of Fourteenth Corps, camped near Black River. That day Ward's division of Twentieth Corps advanced to Averasboro to hold the roads to Raleigh and Smithfield and cover the passage of the trains and wounded. Ward camped at Averasboro that night.[20]

On the morning of March 18 Slocum's four divisions continued their march toward Goldsboro, with Morgan's division of Fourteenth Corps leading the way. Morgan spent most of the afternoon waiting for the rear of the column to come up, and the two divisions camped that night about five miles from the Cole plantation, about two miles south of Bentonville.[21]

That same day Williams' Twentieth Corps followed Davis toward Bentonville, but progress was slow because of the condition of the roads, and it advanced only about twelve miles that day. Ward's division left Averasboro early that morning, with Dustin's brigade marching in the center of the division, moving back in the direction of Fayetteville about a mile, and then turning to the left on a road that ran to the bridge over Black River. In crossing the river, the men were forced to wade through water about two feet deep for some distance at either end of the bridge. Williams' two divisions camped in rear of Fourteenth Corps that night, but Ward did not get into camp until after midnight.[22]

After crossing Black River, Dustin deployed his brigade to guard the train of 125 wagons. The march that day was through an almost continuous swamp, and the trains could be moved only with great difficulty. The brigade advanced very slowly, sometimes waiting for hours for the road to be corduroyed, and then working through the night to get the wagons out of the mud. The head of the train began parking at 10:00 that night, but the rear guard did not come in until 5:00 AM, March 19.[23]

March 15, 1865, General Johnston arrived at Smithfield and established his headquarters there. He then combined the four distinct forces under his command to form the Army of the South. These forces were Hardee's corps, troops of the Army of Tennessee, Major General Robert F. Hoke's division from North Carolina, and Major General Wade Hampton's cavalry. The combined forces totaled roughly 22,000 men. Johnston appointed General P. G. T. Beauregard as second-in-command and assigned Stewart command of what was left of Hood's Army of Tennessee, which had been wrecked at the Battle of Nashville, December 15 and 16, 1864.[24]

When Johnston learned that Sherman's army was marching toward Goldsboro by different routes, he decided to attack Slocum's Left Wing while it was separated from the rest of the army by traveling on another road. He sent Hampton's cavalry to delay Slocum's advance and then managed to get his troops in position along and across the Goldsboro road south of Bentonville before Slocum arrived.[25]

Sherman, who had been marching with the Left Wing, remained with Slocum until the night of March 18, and then, when within about five miles of Bentonville, he moved over to the right and joined Howard's column at Falling Creek Church.[26]

On the morning of March 19 Slocum resumed the march toward Cox's Bridge on the Neuse River as he made his way to Goldsboro. Fourteenth Corps, which was at the head of the column, moved against some opposition until about 10:00 AM, when it arrived at the Cole house, which stood in a large open field. There Carlin's leading division became hotly engaged. Morgan's division, which was following Carlin, arrived at about 11:00 AM and took position on the right of Carlin and south of the Goldsboro road.[27]

When Carlin became engaged, Slocum ordered Williams to hurry forward with his two divisions of Twentieth Corps. Jackson's division, which was leading that morning, went forward immediately and arrived about 11:00 AM at Smithfield Cross Roads. At that point, Slocum ordered Jackson to leave his trains and hurry forward to aid Fourteenth Corps.

Robinson's Third Brigade of Jackson's division took position just in rear of the Cole house, on the left of the Goldsboro road.

Hawley's Second Brigade of Jackson's division was massed in an open field on the left of the Goldsboro road, about a half mile in rear of Robinson's line. Selfridge's First Brigade then came up and moved forward to extend

Hawley's line to the left. Both brigades entrenched on a line about one mile east of the Harper house.[28]

At 8:00 AM, March 19 Ward's Third Division of Twentieth Corps began its march, with Dustin's brigade in front. The 22nd Wisconsin of the brigade had been detailed to help the pioneers repair the road. During the morning, the sounds of heavy cannonading were heard from the front, and about 11:00 AM Williams ordered Ward to hurry forward with his command. At 1:00 PM Ward started forward with Dustin's brigade, moving at the double-quick for about four miles, until he found Davis' Fourteenth Corps heavily engaged. Seeing Davis' left flank threatened, Dustin brought his brigade into line on the run. When the line was completed, it connected with Hawley on the right and the 1st Michigan Engineers on the left. Dustin then moved forward into the edge of a woods and strongly entrenched his position. Case's First Brigade then arrived and was placed on the extreme left and rear of Slocum's line. Cogswell massed his brigade on the left of the main Smithfield road.[29]

That morning the men of the 85th Indiana, after only a half-hour's sleep, had eaten their breakfast and then resumed their march toward Goldsboro, deployed on the trains. Shortly before noon, when Williams informed Ward that Fourteenth Corps was engaged and was being driven, Dustin ordered the regiment to "push forward and let the wagon train go to hell." The 85th Indiana advanced with the rest of Dustin's brigade, but it was not engaged during the day.[30]

By about 2:45 PM Johnston had moved his troops into position for an attack, and a short time later Hardee advanced and drove back the entire left of Davis' line in confusion, including Hobart's and Buell's brigades of Carlin's division of Fourteenth Corps and Robinson's brigade of Jackson's division of Twentieth Corps. They finally halted on Williams' Twentieth Corps, which was just coming into position about a mile to the rear of Davis' original line.[31]

After Carlin's division was driven back, there was a gap between Morgan's division on the right and Williams' corps, but this was soon closed after heavy fighting by Brevet Brigadier General Benjamin D. Fearing's Third Brigade of Morgan's division and Cogswell's Third Brigade of Ward's division. They soon established a continuous line along the Goldsboro road.[32]

When Hardee's attack first broke Carlin's line, Robinson fell back across the fields with a part of his brigade and formed a new line perpendicular to the Goldsboro road, with his right resting on that road and connecting with the left of Fearing's brigade. Hawley's brigade of Jackson's division was in position four hundred yards to the left of Robinson, across an open field, with the interval between covered by a strong line of artillery.[33]

Selfridge's brigade of Jackson's division also fell back from its position on the left of Hawley's brigade and took position across the Goldsboro road, along which the enemy was advancing. Dustin's brigade of Ward's division then moved up and occupied the line vacated by Selfridge. Case's brigade advanced and took position to the left and rear of Slocum's line, and Judson Kilpatrick's cavalry was out beyond Case watching the country to the left.[34]

At 5:00 PM Hardee launched a second attack, this time on the front of Twentieth Corps. Major General William B. Bate led the attacking force, which consisted of his own division (commanded by Colonel Daniel L. Kenan), Cleburne's division (commanded by Brigadier General James A. Smith), and two brigades of Lafayette McLaws' division in support and Taliaferro's division. As Cleburne's and Bate's divisions moved forward, they approached the field that separated the brigades of Robinson and Hawley, where they were stopped by a heavy artillery fire from the guns covering the gap and by musketry fire from the two infantry brigades on their flanks. Five times the Confederates attempted to penetrate the line between Robinson and Hawley, but each time they were driven back. The last attack was made just as the sun was setting, and finally all firing ceased at dark. Confederate losses that day were extremely heavy.[35]

March 19, while Slocum's men were fighting near Bentonville, Howard's Right Wing and the wagon trains continued their march toward Goldsboro, moving on roads to the south of the battlefield. Since early morning, Howard had heard the sounds of Slocum's battle, but at first he was not seriously alarmed. As the day wore on, however, and the sounds of the artillery fire increased, Howard and Sherman, who had joined the Right Wing a short time before, became concerned. Finally, late that evening, Sherman ordered the Right Wing, then about twenty miles east of Bentonville, to march to support Slocum's command. Blair's Seventeenth Corps began its march at 3:00 AM March 20 and was joined by Logan's Fifteenth Corps at Falling Creek Church. By dawn both corps were moving westward on the Goldsboro road toward Bentonville.[36]

Still other help was on the way. At midnight March 19 Geary was ordered to leave one brigade of his division with the Twentieth Corps' trains, and move with his other two brigades and a battery to join Twentieth Corps near Bentonville. General Absalom Baird was also ordered to leave one brigade of his Third Division with the Fourteenth Corps' trains and join Fourteenth Corps. Both divisions reached the battlefield on the morning of March 20 and were placed in reserve.[37]

Skirmishing occured along the front of the armies at Bentonville March 20 but no heavy fighting. By 4:00 PM the troops of Fifteenth Corps and Seventeenth Corps, except those left guarding the trains, had arrived on the field, and Sherman's entire army was reunited. By nightfall it was firmly entrenched.

Fighting erupted again on the morning of March 21, as Howard's troops exerted a steady pressure on the center and right of Sherman's line. Shortly after noon, Major General Joseph A. Mower, with two brigades of his First Division, Seventeenth Corps, advanced around the Confederate left flank and broke through Wheeler's cavalry screen. By 4:00 PM Mower was approaching the bridge over Mill Creek, which was on Johnston's line of retreat. Hardee hurried to the left with such forces as he could collect, and Mower, who was without support, finally fell back to his original position.[38]

There was no further offensive action during the rest of the day, and the men of both armies settled in for the night as best they could, with little shelter and in a driving rain. During the night, Johnston learned that Major General John M. Schofield had occupied Goldsboro with troops of his Department of North Carolina, and sometime after 2:00 AM he drew back from his positions near Bentonville and marched northward toward Smithfield.[39]

Slocum's two corps renewed their march toward Goldsboro March 22. Davis' Fourteenth Corps moved past the rear of Howard's Right Wing but, because of a slow and difficult march did not reach Cox's Bridge on the Neuse River until nightfall. Williams' Twentieth Corps marched back five or six miles on the road toward Fayetteville and then turned to the left on the road to Troublefield's Store. It continued on to the cross roads near Falling Creek, where it went into camp. During the day Dustin's brigade marched alongside the trains, camping at 11:00 that night about six miles from Cox's Bridge. The 85th Indiana arrived in camp at 10:00 PM after a march of only fourteen miles in eighteen hours.[40]

Major General Alfred H. Terry's Provisional Corps of Schofield's Department of North Carolina had arrived at Cox's Bridge March 21, and that evening Lieutenant Colonel Joseph Moore, commanding Slocum's pontoon train, also arrived and reported to Terry. Moore built a bridge across the Neuse River that night and another the next day for the passage of Sherman's army. Terry remained at the bridges until all the army had passed, and, on March 25, 1865, he marched back with his command to Faison's Station on the Wilmington and Weldon Railroad.[41]

On the morning of March 23 Davis' Fourteenth Corps crossed the Neuse River on the pontoon bridges and, marching through Goldsboro, went into camp about two miles north of town. Williams' Twentieth Corps crossed the river in rear of Fourteenth Corps, and, passing through Terry's corps, which was lying on both sides of the river, encamped on Beaver Creek.[42]

Dustin's brigade marched in the center of Ward's division that day and, after crossing the Neuse at 1:00 PM, camped three miles beyond the river at 5:00 PM. Because of a report that rebel cavalry was threatening to get between the army and Goldsboro, however, Dustin moved on and finally encamped at a point about five miles from Goldsboro. He then left a strong camp guard and sent out six companies to guard the approaches from the direction of Smithfield.[43]

At midnight Williams moved the trains toward Goldsboro and followed with his troops at daylight the next morning. Twentieth Corps passed through the city in order of review and took position two or three miles to the north, across the Weldon Railroad, between Fourteenth Corps on the left and Seventeenth Corps on the right. At 6:00 AM March 24, Ward's division moved forward, in advance of the corps, and crossed Little River. It then marched on through Goldsboro and encamped on the right of Fourteenth Corps, two and a half miles north of the town.[44]

Howard's Right Wing had remained on and near the Bentonville battlefield March 22, and the next day followed the Left Wing toward Goldsboro. Two days later, the two corps crossed the Neuse River and the New Berne Railroad and went into camp two miles east of the town. Seventeenth Corps was on the left, next to Ward's division of Twentieth Corps, and Fifteenth Corps was on the right. [45]

Jefferson E. Brant, of the 85th Indiana, has left a description of the army as it entered Goldsboro.

> . . . As we marched into Goldsboro we presented a ragged and dilapidated appearance. Our boys many of them were barefoot. Often marching on icy mornings with their feet bound in old rags, and with clothing of all shades, from butternut and grey to blue. Some of our Bummers were clad in long-tailed butternut overcoats and silk hats of stove-pipe pattern well worn and stove in–a la colored preacher style. One Yankee Bummer clad in this way as we were marching through the well-clad Twenty-Third Corps who lined the roadside; broke loose and declared *"Struck Communication again, I smell Cinnamon."* "Never mind pards, we will have some new clothes ourselves before long." Then to add to the ridiculosity of the scene, came sandwitched between brigades our foragers and pack train, Hugag style, broken down mules and horses loaded from head to tail with camp-kettles, knapsacks and everything of any use or comfort for the boys. On top of these motley loads were game roosters; that had given amusement to their owners, and others as they formed a cockpit and gathered about

in crowds to see the fight. There was one rooster called Billy Sherman, and others called Joe Johnston and Bobby Lee, etc. Billy Sherman was a favorite and was the champion. One evening in South Carolina as a game was on, General Sherman was walking about with his hands folded as usual behind his back. He walked up, and being taller than any of the rest he looked over into the cock pit and saw his namesake at his best, and the boys saying "go in Billy Sherman–give it to him, Billy Sherman."[46]

In addition to the personal appearance of the soldiers, there was also much that was humorous and unmilitary in the passing columns. Many of the men were accompanied by pets that they had picked up along the line of march, such as squirrels and raccoons. Others, who were on foot, were busy tending to the large number of cattle, hogs, and sheep that usually accompanied the army while on the march. Also, in every column there was one or more wagons loaded with chickens, turkeys, and geese, all of which contributed to the general noise generated by the passing army.[47]

At Goldsboro Sherman held a review for the benefit of generals Schofield, Terry, Jacob D. Cox, and other newly arrived officers; but after a few regiments had passed, Sherman decided that it was a failure and called it off.[48]

While at Goldsboro, both Dustin and Crane wrote their reports of the campaign up to that point and included some interesting facts about the march. According to Dustin, in the fifty-four days since leaving Savannah, the brigade was on the march forty-seven days and had covered approximately 475 miles through enemy territory. It had destroyed about five miles of railroad, taken an active part in the Battle of Averasboro March 16, and supported the Fourteenth Corps at the Battle of Bentonville.

The losses sustained by the brigade during this period consisted of two commissioned officers killed, one wounded, and two missing; nine enlisted men killed, forty-six wounded, and thirty missing, for a total of ninety officers and men. It had captured sixty-six prisoners, one piece of artillery, fifteen horses, seventy-seven mules, and 325 head of cattle.[49]

Lieutenant Colonel Alexander B. Crane, commanding the 85th Indiana regiment, stated that upon its arrival at Goldsboro, almost eight weeks after leaving Savannah, the 85th Indiana had marched 459 miles, fought in two battles and many minor skirmishes and engagements, and had destroyed about one mile of railroad track. He further said that there were in the regiment 339 officers and men and that rations and forage received from the Government from February 1, 1865, were as follows: hard bread, sixteen days; sugar, twenty days; coffee, twenty days; meat, three days; and forage, three hundred pounds.

He also estimated that the regiment took from the country forty days' rations of meat, twenty-five rations of breadstuffs, fifteen of sweet pota-toes, and thirty of molasses. He also took quantities of lard, honey, peas, beans, dried fruits, and poultry, which could not be estimated.

In the regiment February 2 were six private animals, six public animals, and thirteen pack mules. Sufficient supplies of forage for these animals were taken from the country. On February 12 the regiment received fourteen other animals for the foragers, which were subsisted for forty days.[50]

Chapter 19

Carolinas Campaign

Goldsboro

William T. Sherman's first important task after arriving at Goldsboro was to equip and supply his command for a continuation of its march northward toward Virginia. He found that neither the railroad from New Berne nor the one from Wilmington had been fully repaired; therefore, no supplies had been accumulated at Goldsboro for him. General Grant at City Point, Virginia, attempted to help this situation by sending south tugboats and barges to carry the supplies from New Berne up as far as Kinston, where they could be moved by wagons to the army camps, but this did not completely solve the problem. Finally, by March 25, 1865, repairs on the railroad had been completed, and the first train from the coast arrived at Goldsboro. Supplies and stores were rapidly brought up from both Morehead City and Wilmington.[1]

Sherman received strong reinforcement when Major General John M. Schofield joined him at Goldsboro with his own Twenty-Third Corps and Major General Alfred H. Terry's Provisional Corps, both from the Department of North Carolina. With the acquisition of these two corps, Sherman decided that some changes were needed in the organization of the army before setting out for Virginia; it might be necessary in the near future to face the combined forces of General Joseph E. Johnston and General Robert E. Lee. There was, however, another reason. Under army regulations, only an army commander could order courts-martial, grant discharges, and perform other acts of discipline and administration; and under the old organization, not all of Sherman's senior officers commanded armies. Sherman arranged with Grant for the necessary changes. On April 2 he announced the final reorganization of his army as follows:

Major General Henry W. Slocum's Left Wing was constituted as a distinct army, to be known as the Army of Georgia, and it was to consist of Brevet Major General Jefferson C. Davis' Fourteenth Corps and Brevet Major General Alpheus S. Williams' Twentieth Corps. On April 6, 1865, Major General Joseph A. Mower was assigned by the President to the permanent command of Twentieth Corps, to date from April 2. He relieved

Williams, who had been serving during the campaign as temporary commander. Williams then again took charge of his First Division, Twentieth Corps, relieving Brigadier General Nathaniel J. Jackson.

Schofield, commander of Twenty-Third Corps, was assigned command of the reorganized Army of the Ohio, which was to consist of Twenty-Third Corps, Department of North Carolina, then commanded by Major General Jacob D. Cox, and Terry's Provisional Corps, whose designation was changed to Tenth Corps, Department of North Carolina. Schofield's Army was designated as the Center of Sherman's Army.

Major General Oliver O. Howard's Right Wing was unchanged, because it had already been designated as the Army of the Tennessee.

At the time of the reorganization, Sherman directed his army commanders to be prepared to move on April 10.[2]

On April 5 Sherman issued orders for the time and manner of the next march. His first objective was to move his army to the north of the Roanoke River, facing west, and establish communication with the Army of the Potomac, then investing Petersburg. This movement was to begin April 11, and for the first stage the three armies were to move by different routes and concentrate at Warrenton in northern North Carolina. The next day, however, Sherman learned that Richmond and Petersburg had been evacuated, and that the Confederate Government and Lee's army had fled in the direction of Danville, Virginia, closely pursued by Grant with Major General George G. Meade's Army of the Potomac. This new development completely changed the military situation, and Sherman immediately discarded his original plan. He issued orders for his entire army to move on April 10 directly against Johnston's forces in North Carolina. After the battle of Bentonville, Johnston had retired with his army to Smithfield, North Carolina, and he had halted there in a position where he could oppose Sherman's march toward Virginia, either by way of Raleigh or by the more direct route through Weldon.[3]

During its stay at Goldsboro, Brevet Major General William T. Ward's Third Division of Twentieth Corps remained in camp, on the right of Fourteenth Corps, about two and a half miles north of the town. Dustin's brigade was encamped on a reserve line along a pleasant wooded ridge about three miles north of the city. This encampment was laid out in a regular pattern, with evergreens added as a decoration. The brigade did not perform any picket duty, but it did supply almost daily all fatigue and miscellaneous details for Ward's division. On one occasion, the 22nd Wisconsin was absent from the brigade for four days when it was sent to Kinston to guard wagon trains that were bringing forward supplies for the army.[4]

While at Goldsboro the troops were reclothed and refitted, drills were again held, and a regular routine of discipline and camp duty was enforced.

Also at Goldsboro, Colonel Daniel Dustin's Second Brigade, with the rest of Ward's division, was reviewed by Mower, the new corps commander.[5]

The 85th Indiana remained relatively inactive in camp with Dustin's brigade during its stay near Goldsboro, but on April 1 ("All Fools Day") it went out on a foraging expedition. Jefferson E. Brant, the regimental historian, described what happened:

> Col. [Alexander B.] Crane being on the sick list, Major Brant was sent out with about 250 men and 16 wagons to forage.
>
> When about ten miles out he was attacked in front by a squad of Guerrillas. After driving them back, the command pushed forward about a half mile, where we came to an old open field. The train was ordered to turn back while the regiment was laying down in deployment across the road.
>
> The first wagon on turning was caught on a sapling and delayed, and while the enemy could be seen—by the five or six officers on horseback—coming out of the fence corners on our front and shooting deliberately at us, one shot struck Capt. [Alphonzo G.] Kellam—(of Gen. Ward's [Colonel Daniel Dustin's] staff, who was acting as pilot)—in the leg. The Major asked the Captain if he was hurt. Throwing up his leg, replied, "No, but my new breeches are ruined". Sure enough, a long rough rent was observed; but no other damage.
>
> Our train was soon turned back toward camp and we came in with men very tired by the march of twenty or more miles. It was said that you might mow that country with a razor, and rake it with a fine tooth comb and you couldn't get enough forage for a grasshopper a week. The Major had orders not to risk the life of any man that day, and saving the above narrow escape returned in good order, but with a feeling that we had been on a "Fool's Errand."[6]

On April 9, the day before the army began its march toward Raleigh, Dustin's Second Brigade received recruits as follows: 33rd Indiana, 120; 85th Indiana, forty; 19th Michigan, one; and 22nd Wisconsin, two In addition, many men of the brigade who had been on detached service returned to their regiments as follows: 33rd Indiana, one-hundred-fifty; 85th Indiana, five; 19th Michigan, thirty-eight and 22nd Wisconsin, thirty-nine. With these additions, the numbers present in the brigade were as follows: 33rd Indiana, 509; 85th Indiana, 408; 19th Michigan, 353; and 22nd Wisconsin, 366, for a total of 1,636 men. Officers of the 85th Indiana on the brigade staff were the following: Dr. Wilson Hobbs, chief surgeon; Lieutenant Henry C. Brown, ambulance officer; and Lieutenant Joseph A. Gurley, pioneer officer.[7]

Finally, on April 10, when all preparations had been completed, Sherman's army left Goldsboro as ordered and began its march toward Raleigh, North Carolina, about fifty miles to the northwest.

Chapter 20
Carolinas Campaign

Advance of the Army

Goldsboro to Raleigh

April 10, 1865, General Sherman's Army of the Military Division of the Mississippi left Goldsboro on its march toward Raleigh, North Carolina. Henry W. Slocum's Left Wing (Army of Georgia), supported by John M. Schofield's Army of the Ohio on the left, was to move by different roads toward Smithfield. Oliver O. Howard's Right Wing (Army of the Tennessee) was to march by roads farther to the right directly toward Raleigh. Judson Kilpatrick's cavalry was to advance on the extreme left of the army.[1]

Jefferson C. Davis' Fourteenth Corps left its camps near Goldsboro early that morning and began its march toward Smithfield. It crossed Little River and moved forward in the direction of Boon Hill on a road south of, and parallel to, the North Carolina Railroad. Fourteenth Corps camped that night near Moccasin Swamp. By moving his corps along the railroad toward Smithfield, Davis left the main river road open for Joseph A. Mower, the new commander of Twentieth Corps, to advance along that road toward Smithfield.[2]

Mower began his march on the morning of April 10 with Alpheus S. Williams' First Division moving out at the head of the column, John W. Geary's Second Division following Williams, and William T. Ward's Third Division bringing up the rear. The corps passed through Goldsboro, crossed Little River about five miles above its mouth at 9:00 AM, and then marched on the road along the Neuse River to Millard, just north of Cox's Bridge. There it turned to the right, crossed Beaver Creek, and took the river road toward Smithfield. Soon after crossing Beaver Creek, Williams' advance met a small body of enemy cavalry pickets and during the rest of the day drove them back, with skirmishing, about eight miles to Moccasin Creek. The march was particularly difficult and disagreeable because of a steady rain that continued to fall all day.[3]

Beyond Moccasin Creek there was a broad swamp, which was heavily tangled with trees, bushes, and brambles. The Confederates had destroyed a dam on the creek, and the ground near the crossing was deeply flooded. The enemy had also destroyed the bridge that spanned the two channels of the creek at this point, both of which were too deep to ford. Several hundred Rebels were in position on the far side of the swamp, keeping up a severe fire on the roadway and on the approaches across the creek. For a time they held up the Federals' advance, but Williams sent forward James L. Selfridge's First Brigade, which drove them back and, in a short time, cleared the road. The entire division then crossed the swamp and went into camp before nightfall on the Atkinson plantation, north of Moccasin Creek and thirteen miles from Goldsboro. That night Twentieth Corps camped to the right and nearly abreast of Fourteenth Corps.[4]

During the march of Twentieth Corps that day, Ward's Third Division marched at the rear of the column, and Daniel Dustin's Second Brigade marched at the rear of the division. Ward's division left its camps that morning, marched through Goldsboro, and then took the road toward Cox's Bridge. It crossed Little River and the North Carolina Railroad, and at Millard turned to the right and camped that night eight miles from Goldsboro, having marched eleven miles. Heavy rains fell during the day, and the brigade made little progress; it was necessary to corduroy much of the road.[5]

Dustin's brigade began its march that day at 6:00 AM, with forty rounds of ammunition per man; ten days ration of sugar, coffee, and salt; five days ration of hard bread; and three days of meat. The 22nd Wisconsin was not with the brigade that day, but was detached and marched in rear of Fourteenth Corps on the road south of and next to the North Carolina Railroad. April 10, 1865, Dustin received his appointment as Brevet Brigadier General, to date from March 16, 1865, the date of the Battle of Averasboro.[6]

Schofield's Army of the Ohio advanced toward Raleigh April 10, on roads to the left of Slocum's Army of Georgia; Howard's Army of the Tennessee also marched toward Raleigh on roads to the right of Slocum.

Major General Jacob D. Cox's Twenty-Third Corps of the Army of the Ohio followed Slocum on the old Neuse road, and Major General Alfred H. Terry's Tenth Corps advanced on the other side of the Neuse River.[7] Major General John A. Logan's Fifteenth Corps, with Major General Frank P. Blair's Seventeenth Corps marching on its left, moved from Goldsboro to Whitley's Mill at Little River.[7]

At 5:00 AM April 11 Davis' Fourteenth Corps arrived at Smithfield but found that Johnston's army had departed for Raleigh. Mower's Twentieth Corps followed Davis, with Geary's division leading, then Ward's division, and finally Williams' division. Mower arrived at Smithfield during the afternoon and evening, after a march of about fifteen miles.[8]

Dustin's brigade, marching with Ward's division, moved out at 7:00 AM, crossed Swift Creek, Moccasin Swamp, and Boorden Creek; and reached Smithfield at 5:00 PM. The day was hot with intermittent showers, and, because the men moved forward rapidly, many were overcome by the heat and excessive exertion.[9]

The rest of Sherman's army also continued its advance April 11, with Schofield's Army of the Ohio marching to Smithfield, and Howard's Army of the Tennessee, still on the right of Slocum's column, moving to Pineville and Moccasin Creek.[10]

During the night of April 11, Sherman received a note from General Grant at Appomattox Court House informing him that Lee had surrendered with his Army of Northern Virginia April 9, 1865. In an order dated April 12, Sherman announced this event to the troops at Smithfield, and the men were, of course, unrestrainedly exuberant. When the march was resumed that morning, they were singing, shouting, and firing muskets into the air.[11]

Fourteenth Corps crossed the Neuse River on the morning of April 12 at Smithfield and marched on the direct road to Raleigh as far as Gulley's Store (present-day Clayton), about fourteen miles from Raleigh. Sherman was at Gulley's Store that day.[12]

Mower's Twentieth Corps also crossed the Neuse on the pontoon bridges and marched to the left of Fourteenth Corps on a road running toward Leachburg. When it arrived at the intersection of that road and the road running from Elevation to Raleigh, eleven miles from Smithfield, the corps turned to the north and camped that night on Swift Creek, about ten miles west and a little north of Gulley's Store.[13]

On the march that day, April 12, Ward's division led the corps, with Dustin's brigade at the head of the division. Dustin's brigade encamped just beyond Swift Creek after a march of fifteen miles. About an hour after going into camp, a general alarm was sounded, and in about ten minutes the brigade was again on the march. After advancing about one mile, however, the movement was called off and the brigade returned to the camp that it had just left.[14]

April 12 Cox's Twenty-Third Corps crossed the Neuse at Turner's Ferry and moved forward on a road to the west of the road used by the Left Wing. Also that day Terry's Tenth Corps moved up to Smithfield, and Howard's Right Wing continued its advance to Pineville.[15]

Late in the afternoon of April 12, while Sherman was at Gulley's Store, a locomotive came down the railroad from Raleigh and passed through Hampton's and Kilpatrick's lines. A boy was on the front end of the locomotive carrying a flag of truce. Also aboard, in addition to the crew, were William H. Graham and David L. Swain, both former governors of the State of North Carolina, and Dr. Edward Warren, Surgeon General of the state. The two commissioners, Graham and Swain, carried a letter from Governor Zebulon B. Vance asking for protection for the citizens of Raleigh. The party remained within the Union lines that night, but the next day Sherman permitted them to return to Raleigh with the locomotive. He asked that the civil authorities in Raleigh remain in office to keep the state government functioning properly.[16]

General William J. Hardee had, that same day, led all Confederate troops except Joseph Wheeler's cavalry out of Raleigh. Wheeler's cavalry began pulling out that evening, and by the next morning all enemy troops had departed. Early on the morning of April 13, in a torrential rain, Mayor William H. Harrison, accompanied by a number of citizens, rode out to meet Sherman's approaching troops. About a mile from the town, he encountered Federal cavalry and surrendered the city to Kilpatrick. Kilpatrick then marched into Raleigh at the head of his cavalry division, with banners and guidons unfurled and a band playing as they rode up Fayetteville Street. He raised the United States flag above the Capitol and then moved on out[17]

Sherman, who was then traveling with Fourteenth Corps, reached Raleigh about 7:30 AM the next day and immediately set up headquarters in the Governor's Mansion. This was done at the request of Governor Vance, who had earlier left the city, in the hope that the Mansion would have a better chance of survival if occupied by General Sherman than if standing vacant or being used by some lesser officer.[18]

Immediately after reaching Raleigh, Slocum ordered Davis to move his Fourteenth Corps to the southwest in an attempt to head off Johnston's army if it should move in that direction. The next day, April 14, the corps moved out from Raleigh toward Aven's Ferry on the Cape Fear River. It traveled on two parallel roads, one that ran through Gray Jones' Cross Roads and the other through Holly Springs. The ferry was just beyond Martha's Vineyard, about twenty-nine miles from Raleigh. Most of the corps reached the Cape Fear River the next day.[19]

Twentieth Corps also arrived at Raleigh during the afternoon of April 13 and camped near the city. Ward's division marched at the rear of the corps that day, and Dustin's brigade at the rear of the division. Dustin reached Raleigh at 3:00 PM, after a march of sixteen miles, and camped with the division near the insane asylum.[20] Schofield's Army of the Ohio also reached Raleigh that day and went into camp.[21]

Meanwhile, Howard's Right Wing pushed on toward Raleigh. It crossed the Neuse River at Hinton's Bridge and Battle's Bridge and then marched through Raleigh and went into camp three or four miles beyond the city.[22]

April 15 Seventeenth Corps marched on to Page's Station, but the rest of the army was inactive that day. Twentieth Corps remained in camp on the south side of Raleigh, with Tenth Corps and Twenty-Third Corps remaining in camp just east of the city.[23]

Up to the time of the occupation of Raleigh, General Joseph E. Johnston had given no indication that he was ready to end the fighting in North Carolina, and on April 14 Sherman issued orders for the army to continue the pursuit of the enemy the next day. His plan was to move in the direction of Ashboro, where he would turn the enemy's position at Hillsboro and also cut Johnston's only available line of retreat through Salisbury and Charlotte.

In accordance with this plan, Sherman directed Kilpatrick to move with his cavalry in the direction of Hillsboro and Graham; Howard to advance with his Right Wing on the road toward Chapel Hill; Slocum to march with his Left Wing from Aven's Ferry on the Cape Fear River by way of Carthage, Caledonia, and Cox's Mill to head off Johnston if he should move south; and Schofield, with his Army of the Ohio, to advance through Holly Springs and New Hill to Haywood, and from there westward to Moffitt's Mills.[24]

Slocum ordered Mower to move with his Twentieth Corps April 14 to the vicinity of Jones' Cross Roads. At 6:00 AM the next day, in a pouring rain, Dustin's brigade, marching with Ward's division, set out on the road to Aven's Ferry to fulfill its part in the marching orders for the day. It had not gone more than a half mile, however, when it was halted and directed to return to its camp. Twentieth Corps remained in camp at Raleigh until April 25.[25]

What had happened was that on the morning of April 14 Sherman had received a report from Kilpatrick, who was at Durham's Station, twenty-six miles up the railroad toward Hillsboro, that a flag of truce had come in from the enemy lines bearing a letter from Johnston and addressed to Sherman. This letter was sent to Sherman at Raleigh; he received it at midnight April 14. In this letter, Johnston asked for a suspension of hostilities and proposed that a meeting be arranged to draw up terms for a surrender that would enable the civil authorities to agree on terms of peace. Sherman agreed to temporarily end all active operations; he sent Major James C. McCoy, aide-de-camp, to Durham's Station with his reply to Johnston, and with instructions to arrange a meeting between the two generals. A meeting was arranged for April 17, 1865, at a point about midway between the picket lines of the two armies. When Sherman agreed to the meeting, he countermanded all march orders for April 15.[26]

Sherman and his staff were preparing to board the train for his meeting with Johnston when he received word of the assassination of President Abraham Lincoln. Sherman ordered that this news not be made public until his return, and he then proceeded up the track to within about five miles of the place selected for the meeting. He then left the train and rode forward on horseback until he met Johnston on the road near Durham's Station. Together they moved over to the log farmhouse of James Bennett on the Hillsboro road, where they began their discussions. They reached no decision that afternoon, but they agreed to meet again the next morning at the same place. That night at Raleigh, Sherman officially announced the death of Lincoln, obviously to the consternation of the officers and men of the army.[27]

Sherman and Johnston again met at the Bennett house the next day, and at this meeting they reached an agreement on the terms of surrender, which both generals signed. Terms of the agreement were then submitted to the civil authorities for approval. President Jefferson Davis, who was nearby, reluctantly agreed with the terms, but there was no immediate news from Washington.[28]

During this waiting period, Sherman's army remained inactive.

Finally, on the morning of April 24 General Grant arrived at Raleigh from Washington, and he informed Sherman that the terms that he had offered Johnston had been disapproved by President Andrew Johnson and his cabinet. Sherman had included civil matters along with military affairs in his negotiations, and Sherman had no authority to discuss civil matters. Grant instructed Sherman to give Johnston the forty-eight hours notice required by the terms of the truce, and then to resume his advance according to the orders of April 14, which directed the army to march on Ashboro.[29]

During the suspension of hostilities, while the terms of surrender were being considered, Mower's Twentieth Corps had remained in its camps near Raleigh. The men of Ward's division had spent their time making the camp more attractive, drilling, and performing the usual routine camp duties. April 22 Dustin's brigade, with the division, passed in review before Sherman in the city of Raleigh and then returned to its camp.[30]

April 25, after the first terms of surrender were rejected, Twentieth Corps broke camp and marched to the southwest toward Jones' Cross Roads. Ward's division marched at the rear of the column, and Dustin's brigade was in the center of the division. The corps reached Jones' Cross Roads at sunset and went into camp, having marched thirteen miles. This was the last march made against the Confederates by Twentieth Corps and by Dustin's brigade.[31]

At 6:15 that evening, Johnston replied to Sherman's earlier communication regarding the ending of the truce, and he proposed a further truce for the purpose of reconsidering the original terms of surrender. Sherman agreed, and the meeting was arranged for noon April 26 at the Bennett house. There, on April 26, 1865, Johnston surrendered his army on the same terms that Grant had given to Lee at Appomattox, and the war in the East was ended.[32]

Dustin's brigade remained in camp at Jones' Cross Roads with Twentieth Corps for a few days, while foraging parties were sent out. They had little success, however, and April 28 the brigade broke camp and marched back with the corps to Raleigh and returned to its old camps. It remained there only one day, and then, on April 30, began its march to Washington and home.[33]

That same day at his headquarters at the Governor's Mansion in Raleigh, Sherman issued orders for the future disposition of his army. Schofield's Twenty-Third Corps, Terry's Tenth Corps, and Kilpatrick's cavalry division were to remain on duty in North Carolina, and the Army of the Tennessee and the Army of Georgia were to march northward in easy stages, under their respective commanders, to Richmond, Virginia. There they were to await the arrival of Sherman, who did not accompany the army on its march.[34]

Shortly after Johnston's surrender, Sherman decided to make a quick trip to Savannah, Georgia. His purpose was to arrange for the feeding and supplying of Major General James H. Wilson's cavalry corps, which had arrived at Macon, Georgia, April 20, after its successful raid on Selma, Alabama, and was then operating in the central part of the state. April 29 Sherman, with a part of his staff, moved by rail to Wilmington, North Carolina, where he embarked on a steamer and proceeded down the coast to Port Royal and the Savannah River. He and his party arrived at Savannah May 1. Wilson was badly in need of food and clothing, and that day Sherman sent a steamer loaded with supplies up the Savannah River to Augusta, Georgia. He also sent upriver a detachment of troops to occupy the arsenal at Augusta and to open communications with Wilson at Macon. The next day he sent a second steamer, this one from Hilton Head, with a full cargo of clothing, sugar, coffee, and bread.[35]

With his work at Savannah thus completed, Sherman began his return to the army May 2. After an overnight stay at Hilton Head and a visit to Charleston, South Carolina, he continued his voyage northward and arrived at Morehead City two days later. He was delayed there by a storm, but on May 7 he continued on to the James River and arrived at Fort Monroe the next day. From there he moved by rail, by way of Suffolk and Petersburg, and reached City Point on the James River about noon May 9. He continued on that day to Manchester, where he resumed command of the army, which had already arrived there from Raleigh.[36]

Marching through the swamps.

Harper's Weekly

Chapter 21

March of Sherman's Army
to Washington, D.C.

On April 30, 1865, General Sherman's army began its march toward Washington, where the men would be mustered out and sent home. The army was to march first to Richmond, Virginia, under the direction of the four corps commanders, and there the corps were to assemble and await the arrival of Sherman, who was absent at Savannah, Georgia, on army business. During the first phase of this march, Oliver O. Howard's Army of the Tennessee was to move to Richmond by way of Petersburg, Virginia, and Henry W. Slocum's Army of Georgia was to move to Richmond by roads farther to the west.[1]

The troops of Joseph A. Mower's Twentieth Corps were in camp near Raleigh, where they made the necessary preparations for the long march north. They lightened their load somewhat by turning in all ammunition except twenty-five rounds per man, and loaded the wagons of the trains with supplies and forage that would be needed as they passed through the country. This march would not be conducted in the same manner as the march across Georgia and through the Carolinas. The war in the east had now ended, and the men were no longer permitted to take what they wanted from the country through which they passed. By that evening the wagons were loaded, and all was in readiness for the march to Washington.[2]

There were some preliminary movements on April 29 when Howard's Right Wing moved up to Rogers' Bridge on the Neuse River and went into camp. It remained there until the morning of May 1.[3]

Early on the morning of April 30 Twentieth Corps moved out of its camps, and, with Alpheus S. Williams' First Division in the lead, passed through Raleigh and marched to Manteo Mills on the Neuse River. John W. Geary's Second Division followed Williams, and William T. Ward's Third Division marched in the rear with the artillery and the pontoon trains. Daniel Dustin's Second Brigade of Ward's division was in charge of the trains. Williams' and Geary's divisions crossed the river on a very unstable bridge and camped a mile or so beyond the river near the Forest Paper Mills. The bridge finally collapsed, leaving Ward's division on the south side of the river. That day, Absalom Baird's and Charles C. Walcutt's divisions of

Jefferson C. Davis' Fourteenth Corps left Raleigh on the road to Louisburg, to the right of the road used by Twentieth Corps. James D. Morgan's division remained in its camps that day.[4]

May 1 with Geary's division leading, Mower resumed his march on the road to Dickerman's Bridge over the Tar River. Geary's and Williams' divisions crossed Cedar Creek at Long's Mill and then the Tar River on a pontoon bridge and finally went into camp near Dickerman's Ferry. The division marched twenty-two miles that day. That morning Dustin's brigade crossed the Neuse River with Ward's division, which followed the other two divisions of the corps during the day.[5]

Fourteenth Corps continued its march in the direction of Taylor's Ferry on the Roanoke River, where it arrived the next day, and Howard's Right Wing began its march, which would take it through Lawrenceville and Petersburg to Richmond, Virginia.[6]

May 2 with Geary's division still in the lead, Twentieth Corps marched toward Williamsboro, North Carolina, by way of Diamond's Cross Roads and Salem Cross Roads. At Salem, Twentieth Corps ran into Fourteenth Corps, which was for some reason moving on the road assigned to Mower. Mower's column then marched northward by a circuitous route and encamped at 2:00 PM near Williamsboro, seventeen miles from Haskin's Ferry on the Roanoke River.[7]

When Davis arrived at Taylor's Ferry he found that the Roanoke River was too wide for his pontoon bridge. Davis reported this to Slocum, who directed Mower to turn off from the Haskin's Ferry road and march to Taylor's Ferry so that the combined pontoons of the two corps could be used to span the river. When completed, the bridge was 675 feet in length.[8]

About noon May 3 Ward's division, leading Twentieth Corps that day, arrived at Taylor's Ferry. Fourteenth Corps was at that time crossing the river, and Ward was forced to wait until the first two divisions were out of the way. Ward's division then began crossing, and at 6:00 PM, Williams' division followed Ward. Morgan's division of Fourteenth Corps was the last to cross that day, and Geary's division of Twentieth Corps remained south of the river that night. As soon as the leading troops of Fourteenth Corps had crossed the river on the morning of May 3, they had marched out through Boydton and Greensboro toward Lewiston, Virginia, and the rest of the corps followed during the day.[9]

On the morning of May 4 Ward's and Williams' divisions of Twentieth Corps marched from Taylor's Ferry, crossed the Boydton Plank Road at Allen's Creek, and then moved on through South Hill to Saffold's Bridge on the Meherrin River in Virginia. Geary's division, which was following the other two divisions, camped that night at South Hill.[10]

Howard's Right Wing crossed the Roanoke at Robinson's Ferry, then marched through Lawrenceville and White Plains to Pennington's Bridge on the Meherrin River. After crossing the river it continued on to the Boydton Plank Road, which it followed toward Petersburg, arriving there the next day.[11]

Twentieth Corps moved on the next day toward Blacks and Whites (present-day Blackstone) on the Southside Railroad. Ward's division, with Dustin's brigade in front, led the corps that day. Williams' division followed Ward, and Geary's division brought up the rear.[12]

Also May 5 Davis' Fourteenth Corps marched from the falls of the Nottoway River through Lewiston and Nottoway Court House to Goode's Bridge on the Appomattox River. It crossed the river there and camped on Swift Creek, about eight miles from Richmond that night.[13]

The next day Twentieth Corps moved toward the Southside Railroad, with the divisions marching in the same order as of the day before. Ward's and Williams' divisions, with Geary's division following, passed through Black's and White's and followed the railroad eastward about six miles to Wellville Station, where they spent the night.[14]

Twentieth Corps continued its march toward Richmond May 7, with the divisions marching in the same order as they did the day before. The corps crossed the Appomattox River on a pontoon bridge at Kidd's Mill; and Ward's division, with Dustin's brigade leading, encamped on Swift Creek. Williams' division camped farther back near the Clover Hill coal mines, and Geary's division halted near the Appomattox River. That day, Fourteenth Corps moved up to Falling Creek about seven miles from Manchester.[15]

May 8 Twentieth Corps moved up and camped on the north side of Falling Creek. Williams marched along the railroad to within two or three miles of Chesterfield Court House, and then turned off to the northeast to Falling Creek. Geary, who was still marching at the rear of the corps, came up and went into camp on Falling Creek.[16]

The three divisions of Twentieth Corps moved on May 9 two or three miles toward Manchester where there were better camp grounds. Fourteenth Corps marched to within two miles of Manchester at Branch Church.[17]

Howard's Army of the Tennessee, which had been in camp near Petersburg, began its march toward Manchester on May 8. Frank P. Blair's Seventeenth Corps marched through Petersburg, crossed the Appomattox River and Swift Creek, and the next day camped near Manchester. John A. Logan's Fifteenth Corps left Petersburg on May 9, passed through the town, crossed Proctor's Creek, and the next day moved on to Manchester.[18]

While at Manchester, Howard received an order from General Grant, dated May 7, 1865, directing him to leave the Army of the Tennessee and to come immediately to Washington and report to the Secretary of War. Grant further instructed Howard to leave Logan and Blair behind and to bring their two corps on to Washington. When he arrived at Washington, Howard was assigned to duty in the War Department as Commissioner of the Bureau of Refugees, Freedmen, and Abandoned Lands.[19]

Sherman rejoined the army at Manchester May 9, after his trip to Savannah, and resumed command. Upon arrival there, he learned that General Henry W. Halleck, then commanding the Military Division of the James, had ordered Davis' Fourteenth Corps to enter Richmond and pass in review before him. When Sherman learned of this, he immediately announced that he would not permit this movement to take place.[20]

The men of Sherman's army were at that time in a near state of rebellion, particularly loud in their denunciation of Secretary of War Edwin M. Stanton, General Henry W. Halleck, and the Army of the Potomac. While still at Raleigh, the soldiers of the army had taken offense at Stanton's and Halleck's actions during the controversy that followed the receipt in Washington of Sherman's first terms of surrender offered to Johnston. It seemed to them that Halleck had acted arrogantly in ordering generals George G. Meade, Philip H. Sheridan, and Horatio G. Wright to send troops into North Carolina to attempt to cut off Johnston's retreat, regardless of any orders except those from General Grant. Halleck also ordered generals George H. Thomas, George Stoneman, and James H. Wilson to disregard Sherman's orders. The men deeply resented the way both Stanton and Halleck had treated their commander.[21]

On April 19, 1865, Halleck had been assigned command of the Military Division of the James, with headquarters at Richmond, Virginia; and he was in command there when Sherman's army arrived across the James River. As the army approached the river, Halleck issued orders that corps should camp not less than three miles from Manchester; no one was to enter Richmond without proper authorization. To enforce this order, he directed that guards be placed on the roads leading into the city. The Western soldiers were highly incensed at thus being forbidden to visit the historic capital of the Confederacy, while citizens and Eastern soldiers were permitted free access to the city. The Western soldiers were ready to use force to have their way. There was some violence, such as throwing stones at the guards, and one squad of the 85th Illinois regiment of Morgan's division, Fourteenth Corps, tossed the provost guard stationed at the pontoon bridge into the James River, and with much shouting and hilarity moved on into the city anyway.[22]

When the Army of Georgia marched through Richmond on May 11 on its way to Washington, the men of the 12th Wisconsin of Seventeenth Corps recognized Halleck's headquarters by the flags and sentries in front of the building. "A splendidly built and equipped guard, very spick and span," stood before the door, and as the regiment passed "a ragged, dirty, westerner, with the devil-may-care swing, sauntered out of the ranks, stared impudently at him, then shot a stream of tobacco juice all over his well blackened shoes."[23]

While at Richmond many of the men of the 85th Indiana visited Libby Prison, where Coburn's brigade had been confined about two years before. At the time of the visit, Dick Turner, whom the men blamed for much of their suffering while in prison, was locked in a cell in the same prison (see Chapter 6). Investigations later revealed that Turner was only a private, taking orders from superiors, and was not responsible for the mistreatment of the prisoners. He was paroled and released June 21, 1866. The men also visited the prisons at Belle Isle and Castle Thunder. They viewed with mixed feelings the scenes of desolation caused by the looting and the fires that had destroyed much of the city after its evacuation. There were feelings of regret but also some satisfaction.[24]

John R. McBride, historian of the 33rd Indiana, had this to say:

> . . . Then [during the confinement of Coburn's brigade in Libby Prison] Richmond was the heart of the Confederacy and the works surrounding it bristled with bayonets. Now what a mighty change! White-winged Peace hovered over the land. The strong works that defended the city were now dismantled and its defenders all gone. The doors of the prison-pens were thrown open, their keepers had disappeared, and the Union soldiers went all through the buildings with freedom. There was no revenge in the hearts of these men. There was no evidence of designs upon men or places. Lovers of law and order, they marched quietly and unostentatiously through the city.[25]

The four corps of Sherman's army remained in their camps near Manchester during the day of May 10, while the men made preparations for the final phase of the march to Washington. General instructions for this movement were issued that day: Slocum's Left Wing was to cross the James River on the pontoon bridges at Manchester and, after passing through Richmond, move on to Hanover Court House. From there it was to march by roads through or to the left of Chilesburg and on by way of Warrenton Junction, Centerville, and Fairfax Court House to a camp near Alexandria, Virginia.

Howard's Right Wing was to follow the Left Wing through Richmond to Hanover Court House, and from there it was to move on by roads to the east of those used by the Left Wing and follow a route that led by Bowling Green, Fredericksburg, Stafford Court House, and Dumfries to a camp near Alexandria.[26]

Slocum's Army of Georgia left its camps near Manchester May 11 and started its march northward toward Washington. Davis' Fourteenth Corps, which moved first, left Manchester, crossed the James River, and, after marching through Richmond, continued on to Hanover Court House, then crossed the Pamunkey River a few miles beyond.[27]

The next day Davis moved on to a church about six miles north of Hanover Court House, where there was a fork in the road. The left-hand road ran through Chilesburg and on to Raccoon Ford on the Rapidan River, and the road to the right ran through Bowling Green to Fredericksburg.[28]

May 13 Fourteenth Corps took the road to Chilesburg, bearing to the left at the church. It was Davis' intention to cross the Rappahannock River at Rappahannock Station.[29]

On the morning of May 11, Mower's Twentieth Corps had left its camps near Manchester and followed Fourteenth Corps across the James River. Williams' First Division marched first, with Geary's Second division following, and Ward's Third Division marching last. In passing through Manchester the troops were reviewed with military honors by Brevet Major General Charles Devens' Twenty-Fourth Corps of the Army of the James, which was drawn up in line on Hull Street, with its left resting on the pontoon bridge.[30]

The corps passed through Richmond with colors displayed and bands playing. The line of march passed Libby Prison, where John Coburn's brigade had been confined after its capture at Thompson's Station March 5, 1863. The troops passed through the principal streets of the city, which were lined with people, including citizens, soldiers, and Negroes. They left the city on the Hanover pike and camped that night in a heavy thunderstorm on Brook Creek, four or five miles north of Richmond and west of Mechanicsville.[31]

Early on the morning of May 12, Twentieth Corps marched toward Ashland in the same order as the day before. It passed through the Chickahominy swamps, where, because of the heavy rain of the night before, the streams were all swollen and the roads in terrible condition. The corps crossed the Chickahominy at Johnston's Bridge and then the South Anna River, encamping near the North Anna after a march of fourteen miles.[32]

May 13 Twentieth Corps marched northward toward Anderson's Bridge over the North Anna River. Williams' division, leading the column, camped that night near Beaver Dam Station on the Virginia Central Railroad. Geary's division, next in line, camped about a mile north of Little River, and Ward's division halted near Little River. Mower's headquarters was at Anderson's Bridge.[33]

Thus, Twentieth Corps, following Fourteenth Corps, was also moving toward Chilesburg. To avoid any confusion that might result if the two corps met on the same road, Fourteenth Corps was directed to cross the Rapidan River at Raccoon Ford and Twentieth Corps to cross the Rappahannock

River at United States Ford.[34]

Davis moved his Fourteenth Corps beyond Chilesburg to allow Twentieth Corps to pass, and then continued on, passing close to the Wilderness battlefield. He arrived on the Rapidan River at Raccoon Ford May 15.[35]

The next day it crossed the Rapidan at the ford and marched on through Stevensburg to the Rappahannock. From there it moved on through Centerville and Fairfax Station and arrived at Bailey's Cross Roads near Alexandria May 19.[36]

Seventeenth Corps left its camps near Manchester May 12, and, after crossing the James River, marched through Richmond and across the Chickahominy swamps. The next day it moved on to Hanover Court House and then crossed the Pamunkey River.[37]

May 13 Fifteenth Corps, the last of the four corps of Sherman's army to move, broke camp and followed Seventeenth Corps north and across the Pamunkey River the next day.[38]

At the church at the forks of the road, the two corps of the Right Wing took the road to the right and headed toward Alexandria. This was the last time the two wings of the army marched together, except during the Grand Review in Washington. After passing the church, the two corps marched through Bowling Green, crossed the Po River, and then continued on northward by way of Fredericksburg, Stafford Court House, Dumfries, and Occoquan and arrived near Alexandria May 20.[39]

Twentieth Corps crossed the North Anna May 14 at Anderson's Bridge and marched on to Chilesburg, where the paths of the two corps of the Left Wing were to cross. When Fourteenth Corps had passed, Twentieth Corps moved on and camped that night near Spottsylvania Court House.[40]

The next day Mower's Twentieth Corps continued its march northward and passed through the Spottsylvania and Chancellorsville battlefields. It reached United States Ford on the Rappahannock River that evening.[41]

Twentieth Corps crossed the river at United States Ford May 16 and marched northward past Hartwood Church to Town Creek, continuing on the next day to Brentsville. Geary's division led the column that day, with Ward's division following with the pontoon train, and Williams' division bringing up the rear. Two days later Twentieth Corps crossed Bull Run and advanced to Fairfax Station on the Orange and Alexandria Railroad. Finally, on May 19 the corps arrived near Alexandria and camped within two to four miles of the city.[42]

Thus, on May 19, 1865, Sherman's entire army was encamped around Alexandria, and George G. Meade's Army of the Potomac occupied the area higher up the Potomac River, opposite Washington and Georgetown. The two great Union armies were finally united.

Chapter 22

In Camp at Washington and Muster Out

The Grand Review at Washington
May 23 and 24, 1865

On May 18, 1865, Lieutenant General Ulysses S. Grant ordered a Grand Review in Washington, with marching salute, of the Army of the Potomac, the Army of the Tennessee, the Army of Georgia, and Major General Philip H. Sheridan's cavalry. The review of the Army of the Potomac, Sheridan's cavalry, and the Ninth Corps, all under the command of Major General George G. Meade, was to take place May 23, and the review of Major General Oliver O. Howard's Army of the Tennessee and Major General Henry W. Slocum's Army of Georgia, both armies commanded by Major General William T. Sherman, was to be held the next day.[1]

A short time before the army passed in review, Sherman made a change in the command of the Army of the Tennessee. On May 12, as the army was moving north toward Alexandria, Howard left the army to become commissioner of the new Freedman's Bureau in Washington, and Major General John A. Logan assumed command of the Army of the Tennessee (Right Wing). Howard was clearly entitled to ride at the head of the Army of the Tennessee, which he had commanded since July 27, 1864, but Sherman asked Howard to let Logan have that honor. Sherman made this request to compensate in part for Logan's disappointment when he selected Howard instead of Logan as commander of the Army of the Tennessee, after the death of Major General James B. McPherson at the Battle of Atlanta.[2]

Sherman assigned Logan to command the Army of the Tennessee and he assumed command May 23, the day before the review of Sherman's army began. Major General William B. Hazen took charge of Logan's Fifteenth Corps. Howard was not forgotten, however, and he was asked to ride with Sherman and his staff at the head of the column during the review.[3]

On May 23 the troops of the Army of the Tennessee moved out from their camps near Alexandria and bivouacked that night in the vicinity of Long Bridge. The two corps of the Army of Georgia remained in their camps that day.[4]

The Army of the Tennessee, which was to march first on the second day of the review, began crossing the Potomac River at the Long Bridge at daylight May 24 and then moved by Maryland Avenue to the north and east of the Capitol, where it massed in the streets adjoining the line of march. Fifteenth Corps formed on Maryland Avenue, with the head of the column near the northern entrance of the Capitol Grounds, and Seventeenth Corps formed on East Capitol Street ready to follow Fifteenth Corps.[5]

At 5:00 AM May 24 Major General Joseph A. Mower's Twentieth Corps left its camps near Alexandria and marched on the road that ran by Fairfax Seminary to Long Bridge. The corps then crossed the river at Long Bridge and marched through the streets of Washington toward the Capitol, where it massed east of the Chesapeake and Ohio Canal, near the Capitol Grounds. Brevet Major General Jefferson C. Davis' Fourteenth Corps also crossed at Long Bridge that day and followed Twentieth Corps.[6]

The order of march of the divisions of Twentieth Corps and of the brigades of Brevet Major General William T. Ward's Third Division of Twentieth Corps in the review was as follows: Brevet Major General Alpheus S. Williams' First Division at the head of the corps, then Brevet Major General John W. Geary's Second Division, and finally Ward's Third Division. Brevet Brigadier General Benjamin Harrison's First Brigade of Ward's division was to march first in Ward's division, Brevet Brigadier General Daniel Dustin's Second Brigade was to follow Harrison, and Brevet Brigadier General William Cogswell's Third Brigade was to follow Dustin.[7]

Perhaps the passing in review of General Sherman's army can best be described in the words of the general himself, because he rode at the head of the column until it reached the reviewing stand. He then moved into the stand, where he watched the entire army pass by. Sherman later wrote of this day as follows:

> The morning of the 24th was extremely beautiful, and the ground was in splendid order for our review. The streets were filled with people to see the pageant, armed with bouquets of flowers for their favorite regiments or heroes, and every thing was propitious. Punctually at 9 am the signal-gun was fired, when in person, attended by General Howard and all my staff, I rode slowly down Pennsylvania Avenue, the crowds of men, women, and children densely lining the sidewalks, and almost obstructing the way. We were followed close by General Logan and the head of Fifteenth Corps. When I reached the Treasury-building, and looked back, the sight was simply magnificent. The column was compact, and the glittering muskets looked like a solid mass of steel, moving with the regularity of a pendulum. We passed the Treasury-building, in front of which and of the White house was an immense throng of people, for whom extensive stands had been prepared on both sides of the avenue. As I neared the brick-house opposite the lower corner of Lafayette Square, some one asked me to

notice Mr. Seward, who, still feeble and bandaged for his wounds, had been removed there that he might behold the troops. I moved in that direction and took off my hat to Mr. Seward, who sat at an upper window. He recognized the salute, and returned it, and we rode on steadily past the President, saluting with our swords. All on his stand arose and acknowledged the salute. Then, turning into the gate of the presidential grounds, we left our horses with orderlies, and went upon the stand, where I found Mrs. Sherman with her father [Thomas Ewing] and son [Tom]. Passing them, I shook hands with the President and General Grant, and each member of the cabinet. As I approached Mr. Stanton, he offered me his hand, but I declined it publicly, and the fact was universally noticed. I then took my post on the left of the President, and for six hours and a half stood, while the army passed in the order of the Fifteenth, Seventeenth, Twentieth, and Fourteenth Corps. It was, in my judgment, the most magnificent army in existence—sixty-five thousand men, in splendid *physique,* who had completed a march of nearly two thousand miles in a hostile country, in good drill, and who realized that they were being closely scrutinized by thousand of their fellow-countrymen and by foreigners. Division after division passed, each commander of an army corps or division coming on the stand during the passage of his command, to be presented to President, cabinet, and spectators. The steadiness and firmness of the tread, the careful dress on the guides, the uniform intervals between the companies, all eyes directly to the front, and the tattered and bullet-riven flags, festooned with flowers, all attracted universal notice.... For six hours and a half that strong tread of the Army of the West resounded along Pennsylvania Avenue; not a soul of that vast crowed of spectators left his place; and, when the rear of the column had passed by, thousands of the spectators still lingered to express their sense of confidence in the strength of a Government which could claim such an army.[8]

Sherman made an additional comment about the review, as follows:

Some little scenes enlivened the day, and called for the laughter and cheers of the crowd. Each division was followed by six ambulances, as a representative of its baggage-train. Some of the division commanders had added, by way of variety, goats, milch-cows and pack mules, whose loads consisted of game-cocks, poultry, hams, etc., and some of them had the families of freed slaves along, with the women leading their children. Each division was preceded by its corps of black pioneers, armed with picks and spades. These marched abreast in double ranks, keeping perfect dress and step, and added much to the interest of the occasion. On the whole, the grand review was a splendid success, and was a fitting conclusion to the campaign and the war.[9]

Jefferson E. Brant, historian of the 85th Indiana, wrote of the Review:

For nearly five days we were preparing for the grand review. Every gun and every button was brightened. Every bayonet and sabre made to shine; so that our army should not suffer in comparison with the army of the Potomac, or any other army.

On the 24th we passed in review and for about eight hours [six and one half hours] the victorious legions of Sherman passed before the reviewing stand near the White House, on Pennsylvania Avenue.

As the 85th passed it looked as if a straight line had been drawn, it would have touched every bayonet point in the division columns. We were proud of our Hoosier boys that day.

Over and against the stalwart marching of Sherman's columns sandwiched in between Brigades and Divisions was our "Hugag" train of Sherman's bummers, made up of old mules and broken down horses, loaded from head to tail, led by our company cooks. Along with these came all sorts of vehicles such as we had used on our long and eventful marches—That was a sight to behold.

The pomp and pageantry of war leading on, with a pageantry behind not splendid but eminently useful. A review of our army would have been a failure without an exhibition of every part of our machinery on that historic day.[10]

A graphic account of the review, written at the time of the review, was published in the *Washington Daily Chronicle,* and McBride included this article in his *History of the of the Thirty-Third Indiana Veteran Infantry:*

The second day of the grand review created perhaps a greater interest than was evoked by the first. The reason is obvious. The Army of the Potomac had been ever near us. Most of the corps have repeatedly passed through the capital. Its nearness and facility of communication rendered its every move known to the country, there never being a week's mystery or doubt about it. Now, Sherman's army, at least those two corps styled the Army of the Tennessee, the Fifteenth and Seventeenth Corps, never before set foot in Washington. [Note. The *Chronicle* should have included Davis' Fourteenth Corps and also Williams' First Division and Henry Case's First Brigade and Dustin's

Second Brigade (Coburn's brigade) of Ward's Third Division of Twentieth Corps.] Down amid the miasmic marshes of the Mississippi, in the slime of the Yazoo and Tennessee, fighting battles above the rolling clouds, disappearing beyond the ken of the telegraph; now supposed to be victorious, and again a cause of apprehension and doubt, marching unrecorded hundreds of miles; supposed to be about Milledgeville or on the road to Macon, when it is compelling the falling of Charleston, seldom authentically heard from save in connection with the news that some new rebel stronghold had surrendered to the general's strategy and its own indomitable energy, . . . The marches it has made, the victory it has won, the difficulties it has surmounted have perhaps never been equaled by any army since the days of Xenophon's Anabasis.

Perhaps no army ever disappointed more people than that of General Sherman. There prevailed a general idea that during its mighty marches, removed far from bases of supplies, the General must have permitted the reins of discipline to slacken; the habit of living on the country, the distances traversed would seem not only to excuse but even to necessitate a disregard of accuracy of detail, and the total negligence of all efforts to gratify many artistic requirements of military criticism; but when the first company front of the leading regiment of the First brigade of the Fifteenth Corps appeared, straight as a tightened string, and rank after rank passed the pavilion in soldierly silence, but one footfall as heard. As the eye took in the massiveness of the column, its compact formation, and passed to the ambulances, meeting no stragglers, seeing nothing awry, but all soldier-like in dress, in manner, in look, in walk, a sudden revelation in the military miracle seemed to burst on the minds of all, and the very welkin rang with cheers. "Distinct as the billows, yet one as the sea," the regiments of Fifteenth Corps passed on, and ere the Seventeenth had reached the corner of Fifteenth Street the conclusion was reached that Sherman had somehow or other managed to turn into uses of discipline the very influences that the past histories of armies had ever considered their bane. As it was with the Fifteenth, so was it with the succeeding corps . . . , and the spectators never tired of expressing their admiration of the demeanor of the men and the beautiful regularity of the marching. The greater number of the men wore hats of felt, black and slouched, which gave to this army a more somber and grave aspect than characterized the Army of the Potomac. The personal appearance of the men was also different, for though youth, unusual youth, was noticeable in the men and officers of both, the western boys seemed larger and more fully developed than the men of Meade's army. This is due, perhaps, to the fact that in the bulk of both armies there are more city men in the Army of the Potomac than in the Army of the West.[11]

When the review finally ended, the troops continued along Pennsylvania Avenue to the Potomac River, where they crossed the Aqueduct Bridge and then returned to their camps. The grounds near Alexandria that had been assigned to Sherman's army when it arrived from Raleigh had been used so often as camps by other forces that they were foul and unfit for further occupancy. Consequently, after the review, the army moved to new camps north of the Potomac River. Mower's Twentieth Corps crossed the Potomac, passed through Washington, and marched out on the Bladensburg road for five miles and went into camp near Fort Lincoln, in an open pine woodland. Daniel Dustin's brigade camped near Fort Lincoln on the Eastern Branch.[12]

Davis' Fourteenth Corps marched northward to the right of Washington and camped near the Soldiers Home, Fort Bunker Hill, and Fort Slemmer.[13]

Seventeenth Corps marched to a new camp four miles north of Washington and camped at Fourteenth Street, near Piney Branch, and Fifteenth Corps camped two miles north of the city at Crystal Spring, Meridian Hill, and Brightwood. Once established in the new camps, the regimental and company officers were soon busy preparing papers and rolls for the muster out of the troops and for the transfer of themselves and their troops to other commands.[14]

Muster Out And Home

On May 18 just as Sherman's army was arriving near Alexandria on its march toward Washington, the War Department issued an order that all white troops in Sherman's command of the Military Division of the Mississippi whose terms of service expired between that date and September 30, 1865, inclusive, were to be mustered out of the service immediately. All men of the same command whose terms of service expired after October 1, 1865, were to be transferred to other organizations from the same state when practicable, and if not practicable, to regiments having the longest times to serve.[15]

On June 4 as a preliminary to muster out, a number of changes were made in the command and composition of Twentieth Corps and Fourteenth Corps. There was a redistribution of the regiments of the two corps so that all Eastern regiments that had come West with Eleventh Corps and Twelfth Corps to reinforce Grant's army near Chattanooga in the fall of 1863, were in Twentieth Corps, and all the Western regiments were in Fourteenth Corps. This was accomplished by transferring two Eastern regiments of Fourteenth Corps to Twentieth Corps, and ten Western regiments of Twentieth Corps to Fourteenth Corps. The latter included the 33rd Indiana of Dustin's (Coburn's) brigade of Ward's division. Fourteenth Corps, then composed of Western regiments, was scheduled to leave soon for Louisville, Kentucky, where the regiments would be mustered out.[16]

June 4 Alpheus S. Williams was relieved from duty with Twentieth Corps and was ordered to report to Jefferson C. Davis, commanding Fourteenth Corps.[17]

June 6 eight Eastern regiments, formerly of Eleventh and Twelfth Corps, of Twentieth Corps, were transferred to Major General Christopher C. Augur's Department of Washington for muster out. During the period June 7-12, an additional five Eastern regiments of Twentieth Corps were mustered out.[18]

Also mustered out on June 10 were three Eastern regiments of Ward's Third Division of Twentieth Corps.[19]

June 8, 1865, 146 recruits of the 27th Indiana, 102 of the 70th Indiana, and 135 of the 85th Indiana, a total of 383 men, were assigned to the 33rd Indiana Regiment of Fourteenth Corps. This corps left Washington June 9-15 and traveled by the Baltimore and Ohio Railroad to Parkersburg, West Virginia. From there it moved by steamer down the Ohio River to Louisville. It arrived there June 14-21 and was attached to Logan's Army of the Tennessee, which had preceded it to Louisville.[20]

The recruits of the 85th Indiana were transferred to the 33rd Indiana June 8 and served with that regiment until it was mustered out at Louisville July 21, and then, with the 33rd Indiana, returned to Indianapolis. The other three regiments of Dustin's brigade were mustered out in Washington as follows: the 19th Michigan on June 10, and the 85th Indiana and the 22nd Wisconsin on June 12.[21]

The men of the 22nd Wisconsin traveled from Washington to Milwaukee, with many continuing on to their homes. They returned to Milwaukee, however, to receive their final pay on June 28.[22]

The 19th Michigan traveled west by rail, by way of Pittsburgh to Cleveland and then crossed Lake Erie to Detroit aboard the *Morning Star*. On

June 25 the men assembled in Detroit to receive their final pay.[23]

The 85th Indiana moved from Washington by rail to Parkersburg, and then down the Ohio River by steamboat to Cincinnati, Ohio. For the men of the 85th, this part of the trip was one grand, unforgettable ovation. From Cincinnati the regiment moved to Indianapolis by rail, and there the men deposited their arms and turned in the government horses and the regimental flag. That done, the men moved on to Terre Haute, from where they had departed for the front so long ago. There they made their last march down the Main Street (also called Wabash Avenue) to the applause and greetings of crowds of men, women, and children of the city. They were home at last.[24]

At the organization of the 85th Indiana regiment in 1862, the following were mustered into service:[25]

Field and staff officers	8
Line officers	30
Enlisted men	883
Enlisted men recruited	194
Total	1115

The final summary for the regiment was as follows:

OFFICERS	Field& Staff	Line Officers	Non-Com Field&Staff	Total
Muster out	6	30	6	42
Resigned	2	6	0	8
Discharged for Disability	3	0	5	8
Died	1	2	0	3
Killed in Action	2	1	3	6
Totals	12	40	12	64

ENLISTED MEN

Killed	17
Died of Wounds	24
Wounded in Battle	147
Died of Disease	164
Discharged by reason of Wounds	18
Discharged for Disability	120
Discharged Expiration of Service	421
Discharged Promoted, etc.	27
Deserted	51
Transferred to other Regiments	209
Totals for Enlisted Men	1051
Totals for Officers and Staff	64
GRAND TOTAL	1115

The officers commanding the 85th Indiana at the time of muster out were as follows:[26]

Lieutenant Colonel Alexander B. Crane	September 4, 1862
Major Jefferson E. Brant	September 14, 1864
Captains	
William T. Crawford	September 2, 1862
Thomas Grimes	May 10, 1863
Josiah H. Sherman	May 12, 1863
Caleb Bales	November 5, 1863
Robert Clarke	October 30, 1864
Orin McAnderson	October 30, 1864
Francis M. Rude	October 30, 1864
George Grimes	October 30, 1864
Francis C. Crawford	November 1, 1864
James D. Este	
Quartermaster, First Lieutenant G. E. Farrington	October 22, 1863
Adjutant, First Lieutenant Lewis W. Wells	November 1, 1864
Surgeon Wilson Hobbs	September 4, 1862
Assistant Surgeon William V. Wiles	September 4, 1862

(Note: The date of each officer's rank is placed after his name.)

Brant concluded his history of the 85th Indiana with the following comment:

It is a remarkable fact that out of the 1115 enrolled, we left behind when mustered out 207 dead, and that of the 908 living at the end of the war about 308 as near as we can learn, are alive—37 years after our muster out. In all 735 have joined the silent majority; since we enlisted forty years ago. It is safe to say that those who still live, average in years not far from sixty. Nearly all of these with shattered health will linger a few more years, when we will sleep in the "windowless home of the dead" and will leave "Old Glory" to float over one country with one flag.[27]

USAMHI

The XX Corps in Grand Review, May 24, 1865. Sherman said his army was "the most magnificent army in existence . . ."

Epilogue

Coburn's brigade was discontinued in June 1865 when the officers and men were mustered out and returned to their homes. There most of them passed into the relative obscurity of civilian life, while others continued on as public figures. In this narrative we have become more or less well acquainted with many of the officers of this brigade, but our knowledge of them ended with the termination of the war. To fill out this missing part of their lives a brief account of their post-war activities is included in this Epilogue.

There are some less prominent officers in the brigade for whom no previous biographies have been given. To rectify these omissions, brief accounts of their pre-war activities are also included in the Epilogue.

The following officers and three privates are included:

DAVID ANDERSON

David Anderson was born in New York in 1824. He started teaching school at the age of twenty and later became interested in business. In 1854 he moved west and settled in Michigan, where he took up farming. He continued in that business until the outbreak of the Civil War. He then joined the 19th Michigan Regiment and was promoted to Major in October 1864. He was the last commander of the regiment.

JOHN PIERSON BAIRD

When John Pierson Baird returned to Terre Haute after his resignation July 20, 1864, he resumed the practice of law. He later formed a partnership with General Charles Cruft after the latter returned from the service in August 1865.

Baird practiced law for the next ten years, and then again he was troubled by failing health—perhaps due, in part, to the work that resulted from the immense clientele the two men maintained. By September 1875 Baird was experiencing serious mental problems and retired to his home. He remained there until April 1, 1876, and then heeded the advice of friends and consented to be taken to the Indianapolis Hospital for the Insane for treatment. In March of that year, his only son was born but lived only a few months. This only added to the anguish John Baird suffered.

He remained at the institution for about five years, and finally kidney failure resulted in his death on March 7, 1881, at the age of fifty-one years. He was buried at the Woodlawn Cemetery at Terre Haute, Indiana.

There is an interesting passage in Baird's obituary, which was published in Terre Haute March 9, 1881, which attests to General Cruft's high regard for Colonel Baird. This refers to Baird's stay at the Insane Asylum:

> . . . His partner, General Cruft, has, throughout, entertained for him the greatest respect and affection, visiting him every week [in Indianapolis], and sometimes more frequently. He has watched over him and cared for him with an affection as great as the fondest mother could lavish on a favorite son, and was with him to minister to his wants until he breathed his last.

Captain Brant of Company E perhaps provides us with the best overview of Colonel Baird the soldier, and how he appeared in his final years, by offering this brief description of Baird after his departure:

> Colonel John P. Baird had his besetting sins, but aside from these he was much admired by the regiment. Exceedingly shrewd and tactful, brave and generous to a fault. We were proud of him. He was one of the handsomest officers in our army, in every way, and brilliant. He might have been a Major General. The last time I saw him he was in the Insane Asylum at Indianapolis. His raven black hair and beard had turned white. He explained to me his mental trouble. His memory was gone. He could not call up the past at the bidding of his will. In a few months after this in the fall of 1875[sic, actually Bed in 1881] he joined the silent majority. General Cruft his old law partner told me [Brant] that the hanging of the spies at Franklin preyed upon his mind and probably accounted in part for his mental trouble.

FRANK D. BALDWIN

Frank D. Baldwin served during the war as captain of Company D of the 19th Michigan Regiment. He was mustered out June 10, 1865, and then entered the regular army. During the rest of his career he served in the West, fighting Indians and keeping the peace, particuarly in Texas and Montana. He rose to the rank of brigadier general June 9, 1902.

CALEB BALES

Caleb Bales was born in 1836 and attended school at Georgetown, Illinois, and Newport, Indiana. He was a farmer for his entire life, except for the three years that he was in California and the time he was in the army during the Civil War. When the war was over, he returned to his home at Toronto, near present day Dana, in Vermillion County, Indiana, and resumed farming. He built a fine two-story farmhouse and lived there the rest of his life. Bales, a successful and prosperous farmer, died May 12, 1901, and was buried on his farm in the Bales Cemetery.

DR. ROBERT F. BENCE

Dr. Robert F. Bence was assistant surgeon and surgeon of the 33rd Indiana Regiment and was the brother-in-law of Colonel John Coburn. He returned to Indianapolis after the war and became Deputy Recorder of Marion county and also worked in the County Auditor's office. He died January 14, 1890, and was buried in the Crown Hill Cemetery at Indianapolis.

EDWARD BLOODGOOD

Colonel Edward Bloodgood was mustered out of the service in Milwaukee, Wisconsin, in June 1865. July 28, 1866, he was commissioned captain in the regular army. Later he was given the rank of brevet major and brevet lieutenant colonel in the regular army for meritorious conduct during the Civil War.

He was married early in 1867 and was then assigned to duty in the West. He was soon in trouble again, as he had been on several occasions during the Civil War when he quarreled with his associates. He would have lost his commission without the intervention of the War Department. Congress reduced the size of the army in the winter of 1870-1871, during President Grant's second administration, and Bloodgood was mustered out January 1, 1871. He was thus forced to begin a new life. He settled at Waukesha, Wisconsin, and then moved to Milwaukee, where he was given a small position at the post office. Bloodgood lived for many years with his son-in-law and daughter in Milwaukee, and he spent the summers with them at their summer home near Mukwonago, not far from Milwaukee. It was there that he died October 22, 1914.

JEFFERSON E. BRANT

After returning home from the army, Jefferson E. Brant resumed the ministry and served as pastor at Brazil, Bedford, Rockport, and Indianapolis in Indiana. In 1876 he became presiding elder of the Evansville, Indiana, District of the Church, and then served as pastor at Martinsville and Bloomington, also in Indiana. In 1885 he transferred to the South Kansas Conference and served in various capacities at Fort Scott, Parsons, and Burlington in that state. After his retirement in 1898, he lived in Bloomington, Indiana, and there completed a *History of the Eighty-Fifth Indiana Volunteer Infantry*, which was published in 1902.

LAWRENCE BURGET

Lawrence Burget served with the 85th Indiana during the war and was wounded during the Atlanta Campaign. After the war he returned to Terre Haute, and in September 1912, when the 85th Indiana held their 50th Reunion at Terre Haute, Burget and his old friend George Farrington were in charge of the local arrangements for the entertainment. Eventually, Burget went into the insurance business, in which he continued until he was about seventy-two years old. After retirement, he spent nearly six months in California and then his health began to fail. He died November 1, 1915, and was buried in the Highland Lawn Cemetery in Terre Haute.

JAMES E. BURTON

When the war ended, James E. Burton returned to his farm in Baker Township, Morgan County, Indiana, and was soon again actively engaged in the business of farming and stock trading. During the Panic of 1873, however, he suffered severe financial losses, and he never recovered his fortune. He then moved to Martinsville, which was nearby in Morgan County, Indiana, and he continued to live there until his death. He was survived by his elderly widow and two sons, David P. Burton of Gosport, Indiana, and

James S. Burton of Martinsville. He died at the home of his son David September 27, 1900.

ALEXANDER BAXTER CRANE

Alexander B. Crane moved to New York after the war, and on July 12, 1865, he was married to Laura Cornelia Mitchell of Charleston, South Carolina. They had six children.

Crane took up the general practice of law in New York in 1865 and established his office at 92 Broadway. He soon moved to Wall Street, however, where his office remained until 1930.

Crane decided to make Scarsdale, New York, his permanent home, and moved there in 1873. He bought "Holmhurst," a home in that town, which later became known as the Crane Manor House and Stone House Farm. During his remaining active years, Colonel Crane was interested in the affairs of his Episcopal Church, the community of Scarsdale, and Westchester county. Crane did not forget his friends back in Indiana, however, and often returned to Terre Haute following the war to attend soldiers reunions. At such events, Crane was typically the center of attention.

Crane died of pneumonia April 16, 1930, at his home in Scarsdale, at the age of ninety-six. He was buried in the churchyard of the Church of St. James the Less (Protestant Episcopal). A number of boulevards in Scarsdale are named for the Crane family.

SAMUEL COBLE

Samuel Coble was born in Ohio in 1838 and moved to Parke County, Indiana, in 1850. At the age of nineteen, he learned to be a blacksmith. He worked on his father's farm and on other farms in the community until he entered the service during the Civil War. When the war was ended, Coble returned to Parke County and became a farmer and stock raiser near Rosedale. He was a staunch Republican, holding the office of County Assessor and County Commissioner. He died March 27, 1927, and was buried in the Rockville Cemetery.

JOHN COBURN

Following his resignation, Coburn returned to Indianapolis and resumed the practice of law. In the spring of 1865, he received an appointment as First Secretary of the Territory of Montana, but he declined. That fall he was elected, without opposition, judge of the Circuit Court of Marion and Hendricks counties. He served in this capacity until nominated for Congress in 1866, and he then resigned and began campaigning for the upcoming election. He was elected and served four consecutive terms. His last term expired March 5, 1875, after he was defeated, along with the Republican ticket. He served with distinction on various committees, including Public Expenditures, Banking and Currency, Military Affairs, the Ku Klux Klan investigation, and the Alabama Election investigation. While Chairman of the Committee on Military Affairs, he successfully advocated before Congress the importance of preserving the records of the Civil War, which were then rapidly deteriorating, and in some instances destroyed. He was aided in his efforts by Adjutant-General Edward D. Townsend and General H. V. Boynton, a prominent newspaper correspondent of the day. Their combined efforts resulted in the publication of the invaluable *War of the Rebellion: Official Records of the Union and Confederate Armies.*

He strongly supported all matters that were of interest to the old soldier. Thus he formulated a bill, which subsequently became law, that made it possible for the grave of every Union soldier to be marked with a head stone.

In 1876 Coburn declined to be a candidate for Congress, and in 1880 he turned down an offer to run as a candidate for Governor of Indiana. After he retired from Congress, he practiced law at Indianapolis, except when he was absent from the state as United States Commissioner at Hot Springs, Arkansas, and as Judge of the Supreme Court of Montana.

During his residence in Indianapolis, he was very active in public affairs. As early as 1851 he began agitation for the building of a United States Post Office. This ended successfully with Indianapolis having one of the few public buildings in the nation, except New Orleans and Detroit. Coburn also served a term as school commissioner of Indianapolis and was a pioneer in introducing manual training in the city schools. He also played an important part in the founding of the Indiana Soldiers' Orphans' Home at Knightstown, Indiana. He was among the first to advocate the building of a soldiers monument, and he later delivered an oration at the laying of the corner stone of the present Soldiers and Sailors Monument in Indianapolis. John Coburn's father, Henry P. Coburn, and his father-in-law, Charles H. Test, were both very active in the early years of the of the Indiana Historical Society. John Coburn also played a very active role in the affairs of the Society and has been referred to as the "mainstay" of the Indiana Historical Society during the 1870's and 1880's. His sister, Caroline Bruce, was married to Dr. Robert Bruce, surgeon for the 33rd Indiana Infantry.

John Coburn died January 28, 1908, and he was buried at Crown Hill Cemetery in Indianapolis, not far from the grave of Governor Morton. At the end of Coburn's life, the Indianapolis newspapers heralded him as perhaps the oldest living native of the city, being born there soon after the state Capital moved from Corydon to Indianapolis.

Frank C. Crawford

Frank C. Crawford was born in Terre Haute, Indiana, and was educated at Kenyon College, Gambier, Ohio. He was on a visit to his father's home in Ireland when the war broke out, but when he returned to Terre Haute he enlisted as a private in the 71st Indiana Regiment. Upon the recommendation of Colonel Richard Thompson, however, he was transferred to the 85th Indiana as the adjutant of that regiment. After the death of Major Robert E. Craig at Murfreesboro, Tennessee, Colonel Thompson again wrote Governor Morton urging him to appoint Frank Crawford major of the regiment. This did not happen, however, but Crawford was later commissioned as major and aide-de-camp on the staff of General William T. Ward. After the war, Frank returned to Terre Haute and became engaged in the wholesale shoe business. In 1870 he left this business and began work in the treasurer's department of the Vandalia Railroad. Soon after, he was made paymaster and served in that capacity until he retired in 1908. Frank Crawford died on May 13, 1919, at Daytona, Florida. He was buried in the Highland Lawn Cemetery in Terre Haute.

William T. Crawford

William T. Crawford moved to Sullivan County, Indiana, in 1860 and soon began work on the Ascension Seminary at Farmersburg. He had been educated at the high school in New Lisbon, Ohio, and Mount Union Seminary in Mount Union, Ohio. In 1862, before the Ascension Academy was completed, he raised a company of men and was made Captain of Company H, 85th Indiana Infantry. After the war, William Crawford resumed his work on the Ascension Seminary, and in 1865 he opened a normal school which he ran quite successfully until 1872. He then moved to Sullivan, Indiana, and consolidated his seminary with the local high school until 1876. Crawford then became a pension agent for soldiers of the Civil War. He died on October 15, 1914, and was buried at Center Ridge Cemetery,

Sullivan County. His honorary pall bearers consisted of men who had been members of Company H, 85th Indiana Regiment.

JOHN B. DOWD

John B. Dowd was born in Cincinnati, Ohio, April 8, 1841. He was educated in the common schools of Cincinnati and taught school for several years. In the summer of 1861 he moved to Parke County. He entered the war as a member of the 85th Indiana Regiment, but on November 1, 1863, he left that regiment to become captain of Company H of the 13th Regular United States Colored Troops. He was permanently disabled in a railroad accident near Waverly, Tennessee, and returned to Rockville, Indiana. In January 1865 he was appointed a member of the court-martial at Nashville, Tennessee, composed of disabled officers, and he served in that capacity until mustered out April 20, 1865. He was married September 22, 1864, to Miss Elizabeth J. Cole, and they had four children.

After the war, Dowd studied law under Colonel John P. Baird and was admitted to the bar at Rockville in September 1867. He moved from Catlin to Rockville that same year and in 1870 became postmaster at Rockville. He was reappointed by President Grant in 1871 and was again reappointed by President Hayes in 1877. Sometime after 1882 he obtained a position in the Pension Department in Washington, D.C., which was at that time, quartered in Ford's Theater. On June 9, 1893, the building collapsed, and many people were killed. Dowd, however, escaped with only a broken leg and other minor injuries. After he retired, he frequently returned to Rockville to visit old friends. Dowd died March 22, 1923, at the home of his daughter, and was buried with his wife in Arlington Cemetery.

JOHN PATRICK DUFFICY

Major John P. Dufficy of the 35th Indiana Regiment, born in Roscommon County, Ireland, was often acclaimed in the *Official Records* for his performance and bravery during engagements with the enemy. John Baird, Alexander Crane, and John Dufficy were friends in Terre Haute before the war, and their reunion at Libby Prison in March 1863 must have been heart-rending. Dufficy was mortally wounded in the left arm at Kennesaw Mountain on June 20, 1864. In November of that year, a local undertaker, Isaac Ball, advertised that he was traveling to Nashville, Chattanooga, and other places throughout the south for the purpose of bringing back the remains of deceased soldiers. Major Dufficy's body had been temporarily interred at Bridgeport, Alabama, and Isaac Ball returned it to Terre Haute. Dufficy's remains were finally interred in the St. Joseph Cemetery, Terre Haute, on January 11, 1865.

DANIEL DUSTIN

After Daniel Dustin was mustered out of the service in Washington June 7, 1865 he returned to his home at Sycamore, west of Chicago, in De Kalb County, Illinois. He soon became active in politics, and in November 1865 he was elected, without opposition, to the office of county clerk on the Republican ticket. He served in that capacity for four years, and then served two years as county treasurer. In 1880 he was elected Circuit Clerk and Recorder. He was reelected in 1884, and he then served in this office for ten years by reelection. He resigned to accept President Benjamin Harrison's appointment May 2, 1890, as sub-treasurer of the United States Treasury at Chicago, and he remained in this office until his death.

After returning home, Dustin was interested in all matters relating to the welfare of Civil War veterans. When the Soldiers and Sailors Home at Quincy, Illinois, was under construction, he was president of the board of trustees.

Dustin was a member of the Masonic Order, and in 1872 he was elected commander of the Knight's Templars of Illinois. He became a staunch Republican at the time of the organization of that party, and he remained an active and influential member until his death. He died at Carthage, Missouri, March 30, 1892, while visiting at his daughter's home.

GEORGE E. FARRINGTON

George E. Farrington was born in Terre Haute, Indiana, and, like his friend Frank Crawford, attended Kenyon College at Gambier, Ohio. Following the war he worked as a clerk to the Secretary of the Vandalia Railroad, and after several promotions he was made general agent. In 1869 he married Mary E. Turner, and they had four children. George Farrington was a Republican, a councilman, and a thirty-third degree Mason. He died February 7, 1920, and was buried in the Highland Lawn Cemetery in Terre Haute.

DAVID W. FINNEY

After the war, in 1866, Private David W. Finney moved to Kansas and was engaged in hardware merchandising and in railroad work. He took a great interest in the political affairs of Kansas during the early days of statehood. He served three terms as lieutenant-governor of the state, was in the state senate and house of representatives, and was also state railroad commissioner.

ABNER FLOYD

It was reported that when Captain Abner Floyd fell mortally wounded at the head of his company at Thompson's Station, Tennessee, he was left on the field nearly alone. Eventually, he was taken to a Negro's cabin near the battlefield and there the black man attended him until he died. Floyd knew that his wounds were mortal, and before he breathed his last, he disposed of his sword and ring and conveyed his final message to his wife. The remains of Captain Floyd were sent home after the battle, and he was buried in the Cashatt Cemetery in northern Parke County in Indiana. Out of respect for Captain Floyd, the G.A.R. post at Annapolis, Indiana, was named in his honor. Before the war, Floyd was a schoolmaster and had taught some of the men of his company.

GORDON GRANGER

Soon after the end of the war, Union troops were dispatched throughout the former Confederate states to advise the populace that all slaves were free. As a part of this mission, Gordon Granger with nearly 1,800 Union soldiers arrived at Galveston, Texas, on June 19, 1865, and there he proclaimed by executive order that all slaves were free and any further connections between former masters and slaves were to be on an employer/free labor basis. To this day, "Juneteenth," as it is called in Texas, is the day of emancipation.

Granger was mustered out of the volunteer service on January 25, 1866, and was appointed colonel of infantry in the regular army, serving in that post for nearly ten years. In 1869 he married Maria, daughter of Dr. Joseph P. Letcher of Lexington, Kentucky.

Though in poor health much of the time during his post-war years, and frequently absent from the service, he commanded the district of Memphis on two occasions during the period 1867-69, also commanded the District of New Mexico. He died in Santa Fe, New Mexico, on January 10, 1876, and was buried in Lexington, Kentucky, the home of his wife's family. His burial place is not far from the graves of John Hunt Morgan, John C. Breckinridge, and Henry Clay.

DR. WILSON HOBBS

Wilson Hobbs was born in Salem in southern Indiana. Both parents had died before he was ten years old, and he was sent to live with his uncle, Elisha Hobbs, at Carthage, in Rush County, Indiana. Hobbs obtained his education at the Friends boarding school at Mount Pleasant, Ohio, and he paid his way by splitting wood for the school. He began teaching in 1842, and four years later married Zalina Williams. In 1848 he began studying medicine, and in 1850 Dr. Hobbs, his wife, and two children, moved to the Shawnee Mission in Kansas, where he took charge of the Mission School. (Shawnee Mission was just across the state line from present day Kansas City, Missouri, on present day Interstate Route 50.) There, among the Shawnee Indians he began the practice of medicine. In 1853 he moved back to Indiana with his family, and at Annapolis, in Parke County, he resumed the practice of medicine. He was also School Examiner of Parke County.

On September 4, 1862, in the second year of the war, Dr. Hobbs was commissioned Surgeon of the 85th Indiana Regiment and served with the regiment until muster out in June 1865. Following his military service, Dr. Hobbs resumed his profession as physician in Carthage, Indiana, but in 1873 he removed his practice to Knightstown. There he became President of the School Board of Knightstown, President of the State Medical Association in 1874, and was a delegate to the International Medical Congress in 1876. Dr. Wilson Hobbs died July 24, 1892, and was buried in the Glen Cove Cemetery, Knightstown, Indiana.

ELWOOD HUNT

Christened Silas Elwood, he used this name during his youth and early manhood, including the time he served in the 85th Indiana Regiment, but later in life he became known as Elwood Hunt. He was a private, and his name appeared on the roster of the 85th Indiana Regiment as Silas E. Hunt. He received a serious gunshot wound in his left arm at Thompson's Station and was unable to perform further service and was discharged June 8, 1863. He later studied at Bloomingdale and Waveland academies, and at Asbury College (now Depauw University). He taught school for a short time, and in 1868 he began to study law. This study was interrupted when he was appointed deputy clerk of the Parke Circuit Court, and in 1870 he was elected County Recorder. In 1874 he declined renomination for this position to devote all his time to the study of law. He eventually opened a successful law practice in Rockville. He died on June 13, 1925 and was buried in the Rockville Cemetery.

SALMON LUSK, JR.

Salmon "Solly" Lusk's body was never returned to Indiana following his death at Thompson's Station. His father, a War of 1812 veteran, came to Indiana from Vermont in 1816 and first settled at Fort Harrison, on the Wabash River. Soon after, he moved to Vermillion County and finally settled at the "Narrows" on Sugar Creek in Parke County by 1826. In 1841 construction was completed on a brick home overlooking the beautiful creek and mill. Before the Civil War, the Lusk home was considered the finest in the area, and it became a meeting place for the young people of the community. Much of the land owned by the Lusk family is now Turkey Run State Park, and their home is maintained by the State of Indiana. There is a monument to Salmon Lusk's memory at the Bethany Cemetery, in Parke County.

EDWARD T. McCREA

Edward T. McCrea was born in Shelby County, Indiana, in 1836. He attended Franklin College and studied law at Hanover College. During the war Captain McCrea served with the 33rd Indiana Regiment, and then moved to Montgomery County in about 1875. He served in the Indiana House of Representatives in 1895 and 1897. He was a teacher, farmer, miller, and breeder of Aberdeen Angus Cattle. He died April 7, 1915.

WILLIAM NEET

Private William Neet was born in Kentucky in 1824, later moving to Parke County, Indiana, where he became a farmer and in 1845 he married Eliza P. Jacks. Following the war, Neet returned to farming near Catlin, Indiana, a few miles southeast of Rockville. William and Eliza had twelve children. William Neet was said to be one of the finest farmers in the area, a devout Methodist, and a devoted patriot. His older brother, John C. Neet, was a musician in the 85th Indiana Regiment. Neet died December 2, 1879, and was buried in Mount Olivet Cemetery, Parke County.

HIRAM L. TILLOTSON

Hiram L. Tillotson, adjutant of the 85th Indiana, resigned while the army was at Savannah, Georgia, and returned to his home at Prairie Creek. There he resumed his old trade as a harness maker. He finally settled in Nevada, Missouri, where he was appointed postmaster by President Grant at the beginning of his first term. He remained in this position for almost nineteen years and then served a term in the Missouri Legislature. He was president of the First National Bank of Nevada and was an active member of the Baptist Church of that city. He died at the age of seventy-three, on June 7, 1902.

William L. Utley

After Utley resigned his commission because of ill health July 5, 1864, while the army was in Georgia, he returned to Racine, Wisconsin. After regaining his health the following year, he purchased the *Racine Journal*, a struggling Democratic paper. He was accompanied in this venture by his son, Hamilton, the only surviving member of his family. He then changed his politics, and by his efforts during the next nine years greatly increased both the circulation and influence of this paper.

In 1869 President Ulysses S. Grant appointed Utley as postmaster at Racine, and he served in his office for eight years. As postmaster Utley was largely responsible for the construction of a fine new post office building for the city.

In 1875 Utley sundered his connection with the *Racine Journal* and on behalf of the Greenback party started *The New Deal* as its political organ. In 1883 he bought the press of the *New Deal*, which had ceased operations, and with his son founded the *Racine Daily Times*, which he edited until his death. He was also editor of *Utley's Dollar Weekly* during this period.

It should be noted that for thirty years, Utley devoted much time in raising fast, blooded horses, and some of these became well known.

Utley's first wife died April 10, 1864, and on February 22, 1866 he married Sarah J. Wooster, by whom he had one son. Utley died of diabetes on March 4, 1887.

William D. Weir

William D. Weir was born August 6, 1827. He was a member of the Second Indiana Volunteer Infantry in the Mexican War and served as captain of Company F, 85th Indiana during the Civil War. Weir was from Prairie Creek, Indiana. His resignation, written July 8, 1864, states that he tendered his "immediate and unconditional resignation . . . for the good of the service." The endorsements of the command were as follows: Colonel Baird's comments stated that "this officer is entirely inefficient & worthless and gets drunk every time he is put on duty and the service requires that he should be either mustered out or dismissed." Coburn approved and added that "I think the service would be greatly benefited by an acceptance of this resignation." General Ward added the observation "approved and strongly recommended." Major General Joseph Hooker also signed the resignation July 9, 1864, and Weir was ordered to Chattanooga for dismissal. This took effect July 14, 1864. Weir died March 27, 1881, and was buried in the West Lawn Cemetery at Prairie Creek, Indiana.

Dr. William V. Wiles

William V. Wiles was born in Ohio and studied medicine at Connersville, Indiana. In 1852 he moved to Indiana, establishing a regular practice at the "Falls of the Eel," near present day Cataract in northern Owen County. He was nominated by the Democratic party to run for the legislature, but he declined so that he could accept the position of Assistant Surgeon of the 85th Indiana Regiment which Governor Oliver P. Morton had offered to him. After the war, Wiles returned home and soon thereafter moved to Spencer in Owen County. He practiced medicine and was a druggist there for the remainder of his career. At Spencer, he married Parthinia I. Jennings, and they had seven children. Dr. Wiles died at his home on October 24, 1892, and was buried in the Riverview Cemetery, Spencer, Indiana.

End Notes

Chapter 1

1. *War of the Rebellion: Official Records of the Union and Confederate Armies*, Series 3, Vol. 2, pp. 316-17, 415-16. Cited hereafter as *OR*,; *Indiana in the War of the Rebellion, Official Report of W. H. H. Terrell, Adjutant General of Indiana*, Indianapolis, 1869: Vol. I, *Appendix, Statistics and Documents*, pp. 39, 333-34. Cited hereafter as Terrell.

2. Don C. Seitz, *Braxton Bragg, General of the Confederacy*, The State Company, Columbia, South Carolina, 1924, pp. 131-32, 138, 148-49, 152-54. Cited hereafter as Seitz.

3. Henry M. Cist, *The Army of the Cumberland*, Charles Scribner's Sons, New York, 1882, pp. 35-40. Cited hereafter as Cist; *OR,* Series I, Vol. 16, Part I, pp. 731-84. Cited hereafter as *OR,* and refers to Series I unless otherwise stated; Seitz, pp. 138-43.

4. *OR,* Vol. 16, Part II, pp. 412, 436, 450, 458, 660; Frederick H. Dyer, *A Compendium of the War of the Rebellion*, Thomas Yoseloff Publisher, New York and London, 1909. A new edition was published in 1959, Vol. 3, pp. 1143-46. Cited hereafter as Dyer's *Compendium*.

5. Terrell, Vol. I, *Appendix, Statistics and Documents*, p. 39.

6. Dyer's *Compendium*, Vol. III, pp. 1147-51.

7. *Indiana History Bulletin*, December 1961, Vol. 38, No. 12, p. 216,The Indiana Historical Bureau, Indianapolis; Jefferson E. Brant, *History of the Eighty-Fifth Indiana Volunteer Infantry*, Cravens Brothers, Printers and Binders, Bloomington, Indiana, 1902, p. 7. Cited hereafter as Brant.

8. Terrell, Vol. III, pp. 65-71 and Vol. 6, pp. 372-87.

9. *Supplement to the Official Records of the Union and Confederate Armies*, Broadfoot Publishing Company, Wilmington, North Carolina, 1995, Part II, Record of Events, Vol. 18, pp. 261. Cited hereafter as *Supplement to the Official Records*; George W. Hawes, *Indiana Gazeteer and Business Directory for 1860 and 1861*, Number Two, Second Edition, p. 12. Cited hereafter as Hawes.

10. *Supplement to the Official Records*, Part II, Vol. 18, p. 263; *The Parke County Republican*, Rockville, Indiana, September 10, 1862.

11. *Supplement to the Official Records*, Part II, Vol. 18, p. 265.

12. Ibid., Part II, Vol. 18, p. 267.

13. Ibid., p. 269.

14. Ibid., p. 271; Brant, p. 134.

15. *Supplement to the Official Records*, Part II, Vol 18, p. 272.

16. Ibid., p. 274.

17. Ibid., p. 276.

18. Ibid., p. 277; Hawes, p. 72.

19. *The Alford Brothers: "We All Must Dye Sooner or Later,"* Richard S. Skidmore, editor, Nugget Publishers, Hanover, Indiana, 1995, pp. 21, 27; Nancy Niblack Baxter, *Gallant Fourteenth, The Story of an Indiana Civil War Regiment*, revised edition, Guild Press, Carmel, Indiana, 1987, pp. 35-36. (William Houghton's description of the camp is given in a letter written to his parents May 12, 1861.)

20. *Indiana History Bulletin*, January 1962, Vol. 39, No. 1, *The Indiana Historical Bureau*, Indianapolis, p. 17.

21. Henry C. Bradsby, *History of Vigo County, Indiana*, S. B. Nelson & Company, Publishers, Chicago, 1891, Part II, pp. 960-64. Cited hereafter as Bradsby; *Encyclopedia of Biography of Indiana*, George Irving Reed, ed., The Century Publishing and Engraving Company, Chicago, 1895, Vol. 1, pp. 1-8. Cited hereafter as George Reed, *Encyclopedia*.

22. Terrell, Vol. I, p. 112.

23. *Indiana History Bulletin*, January 1962, Vol. 39, No. 1, p. 17.

24. Bradsby, Part I, pp. 337-39.

25. Brant, p. 8; *The Parke County Republican*, September 10, 1862.

26. Terrell, Vol. I, p. 154.

27. Joseph H. Parks, *General Edmund Kirby Smith, C.S.A.*, Louisiana State University Press, Baton Rouge, 1954, pp. 205-06. Cited hereafter as Parks.

28. Lew Wallace, *An Autobiography*, Harper and Brothers, New York and London, 1906, Vol. II, pp. 592-94.

29. *OR*, Vol. 16, Part II, p. 375.

30. Ibid., pp. 405, 470.

31. *OR*, Vol. 16, Part I, p. 3.

32. Ibid., pp. 933-34, 939.

33. Henry R. Ingraham, letter to his parents, September 2, 1862, Indiana Historical Society Library; *The Wabash Daily Express*, Terre Haute, Indiana, September 3, 1862.

34. Bradsby, pp. 337-38.

35. Brant, pp. 135-43; Terrell, Vol. 3, pp. 65-71, Vol. 6, pp. 372-87.

36. Brant, p. 8.

37. William M. Anderson, *They Died to Make Men Free*, Morningside House, Inc., Dayton, Ohio, 1994, p. 20. Cited hereafter as Anderson.

38. Ibid., p. 20.

39. Ibid., pp. 21-23.

40. Ibid., pp. 29, 36, 46.

41. Ibid., p. 47.

42. Anderson, pp. 55-57; G. S. Bradley, *The Star Corps; or, Notes of an Army Chaplain during Sherman's "Famous March to the Sea,"* Jermain and Brightman, Book and Job Printers, Sentinel Building, Milwaukee, Wisconsin, 1865, p. 31. Cited hereafter as Bradley, *Star Corps.*

43. Anderson, p. 43.

44. *View from Headquarters: Civil War Letters of Harvey Reid,* Frank L. Byrne, Editor, The Historical Society of Wisconsin, Madison, 1965, p. xii. Cited hereafter as Reid; Bradley, *Star Corps,* p. 21.

45. William DeLoss Love, *Wisconsin in the War of the Rebellion,* Church and Goodman, Publishers, Chicago, 1866, pp. 993; E. B. Quiner, *The Military History of Wisconsin in the War for the Union,* Clarke and Company, Publishers, Chicago, 1886, p. 697. Cited hereafter as Quiner.

46. *The United States Biographical Dictionary,* Wisconsin Volume, American Biographical Publishing Company, Chicago, Cincinnati and New York, 1877, pp. 98-99; *History of Racine County,* S. J. Clarke Publishing Company, Chicago, 1916, V, pp. 445, 447, VI, p. 428; Reid, p. xii.

47. *Indiana History Bulletin,* January 1962, Volume 39, Number 1, p. 14.

48. John R. McBride, *History of the Thirty-Third Indiana Veteran Volunteer Infantry,* William B. Burford, Printer and Binder, Indianapolis, 1900, p. 13. Cited hereafter as McBride.

49. McBride, pp. 8-12.

50. McBride, pp. 13-15; Terrell, Vol. I, *Appendix, Statistics and Documents,* p. 39.

51. George Reed, Vol. 2, pp. 62-66; Anderson, p. 83.

52. *OR,* Vol. 10, Part I, pp. 60-61; Part II, p. 68; Cist,; McBride, pp. 35-37.

53. Cist, p. 52.

Chapter 2

1. Anderson, pp. 67-68.

2. *OR,* Vol. 16, Part II, pp. 491-92.

3. Chester F. Geaslen, *Our Moment of Glory in the Civil War,* Otto Printing Co. Newport, Kentucky, pp. 22, 42-43, 48. Cited hereafter as Gealsen.

4. Brant, p. 8; *Diary and Civil War Letters of Samuel H. Mattox,* Vigo County Public Library, Terre Haute, Indiana, letter to his wife, September 8, 1862. Cited hereafter as Mattox; *The Wabash Daily Express,* Terre Haute, Indiana, September 5, 1862; *The Parke County Republican,* Rockville, Indiana, September 17, 1862.

5. *Terrell,* Vol. 1, p. 159.

6. *The Daily Wabash Express,* Terre Haute, Indiana, September 13, 1862.

7. Ibid., September 16, 1862.

8. Ibid., September 29, 1862.

9. Brant, pp. 8-9.

10. Geaslen, pp. 42-43, 70-71; Andrew McClure, *Letter to The Parke County Republican*, October 1, 1862.

11. Salmon Lusk, letter written to his cousin, Mary Wright, September 26, 1862, Indiana Historical Society; Wilson Hobbs, in a letter to the *Parke County Republican*, Rockville, Indiana, October 16, 1862.

12. Captain Francis Brooks, letter to *The Wabash Daily Express*, September 17, 1862.

13. *The Wabash Daily Express*, September 26, 1862; *The Parke County Republican*, September 17, 1862 and October 1, 1862.

14. Anderson, pp. 55-57; Bradley, *Star Corps*, p. 31.

15. Reid, pp. xiii-xiv.

16. Reid, p. 3; Geaslen, p. 15.

17. Reid, pp. 3-4.

18. Ibid., pp. 4-5; Geaslen, pp. 29, 48.

19. Reid, p. 5.

20. Ibid., pp. 5-7.

21. *OR*, Vol. 16, Part II, pp. 615, 659, 993; *Official Army Register of the Volunteer Force of the United States Army*, Adjutant General's Office Washington, D.C., 1865. Reprinted by Ron Van Sickle Military Books, Gaithersburg, Maryland, 1987, Vol. 7, p. 196, cited hereafter as *Official Army Register*; Bradley, *Star Corps* p. 21.

22. *OR*, Vol. 16, Part II, pp. 506, 510.

23. Ibid., p. 523.

24. *OR*, Vol. 16, Part II, pp. 472, 477; *Personal Memoirs of P. H. Sheridan*, Charles L. Webster & Company, New York, 1888, Vol. 1, pp. 182-84. Cited hereafter as Sheridan's *Memoirs*.

25. Sheridan's *Memoirs*, pp. 182-84.

26. *OR*, Vol. 52, Part I, p. 281.

27. *OR*, Vol. 16, Part II, p. 553.

28. Parks, pp. 221, 226; *OR*, Vol. 16, Part II, pp. 830, 838, 844. 29. Cist, p. 55; *OR*, Vol. 16, Part I, p. 933; *OR*, Vol. 16, Part II, pp. 807, 830, 873.

29. Cist, p. 55; OR Vol 16, Part I, p. 933; OR Vol. 16, Part II, pp.807,830,873.

30. Cist, pp. 42-43; Joseph Wheeler, *Bragg's Invasion of Kentucky, Battles and Leaders of the Civil War*, Edited by Robert U. Johnson and Clarence C. Buel, Volume III, The Century Company, New York, 1884, 1888, pp. 7-9. Cited hereafter as *Battles and Leaders*.

31. Seitz, pp. 178-79, 184.

32. *OR*, Vol. 16, Part II, pp. 558-59, 560.

33. Seitz, pp. 185, 190.

34. *OR*, Vol. 16, Part I, pp. 1093-94.

35. McBride, pp. 49, 53-54, 56-57.

36. *OR,* Vol. 16, Part II, p. 587; *OR,* Vol. 52, Part I, p. 288.

37. *OR,* Vol. 16, Part II, pp. 586-87.

38. Ibid., 586-87, 659; *Bradley, Star Corps* pp. 21, 33; *The Parke County Republican,* October 29, 1862; Letter from Abner Floyd to Mr. E. Robbins, Rockville Public Library.

39. *OR,* Vol. 52, Part I, p. 289.

40. Gil R. Stormont, *History of Gibson County, Indiana, Her People, Industries, and Institutions,* B. F. Bowen & Company, Inc., Indianapolis, 1914, p. 211.

41. *OR,* Vol. 52, Part I, pp. 289-90.

42. Bradley, *Star Corps,* p. 22.

43. Anderson, p. 67.

44. *OR,* Vol. 52, Part I, pp. 289, 291; *OR,* Vol. 16, Part II, p. 617.

45. *OR,* Vol. 16, Part II, p. 659.

46. Ibid., pp. 621, 630; *OR,* Vol. 52, Part I, pp. 291-92; Geaslen, p. 61; *The Parke County Republican,* November 19, 1862.

47. Reid, pp. 9-10.

48. *OR,* Vol. 16, Part, II, p. 626; *OR,* Vol. 52, Part I, pp. 291-92; Bradley, *Star Corps,* p. 22.

49. Anderson, pp. 70-71.

50. Reid, pp. 10-11; Bradley, *Star Corps.* p. 22.

51. Ibid., p. 11; *The Parke County Republican,* November 19, 1862.

52. Reid, p. 12.

53. Anderson, p. 72.

54. *OR,* Vol. 52, Part I, p. 296.

55. McBride, p. 63.

56. *The Wabash Daily Express,* October 13, 1862.

57. Ibid., November 18, 1862.

58. Brant, p. 9; Bradley, *Star Corps,* p. 33.

59. Reid, p. 12.

60. Ibid., p. 12; Bradley, *Star Corps,* p. 22.

61. *OR,* Vol. 16, Part II, p. 656; Reid, p. 12-13.

62. Anderson, pp. 70-72; McBride, p. 17.

63. Brant, p. 9.

64. McBride, p. 68; Rossiter Johnson, *Campfires and Battlefields,* The Blue and Gray Press, New York, 1958, pp. 496-98; Robert Hale Strong, *A Yankee Private's Civil War,* Edited by Ashley Halsey, Henry Regnery Company, Chicago, 1961, p. 10; *Historical Times Illustrated Enclycopedia of the Civil War,* Patricia L. Faust, editor, Harper and Row Publishers, New York, 1986, pp. 687-88.

65. *OR,* Vol. 16, Part II, p. 993.

66. Brant, pp. 9-10.

67. Ibid., p. 10.

68. *OR,* Vol. 16, Part II, pp. 649; *OR,* Vol. 20, Part II, pp. 24, 37.

69. *OR,* Vol. 52, Part I, p. 300.

70. Anderson, pp. 84-85.

71. *OR,* Vol. 16, Part II, p. 593; *OR,* Vol. 20, Part I, p. 181.

72. *Supplement to the Official Records,* Part II, Vol. 14, p. 403.

73. Brant, p. 10.

74. *Civil War Letters of William Neet* (85th Indiana Volunteer Infantry), compiled by Neet McCanliss, Rockville, Indiana, 1933 (copied and distributed by Dale V. Bush, 1980), Rockville Public Library, Rockville, Indiana. Letter of November 29, 1862. Cited hereafter as Neet.

75. *OR,* Vol. 20, Part II, p. 64.

76. Brant, pp. 10-11; John B. Dowd, letter published in *The Parke County Republican,* December 17, 1862.

77. Mattox, Diary, entry of August 15, 1862.

78. *Revised Regulations for the Army of the United States,* by Authority of the War Department, J. G. L. Brown, Printer, Philadelphia, 1861. Republished by *The Civil War Times Illustrated,* Gettysburg, Pennsylvania, 1974, p. 341; Anderson, p. 50.

79. Anderson, 91.

80. *The Wabash Daily Express,* November 20, 1862.

81. Mattox, letter to his family, January 7, 1863; Anderson, pp. 123-24.

82. *OR,* Vol. 20, Part II, p. 174; Anderson, p. 103; Brant, pp. 11-12.

83. *Supplement to the Official Records,* Vol. 18, pp. 258, 275.

84. Brant, pp. 11-12.

85. Terrell, Vol. 3, pp. 65-71, Vol. 6, pp. 372-87.

86. Anderson, pp. 85-86, 88, 420-21.

87. Bradley, *Star Corps,* p. 22.

88. McBride, p. 29; Anderson, p. 86.

89. Basil W. Duke, *Morgan's Cavalry,* The Neal Publishing Company, New York and Washington, 1906, pp. 231-47; *OR,* Vol. 20, Part I, pp. 154-58.

90. Anderson, pp. 119-23; *OR,* Vol. 20, Part I, p. 142.

91. Ibid., pp. 120-21.

92. Ibid., pp. 120-21; *OR,* Vol. 20, Part I, pp. 142; Henry R. Ingraham, letter to his parents, January 6, 1863, Indiana Historical Society; *The Parke County Republican,* January 21, 1863.

93. Anderson, pp. 119-23; McBride, p. 64; *Supplement to the Official Records,* Part II, Vol. 18, p. 258; Bradley, *Star Corps,* p. 22.

94. McBride, p. 64.

95. John B. Dowd, letter to *The Parke County Republican,* January 21, 1863, pp. 1-2; Reid, p. 19; Samuel Coble, *Day Book of the 85th Indiana, Company G,* 1863, Indiana Historical Society. Cited hereafter as Coble *Day Book;* Joseph M. Elphine, *Diary,* Indiana Historical Society.

Chapter 3

1. *OR*, Vol. 20, Part II, pp. 332.
2. Ibid., pp. 342-43.
3. *OR*, Vol. 52, Part I, p. 333.
4. Anderson, pp. 146-47; Brant, p. 12; Coble, *Day Book*.
5. Reid, pp. 20-21.
6. Anderson, p. 147; McBride, 71.
7. McBride, p. 71.
8. McBride, p. 72; Mattox, letter of February 8, 1863; *Supplement to the Official Records*, Vol. 18, p. 258; *The Parke County Republican*, February 25, 1863.
9. Brant, p. 13.
10. McBride, p. 72.
11. Neet, letter of February 24, 1863.
12. McBride, p. 72; Anderson, pp. 147-48; *Supplement to the Official Records*, Part II, Vol. 18, p. 258.
13. Cist, pp. 140-41; *OR*, Vol. 23, Part I, pp. 34-39, 39-41; John B. Dowd, letter to *The Parke County Republican*, February 25, 1863.
14. Anderson, p. 149; Bradley, *Star Corps* p. 25; *The Parke County Republican*, February 25, 1863.
15. Anderson, pp. 149-50.
16. Anderson, pp. 149-50; Bradley, *Star Corps* pp. 29-30.
17. Wilson Hobbs, letter to *The Parke County Republican*, February 25, 1863
18. Bradley, *Star Corps* p. 29.
19. Anderson, p. 156.
20. Mattox, letter to his family, February 24, 1863.
21. James H. Madison, *The Indiana Way: A State History*, Indiana University Press, Bloomington, Indiana, 1986, pp. 197-207; Emma Lou Thornbrough, *Indiana in the Civil War Era: 1850-1880*, Indiana Historical Society, Indianapolis, 1989, pp. 111-23; *The Parke County Republican*, March 4, 1863; *The Wabash Daily Express*, March 4, 1863; *The Indianapolis Journal*, Indianapolis, March 7, 1863.
22. Anderson pp. 157-58; Bradley, *Star Corps* p. 30.
23. *OR*, Vol. 23, Part I, p. 85; Anderson, p. 158; Reid, p. 28
24. Brant, p. 14.

Chapter 4

1. *OR*, Vol. 23, Part I, p. 77.
2. Ibid., pp. 77-78.
3. *OR*, Vol. 23, Part I, pp. 85-86; Brant, p. 15.
4. *OR*, Vol. 23, Part I, p. 84.

5. Reid, p. 28

6. *OR,* Vol. 23, Part I, p. 86; Reid, p. 28.

7. Joseph E. Johnston, *Narrative of Military Operations,* D. Appleton and Company, New York, 1874, pp. 160-61; *OR,* Vol. 23, Part I, p. 116; *OR,* Vol. 23, Part II, p. 634; *OR,* Vol. 52, Part II, p. 425; Charles P. Lincoln, *Engagement at Thompson's Station, Tennessee,* War Paper 14, Military Order of the Loyal Legion of the United States (MOLLUS), Commandery of the District of Columbia. Read November 1893. Note: Broadfoot Publishing Company has published the MOLLUS papers of all the commanderies, and Lincoln's paper appears in Book 42, District of Columbia, Vol. 1, pp. 211-25. Cited hereafter as Lincoln.

8. *OR,* Vol. 23, Part I, p. 116.

9. Ibid., pp. 80, 86.

10. Ibid., pp. 80, 86, 113.

11. Reid, p. 31.

12. Ibid.

13. *OR,* Vol. 23, Part I, p. 86; Reid, p. 31.

14. Lincoln, pp. 213-14.

15. *OR,* Vol. 23, Part I, pp. 76-77, 78, 86, 94, 97-98, 102.

16. Ibid., p. 78.

17. Reid, pp. 31-32.

18. *OR,* Vol. 23, Part I, pp. 86, 98, 100-01, 102; Brant, p. 15; Reid, p. 31.

19. *OR,* Vol. 23, Part I, pp. 76-77, 86-87, 94, 98.

20. Ibid., p. 87; Lincoln, p. 214.

21. *OR,* Vol. 23, Part I, p. 87.

22. Ibid.

23. John P. Baird, letter written while in Libby Prison March 30, 1863. It was carried from the prison by Josiah H. Sherman of Co. A. 85th Indiana Regiment, who gave the letter to Major John P. Dufficy of the 35th Indiana. Dufficy sent the letter on by mail to the editor of *The Daily Wabash Express* for publication. *The Daily Wabash Express* for this period is not known to exist, but the letter was picked up and copied in *The Daily Evansville Journal* on April 11, 1863, and in *The Parke County Republican* on April 15, 1863. Cited hereafter as Baird's Letter.

24. *OR,* Vol. 23, Part I, p. 111; Baird's Letter.

25. Ibid., p. 87; Baird's Letter.

26. Ibid., p. 119; John A. Wyeth, *Life of General Nathan Bedford Forrest,* Harper and Brothers Publishers, New York and London, 1899, p. 155. Cited hereafter as Wyeth.

27. *OR,* Vol. 23, Part I, p. 116; Wyeth, p. 157.

28. *OR,* Vol 23, Part I, pp. 80-81, 106, 113-14; Reid, p. 32.

29. *OR,* Vol 23, Part I, pp. 102, 106-07.

30. Ibid., p. 87.

31. *OR,* Vol. 23, Part I, pp. 87, 100, 102, 104, 106-07; Reid, p. 33.

32. *OR,* Vol. 23, Part I, pp. 87-88; Lincoln p. 215.

33. *OR,* Vol. 23, Part I, p. 88.

34. Ibid., p. 102.

35. Ibid., p. 101.

36. Ibid., p. 88.

37. *OR,* Vol. 23, Part I, p. 102; Baird's Letter.

38. *OR,* Vol. 23, Part I, p. 102.

39. *OR,* Vol. 23, Part I, pp. 101, 116; McBride, p. 75; Baird's Letter; *The Wabash Daily Express,* March 18, 1863.

40. *OR,* Vol. 23, Part I, pp. 88, 99.

41. Ibid., pp. 88, 102, 116; McBride, p. 76.

42. *OR,* Vol. 23, Part I, p. 88.

43. Ibid., p. 103.

44. Ibid., pp. 116-17, 120.

45. Ibid., p. 104.

46. Lincoln, p. 216.

47. *OR,* Vol. 23, Part I, pp. 99, 104; Lincoln, p. 216.

48. *OR,* Vol. 23, Part I, pp. 95, 99.

49. Ibid., p. 104, 107; Reid, p. 34.

50. Anderson, p. 168; Lincoln, pp. 217-18.

51. *OR,* Vol. 23, Part I, p. 107.

52. Ibid., pp. 99, 104, 107.

53. Ibid., p. 116.

54. Ibid., p. 120.

55. Ibid., pp. 116-117; Wyeth, p. 117.

56. *OR,* Vol. 23, Part I p. 120.

57. Ibid., pp. 99, 120.

58. Ibid., pp. 95, 99, 108.

59. Ibid., p. 108.

60. Ibid., p. 103.

61. Ibid.

62. Ibid., p. 117, p. 124; Lincoln, pp. 218-19.

63. Baird's Letter

64. *OR,* Vol. 23, Part I, pp. 89, 104-05, 108-09, 122; Anderson, pp. 169-72; Lincoln, p. 219.

65. Lincoln, p. 219.

66. *OR,* Vol. 23, Part I, p. 89.

67. Ibid., pp. 108-09.

68. Ibid., p. 120.

69. Ibid., p. 89.

70. Ibid., p. 89, p. 103.

71. Ibid., p. 89; Lincoln, pp. 219-20.

72. *OR,* Vol. 23, Part I, pp. 89, 103.

73. *OR,* Vol. 23, Part I, pp. 91, 103; Brant, p. 18; Baird's Letter.

74. *OR,* Vol. 23, Part I, pp. 75, 91.

75. Anderson, p. 174

76. *OR,* Vol. 23, Part I, p. 81.

77. Ibid., pp. 81-82.

78. Ibid., p. 82.

79. Ibid., p. 115.

80. *OR,* Vol. 23. Part I, pp. 80, 83, 91; Anderson, p. 176.

81. *OR,* Vol. 23, Part I, p. 105.

82. Ibid., pp. 82, 116-17.

83. Ibid., p. 82.

84. Ibid., p. 106.

85. Anderson, p. 177.

86. *OR,* Vol. 23, Part I, p. 114.

87. Ibid., pp. 114-15.

88. *OR,* Vol. 23, Part I, p. 91; Anderson, p. 176.

89. *OR,* Vol. 23, Part I, p. 95, 107, 112.

90. Ibid., pp. 95, 114.

91. Ibid., p. 116.

92. Ibid., p. 120.

93. Ibid., p. 105.

94. Baird's Letter

95. *OR,* Vol. 23, Part I, p. 115.

96. Ibid., pp. 108, 112.

97. Ibid., p. 112.

98. Ibid., pp. 95-96.

99. Frank K. Moore, ed., *The Rebellion Record: A Diary of American Events,* Boston, 1900, Vol. 6, pp. 442-43.

100. *OR,* Vol. 23, Part I, p. 108.

101. Anderson, p. 179.

102. *OR,* Vol. 23, Part II, p. 112.

103. Anderson, pp. 179-80.

104. *OR,* Vol. 23, Part II, p. 109.

105. Alexander, pp. 179-99.

106. *The Indianapolis Journal,* March 13, 1863. Reprinted in the *New Albany, Indiana, Ledger,* March 16, 1863.

107. Bradley, *Star Corps,* p. 41.

108. Stewart Stifakis, *Who Was Who in the Civil War,* Facts on File, Inc., New York, 1988, p. 248; Ezra J. Warner, *Generals in Blue,* Louisiana State University Press, Baton Rouge, 1964, p. 174. Cited hereafter as *Generals in Blue.*

109. *OR,* Vol. 23, Part I, pp. 183-85; Anderson, pp. 194-96.

110. *OR,* Vol. 38, Part I, p. 99; Anderson, p. 84.

Chapter 5

1. McBride, p. 79; Brant, pp. 21-22.
2. McBride, p. 88.
3. Brant, p. 22; McBride, p. 79; Baird's Letter; *The Parke County Republican,* April 29, 1863.
4. *OR,* Vol. 23, Part I, p. 91.
5. Brant, p. 22; McBride, p. 79; *The Parke County Republican,* April 29, 1863; Baird's Letter.
6. Anderson, pp. 187-88; McBride, p. 79.
7. *OR,* Vol. 23, Part I, p. 91; Anderson, pp. 186-87; McBride, pp. 79-80; *The Parke County Republican,* April 29, 1863; Baird's Letter.
8. Brant, p. 22; Baird's Letter
9. McBride, p. 80.
10. *OR,* Vol. 23, Part I, p. 110.
11. Anderson, p. 189.
12. *OR,* Vol. 23, Part I, p. 92; Brant, p. 23; McBride, pp. 80-82; *The Parke County Republican,* April 29, 1863.
13. Indiana Scrapbook Collection, Indiana State Library. The name of the Indianapolis newspaper and the date of the article are not given.
14. *OR,* Vol. 23, Part I, p. 92.
15. McBride, p. 83.
16. *OR,* Vol. 23, Part I, p. 92.
17. *OR,* Vol 23, Part I, p. 92; McBride, p. 84.
18. Brant, p. 23; McBride, p. 83.
19. McBride, p. 84.
20. McBride, p. 84; *Libby Prison, Richmond, Virginia,* Official Publication No. 12, Richmond Civil War Centennial Committee, Richmond, Virginia; Coble's *Day Book,* Indiana Historical Society.

Chapter 6

1. Brant, pp. 24, 28. ; McBride, p. 84; *OR,* Series II, Vol. 8, pp. 912, 930.
2. Anderson, p. 196.
3. *OR,* Vol. 23, Part I, p. 93; Anderson, pp. 199-200.
4. Anderson, p. 196; *The Parke County Republican,* March 16, 1863.
5. *OR,* Vol. 23, Part I, p. 93; Brant, pp. 24-25; Anderson, pp. 196-97; McBride, p. 84.
6. *OR,* Vol. 23, Part I, p. 93; McBride, p. 84.

7. Anderson, pp. 197-99.

8. McBride, p. 84.

9. Ibid., p. 87.

10. Brant, p. 24.

11. *OR,* Vol. 23, Part I, p, 93.

12. Ibid.

13. Ibid.

14. Brant, p. 26.

15. Ibid., pp. 23-24.

16. Ibid., p. 26.

17. Ibid., pp. 27-28.

18. Ibid., p. 24.

19. Ibid., pp. 24-25.

20. Ibid.

21. Ibid., p. 25.

22. McBride, pp. 85, 87-88; Coble, *Day Book.*

23. Anderson, p. 201; McBride, p. 85.

24. Brant, pp. 29-30.

25. John Coburn Collection "Memoranda of the early service of the 33rd Regt. Indiana Volunteers" [ca. 1885], Indiana Historical Society.

26. Brant, pp. 30-31.

27. Ibid., p. 36.

28. Ibid., pp. 28-29.

Chapter 7

1. Reid, p. 45; Brant, p. 15; McBride, p. 96; *OR,* Vol. 23, Part II, pp. 82, 106, 115.

2. *OR,* Vol. 23, Part I, p. 102; *The Parke County Republican,* May 6 and May 20, 1863.

3. McBride, p. 96.

4. *OR,* Vol. 23, Part II, pp. 109, 338; Cist, p. 143.

5. Anderson, pp. 190-91.

6. Reid, pp. 41-42.

7. Wyeth, p. 164.

8. Reid pp. 44-45.

9. *OR,* Vol. 23, Part I, pp. 183-84.

10. Ibid., pp. 179, 188.

11. *OR,* Vol. 23, Part I, pp. 179, 185-86.

12. Anderson, p. 194.

13. *Official Army Register,* Vol. 5, p. 326; Anderson, pp. 194-96, 219; Reid, pp. 63-64, 66.

14. Anderson, pp. 166-67.

15. Brant, pp. 36, 139.

16. Ibid., p. 36.

17. Letter from Lieutenant Colonel Alexander B. Crane to the Terre Haute, Indiana, Bar (addressed to General Charles Cruft), dated March 14, 1881, shortly after the death of Colonel Baird. This letter was published in the *Terre Haute Express*, Tuesday, March 22, 1881.

18. Memorandum from *Prisoner of War Records of Camp Morton, Indiana*, Vol. 116, p. 16.

19. *OR*, Vol. 23, Part I, pp. 222-24.

20. Wyeth, p. 178.

21. *OR*, Vol. 23, Part I, pp. 224-26.

22. Ibid., pp. 226-27.

23. Brant, pp. 33-36; William Herron, *Reminiscences of the Eighty-Fifth Regiment of Indiana Volunteer Infantry*, printed at the Sullivan Union Office, Sullivan, Indiana, 1875.

24. Ezra J. Warner, *Generals in Gray*, Louisiana State University Press, 1959, pp. 314-15. Cited hereafter as Warner, *Generals in Gray*

25. *The Parke County Republican*, May 6, 1863.

26. *OR*, Vol. 23, Part II, p. 390.

27. Coble, *Day Book*.

28. *OR*, Vol. 23, Part II, pp. 398-400.

29. Brant, p. 36; *OR*, Vol. 23, Part I, p. 416; Coble, *Day Book*; Reid, p. 75; *The Parke County Republican*, June 17, 1863.

30. McBride, p. 100.

31. Anderson, pp. 202-05.

32. Ibid., pp. 205-06.

33. Ibid., p. 207.

34. Quiner, p. 700; Reid, pp. 70-71.

35. Reid, pp. 71-72.

36. Ibid., pp. 72-73.

37. Ibid., p. 73.

38. Ibid., pp. 74-75.

39. Ibid., pp. 75-76.

40. Ibid., p. 77.

41. Brant, p. 44.

42. Ibid., pp. 44-45.

43. Neet, letter of May 15, 1863.

44. Brant, pp. 44-45.

45. John Bakeless, "Incident at Fort Granger," *Civil War Times Illustrated*, April 1969, p. 10. Cited hereafter as "Incident at Fort Granger";Dr. Wilson Hobbs, letter published in *Harper's Weekly*, July 4, 1863, cited hereafter as Hobbs' letter.

46. *OR*, Vol. 23, Part II, p. 425.

47. *Frank H. Smith's History of Maury County, Tennessee*, published by the Maury County Historical Society, 1969, pp. 177, 181; Partick J. Griffin III, "Tragedy of Two Cousins–Adventurers or Spies?" *The Montgomery County* [Maryland] *Story*. Published by the Montgomery County Historical Society, November 1991. Cited hereafter as "Tragedy of Two Cousins."

48. *OR,* Vol. 23, Part II, pp. 426-27.

49. Hobbs' letter.

50. "Tragedy of Two Cousins," p. 183; Hobbs' letter.

51. *OR,* Vol. 23, Part II, p. 397.

52. Ibid., p. 397.

53. Ibid.

54. Ibid., p. 398.

55. "Incident at Fort Granger," p. 14; "Tragedy of Two Cousins," p. 184.

56. "Incident at Fort Granger," p. 14.

57. *OR,* Vol. 23, Part II, p. 416.

58. Ibid.

59. Ibid., p. 424.

60. Ibid., p. 416.

61. Ibid., p. 425

62. Ibid.

63. *Rockville Tribune*, Army Reminiscences, March 26, 1879.

64. McBride, 98.

65. *OR,* Vol. 23, Part II, p. 425.

66. Ibid., p. 416.

67. Tudor Place Foundation, Inc., Washington, D.C.

68. *OR,* Vol. 23, Part II, pp. 415-16.

69. *The Indianapolis Daily Journal,* June 17, 1863

70. Brant, p. 63.

Chapter 8

1. *OR,* Vol. 23, Part I, p. 404. Thomas B. Van Horne, *History of the Army of the Cumberland*, Robert Clarke and Company, Cincinnati, Ohio, 1875, Vol. I, p. 302. Cited hereafter as Van Horne.

2. *OR,* Vol. 23, Part I, pp. 404-05; *The Parke County Republican*, May 20, 1863.

3. *OR,* Vol. 23, Part I, p. 535; Part II, p. 442.

4. *OR,* Vol. 23, Part II, pp. 398-99.

5. Anderson, p. 209; Reid p. 76.

6. Anderson, pp. 209-10.

7. *OR,* Vol. 23, Part I, pp. 405-06.

8. *OR,* Vol. 23, Part I, pp. 454-55, 457-59; John W. Rowell, *Yankee Artilleryman*,

The University of Tennessee Press, Knoxville, 1975, pp. 76-83.

9. *OR,* Vol. 23, Part I, pp. 462, 469-70, 483-84, 514.

10. Ibid., pp. 451, 514.

11. Dyer's *Compendium,* Vol. I, p. 451.

12. *OR,* Vol. 23, Part I, pp. 451-52; Part II, p. 451.

13. *OR,* Vol. 23, Part I, pp. 442, 465-66.

14. Ibid., pp. 406, 430-31.

15. Ibid., p. 466, 535-36.

16. *OR,* Vol. 23, Part I, p. 583; Cist, pp. 159-63.

17. *OR,* Vol. 23, Part I, pp. 406-07, 456.

18. Ibid., pp. 534, 536-37.

19. Anderson, p. 210.

20. McBride, p. 101.

21. Ibid.

22. *OR,* Vol. 23, Part I, pp. 408, 583; Cist, p. 166; Seitz, pp. 310-12.

23. *OR,* Vol. 23, Part I, pp. 408.

24. Cist, p. 171; Van Horne, Vol. I, pp. 310-12.

25. McBride, pp. 102-03.

26. Brant, p. 45; *The Parke County Republican,* August 19, 1863.

27. Reid, pp. 78, 80.

28. Ibid., pp. 78-79; E. B. Quiner, *The Military History of Wisconsin in the War for the Union,* Clarke and Company, Publishers, Chicago, 1886, p. 700.

29. Reid, pp. 79-80.

30. Ibid., p. 80.

31. Ibid., pp. 81-82, 84.

32. Ibid., pp. 82-83.

33. Reid, p. 82; *The Indianapolis Daily Journal,* July 9, 1863.

34. McBride, pp. 101-02; *The Indianapolis Daily Journal,* July 27, 1863.

35. Anderson, pp. 215-16, 219.

36. Neet, letter of July 18, 1863.

37. Brant, p. 45.

38. Ibid., pp. 124-25.

39. Mattox, letters to his family, May 12, 1863 and June 6, 1863.

40. Neet, letter of August 16, 1863.

41. Mattox, letter to his family, August 12, 1863.

42. *OR,* Vol. 23, Part II, p. 592; Van Horne, Vol. I, pp. 310-13; Kenneth P. Williams, *Lincoln Finds a General,* The Macmillan Company, New York, 1959, Vol. 5, pp. 240-01.

43. Cist, pp. 179-80; Van Horne, Vol. I, pp. 313-14.

44. *OR,* Vol. 30, Part III, p. 4.

45. Ibid., pp. 70, 141, 192.

46. Brant, p. 52.

47. Reid, p. 87; *OR,* Vol. 30, Part III, p. 141.

48. *OR,* Vol. 30, Part III, p. 329.

49. Ibid., pp. 373, 521, 613, 635.

50. Ibid., p. 636.

51. *Supplement to the Official Records,* Part II, Vol. 18, pp. 259, 262, 264, 266, 271, 273, 275, 276; *Official Army Register,* Vol. 6, p. 143; *OR,* Vol. 30, Part III, p. 329; Mattox, letter to his family, September 15, 1863.

52. Mattox, letter to his family, September 15, 1863.

53. DePauw University, *Alumni Register of Officers, Faculties, and Graduates, 1837–1900.* Published by DePauw University, Greencastle, Indiana, 1901.

54. Henry R. Ingraham, letter to his mother, September 14, 1863, Indiana Historical Society.

55. McBride, p. 102; *Supplement to the Official Records,* Part II, Vol. 17, p. 6.

56. Anderson, pp. 230, 237; Reid, p. 90.

57. Anderson, p. 238.

58. *OR,* Vol. 30, Part III, pp. 493-94, 539.

59. *Ibid.,* pp. 539, 541, 545-46; Van Horne, Vol. I, pp. 386-92.

60. Brant, pp. 48-49.

61. Ibid., p. 48.

62. *OR,* Vol. 30, Part IV, p. 710; John P. Dyer, *Joseph Wheeler,* Louisiana State University Press, University, Louisiana, 1941, pp.123-24, 125. Cited hereafter as Dyer's *Wheeler.*

63. *OR,* Vol. 30, Part II, pp. 723-24; Part IV, p. 710; Dyer's *Wheeler,* pp. 126-31.

64. *Ibid.,* pp. 706-07, 724.

65. Brant, p. 49.

66. Ibid., pp. 49-50.

67. Ibid., pp. 51-52.

68. Ibid., pp. 51.

69. Brant, pp. 51-52; Mattox, letter to his family, October 20, 1863.

70. *OR,* Vol. 30, Part II, p. 697; *Supplement to the Official Records,* Part II, Record of Events, Vol. 18, p. 259.

71. *OR,* Vol. 30, Part II, pp. 697-98.

72. Walter H. Hebert, *Fighting Joe Hooker,* The Bobbs-Merrill Company, Indianapolis, 1944, p. 250.

73. *OR,* Vol. 30, Part IV, pp. 90-92.

74. Ibid., pp. 93-95.

75. *OR,* Vol. 30, Part II. pp. 700-03.

76. *OR,* Vol. 30, Part II, p. 702; Part IV, p. 139.

77. *OR,* Vol. 30, Part II, p. 714.

78. *OR,* Vol. 30, Part II, p. 698; Part IV, p. 113.

79. *OR,* Vol. 30, Part II, p. 698.

80. Ibid., pp. 698-99.

81. *OR*, Vol. 30, Part II. p. 699; *Supplement to the Official Records*, Part II, Vol. 18, p. 262.

82. *OR*, Vol. 30, Part II, p. 700.

83. Ibid., pp. 699-700.

84. Ibid., p. 700.

85. *OR*, Vol. 30, Part IV, pp. 135-36.

86. *OR*, Vol. 30, Part II, p. 714.

87. Ibid., p. 716.

88. Ibid., p. 669.

89. Ibid.

90. Ibid., p. 724.

91. Ibid., p. 686.

92. Mark M. Boatner III, *The Civil War Dictionary*, David McKay, Inc., New York, 1959, pp. 910-11. Cited hereafter as Boatner.

93. *OR*, Vol. 30, Part II, pp. 728-30.

94. *OR*, Vol. 30, Part IV, pp. 209-10, 253-54.

95. Ibid., p. 218.

96. Ibid.

97. Ibid., pp. 266-67, 344.

98. Ibid., p. 344.

99. Ibid., pp. 346, 397-99.

100. *OR*, Vol. 31, Part I. p. 669; Ulysses S. Grant, *Personal Memoirs of U. S. Grant*, Charles L. Webster & Company, New York, 1886, Vol. II, pp. 17-19, 27-28. Cited hereafter as Grant's *Memoirs*; *Personal Memoirs of Gen. W. T. Sherman*, Charles L. Webster & Company, New York, 1892, Vol. I. p. 382. Cited hereafter as Sherman's *Memoirs*.

101. Cist, pp. 230-31.

102. Ibid., pp. 237-40.

103. *OR*, Vol. 31, Part I, p. 834; Anderson, p. 246; Robert C. Black, *Railroads of the Confederacy*, The University of North Carolina Press, Chapel Hill, North Carolina, 1952, End Map.

104. Reid, p. 101.

105. *OR*, Vol. 31, Part I, pp. 847-48; Anderson, pp. 246-47.

106. Anderson, pp. 247-49.

107. Ibid., pp. 249-50, 269-70.

108. *OR*, Vol. 31, Part I, p. 841.

109. *OR*, Vol. 31, Part III, pp. 26-27.

110. McBride, pp. 104-05.

111. Ibid., p. 104.

112. Mattox, letter to his family, November 10, 1863; *The Parke County Republican*, December 9, 1863.

113. Mattox, letter to his wife, December 8, 1863.

114. Brant, p. 52; *Supplement to the Official Records*, Part II, Vol. 18, p. 259.

115. Brant, p. 52.

116. Reid, p. 93, 102.

117. Ibid., pp. 105-06.

118. Ibid., p. 110.

119. *OR*, Vol. 31, Part III, pp. 109, 558.

120. *OR*, Vol. 30, Part III, pp. 594, 864; Sherman's *Memoirs*, Vol. I, p. 375.

121. *OR*, Vol. 31, Part II, pp. 573-74; Sherman's *Memoirs*, Vol. I, p. 392.

122. *OR*, Vol. 31, Part II, pp. 315-17.

123. James Lee McDonough, *Chattanooga—A Death Grip on the Confederacy*, The University of Tennessee Press, Knoxville, Tennessee, 1984, pp. 170, 225, 168-78, 201-05; Boatner, pp. 145-46.

124. *OR*, Vol. 32, Part II, p. 11.

125. Brant, p. 52.

126. Reid, pp. 115-16.

127. Ibid., pp. 117-18.

128. File of John P. Baird, National Archives.

129. Ibid.

130. Ibid.

131. *OR*, Vol. 32, Part I, pp. 25-26.

132. Ibid., p. 25.

133. Brant, p. 53.

134. Neet, letter of March 3, 1864.

135. Reid, p. 120.

136. McBride, p. 108.

137. Wilson Hobbs Collection, Wilson Hobbs, letter to his wife, March 13, 1864, Indiana Historical Society.

138. Reid, pp. 120-21.

139. *OR*, Vol. 29, Part II, pp. 556-57, 565, 573-74; *OR*, Series 3, Vol. III, pp. 414-16, 1084, 1179; Boatner, p. 870.

140. *OR*, Vol. 32, Part I, p. 26; Part III, pp. 337-38; William N. Mackinziah, *Civil War Diary*, Indiana Historical Society Library; McBride, p. 106-08.

141. *The Parke County Republican*, April 27, 1864.

142. Neet, letter of April 3, 1864.

143. *OR*, Vol. 32, Part III, p. 291; *Supplement to the Official Records*, Part II, Vol. 18, pp. 261-277.

Chapter 9

1. Grant's *Memoirs* Vol. II, pp. 114-17; *OR*, Vol. 32, Part III. pp. 58, 83.

2. Ibid., pp. 118-19.

3. Ibid., pp. 129-34; *OR,* Vol. 36, Part I, pp. 14-18.

4. Adam Badeau, *Military History of Ulysses S. Grant,* D. Appleton and Company, New York, 1881, Vol. II, pp. 26-28.

5. *OR,* Vol. 32, Part III, pp. 140, 291.

6. Ibid., pp. 290, 337-38.

7. *OR,* Vol. 38, Part I, pp. 99-100; *OR,* Vol. 32, Part III pp. 364-65.

8. *OR,* Vol. 32, Part III, pp. 384-85, 556.

9. Brant, p. 53

10. Ibid., p. 53.

11. Anderson, p. 313.

12. Ibid., pp. 313-15.

13. Reid, pp. 125, 129.

14. Ibid., pp. 129-34.

15. Albert Castel, *Decision in the West, The Atlanta Campaign of 1864,* University Press of Kansas, Lawrence, Kansas, 1992, pp. 117, 123-34. Cited hereafter as Castel; Brant, p. 54.

16. *OR,* Vol. 32, Part III, p. 569; *OR,* Vol. 38, Part II, p. 509.

17. *OR,* Vol. 32, Part III, p. 561; *OR,* Vol. 38, Part III pp. 30, 539.

18. *OR,* Vol. 32, Part III, p. 550; *OR,* Vol. 38, Part I, p. 187.

19. *OR,* Vol. 38, Part I, pp. 518, 625-26, 733.

20. *OR,* Vol. 38, Part II, pp. 27, 113, 322; Part IV, pp. 14, 21

21. *OR,* Vol. 38, Part II, p. 510.

22. *OR,* Vol. 38, Part I, p. 139.

23. *OR,* Vol. 38, Part IV, p. 3.

24. *OR,* Vol. 38, Part I, pp. 626, 732-33; Part II, pp. 428-29; Part IV, pp. 13-14.

25. *OR,* Vol. 38, Part II, pp. 27, 510.

26. Anderson, p. 317; Brant, p. 54; *OR,* Vol. 38, Part IV, p. 21.

27. Wilson Hobbs Collection, Wilson Hobbs, letter to his wife from near Ringgold, Georgia, May 4, 1864, Indiana Historical Society.

28. *OR,* Vol. 38, Part I, pp. 187-88; Part II, pp. 510, 766.

29. *OR,* Vol. 38, Part II, pp. 27, 113-14, 429; Part IV, pp. 21, 37; *Supplement to the Official Records,* Part II, Vol. 4, p. 391

30. *OR,* Vol. 38, Part III, pp. 30, 90, 375.

31. *OR,* Vol. 38, Part II, pp. 27, 114, 424; *Supplement to the Official Records,* Part II, Vol. 4, p. 391.

32. *OR,* Vol. 38, Part IV, p. 44.

33. *OR,* Vol. 38, Part II, p. 415.

34. *OR,* Vol. 38, Part III, p. 30.

35. *OR,* Vol. 38, Part II, p. 510.

36. *OR,* Vol. 38, Part III p. 30; Part IV, p. 66-67.

37. *OR,* Vol. 38, Part I, pp. 188, 505.

38. *OR,* Vol. 38, Part I, pp. 139-40; Part II, pp. 27, 114, 429, 447; Part IV, p. 60.

39. *OR,* Vol. 38, Part I, pp. 139-40; Castel, p. 131.

40. *OR,* Vol. 38, Part III, p. 30.

41. *OR,* Vol. 38, Part II, pp. 114-15; Part IV, p. 76; Castel, pp. 131-34.

42. *OR,* Vol. 38, Part III, pp. 30-31.

43. *OR,* Vol. 38, Part II, pp. 27, 117, 510.

44. McBride, p. 109.

45. Ibid., p. 145.

46. *OR,* Vol. 38, Part II, p. 27.

47. *OR,* Vol. 38, Part IV, pp. 114, 116.

48. *OR,* Vol. 38, Part II, pp. 378, 447-48; Anderson, p. 320; *Supplement to the Official Records,* Part II, Vol. 4, p. 391.

49. *OR,* Vol. 38, Part IV, pp. 135-36, 145; McBride, p. 110.

50. *OR,* Vol. 38, Part I, p. 64; Jacob D. Cox, *Atlanta,* Charles Scribner's Sons, New York, 1882, p. 40. Cited hereafter as Cox, *Atlanta.*

51. *OR,* Vol. 38, Part I, pp. 64, 505; *OR,* Vol. 38, Part II, pp. 117, 510; Cox, *Atlanta,* p. 40.

52. *OR,* Vol. 38, Part III, p. 615; Cox, *Atlanta,* p. 41.

53. *OR,* Vol. 38, Part II, p. 378.

54. *OR,* Vol. 38, Part I, pp. 220, 293, 374; Castel, pp. 150-51.

55. *OR,* Vol. 38, Part I, p. 141.

56. *OR,* Vol. 38, Part II, p. 510.

57. *OR,* Vol. 38, Part IV, pp. 151, 159.

58. *OR,* Vol. 38, Part II, p. 322.

59. Ibid., pp. 322, 339.

60. *OR,* Vol. 38, Part II, p. 378; *The Parke County Republican,* June 1, 1864.

61. *OR,* Vol. 38, Part II, pp. 433-34.

62. Ibid., pp. 322, 339, 378, 434.

63. *OR,* Vol. 38, Part II, pp. 27-28, 117-18; Part III, p. 761.

64. *OR,* Vol. 38, Part II, pp. 378-79, 415; Part IV, p. 178.

65. *OR,* Vol. 38, Part II, pp. 118, 322; Part IV, p. 193.

66. *OR,* Vol. 38, Part, II, p. 322; Part IV, p. 194.

67. *OR,* Vol. 38, Part II, p. 379.

68. Ibid., p. 379.

69. Ibid., p. 340.

70. Ibid., pp. 340, 379, 434.

71. *OR,* Vol. 38, Part II, pp. 352, 371; Henry J. Sievers, *Benjamin Harrison: Hoosier Warrior.* Henry Regnery Company, Chicago, 1952, pp. 247-52. Cited hereafter as Sievers, *Hoosier Warrior.*

72. *OR,* Vol. 38, Part II, pp. 276-78; *The Parke County Republican,* June 1, 1864

73. McBride, pp. 111-12; *OR,* Vol. 38, Part II, p. 379.

74. McBride, p. 111; *OR,* Vol. 38, Part II, p. 379.

75. *OR,* Vol. 38, Part II, p. 380; Anderson, pp. 328-33.

76. *OR*, Vol. 38, Part II, p. 379.

77. *Terre Haute Tribune*, "Memories of the Civil War," June 30, 1912.

78. McBride, pp. 111-12.

79. *OR*, Vol. 38, Part II, pp. 380, 415; *The Parke County Republican*, June 1, 1864.

80. McBride, pp. 112-14.

81. *OR*, Vol. 38, Part III, pp. 32, 615; Castel, pp. 154-56, 162-63, 178, 180; Cox, *Atlanta*, pp. 47-48, 49-50, 70.

82. *OR*, Vol. 38, Part I, p. 142; Cox, *Atlanta*, p. 48.

83. *OR*, Vol. 38, Part II, pp. 64-65; Cox, *Atlanta*, p. 51.

84. Cox, *Atlanta*, p. 52.

85. *OR*, Vol. 38, Part II, p. 191; Cox, *Atlanta*, p. 51.

86. *OR*, Vol. 38, Part II, p. 121.

87. Ibid., p. 29.

88. Ibid., pp. 380, 395.

89. *OR*, Vol. 38, Part I, pp. 191, 222, 522, 736.

90. Ibid., p. 191.

91. *OR*, Vol. 38, Part I, pp. 64-65, 142; Part II, p. 416.

92. *OR*, Vol. 38, Part, I, pp. 522, 736.

93. *OR*, Vol. 38, Part II, pp. 380, 395.

94. Ibid., pp. 380, 395, 416.

95. Ibid., p. 452.

96. Ibid., p. 425.

97. *OR*, Vol. 38, Part II, pp. 29, 121-22; Brant, p. 56.

98. *OR*, Vol. 38, Part II, p. 381.

99. Ibid., p. 381.

100. Ibid., pp. 381, 416.

101. *OR*, Vol. 38, Part I, p. 191.

102. Ibid., p. 191-92.

103. Ibid., pp. 522, 736-37.

104. Ibid., p. 65.

105. *OR*, Vol. 38, Part II, pp. 41, 381.

106. Brant, pp. 55-59.

Chapter 10

1. Sherman's *Memoirs*, Vol. II, pp. 42-43; *OR*, Vol. 38, Part I, p. 65; Castel, p. 209.

2. *OR*, Vol. 38, Part I, p. 65; Castel, pp. 219-20; Cox, *Atlanta*, p. 64.

3. *OR*, Vol. 38, Part I, p. 142; Cox, *Atlanta*, pp. 59, 63.

4. Cox, *Atlanta*, p. 59.

5. Ibid., pp. 59-60.

6. Ibid., p. 60.

7. *OR*, Vol. 38, Part III, pp. 33, 95.

8. *OR*, Vol. 38, Part I, pp. 142-43.

9. Cox, *Atlanta*, pp. 66-67.

10. *OR*, Vol. 38, Part I, pp. 65, 143, 192, 630; Part III, p. 33.

11. *OR*, Vol. 38, Part II, p. 511; Cox, *Atlanta*, pp. 66-67.

12. *OR*, Vol. 38, Part III, p. 34.

13. *OR*, Vol. 38, Part II, pp. 29, 122, 511.

14. Ibid., pp. 382, 452.

15. *OR*, Vol. 38, Part II, pp. 122, 511-12, 680; Cox, *Atlanta*, p. 67

16. Joseph E. Johnston, *Narrative of Military Operations*, D. Appleton and Company, New York, 1874, pp. 325-26. Cited hereafter as Johnston's *Narrative*. Gilbert E. Govan and James W. Livengood, *A Different Kind of Valor*, The Bobbs-Merrill Company, Inc., Indianapolis and New York, 1956, p. 280. Cited hereafter as Govan and Livengood, *Autobiography of Oliver Otis Howard*, The Baker and Taylor Company, New York, 1908, Vol. 1, pp. 541-42. Cited hereafter as Howard's *Autobiography*; Cox, *Atlanta*, p. 68.

17. *OR*, Vol. 38, Part II, pp. 511-12, 542, 567; Part III, p. 34.

18. *OR*, Vol. 38, Part I, p. 143; Cox, *Atlanta*, p. 70; Howard's *Autobiography*, Vol. I, pp. 542-43; Van Horne, Vol. II, pp. 75-76.

19. *OR*, Vol. 38, Part II, 122-23; Cox, *Atlanta*, p. 72; Van Horne, Vol. II, pp. 75-76.

20. Cox, *Atlanta*, p. 68.

21. *OR*, Vol. 38, Part II, pp. 122-23; Howard's *Autobiography*, Vol. I, pp. 544-45.

22. *OR*, Vol. 38, Part II, p. 123; Cox, *Atlanta*, p. 72.

23. *OR*, Vol. 38, Part I, pp. 192-93; Part II, pp. 30, 123.

24. *OR*, Vol. 38, Part II, p. 382.

25. Ibid., p. 438.

26. *OR*, Vol. 38, Part II, p. 382; Correspondence of the *Union Democrat*, Terre Haute, Indiana, July 1, 1864. Files of the Vigo County Public Library, topic "Civil War."

27. *OR*, Vol. 38, Part II, pp. 382, 416.

28. Ibid., p. 382.

29. Ibid., pp. 382, 396, 410.

30. Ibid., p. 324.

31. Cox, *Atlanta*, p. 73; Howard's *Autobiography*, Vol. I, p. 545.

32. Cox, *Atlanta*, pp. 72-73; Howard's *Autobiography*, Vol. I, pp. 546-47.

33. Brant, p. 60.

34. Ibid., pp. 60-61.

35. *OR*, Vol. 38, Part II, p. 383.

36. *OR*, Vol. 38, Part I, pp. 192-93.

37. *OR*, Vol. 38, Part I, pp. 630-31; Part III, p. 34.

38. *OR*, Vol. 38, Part IV, p. 320.

39. *OR*, Vol. 38, Part I, pp. 523, 737.

40. *OR*, Vol. 38, Part II, pp. 383, 396, 416-17, 425.

41. Cox, *Atlanta*, pp. 76-79; Castel, pp. 233-34, 239.

42. *OR*, Vol. 38, Part II, p. 383.

43. *OR*, Vol. 38, Part I, p. 66; Cox, *Atlanta*, pp. 83-84; Sherman's *Memoirs*, Vol. II, pp. 44-45.

44. *OR*, Vol. 38, Part IV, pp. 339, 341-42.

45. *OR*, Vol. 38, Part III, pp. 34-35.

46. *OR*, Vol. 38, Part II, p. 383.

47. *OR*, Vol. 38, Part I, p. 66; Cox, *Atlanta*, p. 89.

48. *OR*, Vol. 38, Part I, p. 147; Part II, pp. 30, 125-26, 324, 383.

49. Cox, *Atlanta*, pp. 91, 97; Castel, p. 256.

50. *OR*, Vol. 38, Part, II, pp. 324, 383, 512, 567-68, 681; Cox, *Atlanta*, pp. 89-91.

51. *OR*, Vol. 38, Part I, p. 737; Cox, *Atlanta*, p. 92.

52. *OR*, Vol. 38, Part II, p. 512; Cox, *Atlanta*, p. 92.

53. *OR*, Vol. 38, Part II, pp. 126, 324; Cox, *Atlanta*, p. 92.

54. *OR*, Vol. 38, Part III, p. 616; Castel, pp. 259-60; Cox, *Atlanta*, pp. 92-93; Johnston's *Narrative*, pp. 334-35.

55. *OR*, Vol. 38, Part II, p. 512; Part III, pp. 35, 97; Part IV, pp. 415, 433.

56. *OR*, Vol. 38, Part II, pp. 30, 126, 324.

57. *OR*, Vol. 38, Part I, pp. 196, 506.

58. Brant, pp. 61-62.

59. *OR*, Vol. 38, Part II, p. 512; Part IV, p. 448.

60. McBride, p. 120.

61. Ibid., pp. 217-20.

62. McBride, p. 230; *The Parke County Republican*, August 19, 1863.

63. McBride, p. 121.

Chapter 11

1. Sherman's *Memoirs*, Vol. II, p. 51.

2. Cox, *Atlanta*, p. 64; Dennis Kelly, "Atlanta Campaign, The Battle of Kennesaw Mountain," *Blue and Gray Magazine*, June 1989, pp. 9, 11. Cited hereafter as Kelly, "Battle of Kennesaw Mountain."

3. *OR*, Vol. 38, Part II, p. 512.

4. OR, Vol. 38, Part III, pp. 35, 97, 381, 552.

5. *OR*, Vol. 38, Part I, pp. 148, 196.

6. *OR*, Vol. 38, Part II, pp. 30-31.

7. Sherman's *Memoirs*, Vol. II, p. 51.

8. *OR*, Vol. 38, Part I, p. 148.

9. *OR*, Vol. 38, Part I, pp. 148-49; Cox, *Atlanta*, p. 97.

10. Castel pp, 275-77; *OR*, Vol. 38, Part I, pp. 223, 243.

11. Cox, *Atlanta*, p. 98; *OR*, Vol. 38, Part I, pp. 149, 196, 223, 243; Johnston's,

Narrative p. 337.

12. *OR,* Vol. 38, Part I, p. 149.

13. Ibid., pp. 149, 196.

14. *OR,* Vol. 38, Part II, p. 127.

15. Ibid., pp. 127-28.

16. *OR,* Vol. 38, Part I, p. 196.

17. *OR,* Vol. 38, Part II, p. 127-28.

18. Ibid., p. 31.

19. Ibid., pp. 324, 374, 384.

20. Ibid., p. 325

21. Ibid.

22. Ibid.

23. Ibid.

24. Ibid., p. 384.

25. *OR,* Vol. 38, Part II, pp. 324-25, 384-85, 411; Anderson, pp. 347-52; McBride, pp. 121-22.

26. *OR,* Vol. 38, Part II, pp. 384-85; McBride, p. 122; Sydney C. Kerksis, "Action at Gilgal Church, Georgia," *The Atlanta Historical Bulletin,* Atlanta, Georgia, Fall 1970, pp. 9-43.

27. *OR,* Vol. 38, Part II, p. 513.

28. *OR,* Vol. 38, Part II, p. 513; Cox, *Atlanta,* p. 100.

29. Cox, *Atlanta,* p. 100; Kelly, "Battle of Kennesaw Mountain," p. 17.

30. Stanley F. Horn, *The Army of Tennessee,* The Bobbs-Merrill Company, Indianapolis, Indiana, 1941, p. 333. Cited hereafter as Horn.

31. *OR,* Vol. 38, Part II, pp. 129-30, 513.

32. Ibid., pp. 130, 513.

33. *OR,* Vol. 38, Part I, p. 149; Part II, p. 31.

34. *OR,* Vol. 38, Part I, p. 149; Part II, pp. 385, 439.

35. *OR,* Vol. 38, Part II, p. 513; Kelly, "Battle of Kennesaw Mountain," p. 18.

36. Cox, *Atlanta,* pp. 103-04; Sherman's *Memoirs,* Vol. II, p. 56.

37. Cox, *Atlanta,* pp. 103-04; Kelly, "Battle of Kennesw Mountain," p. 20.

38. *OR,* Vol. 38, Part I, pp. 68, 150; Part II, p. 513; Cox, *Atlanta,* pp. 104-05.

39. *OR,* Vol. 38, Part II, p. 132; Cox, *Atlanta,* p. 104; Kelly, "Battle of Kennesaw Mountain," pp. 9, 11.

40. *OR,* Vol. 38, Part I, pp. 197-98.

41. *OR,* Vol. 38, Part II, p. 132.

42. Ibid., pp. 132, 385-86, 439.

43. Ibid., p. 31.

44. Ibid., p. 132.

45. Ibid., pp. 386, 439.

46. *OR,* Vol. 38, Part II, pp. 31, 132.

47. Ibid., p. 386.

48. *OR,* Vol. 38, Part I, pp. 150, 198; Cox, *Atlanta,* p. 106; Kelly, "Battle of Kennesaw Mountain," p. 26.

49. Castel, p. 290.

50. *OR,* Vol. 38, Part II, pp. 386, 399, 418; McBride, p. 123.

51. *OR,* Vol. 38, Part II, pp. 31, 132-33; Cox, *Atlanta,* p, 109.

52. *OR,* Vol. 38, Part II, p. 513.

53. Castel, pp. 292-94.

54. Cox, *Atlanta,* pp. 108-09.

55. Kelly, "Battle of Kennesaw Mountain," pp. 23-24; Castel, pp. 289-95; Cox, *Atlanta,* 111-12.

56. *OR,* Vol. 38, Part I, p. 224; Part II, pp. 386-87.

57. *OR,* Vol. 38, Part II, pp. 387.

58. Ibid., p. 440.

59. Cox, *Atlanta,* pp. 117-118; Kelly, "Battle of Kennesaw Mountain," p. 25; Sherman's *Memoirs,* Vol. II, p. 60.

60. *OR,* Vol. 38, Part I, p. 632; Part IV, p. 588.

61. *OR,* Vol. 38, Part I, p. 739; Part II, p. 683; Cox. *Atlanta,* p. 119.

62. Kelly, "Battle of Kennesaw Mountain," p. 25; Cox, *Atlanta,* pp. 118-19.

63. *OR,* Vol. 38, Part I, p. 151; Part II, p. 134; Part III, p. 36.

64. Cox, *Atlanta,* pp. 122-27; Castel, pp. 306-16; Kelly, "Battle of Kennesaw Mountain." pp. 30, 53.

65. *OR,* Vol. 38, Part II, p. 387.

66. *OR,* Vol. 38, Part I, p. 99; Part II, p. 326.

67. Reid, pp. 97-98.

68. *Generals in Blue,* pp. 538-39.

69. *OR,* Vol. 38, Part II, pp. 388, 411, 440.

70. *OR,* Vol. 38, Part II, p. 134; Cox, *Atlanta,* p. 132.

71. *OR,* Vol. 38, Part I, p. 69; Cox, *Atlanta,* pp. 130-31.

72. *OR,* Vol. 38, Part III, pp. 100, 382, 541; Part V, pp. 3, 14, 15, 28.

73. Horn, p. 338; Cox, *Atlanta,* p. 131; Kelly, "Battle of Kennesaw Mountain," p. 53.

74. *OR,* Vol. 38, Part I, p. 69; Cox, *Atlanta,* pp. 132-33.

75. *OR,* Vol. 38, Part I, p. 154.

76. *OR,* Vol. 38, Part II, pp. 32, 135, 326.

77. Ibid., p. 32.

78. *OR,* Vol. 38, Part II, p. 388; McBride, pp. 126-27.

79. *OR,* Vol. 38, Part II, pp. 326-27, 388, 401.

80. *OR,* Vol. 38, Part I, p. 154.

81. *OR,* Vol. 38, Part III, pp. 100, 382, 485; Part V, pp. 28, 50, 56; Cox, *Atlanta,* p. 133; Kelly, "Battle of Kennesaw Mountain," p. 54.

82. *OR,* Vol. 38, Part II, pp. 813, 838.

83. *OR,* Vol. 38, Part I, p. 154; Part II, pp. 33, 327.

84. *OR,* Vol. 38, Part I, p. 69; Part III, p. 37; Cox, *Atlanta,* p. 133; Sherman's

Memoirs, Vol. II, pp. 66-67; Kelly, "Battle of Kennesaw Mountain," pp. 54-55; Johnston's *Narrative*, p. 346.

85. *OR*, Vol. 38, Part I, pp. 69, 154-55; Part II, p. 515; Part III, pp. 37-38; Kelly, "Battle of Kennesaw Mountain," p. 55.

86. *OR*, Vol. 38, Part I, p. 69.

87. *OR*, Vol. 38, Part II, p. 135.

88. Ibid., pp. 33, 327.

89. Sherman's *Memoirs*, Vol. II, p. 67; William S. Harbert, letter to Professor Caleb Mills at Wabash College, Crawfordsville, Indiana, July 31, 1864, Indiana Historical Society.

90. *OR*, Vol. 38, Part II, p. 804; Castel, pp. 335-36; Cox, *Atlanta*, pp. 134, 136-37; Kelly, "Battle of Kennesaw Mountain," p. 55.

91. *OR*, Vol. 38, Part III, pp. 553, 579.

92. *OR*, Vol. 38, Part II, pp. 33, 136, 327, 388, 419, 441.

93. *OR*, Vol. 38, Part II, pp. 33, 136; Cox, *Atlanta*, p. 137.

94. *OR*, Vol. 38, Part II, pp. 515-16, 683-85; Cox, *Atlanta*, pp. 137-40; Castel, pp. 336-39.

95. *OR*, Vol. 38, Part I, pp. 200, 296; Part III, pp. 382-83.

96. Cox, *Atlanta*, p. 141; Kelly, "Battle of Kennesaw Mountain," p. 58.

97. McBride, p. 127.

98. Reid, p. 168.

99. *OR*, Vol. 38, Part III, p. 38.

100. *OR*, Vol. 38, Part I, pp. 200, 201; Part 3, p. 282-83, 553.

101. *OR*, Vol. 38, Part I, pp. 155-56, 524; Cox, *Atlanta*, p. 150.

102. *OR*, Vol. 38, Part II, pp. 388-89; McBride, pp. 127-28.

103. *OR*, Vol. 38, Part III, p. 38.

104. Reid, pp. 167-68.

105. *Milwaukee Morning Sentinel*, October 23, 1914; Francis B. Heitman, *Historical Register and Dictionary of the United States Army, 1789-1903*, Volume I, Government Printing Office, Washington, 1903. Reprinted by The University of Illinois Press, Urbana, 1965, p. 226.

106. *OR*, Vol. 38, Part I, p. 99; Brant, 135, 141; Anderson, p. 84.

107. Personal communication from Joseph W. Quigley, M.D., of Indianapolis, Indiana, based upon an examination of John Bard's Military File, National Archives, pertaining to Baird's health.

108. Harry Hansen, *Scarsdale*, Harper and Brothers, Publishers, New York, 1954, pp. 72-73, 104, 114-15, 170; *The Scarsdale Inquirer*, Scarsdale, New York, April 18, 1930, p. 1, and issue of April 25, 1930, p. 4; *The New York Times*, April 17, 1930, p. 27; *Memorial of Alexander B. Crane*, by Alexander M. Crane. Reprinted from the *1930 Yearbook of the Association of the Bar of the City of New York*.

109. Brant, p. 141.

110. Letter from Horace Maynard, Pro-Union Attorney General of the State

Tennessee, to Major General William S. Rosecrans, June 12, 1863, from John Baird's Military File, National Archives.

111. Harrison Collection, Samuel C. Harrison's *Diary*, entry for June 20, 1864, Indiana Historical Society.

Chapter 12

1. Cox, *Atlanta*, p. 147; Stephen Davis, "Atlanta Campaign," *Blue and Gray Magazine*, Special Issue, August 1989, pp. 9-10. Cited hereafter as Davis, "Atlanta Campaign."

2. *OR,* Vol. 38, Part III, p. 630; Part V, pp. 870, 92; Castel, pp. 361-62, 364.

3. *OR,* Vol. 38, Part V, p. 167.

4. Ibid., p. 168.

5. *OR,* Vol. 38, Part I, p. 156; Cox, *Atlanta*, p. 151; Castel, p. 365.

6. *OR,* Vol. 38, Part II, pp. 33, 136, 327, 389.

7. Ibid., p. 516.

8. *OR,* Vol. 38, Part I, pp. 201-02; Cox, *Atlanta*, p. 150.

9. *OR,* Vol. 38, Part I, pp. 634-35; Cox, *Atlanta*, pp. 150-51.

10. *OR,* Vol. 38, Part II, pp. 136-37.

11. Ibid., pp. 33, 327.

12. *OR,* Vol. 38, Part V, p. 190.

13. *OR,* Vol. 38, Part III, p. 38.

14. *OR,* Vol. 38, Part I, p. 202.

15. *OR,* Vol. 38, Part I, pp. 202, 297; Cox, *Atlanta*, p. 155.

16. *OR,* Vol. 38, Part II, pp. 33, 327.

17. Ibid., pp. 327, 389.

18. Ibid., pp. 389, 404, 413, 441-42.

19. Ibid., pp. 327, 441.

20. Ibid., p. 327.

21. Ibid., p. 389.

22. Ibid., p. 344-45.

23. Ibid., p. 327, 344-45, 442.

24. Ibid., p. 137.

25. Ibid.

26. Ibid., pp. 33-34, 137.

27. Cox, *Atlanta*, pp. 147, 149; Davis, "Atlanta Campaign," pp. 12-13; Castel, pp. 366-68.

28. Castel, pp. 368, 371-72; Davis, "Atlanta Campaign," p. 12.

29. *OR,* Vol. 38, Part II, pp. 426-27.

30. Ibid., p. 427.

31. McBride, p. 128; *OR,* Vol. 38, Part II, pp. 327-28, 389-90.

32. Davis, "Atlanta Campaign," pp. 12-14; Castel, p. 376.

33. Davis, "Atlanta Campaign," pp. 12-14.

34. *OR,* Vol. 38, Part I, pp. 297-98, 306; Part II, pp. 442-43; Davis, "Atlanta Campaign," p. 14; Castel, p. 376.

35. *OR,* Vol. 38, Part II, p. 390.

36. Ibid.

37. Ibid.

38. Ibid., pp. 442-43.

39. Ibid.

40. Ibid., p. 346.

41. Ibid.

42. Davis, "Atlanta Campaign," p. 14; Cox, *Atlanta,* p. 156.

43. *OR,* Vol. 38, Part II. p. 138; Davis, "Atlanta Campaign," p, 17.

44. *OR,* Vol. 38, Part II, pp. 33-34.

45. *OR,* Vol. 38, Part I, pp. 601-02; Part II, p. 62;   Davis, Atlanta Campaign, p. 17.

46. McBride, pp. 130-31.

47. *Terre Haute Tribune,* "Memories of the Civil War," October 15, 1911.

48. Ibid., August 18, 1912.

49. Brant, p. 67; *OR,* Vol. 38, Part, II. pp. 390-91; McBride, p. 132.

50. McBride, p. 133.

51. *OR,* Vol. 38, Part II, p. 390.

Chapter 13

1. *OR,* Vol. 38, Part I, p. 299; Part II, p. 329.

2. *OR,* Vol. 38, Part I, pp. 203, 382; Cox, *Atlanta,* p. 163.

3. Castel, pp. 383-84; Cox, *Atlanta,* p. 163.

4. John B. Hood, *Advance and Retreat,* Press of Burke and M'Fetridge, Philadelphia, 1880, p. 173-74; *OR,* Vol. 38, Part III, p. 631; Cox, *Atlanta,* pp. 164-66; Castel, pp. 385-87.

5. Nathaniel Cheairs Hughes, Jr. *General William J. Hardee, Old Reliable,* Broadfoot Publishing Company, Wilmington, North Carolina, 1987, pp. 225-27; Cox, *Atlanta,* pp. 165-66.

6. *OR,* Vol. 38, Part I, p. 72; Cox, *Atlanta,* p. 166.

7. *OR,* Vol. 38, Part II, p. 516; Cox, *Atlanta,* p. 166.

8. *OR,* Vol. 38, Part I, p. 203.

9. *OR,* Vol. 38, Part II, pp. 348, 391.

10. Ibid., pp. 391, 406-07, 414.

11. Ibid., pp. 141-42.

12. Davis, "Atlanta Campaign,"pp. 20-25; Castel, pp. 395-403; Cox, *Atlanta,* pp. 168-75.

13. *OR*, Vol. 38, Part II, pp. 35, 142, 157, 329.

14. Sherman's *Memoirs*, Vol, II, p. 88; *OR*, Vol. 38, Part, I, pp. 75-76; Part II, pp. 915-19; Part V, p. 255; Castel, pp. 436-40.

15. *OR*, Vol. 38, Part I, pp. 75-77; Part II, pp. 761-64; Castel, pp. 436-40.

16. *OR*, Vol. 38, Part V, pp. 277-78, 307; Cox, *Atlanta*, pp. 177-79; Sherman's *Memoirs*, Vol. II, pp. 85-88.

17. *OR*, Vol. 38, Part V, p. 255; Cox, *Atlanta*, p. 181.

18. *OR*, Vol. 38, Part V, pp 268-69; Cox, *Atlanta*, pp. 182, 184.

19. Davis, "Atlanta Campaign," pp. 30-33; Cox, *Atlanta*, pp. 184-85.

20. *OR*, Vol. 38, Part II, p. 391.

21. *OR*, Vol. 38, Part I, p. 635.

22. *OR*, Vol. 38, Part II, pp. 329, 391, 408.

23. Ibid., 391-92, 408.

24. *OR*, Vol. 38, Part II, pp. 517; Part V, pp. 315, 324; Cox, *Atlanta*, p. 189.

25. *OR*, Vol. 38, Part I, pp. 160-61; Part II, pp. 329, 392; Part V, pp. 331-32.

26. *OR*, Vol. 38, Part I, pp. 525, 744, 790; Part II, pp. 18, 329, 362, 392, 420, 444.

27. *OR*, Vol. 38, Part II, pp. 349, 392, 444.

28. Brant. p. 70.

29. Ibid., p. 71.

30. Sherman's *Memoirs*, Vol. II. pp. 99-101; Cox, *Atlanta*, pp. 189-90; Castel, pp. 454-56.

31. Cox, *Atlanta*, p. 193.

32. *OR*, Vol. 38, Part V, pp. 407, 446, 660.

33. Cox, *Atlanta*, p. 194; Davis, "Atlanta Campaign," p. 45.

34. Brant, p. 70.

35. Brant, pp. 70-71; John Finton, letter to his daughter, August 24, 1864, Indiana Historical Society.

36. Cox, *Atlanta*, pp. 194-95.

37. *OR*, Vol. 38, Part II, p. 392.

38. John Finton, letter to his daughter, August 24, 1864, Indiana Historical Society.

39. Neet, letter of August 14, 1864.

40. *OR*, Vol. 38, Part III, pp. 957-60; Dyer's *Wheeler*, pp. 191-92.

41. *OR*, Vol. 38, Part II, pp. 858-59; Cox, *Atlanta*, pp. 195-96; Castel, pp. 471-75.

42. Cox, *Atlanta*, p. 196.

43. Ibid., pp. 196-97.

44. *OR*, Vol. 38, Part II, p. 18.

45. Ibid., pp. 18-19.

46. *OR*, Vol. 38, Part I, pp. 213, 299; Part II, p. 44.

47. *OR*, Vol. 38, Part II, pp. 44, 340-50.

48. *OR*, Vol. 38, Part II, p. 445; Part III, p. 48.

49. *OR*, Vol. 38, Part II, pp. 392, 408-09, 420.

50. Ibid., pp. 392, 408-09, 420.

51. Ibid., pp. 5, 350.

52. *OR* Vol. 38, Part III, pp. 445, 905-06.

53. *OR,* Vol. 38, Part I, p. 80; Part II, p. 518.

54. *OR,* Vol. 38, Part III, p. 390; Cox, *Atlanta*, p. 197.

55. *OR,* Vol. 38, Part II, p. 165; Part 3, p. 43.

56. Cox, *Atlanta*, p. 198; *OR,* Vol. 38, Part 3, pp. 391, 411, 554.

57. Cox, *Atlanta*, p. 200.

58. Cox, *Atlanta*, p. 201.

59. *OR,* Vol. 38, Part II, pp. 518-19; Cox, *Atlanta*, p. 202.

60. *OR,* Vol. 38, Part II, pp. 518-19; Cox, *Atlanta*, pp. 203-04.

61. *OR,* Vol. 38, Part III, p. 765; Cox, *Atlanta*, pp. 202-03.

62. Cox, *Atlanta*, pp. 204-06.

63. Ibid., p. 207.

64. *OR,* Vol. 38, Part I, p. 82; Part II, pp. 330-31, 392-93.

65. *OR,* Vol. 38, Part II, p. 393; Castel, pp. 528-29.

66. *The Terre Haute Tribune,* "Memories of the Civil War," November 16, 1913.

67. *The American Tribune,* Indianapolis, Indiana, January 4, 1889.

68. *OR,* Vol. 38, Part II, p. 20.

69. Ibid., pp. 409, 428, 445-46.

Chapter 14

1. *OR* Vol. 38, Part I, pp. 97-100.

2. *OR* Vol. 38, Part II, p. 35.

3. Ibid., pp. 146, 219.

4. *OR* Vol. 38, Part II, pp. 393, 428, 446, 455; *OR* Vol. 39, Part I, p. 679; OR Vol. 39, Part II, p. 382.

5. Anderson, p. 376.

6. *OR* Vol. 39, Part I, p. 689.

7. Sherman's *Memoirs* Vol. II, p. 111OR Vol. 38, Part V, pp. 837-38.

8. *OR* Vol. 38, Part V, p. 838.

9. George E. Farrington Collection, George E. Farrington, letter to his mother, Harriet Ewing Farrington, September 23, 1864, Community Archives, Vigo County Public Library, Terre Haute, Indiana.

10. *OR* Vol. 39, Part I, p. 580.

11. Ibid., p. 580.

12. McBride, p. 147; OR Vol. 39, Part II, p. 549.

13. *OR* Vol. 39, Part II, pp. 377, 379.

14. Sievers, *Hoosier Warrior*, p. 265.

15. Sievers, *Hoosier Warrior*, pp. 270-73, 277.

16. Ibid., pp. 278-79.

17. McBride, p. 143; John Coburn's Pension File, National Archives.

18. Ibid., p. 143.

19. *OR* Vol. 39, Part I, p. 693.

20. McBride, p. 145.

21. Ibid., pp. 195-96.

22. *OR* Vol. 39, Part I, p. 581; Part II, p. 880.

23. *OR* Vol. 39, Part II, pp. 440-41, 448-49.

24. *OR* Vol. 39, Part I, pp. 514-15, 585; Robert Dunnavant, Jr., *The Railroad War*, Pea Ridge Press, Athens, Alabama, 1994, pp. 81-84.

25. *OR* Vol. 39, Part I, p. 585; Part II, pp. 465-66; Sherman's *Memoirs*, Vol. II, p. 140-41.

26. *OR* Vol. 39, Part I, p. 585.

27. McBride, 146; *The Parke County Republican*, Rockville, Indiana, October 21, 1864.

28. *OR* Vol. 39, Part II, pp. 548-49.

29. *OR* Vol. 39, Part I, pp. 581, 802.

30. Ibid., p. 581

31. Ibid., p. 802.

32. Ibid., pp. 748-49, 760, 813-14.

33. Ibid., p. 582.

34. *OR* Vol. 39, Part II, p. 159; Part III, p. 401; Sherman's *Memoirs*, Vol. II, p. 159.

35. *OR* Vol. 39, Part III, p. 401; Sherman's *Memoirs*, Vol. II, p. 159.

36. *OR* Vol. 39, Part III, pp. 402, 442.

37. *OR* Vol. 39, Part I, p. 584.

38. *OR* Vol. 39, Part I, pp. 649-50; Charles E. Slocum, *The Life and Services of Major General H. W. Slocum*, The Slocum Publishing Company, Toledo, Ohio, 1913, p. 209. Cited hereafter as Slocum.

39. *OR* Vol. 39, Part I, p. 668.

40. *OR* Vol. 39, Part I, pp. 649, 659.

41. Ibid., p. 668.

42. Ibid., p. 680.

43. Anderson, p. 376.

44. *OR* Vol. 39, Part I, pp. 689, 692.

45. Ibid., pp. 663-64, 668.

46. Ibid., pp. 659-60.

47. Ibid., pp. 689-90.

48. Ibid., pp. 682-83.

49. Ibid., pp. p. 680.

50. Ibid., p, 680.

51. McBride, p. 233.

52. *OR* Vol. 39, Part III, pp. 558-59.

53. *OR* Vol. 39, Part I, p. 691, Brant, p. 75.

54. *OR* Vol. 39, Part I, pp. pp. 689, 691.

55. Joseph Glatthaar, *The March to the Sea and Beyond*, New York University Press, New York and London, 1985, pp. 200, 202.

56. Anderson, pp. 380-81.

57. *OR* Vol. 39, Part I, p. 690.

58. *OR* Vol. 39, Part I, p. 690.

59. Lewis M. Gross, *Past and Present of DeKalb County*, Illinois. Volume I, The Pioneer Publishing Company, Chicago, 1907, pp. 346-51; T*he Biographical Record of DeKalb County, Illustrated*, the S. J. Clarke Publishing Company, Chicago, 1898, pp. 9-12; *Portrait and Biographical Album of DeKalb County*, Illinois, Chapman Brothers, Chicago, 1885, pp. 589-91.

60. *OR* Vol. 39, Part I, p. 688.

61. Ibid., p. 692

62. Sherman's *Memoirs*, Vol. II, pp. 114-15.

63. Ibid., Vol. II, p. 152.

64. Jacob D. Cox, *The March to the Sea—Franklin and Nashville,* Charles Scribner's Sons, New York, 1882, p. 5.

65. *OR* Vol. 39, Part I, p. 584; OR Vol. 39, Part III, p. 679; Sherman's *Memoirs*, Vol. II, p. 166; Lloyd Lewis, *Sherman, Fighting Prophet*, Harcourt, Brace and Company, New York, 1932, pp. 429-32. Cited hereafter as Lewis, *Fighting Prophet*.

66. *OR* Vol. 39, Part III, p. 713; Slocum, pp. 219, 222 .

67. *OR* Vol. 39, Part I, pp. 688, 691-92

68. Ibid., p. 584

69. *OR* Vol. III, Part I, p. 562; Sherman's *Memoirs*, Vol. II, p. 177; Lewis, *Fighting Prophet*, p. 435.

70. *OR* Vol. 39, Part I, pp. 616, 637.

71. *OR* Vol. 39, Part III, 762, 763.

72. Ibid., pp. 750-51.

73. *OR* Vol. 39, Part I, p. 688.

Chapter 15

1. Sherman's *Memoirs*, Vol. II. p. 177; *OR*, Vol. 44, pp. 8, 451-52; Cox, *The March to the Sea*, pp. 25-28.

2. Sherman's *Memoirs*, Vol. II, p. 177; Jim Miles, *To the Sea*, Rutledge Hill Press, Nashville, Tennessee, 1989, p. 32. Cited hereafter as Miles, *To the Sea*; William R. Scaife, "The March to the Sea," *Blue and Gray Magazine*, Special Issue, December 1989, pp. 20-21. Cited hereafter as Scaife, "The March to the Sea."

3. Miles, *To The Sea*, p. 32.

4. *OR*, Vol. 44, pp. 65-66, 157, 461, 471.

5. Ibid., pp. 8, 65-66.

6. *OR,* Vol. 44, pp. 216, 269, 326, 334; Letter from Lieutenant Henry C. Brown of the 85th Indiana, *The Parke County Republican,* January 11, 1865. Written December 18, 1864. Cited hereafter as Brown's Letter, January 11, 1865.

7. *OR,* Vol. 44, p. 56; Miles, *To the Sea,* pp. 17-28; Scaife, p. 18; Henry Hitchcock, *Marching with Sherman,* University of Nebraska Press, Lincoln and London, 1995, pp. 56-58. Cited hereafter as Hitchcock.

8. *OR,* Vol. 44, pp. 326, 334.

9. Brant, p. 76.

10. Ibid., pp. 76-77.

11. *OR,* Vol. 44, p. 163.

12. *OR,* Vol. 44, pp. 326, 334; Brant, p. 76.

13. *OR,* Vol. 44, pp. 213, 270, 326, 334; Brant, p. 76.

14. Slocum, pp. 230-31; Oliver O. Howard, "Sherman's Advance from Atlanta," *Battles and Leaders,* Vol. 4, pp. 663-65.

15. *OR,* Vol. 44, p. 334; McBride, pp. 151-52.

16. *OR,* Vol. 44, pp. 206-07, 270; Miles, *To the Sea,* pp. 62-63.

17. *OR,* Vol. 44, pp. 326, 334, 347; Brown's Letter, January 11, 1865.

18. Brant, p. 77; McBride, p. 152.

19. *OR,* Vol. 44, pp. 207, 214.

20. *OR,* Vol. 44, p. 334; McBride, pp. 152-53.

21. *OR,* Vol. 44, p. 214.

22. Brown's Letter, January 11, 1865.

23. *OR,* Vol. 44, p. 326; McBride, p. 153; Brown's Letter, January 11, 1865.

24. *OR,* Vol. 44, pp. 207, 271; Miles, *To The Sea,* p. 63.

25. *OR,* Vol. 44, pp. 207, 214, 217, 271; Brant, p. 78.

26. *OR,* Vol. 44, pp. 326, 334, 342; Brant, p. 78.

27. *OR,* Vol. 44, p. 271.

28. *OR,* Vol. 44, pp. 163-64; Hitchcock, p. 78.

29. Slocum, p. 228.

30. *OR,* Vol. 44, pp. 65-67, 81-82, 147.

31. *OR,* Vol. 44, pp. 97-98; Cox, *The March to the Sea,* pp. 30-31.

32. *OR,* Vol. 44, p. 527.

33. Ibid., p. 527.

34. *OR,* Vol. 44, p. 207; Hitchcock, pp. 86-88; Brown's Letter January 11, 1865.

35. Brant, pp. 78-79; McBride, p. 153.

36. Brant, p. 79.

37. *OR,* Vol. 44, pp. 207, 214, 334-35.

38. *OR,* Vol. 44, p. 342; Brant, p. 80; McBride, p. 153.

39. *OR,* Vol. 44, p. 363.

40. *OR,* Vol. 44, p. 164; Scaife, "The March to the Sea," pp. 23, 26.

41. *OR,* Vol. 44, pp. 214, 335; McBride, p. 153; Miles, *To the Sea,* p. 86.

42. *OR,* Vol. 44, pp. 57, 207, 214; Brant, p. 80.

43. *OR,* Vol. 44, p. 335.

44. Ibid., p. 164.

45. Ibid., pp. 207, 214.

46. Ibid., pp. 157-58, 207, 214, 272, 335.

47. Sherman's *Memoirs,* Vol. II, p. 191; Hitchcock, pp. 98-99.

48. *OR,* Vol. 44, pp. 217, 272-73.

49. Ibid., pp. 157-58, 207, 326.

50. McBride, p. 154.

51. *OR,* Vol. 44, pp. 44, 326-27, 335.

52. *OR,* Vol. 44, pp. 214-15; Brant, p. 81.

53. *OR,* Vol. 44, pp. 335, 342; McBride, p. 155.

54. *OR,* Vol. 44, pp. 335, 342; Brant, pp. 81-82.

55. *OR,* Vol. 44, pp. 207, 215, 273.

56. Ibid., p. 327.

57. *OR,* Vol. 44, p. 335; Brant, p. 82.

58. *OR,* Vol. 44, pp. 215, 335; McBride, p. 155; Miles, *To the Sea,* p. 111; Sherman's *Memoirs,* Vol. II, pp. 192-93.

59. Miles, p. 111.

60. *OR,* Vol. 44, p. 48; Miles, *To the Sea,* p. 112; Brant, p. 83.

61. *OR,* Vol. 44, p. 327.

62. *OR,* Vol. 44, pp. 327, 335; McBride, p. 156.

63. *OR,* Vol. 44, pp. 363-64; Dyer's *Wheeler,* pp. 208-09; Scaife, "The March to the Sea," p. 28.

64. *OR,* Vol. 44, pp. 37, 180, 183, 551-52.

65. Ibid., pp. 9, 165.

66. Ibid., pp. 67-68.

67. Ibid., pp. 69-70.

68. Ibid., pp. 70-72.

69. Ibid., p. 9.

70. Scaife, "The March to the Sea," p. 28.

71. *OR,* Vol. 44, pp. 612-15, 617-18; Cox, *The March to the Sea,* p. 34; Miles, *To the Sea,* p. 173.

72. *OR,* Vol. 44, pp. 275, 327, 335; Brant, p. 83; McBride, p. 157.

73. *OR,* Vol. 44, pp. 218, 275, 327, 335, 365.

74. Ibid., pp. 207, 215, 327, 335.

75. Ibid., p. 218.

76. Ibid., pp. 327, 335-36.

77. Ibid., p. 218.

78. Ibid., pp. 208, 218, 276.

79. *OR,* Vol. 44, pp. 276, 336; McBride, pp. 157-58.

80. Brant, pp. 83-84.

81. Ibid., p. 84.

82. *OR,* Vol. 44, p. 327; Brant, p. 84.

83. Ibid., pp. 327, 347.

84. Ibid., pp. 327, 336.

85, Ibid., p. 276.

86. Ibid., pp. 158, 208.

87. Ibid., p. 208.

88. Ibid., pp. 208, 327-28, 336, 357.

89. Ibid., pp. 336, 341, 347.

90. Ibid., p. 165.

91. Ibid., pp. 165, 166, 204.

92. Ibid., p. 166.

93. Cox, *The March to the Sea,* p. 52.

94. *OR,* Vol. 44, pp. 9-10.

95. *OR,* Vol. 44, p. 336; Cox, *The March to the Sea,* p. 52; McBride, pp. 158-59; Brant, pp. 84-85.

96. *OR,* Vol. 44, p. 357.

97. Cox, *The March to the Sea,* pp. 52-55.

98. *OR,* Vol. 44, p. 343.

99. Ibid., pp. 218-19, 328, 336-37.

100. Brant, p. 86.

101. *OR,* Vol. 44, p. 337; Brant, pp. 86-87.

102. *OR,* Vol. 44, pp. 279-80.

103. Ibid., pp. 328, 337, 341.

104. Ibid., p. 328.

105. Ibid., p. 783.

106. Ibid., p. 280.

107. Ibid., p. 343.

108. Ibid., p. 338.

109. Glatthaar, p. 54; Henry W. Slocum, "Sherman's March from Savannah to Bentonville," *Battles and Leaders of the Civil War,* The Century Company, New York, 1884, 1888, Vol. IV, pp. 688-90. Cited hereafter as *Battles and Leaders;* Lewis, *Fighting Prophet,* pp. 438-40.

110. McBride, p. 154.

111. Ibid., Brown's Letter, January 11, 1865.

112. Brant, p. 111.

113. Ibid., pp. 110-11.

114. *OR,* Vol. 47, Part I, p. 809.

115. Brant, pp. 94-96.

116. *OR,* Vol. 44, p. 338.

Chapter 16

1. Sherman's *Memoirs*, Vol. II, p. 218; Miles, *To the Sea*, p. 231; Hitchcock, pp. 198-99.
2. Hitchcock, p. 199.
3. Brant, p. 89.
4. Ibid., pp. 88.
5. Hitchcock, pp. 199-200.
6. Sherman's *Memoirs*, Vol. II, pp. 236-37.
7. Brant, p. 134.
8. Anderson, p. 393; Brant, pp. 88-89.
9. *OR*, Vol. 44, pp. 777-78, 794.
10. *OR*, Vol. 44, p. 62.
11. Sherman's *Memoirs*, Vol. II, p. 237, 793-94, 811-12.

Chapter 17

1. *OR*, Vol. 44, pp. 636-37, 726, 728.
2. Sherman's *Memoirs*. Vol. II, pp. 213, 225-26. *OR*, Vol. 44, pp. 727-28, 820-21.
3. Sherman's *Memoirs*, Vol. II, p. 240.
4. *OR*, Vol. 47, Part I, pp. 46-55.
5. Frederick Phisterer, *Statistical Records of the Armies of the United States*, Charles Scribner's Sons, New York, 1883, pp. 301-02, 308, 310-11; *OR*, Vol. 47, Part II, pp. 42, 64.
6. Sherman's *Memoirs*, Vol. II, pp. 269.
7. Ibid., pp. 239-40; *OR*, Vol. 47, Part I, pp. 17-18.
8. *OR*, Vol. 47, Part I, pp. 581, 782.
9. Ibid., p. 782.
10. McBride, p. 233.
11. *OR*, Vol. 44, pp. 823, 838; *OR*, Vol. 47, Part I, p. 782.
12. *OR*, Vol. 47, Part I, p. 802; McBride, p. 162.
13. Sherman's *Memoirs*, Vol. 2, pp. 238, 240.
14. *OR*, Vol. 47, Part I, pp. 782, 788, 802.
15. Ibid., pp. 220-21, 336-37, 374.
16. Sherman's *Memoirs*, Vol. II, pp. 253, 255-56.
17. *OR*, Vol. 47, Part I, p. 782; Anderson, pp. 395, 397.
18. Brant, pp. 91-92.
19. Ibid., p. 92.
20. *OR*, Vol. 47, Part I, p. 819; Anderson, p. 397; Reid, pp. 221, 241.
21. *OR*, Vol. 47, Part I, pp. 782, 802-03.
22. Ibid., p. 803.
23. Ibid., pp. 597-98.

24. Sherman's *Memoirs*, Vol. II, p. 253.

25. *OR*, Vol. 47, Part I, pp. 429, 582-83, 680-81.

26. Ibid., p. 681-82.

27. Reid, p. 223.

28. *OR*, Vol. 47, Part I, pp. 782, 803.

29. *OR*, Vol. 47, Part I, p. 803; Brant, p. 92.

30. *OR*, Vol. 47, Part I, pp. 419, 429, 682, 857.

31. Ibid., pp. 419, 429, 582, 592.

32. Ibid., pp. 169-70, 426, 429, 682.

33. *OR*, Vol. 47, Part II, pp. 181, 194-95, 207-08; Sherman's *Memoirs*, Vol. II, pp. 272-73.

34. *OR*, Vol. 47, Part I, pp. 194-95; Sherman's *Memoirs*, Vol. II, pp. 272-73.

35. *OR*, Vol. 47, Part I, p. 592.

36. Ibid., pp. 142, 788, 803, 821.

37. Brant, p. 93.

38. Reid, p. 229..

39. *OR*, Vol. 47, Part I, p. 803.

40. Brant, pp. 93-94.

41. *OR*, Vol. 47, Part I, pp. 582, 803.

42. Ibid., pp. 170, 582.

43. Ibid., pp. 582, 803-04.

44. Ibid.

45. Ibid., pp. 420, 682, 857.

46. Ibid., p. 858.

47. Ibid., pp. 429-30, 445, 482, 550.

48. Ibid., pp. 682-84.

49. Ibid., p. 337.

50. Ibid., pp. 195, 592.

51. Ibid., p. 804.

52. Brant, p. 96.

53. *OR*, Vol. 47, Part I, p. 804

54. Ibid., pp. 788, 804, 817, 822.

55. Slocum. p. 260.

56. *OR*, Vol. 47, Part I, p. 684.

57. *OR*, Vol. 47, Part I, pp. 788, 804, 817, 822; Brant, p. 97.

58. *OR*, Vol. 47, Part I, pp. 598, 660, 684.

59. Ibid., pp. 858-59.

60. *OR*, Vol. 47, Part II, p. 343; Sherman's *Memoirs*, Vol. II, pp. 274-75.

61. *OR*, Vol. 47, Part I, pp. 92, 195-98, 224-25, 338, 378-79.

62. Ibid., p. 225.

63. *OR*, Vol. 47, Part I, pp. 592, 804; Brant, p. 97.

64. *OR*, Vol. 47, Part I, pp. 684-85.

65. *OR*, Vol. 47, Part I, pp. 593, 783, 804-05; Brant, p. 97.

66. *OR*, Vol. 47, Part I, pp. 583, 585, 593.

67. Ibid., p. 430.

68. Ibid., p. 805.

69. Brant, pp. 98-99.

70. *OR*, Vol. 47, Part I, pp. 198-99, 227-28, 379.

71. Howard's *Autobiography*, Vol. II, pp. 120-21.

72. *OR*, Vol. 47, Part I, p. 198.

73. Ibid., p. 265.

74. Ibid., pp. 198-99.

75. Ibid., pp. 92, 199-200, 380.

76. *Chaplain John J. Hight's History of the 58th Indiana Regiment*, compiled and published by Gilbert R. Stormont, Press of the Clarion, Princeton, Indiana, 1895, pp. 478-79; *OR*, Vol. 47, Part I, pp. 21, 426, 430; Part II, p. 444; Slocum, pp. 261-62.

77. *OR*, Vol. 47, Part I, p. 859.

78. Ibid., pp. 583, 805.

79. Ibid., pp. 430-31.

80. Ibid., pp. 583, 593, 805.

81. Ibid.

82. Ibid., pp. 583, 687, 783.

83. Ibid., p. 859.

84. Ibid., pp. 599, 783, 805-06.

85. *OR*, Vol. 47, Part I, pp. 583, 593-94, 599, 805-05; McBride, pp. 167-68; Brant, pp. 99-100.

86. *OR*, Vol. 47, Part I, pp. 594, 806.

87. Ibid., pp. 22, 866.

88. Ibid., p. 431.

89. Ibid., pp. 200, 229, 380.

90. Ibid., pp. 201-02, 229-30, 380-81.

91. Sherman's *Memoirs*, Vol. II, pp. 290-93.

92. *OR*, Vol. 47, Part I, pp. 421, 583-84, 594; Brant, p. 100.

93. *OR*, Vol. 47, Part I, pp. 421, 427, 431, 550-51.

94. Ibid., p. 431.

95. Ibid., pp. 431-32.

96. *OR*, Vol. 47, Part I, p. 146; Sherman's *Memoirs*, Vol. II, p. 293.

97. *OR*, Vol. 47, Part I, pp. 583-84.

98. Ibid., p. 584.

99. Ibid.

100. Ibid., pp. 584, 806.

101. Brant, p. 101; McBride, p, 169.

102. Brant, pp. 101-02.

103. Ibid., p. 101.

104. Ibid.

105. *OR,* Vol. 47, Part I, pp. 584, 594, 690.

106. Ibid., pp. 432, 447.

107. Ibid., pp. 79, 92, 116, 202, 381-82.

108. *OR,* Vol. 47, Part I, p. 202; Sherman's *Memoirs,* Vol. II, p. 292.

109. *OR,* Vol. 47, Part I, pp. 202-04, 231-32.

110. Ibid., p. 432.

111. *OR,* Vol. 47, Part I, p. 584; Sherman's *Memoirs,* Vol. II, pp. 292-93.

112. *OR,* Vol. 47, Part I, p. 806; Brant, p. 102.

113. *OR,* Vol. 47, Part I, pp. 584, 594, 690.

114. *OR,* Vol. 47, Part I, pp. 584, 806; Brant, p. 102.

115. *OR,* Vol. 47, Part I, pp. 584-85; Brant, pp. 102-03.

116. *OR,* Vol. 47, Part I, pp. 584-85, 807.

117. Brant, p. 103.

118. *OR,* Vol. 47, Part I, pp. 104, 585; Brant, p. 103.

119. Brant, p. 103.

120. *OR,* Vol. 47, Part I, p. 204.

121. *OR,* Vol. 47, Part I, p. 585; Brant, pp. 103-04.

122. *OR,* Vol. 47, Part I, pp. 204, 432.

123. Ibid.

Chapter 18

1. Sherman's *Memoirs,* Vol. II, p. 300; *OR,* Vol. 47, Part I, pp. 171-72, 551.

2. *OR,* Vol. 47, Part I, p. 1050; Govan and Livengood, pp. 348-50; Sherman's *Memoirs,* Vol. II, p. 299.

3. *OR,* Vol. 47, Part II, pp. 1386, 1387; Mark L. Bradley, *The Battle of Bentonville,* Savas Woodbury Publishers, Campbell, California, 1996, p. 136. Cited hereafter as Bradley, *Bentonville.*

4. *OR,* Vol. 47, Part I, p. 204; Sherman's *Memoirs,* Vol. II. p. 300.

5. *OR,* Vol. 47, Part I, pp. 204-05, 422.

6. Ibid., p. 205.

7. Bradley, *Bentonville.* pp. 199-200; *OR,* Vol. 47, Part I, pp. 422, 599, 637, 783, 862.

8. *OR,* Vol. 47, Part I, pp. 205, 422.

9. Ibid., p. 862.

10. Ibid., pp. 585, 595, 611, 807-08.

11. *OR,* Vol. 47, Part I, p. 600; *Bradley, Bentonville,* p. 122-23.

12. *OR,* Vol. 47, Part I, pp. 807-08; *Bradley, Bentonville,* p. 123.

13. *OR,* Vol. 47, Part I, pp. 789, 807, 846-47.

14. Ibid., p. 808.

15. Ibid., p. 784.

16. Ibid., pp. 586, 808.

17. *OR,* Vol. 47, Part I, p. 586; Slocum, p. 271.

18. *OR,* Vol. 47, Part I, p. 808.

19. Brant, pp. 105-06; McBride, p. 172.

20. *OR,* Vol. 47, Part I, pp. 123, 434, 784.

21. Ibid., pp. 423, 434, 634.

22. Ibid., pp. 586, 784, 808-09.

23. *OR,* Vol. 47, Part I, p. 809; Brant, p. 106.

24. Bradley, *Bentonville*, p. 137.

25. John G. Barrett, *The Civil War in North Carolina*, The University of North Carolina Press, Chapel Hill, North Carolina, 1963, p. 325. Cited hereafter as Barrett; Bradley, *Bentonville*, pp. 142-44.

26. Sherman's *Memoirs*, Vol. 2, p. 303.

27. *OR,* Vol. 47, Part I, pp. 434-35, 448-49, 485; Jay Luvaas, *The Battle of Bentonville*, booklet, Harper House, Bentonville Chapter U. D. C., pp. 6-7, 10. Cited hereafter as Luvaas; Barrett, pp. 329-31; Bradley, *Bentonville*. pp. 146, 161-63, 174-76, 178-79.

28. *OR,* Vol. 47, Part I, pp. 587, 601, 637.

29. *OR,* Vol. 47, Part I, pp. 784, 809, 826; *Bradley, Bentonville,* pp. 275-78, 286-87.

30. *OR,* Vol. 47, Part I, pp. 784-85. 817-18; Brant, p. 106.

31. Luvaas, pp. 12-13; Barrett, pp. 332-33; Bradley, Bentonville, pp. 213-14, 216.

32. *OR,* Vol. 47, Part I, p. 435; Barrett, pp. 334-35; Luvaas, pp. 15-16.

33. *OR,* Vol. 47, Part I, pp. 587, 666-67.

34. *OR,* Vol. 47, Part I, pp. 587, 601, 612; Luvaas, pp. 16-17.

35. *OR,* Vol. 47, Part I, pp. 1106-07; Barrett, p. 335; Bradley, *Bentonville*, pp. 290-92; Luvaas, pp. 17-18.

36. *OR,* Vol. 47, Part I, pp. 25-27, 205-06.

37. Ibid., pp. 551-52, 588, 694.

38. *OR,* Vol. 47, Part I, pp. 383, 391; Luvaas, pp. 21-22; Bradley, Bentonville. pp. 391-93.

39. Luvaas, p. 24.

40. *OR,* Vol. 47, Part I, pp. 436, 809; Brant, pp. 107-08.

41. *OR,* Vol. 47, Part II, pp. 930, 937, 962-63; Part III, pp. 13-14.

42. *OR,* Vol. 47. Part I, pp. 436, 588.

43. Ibid., p. 809.

44. Ibid., pp. 588, 785.

45. Ibid., p. 207.

46. Brant, pp. 109-10.

47. Barrett, p. 344.

48. Barrett, pp. 344-45.

49. *OR,* Vol. 47, Part I, pp. 785, 809-10.

50. Ibid., p. 818.

Chapter 19

1. Sherman's *Memoirs*, Vol. II, p. 331. *OR*, Vol. 47, Part I, pp. 27-28.
2. *OR*, Vol. 47, Part III, pp. 84, 86; Sherman's *Memoirs*, Vol. II, p. 333.
3. *OR*, Vol. 47, Part III, pp. 95, 102-03, 111-12, 119, 121-22.
4. *OR*, Vol. 47, Part I, pp. 785, 810-11.
5. Ibid., pp. 810-11.
6. Brant, pp. 113-14.
7. *OR*, Vol. 47, Part I, p. 811.

Chapter 20

1. *OR*, Vol. 47, Part III, pp. 102-03, 121-22, 103, 141, 145; Slocum, p. 306.
2. *OR*, Vol. 47, Part I, p. 145.
3. Ibid., pp. 138, 144, 596, 603.
4. Ibid., pp. 603, 614-15.
5. Ibid., p. 811.
6. *OR*, Vol. 47, Part I, pp. 142, 811; *Historical Register of the United States Army*, Francis B. Heitman, Government Printing Office, Washington, 1903, Facsimile reprint, University of Illinois, Urbana, 1965, Vol. I, p. 391.
7. *OR*, Vol. 47, Part III, pp. 141, 158-60; Slocum, p. 306.
8. *OR*, Vol. 47, Part I, pp. 30, 116, 603, 699-700; Part III, p. 157.
9. Ibid., p. 811.
10. *OR*, Vol. 47, Part III, p. 153.
11. *OR*, Vol. 47, Part III, p. 140; Sherman's *Memoirs*, Vol. 2, pp. 343-44.
12. Ibid., p. 170.
13. *OR*, Vol. 47, Part I, p. 786; Part III, pp. 170-71, 185.
14. Ibid., p. 811.
15. *OR*, Vol. 47, Part III, pp. 173-74, 174-75, 180.
16. Lewis, *Fighting Prophet*, pp. 528-32; Barrett, pp. 372-77; Sherman's *Memoirs*, Vol. II, pp. 344-45.
17. *OR*, Vol. 47, Part I, p. 1132; Barrett, p. 377.
18. Barrett, p. 377
19. *OR*, Vol. 47, Part I, pp. 386, 786, 811.
20. Ibid., p. 156.
21. *OR*, Vol. 47, Part III, pp. 193, 194-95.
22. Ibid., pp. 196-97, 213-14, 232-33.
23. *OR*, Vol. 47, Part I, pp. 123, 131; Part III, p. 210.
24. *OR*, Vol. 47, Part III, pp. 208-09.
25. *OR*, Vol. 47, Part I, p. 811; Part III, 123, 131, 213.
26. Sherman's *Memoirs*, Vol. II, pp. 346-47.

27. Ibid., pp. 347-50.

28. Ibid., pp. 352-54.

29. *OR,* Vol. 47, Part III, p. 304; Lewis, *Fighting Prophet,* p. 555; Grant's *Memoirs,* Vol. II, pp. 514-17.

30. *OR,* Vol. 47, Part I, p. 811.

31. Ibid., pp. 811-12.

32. *OR,* Vol. 47, Part III, pp. 303, 304, 312-13.

33. *OR,* Vol. 47, Part I, p. 812.

34. *OR,* Vol. 47, Part III, p. 323; Sherman's *Memoirs,* Vol. II, p. 368.

35. Sherman's *Memoirs,* Vol. II, pp. 368-69.

36. Ibid., pp. 369, 374.

Chapter 21

1. *OR,* Vol. 47, Part III, pp. 324-25, 327.

2. *OR,* Vol. 47, Part I, p. 812; Part III, p. 341.

3. *OR,* Vol. 47, Part I, pp. 210-11; Part III, pp. 340, 352.

4. *OR,* Vol. 47, pp. 604, 700; Part III, p. 347-48.

5. *OR,* Vol. 47, Part I, pp. 604, 701.

6. *OR,* Vol. 47, Part I, p. 77; Part III, p. 365.

7. *OR,* Vol. 47, Part I, pp. 108, 701.

8. *OR,* Vol. 47, Part III, pp. 374-75.

9. Ibid., pp. 382-84.

10. *OR,* Vol. 47, Part I, pp. 604, 701.

11. Ibid., p. 94; Part III, pp. 390, 401-02, 413, 421.

12. *OR,* Vol. 47, Part I, p. 139; Part III, p. 391, 403-04.

13. Ibid., pp. 108, 113, 117; Part III, p. 403.

14. *OR,* Vol. 47, Part I, pp. 125, 132, 139, 701.

15. Ibid., pp. 604, 701.

16. Ibid.

17. Ibid.

18. *OR,* Vol. 47, Part III, pp. 421, 448.

19. Howard's *Autobiography,* Vol. 2, pp. 206-07; *OR,* Vol. 47, Part III, pp. 421, 477, 562.

20. *OR,* Vol. 47, Part III, pp. 438, 446, 459; Sherman's *Memoirs,* Vol. 2, p. 374

21. Lewis, *Fighting Prophet,* pp. 564-65; Benjamin P. Thomas and Harold M. Hyman, *Stanton, The Life and Times of Lincoln's Secretary of War,* Alfred A. Knopf, New York, 1962, pp. 405-12.

22. *OR,* Vol. 47, Part III, pp. 250, 421, 424, 425; Lewis, *Fighting Prophet,* pp. 564-65; Henry J. Aten, *History of the 85th Illinois Volunteer Infantry,* Hiawatha, Kansas, 1901.

23. Lewis, *Fighting Prophet*, pp. 565-66; *Reunion Story of Company E, of the 12th Wisconsin Infantry*, privately printed.

24. *OR* Series II, Vol. 8, pp. 912, 930; Brant, p. 116.

25. McBride, pp. 183-184.

26. *OR*, Vol. 47, Part III, p. 455.

27. *OR*, Vol. 47, Part I, pp. 108, 117; Part III, p. 469; Slocum, pp. 314-16.

28. *OR*, Vol. 47, Part III, p. 480.

29. Ibid., pp. 458-59, 480.

30. Ibid., pp. 469, 487-88.

31. *OR*, Vol. 47, Part I, pp. 605, 793; *OR*, Vol. 47, Part III, pp. 458-59.

32. *OR*, Vol. 47, Part III, pp. 605, 701; Lewis, *Fighting Prophet*, p. 565.

33. Ibid., pp. 605, 701-02.

34. Ibid., pp. 132, 134, 140; Part III, pp. 481, 489.

35. *OR*, Vol. 47, Part III, pp. 125-605, 702; Part III, pp. 487-88; Slocum, p. 316.

36. Ibid., pp. 108, 113, 117.

37. Ibid., p. 94; Part III, p. 479.

38. *OR*, Vol. 47, Part III, pp. 487, 495, 501.

39. *OR*, Vol. 47, Part I, pp. 78, 83, 89, 94; Part III, pp. 500-01, 508-09.

40. Ibid., pp. 125, 132, 140, 605, 702; Part III, pp. 488-89, 501.

41. Ibid., pp. 606, 702; Slocum, p. 316.

42. Slocum, pp. 605, 702, 786.

Chapter 22

1. *OR*, Vol. 47, Part III, pp. 526, 539.

2. *OR*, Vol. 47, Part III p. 477; Lewis, *Fighting Prophet*, p. 573.

3. *OR*, Vol. 47, Part III, pp. 532, 562, 563.

4. Ibid., pp. 539, 558.

5. Ibid., pp. 539, 554-55.

6. Ibid., pp. 558, 559, 563.

7. Ibid., pp. 563, 564.

8. Sherman's *Memoirs*, Vol. II, pp. 377-78; Lewis, *Fighting Prophet*, pp. 573-77.

9. Sherman's *Memoirs*, Vol. II, pp. 378.

10. Brant, pp. 116-17.

11. McBride, pp. 185-86.

12. *OR*, Vol. 47, Part I, p. 812.

13. Ibid., pp. 107, 112, 113; Part III, pp. 566-67.

14. *OR*, Vol. 47, Part III, p. 584.

15. Ibid., pp. 525-26.

16. Ibid., pp. 620.

17. Ibid.

18. *OR,* Vol. 47, Part I, p. 134.

19. Ibid., pp. 142, 145.

20. *OR,* Vol. 47, Part I, pp. 107, 108, 112, 113, 118, 120; McBride, p. 190; Terrell, Vol. I, *Appendix, Statistics and Documents,* p. 47.

21. Ibid., p. 142; McBride, p. 190; Terrell, Vol. I, *Appendix, Statistics and Documents,* p. 47.

22. Reid, p. 248.

23. Anderson, pp. 416.

24. Brant, p. 117.

25. Ibid., pp. 122-23.

26. *Official Army Register,* Vol. 6, p. 143

27. Brant, p. 124.

Index

Burget, Lawrence, 392.
Burnt Hickory, Ga., 188, 189, 190, 194, 196, 197.
Burton, Cynthia A. Biskirk (Mrs. James E. Burton), 266.
Burton, James E., 266, 269, 276, 278, 301, 316, 326, 348, 392-93.
Buschbeck, Adolphus, 161, 171.
Butler, Benjamin F., 157.
Butler, Matthew, C., 338.
Butterfield, Daniel, 141, 143, 144, 158, 161, 162, 167, 172, 179, 180, 191, 198, 201, 212, 213, 214, 216, 217, 218.
Butterfield's Division, 162, 165, 166, 167, 168, 169, 171, 172-73, 177, 179, 180, 188, 189, 190, 191, 192, 194, 195, 196, 197, 206, 209, 210, 211, 212, 213, 214, 215, 217.
Buzzard's Roost Gap, Ga., 165, 166, 167.

C

Calhoun, Ga. 176, 177, 179, 252.
Mayor James M., 257, 263.
Camp Bloodgood, Ky., 26.
Chase, Columbus, Ohio, 97, 107, 108, 139.
Dick Robinson, 42.
Dick Thompson, Terre Haute, Ind., 5-6, 15, 39, 40, 259.
Gamble, St. Louis, Mo., 108.
Gilmer, Ky., 31.
King, Ky., 21, 23
Lew Wallace, Ky., 23.
Mitchel, Ky., 20, 21, 22.
Morton, Indianapolis, Ind., 12-13, 103, 107.
Parole, near Annapolis, Md., 98, 103.
Smith, Ky., 26.
Sullivan, Indianapolis, Ind., 14.
Vigo, Terre Haute, Ind., 5.
Willcox, Dowagiac, Mich., 10.
Campbell, Archibald P., 52.
Candy, Charles, 141, 161, 171.
Cape Fear River, N.C., 315, 342, 344, 350, 367.
Caperton's Ferry, Ala., 133.
Capron, Horace, 257.
William P. Carlin, 171, 295, 296, 333, 337, 340, 342, 344, 352, 353.
Carman, Ezra A., 303, 316.

Case, Henry, 316, 318, 348, 350, 353, 354.
Cassville, Ga., 179, 181, 183, 185, 188.
Catawba River, 334, 335, 337.
Central Alabama Railroad, 56.
Central Railroad of Georgia, 288, 290, 293, 294, 297, 298, 301, 305.
Champion, Thomas E., 107, 133.
Champion, transport, 47, 48.
Chapman, Warren, 10.
Charleston and Savannah Railroad, 299, 300, 301, 302, 303, 320.
Charleston and Wilmington Railroad, 315.
Charlotte and South Carolina Railroad, 332, 334.
Chattahoochee River, Ga., 198, 203, 220, 222, 227, 228, 253, 254, 256, 258, 262, 278, 279.
Chattanooga, Tenn., 91, 156, 159, 160, 164.
Cheatham, Benjamin F., 216, 227, 230, 234, 243, 246, 267, 343.
Cheraw, S.C., 334, 337, 338, 339, 340, 343.
Chesterfield, S.C., 35, 337, 338.
Court House, 373.
Cheves' plantation, S.C., 318, 320, 322.
Chicago and New Albany Railroad, 108.
Chickahominy River, Va., 376.
Chickamauga, Ga., Battle of, 132, 133, 135, 136, 147.
Creek, 135, 151.
Chilesburg, Va. 375, 376, 377.
Christ, Henry, 235.
Christiana, Tenn., 123, 125, 126, 133, 134, 136, 137, 138, 139, 141, 146, 149, 154, 155.
Cincinnati and Southern Railroad, 38.
City Point, Va., 96, 97, 276, 277.
Clark, E., 10.
Clarke, Robert, 387.
Cleburne, Patrick R., 254, 255.
Cobham, George A., 172, 174, 175.
Coble, Samuel, 107, 393.
Coburn, John, 14, 15, 30, 31, 35,37, 38, 40, 49, 50, 51, 53, 54, 55, 57, 58, 60, 62, 63, 64, 65, 68, 69, 71, 72, 73, 74, 75, 77, 78, 79, 87, 90, 91, 95, 97, 107, 108, 122, 123, 129, 130, 131, 138, 139, 141, 142, 143, 144, 146, 147, 149, 150, 152, 155, 156, 158, 162, 166, 172, 174,

179, 180, 182, 191, 192, 195, 207, 209, 211, 213, 215, 216, 219, 223, 233, 235, 236, 238, 244, 252, 254, 258, 261, 265, 266, 268, 272, 276, 394-95.

Coburn's brigade, 3, 27, 35, 39, 40, 42, 43, 45, 46, 47, 48, 49, 52, 56, 68, 69, 70, 71, 73, 80, 87, 92, 96, 99, 104, 106, 107, 108, 109, 110, 111, 122, 126, 127, 130, 133, 135, 140, 143, 145, 146, 148, 151, 152, 154, 158, 159, 160, 161, 167, 168, 169, 171, 172, 174, 175, 177, 179, 180, 183, 188, 189, 190, 191, 192, 193, 194, 195, 196, 198, 199, 201, 207, 208, 210, 211, 212, 213, 214, 215, 217, 218, 219, 221, 222, 225, 229, 232, 233, 235, 237, 239, 240, 244, 245, 248, 249, 251, 253, 254, 256, 257, 258, 259, 262, 265, 274, 299, 305, 317, 346, 350, 375, 376, 383.

Coburn, Caroline Test (Mrs. John Coburn), 46.

Cochran, John C., 15, 38.

Cogshall, Israel, 10.

Cogswell, William, 149, 317, 324, 328, 346, 348, 350, 353, 380.

Collier's Mill, Ga., 230, 232, 233, 235, 237, 238, 239.

Ridge and Road, 232, 235, 237, 238.

Columbia, Tenn., 49, 51, 87.

Columbia, S.C., 317, 328, 329, 330, 331, 332, 333.

Columbia Pike, Tenn., 50, 51, 52, 55, 56, 103, 104.

Conaway, Lloyd W., 69.

Connecticut Troops

5th Conn., 159; **20th Conn.**, 158, 159, 160, 166, 167, 172, 174, 175, 179, 186, 236, 237.

Congaree River, S.C., 328, 330.

Connesauga River, Ga., 177.

Conrick, J. Oscar, 152.

Cook, Philip B., 8.

Coosawhatchie River, S.C., 176, 177.

Swamp, S.C., 325.

Corse, John M., 267, 278, 320, 323, 328, 339.

Cosby, George B., 56, 68, 87.

Covington, Ky., 19, 29, 36, 38.

Cowan, Tenn., 134, 140, 146, 159, 160.

Tunnel, Tenn., 135.

Cowpens Creek, Ga., 298.

Cox, Jacob D., 30, 186, 208, 213, 215, 221, 228, 256, 265, 270, 357, 360, 364, 365.

Cox, N. N., 64.

Cox's Bridge, N.C., 351, 352, 355, 363, 364.

Crabb, James H., 239.

Craig, Robert, E., 8, 156.

Crane, Abiel Briggs, 224.

Crane, Alexander B., 5, 8, 23, 38, 102, 103, 133, 152, 153, 223, 224, 244, 245, 251, 274, 275, 276, 278, 286, 292, 299, 301, 303, 304, 316, 320, 321, 324, 327, 329, 348, 357, 361, 387, 393.

Crane, Emma Tisdale, 224.

Crane, Nirom N., 262.

Crawford, Francis (Frank) C., 60, 145, 146, 180, 183, 224, 258, 308, 309, 329, 387, 395.

Crawford, Jesse Burr (Mrs. Francis Crawford), 39.

Crawford, William T., 5, 8, 37, 104, 105, 106, 113, 116, 134, 240, 257, 387, 395-96.

Crittenden, Thomas L., 28, 123, 125, 135.

Crook, George, 45, 143, 144, 145.

Cruft, Charles, 102, 119, 151, 390.

Cumberland Gap, Tenn., 265.

Mountains, Tenn., 137, 147, 160.

Custis, Martha Parke, 118.

Mary Anne (Mrs. Robert E. Lee), 118.

D

Dahlgren, John A., 303.

Dallas, Ga., 185, 186, 188, 189, 190, 193, 195, 196, 265.

Dalton, Ga., 151, 161, 165, 168.

Danville, Ky., 40.

Danville, Va., 360.

Darby House, Ga., 209, 210.

Davidson, Henry B., 137, 145.

Davis, Edward, 116.

Ellery C., 8, 134, 224.

President Jefferson, 227, 311, 368.

Jefferson C., 161, 162, 175, 188, 193, 195, 215, 216, 229, 248, 249, 250, 251, 254, 256, 270, 277, 278, 285, 289, 292, 297, 302, 313, 316, 317, 322, 323, 329,

Fosterville, Tenn., 126, 130, 134, 139, 149, 152, 158, 159.
Franklin, Tenn., 49, 99, 104, 106, 108, 109.
Fredericksburg, Va., 375, 376, 377.
Freeland, John T., 99, 100.
Freeman, Samuel L., 62.
Freeman's Battery, 63, 64, 71, 75, 76, 101, 103, 104.
French, Samuel G., 234, 254, 269.

G

Galbraith, Robert, 141, 142, 143.
Garfield, James A., 51, 78, 112, 114, 115, 118,
Garrard, Israel, 373
Garrrard, Kenner, 180, 195, 219, 220, 228, 246.
Garrison's Fork (Creek) of Duck River, Tenn., 134, 142, 143, 144, 145, 146.
Geary, John W., 140, 141, 146, 147, 151, 158, 161, 166, 167, 168, 169, 171, 172, 177, 190, 206, 207, 208, 209, 244, 246, 254, 261, 272, 273, 274, 296, 298, 301, 304, 305, 316, 317, 334, 363, 364, 371, 372, 373, 376, 377, 380.
Geary's Division, 164, 165, 169, 171, 172, 174, 175, 176, 179, 188, 189, 190, 191, 196, 197, 210, 211, 212, 213, 214, 217, 218, 219, 220, 221, 228, 229, 230, 232, 233, 234, 235, 236, 238, 245, 246, 248, 253, 259, 262, 271, 272, 274, 278, 284, 285, 287, 288, 289, 293, 294, 295, 296, 298, 299, 301, 304, 305, 312, 313, 322, 323, 326, 327, 328, 329, 333, 335, 337, 338, 339, 241, 342.
General Lee, steamer tug, 322.
Georgia Central Railroad (Central Railroad of Georgia), 294.
Georgia Railroad, 227, 228, 285.
Gilbert, Charles C., 28, 50, 51, 52, 54, 55, 76, 78, 79, 80, 100, 103.
Gilbert, Henry C., 9, 10, 39, 52, 62, 63, 65, 72, 75, 76, 78, 90, 108, 123, 129, 147, 148, 167, 172, 174.
Gilbert, Samuel A., 37.
Gilgal Church, Ga., 207.
Gillmore, Quincy A., 27, 30, 31, 34, 36.
Goldsboro, N.C., 309, 343, 344, 351, 352,

353, 354, 355, 356, 357, 359, 360, 361, 362, 363.
Goodrich, Gustavus, 11.
Goodspeed, Wilbur A., 236.
Gordon, James, 82, 90.
Graham, William H., 365.
Granger, Gordon, 18, 26, 29, 30, 31, 34, 36, 37, 38, 39, 42, 45, 46, 47, 71, 78, 99, 100, 101, 103, 104, 106, 107, 109, 111, 121, 122, 123, 125, 126, 129, 131, 133, 138, 139, 142, 144, 145, 146, 398.
Granger, Robert S., 107, 140, 146.
Grant, Ulysses S., 1, 131, 146, 147, 151, 157, 276, 277, 315, 320, 359, 360, 365, 373. 374, 379, 381.
Gravel Pit, Ohio, 24.
Gravelly Plateau, Ga., 179, 181.
Green, Charles, 311.
Greenberry, Marks, 295.
Greensboro, N.C., 372.
Greenville and Columbia Railroad, 333.
Griffin, Eli A., 174, 191, 208.
Grimes, George, 387.
Grimes, Thomas, 387.
Griffith, Owen, 11, 99, 152.
Griswold, William D., 6.
Griswoldville, Ga., Battle of, 290.
Grose, William, 246.
Grover, Cuvier, 322.
Guignard's Bridge, S.C., 329.
Gunn, John, 139.
Gunn, Otis J., 138.
Gurley, Joseph A., 361.
Guy's Gap, Tenn., 125, 126, 128, 129, 137, 139.

H

Hale, Bradford, 323.
Halleck, Henry W., 45, 106, 121, 131, 132, 374.
Hampton, Wade, 331, 365, 377.
Hanover Court House, Va., 375, 376, 377.
Harbert, William S., 201, 279, 302, 305.
Hardee, William J., 122, 123, 125, 189, 193, 195, 205, 206, 209, 210, 213, 214, 216, 227, 234, 235, 236, 238, 243, 244, 245, 250, 255, 256, 267, 283, 304, 313, 343, 344, 346, 350, 351, 352, 353, 354, 366.

X

no entries

Y

Z
no entries